A Documentary History
of the
American Civil War Era

A Documentary History *of the* American Civil War Era

VOLUME 3

Judicial Decisions, 1857–1866

Edited by Thomas C. Mackey

Voices of the Civil War

The University of Tennessee Press / Knoxville

 The Voices of the Civil War series makes available a variety of primary source materials that illuminate issues on the battlefield, the home front, and the western front, as well as other aspects of this historic era. The series contextualizes the personal accounts within the framework of the latest scholarship and expands established knowledge by offering new perspectives, new materials, and new voices.

 Copyright © 2014 by The University of Tennessee Press / Knoxville.
All Rights Reserved. Manufactured in the United States of America.
First Edition.

The paper in this book meets the requirements of American National Standards Institute / National Information Standards Organization specification Z39.48-1992 (Permanence of Paper). It contains 30 percent post-consumer waste and is certified by the Forest Stewardship Council.

Library of Congress Cataloging-in-Publication Data

A documentary history of the American Civil War era / edited by Thomas C. Mackey. — 1st ed.
    p. cm.
Includes bibliographical references and index.
ISBN 978-1-62190-005-4 (hardcover) — ISBN 1-62190-005-3 (hardcover)
1. United States—Politics and government—1861–1865—Sources.
2. United States—History—Civil War, 1861–1865—Sources.
I. Mackey, Thomas C., 1956–

E459.D53 2013
973.7—dc23
2012026779

*For Harold M. Hyman
and
William E. Nelson*

With gratitude and thanks

Contents

Acknowledgments ix
Introduction: A Documentary History of the American Civil War Era xi

Volume 3
Judicial Decisions, 1857–1866

Dred Scott v. Sandford, 19 Howard (60 U.S.) 393 (1857). 5
Ableman v. Booth, 21 How. (62 U.S.) 506 (1859). 203
Grand Jury Indictment of John Brown, October 26, 1859 219
Lemmon v. People, 20 N.Y. 562 (1860) 225
Kentucky v. Dennison, 24 How. (65 U.S. 10) 66 (1861). 283
Ex parte Merryman, 17 Fed. Cas. 144, Case # 9,487 (1861). 317
Prize Cases, 2 Black (67 U.S.) 635 (1863) 335
Ex parte Vallandigham, 1 Wallace (68 U.S.) 243 (1864) 379
Gelpcke v. City of Dubuque, 1 Wallace (68 U.S.) 175 (1864). 389
Ex parte Milligan, 4 Wallace (71 U.S.) 2 (1866) 419
United States v. Rhodes, 27 Fed. Cas. 785, Case # 16,151 (1866). 515

Chronology 533
Selected Readings 539
Index. 547

Acknowledgments

This project did not happen without the help of numerous people and they have earned mention and thanks in this acknowledgment. Of course, all errors of omission and commission in this work are mine alone. A good place to start (and a good place to work) would be the University of Tennessee Press. Scot Danforth, director of the Press and specialist in the era of the United States Civil War, has offered encouragement and been patient with this project and with me. He has cheerfully answered all questions while always nudging the project forward. The former editor of the Voices of the Civil War series for the University of Tennessee Press, Peter Carmichael, has assisted from first discussions to final draft. His help and insights have been most welcome, and the overall project is better because of his suggestions and editor's eye. A special thanks to the anonymous readers is due; their honest, blunt assessments and recommendations improved the manuscript and assisted in developing my understanding of what this project could and could not achieve.

I have had the good fortune to receive assistance on this project from graduate students at the University of Louisville and summer undergraduate research assistants as well. Working on the document collection and editing became a "teaching moment" for graduate students James D. Kendall, William E. Hardy, James Osborne, and John Spenlau, and undergraduates Sarah J. Bodell and, especially, James B. "Ben" Shepard.

In the History Department at the University of Louisville, John McLeod should be singled out for his continual good humor and encouragement when he served as chair of the department and since. At the Brandeis School of Law at the University of Louisville, Dean James Chen and Associate Deans Tom Blackburn and Tony Arnold support my field of United States legal history as both a research endeavor and as a teaching area. The History Department staff of Jon-Paul Moody and Lee Keeling has been their normal helpful, professional, and supportive selves.

July 2011 marks thirty years that I have known Kelly Kane, even though we only reconnected and married twelve years ago. To her and for her support, encouragement, fussing, help, and good sense, I cannot offer enough thanks nor express my wide and deep gratitude for her agreeing to be us. For how she managed to hold down a full-time job, attend four years of law school at night, pass the bar, and now work as an attorney-at-law, all the while dealing with me, she should receive all accolades, huzzas, honors, and thanks.

In academia, students do not thank master professors enough. As a result, these volumes are dedicated to the two extraordinary professors, critics, mentors, and friends with whom I have had the great good fortune to work and to learn from: Dr. Harold M. Hyman, the William P. Hobby Professor of History, Emeritus, at Rice University, and Dr. William E. Nelson, the Judge Edward Weinfeld Professor of Law at the New York University School of Law. Each a New Yorker, both personify the best that the history profession offers to students willing to be challenged and changed. My good kismet to work with Harold Hyman both enriched and reshaped me in graduate school many years ago. And my professional and personal debts to Bill Nelson and his family (Elaine, Leila, and Greg) are far too numerous to list. To Harold and Bill, I dedicate these volumes as a token of my highest esteem and respect. Thanks guys.

Introduction:
A Documentary History of the American Civil War Era

I

In 1881, Union Civil War veteran, distinguished law author and attorney, and later Associate Justice of the United States Supreme Court, Oliver Wendell Holmes Jr. published a little book entitled, *The Common Law*. Although little read in its entirety today, the point of the book continues to influence law academics, historians of the law, and jurisprudents to the current day. Holmes possessed a deep understanding of law and of history and he understood those two topics of intellectual endeavor to be symbiotic—mutually reinforcing. In the famous first paragraph of *The Common Law*, Holmes wrote, " . . . The life of the law has not been logic: it has been experience. The felt necessities of the time, the prevalent moral and political theories, intuitions of public policy, avowed or unconscious, even the prejudices which judges share with their fellow-men, have had a good deal more to do than the syllogism in determining the rules by which men should be governed." Holmes argued that law is, and was, embedded in culture, and that law and public policy were not some set of eternal rules that could only be divined through case law and statutes. He then shifted his focus a bit and argued for the need to understand history to understand law and public policy. Holmes explained:

> The law embodies the story of a nation's development through many centuries, and it cannot be dealt with as if it contained only the axioms and corollaries of a book of mathematics. In order to know what it is, we must know what it has been, and what it tends to become. We must alternately consult history and existing theories of legislation. But the most difficult labor will be to understand the combination of the two new products at every stage. The substances of the law at any given time pretty nearly corresponds, so far as it goes, with what is then understood to be convenient; but its form and machinery, and the degree to which it is able to work out desired results, depends very much upon its past.[1]

This collection of documents, headnotes, and introductory essays enriches the study of the middle period of the nineteenth-century United States by providing students and scholars access to the most important (and sometimes overlooked and difficult to locate) public policy and judicial decisions in the era of Abraham Lincoln. If, as Holmes says, the law embodies a nation's history, then it is necessary for students of history to confront and consider the law and the public policies that defined each era. This set of documents defines not only the historical context of that past era but also in at least a few instances—the Thirteenth Amendment, the Civil Rights Act of 1866, the Fourteenth Amendment, and the 1873 decision by the United States Supreme Court in the *Slaughter-House Cases*—that these public policies established a new baseline for federalism and for individual and group rights in the post–Civil War/Reconstruction United States. But documents and evidence do not speak for themselves; thus, the introductory headnotes before each document explain the historical significance of that document within its context and trace the lasting significance of each. Further, the introductory notes explain why modern audiences will find these documents relevant to their current interests and researches.

In "historical methods" courses taught at colleges and universities, historians stress to students just how foreign the past is, even telling their students that "the past is a foreign country."[2] One approach to understanding the past is to consider the legal and public policy choices each generation made and to explore why they made those choices. To modern audiences, it is difficult to grasp and understand just how breathtaking, how extreme ("radical" in the parlance of the day) the April 16, 1862, abolition of slavery in the District of Columbia really was for that generation within its historical context. With a wave of the hand and a dismissive "whatever," today's students too often ignore the past. But that decision, which appears to moderns as nothing more than simple justice, thrilled large parts of the white majority northern and midwestern populations and confirmed the worst fears of the white southerner population. That decision instilled hope in the African American population and their allies that maybe, just perhaps maybe, the administration of President Lincoln was not as inept and slow on the issue of race relations and slavery as they had led themselves to believe. Thus, that understanding—that recapturing, of the excitement and fear of new public policies—is the challenge of history in general, and one of the particular challenges confronting political and legal historians.

It is a truism that change happens. But, in the worst of times in a nation's history, a time of civil war, change occurred. Not just cultural or social change, but important political and legal change occurred and added a new war goal for the Union, such as President Lincoln's January 1, 1863, addition of uncompensated emancipation to the primary Union goal of preserving the nation. The addition of the Fourteenth Amendment to the 1787 Constitution changed the very foundation of the nation, and most legal and historical scholars now consider the document and its amendments a second United States Constitution. Though not denying the importance of the military events (as Lincoln himself stated in his second inaugural, "The progress of our arms, upon which all else chiefly depends"), the war did not endure. However, in contrast to the war, these political, legal, and judicial decisions chronicling change from that era lasted well past their immediate political and legal moment and affected and affect Americans from their times to the present; change happened, and those changes mattered, and still matter.

II

Some persons embraced the changes and reforms that rattled within the United States before, during, and after the four years of Civil War, while other persons resisted those changes. The pace of change and the unexpected directions of reform bewildered many, perhaps even the majority of, the sensitive and acute observers of the time. Starting in March 1861, residing in the Executive Mansion at the center of that destructive and constructive hurricane of war and change, was the Kentucky-born, Indiana-raised, Illinois attorney, Abraham Lincoln. Popular-culture writers and textbooks do not credit Lincoln enough for his appreciation of history and history's random nature. As a regional politician, a senatorial candidate, a presidential candidate, a president-elect, and the president, Lincoln understood that his every action, word, clause, sentence, paragraph, and speech would be analyzed and parsed for meaning and nuance. For this reason, Lincoln rarely spoke informally or off-the-cuff, preferring to explain himself and his political positions through his writings, which he pored over, wrote, and rewrote.

Although Lincoln had his occasional internal doubts as his moods rose and fell and as the Union's fortunes rose and fell and rose again, the president possessed the ability to grasp the significance of his unique historical moment. This appreciation can be gathered from the closing of his much underappreciated (and included in this collection) December 1, 1862, message to Congress. He began the last paragraph of that message saying, "Fellow-citizens, *we* cannot escape history." Lincoln continued, "We of this Congress and this administration, will be remembered in spite of ourselves. No personal significance, or insignificance, can spare one or another of us. The fiery trial through which we pass, will light us down, in honor or dishonor, to the latest generation." He closed that message by explaining and defending his September 1862 decision to issue a preliminary emancipation proclamation; by doing so, he educated the country about the benefits of adding this second war goal to the Union cause. Lincoln understood that emancipation was not popular in the North and Midwest, but he also understood that emancipation aided his cause and hurt the southern cause. For the President, these long-term benefits outweighed the short-term costs. Escaping history and the analysis and assessments of historians was not possible, and Lincoln knew it. So, regardless of later assessments, Lincoln acted both to preserve the country while, in time, adding emancipation to the Union's war goals.

He also at least suspected, perhaps knew, that foundation-shattering political and legal change engulfed him and his contemporaries. In that same message to Congress, Lincoln pointed out that, "The dogmas of the quiet past, are inadequate to the stormy present." In such difficult times, change constituted the only constant. "The occasion is piled high with difficulty, and we must rise with the occasion," Lincoln continued. He also understood that the new context and the new times brought about by all of the changes required—perhaps demanded—new imagination. As Lincoln put the issue: "As our case is new, so we must think anew, and act anew."

This document collection presents the raw "stuff" of Lincoln's era, full-text documents of the political, public policy, and judicial voices of the Civil War era so that students, scholars, and interested readers can measure and gauge how that generation met Lincoln's challenge to "think anew, and act anew."

III

These four volumes of statutes, speeches, letters, party platforms, and judicial decisions from the era of the Civil War and Reconstruction fill a gap in the current literature of the period; it also provides modern researchers, graduate students, undergraduate students, and the general public with access to key public policy documents of that crucial era in United States history. In the last thirty to forty years, social, cultural, and military historians of the United States have done a fine job of interpreting and broadening the scope of topics and insights into the era of the Civil War and Reconstruction. At the same time, the political, legal, and constitutional history of that era has suffered and become a bit (actually more than a bit) lost. With the recent successful bicentennial celebration of Abraham Lincoln's birth, a new wave of interest in Lincoln and his times has emerged in both the popular and the scholarly press. Lincoln's bicentennial has been followed by sesquicentennial remembrances, conferences, and publications focused on the Civil War years as well. This collection of documents contributes to the Lincoln bicentennial outburst of publications as well as highlights the public policy and judicial decisions of the Civil War era during the sesquicentennial. These primary sources provide an indispensable resource for scholars, teachers, students, and the general public. One goal for this book is to make available to a wide audience public policy documents that are known and appreciated by legal historians and associated scholars of the era. For example, documents such as the Civil Rights Act of 1866 or the key United States Supreme Court decision by Chief Justice Salmon P. Chase in *Texas v. White* (1869) that defined the nature of the nation are included, but these documents are seldom, if ever, reprinted. As a result, these sources are often difficult to access for the average historian, much less the general reader.

Each document is cited to its source and a headnote essay is included with each. The headnote essay places the document within its historical context and comments on the significance of the document as well. These volumes bring back into the mainstream of the middle period of nineteenth-century United States studies the political, legal, and constitutional issues of public policy over which that generation of Americans fought and died. As a result, this collection introduces readers and students to the richness of the Civil War/Reconstruction–era primary sources and provides an overview of the major, minor, better-known, and lesser-known documents of that era and of the issues that confronted policymakers and their publics.

IV

It is important to state what these volumes are not: it is not a definitive compilation of documents from the Civil War era. To include all federal, all state, all county, all local, and then all of the personal documents of the general public and leaders of that era would entail publishing whole archives—and then some. Instead, this collection is much more humble. It focuses on the most important political, judicial, and public policy decisions of that time. Another scholar might choose a slightly different list of documents to include and yet another might shift the focus of the headnote essays, all of which are understandable. Instead, this set of documents reflects some best known then, and best known now (at least to specialists), documents and decisions, knowing that even in the area of public policy and judicial decisions, this list is not complete. It is not meant to be complete, just representative. For example, some might argue that the Judicial Circuits Act of 1866 or Kentucky Governor Beriah Magoffin's April 16, 1861, response to President Abraham Lincoln's call for troops from all of the states including Kentucky to put down the insurrection are minor documents; well, that is the point. Such statutes and policies mattered at the time and their inclusion here is aimed to help readers recapture the obvious and some of the less obvious yet significant and emotional points of contention of that crucial era.

To make sense of this jumble of public policies, political statements, and judicial decisions, these primary sources are divided into three thematic groupings, and then arranged chronologically within each group: volume 1, Legislative Achievements, contains legislation passed in response to the turmoil churning through the country on the brink of, during, and in the wake of the Civil War; volume 2, Political Arguments, contains voices of politicians, political party platforms, and administrative speeches; and volume 3, Judicial Decisions, provides the reader with a plethora of judicial opinions and verdicts as the Civil War raged on the battlefield and in the courtroom. Each of these three volumes includes well-known documents such as the Homestead Act of 1862, Jefferson Davis's inaugural address, Lincoln's two inaugural addresses, and the majority decision and dissents in the 1857 *Dred Scott* decision. Such documents are included because students and scholars will want to find these "greatest hits" in such a volume. Also included in this collection are important, even fundamental, documents and public policy decisions that are far less well known to most general readers and even some scholars of the period. For example, the previously mentioned April 16, 1862, abolishment of slavery in the District of Columbia Act overjoyed the Radical Republicans, worried the moderates, and horrified the Democrats and the South even though it occurred at a low point in the war for the Union. Although the abolition of slavery in the District may have been more symbolic than substantive (unless one was an African American freed by the statute, of course), nevertheless, it was an important symbol of the shifting goals of the war, and a hint of what race relations might look like in the future should the Union be successful. Party platforms were far more important public policy documents in the nineteenth century than they are in the early twenty-first century, and they need to be read for the stances the political parties took (and did not take) on the pressing issues of the day. President Andrew Johnson's May 29, 1865, Proclamations of Amnesty and Reconstruction constituted a major turning point in the Reconstruction of the nation, and yet it remains little known, read, analyzed, or appreciated. Judicial decisions, too, mattered more to that generation than they do now, and perhaps no decision of the United States Supreme Court needs to be better known and appreciated than *Texas v. White* (1869). In that decision, the majority of the justices redefined the nature of the nation and settled a political and constitutional debate that had raged in United States political theory since the 1787-1788 political battles over the ratification of the Constitution. By raising the Lincoln administration's belief in a perpetual Union/nation and the idea that the nation of the United States existed prior to the formation of the 1781 Articles of Confederation to constitutional principle, Chief Justice Chase and the Supreme Court's majority provided a new constitutional basis for the building of modern America. Then add in section one of the 1868 Fourteenth Amendment, which reconstituted and rebalanced the powers and duties of the states and the nation (United States federalism), as well as established a new basis and definition of national and state citizenship, and modern nationalism comes into view. Of course not everyone everywhere accepted these decisions and changes; each decision met with stiff resistance and, at times, fierce debate. But, standing back, historians have discerned a pattern of political, legal, and constitutional changes that these public policies and judicial decisions reflect. These volumes make these primary sources accessible for further analysis.

Volume One, Legislative Achievements, contains some of the most significant and lasting public policy documents from the era of the Civil War, beginning with the controversial September 18, 1850, Fugitive Slave Act and concluding with the June 18, 1878, Posse Comitatus Act. Both military and nonmilitary legislation is included in this section, such as the April 19, 1861, proclamations by President Abraham Lincoln declaring a naval blockade of Southern ports and, ironically on the same day, the president of the so-called Confederate States of America, Jefferson Davis's proclamation offering Letters of Marque authorizing blockade runners and privateers to attack Northern shipping and trade. Other important pieces of legislation are included, such as the Confiscation Acts of 1861 and 1862, the 1862 Confederate Conscription Act (with the later "20 Negro" exemption), and the 1863 Federal Conscription Act. Nonmilitary legislation includes statutes that looked forward in time to the world after the war, such as the 1862 Homestead Act, the Pacific Railroad Act, the Civil Rights Act of 1866, and the text of all four of the Reconstruction Acts. Also included are the three constitutional amendments added in the era—the 1865 Thirteenth Amendment, the 1868 Fourteenth Amendment (the second American Constitution), and the 1870 Fifteenth Amendment.

Volume Two, Political Arguments, contains the party platforms of the major and some minor parties from 1856 to 1876. Also included in this section are documents such as Robert Edward Lee's April 20, 1861, letter of resignation from the U.S. Army, a few of the key speeches by the rising attorney-politician from Illinois, Abraham Lincoln, and (completely consistently) a selected letter on the "American Question" written by a European observer of the events in the United States, Karl Marx. Other documents include examples of the 1860-1861 state ordinances of secession and key speeches by Jefferson Davis and, on the other side of the coin, speeches by the Republican leader in the House of Representatives from Pennsylvania, Thaddeus Stevens, on emancipation and Reconstruction.

Volume Two also divides the documents into presidential administrations, including one document from Confederate President Jefferson Davis telling his congress that the Southern cause was "just and holy." This section includes documents from the presidencies of James Buchanan, Abraham Lincoln, Andrew Johnson, Ulysses S. Grant, and Rutherford B. Hayes. Classic documents such as Lincoln's September 22, 1862, announcement of forthcoming emancipation and the January 1, 1863, Emancipation Proclamation, are included, as well as lesser-known but important documents such as Francis Lieber's April 23, 1863, revised law code for war, General Order 100, and Attorney General James Speed's 1865 opinion supporting the Andrew Johnson administration's decision to try the Lincoln murder conspirators by special military commission and not in the civilian courts.

Volume Three and *Volume Four, Judicial Decisions,* constitute the most unexpected section of documents from the era of the Civil War and Reconstruction for many readers. It may seem odd to include a section on judicial opinions because of the old rule of thumb in wartime, *inter arma [enim] silent leges*—in times of war, the law falls silent. But in the United States, the federal courts are not just courts of law; rather, they constitute a third branch of government. Thus, the judiciary generally, and, in particular, the United States Supreme Court, is a policy-making institution. However, unlike Congress and the President, which are accountable to the country through calendared elections and which actively make policy, courts are passive. Cases and disputes have to make their way through the judicial process to reach decision by higher appellate courts. As a result, a time lag exists between the moment an action is taken or decided upon by Congress, by a president, by a state, or by an individual and the moment that issue reaches a trial court. Only after all of those actions are taken and a decision rendered at trial can the issues become ripe for an appellate court decision. In times of crisis, like war, judges and justices prefer to leave the "hot" issues of the day to the more accountable political branches and delay or refuse to involve themselves in controversial issues that might affect or hinder the nation's war efforts. But once the fighting has ceased and genuine legal and constitutional issues reach their trial and appellate dockets for argument and decision, judges and justices are much more apt to take cases for hearing and, on occasion, rebuke the other branches for their actions during wartime. Judicial decisions, especially those of the United States Supreme Court, in turn, become national public policy. This pattern of judicial decision making can be discerned before, during, and after the United States Civil War. As a result, it is proper that this collection contains a series of state and federal judicial appellate opinions. Like the previous sections, this section contains some of the classic judicial decisions of the time, such as the 1857 decision in *Dred Scott*, the 1861 *Ex parte Merryman* decision, the 1869 decision in *Texas* v. *White*, and the first judicial interpretation of the 1868 Fourteenth Amendment, the 1873 *Slaughter-House Cases*. Other decisions are well known to specialists but deserve wider readership and discussion; decisions such as the October 1859 Jefferson County, Virginia, indictment of John Brown, the decision in the 1864 case of political and seditious activity in *Ex parte Vallandigham*, and the 1867 state and 1878 federal case that upheld the separation of the races in public accommodations (and thus constituted the common law of common commerce) long before the more notorious, also included, 1896 case of *Plessy v. Ferguson*. These judicial voices constitute a lasting and often overlooked aspect of the age of Abraham Lincoln.[3] This volume remedies the lack of access to judicial decision making of the era and adds back into the larger literature these judicial decisions as part of the political voices of the middle period of United States history.

 Readers will notice that more Union documents are present in this work than Confederate documents. To "think anew, and act new," as Lincoln argued, guided the selection of documents because some public policy decisions, like the Fourteenth Amendment, have cast long, important shadows on United States law and culture. While the Confederate Congress and the state legislatures in the Southern states debated numerous issues, their efforts often came to naught. For example, on January 18, 1862, Confederate President Jefferson Davis signed a January 13 act that the Confederate Congress had passed to organize the Confederate "Territory of Arizona."[4] This pipe dream never became a reality. In fact, this act demonstrates the falsehood of Southerners' claims (and modern apologists for the Confederacy) that they did not seek to expand the Confederacy with slavery. Members of the Confederate Congress considered and proposed westward expansion, and it was an open Southern "secret" that Cuba formed a tempting target for

Southern expansion for the purpose of protecting their "domestic institutions," the polite euphemism for slavery as a form of race relations. But this Confederate public policy proved to be but a paper tiger; no such Confederate territory of Arizona ever emerged and breathed political life. Thus, this Confederate statute changed nothing, had no effect, and it is not included. Should a later supplement to this volume be appropriate, then such a document might be included; for now, this collection limits itself to those policies and statements that actually made a difference at the time, resonated among the people, and created public policy ripples through United States politically, constitutionally, and culturally.

Several groups of readers will find this work useful. It complements and expands upon every public and private college and university and law school library's collection of nineteenth-century United States history and law. Specialists on the middle period of the nineteenth century will consult this work to support their ongoing research projects. Scholars in United States history, legal and constitutional historians, law professors, and political science and public policy programs at the college and university levels will be interested in this collection for access to primary sources. It can serve as a reference work and a document book to support either an undergraduate course in colleges or universities or graduate seminars in the era of the Civil War and Reconstruction. These volumes differ from other collections of documents because it focuses only on public policy and judicial issues. Further, for a group of nonspecialist readers that can be called better-than-the-usual–Civil War/Reconstruction "buffs" as well as members of the numerous Civil War roundtables that exist across the country (and even Europe), these volumes will be useful because they include difficult to locate primary sources on public policy. These nonprofessional historians do creative work and possess a serious interest in the field larger than the old-fashioned "drum and trumpet" military history too often solely associated with the Civil War. Thus, all of these different groups will find material here that will challenge and enrich their work and understanding of the period.

V

Editing of the documents has been as minimal and as unobtrusive as possible. Nevertheless, one issue arose from the decision to include the full text of the selected documents. Historians and other scholars understand that acceptable spelling has varied over time; but, spelling variations may surprise contemporary readers and students. For example, in the nineteenth century, "defence" constituted acceptable spelling of the modern "defense." Other examples include "unfrequent" and "infrequent"; "practise," and "practice"; and, "intrusted," and "entrusted." As a result, I have left the original spelling in place, only occasionally employing the editors' notation of "[sic]" when needed to indicate that the irregular spelling is in the original document.

Notes

1. Oliver Wendell Holmes Jr., *The Common Law* (Boston: Little, Brown, 1881), 1-2.

2. See David Lowenthal, *The Past is a Foreign Country* (New York: Cambridge University Press, 1985).

3. See Orville Vernon Burton, *The Age of Lincoln* (New York: Hill & Wang, 2007).

4. *Journal of the Congress of the Confederate States of America, 1861-1865* (Washington, D.C.: Government Printing Office, 1904-1905), vol. 1: 475, 551, 612-20, 635, 660-91.

VOICES OF THE JUDICIARY
1857–1866

INTRODUCTION

Readers should not feel surprise in finding a section on how the federal and state courts responded to the events and issues that arose before, during, and after the era of the Civil War and Reconstruction. One of the rules of thumb in United States history is that in one form or another, all significant issues in public policy history end up being challenged and analyzed in and before the courts, especially the federal courts. In fact, the federal judiciary had the last word on the great issues of the Civil War and on the constitutionality of Reconstruction and the composition and permanence of the nation. Federal legislators and judges set the parameters and standards for defining citizenship and struggled with the difficult issues of black rights and liberties in light of the Thirteenth, Fourteenth, and Fifteenth Amendments and the 1866 and 1875 Civil Rights Acts. But the story of "Voices of the Judiciary" is less straightforward than it might appear. No one in the United States, much less the justices of the Supreme Court or any of the lower federal and state courts, had any experience reconstructing loyal state governments or knew how to go about recognizing and enforcing national "rights" for racial minorities as they lived their lives in their localities and their states. Thus, it is not surprising that the justices made the decisions that they did, or that Reconstruction did not achieve its full potential even by the standards of that era; rather, what may be surprising is just how much changed, altered, adapted, and accommodated in United States law and society.

Not only does this section contain one of the most infamous decisions handed down by the United States Supreme Court, *Dred Scott v. Sandford* (1857), but it also contains one of the most important decisions, *The Slaughter-House Cases* (1873). This section also includes cases that ought to be better known, such as *Texas v. White* (1869), which raised to constitutional principle President Abraham Lincoln's understanding of the fundamental nature of the nation, "an indestructible Union of indestructible states." Further, this section contains decisions on "hard" issues such as internal security and the breadth and possible limits of the president's war powers in crisis time: *Ex parte Merryman* (1861) and *Ex parte Milligan* (1866). Reconstruction issues abound, from a federal circuit court opinion regarding the meaning of the Thirteenth Amendment to the rise of the "state action doctrine" that limited federal oversight of "rights" of all Americans and left the remedy for any rights violations with the states and majority populations within their localities. This traditional location for enforcing rights at the local level proved problematic for the African American population as they struggled to exercise civil and political rights in the face of hostile white majorities. Indicating the hurdles they faced, the leading case law on the common law of common commerce (the transportation cases from *West Chester and Philadelphia Railroad Co. v. Miles* [1867] to the federal cases of *Hall v. DeCuir* [1878] to *Plessy v. Ferguson* [1896]) are also included here. This case law suggests that the ripples from the judicial public policy decisions reverberated long after the Civil War ended. These judicial voices of the Civil War constitute a too often overlooked aspect of the important public policy decisions of the era of the Civil War and Reconstruction.

DRED SCOTT, PLAINTIFF IN ERROR, v. JOHN F. A. SANDFORD

Supreme Court of the United States
March 6–7, 1857
19 Howard (60 U.S.) 393 (1857)

> One of the most famous and infamous decisions in all United States Supreme Court history, *Dred Scott v. Sandford* forms one of the turning points in the crisis of the 1850s. In what began as a routine freedom suit by a slave in Missouri, *Dred Scott* became a vehicle for Chief Justice Roger B. Taney to declare the Missouri Compromise of 1820 unconstitutional, to declare that all blacks—free and slave—had no rights that whites were bound to respect, and that the federal government could not act to limit the expansion of slavery but had to act positively in protecting a person's right to take their property in persons into the federal territories. In this difficult 7–2 decision, Taney wrote the "Opinion of the Court," but all nine justices filed their own individual decisions; the most separate decisions in a United States Supreme Court ruling to that point in United States history. What was clear when all the decisions were read and considered was that Dred Scott was still a slave, and instead of taking the slavery issue *out* of the national political debate, this decision and especially Taney's "Opinion of the Court" *itself* became part of the debate. Much of the famous 1858 Abraham Lincoln/Stephen Douglas Illinois Senate debates dealt with the issues raised in *Dred Scott* and fears of a second *Dred Scott* decision, one where the Supreme Court might decide that free states could not prevent slavery on their soil, sharpened in light of this decision. Overcoming *Dred Scott* proved not an easy task. In June 1862, Congress prohibited slavery in the federal territories. The Thirteenth Amendment (1865) abolished slavery, and the Civil Rights Act of 1866 began the process of enunciating what rights free persons possessed, which Congress constitutionalized in the Fourteenth Amendment (1868). But the use of racial

categories to craft public policies continues and constitutes part of the enduring legacy of *Dred Scott v. Sandford*.

Pleading—Status of the Negro—Citizenship—Missouri Compromise Unconstitutional—
Rights of Slave Owners under the Constitution

1. A plea of abatement, as to the citizenship of the plaintiff below and plaintiff here, was ruled bad on demurrer in the circuit court: Held, that this court can revise and reverse the case on that ground, though the decision was in favor of plaintiff in error, who does not complain of it, and the defendant had pleaded over to the merits.
2. This question, on the ground of the limited jurisdiction of the circuit court, is always a subject of inquiry in this court, where the record shows the want of it.
3. Persons whose ancestors were negroes of the African race, imported into this country and held as slaves, cannot, though they be emancipated, or born of parents who were free at their birth, become citizens of a State, in sense in which that word is used in the constitution of the United States.
4. Therefore such persons cannot, though free, sustain a suit in the circuit courts of the United States, on the ground of being citizens of a State different from the adverse party.
5. The clause of the constitution, which confers on congress the power to dispose of and make all needful rules and regulations respecting the territory or other property of the United States, is confined to the territory which at that time belonged to or was claimed by the United States, and can have no influence on territory afterwards acquired from a foreign government.
6. The constitution confers no express power to acquire new territory to be governed as colonies or as territories, but it confers a power to admit new States into the Union, and, under this power, territory may be acquired which is intended to be admitted as new States, and which from the necessity of the case, may be governed by congress until fitted to be so admitted.
7. But congress holds this territory in trust for the benefit of the people of the United States, and is limited in its exercise of legislative power in such territory, by all the restrictions which the constitution has imposed upon that body, in regard to the rights of persons and property generally.
8. It follows that congress cannot, by an attempt at legislation, deprive a person of his property in such territory without due process of law or without compensation; and in this regard the right of property in slaves is as much protected by the constitution as other property.
9. Therefore the act of congress of 1821, prohibiting slavery in the territory ceded by France, north of thirty-six degrees thirty minutes north latitude, is unconstitutional and void.

10. The plaintiff in this case did not acquire freedom by being carried into that territory by his owner voluntarily.
11. Nor did a similar residence in the State of Illinois, where slavery was forbidden by law, discharge him from slavery after his return to Missouri, the law of this latter State on that subject being conclusive of his status as to freedom or slavery.

This was a writ of error to the circuit court for the district of Missouri.

The pleadings and facts are fully stated in the opinion of the court and in several opinions of the justices.

It was argued at the proceeding term, and was then ordered for reargument at the present term.

It was now argued by *Mr. Blair* and *Mr. G. F. Curtis*, for the plaintiff in error, and by *Mr. Geyer* and *Mr. Reverdy Johnson*, for the defendant.

Mr. Chief Justice TANEY delivered
the opinion of the court.

This case has been twice argued. After the argument at the last term, differences of opinion were found to exist among the members of the court; and as the questions in controversy are of the highest importance, and the court was at that time much pressed by the ordinary business of the term, it was deemed advisable to continue the case, and direct a reargument on some of the points, in order that we might have an opportunity of giving to the whole subject a more deliberate consideration. It has accordingly been again argued by counsel, and considered by the court; and I now proceed to deliver its opinion.

There are two leading questions presented by the record:
1. Had the circuit court of the United States jurisdiction to hear and determine the case between these parties? And
2. If it had jurisdiction, is the judgment it has given erroneous or not?

The plaintiff in error, who was also the plaintiff in the court below, was, with his wife and children, held as slaves by the defendant, in the State of Missouri; and he brought this action in the circuit court of the United States for that district, to assert the title of himself and his family to freedom.

The declaration is in the form usually adopted in that State to try questions of this description, and contains the averment necessary to give the court jurisdiction; that he and the defendant are citizens of different States; that is, that he is a citizen of Missouri, and the defendant a citizen of New York.

The defendant pleaded in abatement to the jurisdiction of the court, that the plaintiff was not a citizen of the State of Missouri, as alleged in his declaration, being a negro of African descent, whose ancestors were of pure African blood, and who were brought into this country and sold as slaves.

To this plea the plaintiff demurred, and the defendant joined in demurrer. The court overruled the plea, and gave judgment that the defendant should answer over. And he thereupon put in sundry pleas in bar, upon which issues were joined; and at the trial the verdict and judgment were in his favor. Whereupon the plaintiff brought this writ of error.

Before we speak of the pleas in bar, it will be proper to dispose of the questions which have arisen on the plea in abatement.

That plea denies the right of the plaintiff to sue in a court of the United States, for the reasons therein stated.

If the question raised by it is legally before us, and the court should be of opinion that the facts stated in it disqualify the plaintiff from becoming a citizen, in the sense in which that word is used in the constitution of the United States, then the judgment of the circuit court is erroneous, and must be reversed.

It is suggested, however, that this plea is not before us; and that as the judgment in the court below on this plea was in favor of the plaintiff, he does not seek to reverse it, or bring it before the court for revision by his writ of error; and also that the defendant waived this defence by pleading over, and thereby admitted the jurisdiction of the court.

But, in making this objection, we think the peculiar and limited jurisdiction of courts of the United States has not been adverted to. This peculiar and limited jurisdiction has made it necessary, in these courts, to adopt different rules and principles of pleading, so far as jurisdiction is concerned, from those which regulate courts of common law in England, and in the different States of the Union which have adopted the common-law rules.

In these last-mentioned courts, where their character and rank are analogous to that of a circuit court of the United States; in other words, where they are what the law terms courts of general jurisdiction; they are presumed to have jurisdiction, unless the contrary appears. No averment in the pleadings of the plaintiff is necessary, in order to give jurisdiction. If the defendant objects to it, he must plead it specially, and unless the fact on which he relies is found to be true by a jury, or admitted to be true by the plaintiff, the jurisdiction cannot be disputed in an appellate court.

Now, it is not necessary to inquire whether in courts of that description a party who pleads over in bar, when a plea to the jurisdiction has been ruled against him, does or does not waive his plea; nor whether upon a judgment in his favor on the pleas in bar, and a writ of error brought by the plaintiff, the question upon the plea in abatement would be open for revision in the appellate court. Cases that may have been decided in such courts, or rules that may have been laid down by common-law pleaders, can have no influence in the decision in this court. Because, under the constitution and laws of the United States, the rules which govern the pleadings in its courts, in questions of jurisdiction, stand on different principles and are regulated by different laws.

This difference arises, as we have said, from the peculiar character of the government of the United States. For although it is sovereign and supreme in its appropriate sphere of action, yet it does not possess all the powers which usually belong to the sovereignty of a nation. Certain specified powers, enumerated in the constitution, have been conferred upon it; and neither the legislative, executive, nor judicial departments of the government can lawfully exercise any authority beyond the limits marked out by the constitution. And in regulating the judicial department, the cases in which the courts of the United States shall have jurisdiction are particularly and specifically enumerated and defined; and they are not authorized to take cognizance of any case which does not come within the description therein specified. Hence, when a plaintiff sues in a court of the United States, it is necessary that he should show, in his pleading, that the suit he brings is within the jurisdiction of the court, and that he is entitled to sue there. And if he omits to do this, and should, by any oversight of the circuit court, obtain a judgment in his favor, the judgment would be reversed in the appellate court for want of jurisdiction in the court below. The jurisdiction would not be presumed, as in the case of a common-law English or State court, unless the contrary appeared. But the record, when it comes before the appellate court, must show, affirmatively, that the inferior court had authority, under the constitution, to hear and determine the case. And if the plaintiff claims a right to sue in a circuit court of the United States, under that provision of the constitution which gives jurisdiction in controversies between citizens of different States, he must distinctly aver in his pleading that they are citizens of different States; and he cannot maintain his suit without showing that fact in the pleadings.

This point was decided in the case of Bingham *v.* Cabot, (in 3 Dall., 382,) and ever since adhered to by the court. And in Jackson *v.* Ashton, (8 Pet., 148,) it was held that the objection to which it was open could not be waived by the opposite party, because consent of parties could not give jurisdiction.

It is needless to accumulate cases on this subject. Those already referred to, and the cases of Capron *v.* Van Noorden, (in 2 Cr., 126,) and Montalet *v.* Murray, (4 Cr., 46,) are sufficient to show the rule of which we have spoken. The case of Capron *v.* Van Noorden strikingly illustrates the difference between a common-law court and a court of the United States.

If, however, the fact of citizenship is averred in the declaration, and the defendant does not deny it, and put it in issue by plea in abatement, he cannot offer evidence at the trial to disprove it, and consequently cannot avail himself of the objection in the appellate court, unless the defect should be apparent in some other part of the record. For if there is no plea in abatement, and the want of jurisdiction does not appear in any other part of the transcript brought up by the writ of error, the undisputed averment of citizenship in the declaration must be taken in this court to be true. In this case, the citizenship is averred, but it is denied by the defendant in the manner required by the rules of pleading, and the fact upon which the denial is based is admitted by the demurrer. And, if the plea and demurrer, and judgment of the court below upon it, are before us upon this record, the question to be decided is, whether the facts stated in the plea are sufficient to show that the plaintiff is not entitled to sue as a citizen in a court of the United States.

We think they are before us. The plea in abatement and the judgment of the court upon it, are a part of the judicial proceedings in the circuit court, and are there recorded as such; and a writ of error always brings up to the superior court the whole record of the proceedings in the court below. And in the case of the United States *v.* Smith, (11 Wheat., 172,) this court said, that the case being brought up by writ of error, the whole record was under the consideration of this court. And this being the case in the present instance, the plea in abatement is necessarily under consideration; and it becomes, therefore, our duty to decide whether the facts stated in the plea are or are not sufficient to show that the plaintiff is not entitled to sue as a citizen in a court of the United States.

This is certainly a very serious question, and one that now for the first time has been brought for decision before this court. But it is brought here by those who have a right to bring it, and it is our duty to meet it and decide it.

The question is simply this: Can a negro, whose ancestors were imported into this country, and sold as slaves, become a member of the political community formed and brought into existence by the constitution of the United States, and as such become entitled to all the rights, and privileges, and immunities, guarantied by that instrument to the citizen? One of which rights is the privilege of suing in a court of the United States in the cases specified in the constitution.

It will be observed, that the plea applies to that class of persons only whose ancestors were negroes of the African race, and imported into this country, and sold and held as slaves. The only matter in issue before the court, therefore, is, whether the descendants of such slaves, when they shall be emancipated, or who are born of parents who had become free before their birth, are citizens of a State, in the sense in which the word citizen is used in the constitution of the United States. And this being the only matter in dispute on the pleadings, the court must be understood as speaking in this opinion of that class only, that is, of those persons who are the descendants of Africans who were imported into this country, and sold as slaves.

The situation of this population was altogether unlike that of the Indian race. The latter, it is true, formed no part of the colonial communities, and never amalgamated with them in social connections or in government. But although they were uncivilized, they were yet a free and independent people, associated together in nations or tribes, and governed by their own laws. Many of these political communities were situated in territories to which the white race claimed the ultimate right of dominion. But that claim was acknowledged to be subject to the right of the Indians to occupy it as long as they thought proper, and neither the English nor colonial governments claimed or exercised any dominion over the tribe or nation by whom it was occupied, nor claimed the right to the possession of the territory, until the tribe or nation consented to cede it. These Indian governments were regarded and treated as foreign governments, as much so as if an ocean had separated the red man from the white; and their freedom has constantly been acknowledged, from the time of the first emigration to the English colonies to the present day, by the different governments which succeeded each other. Treaties have been negotiated with them, and their alliance sought for in war; and the people who compose these Indian political communities have always been treated as foreigners not living under our government. It is true that the course of events has brought the Indian tribes within the limits of the United States under subjection to the white race; and it has been found necessary, for their sake as well as our own, to regard them as in a state of pupilage, and to legislate to a certain extent over them and the territory they occupy. But they may, without doubt, like the subjects of any other foreign government, be naturalized by the authority of congress, and become citizens of a State, and of the United States; and if an individual should leave his nation or tribe, and take up his abode among the white population, he would be entitled to all the rights and privileges which would belong to an emigrant from any other foreign people.

We proceed to examine the case as presented by the pleadings.

The words "people of the United States" and "citizens" are synonymous terms, and mean the same thing. They both describe the political body who, according to our republican institutions, form the sovereignty, and who hold the power and conduct the government through their representatives. They are what we familiarly call the "sovereign people," and every citizen is one of this people, and a constituent member of this sovereignty. The question before us is, whether the class of persons described in the plea in abatement compose a portion of this people, and are constituent members of this sovereignty? We think they are not, and that they are not included, and were not intended to be included, under the word "citizens" in the constitution, and can therefore claim none of the rights and privileges which that instrument provides for and secures to citizens of the United States. On the contrary, they were at that time considered as a subordinate and inferior class of beings, who had been subjugated by the dominant race, and, whether emancipated or not, yet remained subject to their authority, and had no rights or privileges but such as those who held the power and the government might choose to grant them.

It is not the province of the court to decide upon the justice or injustice, the policy or impolicy, of these laws. The decision of that question belonged to the political or law-making power; to those who formed the sovereignty and framed the constitution. The duty of the court is, to interpret the instrument they have framed, with the best lights we can obtain on the subject, and to administer it as we find it, according to its true intent and meaning when it was adopted.

In discussing this question, we must not confound the rights of citizenship which a State may confer within its own limits, and the rights of citizenship as a member of the Union. It does not by any means follow, because he has all the rights and privileges of a citizen of a State, that he must be a citizen of the United States. He may have all of the rights and privileges of the citizen of a State, and yet not be entitled to the rights and privileges of a citizen in any other State. For, previous to the adoption of the constitution of the United States, every State had the undoubted right to confer on whomsoever it pleased the character of citizen, and to endow him with all its rights. But this character of course was confined to the boundaries of the State, and gave him no rights or privileges in other States beyond those secured to him by the laws of nations and the comity of States. Nor have the several States surrendered the power of conferring these rights and privileges by adopting the constitution of the United States. Each State may still confer them upon an alien, or any one it thinks proper, or upon any class or description of persons; yet he would not be a citizen in the sense in which that word is used in the constitution of the United States, nor entitled to sue as such in one of its courts, nor to the privileges and immunities of a citizen in the other States. The rights which he would acquire would be restricted to the State which gave them. The constitution has conferred on congress the right to establish an uniform rule of naturalization, and this right is evidently exclusive, and has always been held by this court to be so. Consequently, no State, since the adoption of the constitution, can by naturalizing an alien invest him with the rights and privileges secured to a citizen of a State under the federal government, although, so far as the State alone was concerned, he would undoubtedly be entitled to the rights of a citizen, and clothed with all the rights and immunities which the constitution and laws of the State attached to that character.

It is very clear, therefore, that no State can, by any act or law of its own, passed since the adoption of the constitution, introduce a new member into the political community created by the constitution of the United States. It cannot make him a member of this community by making him a member of its own. And for the same reason it cannot introduce any person, or description of persons, who were not intended to be embraced in this new political family, which the constitution brought into existence, but were intended to be excluded from it.

The question then arises, whether the provisions of the constitution, in relation to the personal rights and privileges to which the citizen of a State should be entitled, embraced the negro African race, at that time in this country, or who might afterwards be imported, who had then or should afterwards be made free in any State; and to put it in the power of a single State to make him a citizen of the United States, and endue him with the full rights of citizenship in every other State without their consent? Does the constitution of the United States act upon him whenever he shall be made free under the laws of a State, and raised there to the rank of a citizen, and immediately clothe him with all the privileges of a citizen in every other State, and in its own courts?

The court think the affirmative of these propositions cannot be maintained. And if it cannot, the plaintiff in error could not be a citizen of the State of Missouri, within the meaning of the constitution of the United States, and, consequently, was not entitled to sue in its courts.

It is true, every person, and every class and description of persons, who were at the time of the adoption of the constitution recognized as citizens in the several States, became also citizens of this new political body; but none other; it was formed by them, and for them and their posterity, but for no one else. And the personal rights and privileges guaranteed to citizens of this new sovereignty were intended to embrace those only who were then members of the several State communities, or who should afterwards by birthright or otherwise become members, according to the provisions of the constitution and the principles on which it was founded. It was the union of those who were at that time members of distinct and separate political communities into one political family, whose power, for certain specified purposes, was to extend over the whole territory of the United States. And it gave to each citizen rights and privileges outside of his State which he did not before possess, and placed him in every other State upon a perfect equality with its own citizens as to rights of person and rights of property; it made him a citizen of the United States.

It becomes necessary, therefore, to determine who were citizens of the several States when the constitution was adopted. And in order to do this, we must recur to the governments and institutions of the thirteen colonies, when they separated from Great Britain and formed new sovereignties, and took their places in the family of independent nations. We must inquire who, at that time, were recognized as the people or citizens of a State, whose rights and liberties had been outraged by the English government; and who declared their independence, and assumed the powers of government to defend their rights by force of arms.

In the opinion of the court, the legislation and histories of the times, and the language used in the declaration of independence, show, that neither the class of persons who had been imported as slaves, nor their descendants, whether they had become free or not, were then acknowledged as a part of the people, nor intended to be included in the general words used in that memorable instrument.

It is difficult at this day to realize the state of public opinion in relation to that unfortunate race, which prevailed in the civilized and enlightened portions of the world at the time of the declaration of independence, and when the constitution of the United States was framed and adopted. But the public history of every European nation displays it in a manner too plain to be mistaken.

They had for more than a century before been regarded as beings of an inferior order, and altogether unfit to associate with the white race, either in social or political relations; and so far inferior, that they had no rights which the white man was bound to respect; and that the negro might justly and lawfully be reduced to slavery for his benefit. He was bought and sold, and treated as an ordinary article of merchandise and traffic, whenever a profit could be made by it. This opinion was at that time fixed and universal in the civilized portion of the white race. It was regarded as an axiom in morals as well as in politics, which no one thought of disputing, or supposed to be open to dispute; and men in every grade and position in society daily and habitually acted upon it in their private pursuits, as well as in matters of public concern, without doubting for a moment the correctness of this opinion.

And in no nation was this opinion more firmly fixed or more uniformly acted upon than by the English government and English people. They not only seized them on the coast of Africa, and sold them or held them in slavery for their own use; but they took them as ordinary articles of merchandise to every country where they could make a profit on them, and were far more extensively engaged in this commerce than any other nation in the world.

The opinion thus entertained and acted upon in England was naturally impressed upon the colonies they founded on this side of the Atlantic. And, accordingly, a negro of the African race was regarded by them as an article of property, and held, and bought and sold as such, in every one of the thirteen colonies which united in the declaration of independence, and afterwards formed the constitution of the United States. The slaves were more or less numerous in the different colonies, as slave labor was found more or less profitable. But no one seems to have doubted the correctness of the prevailing opinion of the time.

The legislation of the different colonies furnishes positive and indisputable proof of this fact.

It would be tedious, in this opinion, to enumerate the various laws they passed upon this subject. It will be sufficient, as a sample of the legislation which then generally prevailed throughout the British colonies, to give the laws of two of them; one being still a large slaveholding State, and the other the first State in which slavery ceased to exist.

The province of Maryland, in 1717, (ch. 13, s. 5,) passed a law declaring "that if any free negro or mulatto intermarry with any white woman, or if any white man shall intermarry with any negro or mulatto woman, such negro or mulatto shall become a slave during life, excepting mulattoes born of white women, who, for such intermarriage, shall only become servants for seven years, to be disposed of as the justices of the county court, where such marriage so happens, shall think fit; to be applied by them towards the support of a public school within the said county. And any white man or white woman who shall intermarry as aforesaid, with any negro or mulatto, such white man or white woman shall become servants during the term of seven years, and shall be disposed of by the justices as aforesaid, and be applied to the uses aforesaid."

The other colonial law to which we refer was passed by Massachusetts in 1705, (chap. 6.) It is entitled "An act for the better preventing of a spurious and mixed issue," &c.; and it provides, that "if any negro or mulatto shall presume to smite or strike any person of the English or other Christian nation, such negro or mulatto shall be severely whipped, at the discretion of the justices before whom the offender shall be convicted."

And "that none of her Majesty's English or Scottish subjects, nor of any other Christian nation, within this province, shall contract matrimony with any negro or mulatto; nor shall any person, duly authorized to solemnize marriage, presume to join any such in marriage, on pain of forfeiting the sum of fifty pounds; one moiety thereof to her Majesty, for and towards the support of the government within this province, and the other moiety to him or them that shall inform and sue for the same, in any of her Majesty's courts of record within the province, by bill, plaint, or information."

We give both of these laws in the words used by the respective legislative bodies, because the language in which they are framed, as well as the provisions contained in them, show, too plainly to be misunderstood, the degraded condition of this unhappy race. They were still in force when the revolution began, and are a faithful index to the state of feeling towards the class of persons of whom they speak, and of the position they occupied throughout the thirteen colonies, in the eyes and thoughts of the men who framed the declaration of independence and established the State constitutions and governments. They show that a perpetual and impassable barrier was intended to be erected between the white race and the one which they had reduced to slavery, and governed as subjects with absolute and despotic power, and which they then looked upon as so far below them in the scale of created beings, that intermarriages between white persons and negroes or mulattoes were regarded as unnatural and immoral, and punished as crimes, not only in the parties, but in the person who joined them in marriage. And no distinction in this respect was made between the free negro or mulatto and the slave, but this stigma, of the deepest degradation, was fixed upon the whole race.

We refer to these historical facts for the purpose of showing the fixed opinions concerning that race, upon which the statesmen of that day spoke and acted. It is necessary to do this, in order to determine whether the general terms used in the constitution of the United States, as to the rights of man and the rights of the people, was intended to include them, or to give to them or their posterity the benefit of any of its provisions.

The language of the declaration of independence is equally conclusive:

It begins by declaring that, "when in the course of human events it becomes necessary for one people to dissolve the political bands which have connected them with another, and to assume among the powers of the earth the separate and equal station to which the laws of nature and nature's God entitle them, a decent respect for the opinions of mankind requires that they should declare the causes which impel them to the separation."

It then proceeds to say: "We hold these truths to be self-evident: that all men are created equal; that they are endowed by their Creator with certain unalienable rights; that among them is life, liberty, and the pursuit of happiness; that to secure these rights, governments are instituted, deriving their just powers from the consent of the governed."

The general words above quoted would seem to embrace the whole human family, and if they were used in a similar instrument at this day would be so understood. But it is too clear for dispute, that the enslaved African race were not intended to be included, and formed no part of the people who framed and adopted this declaration; for if the language, as understood in that day, would embrace them, the conduct of the distinguished men who framed the declaration of independence would have been utterly and flagrantly inconsistent with the principles they asserted; and instead of the sympathy of mankind, to which they so confidently appealed, they would have deserved and received universal rebuke and reprobation.

Yet the men who framed this declaration were great men—high in literary acquirements—high in their sense of honor, and incapable of asserting principles inconsistent with those on which they were acting. They perfectly understood the meaning of the language they used, and how it would be understood by others; and they knew that it would not in any part of the civilized world be supposed to embrace the negro race, which, by common consent, had been excluded from civilized governments and the family of nations, and doomed to slavery. They spoke and acted according to the then established doctrines and principles, and in the ordinary language of the day, and no one misunderstood them. The unhappy black race were separated from the white by indelible marks, and laws long before established, and were never thought of or spoken of except as property, and when the claims of the owner or the profit of the trader were supposed to need protection.

This state of public opinion had undergone no change when the constitution was adopted, as is equally evident from its provisions and language.

The brief preamble sets forth by whom it was formed, for what purposes, and for whose benefit and protection. It declares that it is formed by the *people* of the United States; that is to say, by those who were members of the different political communities in the several States; and its great object is declared to be to secure the blessings of liberty to themselves and their posterity. It speaks in general terms of the *people* of the United States, and of *citizens* of the several States, when it is providing for the exercise of the powers granted or the privileges secured to the citizen. It does not define what description of persons are intended to be included under these terms, or who shall be regarded as a citizen and one of the people. It uses them as terms so well understood, that no further description or definition was necessary.

But there are two clauses in the constitution which point directly and specifically to the negro race as a separate class of persons, and show clearly that they were not regarded as a portion of the people or citizens of the government then formed.

One of these clauses reserves to each of the thirteen States the right to import slaves until the year 1808, if it thinks proper. And the importation which it thus sanctions was unquestionably of persons of the race of which we are speaking, as the traffic in slaves in the United States had always been confined to them. And by the other provision the States pledge themselves to each other to maintain the right of property of the master, by delivering up to him any slave who may have escaped from his service, and be found within their respective territories. By the first above-mentioned clause, therefore, the right to purchase and hold this property is directly sanctioned and authorized for twenty years by the people who framed the constitution. And by the second, they pledge themselves to maintain and uphold the right of the master in the manner specified, as long as the government they then formed should endure. And these two provisions show, conclusively, that neither the description of persons therein referred to, nor their descendants, were embraced in any of the other provisions of the constitution; for certainly these two clauses were not intended to confer on them or their posterity the blessings of liberty, or any of the personal rights so carefully provided for the citizen.

No one of that race had ever migrated to the United States voluntarily; all of them had been brought here as articles of merchandise. The number that had been emancipated at that time were but few in comparison with those held in slavery; and they were identified in the public mind with the race to which they belonged, and regarded as a part of the slave population rather than the free. It is obvious that they were not even in the minds of the framers of the constitution when they were conferring special rights and privileges upon the citizens of a State in every other part of the Union.

Indeed, when we look to the condition of this race in the several States at the time, it is impossible to believe that these rights and privileges were intended to be extended to them.

It is very true, that in that portion of the Union where the labor of the negro race was found to be unsuited to the climate and unprofitable to the master, but few slaves were held at the time of the declaration of independence; and when the constitution was adopted, it had entirely worn out in one of them, and measures had been taken for its gradual abolition in several others. But this change had not been produced by any change of opinion in relation to this race; but because it was discovered, from experience, that slave labor was unsuited to the climate and productions of these States: for some of the States, where it had ceased or nearly ceased to exist, were actively engaged in the slave trade, procuring cargoes on the coast of Africa, and transporting them for sale to those parts of the Union where their labor was found to be profitable, and suited to the climate and productions. And this traffic was openly carried on, and fortunes accumulated by it, without reproach from the people of the States where they resided. And it can hardly be supposed that, in the States where it was then countenanced in its worst form—that is, in the seizure and transportation—the people could have regarded those who were emancipated as entitled to equal rights with themselves.

And we may here again refer, in support of this proposition, to the plain and unequivocal language of the laws of the several States, some passed after the declaration of independence and before the constitution was adopted, and some since the government went into operation.

We need not refer, on this point, particularly to the laws of the present slaveholding States. Their statute books are full of provisions in relation to this class, in the same spirit with the Maryland law which we have before quoted. They have continued to treat them as an inferior class, and to subject them to strict police regulations, drawing a broad line of distinction between the citizen and the slave races, and legislating in relation to them upon the same principle which prevailed at the time of the declaration of independence. As relates to these States, it is too plain for argument, that they have never been regarded as a part of the people or citizens of the State, nor supposed to possess any political rights which the dominant race might not withhold or grant at their pleasure. And as long ago as 1822, the court of appeals of Kentucky decided that free negroes and mulattoes were not citizens within the meaning of the constitution of the United States; and the correctness of this decision is recognized, and the same doctrine affirmed, in 1 Meigs's Tenn. Reports, 331.

And if we turn to the legislation of the States where slavery had worn out, or measures taken for its speedy abolition, we shall find the same opinions and principles equally fixed and equally acted upon.

Thus, Massachusetts, in 1786, passed a law similar to the colonial one of which we have spoken. The law of 1786, like the law of 1705, forbids the marriage of any white person with any negro, Indian, or mulatto, and inflicts a penalty of fifty pounds upon any one who shall join them in marriage; and declares all such marriage absolutely null and void, and degrades thus the unhappy issue of the marriage by fixing upon it the stain of bastardy. And this mark of degradation was renewed, and again impressed upon the race, in the careful and deliberate preparation of their revised code published in 1836. This code forbids any person from joining in marriage any white person with any Indian, negro, or mulatto, and subjects the party who shall offend in this respect, to imprisonment, not exceeding six months, in the common jail, or to hard labor, and to a fine of not less than fifty nor more than two hundred dollars; and, like the law of 1786, it declares the marriage to be absolutely null and void. It will be seen that the punishment is increased by the code upon the person who shall marry them, by adding imprisonment to a pecuniary penalty.

So, too, in Connecticut. We refer more particularly to the legislation of this State, because it was not only among the first to put an end to slavery within its own territory, but was the first to fix a mark of reprobation upon the African slave trade. The law last mentioned was passed in October, 1788, about nine months after the State had ratified and adopted the present constitution of the United States; and by that law it prohibited its own citizens, under severe penalties, from engaging in the trade, and declared all policies of insurance on the vessel or cargo made in the State to be null and void. But, up to the time of the adoption of the constitution, there is nothing in the legislation of the State indicating any change of opinion as to the relative rights and position of the white and black races in this country, or indicating that it meant to place the latter, when free, upon a level with its citizens. And certainly nothing which would have led the slaveholding States to suppose, that Connecticut designed to claim for them, under the new constitution, the equal rights and privileges and rank of citizens in every other State.

The first step taken by Connecticut upon this subject was as early as 1774, when it passed an act forbidding the further importation of slaves into the State. But the section containing the prohibition is introduced by the following preamble:

"And whereas the increase of slaves in this State is injurious to the poor, and inconvenient."

This recital would appear to have been carefully introduced, in order to prevent any misunderstanding of the motive which induced the legislature to pass the law, and places it distinctly upon the interest and convenience of the white population—excluding the inference that it might have been intended in any degree for the benefit of the other.

And in the act of 1784, by which the issue of slaves, born after the time therein mentioned, were to be free at a certain age, the section is again introduced by a preamble assigning a similar motive for the act. It is in these words:

"Whereas sound policy requires that the abolition of slavery should be effected as soon as may be consistent with the rights of individuals, and the public safety and welfare"—showing that the right of property in the master was to be protected, and that the measure was one of policy, and to prevent the injury and inconvenience, to the whites, of a slave population in the State.

And still further pursuing its legislation, we find that in the same statute passed in 1774, which prohibited the further importation of slaves into the State, there is also a provision by which any negro, Indian, or mulatto servant, who was found wandering out of the town or place to which he belonged, without a written pass such as is therein described, was made liable to be seized by any one, and taken before the next authority to be examined and delivered up to his master—who was required to pay the charge which had accrued thereby. And a subsequent section of the same law provides, that if any free negro shall travel without such pass, and shall be stopped, seized, or taken up, he shall pay all charges arising thereby. And this law was in full operation when the constitution of the United States was adopted, and was not repealed till 1797. So that up to that time free negroes and mulattoes were associated with servants and slaves in the police regulations established by the laws of the State.

And again, in 1833, Connecticut passed another law, which made it penal to set up or establish any school in that State for the instruction of persons of the

African race not inhabitants of the State, or to instruct or teach in any such school or institution, or board or harbor for that purpose, any such person, without the previous consent in writing of the civil authority of the town in which such school or institution might be.

And it appears by the case of Crandall *v.* The State, reported in 10 Conn. Rep., 340, that upon an information filed against Prudence Crandall for a violation of this law, one of the points raised in the defence was, that the law was a violation of the constitution of the United States; and that the persons instructed, although of the African race, were citizens of other States, and therefore entitled to the rights and privileges of citizens in the State of Connecticut. But Chief Justice Dagget, before whom the case was tried, held, that persons of that description were not citizens of a State, within the meaning of the word citizen in the constitution of the United States, and were not therefore entitled to the privileges and immunities of citizens in other States.

The case was carried up to the supreme court of errors of the State, and the question fully argued there. But the case went off upon another point, and no opinion was expressed on this question.

We have made this particular examination into the legislative and judicial action of Connecticut, because, from the early hostility it displayed to the slave trade on the coast of Africa, we may expect to find the laws of that State as lenient and favorable to the subject race as those of any other State in the Union; and if we find that at the time the constitution was adopted, they were not even there raised to the rank of citizens, but were still held and treated as property, and the laws relating to them passed with reference altogether to the interest and convenience of the white race, we shall hardly find them elevated to a higher rank anywhere else.

A brief notice of the laws of two other States, and we shall pass on to other considerations.

By the laws of New Hampshire, collected and finally passed in 1815, no one was permitted to be enrolled in the militia of the State, but free white citizens; and the same provision is found in a subsequent collection of the laws, made in 1855. Nothing could more strongly mark the entire repudiation of the African race. The alien is excluded, because, being born in a foreign country, he cannot be a member of the community until he is naturalized. But why are the African race, born in the State, not permitted to share in one of the highest duties of the citizen? The answer is obvious; he is not, by the institutions and laws of the State, numbered among its people. He forms no part of the sovereignty of the State, and is not therefore called on to uphold and defend it.

Again, in 1822, Rhode Island, in its revised code, passed a law forbidding persons who were authorized to join persons in marriage, from joining in marriage any white person with any negro, Indian, or mulatto, under the penalty of two hundred dollars, and declaring all such marriages absolutely null and void;

and the same law was again re-enacted in its revised code of 1844. So that, down to the last-mentioned period, the strongest mark of inferiority and degradation was fastened upon the African race in that State.

It would be impossible to enumerate and compress in the space usually allotted to an opinion of a court, the various laws, marking the condition of this race, which were passed from time to time after the revolution, and before and since the adoption of the constitution of the United States. In addition to those already referred to, it is sufficient to say, that Chancellor Kent, whose accuracy and research no one will question, states in the sixth edition of his Commentaries, (published in 1848, 2 vol., 258, note *b*,) that in no part of the country except Maine, did the African race, in point of fact, participate equally with the whites in the exercise of civil and political rights.

The legislation of the States therefore shows, in a manner not to be mistaken, the inferior and subject condition of that race at the time the constitution was adopted, and long afterwards, throughout the thirteen States by which that instrument was framed; and it is hardly consistent with the respect due to these States, to suppose that they regarded at that time, as fellow-citizens and members of the sovereignty, a class of beings whom they had thus stigmatized; whom, as we are bound, out of respect to the State sovereignties, to assume they had deemed it just and necessary thus to stigmatize, and upon whom they had impressed such deep and enduring marks of inferiority and degradation; or, that when they met in convention to form the constitution, they looked upon them as a portion of their constituents, or designed to include them in the provisions so carefully inserted for the security and protection of the liberties and rights of their citizens. It cannot be supposed that they intended to secure to them rights, and privileges, and rank, in the new political body throughout the Union, which every one of them denied within the limits of its own dominion. More especially, it cannot be believed that the large slaveholding States regarded them as included in the word citizens, or would have consented to a constitution which might compel them to receive them in that character from another State. For if they were so received, and entitled to the privileges and immunities of citizens, it would exempt them from the operation of the special laws and from the police regulations which they considered to be necessary for their own safety. It would give to persons of the negro race, who were recognized as citizens in any one State of the Union, the right to enter every other State whenever they pleased, singly or in companies, without pass or passport, and without obstruction, to sojourn there as long as they pleased, to go where they pleased at every hour of the day or night without molestation, unless they committed some violation of law for which a white man would be punished; and it would give them the full liberty of speech in public and in private upon all subjects upon which its own citizens might speak; to hold public meetings upon political affairs, and to keep and carry arms wherever they went. And all of this would be done in the face of the subject race of the same color, both free and slaves, and inevitably producing discontent and insubordination among them, and endangering the peace and safety of the State.

It is impossible, it would seem, to believe that the great men of the slaveholding States, who took so large a share in framing the constitution of the United States, and exercised so much influence in procuring its adoption, could have been so forgetful or regardless of their own safety and the safety of those who trusted and confided in them.

Besides, this want of foresight and care would have been utterly inconsistent with the caution displayed in providing for the admission of new members into this political family. For, when they gave to the citizens of each State the privileges and immunities of citizens in the several States, they at the same time took from the several States the power of naturalization, and confined that power exclusively to the federal government. No State was willing to permit another State to determine who should or should not be admitted as one of its citizens, and entitled to demand equal rights and privileges with their own people, within their own territories. The right of naturalization was therefore, with one accord, surrendered by the States, and confided to the federal government. And this power granted to congress to establish an uniform rule of *naturalization* is, by the well-understood meaning of the word, confined to persons born in a foreign country, under a foreign government. It is not a power to raise to the rank of a citizen any one born in the United States, who, from birth or parentage, by the laws of the country, belongs to an inferior and subordinate class. And when we find the States guarding themselves from the indiscreet or improper admission by other States of emigrants from other countries, by giving the power exclusively to congress, we cannot fail to see that they could never have left with the States a much more important power—that is, the power of transforming into citizens a numerous class of persons, who in that character would be much more dangerous to the peace and safety of a large portion of the Union, than the few foreigners one of the States might improperly naturalize. The constitution upon its adoption obviously took from the States all power by any subsequent legislation to introduce as a citizen into the political family of the United States any one, no matter where he was born, or what might be his character or condition; and it gave to congress the power to confer this character upon those only who were born outside of the dominions of the United States. And no law of a State, therefore, passed since the constitution was adopted, can give any right of citizenship outside of its own territory.

A clause similar to the one in the constitution, in relation to the rights and immunities of citizens of one State in the other States, was contained in the articles of confederation. But there is a difference of language, which is worthy of note. The provision in the articles of confederation was, "that the *free inhabitants* of each of the States, paupers, vagabonds, and fugitives from justice, excepted, should be entitled to all the privileges and immunities of free citizens in the several States."

It will be observed, that under this confederation, each State had the right to decide for itself, and in its own tribunals, whom it would acknowledge as a free inhabitant of another State. The term *free inhabitant*, in the generality of its terms, would certainly include one of the African race who had been manumitted. But no example, we think, can be found of his admission to all the privileges of citizenship in any State of the Union after these Articles were formed, and while they continued in force. And, notwithstanding the generality of the words "free inhabitants," it is very clear that, according to their accepted meaning in that day, they did not include the African race, whether free or not: for the fifth section of the ninth article provides that congress should have the power "to agree upon the number of land forces to be raised, and to make requisitions from each State for its quota in proportion to the number of *white* inhabitants in such State, which requisition should be binding."

Words could hardly have been used which more strongly mark the line of distinction between the citizen and the subject; the free and the subjugated races. The latter were not even counted when the inhabitants of a State were to be embodied in proportion to its numbers for the general defence. And it cannot for a moment be supposed, that a class of persons thus separated and rejected from those who formed the sovereignty of the States, were yet intended to be included under the words "free inhabitants," in the preceding article, to whom privileges and immunities were so carefully secured in every State.

But although this clause of the articles of confederation is the same in principle with that inserted in the constitution, yet the comprehensive word *inhabitant*, which might be construed to include an emancipated slave, is omitted; and the privilege is confined to *citizens* of the State. And this alteration in words would hardly have been made, unless a different meaning was intended to be conveyed, or a possible doubt removed. The just and fair inference is, that as this privilege was about to be placed under the protection of the general government, and the words expounded by its tribunals, and all power in relation to it taken from the State and its courts, it was deemed prudent to describe with precision and caution the persons to whom this high privilege was given—and the word *citizen* was on that account substituted for the words *free inhabitant*. The word citizen excluded, and no doubt intended to exclude, foreigners who had not become citizens of some one of the States when the constitution was adopted; and also every description of persons who were not fully recognized as citizens in the several States. This, upon any fair construction of the instruments to which we have referred, was evidently the object and purpose of this change of words.

To all this mass of proof we have still to add, that congress has repeatedly legislated upon the same construction of the constitution that we have given. Three laws, two of which were passed almost immediately after the government went into operation, will be abundantly sufficient to show this. The two first are particularly worthy of notice, because many of the men who assisted in framing the constitution, and took an active part in procuring its adoption, were then in the halls of legislation, and certainly understood what they meant when they used the words "people of the United States" and "citizen" in that well-considered instrument.

The first of these acts is the naturalization law, which was passed at the second session of the first congress, March 26, 1790, and confines the right of becoming citizens *"to aliens being free white persons."*

Now, the constitution does not limit the power of congress in this respect to white persons. And they may, if they think proper, authorize the naturalization of any one, of any color, who was born under allegiance to another government. But the language of the law above quoted, shows that citizenship at that time was perfectly understood to be confined to the white race; and that they alone constituted the sovereignty in the government.

Congress might, as we before said, have authorized the naturalization of Indians, because they were aliens and foreigners. But, in their then untutored and savage state, no one would have thought of admitting them as citizens in a civilized community. And, moreover, the atrocities they had but recently committed, when they were the allies of Great Britain in the Revolutionary war, were yet fresh in the recollection of the people of the United States, and they were even then guarding themselves against the threatened renewal of Indian hostilities. No one supposed then that any Indian would ask for, or was capable of enjoying, the privileges of an American citizen, and the word white was not used with any particular reference to them.

Neither was it used with any reference to the African race imported into or born in this country; because congress had no power to naturalize them, and therefore there was no necessity for using particular words to exclude them.

It would seem to have been used merely because it followed out the line of division which the constitution has drawn between the citizen race, who formed and held the government, and the African race, which they held in subjection and slavery, and governed at their own pleasure.

Another of the early laws of which we have spoken, is the first militia law, which was passed in 1792, at the first session of the second congress. The language of this law is equally plain and significant with the one just mentioned. It directs that every "free able-bodied white male citizen" shall be enrolled in the militia. The word *white* is evidently used to exclude the African race, and the word "citizen" to exclude unnaturalized foreigners; the latter forming no part of the sovereignty, owing it no allegiance, and therefore under no obligation to defend it. The African race, however, born in the country, did owe allegiance to the government, whether they were slave or free; but it is repudiated, and rejected from the duties and obligations of citizenship in marked language.

The third act to which we have alluded is even still more decisive; it was passed as late as 1813, (2 Stat., 809,) and it provides: "That from and after the termination of the war in which the United States are now engaged with Great Britain, it shall not be lawful to employ, on board of any public or private vessels of the United States, any person or persons except citizens of the United States, *or persons of color, natives of the United States.*

Here the line of distinction is drawn in express words. Persons of color, in the judgment of congress, were not included in the word citizens, and they are described as another and different class of persons, and authorized to be employed, if born in the United States.

And even as late as 1820, (chap. 104, sec. 8,) in the charter to the city of Washington, the corporation is authorized "to restrain and prohibit the nightly and other disorderly meetings of slaves, free negroes, and mulattoes," thus associating them together in its legislation; and after prescribing the punishment that may be inflicted on the slaves, proceeds in the following words: "And to punish such free negroes and mulattoes by penalties not exceeding twenty dollars for any one offence; and in case of the inability of any such free negro or mulatto to pay any such penalty and cost thereon, to cause him or her to be confined to labor for any time not exceeding six calendar months." And in a subsequent part of the same section, the act authorizes the corporation "to prescribe the terms and conditions upon which free negroes and mulattoes may reside in the city."

This law, like the laws of the States, shows that this class of persons were governed by special legislation directed expressly to them, and always connected with provisions for the government of slaves, and not with those for the government of free white citizens. And after such an uniform course of legislation as we have stated, by the colonies, by the States, and by congress, running through a period of more than a century, it would seem that to call persons thus marked and stigmatized, "citizens" of the United States, "fellow-citizens," a constituent part of the sovereignty, would be an abuse of terms, and not calculated to exalt the character of an American citizen in the eyes of other nations.

The conduct of the executive department of the government has been in perfect harmony upon this subject with this course of legislation. The question was brought officially before the late William Wirt, when he was the attorney general of the United States, in 1821, and he decided that the words "citizens of the United States" were used in the acts of congress in the same sense as in the constitution; and that free persons of color were not citizens, within the meaning of the constitution and laws; and this opinion has been confirmed by that of the late attorney general, Caleb Cushing, in a recent case, and acted upon by the secretary of state, who refused to grant passports to them as "citizens of the United States."

But it is said that a person may be a citizen, and entitled to that character, although he does not possess all the rights which may belong to other citizens; as, for example, the right to vote, or to hold particular offices; and that yet, when he goes into another State, he is entitled to be recognized there as a citizen, although the State may measure his rights by the rights which it allows to persons of a like character or class resident in the State, and refuse to him the full rights of citizenship.

This argument overlooks the language of the provision in the constitution of which we are speaking.

Undoubtedly, a person may be a citizen, that is, a member of the community who form the sovereignty, although he exercises no share of the political power, and is incapacitated from holding particular offices. Women and minors, who form a part of the political family, cannot vote; and when a property qualification is required to vote or hold a particular office, those who have not the necessary qualification cannot vote or hold the office, yet they are citizens.

So, too, a person may be entitled to vote by the law of the State, who is not a citizen even of the State itself. And in some of the States of the Union foreigners not naturalized are allowed to vote. And the State may give the right to free negroes and mulattoes, but that does not make them citizens of the State, and still less of the United States. And the provision in the constitution giving privileges and immunities in other States, does not apply to them.

Neither does it apply to a person who, being the citizen of a State, migrates to another State. For then he becomes subject to the laws of the State in which he lives, and he is no longer a citizen of the State from which he removed. And the State in which he resides may then, unquestionably, determine his *status* or condition, and place him among the class of persons who are not recognized as citizens, but belong to an inferior and subject race; and may deny him the privileges and immunities enjoyed by its citizens.

But so far as mere rights of person are concerned, the provision in question is confined to citizens of a State who are temporarily in another State without taking up their residence there. It gives them no political rights in the State, as to voting or holding office, or in any other respect. For a citizen of one State has no right to participate in the government of another. But if he ranks as a citizen in the State to which he belongs, within the meaning of the constitution of the United States, then, whenever he goes into another State, the constitution clothes him, as to the rights of person, with all the privileges and immunities which belong to citizens of the State. And if persons of the African race are citizens of a State, and of the United States, they would be entitled to all of these privileges and immunities in every State, and the State could not restrict them; for they would hold these privileges and immunities under the paramount authority of the federal government, and its courts would be bound to maintain and enforce them, the constitution and laws of the State to the contrary notwithstanding. And if the States could limit or restrict them, or place the party in an inferior grade, this clause of the constitution would be unmeaning, and could have no operation; and would give no rights to the citizen when in another State. He would have none but what the State itself chose to allow him. This is evidently not the construction or meaning of the clause in question. It guarantees rights to the citizen, and the

State cannot withhold them. And these rights are of a character and would lead to consequences which make it absolutely certain that the African race were not included under the name of citizens of a State, and were not in the contemplation of the framers of the constitution when these privileges and immunities were provided for the protection of the citizen in other States.

The case of Legrand *v.* Darnall (2 Peters, 664) has been referred to for the purpose of showing that this court has decided that the descendant of a slave may sue as a citizen in a court of the United States; but the case itself shows that the question did not arise and could not have arisen in the case.

It appears from the report, that Darnall was born in Maryland, and was the son of a white man by one of his slaves, and his father executed certain instruments to manumit him, and devised to him some landed property in the State. This property Darnall afterwards sold to Legrand, the appellant, who gave his notes for the purchase-money. But becoming afterwards apprehensive that the appellee had not been emancipated according to the laws of Maryland, he refused to pay the notes until he could be better satisfied as to Darnall's right to convey. Darnall, in the mean time, had taken up his residence in Pennsylvania, and brought suit on the notes, and recovered judgment in the circuit court for the district of Maryland.

The whole proceeding, as appears by the report, was an amicable one; Legrand being perfectly willing to pay the money, if he could obtain a title, and Darnall not wishing him to pay unless he could make him a good one. In point of fact, the whole proceeding was under the direction of the counsel who argued the case for the appellee, who was the mutual friend of the parties, and confided in by both of them, and whose only object was to have the rights of both parties established by judicial decision in the most speedy and least expensive manner.

Legrand, therefore, raised no objection to the jurisdiction of the court in the suit at law, because he was himself anxious to obtain the judgment of the court upon his title. Consequently, there was nothing in the record before the court to show that Darnall was of African descent, and the usual judgment and award of execution was entered. And Legrand thereupon filed his bill on the equity side of the circuit court, stating that Darnall was born a slave, and had not been legally emancipated, and could not therefore take the land devised to him, nor make Legrand a good title; and praying an injunction to restrain Darnall from proceeding to execution on the judgment, which was granted. Darnall answered, averring in his answer that he was a free man, and capable of conveying a good title. Testimony was taken on this point, and at the hearing the circuit court was of opinion that Darnall was a free man and his title good, and dissolved the injunction and dismissed the bill; and that decree was affirmed here, upon the appeal of Legrand.

Now, it is difficult to imagine how any question about the citizenship of Darnall, or his right to sue in that character, can be supposed to have arisen or been decided in that case. The fact that he was of African descent was first brought before the court upon the bill in equity. The suit at law had then passed into judgment and award of execution, and the circuit court, as a court of law, had no longer any authority over it. It was a valid and legal judgment, which the court that rendered it had not the power to reverse or set aside. And unless it had jurisdiction as a court of equity to restrain him from using its process as a court of law, Darnall, if he thought proper, would have been at liberty to proceed on his judgment, and compel the payment of the money, although the allegations in the bill were true, and he was incapable of making a title. No other court could have enjoined him, for certainly no State equity court could interfere in that way with the judgment of a circuit court of the United States.

But the circuit court as a court of equity certainly had equity jurisdiction over its own judgment as a court of law, without regard to the character of the parties; and had not only the right, but it was its duty—no matter who were the parties in the judgment—to prevent them from proceeding to enforce it by execution, if the court was satisfied that the money was not justly and equitably due. The ability of Darnall to convey did not depend upon his citizenship, but upon his title to freedom. And if he was free, he could hold and convey property, by the laws of Maryland, although he was not a citizen. But if he was by law still a slave, he could not. It was therefore the duty of the court, sitting as a court of equity in the latter case, to prevent him from using its process, as a court of common law, to compel the payment of the purchase-money, when it was evident that the purchaser must lose the land. But if he was free, and could make a title, it was equally the duty of the court not to suffer Legrand to keep the land, and refuse the payment of the money, upon the ground that Darnall was incapable of suing or being sued as a citizen in a court of the United States. The character or citizenship of the parties had no connection with the question of jurisdiction, and the matter in dispute had no relation to the citizenship of Darnall. Nor is such a question alluded to in the opinion of the court.

Besides, we are by no means prepared to say that there are not many cases, civil as well as criminal, in which a circuit court of the United States may exercise jurisdiction, although one of the African race is a party; that broad question is not before the court. The question with which we are now dealing is, whether a person of the African race can be a citizen of the United States, and become thereby entitled to a special privilege, by virtue of his title to that character, and which, under the constitution, no one but a citizen can claim. It is manifest that the case of Legrand and Darnall has no bearing on that question, and can have no application to the case now before the court.

This case, however, strikingly illustrates the consequences that would follow the construction of the constitution which would give the power contended for to a State. It would in effect give it also to an individual. For if the father of young Darnall had manumitted him in his lifetime, and sent him to reside in a

State which recognized him as a citizen, he might have visited and sojourned in Maryland when he pleased, and as long as he pleased, as a citizen of the United States; and the State officers and tribunals would be compelled, by the paramount authority of the constitution, to receive him and treat him as one of its citizens, exempt from the laws and police of the State in relation to a person of that description, and allow him to enjoy all the rights and privileges of citizenship, without respect to the laws of Maryland, although such laws were deemed by it absolutely essential to its own safety.

The only two provisions which point to them and include them, treat them as property, and make it the duty of the government to protect it; no other power, in relation to this race, is to be found in the constitution; and as it is a government of special, delegated, powers, no authority beyond these two provisions can be constitutionally exercised. The government of the United States had no right to interfere for any other purpose but that of protecting the rights of the owner, leaving it altogether with the several States to deal with this race, whether emancipated or not, as each State may think justice, humanity, and the interests and safety of society, require. The States evidently intended to reserve this power exclusively to themselves.

No one, we presume, supposes that any change in public opinion or feeling, in relation to this unfortunate race, in the civilized nations of Europe or in this country, should induce the court to give to the words of the constitution a more liberal construction in their favor than they were intended to bear when the instrument was framed and adopted. Such an argument would be altogether inadmissible in any tribunal called on to interpret it. If any of its provisions are deemed unjust, there is a mode prescribed in the instrument itself by which it may be amended; but while it remains unaltered, it must be construed now as it was understood at the time of its adoption. It is not only the same in words, but the same in meaning, and delegates the same powers to the government, and reserves and secures the same rights and privileges to the citizen; and as long as it continues to exist in its present form, it speaks not only in the same words, but with the same meaning and intent with which it spoke when it came from the hands of its framers, and was voted on and adopted by the people of the United States. Any other rule of construction would abrogate the judicial character of this court, and make it the mere reflex of the popular opinion or passion of the day. This court was not created by the constitution for such purposes. Higher and graver trusts have been confided to it, and it must not falter in the path of duty.

What the construction was at that time, we think can hardly admit of doubt. We have the language of the declaration of independence and of the articles of confederation, in addition to the plain words of the constitution itself; we have the legislation of the different States, before, about the time, and since, the constitution was adopted; we have the legislation of congress, from the time of its adoption to a recent period; and we have the constant and uniform action of the executive department, all concurring together, and leading to the same result. And if anything in relation to the construction of the constitution can be regarded as settled, it is that which we now give to the word "citizen" and the word "people."

And upon a full and careful consideration of the subject, the court is of opinion, that, upon the facts stated in the plea in abatement, Dred Scott was not a citizen of Missouri within the meaning of the constitution of the United States, and not entitled as such to sue in its courts; and, consequently, that the circuit court had no jurisdiction of the case, and that the judgment on the plea in abatement is erroneous.

We are aware that doubts are entertained by some of the members of the court, whether the plea in abatement is legally before the court upon this writ of error; but if that plea is regarded as waived, or out of the case upon any other ground, yet the question as to the jurisdiction of the circuit court is presented on the face of the bill of exception itself, taken by the plaintiff at the trial; for he admits that he and his wife were born slaves, but endeavors to make out his title to freedom and citizenship by showing that they were taken by their owner to certain places, hereinafter mentioned, where slavery could not by law exist, and that they thereby became free, and upon their return to Missouri became citizens of that State.

Now, if the removal of which he speaks did not give them their freedom, then by his own admission he is still a slave; and whatever opinions may be entertained in favor of the citizenship of a free person of the African race, no one supposes that a slave is a citizen of the State or of the United States. If, therefore, the acts done by his owner did not make them free persons, he is still a slave, and certainly incapable of suing in the character of a citizen.

The principle of law is too well settled to be disputed, that a court can give no judgment for either party, where it has no jurisdiction; and if, upon the showing of Scott himself, it appeared that he was still a slave, the case ought to have been dismissed, and the judgment against him and in favor of the defendant for costs, is, like that on the plea in abatement, erroneous, and the suit ought to have been dismissed by the circuit court for want of jurisdiction in that court.

But, before we proceed to examine this part of the case, it may be proper to notice an objection taken to the judicial authority of this court to decide it; and it has been said, that as this court has decided against the jurisdiction of the circuit court on the plea in abatement, it has no right to examine any question presented by the exception; and that anything it may say upon that part of the case will be extra-judicial, and mere *obiter dicta*.

This is a manifest mistake; there can be no doubt as to the jurisdiction of this court to revise the judgment of a circuit court, and to reverse it for any error apparent on the record, whether it be the error of giving judgment in a case over which it had no jurisdiction, or any other material error; and this, too, whether there is a plea in abatement or not.

The objection appears to have arisen from confounding writs of error to a State court, with writs of error to a circuit court of the United States. Undoubtedly, upon a writ of error to a State court, unless the record shows a case that gives jurisdiction, the case must be dismissed for want of jurisdiction in *this court*. And if it is dismissed on that ground, we have no right to examine and decide upon any question presented by the bill of exceptions, or any other part of the record. But writs of error to a State court, and to a circuit court of the United States, are regulated by different laws, and stand upon entirely different principles. And in a writ of error to a circuit court of the United States, the whole record is before this court for examination and decision; and if the sum in controversy is large enough to give jurisdiction, it is not only the right, but it is the judicial duty of the court, to examine the whole case as presented by the record; and if it appears upon its face that any material error or errors have been committed by the court below, it is the duty of this court to reverse the judgment, and remand the case. And certainly an error in passing a judgment upon the merits in favor of either party, in a case which it was not authorized to try, and over which it had no jurisdiction, is as grave an error as a court can commit.

The plea in abatement is not a plea to the jurisdiction of this court, but to the jurisdiction of the circuit court. And it appears by the record before us, that the circuit court committed an error, in deciding that it had jurisdiction, upon the facts in the case, admitted by the pleadings. It is the duty of the appellate tribunal to correct this error; but that could not be done by dismissing the case for want of jurisdiction here—for that would leave the erroneous judgment in full force, and the injured party without remedy. And the appellate court therefore exercises the power for which alone appellate courts are constituted, by reversing the judgment of the court below for this error. It exercises its proper and appropriate jurisdiction over the judgment and proceedings of the circuit court, as they appear upon the record brought up by the writ of error.

The correction of one error in the court below does not deprive the appellate court of the power of examining further into the record, and correcting any other material errors which may have been committed by the inferior court. There is certainly no rule of law—nor any practice—nor any decision of a court—which even questions this power in the appellate tribunal. On the contrary, it is the daily practice of this court, and of all appellate courts where they reverse the judgment of an inferior court for error, to correct by its opinions whatever errors may appear on the record material to the case; and they have always held it to be their duty to do so where the silence of the court might lead to misconstruction or future controversy, and the point has been relied on by either side, and argued before the court.

In the case before us, we have already decided that the circuit court erred in deciding that it had jurisdiction upon the facts admitted by the pleadings. And it appears that, in the further progress of the case, it acted upon the erroneous principle it had decided on the pleadings, and gave judgment for the defendant, where, upon the facts admitted in the exception, it had no jurisdiction.

We are at a loss to understand upon what principle of law, applicable to appellate jurisdiction, it can be supposed that this court has not judicial authority to correct the last-mentioned error, because they had before corrected the former; or by what process of reasoning it can be made out, that the error of an inferior court in actually pronouncing judgment for one of the parties, in a case in which it had no jurisdiction, cannot be looked into or corrected by this court, because we have decided a similar question presented in the pleadings. The last point is distinctly presented by the facts contained in the plaintiff's own bill of exceptions, which he himself brings here by this writ of error. It was the point which chiefly occupied the attention of the counsel on both sides in the argument—and the judgment which this court must render upon both errors is precisely the same. It must, in each of them, exercise jurisdiction over the judgment, and reverse it for the errors committed by the court below; and issue a mandate to the circuit court to conform its judgment to the opinion pronounced by this court, by dismissing the case for want of jurisdiction in the circuit court. This is the constant and invariable practice of this court, where it reverses a judgment for want of jurisdiction in the circuit court.

It can scarcely be necessary to pursue such a question further. The want of jurisdiction in the court below may appear on the record without any plea in abatement. This is familiarly the case where a court of chancery has exercised jurisdiction in a case where the plaintiff had a plain and adequate remedy at law, and it so appears by the transcript when brought here by appeal. So also where it appears that a court of admiralty has exercised jurisdiction in a case belonging exclusively to a court of common law. In these cases there is no plea in abatement. And for the same reason, and upon the same principles, where the defect of jurisdiction is patent on the record, this court is bound to reverse the judgment, although the defendant has not pleaded in abatement to the jurisdiction of the inferior court.

The cases of Jackson *v.* Ashton and of Capron *v.* Van Noorden, to which we have referred in a previous part of this opinion, are directly in point. In the last-mentioned case, Capron brought an action against Van Noorden in a circuit court of the United States, without showing, by the usual averments of citizenship, that the court had jurisdiction. There was no plea in abatement put in, and the parties went to trial upon the merits. The court gave judgment in favor of the defendant with costs. The plaintiff thereupon brought his writ of error, and this court reversed the judgment given in favor of the defendant, and remanded the case with directions to dismiss it, because it did not appear by the transcript that the circuit court had jurisdiction.

The case before us still more strongly imposes upon this court the duty of examining whether the court below has not committed an error, in taking jurisdiction and giving a judgment for costs in favor of the defendant; for in Capron *v.*

Van Noorden the judgment was reversed, because it did *not appear* that the parties were citizens of different States. They might or might not be. But in this case it *does appear* that the plaintiff was born a slave; and if the facts upon which he relies have not made him free, then it appears affirmatively on the record that he is not a citizen, and consequently his suit against Sandford was not a suit between citizens of different States, and the court had no authority to pass any judgment between the parties. The suit ought, in this view of it, to have been dismissed by the circuit court, and its judgment in favor of Sandford is erroneous, and must be reversed.

It is true that the result either way, by dismissal or by a judgment for the defendant, makes very little, if any, difference in a pecuniary or personal point of view to either party. But the fact that the result would be very nearly the same to the parties in either form of judgment, would not justify this court in sanctioning an error in the judgment which is patent on the record, and which, if sanctioned, might be drawn into precedent, and lead to serious mischief and injustice in some future suit.

We proceed, therefore, to inquire whether the facts relied on by the plaintiff entitled him to his freedom.

The case, as he himself states it, on the record brought here by his writ of error, is this:

The plaintiff was a negro slave, belonging to Dr. Emerson, who was a surgeon in the army of the United States. In the year 1834, he took the plaintiff from the State of Missouri to the military post at Rock Island, in the State of Illinois, and held him there as a slave until the month of April or May, 1836. At the time last mentioned, said Dr. Emerson removed the plaintiff from said military post at Rock Island to the military post at Fort Snelling, situate on the west bank of the Mississippi river, in the territory known as upper Louisiana, acquired by the United States of France [*sic*], and situate north of the latitude of thirty-six degrees thirty minutes north, and north of the State of Missouri. Said Dr. Emerson held the plaintiff in slavery at said Fort Snelling, from said last-mentioned date until the year 1838.

In the year 1835, Harriet, who is named in the second count of the plaintiff's declaration, was the negro slave of Major Taliaferro, who belonged to the army of the United States. In that year, 1835, said Major Taliaferro took said Harriet to said Fort Snelling, a military post, situated as hereinbefore stated, and kept her there as a slave until the year 1836, and then sold and delivered her as a slave, at said Fort Snelling, unto the said Dr. Emerson hereinbefore named. Said Dr. Emerson held said Harriet in slavery at said Fort Snelling until the year 1838.

In the year 1836, the plaintiff and Harriet intermarried, at Fort Snelling, with the consent of Dr. Emerson, who then claimed to be their master and owner. Eliza and Lizzie, named in the third count of the plaintiff's declaration, are the fruit of that marriage. Eliza is about fourteen years old, and was born on board the steamboat Gipsey, north of the north line of the State of Missouri, and upon the river Mississippi. Lizzie is about seven years old, and was born in the State of Missouri, at the military post called Jefferson Barracks.

In the year 1838, said Dr. Emerson removed the plaintiff and said Harriet, and their said daughter Eliza, from said Fort Snelling to the State of Missouri, where they have ever since resided.

Before the commencement of this suit, said Dr. Emerson sold and conveyed the plaintiff, and Harriet, Eliza, and Lizzie, to the defendant, as slaves, and the defendant has ever since claimed to hold them, and each of them, as slaves.

In considering this part of the controversy, two questions arise: 1. Was he, together with his family, free in Missouri by reason of the stay in the territory of the United States hereinbefore mentioned? And 2. If they were not, is Scott himself free by reason of his removal to Rock Island, in the State of Illinois, as stated in the above admissions?

We proceed to examine the first question.

The act of Congress, upon which the plaintiff relies, declares that slavery and involuntary servitude, except as a punishment for crime, shall be forever prohibited in all that part of the territory ceded by France, under the name of Louisiana, which lies north of thirty-six degrees thirty minutes north latitude, and not included within the limits of Missouri. And the difficulty which meets us at the threshold of this part of the inquiry is, whether Congress was authorized to pass this law under any of the powers granted to it by the constitution; for if the authority is not given by that instrument, it is the duty of this court to declare it void and inoperative, and incapable of conferring freedom upon any one who is held as a slave under the have [laws] of any one of the States.

The counsel for the plaintiff has laid much stress upon that article in the constitution which confers on congress the power "to dispose of and make all needful rules and regulations respecting the territory or other property belonging to the United States;" but, in the judgment of the court, that provision has no bearing on the present controversy, and the power there given, whatever it may be, is confined, and was intended to be confined, to the territory which at that time belonged to, or was claimed by, the United States, and was within their boundaries as settled by the treaty with Great Britain, and can have no influence upon a territory afterwards acquired from a foreign government. It was a special provision for a known and particular territory, and to meet a present emergency, and nothing more.

A brief summary of the history of the times, as well as the careful and measured terms in which the article is framed, will show the correctness of this proposition.

It will be remembered that, from the commencement of the revolutionary war, serious difficulties existed between the States, in relation to the disposition of large and unsettled territories which were included in the chartered limits of some of the States. And some of the other States, and more especially Maryland, which had no unsettled lands, insisted that as the unoccupied lands, if wrested from Great Britain, would owe their preservation to the common purse and the common sword, the money arising from them ought to be applied in just proportion among the several States to pay the expenses of the war, and ought not to be appropriated to the use of the State in whose chartered limits they might happen to lie, to the exclusion of the other States, by whose combined efforts and common expense the territory was defended and preserved against the claim of the British government.

These difficulties caused much uneasiness during the war, while the issue was in some degree doubtful, and the future boundaries of the United States yet to be defined by treaty, if we achieved our independence.

The majority of the congress of the confederation obviously concurred in opinion with the State of Maryland, and desired to obtain from the States which claimed it a cession of this territory, in order that congress might raise money on this security to carry on the war. This appears by the resolution passed on the 6th of September, 1780, strongly urging the States to cede these lands to the United States, both for the sake of peace and union among themselves, and to maintain the public credit; and this was followed by the resolution of October 10th, 1780, by which congress pledged itself, that if the lands were ceded, as recommended by the resolution above mentioned, they should be disposed of for the common benefit of the United States, and be settled and formed into distinct republican States, which should become members of the federal Union, and have the same rights of sovereignty, and freedom, and independence, as other States.

But these difficulties became much more serious after peace took place, and the boundaries of the United States were established. Every State, at that time, felt severely the pressure of its war debt; but in Virginia, and some other States, there were large territories of unsettled lands, the sale of which would enable them to discharge their obligations without much inconvenience; while other States, which had no such resource, saw before them many years of heavy and burdensome taxation; and the latter insisted, for the reasons before stated, that these unsettled lands should be treated as the common property of the States, and the proceeds applied to their common benefit.

The letters from the statesmen of that day will show how much this controversy occupied their thoughts, and the dangers that were apprehended from it. It was the disturbing element of the time, and fears were entertained that it might dissolve the confederation by which the States were then united.

These fears and dangers were, however, at once removed, when the State of Virginia, in 1784, voluntarily ceded to the United States the immense tract of country lying northwest of the river Ohio, and which was within the acknowledged limits of the State. The only object of the State, in making this cession, was to put an end to the threatening and exciting controversy, and to enable the congress of that time to dispose of the lands, and appropriate the proceeds as a common fund for the common benefit of the States. It was not ceded, because it was inconvenient to the State to hold and govern it, nor from any expectation that it could be better or more conveniently governed by the United States.

The example of Virginia was soon afterwards followed by other States, and, at the time of the adoption of the constitution, all of the States, similarly situated, had ceded their unappropriated lands, except North Carolina and Georgia. The main object for which these cessions were desired and made, was on account of their money value, and to put an end to a dangerous controversy, as to who was justly entitled to the proceeds when the lands should be sold. It is necessary to bring this part of the history of these cessions thus distinctly into view, because it will enable us the better to comprehend the phraseology of the article in the constitution, so often referred to in the argument.

Undoubtedly the powers of sovereignty and the eminent domain were ceded with the land. This was essential, in order to make it effectual, and to accomplish its objects. But it must be remembered that, at that time, there was no government of the United States in existence with enumerated and limited powers; what was then called the United States, were thirteen separate, sovereign, independent States, which had entered into a league or confederation for their mutual protection and advantage, and the congress of the United States was composed of the representatives of these separate sovereignties, meeting together, as equals, to discuss and decide on certain measures which the States, by the articles of confederation, had agreed to submit to their decision. But this confederation had none of the attributes of sovereignty in legislative, executive, or judicial power. It was little more than a congress of ambassadors, authorized to represent separate nations, in matters in which they had a common concern.

It was this congress that accepted the cession from Virginia. They had no power to accept it under the articles of confederation. But they had an undoubted right, as independent sovereignties, to accept any cession of territory for their common benefit, which all of them assented to; and it is equally clear, that as their common property, and having no superior to control them, they had the right to exercise absolute dominion over it, subject only to the restrictions which Virginia had imposed in her act of cession. There was, as we have said, no government of the United States then in existence with special enumerated and limited powers. The territory belonged to sovereignties, who, subject to the limitations above mentioned, had a right to establish any form of government they pleased, by compact or treaty among themselves, and to regulate rights of person and rights of property in the territory, as they might deem proper. It was by a congress, representing the authority of these several and separate sovereignties, and acting under their authority and command, (but not from any authority derived from the articles of confederation,) that the instrument usually called the ordinance of 1787 was adopted; regulating in much detail the principles and the laws by which this territory should be governed; and among other provisions, slavery is prohibited in it. We do not question the power of the States, by agreement among themselves, to pass this ordinance, nor its obligatory force in the territory, while the confederation or league of the States in their separate sovereign character continued to exist.

This was the state of things when the constitution of the United States was formed. The territory ceded by Virginia belonged to the several confederated States as common property, and they had united in establishing in it a system of government and jurisprudence, in order to prepare it for admission as States, according to the terms of the cession. They were about to dissolve this federative Union, and to surrender a portion of their independent sovereignty to a new government, which, for certain purposes, would make the people of the several States one people, and which was to be supreme and controlling within its sphere of action throughout the United States; but this government was to be carefully limited in its powers, and to exercise no authority beyond those expressly granted by the constitution, or necessarily to be implied from the language of the instrument, and the objects it was intended to accomplish; and as this league of States would, upon the adoption of the new government, cease to have any power over the territory, and the ordinance they had agreed upon be incapable of execution, and a mere nullity, it was obvious that some provision was necessary to give the new government sufficient power to enable it to carry into effect the objects for which it was ceded, and the compacts and agreements which the States had made with each other in the exercise of their powers of sovereignty. It was necessary that the lands should be sold to pay the war debt; that a government and system of jurisprudence should be maintained in it, to protect the citizens of the United States who should migrate to the territory, in their rights of person and of property. It was also necessary that the new government, about to be adopted, should be authorized to maintain the claim of the United States to the unappropriated lands in North Carolina and Georgia, which had not then been ceded, but the cession of which was confidently anticipated upon some terms that would be arranged between the general government and these two States. And, moreover, there were many articles of value besides this property in land, such as arms, military stores, munitions, and ships of war, which were the common property of the States, when acting in their independent characters as confederates, which neither the new government nor any one else would have a right to take possession of, or control, without authority from them; and it was to place these things under the guardianship and protection of the new government, and to clothe it with the necessary powers, that the clause was inserted in the constitution which gives congress the power "to dispose of and make all needful rules and regulations respecting the territory or other property belonging to the United States." It was intended for a specific purpose, to provide for the things we have mentioned. It was to transfer to the new government the property then held in common by the

States, and to give to that government power to apply it to the objects for which it had been destined by mutual agreement among the States before their league was dissolved. It applied only to the property which the States held in common at that time, and has no reference whatever to any territory or other property which the new sovereignty might afterwards itself acquire.

The language used in the clause, the arrangement and combination of the powers, and the somewhat unusual phraseology it uses, when it speaks of the political power to be exercised in the government of the territory, all indicate the design and meaning of the clause to be such as we have mentioned. It does not speak of *any* territory, nor of *territories*, but uses language which, according to its legitimate meaning, points to a particular thing. The power is given in relation only to *the* territory of the United States—that is, to a territory then in existence, and then known or claimed as the territory of the United States. It begins its enumeration of powers by that of disposing, in other words, making sale of the lands, or raising money from them, which, as we have already said, was the main object of the cession, and which is accordingly the first thing provided for in the article. It then gives the power which was necessarily associated with the disposition and sale of the lands—that is, the power of making needful rules and regulations respecting the territory. And whatever construction may now be given to these words, every one, we think, must admit that they are not the words usually employed by statesmen in giving supreme power of legislation. They are certainly very unlike the words used in the power granted to legislate over territory which the new government might afterwards itself obtain by cession from a State, either for its seat of government, or for forts, magazines, arsenals, dock yards, and other needful buildings.

And the same power of making needful rules respecting the territory is, in precisely the same language, applied to the *other* property belonging to the United States—associating the power over the territory in this respect with the power over movable or personal property—that is, the ships, arms, and munitions of war, which then belonged in common to the State sovereignties. And it will hardly be said, that this power, in relation to the last-mentioned objects, was deemed necessary to be thus specially given to the new government, in order to authorize it to make needful rules and regulations respecting the ships it might itself build, or arms and munitions of war it might itself manufacture or provide for the public service. No one, it is believed, would think a moment of deriving the power of congress to make needful rules and regulations in relation to property of this kind from this clause of the constitution. Nor can it, upon any fair construction, be applied to any property but that which the new government was about to receive from the confederated States. And if this be true as to this property, it must be equally true and limited as to the territory, which is so carefully and precisely coupled with it—and like it referred to as property in the power granted. The concluding words of the clause appear to render this construction irresistible;

for, after the provisions we have mentioned, it proceeds to say, "that nothing in the constitution shall be so construed as to prejudice any claims of the United States, or of any particular State."

Now, as we have before said, all of the States, except North Carolina and Georgia, had made the cession before the constitution was adopted, according to the resolution of congress of October 10, 1780. The claims of other States, that the unappropriated lands in these two States should be applied to the common benefit, in like manner, was still insisted on, but refused by the States. And this member of the clause in question evidently applies to them, and can apply to nothing else. It was to exclude the conclusion that either party, by adopting the constitution, would surrender what they deemed their rights. And when the latter provision relates so obviously to the unappropriated lands not yet ceded by the States, and the first clause makes provision for those then actually ceded, it is impossible, by any just rule of construction, to make the first provision general, and extend to all territories, which the federal government might in any way afterwards acquire, when the latter is plainly and unequivocally confined to a particular territory; which was a part of the same controversy, and involved in the same dispute, and depended upon the same principles. The union of the two provisions in the same clause shows that they were kindred subjects; and that the whole clause is local, and relates only to lands, within the limits of the United States, which had been or then were claimed by a State; and that no other territory was in the mind of the framers of the constitution, or intended to be embraced in it. Upon any other construction it would be impossible to account for the insertion of the last provision in the place where it is found, or to comprehend why, or for what object, it was associated with the previous provision.

This view of the subject is confirmed by the manner in which the present government of the United States dealt with the subject as soon as it came into existence. It must be borne in mind that the same States that formed the confederation also formed and adopted the new government, to which so large a portion of their former sovereign powers were surrendered. It must also be borne in mind that all of these same States which had then ratified the new constitution were represented in the congress which passed the first law for the government of this territory; and many of the members of that legislative body had been deputies from the States under the confederation—had united in adopting the ordinance of 1787, and assisted in forming the new government under which they were then acting, and whose powers they were then exercising. And it is obvious from the law they passed to carry into effect the principles and provisions of the ordinance, that they regarded it as the act of the States done in the exercise of their legitimate powers at the time. The new government took the territory as it found it, and in the condition in which it was transferred, and did not attempt to undo anything that had been done. And, among the earliest laws passed under the new government, is one reviving the ordinance of 1787, which had become inoperative and a nullity upon the adoption of the constitution. This law introduces no new form or principles for its government, but recites, in the preamble, that it is passed in order that this ordinance may continue to have full effect, and proceeds to make only those rules and regulations which were needful to adapt it to the new government, into whose hands the power had fallen. It appears, therefore, that this congress regarded the purposes to which the land in this Territory was to be applied, and the form of government and principles of jurisprudence which were to prevail there, while it remained in the territorial state, as already determined on by the States when they had full power and right to make the decision; and that the new government, having received it in this condition, ought to carry substantially into effect the plans and principles which had been previously adopted by the States, and which no doubt the States anticipated when they surrendered their power to the new government. And if we regard this clause of the constitution as pointing to this territory, with a territorial government already established in it, which had been ceded to the States for the purposes hereinbefore mentioned—every word in it is perfectly appropriate and easily understood, and the provisions it contains are in perfect harmony with the objects for which it was ceded, and with the condition of its government as a territory at the time. We can, then, easily account for the manner in which the first congress legislated on the subject—and can also understand why this power over the territory was associated in the same clause with the other property of the United States, and subjected to the like power of making needful rules and regulations. But if the clause is construed in the expanded sense contended for, so as to embrace any territory acquired from a foreign nation by the present government, and to give it in such territory a despotic and unlimited power over persons and property, such as the confederated States might exercise in their common property, it would be difficult to account for the phraseology used, when compared with other grants of power—and also for its association with the other provisions in the same clause.

The constitution has always been remarkable for the felicity of its arrangement of different subjects, and the perspicuity and appropriateness of the language it uses. But if this clause is construed to extend to territory acquired by the present government from a foreign nation, outside of the limits of any charter from the British government to a colony, it would be difficult to say, why it was deemed necessary to give the government the power to sell any vacant lands belonging to the sovereignty which might be found within it; and if this was necessary, why the grant of this power should precede the power to legislate over it and establish a government there; and still more difficult to say, why it was deemed necessary so specially and particularly to grant the power to make needful rules and regulations in relation to any personal or movable property it might acquire there. For the words, *other property* necessarily, by every known rule of interpretation, must mean property of a different description from territory or land. And the difficulty would perhaps be insurmountable in endeavoring to account for the last member of the sentence, which provides that "nothing in this constitution shall be so construed as to prejudice any claims of the United States or any particular State," or to say how any particular State could have claims in or to a territory ceded by a foreign government, or to account for associating this provision with the preceding provisions of the clause, with which it would appear to have no connection.

The words "needful rules and regulations" would seem, also, to have been cautiously used for some definite object. They are not the words usually employed by statesmen, when they mean to give the powers of sovereignty, or to establish a government, or to authorize its establishment. Thus, in the law to renew and keep alive the ordinance of 1787, and to re-establish the government, the title of the law is: "An act to provide for the government of the territory northwest of the river Ohio." And in the constitution, when granting the power to legislate over the territory that may be selected for the seat of government independently of a State, it does not say congress shall have power "to make all needful rules and regulations respecting the territory;" but it declares that "congress shall have power to exercise exclusive legislation in all cases whatsoever over such district (not exceeding ten miles square) as may, by cession of particular States and the acceptance of congress, become the seat of the government of the United States."

The words "rules and regulations" are usually employed in the constitution in speaking of some particular specified power which it means to confer on the government, and not, as we have seen, when granting general powers of legislation. As, for example, in the particular power to congress "to make rules for the government and regulation of the land and naval forces, or the particular and specific power to regulate commerce;" "to establish an uniform *rule* of naturalization;" "to coin money and *regulate* the value thereof." And to construe the words of which we are speaking as a general and unlimited grant of sovereignty over territories which the government might afterwards acquire, is to use them in a sense and for a purpose for which they were not used in any other part of the instrument. But if confined to a particular territory, in which a government and laws had already been established, but which would require some alterations to adapt it to the new government, the words are peculiarly applicable and appropriate for that purpose.

The necessity of this special provision in relation to property and the rights or property held in common by the confederated States, is illustrated by the first clause of the sixth article. This clause provides that "all debts, contracts, and engagements entered into before the adoption of this constitution, shall be as valid against the United States under this government as under the confederation." This provision, like the one under consideration, was indispensable if the new constitution was adopted. The new government was not a mere change in a dynasty, or in a form of government, leaving the nation or sovereignty the same, and clothed with all the rights, and bound by all the obligations of the preceding one. But, when the present United States came into existence under the new government, it was a new political body, a new nation, then for the first time taking its place in the family of nations. It took nothing by succession from the confederation. It had no right, as its successor, to any property or rights of property which it had acquired, and was not liable for any of its obligations. It was evidently viewed in this light by the framers of the constitution. And as the several States would cease to exist in their former confederated character upon the adoption of the constitution, and could not, in that character, again assemble together, special provisions were indispensable to transfer to the new government the property and rights which at that time they held in common; and at the same time to authorize it to lay taxes and appropriate money to pay the common debt which they had contracted; and this power could only be given to it by special provisions in the constitution. The clause in relation to the territory and other property of the United States provided for the first, and the clause last quoted provided for the other. They have no connection with the general powers and rights of sovereignty delegated to the new government, and can neither enlarge nor diminish them. They were inserted to meet a present emergency, and not to regulate its powers as a government.

Indeed, a similar provision was deemed necessary, in relation to treaties made by the confederation; and when in the clause next succeeding the one of which we have last spoken, it is declared that treaties shall be the supreme law of the land, care is taken to include, by express words, the treaties made by the confederated States. The language is: "and all treaties made, or which shall be made, under the authority of the United States, shall be the supreme law of the land."

Whether, therefore, we take the particular clause in question, by itself, or in connection with the other provisions of the constitution, we think it clear, that it applies only to the particular territory of which we have spoken, and cannot, by any just rule of interpretation, be extended to territory which the new government might afterwards obtain from a foreign nation. Consequently, the power which congress may have lawfully exercised in this territory, while it remained under a territorial government, and which may have been sanctioned by judicial decision, can furnish no justification and no argument to support a similar exercise of power over territory afterwards acquired by the federal government. We put aside, therefore, any argument, drawn from precedents, showing the extent of the power which the general government exercised over slavery in this territory, as altogether inapplicable to the case before us.

But the case of the American and Ocean Insurance Companies *v.* Canter (1 Pet. 511) has been quoted as establishing a different construction of this clause of the constitution. There is, however, not the slightest conflict between the opinion now given and the one referred to; and it is only by taking a single sentence out of the latter and separating it from the context, that even an appearance of conflict can be shown. We need not comment on such a mode of expounding an opinion of the court. Indeed it most commonly misrepresents instead of expounding it. And this is fully exemplified in the case referred to, where, if one sentence is taken by itself, the opinion would appear to be in direct conflict with that now given; but the words which immediately follow that sentence show that the court did not mean to decide the point, but merely affirmed the power of congress to establish a government in the territory, leaving it an open question, whether that power was derived from this clause in the constitution, or was to be necessarily inferred from a power to acquire territory by cession from a foreign government. The opinion on this part of the case is short, and we give the whole of it to show how well the selection of a single sentence is calculated to mislead.

The passage referred to is in page 542, in which the court, in speaking of the power of congress to establish a territorial government in Florida until it should become a State, uses the following language:

"In the meantime Florida continues to be a territory of the United States, governed by that clause of the constitution which empowers congress to make all needful rules and regulations respecting the territory or other property of the United States. Perhaps the power of governing a territory belonging to the United States, which has not, by becoming a State, acquired the means of self-government, may result, necessarily, from the facts that it is not within the jurisdiction of any particular State, and is within the power and jurisdiction of the United States. The right to govern may be the inevitable consequence of the right to acquire territory. *Whichever may be the source from which the power is derived, the possession of it is unquestionable.*"

It is thus clear, from the whole opinion on this point, that the court did not mean to decide whether the power was derived from the clause in the constitution, or was the necessary consequence of the right to acquire. They do decide that the power in congress is unquestionable, and in this we entirely concur, and nothing will be found in this opinion to the contrary. The power stands firmly on the latter alternative put by the court—that is, as *"the inevitable consequence of the right to acquire territory."*

And what still more clearly demonstrates that the court did not mean to decide the question, but leave it open for future consideration, is the fact that the case was decided in the circuit court by Mr. Justice Johnson, and his decision was affirmed by the supreme court. His opinion at the circuit is given in full in a note to the case, and in that opinion he states, in explicit terms, that the clause of the constitution applies only to the territory then within the limits of the United States, and not to Florida, which had been acquired by cession from Spain. This part of his opinion will be found in the note in page 517 of the report. But he does not dissent from the opinion of the supreme court; thereby showing that, in his judgment, as well as that of the court, the case before them did not call for a decision on that particular point, and the court abstained from deciding it. And in a part of its opinion subsequent to the passage we have quoted, where the court speak of the legislative power of congress in Florida, they still speak with the same reserve. And in page 546, speaking of the power of congress to authorize the territorial legislature to establish courts there, the court say: "They are legislative courts, created in virtue of the general right of sovereignty which exists in the government, or in virtue of that clause which enables congress to make all needful rules and regulations respecting the territory belonging to the United States."

It has been said that the construction given to this clause is new, and now for the first time brought forward. The case of which we are speaking, and which has been so much discussed, shows that the fact is otherwise. It shows that precisely the same question came before Mr. Justice Johnson, at his circuit, thirty years ago—was fully considered by him, and the same construction given to the clause in the constitution which is now given by this court. And that upon an appeal from his decision the same question was brought before this court, but was not decided because a decision upon it was not required by the case before the court.

There is another sentence in the opinion which has been commented on, which even in a still more striking manner shows how one may mislead or be misled by taking out a single sentence from the opinion of a court, and leaving out of view what precedes and follows. It is in page 546, near the close of the opinion, in which the court say: "In legislating for them," (the territories of the United States,) "congress exercises the combined powers of the general and of a State government." And it is said, that as a State may unquestionably prohibit slavery within its territory, this sentence decides in effect that congress may do the same in a territory of the United States, exercising there the powers of a State, as well as the power of the general government.

The examination of this passage in the case referred to, would be more appropriate when we come to consider in another part of this opinion what power congress can constitutionally exercise in a territory, over the rights of person or rights of property of a citizen. But, as it is in the same case with the passage we have before commented on, we dispose of it now, as it will save the court from the necessity of referring again to the case. And it will be seen upon reading the page in which this sentence is found, that it has no reference whatever to the power of congress over rights of person or rights of property—but relates altogether to the power of establishing judicial tribunals to administer the laws constitutionally passed, and defining the jurisdiction they may exercise.

The law of congress establishing a territorial government in Florida, provided that the legislature of the territory should have legislative powers over "all rightful objects of legislation; but no law should be valid which was inconsistent with the laws and constitution of the United States."

Under the power thus conferred, the legislature of Florida passed an act, erecting a tribunal at Key West to decide cases of salvage. And in the case of which we are speaking, the question arose whether the territorial legislature could be authorized by congress to establish such a tribunal, with such powers;

and one of the parties, among other objections, insisted that congress could not under the constitution authorize the legislature of the territory to establish such a tribunal with such powers, but that it must be established by congress itself; and that a sale of cargo made under its order, to pay salvors, was void, as made without legal authority, and passed no property to the purshaser.

It is in disposing of this objection that the sentence relied on occurs, and the court begin[s] that part of the opinion by stating with great precision the point which they are about to decide.

They say: "It has been contended that by the constitution of the United States, the judicial power of the United States extends to all cases of admiralty and maritime jurisdiction; and that the whole of the judicial power must be vested 'in one supreme court, and in such inferior courts as congress shall from time to time ordain and establish.' Hence it has been argued that congress cannot vest admiralty jurisdiction in courts created by the territorial legislature."

And after thus clearly stating the point before them, and which they were about to decide, they proceed to show that these territorial tribunals were not constitutional courts, but merely legislative, and that congress might, therefore, delegate the power to the territorial government to establish the court in question; and they conclude that part of the opinion in the following words: "Although admiralty jurisdiction can be exercised in the States in those courts only which are established in pursuance of the third article of the constitution, the same limitation does not extend to the territories. In legislating for them, congress exercises the combined powers of the general and State governments."

Thus it will be seen by these quotations from the opinion, that the court, after stating the question it was about to decide in a manner too plain to be misunderstood, proceeded to decide it, and announced, as the opinion of the tribunal, that in organizing the judicial department of the government in a territory of the United States, congress does not act under, and is not restricted by, the third article in the constitution, and is not bound, in a territory, to ordain and establish courts in which the judges hold their offices during good behaviour, but may exercise the discretionary power which a State exercises in establishing its judicial department, and regulating the jurisdiction of its courts, and may authorize the territorial government to establish, or may itself establish, courts in which the judges hold their offices for a term of years only; and may vest in them judicial power upon subjects confided to the judiciary of the United States. And in doing this, congress undoubtedly exercises the combined power of the general and a State government. It exercises the discretionary power of a State government in authorizing the establishment of a court in which the judges hold their appointments for a term of years only, and not during good behaviour; and it exercises the power of the general government in investing that court with admiralty jurisdiction, over which the general government had exclusive jurisdiction in the territory.

No one, we presume, will question the correctness of that opinion; nor is there anything in conflict with it in the opinion now given. The point decided in the case cited has no relation to the question now before the court. That depended on the construction of the third article of the constitution, in relation to the judiciary of the United States, and the power which congress might exercise in a territory in organizing the judicial department of the government. The case before us depends upon other and different provisions of the constitution, altogether separate and apart from the one above mentioned. The question as to what courts congress may ordain or establish in a territory to administer laws which the constitution authorizes it to pass, and what laws it is or is not authorized by the constitution to pass, are widely different—are regulated by different and separate articles of the constitution, and stand upon different principles. And we are satisfied that no one who reads attentively the page in Peters's Reports to which we have referred, can suppose that the attention of the court was drawn for a moment to the question now before this court, or that it meant in that case to say that congress had a right to prohibit a citizen of the United States from taking any property which he lawfully held into a territory of the United States.

This brings us to examine by what provision of the constitution the present federal government, under its delegated and restricted powers, is authorized to acquire territory outside of the original limits of the United States, and what powers it may exercise therein over the person or property of a citizen of the United States, while it remains a territory, and until it shall be admitted as one of the States of the Union.

There is certainly no power given by the constitution to the federal government to establish or maintain colonies bordering on the United States or at a distance, to be ruled and governed at its own pleasure; nor to enlarge its territorial limits in any way, except by the admission of new States. That power is plainly given; and if a new State is admitted, it needs no further legislation by congress, because the constitution itself defines the relative rights and powers, and duties of the State, and the citizens of the State, and the federal government. But no power is given to acquire a territory to be held and governed permanently in that character.

And indeed the power exercised by congress to acquire territory and establish a government there, according to its own unlimited discretion, was viewed with great jealousy by the leading statesmen of the day. And in the Federalist, (No. 38,) written by Mr. Madison, he speaks of the acquisition of the northwestern territory by the confederated States, by the cession from Virginia, and the establishment of a government there, as an exercise of power not warranted by the articles of confederation, and dangerous to the liberties of the people. And he urges the adoption of the constitution as a security and safeguard against such an exercise of power.

We do not mean, however, to question the power of congress in this respect. The power to expand the territory of the United States by the admission of new

States is plainly given; and in the construction of this power by all the departments of the government, it has been held to authorize the acquisition of territory, not fit for admission at the time, but to be admitted as soon as its population and situation would entitle it to admission. It is acquired to become a State, and not to be held as a colony and governed by congress with absolute authority; and as the propriety of admitting a new State is committed to the sound discretion of congress, the power to acquire territory for that purpose, to be held by the United States until it is in a suitable condition to become a State upon an equal footing with the other States, must rest upon the same discretion. It is a question for the political department of the government, and not the judicial; and whatever the political department of the government shall recognize as within the limits of the United States, the judicial department is also bound to recognize, and to administer in it the laws of the United States, so far as they apply, and to maintain in the territory the authority and rights of the government, and also the personal rights and rights of property of individual citizens, as secured by the constitution. All we mean to say on this point is, that, as there is no express regulation in the constitution defining the power which the general government may exercise over the person or property of a citizen in a territory thus acquired, the court must necessarily look to the provisions and principles of the constitution, and its distribution of powers, for the rules and principles by which its decision must be governed.

Taking this rule to guide us, it may be safely assumed that citizens of the United States who migrate to a territory belonging to the people of the United States, cannot be ruled as mere colonists, dependent upon the will of the general government, and to be governed by any laws it may think proper to impose. The principle upon which our governments rest, and upon which alone they continue to exist, is the union of States, sovereign and independent within their own limits in their internal and domestic concerns, and bound together as one people by a general government, possessing certain enumerated and restricted powers, delegated to it by the people of the several States, and exercising supreme authority within the scope of the powers granted to it, throughout the dominion of the United States. A power, therefore, in the general government to obtain and hold colonies and dependent territories, over which they might legislate without restriction, would be inconsistent with its own existence in its present form. Whatever it acquires, it acquires for the benefit of the people of the several States who created it. It is their trustee acting for them, and charged with the duty of promoting the interests of the whole people of the Union in the exercise of the powers specifically granted.

At the time when the territory in question was obtained by cession from France, it contained no population fit to be associated together and admitted as a State; and it therefore was absolutely necessary to hold possession of it, as a territory belonging to the United States, until it was settled and inhabited by a civilized community capable of self-government, and in a condition to be admitted on equal terms with the other States as a member of the Union. But, as we have before said, it was acquired by the general government, as the representative and trustee of the people of the United States, and it must therefore be held in that character for their common and equal benefit; for it was the people of the several States, acting through their agent and representative, the federal government, who in fact acquired the territory in question, and the government holds it for their common use until it shall be associated with the other States as a member of the Union.

But until that time arrives, it is undoubtedly necessary that some government should be established, in order to organize society, and to protect the inhabitants in their persons and property; and as the people of the United States could act in this matter only through the government which represented them, and through which they spoke and acted when the territory was obtained, it was not only within the scope of its powers, but it was its duty to pass such laws and establish such a government as would enable those by whose authority they acted to reap the advantages anticipated from its acquisition, and to gather there a population which would enable it to assume the position to which it was destined among the States of the Union. The power to acquire necessarily carries with it the power to preserve and apply to the purposes for which it was acquired. The form of government to be established necessarily rested in the discretion of congress. It was their duty to establish the one that would be best suited for the protection and security of the citizens of the United States, and other inhabitants who might be authorized to take up their abode there, and that must always depend upon the existing condition of the territory, as to the number and character of its inhabitants, and their situation in the territory. In some cases a government, consisting of persons appointed by the federal government, would best subserve [serve] the interests of the territory, when the inhabitants were few and scattered, and new to one another. In other instances, it would be more advisable to commit the powers of self-government to the people who had settled in the territory, as being the most competent to determine what was best for their own interests. But some form of civil authority would be absolutely necessary to organize and preserve civilized society, and prepare it to become a State; and what is the best form must always depend on the condition of the territory at the time, and the choice of the mode must depend upon the exercise of a discretionary power by congress, acting within the scope of its constitutional authority, and not infringing upon the rights of person or rights of property of the citizen who might go there to reside, or for any other lawful purpose. It was acquired by the exercise of this discretion, and it must be held and governed in like manner, until it is fitted to be a State.

But the power of congress over the person or property of a citizen can never be a mere discretionary power under our constitution and form of government. The powers of the government and the rights and privileges of the citizen are regulated and plainly defined by the constitution itself. And when the territory becomes a part of the United States, the federal government enters into possession in the character impressed upon it by those who created it. It enters upon it with its powers over the citizen strictly defined, and limited by the constitution, from which it derives its own existence, and by virtue of which alone it continues to exist and act as a government and sovereignty. It has no power of any kind beyond it; and it cannot, when it enters a territory of the United States, put off its character, and assume discretionary or despotic powers which the constitution has denied to it. It cannot create for itself a new character separated from the citizens of the United States, and the duties it owes them under the provisions of the constitution. The territory being a part of the United States, the government and the citizen both enter it under the authority of the constitution, with their respective rights defined and marked out; and the federal government can exercise no power over his person or property, beyond what that instrument confers, nor lawfully deny any right which it has reserved.

A reference to a few of the provisions of the constitution will illustrate this proposition.

For example, no one, we presume, will contend that congress can make any law in a territory respecting the establishment of religion, or the free exercise thereof, or abridging the freedom of speech or of the press, or the right of the people of the territory peaceably to assemble, and to petition the government for the redress of grievances.

Nor can congress deny to the people the right to keep and bear arms, nor the right to trial by jury, nor compel any one to be a witness against himself in a criminal proceeding.

These powers, and others, in relation to rights of person, which it is not necessary here to enumerate, are, in express and positive terms, denied to the general government; and the rights of private property have been guarded with equal care. Thus the rights of property are united with the rights of person, and placed on the same ground by the fifth amendment to the constitution, which provides that no person shall be deprived of life, liberty, and property, without due process of law. And an act of congress which deprives a citizen of the United States of his liberty or property, merely because he came himself or brought his property into a particular territory of the United States, and who had committed no offence against the laws, could hardly be dignified with the name of due process of law.

So, too, it will hardly be contended that congress could by law quarter a soldier in a house in a territory without the consent of the owner, in time of peace; nor in time of war, but in a manner prescribed by law. Nor could they by law forfeit the property of a citizen in a territory who was convicted of treason, for a longer period than the life of the person convicted; nor take private property for public use without just compensation.

The powers over person and property of which we speak are not only not granted to congress, but are in express terms denied, and they are forbidden to exercise them. And this prohibition is not confined to the States, but the words are general, and extend to the whole territory over which the constitution gives it power to legislate, including those portions of it remaining under territorial government, as well as that covered by States. It is a total absence of power everywhere within the dominion of the United States, and places the citizens of a territory, so far as these rights are concerned, on the same footing with citizens of the States, and guards them as firmly and plainly against any inroads which the general government might attempt, under the plea of implied or incidental powers. And if congress itself cannot do this—if it is beyond the powers conferred on the federal government—it will be admitted, we presume, that it could not authorize a territorial government to exercise them. It could confer no power on any local government, established by its authority, to violate the provisions of the constitution.

It seems, however, to be supposed, that there is a difference between property in a slave and other property, and that different rules may be applied to it in expounding the constitution of the United States. And the laws and usages of nations, and the writings of eminent jurists upon the relation of master and slave and their mutual rights and duties, and the powers which governments may exercise over it, have been dwelt upon in the argument.

But in considering the question before us, it must be borne in mind that there is no law of nations standing between the people of the United States and their government, and interfering with their relation to each other. The powers of the government, and the rights of the citizen under it, are positive and practical regulations plainly written down. The people of the United States have delegated to it certain enumerated powers, and forbidden it to exercise others. It has no power over the person or property of a citizen but what the citizens of the United States have granted. And no laws or usages of other nations, or reasoning of statesmen or jurists upon the relations of master and slave, can enlarge the powers of the government, or take from the citizens the rights they have reserved. And if the constitution recognizes the right of property of the master in a slave, and makes no distinction between that description of property and other property owned by a citizen, no tribunal, acting under the authority of the United States, whether it be legislative, executive, or judicial, has a right to draw such a distinction, or deny to it the benefit of the provisions and guarantees which have been provided for the protection of private property against the encroachments of the government.

Now, as we have already said in an earlier part of this opinion, upon a different point, the right of property in a slave is distinctly and expressly affirmed in the constitution. The right to traffic in it, like an ordinary article of merchandise and property, was guaranteed to the citizens of the United States, in every State that might desire it, for twenty years. And the government in express terms is pledged to protect it in all future time, if the slave escapes from his owner. This is done in plain words—too plain to be misunderstood. And no word can be found in the constitution which gives congress a greater power over slave property, or which entitles property of that kind to less protection that property of any other description. The only power conferred is the power coupled with the duty of guarding and protecting the owner in his rights.

Upon these considerations, it is the opinion of the court that the act of congress which prohibited a citizen from holding and owning property of this kind in the territory of the United States north of the line therein mentioned, is not warranted by the constitution, and is therefore void; and that neither Dred Scott himself, nor any of his family, were made free by being carried into this territory; even if they had been carried there by the owner, with the intention of becoming a permanent resident.

We have so far examined the case, as it stands under the constitution of the United States, and the powers thereby delegated to the federal government.

But there is another point in the case which depends on State power and State law. And it is contended, on the part of the plaintiff, that he is made free by being taken to Rock Island, in the State of Illinois, independently of his residence in the territory of the United States; and being so made free, he was not again reduced to a state of slavery by being brought back to Missouri.

Our notice of this part of the case will be very brief; for the principle on which it depends was decided in this court, upon much consideration, in the case of Strader *et al. v.* Graham, reported in 10th Howard, 82. In that case, the slaves had been taken from Kentucky to Ohio, with the consent of the owner, and afterwards brought back to Kentucky. And this court held that their *status* or condition, as free or slave, depended upon the laws of Kentucky, when they were brought back into that State, and not of Ohio; and that this court had no jurisdiction to revise the judgment of a State court upon its own laws. This was the point directly before the court, and the decision that this court had not jurisdiction turned upon it, as will be seen by the report of the case.

So in this case. As Scott was a slave when taken into the State of Illinois by his owner, and was there held as such, and brought back in that character, his *status*, as free or slave, depended on the laws of Missouri, and not of Illinois.

It has, however, been urged in the argument, that by the laws of Missouri he was free on his return, and that this case, therefore, cannot be governed by the case of Strader *et al. v.* Graham, where it appeared, by the laws of Kentucky, that the plaintiffs continued to be slaves on their return from Ohio. But whatever doubts or opinions may, at one time, have been entertained upon this subject, we are satisfied, upon a careful examination of all the cases decided in the State courts of Missouri referred to, that it is now firmly settled by the decisions of the highest court in the State, that Scott and his family upon their return were not free, but were, by the laws of Missouri, the property of the defendant; and that the circuit court of the United States had no jurisdiction, when, by the laws of the State, the plaintiff was a slave, and not a citizen.

Moreover, the plaintiff, it appears, brought a similar action against the defendant in the State court of Missouri, claiming the freedom of himself and his family upon the same grounds and the same evidence upon which he relies in the case before the court. The case was carried before the supreme court of the State; was fully argued there; and that court decided that neither the plaintiff nor his family were entitled to freedom, and were still the slaves of the defendant; and reversed the judgment of the inferior State court, which had given a different decision. If the plaintiff supposed that this judgment of the supreme court of the State was erroneous, and that this court had jurisdiction to revise and reverse it, the only mode by which he could legally bring it before this court was by writ of error directed to the supreme court of the State, requiring it to transmit the record to this court. If this had been done, it is too plain for argument that the writ must have been dismissed for want of jurisdiction in this court. The case of Strader and others *v.* Graham is directly in point; and, indeed, independent of any decision, the language of the 25th section of the act of 1789 is too clear and precise to admit of controversy.

But the plaintiff did not pursue the mode prescribed by law for bringing the judgment of a State court before this court for revision, but suffered the case to be remanded to the inferior State court, where it is still continued, and is, by agreement of parties, to await the judgment of this court on the point. All of this appears on the record before us, and by the printed report of the case.

And while the case is yet open and pending in the inferior State court, the plaintiff goes into the circuit court of the United States, upon the same case and the same evidence, and against the same party, and proceeds to judgment, and then brings here the same case from the circuit court, which the law would not have permitted him to bring directly from the State court. And if this court takes jurisdiction in this form, the result, so far as the rights of the respective parties are concerned, is in every respect substantially the same as if it had in open violation of law entertained jurisdiction over the judgment of the State court upon a writ of error, and revised and reversed its judgment upon the ground that its opinion upon the question of law was erroneous. It would ill become this court to sanction such an attempt to evade the law, or to exercise an appellate power in this circuitous way, which it is forbidden to exercise in the direct and regular and invariable forms of judicial proceedings.

Upon the whole, therefore, it is the judgment of this court, that it appears by the record before us that the plaintiff in error is not a citizen of Missouri, in the sense in which that word is used in the constitution; and that the circuit court of the United States, for that reason, had no jurisdiction in the case, and could give no judgment in it. Its judgment for the defendant must, consequently, be reversed, and a mandate issued, directing the suit to be dismissed for want of jurisdiction.

Mr. Justice WAYNE.

Concurring as I do entirely in the opinion of the court, as it has been written and read by the chief justice—without any qualification of its reasoning or its conclusions—I shall neither read nor file an opinion of my own in this case, which I prepared when I supposed it might be necessary and proper for me to do so.

The opinion of the court meets fully and decides every point which was made in the argument of the case by the counsel on either side of it. Nothing belonging to the case has been left undecided, nor has any point been discussed and decided which was not called for by the record, or which was not necessary for the judicial disposition of it, in the way that it has been done, by more than a majority of the court.

In doing this, the court neither sought nor made the case. It was brought to us in the course of that administration of the laws which congress has enacted, for the review of cases from the circuit courts by the supreme court.

In our action upon it, we have only discharged our duty as a distinct and efficient department of the government, as the framers of the constitution meant the judiciary to be, and as the States of the Union and the people of those States intended it should be, when they ratified the constitution of the United States.

The case involves private rights of value, and constitutional principles of the highest importance, about which there had become such a difference of opinion, that the peace and harmoney of the country required the settlement of them by judicial decision.

It would certainly be a subject of regret, that the conclusions of the court have not been assented to by all of its members, if I did not know from its history and my own experience how rarely it has happened that the judges have been unanimous upon constitutional questions of moment, and if our decision in this case had not been made by as large a majority of them as has been usually had on constitutional questions of importance.

Two of the judges, Mr. Justices McLean and Curtis, dissent from the opinion of the court. A third, Mr. Justice Nelson, gives a separate opinion upon a single point in the case, with which I concur, assuming that the circuit court had jurisdiction; but he abstains altogether from expressing any opinion upon the eighth section of the act of 1820, known commonly as the Missouri Compromise law, and six of us declare that it was unconstitutional.

But it has been assumed, that this court has acted extra-judicially in giving an opinion upon the eighth section of the act of 1820, because, as it has decided that the circuit court had no jurisdiction of the case, this court had no jurisdiction to examine the case upon its merits.

But the error of such an assertion has arisen in part from a misapprehension of what has been heretofore decided by the supreme court, in cases of a like kind with that before us; in part, from a misapplication to the circuit courts of the United States, of the rules of pleading concerning pleas to the jurisdiction which prevail in common-law courts; and from its having been forgotten that this case was not brought to this court by appeal or writ of error from a State court, but by a writ of error to the circuit court of the United States.

The cases cited by the chief justice to show that this court has now only done what it has repeatedly done before in other cases, without any question of its correctness, speak for themselves. The differences between the rules concerning pleas to the jurisdiction in the courts of the United States and common-law courts have been stated and sustained by reasoning and adjudged cases; and it has been shown that writs of error to a State court and to the circuit courts of the United States are to be determined by different laws and principles. In the first, it is our duty to ascertain if this court has jurisdiction, under the twenty-fifth section of the judiciary act, to review the case *from the State court;* and if it shall be found that it has not, the case is at end, so far as this court is concerned; for our power to review the case upon its merits has been made, by the twenty-fifth section, to depend upon its having jurisdiction; when it has not, this court cannot criticise, controvert, or give any opinion upon the merits of a case from a State court.

But in a case brought to this court, by appeal or by writ of error from *a circuit court of the United States,* we begin a review of it, *not by inquiring if this court has jurisdiction,* but if that court has it. If the case has been decided by that court upon its merits, but the record shows it to be deficient in those averments which by the law of the United States must be made by the plaintiff in the action, to give the court jurisdiction of his case, we send it back to the court from which it was brought, with directions to be dismissed, though it has been decided there upon its merits.

So, in a case containing the averments by the plaintiff which are necessary to give the circuit court jurisdiction, if the defendant shall file his plea in abatement denying the truth of them, and the plaintiff shall demur to it, and the court should *erroneously sustain the plaintiff's demurrer, or declare the plea to be insufficient, and by doing so require the defendant to answer over by a plea to the merits, and shall decide the case upon such pleading,* this court has the same authority to inquire into the jurisdiction of that court to do so, and to correct its error in that regard, that it had in the other case to correct its error, in trying a case in which the plaintiff had not made those averments which were necessary to give the court jurisdiction. In both cases the record is resorted to, be determine [to determine] the point of jurisdiction; but, as the power of review of cases from a federal court, by this court, is not limited by the law to a part of the case, this court may correct an error upon the merits; and there is the same reason for correcting an erroneous judgment of the circuit court, where the want of jurisdiction appears from any part of the record, that there is for declaring a want of jurisdiction for a want of necessary averments. And attempt to control the court from doing so by the technical common-law rules of pleading in cases of jurisdiction, when a defendant has been denied his plea to it, would tend to enlarge the jurisdiction of the circuit court, by limiting this court's review of its judgments in that particular. But I will not argue a point already so fully discussed. I have every confidence in the opinion of the court upon the point of jurisdiction, and do not allow myself to doubt that the error of a contrary conclusion will be fully understood by all who shall read the argument of the chief justice.

I have already said that the opinion of the court has my unqualified assent.

Mr. Justice NELSON.

I shall proceed to state the grounds upon which I have arrived at the conclusion, that the judgment of the court below should be affirmed. The suit was brought in the court below by the plaintiff, for the purpose of asserting his freedom, and that of Harriet, his wife, and two children.

The defendant plead, in abatement to the suit, that the cause of action, if any, accrued to the plaintiff out of the jurisdiction of the court, and exclusively within the jurisdiction of the courts of the State of Missouri; for, that the said plaintiff is not a citizen of the State of Missouri, as alleged in the declaration, because he is a negro of African descent; his ancestors were of pure African blood, and were brought into this country and sold as negro slaves.

To this plea the plaintiff demurred, and the defendant joined in demurrer. The court below sustained the demurrer, holding that the plea was insufficient in law to abate the suit.

The defendant then plead over in bar of the action:

1. The general issue. 2. That the plaintiff was a negro slave, the lawful property of the defendant. And 3. That Harriet, the wife of said plaintiff, and the two children, were the lawful slaves of the said defendant. Issue was taken upon these pleas, and the cause went down to trial before the court and jury, and an agreed state of facts was presented, upon which the trial proceeded, and resulted in a verdict for the defendant, under the instructions of the court.

The facts agreed upon were substantially as follows:

That in the year 1834, the plaintiff, Scott, was a negro slave of Dr. Emerson, who was a surgeon in the army of the United States; and in that year he took the plaintiff from the State of Missouri to the military post at Rock Island, in the State of Illinois, and held him there as a slave until the month of April or May, 1836. At this date, Dr. Emerson removed, with the plaintiff, from the Rock Island post to the military post at Fort Snelling, situate on the west bank of the Mississippi river, in the Territory of Upper Louisiana, and north of the latitude thirty-six degrees thirty minutes, and north of the State of Missouri. That he held the plaintiff in slavery, at Fort Snelling, from the last-mentioned date until the year 1838.

That in the year 1835, Harriet, mentioned in the declaration, was a negro slave of Major Taliaferro, who belonged to the army of the United States; and in that year he took her to Fort Snelling, already mentioned, and kept her there as a slave until the year 1836, and then sold and delivered her to Dr. Emerson, who held her in slavery, at Fort Snelling, until the year 1838. That in the year 1836, the plaintiff and Harriet were married, at Fort Snelling, with the consent of their master. The two children, Eliza and Lizzie, are the fruit of this marriage. The first is about fourteen years of age, and was born on board the steamboat Gipsey, north of the State of Missouri, and upon the Mississippi river; the other, about seven years of age, was born in the State of Missouri, at the military post called Jefferson Barracks.

In 1838, Dr. Emerson removed the plaintiff, Harriet, and their daughter Eliza, from Fort Snelling to the State of Missouri, where they have ever since resided. And that, before the commencement of this suit, they were sold by the Doctor to Sandford, the defendant, who has claimed and held them as slaves ever since.

The agreed case also states that the plaintiff brought a suit for his freedom, in the circuit court of the State of Missouri, on which a judgment was rendered in his favor; but that, on a writ of error from the supreme court of the State, the judgment of the court below was reversed, and the cause remanded to the circuit for a new trial.

On closing the testimony in the court below, the counsel for the plaintiff prayed the court to instruct the jury, upon the agreed state of facts, that they ought to find for the plaintiff; when the court refused, and instructed them that, upon the facts, the law was with the defendant.

With respect to the plea in abatement, which went to the citizenship of the plaintiff, and his competency to bring a suit in the federal courts, the common-law rule of pleading is, that upon a judgment against the plea on demurrer, and that the defendant answer over, and the defendant submits to the judgment, and pleads over to the merits, the plea in abatement is deemed to be waived, and is not afterwards to be regarded as a part of the record in deciding upon the rights regarded as a part of the record in deciding upon the rights of the parties. There is some question, however, whether this rule of pleading applies to the peculiar system and jurisdiction of the federal courts. As, in these courts, if the facts appearing on the record show that the circuit court had no jurisdiction, its judgment will be reversed in the appellate court for that cause, and the case remanded with directions to be dismissed.

In the view we have taken of the case, it will not be necessary to pass upon this question, and we shall therefore proceed at once to an examination of the case upon its merits. The question upon the merits, in general terms, is, whether or not the removal of the plaintiff, who was a slave, with his master, from the State of Missouri to the State of Illinois, with a view to a temporary residence, and after such residence and return to the slave State, such residence in the free State works an emancipation.

As appears from an agreed statement of facts, this question has been before the highest court of the State of Missouri, and a judgment rendered that this residence in the free State has no such effect; but, on the contrary, that his original condition continued unchanged.

The court below, the circuit court of the United States for Missouri, in which this suit was afterwards brought, followed the decision of the State court, and rendered a like judgment against the plaintiff.

The argument against these decisions is, that the laws of Illinois, forbidding slavery within her territory, had the effect to set the slave free while residing in that State, and to impress upon him the condition and status of a freeman; and that, by force of these laws, this status and condition accompanied him on his return to the slave State, and of consequence he could not be there held as a slave.

This question has been examined in the courts of several of the slaveholding States, and different opinions expressed and conclusions arrived at. We shall hereafter refer to some of them, and to the principles upon which they are founded. Our opinion is, that the question is one which belongs to each State to decide for itself, either by its legislature or courts of justice; and hence, in respect to the case before us, to the State of Missouri—a question exclusively of Missouri law, and which, when determined by that State, it is the duty of the Federal courts to follow it. In other words, except in cases where the power is restrained by the constitution of the United States, the law of the State is supreme over the subject of slavery within its jurisdiction.

As a practical illustration of the principle, we may refer to the legislation of the free States in abolishing slavery, and prohibiting its introduction into their territories. Confessedly, except as restrained by the federal constitution, they exercised, and rightfully, complete and absolute power over the subject. Upon what principle, then, can it be denied to the State of Missouri? The power flows from the sovereign character of the States of the Union; sovereign, not merely as respects the federal government—except as they have consented to its limitation—but sovereign as respects each other. Whether, therefore, the State of Missouri will recognize or give effect to the laws of Illinois within her territories on the subject of slavery, is a question for her to determine. Nor is there any constitutional power in this government that can rightfully control her.

Every State or nation possesses an exclusive sovereignty and jurisdiction within her own territory; and, her laws affect and bind all property and persons residing within it. It may regulate the manner and circumstances under which property is held, and the condition, capacity, and state, of all persons therein; and, also, the remedy and modes of administering justice. And it is equally true, that no State or nation can affect or bind property out of its territory, or persons not residing within it. No State, therefore, can enact laws to operate beyond its own dominions, and, if it attempts to do so, it may be lawfully refused obedience. Such laws can have no inherent authority extra-territorially. This is the necessary result of the independence of distinct and separate sovereignties.

Now, it follows from these principles, that whatever force or effect the laws of one State or nation may have in the territories of another, must depend solely upon the laws and municipal regulations of the latter, upon its own jurisprudence and polity, and upon its own express or tacit consent.

Judge Story observes, in his Conflict of Laws, (p. 24,) "that a State may prohibit the operation of all foreign laws, and the rights growing out of them, within its territories." "And that when its code speaks positively on the subject, it must be obeyed by all persons who are within reach of its sovereignty; when its customary unwritten or common law speaks directly on the subject, it is equally to be obeyed."

Nations, from convenience and comity, and from mutual interest, and a sort of moral necessity to do justice, recognize and administer the laws of other countries. But, of the nature, extent, and utility, of them, respecting property, or the state and condition of persons within her territories, each nation judges for itself; and is never bound, even upon the ground of comity, to recognize them, if prejudicial to her own interests. The recognition is purely from comity, and not from any absolute or paramount obligation.

Judge Story again observes, (398,) "that the true foundation and extent of the obligation of the laws of one nation within another is the voluntary consent of the latter, and is inadmissible when they are contrary to its known interests." And he adds, "in the silence of any positive rule affirming or denying or restraining the operation of the foreign laws, courts of justice presume the tacit adoption of them by their own government, unless they are repugnant to its policy or prejudicial to its interests." (See also 2 Kent Com., p. 457; 13 Peters, 519, 589.)

These principles fully establish, that it belongs to the sovereign State of Missouri to determine by her laws the question of slavery within her jurisdiction, subject only to such limitations as may be found in the federal constitution; and, further, that the laws of other States of the confederacy, whether enacted by their legislatures or expounded by their courts, can have no operation within her territory, or affect rights growing out of her own laws on the subject. This is the necessary result of the independent and sovereign character of the State. The principle is not peculiar to the State of Missouri, but is equally applicable to each State belonging to the confederacy. The laws of each have no extra-territorial operation within the jurisdiction of another, except such as may be voluntarily conceded by her laws or courts of justice. To the extent of such concession upon the rule of comity of nations, the foreign law may operate, as it then becomes a part of the municipal law of the State. When determined that the foreign law shall have effect, the municipal law of the State retires, and gives place to the foreign law.

In view of these principles, let us examine a little more closely the doctrine of those who maintain that the law of Missouri is not to govern the status and condition of the plaintiff. They insist that the removal and temporary residence with his master in Illinois, where slavery is inhibited, had the effect to set him free, and that the same effect is to be given to the law of Illinois, within the State of Missouri, after his return. Why was he set free in Illinois? Because the law of Missouri, under which he was held as a slave, had no operation by its own force extra-territorially; and the State of Illinois refused to recognize its effect within her limits, upon principles of comity, as a state of slavery was inconsistent with her laws, and contrary to her policy. But, how is the case different on the return of the plaintiff to the State of Missouri? Is she bound to recognize and enforce the law of Illinois? For, unless she is, the status and condition of the slave upon his return remains the same as originally existed. Has the law of Illinois any greater force within the jurisdiction of Missouri, than the laws of the latter within that of the former? Certainly not. They stand upon an equal footing. Neither has any force extra-territorially, except what may be voluntarily conceded to them.

It has been supposed, by the counsel for the plaintiff, that a rule laid down by Huberus had some bearing upon this question. Huberus observes that "personal qualities, impressed by the laws of any place, surround and accompany the person wherever he goes, with this effect: that in every place he enjoys and is subject to the same law which other persons of his class elsewhere enjoy or are subject to." (De Confl. Leg., lib. 1, tit. 3, sec. 12; 4 Dallas, 375 n.; 1 Story Con. Laws, pp. 59, 60.)

The application sought to be given to the rule was this: that as Dred Scott was free while residing in the State of Illinois, by the laws of that State, on his return to the State of Missouri he carried with him the personal qualities of freedom, and that the same effect must be given to his status there as in the former State. But the difficulty in the case is in the total misapplication of the rule.

These personal qualities, to which Huberus refers, are those impressed upon the individual by the law of the domicile; it is this that the author claims should be permitted to accompany the person into whatever country he might go, and should supersede the law of the place where he had taken up a temporary residence.

Now, as the domicile of Scott was in the State of Missouri, where he was a slave, and from whence he was taken by his master into Illinois for a temporary residence, according to the doctrine of Huberus, the law of his domicile would have accompanied him, and during his residence there he would remain in the same condition as in the State of Missouri. In order to have given effect to the rule, as claimed in the argument, it should have been first shown that a domicile had been acquired in the free State, which cannot be pretended upon the agreed facts in the case. But the true answer to the doctrine of Huberus is, that the rule, in any aspect in which it may be viewed, has no bearing upon either side of the question before us, even if conceded to the extent laid down by the author; for he admits that foreign governments give effect to these laws of the domicile no further than they are consistent with their own laws, and not prejudicial to their own subjects; in other words, their force and effect depend upon the law of comity of the foreign government. We should add, also, that this general rule of Huberus, referred to, has not been admitted in the practice of nations, nor is it sanctioned by the most approved jurists of international law. (Story Con. secs. 91, 96, 103, 104; 2 Kent Com. pp. 457, 458; 1 Burge Con. Laws, pp. 12, 127.)

We come now to the decision of this court in the case of Strader *et al. v.* Graham, (10 How. p. 2.) The case came up from the court of appeals, in the State of Kentucky. The question in the case was, whether certain slaves of Graham, a resident of Kentucky, who had been employed temporarily at several places in the

State of Ohio, with their master's consent, and had returned to Kentucky into his service, had thereby become entitled to their freedom. The court of appeals held that they had not. The case was brought to this court under the twenty-fifth section of the judiciary act. This court held that it had no jurisdiction, for the reason, the question was one that belonged exclusively to the State of Kentucky. The chief justice, in delivering the opinion of the court, observed that "every State has an undoubted right to determine the status or domestic and social condition of the persons domiciled within its territory, except in so far as the powers of the States in this respect are restrained, or duties and obligations imposed upon them, by the constitution of the United States. There is nothing in the constitution of the United States, he observes, that can in any degree control the law of Kentucky upon this subject. And the condition of the negroes, therefore, as to freedom or slavery, after their return, depended altogether upon the laws of that State, and could not be influenced by the laws of Ohio. It was exclusively in the power of Kentucky to determine, for herself, whether their employment in another State should or should not make them free on their return."

It has been supposed, in the argument on the part of the plaintiff, that the eighth section of the act of congress passed March 6, 1820, (3 St. at Large, p. 544,) which prohibited slavery north of thirty-six degrees thirty minutes, within which the plaintiff and his wife temporarily resided at Fort Snelling, possessed some superior virtue and effect, extra-territorially, and within the State of Missouri, beyond that of the laws of Illinois, or those of Ohio in the case of Strader *et al. v.* Graham. A similar ground was taken and urged upon the court in the case just mentioned, under the ordinance of 1787, which was enacted during the time of the confederation, and reenacted by congress after the adoption of the constitution, with some amendments adapting it to the new government. (1 St. at Large, p. 50.)

In answer to this ground, the chief justice, in delivering the opinion of the court, observed: "The argument assumes that the six articles which that ordinance declares to be perpetual, are still in force in the States since formed within the territory, and admitted into the Union. If this proposition could be maintained, it would not alter the question; for the regulations of congress, under the old confederation or the present constitution, for the government of a particular territory, could have no force beyond its limits. It certainly could not restrict the power of the States, within their respective territories, nor in any manner interfere with their laws and institutions, nor give this court control over them.

"The ordinance in question, he observes, if still in force, could have no more operation than the laws of Ohio in the State of Kentucky, and could not influence the decision upon the rights of the master or the slaves in that State."

This view, thus authoritatively declared, furnishes a conclusive answer to the distinction attempted to be set up between the extra-territorial effect of a State law and the act of congress in question.

It must be admitted that congress possesses no power to regulate or abolish slavery within the States; and that, if this act had attempted any such legislation, it would have been a nullity. And yet the argument here, if there be any force in it, leads to the result, that effect may be given to such legislation; for it is only by giving the act of congress operation within the State of Missouri, that it can have any effect upon the question between the parties. Having no such effect directly, it will be difficult to maintain, upon any consistent reasoning, that it can be made to operate indirectly upon the subject.

The argument, we think, in any aspect in which it may be viewed, is utterly destitute of support upon any principles of constitutional law, as, according to that, congress has no power whatever over the subject of slavery within the State; and is also subversive of the established doctrine of international jurisprudence, as, according to that, it is an axiom that the laws of one government have no force within the limits of another, or extra-territorially, except from the consent of the latter.

It is perhaps not unfit to notice, in this connection, that many of the most eminent statesmen and jurists of the country entertain the opinion that this provision of the act of congress, even within the territory to which it relates, was not authorized by any power under the constitution. The doctrine here contended for, not only upholds its validity in the territory, but claims for it effect beyond and within the limits of a sovereign State—an effect, as insisted, that displaces the laws of the State, and substitutes its own provisions in their place.

The consequences of any such construction are apparent. If congress possesses the power, under the constitution, to abolish slavery in a territory, it must necessarily possess the like power to establish it. It cannot be a one-sided power, as may suit the convenience or particular views of the advocates. It is a power, if it exists at all, over the whole subject; and then, upon the process of reasoning which seeks to extend its influence beyond the territory, and within the limits of a State, if congress should establish, instead of abolish, slavery, we do not see but that, if a slave should be removed from the territory into a free State, his status would accompany him, and continue, notwithstanding its laws against slavery. The laws of the free State, according to the argument, would be displaced, and the act of congress, in its effect, be substituted in their place. We do not see how this conclusion could be avoided, if the construction against which we are contending should prevail. We are satisfied, however, it is unsound, and that the true answer to it is, that even conceding, for the purposes of the argument, that this provision of the act of congress is valid within the territory for which it was enacted, it can have no operation or effect beyond its limits, or within the jurisdiction of a State. It can neither displace its laws, nor change the status or condition of its inhabitants.

Our conclusion, therefore, is, upon this branch of the case, that the question involved is one depending solely upon the law of Missouri, and that the federal court sitting in the State, and trying the case before us, was bound to follow it.

The remaining question for consideration is, What is the law of the State of Missouri on this subject? And it would be a sufficient answer to refer to the judgment of the highest court of the State in the very case, were it not due to that tribunal to state somewhat at large the course of decision and the principles involved, on account of some diversity of opinion in the cases. As we have already stated, this case was originally brought in the circuit court of the State, which resulted in a judgment for the plaintiff. The case was carried up to the supreme court for revision. That court reversed the judgment below, and remanded the cause to the circuit, for a new trial. In that state of the proceeding, a new suit was brought by the plaintiff in the circuit court of the United States, and tried upon the issues and agreed case before us, and a verdict and judgment for the defendant, that court following the decision of the supreme court of the State. The judgment of the supreme court is reported in the 15 Misso. R. p. 576. The court placed the decision upon the temporary residence of the master with the slaves in the State and Territory to which they removed, and their return to the slave State; and upon the principles of international law, that foreign laws have no extra-territorial force, except such as the State within which they are sought to be enforced may see fit to extend to them, upon the doctrine of comity of nations.

This is the substance of the grounds of the decision.

The same question has been twice before that court since, and the same judgment given, (15 Misso. R. 595; 17 Ib. 434.) It must be admitted, therefore, as the settled law of the State, and, according to the decision in the case of Strader *et al. v.* Graham, is conclusive of the case in this court.

It is said, however, that the previous cases and course of decision in the State of Missouri on this subject were different, and that the courts had held the slave to be free on his return from a temporary residence in the free State. We do not see, were this to be admitted, that the circumstance would show that the settled course of decision, at the time this case was tried in the court below, was not to be considered the law of the State. Certainly, it must be, unless the first decision of a principle of law by a State court is to be permanent and irrevocable. The idea seems to be, that the courts of a State are not to change their opinions, or, if they do, the first decision is to be regarded by this court as the law of the State. It is certain, if this be so, in the case before us, it is an exception to the rule governing this court in all other cases. But what court has not changed its opinions? What judge has not changed his?

Waiving, however, this view, and turning to the decisions of the courts of Missouri, it will be found that there is no discrepancy between the earlier and the present cases upon this subject. There are some eight of them reported previous to the decision in the case before us, which was decided in 1852. The last of the earlier cases was decided in 1836. In each one of these, with two exceptions, the master or mistress removed into the free State with the slave, with a view to a permanent residence—in other words, to make that his or her domicile. And in several of the cases, this removal and permanent residence were relied on, as the ground of the decision in favor of the plaintiff. All these cases, therefore, are not necessarily in conflict with the decision in the case before us, but consistent with it. In one of the two excepted cases, the master had hired the slave in the State of Illinois from 1817 to 1825. In the other, the master was an officer in the army, and removed with his slave to the military post of Fort Snelling, and at Prairie du Chien, in Michigan, temporarily, while acting under the orders of his government. It is conceded the decision in this case was departed from in the case before us, and in those that have followed it. But it is to be observed that these subsequent cases are in conformity with those in all the slave States bordering on the free—in Kentucky, (2 Marsh. 476; 5 B. Munroe, 176; 9 Ib. 565)—in Virginia, (1 Rand. 15; 1 Leigh, 172; 10 Grattan, 495)—in Maryland, (4 Harris and McHenry, 295, 322, 325.) In conformity, also, with the law of England on this subject, *Ex parte* Grace, (2 Hagg. Adm. R. 94,) and with the opinions of the most eminent jurists of the country. (Story's Confl. 396 *a;* 2 Kent Com. 258 n; 18 Pick. 193, Chief Justice Shaw. See Corresp. between Lord Stowell and Judge Story, 1 vol. Life of Story, p. 552, 558.)

Lord Stowell, in communicating his opinion in the case of the slave Grace to Judge Story, states, in his letter, what the question was before him, namely: "Whether the emancipation of a slave brought to England insured a complete emancipation to him on his return to his own country, or whether it only operated as a suspension of slavery in England, and his original character devolved on him again upon his return." He observed, "the question had never been examined since an end was put to slavery fifty years ago," having reference to the decision of Lord Mansfield in the case of Somersett; but the practice, he observed, "has regularly been, that on his return to his own country, the slave resumed his original character of slave." And so Lord Stowell held in the case.

Judge Story, in his letter in reply, observes: "I have read with great attention your judgment in the slave case, &c. Upon the fullest consideration which I have been able to give the subject, I entirely concur in your views. If I had been called upon to pronounce a judgment in a like case, I should have certainly arrived at the same result." Again he observes: "In my native State, (Massachusetts,) the state of slavery is not recognized as legal; and yet, if a slave should come hither, and afterwards return to his own home, we should certainly think that the local law attached upon him, and that his servile character would be reintegrated."

We may remark, in this connection, that the case before the Maryland court, already referred to, and which was decided in 1799, presented the same question as that before Lord Stowell, and received a similar decision. This was nearly thirty years before the decision in that case, which was in 1828. The court of appeals observed, in deciding the Maryland case, that "however the laws of Great Britain in such instances, operating upon such persons there, might interfere so as to prevent the exercise of certain acts by the masters, not permitted, as in the case of

Somersett, yet, upon the bringing Ann Joice into this State, (then the province of Maryland,) the relation of master and slave continued in its extent, as authorized by the laws of this State." And Luther Martin, one of the counsel in that case, stated, on the argument, that the question had been previously decided the same way in the case of slaves returning from a residence in Pennsylvania, where they had become free under her laws.

The State of Louisiana, whose courts had gone further in holding the slave free on his return from a residence in a free State than the courts of her sister States, has settled the law, by an act of her legislature, in conformity with the law of the court of Missouri in the case before us. (Sess. Law, 1846.)

The case before Lord Stowell presented much stronger features for giving effect to the law of England in the case of the slave Grace than exists in the cases that have arisen in this country, for in that case the slave returned to a colony of England over which the imperial government exercised supreme authority. Yet, on the return of the slave to the colony, from a temporary residence in England, he held that the original condition of the slave attached. The question presented in cases arising here is as to the effect and operation to be given to the laws of a foreign State, on the return of the slave within an independent sovereignty.

Upon the whole, it must be admitted that the current of authority, both in England and in this country, is in accordance with the law as declared by the courts of Missouri in the case before us, and we think the court below was not only right, but bound to follow it.

Some question has been made as to the character of the residence in this case in the free State. But we regard the facts as set forth in the agreed case as decisive. The removal of Dr. Emerson from Missouri to the military posts was in the discharge of his duties as surgeon in the army, and under the orders of his government. He was liable at any moment to be recalled, as he was in 1838, and ordered to another post. The same is also true as it respects Major Taliaferro. In such a case, the officer goes to his post for a temporary purpose, to remain there for an uncertain time, and not for the purpose of fixing his permanent abode. The question we think too plain to require argument. The case of the Attorney General *v.* Napier, (6 Welsh, Hurtst. and Gordon Exch. Rep. 217) illustrates and applies the principle in the case of an officer of the English army.

A question has been alluded to, on the argument, namely: the right of the master with his slave of transit into or through a free State, on business or commercial pursuits, or in the exercise of a federal right, or the discharge of a federal duty, being a citizen of the United States, which is not before us. This question depends upon different considerations and principles from the one in hand, and turns upon the rights and privileges secured to a common citizen of the republic under the constitution of the United States. When that question arises, we shall be prepared to decide it.

Our conclusion is, that the judgment of the court below should be affirmed.

Mr. Justice GRIER.

I concur in the opinion delivered by Mr. Justice Nelson on the questions discussed by him.

I also concur with the opinion of the court as delivered by the chief justice, that the act of congress of 6th March, 1820, is unconstitutional and void; and that, assuming the facts as stated in the opinion, the plaintiff cannot sue as a citizen of Missouri in the courts of the United States. But, that the record shows a prima facie case of jurisdiction, requiring the court to decide all the questions properly arising in it; and as the decision of the pleas in bar shows that the plaintiff is a slave, and therefore not entitled to sue in a court of the United States, the form of the judgment is of little importance; for, whether the judgment be affirmed or dismissed for want of jurisdiction, it is justified by the decision of the court, and is the same in effect between the parties to the suit.

Mr. Justice DANIEL.

It may with truth be affirmed, that since the establishment of the several communities now constituting the States of this confederacy, there never has been submitted to any tribunal within its limits questions surpassing in importance those now claiming the consideration of this court. Indeed it is difficult to imagine, in connection with the systems of polity peculiar to the United States, a conjuncture of graver import than that must be, within which it is aimed to comprise, and to control, not only the faculties and practical operation appropriate to the American confederacy as such, but also the rights and powers of its separate and independent members, with reference alike to their internal and domestic authority and interests, and the relations they sustain to their confederates.

To my mind it is evident, that nothing less than the ambitious and far-reaching pretension to [en]compass these objects of vital concern, is either directly essayed or necessarily implied in the positions attempted in the argument for the plaintiff in error.

How far these positions have any foundation in the nature of the rights and relations of separate, equal, and independent governments, or in the provisions of our own federal compact, or the laws enacted under and in pursuance of the authority of that compact, will be presently investigated.

In order correctly to comprehend the tendency and force of those positions, it is proper here succinctly to advert to the facts upon which the questions of law propounded in the argument have arisen.

This was an action of trespass *vi et armis*, instituted in the circuit court of the United States for the district of Missouri, in the name of the plaintiff in error, *a negro* held as a slave, for the recovery of freedom for himself, his wife, and two children, *also negroes*.

To the declaration in this case the defendant below, who is also the defendant in error, pleaded in abatement that the court could not take cognizance of the cause, because the plaintiff was not *a citizen* of the State of Missouri, as averred in the declaration, but was a *negro of African descent,* and that his ancestors were of pure African blood, and were brought into this country and sold as *negro slaves;* and hence it followed, from the second section of the third article of the constitution, which creates the judicial power of the United States, with respect to controversies between citizens of different States, that the circuit court could not take cognizance of the action.

To this plea in abatement, a demurrer having been interposed on behalf of the plaintiff, it was sustained by the court. After the decision sustaining the demurrer, the defendant, in pursuance of a previous agreement between counsel, and with the leave of the court, pleaded in bar of the action: 1*st, not guilty;* 2*dly, that the plaintiff was a negro slave, the lawful property of the defendant, and as such the defendant gently laid his hands upon him, and thereby had only restrained him, as the defendant had a right to do;* 3*dly, that with respect to the wife and daughters of the plaintiff, in the second and third counts of the declaration mentioned, the defendant had, as to them, only acted in the same manner, and in virtue of the same legal right.*

Issues having been joined upon the above pleas in bar, the following statement, comprising all the evidence in the cause, was agreed upon and signed by the counsel of the respective parties, viz:

"In the year 1834, the plaintiff was a negro slave belonging to Doctor Emerson, who was a surgeon in the army of the United States. In that year, 1834, said Dr. Emerson took the plaintiff from the State of Missouri to the military post at Rock Island, in the State of Illinois, and held him there as a slave until the month of April or May, 1836. At the time last mentioned, said Dr. Emerson removed the plaintiff from said military post at Rock Island to the military post at Fort Snelling, situate on the west bank of the Mississippi river, in the territory known as upper Louisiana, acquired by the United States of France, and situate north of the latitude of thirty-six degrees thirty minutes north, and north of the State of Missouri. Said Dr. Emerson held the plaintiff in slavery at said Fort Snelling, from said last-mentioned date until the year 1838.

"In the year 1835, Harriet, who is named in the second count of the plaintiff's declaration, was the negro slave of Major Taliaferro, who belonged to the army of the United States. In that year, 1835, said Major Taliaferro took said Harriet to said Fort Snelling, a military post situated as hereinbefore stated, and kept her there as a slave until the year 1836, and then sold and delivered her as a slave at said Fort Snelling unto the said Dr. Emerson, hereinbefore named. Said Dr. Emerson held said Harriet in slavery at said Fort Snelling until the year 1838.

"In the year 1836, the plaintiff and said Harriet, at said Fort Snelling, with the consent of said Dr. Emerson, who then claimed to be their master and owner, intermarried, and took each other for husband and wife. Eliza and Lizzie, named in the third count of the plaintiff's declaration, are the fruit of that marriage. Eliza is about fourteen years old, and was born on board the steamboat Gipsey, north of the north line of the State of Missouri, and upon the river Mississippi. Lizzie is about seven years old, and was born in the State of Missouri, at a military post called Jefferson Barracks.

"In the year 1838, said Dr. Emerson removed the plaintiff and said Harriet, and their said daughter Eliza, from said Fort Snelling to the State of Missouri, where they have ever since resided.

"Before the commencement of this suit, said Dr. Emerson sold and conveyed the plaintiff, said Harriet, Eliza, and Lizzie, to the defendant, as slaves, and the defendant has ever since claimed to hold them and each of them as slaves.

"At the times mentioned in the plaintiff's declaration, the defendant, claiming to be owner as aforesaid, laid his hands upon said plaintiff, Harriet, Eliza, and Lizzie, and imprisoned them, doing in this respect, however, no more than what he might lawfully do if they were of right his slaves at such times.

"Further proof may be given on the trial for either party.

"R. M. FIELD, *for Plaintiff.*
"H. A. GARLAND, *for Defendant.*

"It is agreed that Dred Scott brought suit for his freedom in the circuit court of St. Louis county; that there was a verdict and judgment in his favor; that on a writ of error to the supreme court, the judgment below was reversed, and the cause remanded to the circuit court, where it has been continued to await the decision of this case.

"FIELD, *for Plaintiff.*
"GARLAND, *for Defendant.*"

Upon the aforegoing agreed facts, the plaintiff prayed the court to instruct the jury that they ought to find for the plaintiff, and upon the refusal of the instruction thus prayed for, the plaintiff excepted to the court's opinion. The court then, upon the prayer of the defendant, instructed the jury, that upon the facts of this case agreed as above, the law was with the defendant. To this opinion, also, the plaintiff's counsel excepted, as he did to the opinion of the court denying to the plaintiff a new trial after the verdict of the jury in favor of the defendant.

The question first in order presented by the record in this cause, is that which arises upon the plea in abatement, and the demurrer to that plea; and upon this question it is my opinion that the demurrer should have been overruled, and the plea sustained.

On behalf of the plaintiff it has been urged, that by the pleas interposed in bar of a recovery in the court below, (which pleas both in fact and in law are essentially the same with the objections averred in abatement,) the defence in abatement has been displaced or waived; that it could therefore no longer be relied on in the circuit court, and cannot claim the consideration of this court in reviewing this cause. This position is regarded as wholly untenable. On the contrary, it would seem to follow conclusively from the peculiar character of the courts of the United States, as organized under the constitution and the statutes, and as defined by numerous and unvarying adjudications from this bench, that there is not one of those courts whose jurisdiction and powers can be deduced from mere custom or tradition; not one, whose jurisdiction and powers must not be traced palpably to, and invested exclusively by, the constitution and statutes of the United States; not one that is not bound, therefore, at all times, and at all stages of its proceedings, to look to and to regard the special and declared extent and bounds of its commission and authority. There is no such tribunal of the United States as a court of *general jurisdiction*, in the sense in which that phrase is applied to the superior courts under the common law; and even with respect to the courts existing under that system, it is a well-settled principle, that *consent* can never give jurisdiction.

The principles above stated, and the consequences regularly deducible from them, have, as already remarked, been repeatedly and unvaryingly propounded from this bench. Beginning with the earliest decisions of this court, we have the cases of Bingham *v.* Cabot *et al.* (3 Dallas, 382;) Turner *v.* Eurille, (4 Dallas, 7;) Abercrombie *v.* Dupuis *et al.* (1 Cranch, 343;) Wood *v.* Wagnon, (2 Cranch, 9;) The United States *v.* The Brig Union *et al.* (4 Cranch, 216;) Sullivan *v.* The Fulton Steamboat Company, (6 Wheaton, 450;) Mollan *et al. v.* Torrence, (9 Wheaton, 537;) Brown *v.* Keene, (8 Peters, 112,) and Jackson *v.* Ashton, (8 Peters, 148;) ruling, in uniform and unbroken current, the doctrine that it is essential to the jurisdiction of the courts of the United States, that the facts upon which it is founded should appear upon the record. Nay, to such an extent and so inflexibly has this requisite to the jurisdiction been enforced, that in the case of Capron *v.* Van Noorden, (2 Cranch, 126,) it is declared, that the plaintiff in this court may assign for error his own omission in the pleadings in the court below, where they go to the jurisdiction. This doctrine has been, if possible, more strikingly illustrated in a later decision, the case of The State of Rhode Island *v.* The State of Massachusetts, in the 12th of Peters.

In this case, on page 718 of the volume, this court, with reference to a motion to dismiss the cause *for want of jurisdiction*, have said: "*However late this objection has been made, or may be made, in any cause in an inferior or appellate court of the United States*, it must be considered and decided before any court can move one farther step in the cause, as any movement is necessarily to exercise the jurisdiction. Jurisdiction is the power to hear and determine the subject-matter in controversy between the parties to a suit; to adjudicate or exercise any judicial power over them. The question is, whether on the case before the court their action is judicial or extra-judicial; with or without the authority of law to render a judgment or decree upon the rights of the litigant parties. A motion to dismiss a cause pending in the courts of the United States, is not analogous to a plea to the jurisdiction of a court of common law or equity in England; there, the superior courts have a general jurisdiction over all persons within the realm, and all causes of action between them. It depends on the subject-matter, whether the jurisdiction shall be exercised by a court of law or equity; but that court to which it appropriately belongs can act judicially upon the party and the subject of the suit, unless it shall be made apparent to the court that the judicial determination of the case has been withdrawn from the court of general jurisdiction to an inferior and limited one. It is a necessary presumption that the court of general jurisdiction can act upon the given case, when nothing to the contrary appears; hence has arisen the rule that the party claiming an exemption from its process must set out the reason by a special plea in abatement, and show that some inferior court of law or equity has the exclusive cognizance of the case, otherwise the superior court must proceed in virtue of its general jurisdiction. A motion to dismiss, therefore, cannot be entertained, as it does not disclose a case of exception; and if a plea in abatement is put in, it must not only make out the exception, but point to the particular court to which the case belongs. There are other classes of cases where the objection to the jurisdiction is of a different nature, as on a bill in chancery, that the subject-matter is cognizable only by the king in council, or that the parties['] defendant cannot be brought before any municipal court on account of their sovereign character or the nature of the controversy; or to the very common cases which present the question, whether the cause belong to a court of law or equity. To such cases, a plea in abatement would not be applicable, because the plaintiff could not sue in an inferior court. The objection goes to a denial of any jurisdiction of a municipal court in the one class of cases, and to the jurisdiction of any court of equity or of law in the other, on which last the court decides according to its discretion.

"An objection to jurisdiction on the ground of exemption from the process of the court in which the suit is brought, or the manner in which a defendant is brought into it, is waived by appearance and pleading to issue; but when the objection goes to the power of the court over the parties or the subject-matter, the defendant need not, for he cannot, give the plaintiff a better writ. Where an inferior court can have no jurisdiction of a case of law or equity, the ground of objection is not taken by plea in abatement, as an exception of the given case from the otherwise general jurisdiction of the court; appearance does not cure the defect of judicial power, and it may be relied on by plea, answer, demurrer, *or at the trial or hearing.* As a denial of jurisdiction over the subject-matter of a suit between parties within the realm, over which and whom the court has power to act, cannot be successful in an English court of general jurisdiction, a motion like the present could not be sustained consistently with the principles of its constitution. *But as this court is one of limited and special original jurisdiction,* its action must be confined to the particular cases, controversies, and parties, over which the constitution and laws have authorized it to act; any proceeding without the limits prescribed is *coram non judice,* and its action a nullity. And whether the want or excess of power is objected by a party, or is apparent to the court, it must surcease its action or proceed extra-judicially."

In the constructing of pleadings either in abatement or in bar, every fact or position constituting a portion of the public law, or of known or general history, is necessarily implied. Such fact or position need not be specially averred and set forth; it is what the world at large and every individual are presumed to know— nay, are bound to know and to be governed by.

If, on the other hand, there exist facts or circumstances by which a particular case would be withdrawn or exempted from the influence of public law or necessary historical knowledge, such facts and circumstances form an exception to the general principle, and these must be specially set forth and *established* by those who would avail themselves of such exception.

Now, the following are truths which a knowledge of the history of the world, and particularly of that of our own country, compels us to know—that the African negro race never have been acknowledged as belonging to the family of nations; that as amongst them there never has been known or recognized by the inhabitants of other countries anything partaking of the character of nationality, or civil or political polity; that this race has been by all the nations of Europe regarded as subjects of capture or purchase; as subjects of commerce or traffic; and that the introduction of that race into every section of this country was not as members of civil or political society, but as slaves, as *property* in the strictest sense of the term.

In the plea in abatement, the character or capacity of citizen on the part of the plaintiff is denied; and the causes which show the absence of that character or capacity are set forth by averment. The verity of those causes, according to the settled rules of pleading, being admitted by the demurrer, it only remained for the circuit court to decide upon their legal sufficiency to abate the plaintiff's action. And it now becomes the province of this court to determine whether the plaintiff below, (and in error here,) admitted to be a *negro* of African descent, whose ancestors were of pure African blood, and were brought into this country and sold as negro slaves—such being his *status,* and such the circumstances surrounding his position—whether he can, by correct legal induction from that *status* and those circumstances, be clothed with the character and capacities of a citizen of the State of Missouri?

It may be assumed as a postulate, that to a slave, as such, there appertains and can appertain no relation, civil or political, with the State or the government. He is himself strictly *property,* to be used in subserviency to the interests, the convenience, or the will, of his owner; and to suppose, with respect to the former, the existence of any privilege or discretion, or of any obligation to others incompatible with the magisterial rights just defined, would be by implication, if not directly, to deny the relation of master and slave, since none can possess and enjoy, as his own, that which another has a paramount right and power to withhold. Hence it follows, necessarily, that a slave, the *peculium* or property of a master, and possessing within himself no civil nor political rights or capacities, cannot be a CITIZEN. For who, it may be asked, is a citizen? What do the character and *status* of citizen import? Without fear of contradiction, it does not import the condition of being private property, the subject of individual power and ownership. Upon a principle of etymology alone, the term *citizen*, as derived from *civitas*, conveys the ideas of connection or identification with the State or government, and a participation of its functions. But beyond this, there is not, it is believed, to be found, in the theories of writers on government, or in any actual experiment heretofore tried, an exposition of the term *citizen*, which has not been understood as conferring the actual possession and enjoyment, or the perfect right of acquisition and enjoyment, of an entire equality of privileges, civil and political.

Thus Vattel, in the preliminary chapter to his Treatise on the Law of Nations, says: "Nations or states are bodies politic; societies of men united together for the purpose of promoting their mutual safety and advantage, by the joint efforts of their mutual strength. Such a society has her affairs and her interests; she deliberates and takes resolutions *in common;* thus becoming a moral person, who possesses an understanding and a will peculiar to herself." Again, in the first chapter of the first book of the Treatise just quoted, the same writer, after repeating his definition of a State, proceeds to remark, that, "from the very design that induces a number of men to form a society, which has its common interests and which is to act in concert, it is necessary that there should be established a public authority, to order and direct what is to be done by each, in relation to the end of the association. This political authority is the *sovereignty*." Again this writer remarks: "The authority of *all* over each member essentially belongs to the body politic or the State."

By this same writer it is also said: "The citizens are the members of the civil society; bound to this society by certain duties, and subject to its authority; they *equally* participate in its advantages. The natives, or natural-born citizens, are those born in the country, of parents who are citizens. As society cannot perpetuate itself otherwise than by the children of the citizens, those children naturally follow the condition of their parents, and succeed to all their rights." Again: "I say, to be *of the country*, it is necessary to be born of a person who is a *citizen;* for if he be born there of a foreigner, it will be only the place of his *birth*, and not his *country*. The inhabitants, as distinguished from citizens, are foreigners who are permitted to settle and stay in the country." (Vattel, book 1, cap. 19, p. 101.)

From the views here expressed, and they seem to be unexceptionable, it must follow, that with the *slave*, with one devoid of rights or capacities, *civil or political*, there could be no pact; that one thus situated could be no party to, or actor in, the association of those possessing free will, power, discretion. He could form no part of the design, no constituent ingredient or portion of a society based upon *common,* that is, upon *equal* interests and powers. He could not at the same time be the sovereign and the slave.

But it has been insisted, in argument, that the emancipation of a slave, effected either by the direct act and assent of the master, or by causes operating in contravention of his will, produces a change in the *status* or capacities of the slave, such as will transform him from a mere subject of property, into a being possessing a social, civil, and political equality with a citizen. In other words, will make him a citizen of the State within which he was, previously to his emancipation, a slave.

It is difficult to conceive by what magic the mere *surcease* or renunciation of an interest in a subject of *property,* by an individual possessing that interest, can alter the essential character of that property with respect to persons or communities unconnected with such renunciation. Can it be pretended that an individual in any State, by his single act, though voluntarily or designedly performed, yet without the co-operation or warrant of the government, perhaps in opposition to its policy or its guaranties, can create a citizen of that State? Much more emphatically may it be asked, how such a result could be accomplished by means wholly extraneous, and entirely foreign to the government of the State? The argument thus urged must lead to these extraordinary conclusions. It is regarded at once as wholly untenable, and as unsustained by the direct authority or by the analogies of history.

The institution of slavery, as it exists and has existed from the period of its introduction into the United States, though more humane and mitigated in character than was the same institution, either under the republic or the empire of Rome, bears, both in its tenure and in the simplicity incident to the mode of its exercise, a closer resemblance to Roman slavery than it does to the condition of *villanage,* as it formerly existed in England. Connected with the latter, there were peculiarities, from custom or positive regulation, which varied it materially from the slavery of the Romans, or from slavery at any period within the United States.

But with regard to slavery amongst the Romans, it is by no means true that emancipation, either during the republic or the empire, conferred, by the act itself, or implied, the *status* or the rights of citizenship.

The proud title of Roman citizen, with the immunities and rights incident thereto, and as contradistinguished alike from the condition of conquered subjects or of the lower grades of native domestic residents, was maintained throughout the duration of the republic, and until a late period of the eastern empire, and at last was in *effect* destroyed less by an elevation of the inferior classes than by the degradation of the free, and the previous possessors of rights and immunities civil and political, to the indiscriminate abasement incident to absolute and simple despotism.

By the learned and elegant historian of the Decline and Fall of the Roman Empire, we are told that "In the *decline* of the Roman empire, the proud distinctions of the republic were gradually abolished; and the reason or instinct of Justinian completed the simple form of an absolute monarchy. The emperor could not eradicate the popular reverence which always waits on the possession of hereditary wealth or the memory of famous ancestors. He delighted to honor with titles and emoluments his generals, magistrates, and senators, and his precarious indulgence communicated some rays of their glory to their wives and children. But in the eye of the law all Roman citizens were equal, and all subjects of the empire were citizens of Rome. That inestimable character was *degraded* to an obsolete and empty name. The voice of a Roman could no longer enact his laws, or create the annual ministers of his powers; his constitutional rights might have checked the arbitrary will of a master; and the bold adventurer from Germany or Arabia was admitted with equal favor to the civil and military command which the *citizen* alone had been once entitled to assume over the conquests of his fathers. The first Caesars had scrupulously guarded the distinction of *ingenuous* and *servile* birth, which was decided by the condition of the mother. The slaves who were liberated by a generous master immediately entered into the middle class of *libertini* or freedmen; but they could never be enfranchised from the duties of obedience and gratitude; whatever were the fruits of their industry, their patron and his family inherited the third part, or even the whole of their fortune, if they died without children and without a testament. Justinian respected the rights of patrons, but his indulgence removed the badge of disgrace from the two inferior orders of freedmen; whoever ceased to be a slave, obtained without reserve or delay the station of a citizen; and at length the dignity of an ingenuous birth *was created* or *supposed* by the omnipotence of the emperor."[1]

The above account of slavery and its modifications will be found in strictest conformity with the Institutes of Justinian. Thus, book 1st, title 3d, it is said: "The first general division of persons in respect to their rights is into freemen and slaves." The same title, sec. 4th: "Slaves are born such, or become so. They are born such of bondwomen; they become so either by *the law of nations,* as by capture, or by the civil law." Section 5th: "In the condition of slaves there is no diversity; but among free persons there are many. Thus some are *ingenui* or freemen, others *libertini* or freedmen."

Tit. 4th. DE INGENUIS.—"A freeman is one who is born free by being born in matrimony, of parents who both are free, or both freed; or of parents one free and the other freed. But one born of a free mother, although the father be a slave or unknown, is free."

Tit. 5th. DE LIBERTINIS.—"Freedmen are those who have been manumitted from just servitude."

Section third of the same title states that "freedmen were formerly distinguished by a threefold division." But the emperor proceeds to say: "Our *piety* leading us to reduce all things into a better state, we have amended our laws, and reestablished the ancient usage; for anciently liberty was simple and undivided—that is, was conferred upon the slave as his manumittor possessed it, admitting this single difference, that the person manumitted became only a *freed man,* although his manumittor was a *free* man." And he further declares: "We have made all freed men in general become citizens of Rome, regarding neither the age of the manumitted, nor the manumittor, nor the ancient forms of manumission. We have also introduced many new methods by which *slaves* may become Roman citizens."

By the references above given it is shown, from the nature and objects of civil and political associations, and upon the direct authority of history, that citizenship was not conferred by the simple fact of emancipation, but that such a result was deduced therefrom in violation of the fundamental principles of free political association; by the exertion of despotic will to establish, under a false and misapplied denomination, one equal and universal slavery; and to effect this result required the exertions of absolute power—of a power both in theory and practice, being in its most plenary acceptation the SOVEREIGNTY, THE STATE ITSELF—it could not be produced by a less or inferior authority, much less by the will or the act of one who, with reference to civil and political rights, was himself a *slave.* The master might abdicate or abandon his interest or ownership in his property, but his act would be a mere abandonment. It seems to involve an absurdity to impute to it the investiture of rights which the sovereignty alone had power to impart. There is not perhaps a community in which slavery is recognized, in which the power of emancipation and the modes of its exercise are not regulated by law—that is, by the sovereign authority; and none can fail to comprehend the necessity for such regulation, for the preservation of order, and even of political and social existence.

By the argument for the plaintiff in error, a power equally despotic is vested in every member of the association, and the most obscure or unworthy individual it comprises may arbitrarily invade and derange its most deliberate and solemn ordinances. At assumptions anomalous as these, so fraught with mischief and ruin, the mind at once is revolted, and goes directly to the conclusions, that to change or to abolish a fundamental principle of the society, must be the act of the society itself—of the *sovereignty;* and that none other can admit to a participation of that high attribute. It may further expose the character of the argument urged for the plaintiff, to point out some of the revolting consequences which it would authorize. If that argument possesses any integrity, it asserts the power in any citizen, or *quasi* citizen, or a resident foreigner of any one of the States, from a motive either of corruption or caprice, not only to infract the inherent and necessary authority of such State, but also materially to interfere with the organization of the federal government, and with the authority of the separate and independent States. He may emancipate his negro slave, by which process he first transforms that slave into a citizen of his own State; he may next, under color of article fourth, section second, of the constitution of the United States, obtrude him, and on terms of civil and political equality, upon any and every State in this Union, in defiance of all regulations of necessity or policy, ordained by those States for their internal happiness or safety. Nay, more: this manumitted slave may, by a proceeding springing from the will or act of his master alone, be mixed up with the institutions of the federal government, to which he is not a party, and in opposition to the laws of that government which, in authorizing the extension by naturalization of the rights and immunities of citizens of the United States to those not originally parties to the Federal compact, have restricted that boon to *free white aliens alone*. If the rights and immunities connected with or practiced under the institutions of the United States can by any indirection be claimed or deduced from sources or modes other than the constitution and laws of the United States, it follows that the power of naturalization vested in congress is not exclusive—that it has *in effect* no existence, but is repealed or abrogated.

But it has been strangely contended that the jurisdiction of the circuit court might be maintained upon the ground that the plaintiff was a *resident* of Missouri, and that, for the purpose of vesting the court with jurisdiction over the parties, *residence* within the State was sufficient.

The first, and to my mind a conclusive reply to this singular argument is presented in the fact, that the language of the constitution restricts the jurisdiction of the courts to cases in which the parties shall be *citizens,* and is entirely silent with respect to residence. A second answer to this strange and latitudinous notion is, that it so far stultifies the sages by whom the constitution was framed, as to impute to them ignorance of the material distinction existing between *citizenship* and mere *residence* or *domicil,* and of the well-known facts, that a person confessedly an *alien* may be permitted to reside in a country in which he can possess no civil or political rights, or of which he is neither a citizen nor subject; and that for certain purposes a man may have a *domicil* in different countries, in no one of which he is an actual personal resident.

The correct conclusions upon the question here considered would seem to be these:

That in the establishment of the several communities now the States of this Union, and in the formation of the federal government, the African was not deemed politically a person. He was regarded and owned in every State in the Union as *property* merely, and as such was not and could not be a party or an actor, much less a *peer* in any compact or form of government established by the States or the United States. That if, since the adoption of the State governments, he has been or could have been elevated to the po[s]session of political rights or powers, this result could have been effected by no authority less potent than that of the sovereignty—the State—exerted to that end, either in the form of legislation, or in some other mode of operation. It could certainly never have been accomplished by the will of an individual operating independently of the sovereign power, and even contravening and controlling that power. That so far as rights and immunities appertaining to citizens have been defined and secured by the constitution and laws of the United States, the African race is not and never was recognized either by the language or purposes of the former; and it has been expressly excluded by every act of congress providing for the creation of citizens by *naturalization*, these laws, as has already been remarked, being restricted to *free white aliens* exclusively.

But it is evident that, after the formation of the federal government by the adoption of the constitution, the highest exertion of State power would be incompetent to bestow a character or status created by the constitution, or conferred in virtue of its authority only. Upon those, therefore, who were not originally parties to the federal compact, or who are not admitted and adopted as parties thereto, in the mode prescribed by its paramount authority, no State could have power to bestow the character or the rights and privileges exclusively reserved by the States for the action of the federal government by that compact.

The States, in the exercise of their political power, might, with reference to their peculiar government and jurisdiction, guaranty the rights of person and property, and the enjoyment of civil and political privileges, to those whom they should be disposed to make the objects of their bounty; but they could not reclaim or exert the powers which they had vested exclusively in the government of the United States. They could not add to or change in any respect the class of persons to whom alone the character of citizen of the United States appertained at the time of the adoption of the federal constitution. They could not create citizens of the United States by any direct or indirect proceeding.

According to the view taken of the law, as applicable to the demurrer to the plea in abatement in this cause, the questions subsequently raised upon the several pleas in bar might be passed by, as requiring neither a particular examination, nor an adjudication directly upon them. But as these questions are intrinsically of primary interest and magnitude, and have been elaborately discussed in argument, and as with respect to them the opinions of a majority of the court, including my own, are perfectly coincident, to me it seems proper that they should here be fully considered, and, so far as it is practicable for this court to accomplish such an end, finally put to rest.

The questions then to be considered upon the several pleas in bar, and upon the agreed statement of facts between the counsel, are: 1st. Whether the admitted master and owner of the plaintiff, holding him as his slave in the State of Missouri, and in conformity with his rights guaranteed to him by the laws of Missouri then and still in force, by carrying with him for his own benefit and accommodation, and as his own slave, the person of the plaintiff into the State of Illinois, within which State slavery had been prohibited by the constitution thereof, and by retaining the plaintiff during the commorancy of the master within the State of Illinois, had, upon his return with his slave into the State of Missouri, forfeited his rights as master, by reason of any supposed operation of the prohibitory provision in the Constitution of Illinois, beyond the proper territorial jurisdiction of the latter State? 2d. Whether a similar removal of the plaintiff by his master from the State of Missouri, and his retention in service at a point included within no State, but situated north of thirty-six degrees thirty minutes of north latitude, worked a forfeiture of the right of property of the master, and the manumission of the plaintiff?

In considering the first of these questions, the acts or declarations of the master, as expressive of his purpose to emancipate, may be thrown out of view, since none will deny the right of the owner to relinquish his interest in any subject of property, at any time or in any place. The inquiry here bears no relation to acts or declarations of the owner as expressive of his intent or purpose to make such a relinquishment; it is simply a question whether, irrespective of such purpose, and in opposition thereto, that relinquishment can be enforced against the owner of property within his own country, in defiance of every guaranty promised by its laws; and this through the instrumentality of a claim to power entirely foreign and extraneous with reference to himself, to the origin and foundation of his title, and to the independent authority of his country. A conclusive negative answer to such an inquiry is at once supplied, by announcing a few familiar and settled principles and doctrines of public law.

Vattel, in his chapter of the general principles of the laws of nations, section 15th, tells us, that "nations being free and independent of each other in the same manner that men are naturally free and independent, the second general law of their society is, that each nation should be left in the peaceable enjoyment of that liberty which she inherits from nature."

"The natural society of nations," says this writer, "cannot subsist unless the natural rights of each be respected." In section 16th he says, "as a consequence of that liberty and independence, it exclusively belongs to each nation to form her own judgment of what her conscience prescribes for her—of what it is proper or improper for her to do; and of course it rests solely with her to examine and determine whether she can perform any office for another nation without neglecting the duty she owes to herself. In all cases, therefore, in which a nation has the right of judging what her duty requires, no other nation can compel her to act in such or such a particular manner, for any attempt at such compulsion would be an infringement on the liberty of nations." Again, in section 18th, of the same chapter, "nations composed of men, and considered as so many free persons living together in a state of nature, are naturally equal, and inherit from nature the same obligations and rights. Power or weakness does not produce any difference. A small republic is no less a sovereign state than the most powerful kingdom."

So, in section 20: "A nation, then, is mistress of her own actions, so long as they do not affect the proper and *perfect rights* of any other nation—so long as she is only *internally* bound, and does not lie under any *external* and *perfect* obligation. If she makes an ill use of her liberty, she is guilty of a breach of duty; but other nations are bound to acquiesce in her conduct, since they have no right to dictate to her. Since nations are *free, independent,* and *equal,* and since each possesses the right of judging, according to the dictates of her conscience, what conduct she is to pursue, in order to fulfil her duties, the effect of the whole is to produce, at least externally, in the eyes of mankind, a perfect equality of rights between nations, in the administration of their affairs, and in the pursuit of their pretensions, without regard to the intrinsic justice of their conduct, of which others have no right to form a definitive judgment."

Chancellor Kent, in the 1st volume of his Commentaries, lecture 2d, after collating the opinions of Grotius, Heineccius, Vattel, and Rutherford, enunciates the following positions as sanctioned by these and other learned publicists, viz: that "nations are equal in respect to each other, and entitled to claim equal consideration for their rights, whatever may be their relative dimensions or strength, or however greatly they may differ in government, religion, or manners. This perfect equality and entire independence of all distinct States is a fundamental principle of public law. It is a necessary consequence of this equality, that each nation has a right to govern itself as it may think proper, and no one nation is entitled to dictate a form of government or religion, or a course of internal policy, to another." This writer gives some instances of the violation of this great national immunity, and amongst them the constant interference by the ancient Romans, under the pretext of settling disputes between their neighbors, but with the real purpose of reducing those neighbors to bondage; the interference of Russia, Prussia, and Austria, for the dismemberment of Poland; the more recent invasion of Naples by Austria in 1821, and of Spain by the French government in 1823, under the excuse of suppressing a dangerous spirit of internal revolution and reform.

With reference to this right of self-government in independent sovereign States, an opinion has been expressed, which, whilst it concedes this right as inseparable from and as a necessary attribute of sovereignty and independence, asserts nevertheless some implied and paramount authority of a supposed international law, to which this right of self-government must be regarded and exerted as subordinate; and from which independent and sovereign States can be exempted only by a protest, or by some public and formal rejection of that authority. With all respect for those by whom this opinion has been professed, I am constrained to regard it as utterly untenable, as palpably inconsistent, and as presenting in argument a complete *felo de se.*

Sovereignty, independence, and a perfect right of self-government, can signify nothing less than a superiority to and an exemption from all claims by any extraneous power, however expressly they may be asserted, and render all attempts to enforce such claims merely attempts at usurpation. Again, could such claims from extraneous sources be regarded as legitimate, the effort to resist or evade them, by protest or denial, would be as irregular and unmeaning as it would be futile. It could in no wise affect the question of superior right. For the position here combatted, no respectable authority has been, and none it is thought can be adduced. It is certainly irreconcilable with the doctrines already cited from the writers upon public law.

Neither the case of Lewis Somersett, (Howell's State Trials, vol. 20,) so often vaunted as the proud evidence of devotion to freedom under a government which has done as much perhaps to extend the reign of slavery as all the world besides; nor does any decision founded upon the authority of Somersett's case, when correctly expounded, assail or impair the principle of national equality enunciated by each and all of the publicists already referred to. In the case of Somersett, although the applicant for the *habeas corpus* and the individual claiming property in that applicant were both subjects and residents within the British empire, yet the decision cannot be correctly understood as ruling absolutely and under all circumstances against the right of property in the claimant. That decision goes no farther than to determine, that *within the realm of England* there was no authority to justify the detention of an individual in private bondage. If the decision in Somersett's case had gone beyond this point, it would have presented the anomaly of a repeal by laws enacted for and limited in their operation to the realm alone, of other laws and institutions established for places and subjects without the limits of the realm of England; laws and institutions at that very time, and long subsequently, sanctioned and maintained under the authority of the British government, and which the full and combined action of the king and parliament was required to abrogate.

But could the decision in Somersett's case be correctly interpreted as ruling the doctrine which it has been attempted to deduce from it, still that doctrine must be considered as having been overruled by the lucid and able opinion of Lord Stowell in the more recent case of the slave Grace, reported in the second volume of Haggard, p. 94; in which opinion, whilst it is conceded by the learned judge that there existed no power to coerce the slave whilst in England, that yet, upon her return to the island of Antigua, her *status* as a slave was revived, or, rather, that the title of the owner to the slave as property had never been extinguished, but had always existed in that island. If the principle of this decision be applicable as between different portions of one and the same empire, with how much more force does it apply as between nations or governments entirely separate, and absolutely independent of each other? For in this precise attitude the States of this Union stand with reference to this subject, and with reference to the tenure of every description of property vested under their laws and held within their territorial jurisdiction.

A strong illustration of the principle ruled by Lord Stowell, and of the effect of that principle even in a case of express *contract*, is seen in the case of Lewis *v.* Fullerton, decided by the supreme court of Virginia, and reported in the first volume of Randolph, p. 15. The case was this: A female slave, the property of a citizen of Virginia, whilst with her master in the State of Ohio, was taken from his possession under a writ of *habeas corpus,* and set at liberty. Soon, or immediately after, by agreement between this slave and her master, a deed was executed in Ohio by the latter, containing a stipulation that this slave should return to Virginia, and, after a service of two years in that State, should there be free. The law of Virginia regulating emancipation required that deeds of emancipation should, within a given time from their date, be recorded in the court of the county in which the grantor resided, and declared that deeds with regard to which this requisite was not complied with should be void. Lewis, an infant son of this female, under the rules prescribed in such cases, brought an action, *in forma pauperis,* in one of the courts of Virginia, for the recovery of his freedom, claimed in virtue of the transactions above mentioned. Upon an appeal to the supreme court from a judgment against the plaintiff, Roane, justice, in delivering the opinion of the court, after disposing of other questions discussed in that case, remarks:

"As to the deed of emancipation contained in the record, that deed, taken in connection with the evidence offered in support of it, shows that it had a reference to the State of Virginia; and the testimony shows that it formed a part of this contract, whereby the slave Milly was to be brought back (as she was brought back) into the State of Virginia. Her object was therefore to secure her freedom by the deed within the State of Virginia, after the time should have expired for which she had indented herself, and when she should be found abiding within the State of Virginia.

"If, then, this contract had an eye to the State of Virginia for its operation and effect, the *lex loci* ceases to operate. In that case it must, to have its effect, conform to the laws of Virginia. It is insufficient under those laws to effectuate an emancipation, for what of a due recording in the county court, as was decided in the case of Givens *v.* Mann, in this court. It is also ineffectual within the commonwealth of Virginia for another reason. The *lex loci* is also to be taken subject to the exception, that it is not to be enforced in another country, when it violates some moral duty or the policy of that country, or is not consistent with a positive right secured to a third person or party by the laws of that country in which it is sought to be enforced. In such a case we are told, "*magis jus nostrum, quam jus alienum servemus.*" (Huberus, tom. 2, lib. 1, tit. 3; 2 Fontblanque, p. 444.) "That third party in this instance is the commonwealth of Virginia, and her policy and interests are also to be attended to. These turn the scale against the *lex loci* in the present instance."

The second or last-mentioned position assumed for the plaintiff under the pleas in bar, as it rests mainly if not solely upon the provision of the act of congress of March 6, 1820, prohibiting slavery in upper Louisiana north of thirty-six degrees thirty minutes north latitude, popularly called the *Missouri Compromise,* that assumption renews the question, formerly so zealously debated, as to the validity of the provision in the act of congress, and upon the constitutional competency of congress to establish it.

Before proceeding, however, to examine the validity of the prohibitory provision of the law, it may, so far as the rights involved in this cause are concerned, be remarked, that conceding to that provision the validity of a legitimate exercise of power, still this concession could by no rational interpretation imply the slightest authority for its operation beyond the territorial limits comprised within its terms; much less could there be inferred from it a power to destroy or in any degree to control rights, either of person or property, entirely within the bounds of a distinct and independent sovereignty—rights invested and fortified by the guaranty of that sovereignty. These surely would remain in all their integrity, whatever effect might be ascribed to the prohibition within the limits defined by its language.

But, beyond and in defiance of this conclusion, inevitable and undeniable as it appears, upon every principle of justice or sound induction, it has been attempted to convert this prohibitory provision of the act of 1820 not only into a weapon with which to assail the inherent—the *necessarily* inherent—powers of independent sovereign governments, but into a mean[s] of forfeiting that equality of rights and immunities which are the birthright or the donative from the constitution of every citizen of the United States within the length and breadth of the nation. In this attempt, there is asserted a power in congress, whether from incentives of interest, ignorance, faction, partiality, or prejudice, to bestow upon a portion of the citizens of this nation that which is the common property and privilege of all—the power, in fine, of confiscation, in retribution for no offence, or, if for an offence, for that of accidental locality only.

It may be that, with respect to future cases, like the one now before the court, there is felt an assurance of the impotence of such a pretension; still, the fullest conviction of that result can impart to it no claim to forbearance, nor disperse with the duty of antipathy and disgust at its sinister aspect, whenever it may be seen to scowl upon the justice, the order, the tranquillity, and fraternal feeling, which are the surest, nay, the only means, of promoting or preserving the happiness and prosperity of the nation, and which were the great and efficient incentives to the formation of this government.

The power of congress to impose the prohibition in the eighth section of the act of 1820 has been advocated upon an attempted construction of the second clause of the third section of the fourth article of the constitution, which declares that "congress shall have power to dispose of and to make all needful rules and regulations respecting the *territory* and *other property belonging* to the United States."

In the discussions in both houses of congress, at the time of adopting this eighth section of the act of 1820, great weight was given to the peculiar language of this clause, viz: *territory* and *other property belonging* to the United States, as going to show that the power of disposing of and regulating, thereby vested in congress, was restricted to a *proprietary interest in the territory or land* comprised therein, and did not extend to the personal or political rights of citizens or settlers, inasmuch as this phrase in the constitution, *"territory or other property,"* identified *territory* with *property,* and inasmuch as *citizens* or *persons* could not be property, and especially were not property *belonging* to the United States. And upon every principle of reason or necessity, this power to dispose of and to regulate the *territory* of the nation could be designed to extend no farther than to its preservation and appropriation to the uses of those to whom it belonged, viz: the nation. Scarcely anything more illogical or extravagant can be imagined than the attempt to deduce from this provision in the constitution a power to destroy or in any wise to impair the civil and political rights of the citizens of the United States, and much more so the power to establish inequalities amongst those citizens by creating privileges in one class of those citizens, and by the disfranchisement of other portions or classes, by degrading them from the position they previously occupied.

There can exist no rational or natural connection or affinity between a pretension like this and the power vested by the constitution in congress with regard to the territories; on the contrary, there is an absolute incongruity between them.

But whatever the power vested in congress, and whatever the precise subject to which that power extended, it is clear that the power related to a subject appertaining to the *United States,* and one to be disposed of and regulated for the benefit and under the authority of the *United States.* Congress was made simply the agent or *trustee* for the United States, and could not, without a breach of trust and a fraud, appropriate the subject of the trust to any other beneficiary or *cestui que trust* than the United States, or to the people of the United States, upon equal grounds, legal or equitable. Congress could not appropriate that subject to any one class or portion of the people, to the exclusion of others, politically and constitutionally equals; but every citizen would, if any *one* could claim it, have the like rights of purchase, settlement, occupation, or any other right, in the national territory.

Nothing can be more conclusive to show the equality of this with every other right in all the citizens of the United States, and the iniquity and absurdity of the pretension to exclude or to disfranchise a portion of them because they are the owners of slaves, than the fact that the same instrument, which imparts to congress its very existence and its every function, guaranties to the slaveholder the title to his property, and gives him the right to its reclamation throughout the entire extent of the nation; and, farther, that the only private property which the constitution has *specifically recognized,* and has imposed it as a direct obligation both on the States and the federal government to protect and *enforce,* is the property of the master in his slave; no other right of property is placed by the constitution upon the same high ground, nor shielded by a similar guaranty.

Can there be imputed to the sages and patriots by whom the constitution was framed, or can there be detected in the text of that constitution, or in any rational construction or implication deducible therefrom, a contradiction so palpable as would exist between a pledge to the slaveholder of an equality with his fellow-citizens, and of the formal and solemn assurance for the security and enjoyment of his property, and a warrant given, as it were *uno flatu,* to another, to rob him of that property, or to subject him to proscription and disfranchisement for possessing or for endeavoring to retain it? The injustice and extravagance necessarily implied in a supposition like this, cannot be rationally imputed to the patriotic or the honest, or to those who were merely sane.

A conclusion in favor of the prohibitory power in congress, as asserted in the eighth section of the act of 1820, has been attempted, as deducible from the precedent of the ordinance of the convention of 1787, concerning the cession by Virginia of the territory northwest of the Ohio; the provision in which ordinance, relative to slavery, it has been attempted to impose upon other and subsequently-acquired territory.

The first circumstance which, in the consideration of this provision, impresses itself upon my mind, is its utter futility and want of authority. This court has, in repeated instances, ruled, that whatever may have been the force accorded to this ordinance of 1787 at the period of its enactment, its authority and effect ceased, and yielded to the paramount authority of the constitution, from the period of the adoption of the latter. Such is the principle ruled in the cases of Pollard's Lessee *v.* Hagan, (3 How. 212,) Parmoli *v.* The First Municipality of New Orleans, (3 How. 589,) Strader *v.* Graham, (16 How. 82.) But apart from the superior control of the constitution, and anterior to the adoption of that instrument, it is obvious that the inhibition in question never had and never could have any legitimate and binding force. We may seek in vain for any power in the convention, either to require or to accept a condition or restriction upon the cession like that insisted on; a condition inconsistent with, and destructive of, the object of the grant. The cession was, as recommended by the old congress in 1780, made originally and completed *in terms* to *the United States,* and for the benefit of the United States, i. e., for *the people, all the people,* of the United States. The condition subsequently sought to be annexed in 1787, (declared, too, to be perpetual and immutable,) being contradictory to the terms and destructive of the purposes of the cession, and after the cession was consummated, and the powers of the ceding party terminated, and the rights of the grantees, *the people of the United States,* vested, must necessarily, so far, have been *ab initio* void. With respect to the power of the convention to impose this inhibition, it seems to be pertinent in this place to recur to the opinion of one co[n]temporary with the establishment of the government, and whose distinguished services in the formation and adoption of our national charter, point him out as the *artifex maximus* of our federal system. James Madison, in the year 1819, speaking with reference to the prohibitory power claimed by congress, then threatening the very existence of the Union, remarks of the language of the second clause of the third section of article fourth of the constitution, "that it cannot be well extended beyond a power over the territory *as property,* and the power to make provisions really needful or necessary for the government of settlers, until ripe for admission into the Union."

Again he says, "with respect to what has taken place in the northwest territory, it may be observed that the ordinance giving it is distinctive character on the subject of slaveholding proceeded from the old congress, acting with the best intentions, but under a charter which contains no shadow of the authority exercised; and it remains to be decided how far the States formed within that territory, and admitted into the Union, are on a different footing from its other members as to their legislative sovereignty. As to the power of admitting new States into the federal compact, the questions offering themselves are, whether congress can attach conditions, or the new States concur in conditions, which after admission would *abridge* or *enlarge* the constitutional rights of legislation common to other States; whether congress can, by a compact with a new State, take power either to or from itself, or place the new member above or below the equal rank and rights possessed by the others; whether all such stipulations expressed or implied would not be nullities, and be so pronounced when brought to a practical test. It falls within the scope of your inquiry to state the fact, that there was a proposition in the convention to discriminate between the old and the new States by an article in the constitution. The proposition, happily, was rejected. The effect of such a discrimination is sufficiently evident."[2]

In support of the ordinance of 1787, there may be adduced the semblance at least of obligation deductible from *compact*, the *form* of assent or agreement between the grantor and grantee; but this form or similitude, as is justly remarked by Mr. Madison, is rendered null by the absence of power or authority in the contracting parties, and by the more intrinsic and essential defect of incompatibility with the rights and avowed purposes of those parties, and with their relative duties and obligations to others. If, then, with the attendant *formalities* of assent or compact, the restrictive power claimed was void as to the immediate subject of the ordinance, how much more unfounded must be the pretension to such a power as derived from that source, (viz: the ordinance of 1787,) with respect to territory acquired by purchase or conquest under the supreme authority of the constitution—territory not the subject of *mere donation*, but obtained *in the name of all, by the combined efforts and resources of all,* and with no condition annexed or pretended.

In conclusion, my opinion is, that the decision of the circuit court, upon the law arising upon the several pleas in bar, is correct, but that it is erroneous in having sustained the demurrer to the plea in abatement of the jurisdiction; that for this error the decision of the circuit court should be reversed, and the cause remanded to that court, with instructions to abate the action, for the reason set forth and pleaded in the plea in abatement.

In the aforegoing examination of this cause, the circumstance that the questions involved therein had been previously adjudged between these parties by the court of the State of Missouri, has not been adverted to; for although it has been ruled by this court, that in instances of concurrent jurisdiction, the court first obtaining possession or cognizance of the controversy should retain and decide it, yet, as in this case there had been no plea, either of a former judgment or of *autre action pendent,* it was thought that the fact of a prior decision, however conclusive it might have been if regularly pleaded, could not be incidentally taken into view.

Mr. Justice CAMPBELL.

I concur in the judgment pronounced by the chief justice, but the importance of the cause, the expectation and interest it has awakened, and the responsibility involved in its determination, induce me to file a separate opinion.

The case shows that the plaintiff, in the year 1834, was a negro slave in Missouri, the property of Dr. Emerson, a surgeon in the army of the United States. In 1834, his master took him to the military station at Rock Island, on the border of Illinois, and in 1836 to Fort Snelling, in the present Minnesota, then Wisconsin, territory. While at Fort Snelling, the plaintiff married a slave who was there with her master, and two children have been born of this connection; one during the journey of the family in returning to Missouri, and the other after their return to that State.

Since 1838, the plaintiff and the members of his family have been in Missouri in the condition of slaves. The object of this suit is to establish their freedom. The defendant, who claims the plaintiff and his family, under the title of Dr. Emerson, denied the jurisdiction of the circuit court, by the plea that the plaintiff was a negro of African blood, the descendant of Africans who had been imported and sold in this country as slaves, and thus he had no capacity as a citizen of Missouri to maintain a suit in the circuit court. The court sustained a demurrer to this plea, a trial was then had upon the general issue, and special pleas to the effect that the plaintiff and his family were slaves belonging to the defendant.

My opinion in this case is not affected by the plea to the jurisdiction, and I shall not discuss the questions it suggests. The claim of the plaintiff to freedom depends upon the effect to be given to his absence from Missouri, in company with his master, in Illinois and Minnesota, and this effect is to be ascertained by a reference to the laws of Missouri. For the trespass complained of was committed upon one claiming to be a freeman and a citizen, in that State, and who had been living for years under the dominion of its laws. And the rule is, that whatever is a justification where the thing is done, must be a justification in the forum where the case is tried. (20 How. St. Tri., 234; Cowp. S. C., 161.)

The constitution of Missouri recognizes slavery as a legal condition, extends guaranties to the masters of slaves, and invites immigrants to introduce them, as property, by a promise of protection. The laws of the State charge the master with the custody of the slave, and provide for the maintenance and security of their relation.

The federal constitution and the acts of congress provide for the return of escaping slaves within the limits of the Union. No removal of the slave beyond the limits of the State, against the consent of the master, nor residence there in another condition, would be regarded as an effective manumission by the courts of Missouri, upon his return to the State. *"Sicut liberis captis status restituitur sic servus domino."* Nor can the master emancipate the slave within the State, except through the agency of a public authority. The inquiry arises, whether the manumission of the slave is effected by his removal, with the consent of the master, to a community where the law of slavery does not exist, in a case where neither the master nor slave discloses a purpose to remain permanently, and where both parties have continued to maintain their existing relations. What is the law of Missouri in such a case? Similar inquiries have arisen in a great number of suits, and the discussions in the State courts have relieved the subject of much of its difficulty. (12 B. M. Ky. R. 545; Foster *v.* Foster, 10 Gratt. Va. R. 485; 4 Har. and McH. Md. R. 295; Scott *v.* Emerson, 15 Misso. 576; 4 Rich. S. C. R. 186; 17 Misso. 434; 15 Misso. 596; 5 B. M. 173; 8 B. M. 540, 633; 9 B. M. 565; 5 Leigh, 614; 1 Raud. 15; 18 Pick. 193.)

The result of these discussions is, that in general, the *Status,* or civil and political capacity of a person, is determined, in the first instance, by the law of the domicile where he is born; that the legal effect on persons, arising from the operation of the law of that domicile, is not indelible, but that a new capacity or *status* may be acquired by a change of domicile. That questions of *status* are closely connected with considerations arising out of the social and political organization of the State where they originate, and each sovereign power must determine them within its own territories.

A large class of cases has been decided upon the second of the propositions above stated, in the southern and western courts—cases in which the law of the actual domicile was adjudged to have altered the native condition and *status* of the slave, although he had never actually possessed the *status* of freedom in that domicile. (Rankin *v.* Lydia, 2 A. K. M.; Herny *v.* Decker, Walk. 36; 4 Mart. 385; 1 Misso. 472; Hunter *v.* Fulcher, 1 Leigh.)

I do not impugn the authority of these cases. No evidence is found in the record to establish the existence of a domicile acquired by the master and slave, either in Illinois or Minnesota. The master is described as an officer of the army, who was transferred from one station to another, along the Western frontier, in the line of his duty, and who, after performing the usual tours of service, returned to Missouri; these slaves returned to Missouri with him, and had been there for near fifteen years, in that condition, when this suit was instituted. But absence, in the performance of military duty, without more, is a fact of no importance in determining a question of a change of domicile. Questions of that kind depend upon acts and intentions, and are ascertained from motives, pursuits, the condition of the family, and fortune of the party, and no change will be inferred, unless evidence shows that one domicile was abandoned, and there was an intention to acquire another. (11 L. and Eq. 6; 6 Exch. 217; 6 M. and W. 511; 2 Curt. Ecc. R. 368.)

The cases first cited deny the authority of a foreign law to dissolve relations which have been legally contracted in the State where the parties are, and have their actual domicile—relations which were never questioned during their absence from that State—relations which are consistent with the native capacity and condition of the respective parties, and with the policy of the State where they reside; but which relations were inconsistent with the policy or laws of the State or territory within which they had been for a time, and from which they had returned, with these relations undisturbed. It is upon the assumption, that the law of Illinois or Minnesota was indelibly impressed upon the slave, and its consequences carried into Missouri, that the claim of the plaintiff depends. The importance of the case entitles the doctrine on which it rests to a careful examination.

It will be conceded, that in countries where no law or regulation prevails, opposed to the existence and consequences of slavery, persons who are born in that condition in a foreign State would not be liberated by the accident of their introgression. The relation of domestic slavery is recognized in the law of nations, and the interference of the authorities of one State with the rights of a master belonging to another, without a valid cause, is a violation of that law. (Wheat. Law of Na. 724; 5 Stats. at Large, 601; Calh. Sp. 378; Reports of the Com. U. S. and G. B. 187, 238, 241.)

The public law of Europe formerly permitted a master to reclaim his bondsman, within a limited period, wherever he could find him, and one of the capitularies of Charlemagne abolishes the rule of prescription. He directs, "that wheresoever, within the bounds of Italy, either the runaway slave of the king, or of the church, or of any other man, shall be found by his master, he shall be restored without any bar or prescription of years; yet upon the provision that the master be a Frank or German, or of any other nation (foreign;) but if he be a Lombard or a Roman, he shall acquire or receive his slaves by that law which has been established from ancient times among them." Without referring for precedents abroad, or to the colonial history, for similar instances, the history of the confederation and Union affords evidence to attest the existence of this ancient law. In 1783, congress directed General Washington to continue his remonstrances to the commander of the British forces respecting the permitting [of] negroes belonging to the citizens of these States to leave New York, and to insist upon the discontinuance of that measure. In 1788, the resident minister of the United States at Madrid was instructed to obtain from the Spanish crown orders to its governors in Louisiana and Florida, "to permit and facilitate the apprehension of fugitive slaves from the States, promising that the States would observe the like conduct respecting fugitives from Spanish subjects." The committee that made the report of this resolution consisted of Hamilton, Madison, and Sedgwick, (2 Hamilton's Works, 473;) and the clause in the federal constitution providing for the restoration of fugitive slaves is a recognition of this ancient right, and of the principle that a change of place does not effect a change of condition. The diminution of the power of a master to reclaim his escaping bondsman in Europe commenced in the enactment of laws of prescription in favor of privileged communes. Bremen, Spire, Worms, Vienna, and Ratisbon, in Germany; Carcassonne, Béziers, Toulouse, and Paris, in France, acquired privileges on this subject at an early period. The ordinance of William the Conqueror, that a residence of any of the servile population of England, for a year and a day, without being claimed, in any city, burgh, walled town, or castle of the king, should entitle them to perpetual liberty, is a specimen of these laws.

The earliest publicist who has discussed this subject is Bodin, a jurist of the sixteenth century, whose work was quoted in the early discussions of the courts in France and England on this subject. He says: "In France, although there be some remembrance of old servitude, yet it is not lawful here to make a slave or to buy any one of others, insomuch as the slaves of strangers, so soon as they set their foot within France, become frank and free, as was determined by an old decree of the court of Paris against an ambassador of Spain, who had brought a slave with him into France." He states another case, which arose in the city of Toulouse, of a Genoese merchant, who had carried a slave into that city on his voyage from Spain; and when the matter was brought before the magistrates, the "procureur of the city, out of the records, showed certain ancient privileges given unto them of Tholouse, wherein it was granted that slaves, so soon as they should come into Tholouse, should be free." These cases were cited with much approbation in the discussion of the claims of the West India slaves of Verdelin for freedom, in 1738, before the judges in admiralty, (15 Causes Celébrés, p. 1; 2 Masse Droit Com. sec. 58,) and were reproduced before Lord Mansfield, in the cause of Somersett, in 1772. Of the cases cited by Bodin, it is to be observed that Charles V of France exempted all the inhabitants of Paris from serfdom, or other feudal incapacities, in 1371, and this was confirmed by several of his successors, (3 Dulaire Hist. de Par., 546; Broud. Cout. de Par. 21,) and the ordinance of Toulouse is preserved as follows: *"Civitas Tholosana fuit et erit sine fine libera, adeo ut servi et ancillae, sclavi et sclavae, dominos sive dominas habentes, cum rebus vel sine rebus suis, ad Tholosam vel infraà terminos extra urbem terminatos accedentes acquirant libertatem."* (Hist. de Langue, tome 3, p. 69; Ibid. 6, p. 8; Loysel Inst. b. 1, sec. 6.)

The decisions were made upon special ordinances, or charters, which contained positive prohibitions of slavery, and where liberty had been granted as a privilege; and the history of Paris furnishes but little support for the boast that she was a *"sacro sancta civitas,"* where liberty always had an asylum, or for the "self-complacent rhapsodies" of the French advocates in the case of Verdelin, which amused the grave lawyers who argued the case of Somersett. The case of Verdelin was decided upon a special ordinance, which prescribed the conditions on which West India slaves might be introduced into France, and which had been disregarded by the master.

The case of Somersett was that of a Virginia slave carried to England by his master in 1770, and who remained there two years. For some cause, he was confined on a vessel destined to Jamaica, where he was to be sold. Lord Mansfield, upon a return to a *habeas corpus*, states the question involved. "Here, the person of the slave himself," he says, "is the immediate subject of inquiry. Can any dominion, authority, or coercion, be exercised in this country, according to the American laws?" He answers: "The difficulty of adopting the relation, without adopting it in all its consequences, is indeed extreme, and yet many of those consequences are absolutely contrary to the municipal law of England." Again, he says: "The return states that the slave departed, and refused to serve; whereupon, he was kept to be sold abroad." "So high an act of dominion must be recognized by the law of the country where it is used. The power of the master over his slave has been extremely different in different countries." "The state of slavery is of such a nature, that it is incapable of being introduced on any reasons, moral or political, but only by positive law, which preserves its force long after the reasons, occasion, and time itself, from whence it was created, are erased from the memory. It is so odious, that nothing can be suffered to support it but positive law." That there is a difference in the systems of States, which recognize and which do not recognize the institution of slavery, cannot be disguised. Constitutional law, punitive law, police, domestic economy, industrial pursuits, and amusements, the modes of thinking and of belief of the population of the respective communities, all show the profound influence exerted upon society by this single arrangement. This influence was discovered in the federal convention, in the deliberations on the plan of the constitution. Mr. Madison observed, "that the States were divided into different interests, not by their difference of size, but by other different interests, not by their difference of size, but by other circumstances; the most material of which resulted partly from climate, but principally from the effects of their having or not having slaves. These two causes concur in forming the great division of interests in the United States."

The question to be raised with the opinion of Lord Mansfield, therefore, is not in respect to the incongruity of the two systems, but whether slavery was absolutely contrary to the law of England; for if it was so, clearly, the American laws could not operate there. Historical research ascertains that at the date of the conquest the rural population of England were generally in a servile condition, and under various names, denoting slight variances in condition, they were sold with the land like cattle, and were a part of its living money. Traces of the existence of African slaves are to be found in the early chronicles. Parliament in the time of Richard II, and also of Henry VIII, refused to adopt a general law of emancipation. Acts of emancipation by the last-named monarch and by Elizabeth are preserved.

The African slave trade had been carried on, under the unbounded protection of the crown, for near two centuries, when the case of Somersett was heard, and no motion for its suppression had ever been submitted to parliament; while it was forced upon and maintained in unwilling colonies by the parliament and crown of England at that moment. Fifteen thousand negro slaves were then living in that island, where they had been introduced under the counsel of the most illustrious jurists of the realm, and such slaves had been publicly sold for near a century in the markets of London. In the northern part of the kingdom of Great Britain there existed a class of from 30,000 to 40,000 persons, of whom the parliament said, in 1775, (15 George III, chap. 28,) "many colliers, coal-heavers, and salters, are in a state of slavery or bondage, bound to the collieries and salt works, where they work for life, transferable with the collieries and salt works when their original masters have no use for them; and whereas the emancipating or setting free the colliers, coal-heavers, and salters, in Scotland, who are now in a state of servitude, gradually and upon reasonable conditions, would be the means of increasing the number of colliers, coal-heavers, and salters, to the great benefit of the public, without doing any injury to the present masters, and would remove the reproach of allowing such a state of servitude to exist in a free country," &c.; and again, in 1799, "they declare that many colliers and coal-heavers still continue in a state of bondage." No statute, from the conquest till the 15 George III, had been passed upon the subject of personal slavery. These facts have led the most eminent civilian of England to question the accuracy of this judgment, and to insinuate that in this judgment the offence of *ampliare jurisdictionem* by private authority was committed by the eminent magistrate who pronounced it.

This sentence is distinguishable from those cited from the French courts in this: that there positive prohibitions existed against slavery, and the right to freedom was conferred on the immigrant slave by positive law; whereas here the consequences of slavery merely—that is, the public policy—were found to be contrary to the law of slavery. The case of the slave Grace, (2 Hagg.,) with four others, came before Lord Stowell in 1827, by appeals from the West India vice admiralty courts. They were cases of slaves who had returned to those islands, after a residence in Great Britain, and where the claim to freedom was first presented in the colonial forum. The learned judge in that case said: "This suit fails in its foundation. She (Grace) was not a free person; no injury is done her by her continuance in slavery, and she has no pretensions to any other station than that which was enjoyed by every slave of a family. If she depends upon such freedom conveyed by a mere residence in England, she complains of a violation of right which she possessed no longer than whilst she resided in England, but which totally expired when that residence ceased, and she was imported into Antigua."

The decision of Lord Mansfield was, "that so high an act of dominion" as the master exercises over his slave, in sending him abroad for sale, could not be exercised in England under the American laws, and contrary to the spirit of their own.

The decision of Lord Stowell is, that the authority of the English laws terminated when the slave departed from England. That the laws of England were not imported into Antigua, with the slave, upon her return, and that the colonial forum had no warrant for applying a foreign code to dissolve relations which had existed between persons belonging to that island, and which were legal according to its own system. There is no distinguishable difference between the case before us and that determined in the admiralty of Great Britain.

The complaint here, in my opinion, amounts to this: that the judicial tribunals of Missouri have not denounced as odious the constitution and laws under which they are organized, and have not superseded them on their own private authority, for the purpose of applying the laws of Illinois, or those passed by congress for Minnesota, in their stead. The eighth section of the act of congress of the 6th of March, 1820, (3 Statutes at Large, 545,) entitled, "An act to authorize the people of Missouri to form a State government," &c., &c., is referred to, as affording the authority to this court to pronounce the sentence which the supreme court of Missouri felt themselves constrained to refuse. That section of the act prohibits slavery in the district of country west of the Mississippi, north of thirty-six degrees thirty minutes north latitude, which belonged to the ancient province of Louisiana, not included in Missouri.

It is a settled doctrine of this court, that the federal government can exercise no power over the subject of slavery within the States, nor control the intermigration of slaves, other than fugitives, among the States. Nor can that government affect the duration of slavery within the States, other than by a legislation over the foreign slave trade. The power of congress to adopt the section of the act above cited must therefore depend upon some condition of the territories which distinguishes them from States, and subjects them to a control more extended. The third section of the fourth article of the constitution is referred to as the only and all-sufficient grant to support this claim. It is, that "new States may be admitted by the congress to this Union; but no new State shall be formed or erected within the jurisdiction of any other State, nor any State be formed by the junction of two or more States, or parts of State, without the consent of the legislatures of the States concerned, as well as of the congress. The congress shall have power to dispose of and make all needful rules and regulations respecting the territory or other property belonging to the United States; and nothing in this constitution shall be so construed as to prejudice any claims of the United States, or of any particular State."

It is conceded, in the decisions of this court, that congress may secure the rights of the United States in the public domain, provide for the sale or lease of any part of it, and establish the validity of the titles of the purchasers, and may organize territorial governments, with powers of legislation. (3 How. 212; 12 How. 1; 1 Pet. 511; 13 P. 436; 16 H. 164.)

But the recognition of a plenary power in congress to dispose of the public domain, or to organize a government over it, does not imply a corresponding authority to determine the internal polity, or to adjust the domestic relations, or the persons who may lawfully inhabit the territory in which it is situated. A supreme power to make needful rules respecting the public domain, and a similar power of framing laws to operate upon persons and things within the territorial limits where it lies, are distinguished by broad lines of demarcation in American history. This court has assisted us to define them. In Johnson *v.* McIntosh (8 Wheat. 595–[6]43,) they say: "According to the theory of the British constitution, all vacant lands are vested in the Crown; and the exclusive power to grant them is admitted to reside in the Crown, as a branch of the royal prerogative.

"All the lands we hold were originally granted by the crown, and the establishment of a royal government has never been considered as impairing its right to grant lands within the chartered limits of such colony."

And the British parliament did claim a supremacy of legislation coextensive with the absoluteness of the dominion of the sovereign over the crown lands. The American doctrine, to the contrary, is embodied in two brief resolutions of the people of Pennsylvania, in 1774: 1st. "That the inhabitants of these colonies are entitled to the same rights and liberties, within the colonies, that the subjects born in England are entitled within the realm." 2d. "That the power assumed by parliament to bind the people of these colonies by statutes, in all cases whatever, is unconstitutional, and therefore the source of these unhappy difficulties." The congress of 1774, in their statement of rights and grievances, affirm "a free and exclusive power of legislation" in their several provincial legislatures, "in all cases of taxation and internal polity, subject only to the negative of their sovereign, in such manner as has been heretofore used and accustomed." (1 Jour. Cong., 32.)

The unanimous consent of the people of the colonies, then, to the power of their sovereign, "to dispose of and make all needful rules and regulations respecting the territory" of the crown, in 1774, was deemed by them as entirely consistent with opposition, remonstrance, the renunciation of allegiance, and proclamation of civil war, in preference to submission to his claim of supreme power in the territories.

I pass now to the evidence afforded during the revolution and confederation. The American revolution was not a social revolution. It did not alter the domestic condition or capacity of persons within the colonies, nor was it designed to disturb the domestic relations existing among them. It was a political revolution, by which thirteen dependent colonies became thirteen independent States. "The declaration of independence was not," says Justice Chase, "a declaration that the united colonies jointly, in a collective capacity, were independent States, &c., &c., &c., but that each of them was a sovereign and independent State; that is, that each of them had a right to govern itself by its own authority and its own laws, without any control from any other power on earth." (3 Dall. 199; 4 Cr. 212.)

These sovereign and independent States, being united as a confederation, by various public acts of cession, became jointly interested in territory, and concerned to dispose of and make all needful rules and regulations respecting it. It is a conclusion not open to discussion in this court, "that there was no territory within the (original) United States, that was claimed by them in any other right than that of some of the confederate States." (Harcourt *v.* Gaillord, 12 Wh., 523.) "The question whether the vacant lands within the United States," says Chief Justice Marshall, "became joint property, or belonged to the separate States, was a momentous question, which threatened to shake the American confederacy to its foundations. This important and dangerous question has been compromised, and the compromise is not now to be contested." (6 C. R., 87.)

The cessions of the States to the confederation were made on the condition that the territory ceded should be laid out and formed into distinct republican States, which should be admitted as members to the federal Union, having the same rights of sovereignty, freedom, and independence, as the other States. The first effort to fulfil this trust was made in 1785, by the offer of a charter or compact to the inhabitants who might come to occupy the land.

Those inhabitants were to form for themselves temporary State governments, founded on the constitutions of any of the States, but to be alterable at the will of their legislature; and permanent governments were to succeed these, whenever the population became sufficiently numerous to authorize the State to enter the confederacy; and congress assumed to obtain powers from the States to facilitate this object. Neither in the deeds of cession of the States, nor in this compact, was a sovereign power for congress to govern the territories asserted. Congress retained power, by this act, "to dispose of and to make rules and regulations respecting the public domain," but submitted to the people to organize a government harmonious with those of the confederate States.

The next stage in the progress of colonial government was the adoption of the ordinance of 1787, by eight States, in which the plan of a territorial government, established by act of congress, is first seen. This was adopted while the federal convention to form the constitution was sitting. The plan placed the government in that [the] hands of a governor, secretary, and judges, appointed by congress, and conferred power on them to select suitable laws from the codes of the States, until the population should equal 5,000. A legislative council, elected by the people, was then to be admitted to a share of the legislative authority, under the supervision of congress; and States were to be formed whenever the number of the population should authorize the measure.

This ordinance was addressed to the inhabitants as a fundamental compact, and six of its articles define the conditions to be observed in their constitution and laws. These conditions were designed to fulfil the trust in the agreements of cession, that the States to be formed of the ceded territories should be "distinct republican States." This ordinance was submitted to Virginia in 1788, and the 5th article, embodying as it does a summary of the entire act, was specifically ratified and confirmed by that State. This was an incorporation of the ordinance into her act of cession. It was conceded, in the argument, that the authority of congress was not adequate to the enactment of the ordinance, and that it cannot be supported upon the articles of confederation. To a part of the engagements, the assent of nine States was required, and for another portion no provision had been made in those articles. Mr. Madison said, in a writing nearly contemporary, but before the confirmatory act of Virginia, "congress have proceeded to form new States, to erect temporary governments, to appoint officers for them, and to prescribe the conditions on which such States shall be admitted into the confederacy; all this has been done, and done without the least color of constitutional authority." (Federalist, No. 38.) Richard Henry Lee, one of the committee who reported the ordinance to congress, transmitted it to General Washington, (15th July, 1787,) saying, "It seemed necessary, for the security of property among uninformed and perhaps licentious people, as the greater part of those who go there are, that a strong-toned government should exist, and the rights of property be clearly defined." The consent of all the States represented in congress, the consent of the legislature of Virginia, the consent of the inhabitants of the territory, all concur to support the authority of this enactment. It is apparent, in the frame of the constitution, that the convention recognized its validity, and adjusted parts of their work with reference to it. The authority to admit new States into the Union, the omission to provide distinctly for territorial governments, and the clause limiting the foreign slave trade to States then existing, which might not prohibit it, show that they regarded this territory as provided with government, and organized permanently with a restriction on the subject of slavery. Justice Chase, in the opinion already cited, says of the government before, and it is in some measure true during the confederation, that "the powers of congress originated from necessity, and arose out of and were only limited by events, or, in other words, they were revolutionary in their very nature. Their extent depended upon the exigencies and necessities of public affairs;" and there is only one rule of construction, in regard to the acts done, which will fully support them, viz: that the powers actually exercised were rightfully exercised, wherever they were supported by the implied sanction of the State legislatures, and by the ratifications of the people.

The clauses in the 3d section of the 4th article of the constitution, relative to the admission of new States, and the disposal and regulation of the territory of the United States, were adopted without debate in the convention.

There was a warm discussion on the clauses that relate to the subdivision of the States, and the reservation of the claims of the United States and each of the States from any prejudice. The Maryland members revived the controversy in regard to the crown lands of the southwest. There was nothing to indicate any reference to a government of territories not included within the limits of the Union; and the whole discussion demonstrates that the convention was consciously dealing with a territory whose condition, as to government, had been arranged by a fundamental and unalterable compact.

An examination of this clause of the constitution, by the light of the circumstances in which the convention was placed, will aid us to determine its significance. The first clause is, "that new States may be admitted by the congress to this Union." The condition of Kentucky, Vermont, Rhode Island, and the new States to be formed in the northwest, suggested this, as a necessary addition to the powers of congress. The next clause, providing for the subdivision of States, and the parties to consent to such an alteration, was required, by the plans on foot, for changes in Massachusetts, New York, Pennsylvania, North Carolina, and Georgia. The clause which enables congress to dispose of and make regulations respecting the public domain, was demanded by the exigencies of an exhausted treasury and a disordered finance, for relief by sales, and the preparation for sales, of the public lands; and the last clause, that nothing in the constitution should prejudice the claims of the United States or a particular State, was to quiet the jealousy and irritation of those who had claimed for the United States all the unappropriated lands. I look in vain, among the discussions of the time, for the assertion of a supreme sovereignty for congress over the territory then belonging to the United States, or that they might thereafter acquire. I seek in vain for an annunciation that a consolidated power had been inaugurated, whose subject comprehended an empire, and which had no restriction but the discretion of congress. This disturbing element of the Union entirely escaped the apprehensive previsions of Samuel Adams, George Clinton, Luther Martin, and Patrick Henry; and, in respect to dangers from power vested in a central government over distant settlements, colonies, or provinces, their instincts were always alive. Not a word escaped them, to warn their countrymen, that here was a power to threaten the landmarks of this federative Union, and with them the safeguards of popular and constitutional liberty; or that under this article there might be introduced, on our soil, a single government over a vast extent of country—a government foreign to the persons over whom it might be exercised, and capable of binding those not represented, by statutes, in all cases whatever. I find nothing to authorize these enormous pretensions, nothing in the expositions of the friends of the constitution, nothing in the expressions of alarm by its opponents—expressions which have since been developed as prophecies. Every portion of the United States was then provided with a municipal government, which this constitution was not designed to supersede, but merely to modify as to its conditions.

The compacts of cession by North Carolina and Georgia are subsequent to the constitution. They adopt the ordinance of 1787, except the clause respecting slavery. But the precautionary repudiation of that article forms an argument quite as satisfactory to the advocates for federal power, as its introduction would have done. The refusal of a power to congress to legislate in one place, seems to justify the seizure of the same power when another place for its exercise is found.

This proceeds from a radical error, which lies at the foundation of much of this discussion. It is, that the federal government may lawfully do whatever is not directly prohibited by the constitution. This would have been a fundamental error, if no amendments to the constitution had been made. But the final expression of the will of the people of the States, in the 10th amendment, is, that the powers of the federal government are limited to the grants of the constitution.

Before the cession of Georgia was made, congress asserted rights, in respect to a part of her territory, which require a passing notice. In 1798 and 1800, acts for the settlement of limits with Georgia, and to establish a government in the Mississippi territory, were adopted. A territorial government was organized, between the Chattahoochee and Mississippi rivers. This was within the limits of Georgia. These acts dismembered Georgia. They established a separate government upon her soil, while they rather derisively professed, "that the establishment of that government shall in no respects impair the rights of the State of Georgia, either to the jurisdiction or soil of the territory." The constitution provided that the importation of such persons as any of the existing States shall think proper to admit, shall not be prohibited by congress before 1808. By these enactments, a prohibition was placed upon the importation of slaves into Georgia, although her legislature had made none.

This court have repeatedly affirmed the paramount claim of Georgia to this territory. They have denied the existence of any title in the United States. (6 C. R. 87; 12 Wh. 523; 3 How. 212; 13 How. 381.) Yet these acts were cited in the argument as precedents to show the power of congress in the territories. These statutes were the occasion of earnest expostulation and bitter remonstrance on the part of the authorities of the State, and the memory of their injustice and wrong remained long after the legal settlement of the controversy by the compact of 1802. A reference to these acts terminates what I have to say upon the constitutions of the territory within the original limits of the United States. These constitutions were framed by the concurrence of the States making the cessions, and congress, and were tendered to immigrants who might be attracted to the vacant territory. The legislative powers of the officers of this government were limited to the selection of laws from the States; and provision was made for the introduction of popular institutions, and their emancipation from federal control, whenever a suitable opportunity occurred. The limited reservation of legislative power to the officers of the federal government was excused, on the plea of *necessity;* and the probability is, that the clauses respecting slavery embody some compromise among the statesmen of that time; beyond these, the distinguishing features of the system which the patriots of the revolution had claimed as their birthright, from Great Britain, predominated in them.

The acquisition of Louisiana, in 1803, introduced another system into the United States. This vast province was ceded by Napoleon, and its population had always been accustomed to a viceroyal government, appointed by the crowns of France or Spain. To establish a government constituted on similar principles, and with like conditions, was not an unnatural proceeding.

But there was great difficulty in finding constitutional authority for the measure. The third section of the fourth article of the constitution was introduced into the constitution, on the motion of Mr. Gouverneur Morris. In 1803, he was appealed to for information in regard to its meaning. He answers: "I am very certain I had it not in contemplation to insert a decree *de coercendo imperio* in the constitution of America. * * * I knew then, as well as I do now, that all North America must at length be annexed to us. Happy indeed, if the lust of dominion stop here. It would therefore have been perfectly utopian to oppose a paper restriction to the violence of popular sentiment, in a popular government." (3 Mor. Writ. 185.) A few days later, he makes another reply to his correspondent. "I perceive," he says, "I mistook the drift of your inquiry, which substantially is, whether congress can admit, as a new State, territory which did not belong to the United States when the constitution was made. In my opinion, they cannot. I always thought, when we should acquire Canada and Louisiana, it would be proper to GOVERN THEM AS PROVINCES, AND ALLOW THEM NO VOICE *in our councils. In wording the third* SECTION OF THE *fourth article, I went as far as circumstances would permit, to establish the exclusion.* CANDOR OBLIGES ME TO ADD MY BELIEF, THAT HAD IT BEEN MORE POINTEDLY EXPRESSED, A STRONG OPPOSITION WOULD HAVE BEEN MADE." (3 Mor. Writ., 192.) The first territorial government of Louisiana was an imperial one, founded upon a French or Spanish model. For a time, the governor, judges, legislative council, marshal, secretary, and officers of the militia, were appointed by the president.[3]

Besides these anomalous arrangements, the acquisition gave rise to jealous inquiries, as to the influence it would exert in determining the men and States that were to be "the arbiters and rulers" of the destinies of the Union; and unconstitutional opinions, having for their aim to promote sectional divisions, were announced and developed. "Something," said an eminent statesman, "something has suggested to the members of Congress the policy of acquiring geographical majorities. This is a very direct step towards disunion, for it must foster the geographical enmities by which alone it can be effected. This something must be a contemplation of particular advantages to be derived from such majorities; and is it not notorious that they consist of nothing else but usurpations over persons and property, by which they can regulate the internal *wealth and prosperity of States and individuals?*"

The most dangerous of the efforts to employ a geographical political power, to perpetuate a geographical preponderance in the Union, is to be found in the deliberations upon the act of the 6th of March, 1820, before cited. The attempt consisted of a proposal to exclude Missouri from a place in the Union, unless her people would adopt a constitution containing a prohibition upon the subject of slavery, according to a prescription of congress. The sentiment is now general, if not universal, that congress had no constitutional power to impose the restriction. This was frankly admitted at the bar, in the course of this argument. The principles which this court have pronounced condemn the pretension then made on behalf of the legislative department. In Groves *v.* Slaughter, (15 Pet.) the chief justice said: "The power over this subject is exclusively with the several States, and each of them has a right to decide for itself whether it will or will not allow persons of this description to be brought within its limits." Justice McLean said: "The constitution of the United States operates alike in all the States, and one State has the same power over the subject of slavery as every other State." In Pollard's Lessee *v.* Hagan, (3 How. 212,) the court say: "The United States have no constitutional capacity to exercise municipal jurisdiction, sovereignty, or eminent domain, within the limits of a State or elsewhere, except in cases where it is delegated, and the court denies the faculty of the federal government to add to its powers by treaty or compact."

This is a necessary consequence, resulting from the nature of the federal constitution, which is a federal compact among the States, establishing a limited government, with powers delegated by the people of distinct and independent communities, who reserved to their State governments, and to themselves, the powers they did not grant. This claim to impose a restriction upon the people of Missouri involved a denial of the constitutional relations between the people of the States and congress, and affirmed a concurrent right for the latter, with their people, to constitute the social and political system of the new States. A successful maintenance of this claim would have altered the basis of the constitution. The new States would have become members of a Union defined in part by the constitution and in part by congress. They would not have been admitted to "this Union." Their sovereignty would have been restricted by congress as well as the constitution. The demand was unconstitutional and subversive, but was prosecuted with an energy, and aroused such animosities among the people, that patriots, whose confidence had not failed during the revolution, began to despair for the constitution.[4] Amid the utmost violence of this extraordinary contest, the expedient contained in the eighth section of this act was proposed, to moderate it, and to avert the catastrophe it menaced. It was not seriously debated, nor were its constitutional aspects severely scrutinized by congress. For the first time, in the history of the country, has its operation been embodied in a case at law, and been presented to this court for their judgment. The inquiry is, whether there are conditions in the constitutions of the territories which subject the capacity and *status* of persons within their limits to the direct action of congress. Can congress determine the condition and *status* of persons who inhabit the territories?

The constitution permits congress to dispose of and to make all needful rules and regulations respecting the territory or other property belonging to the United States. This power applies as well to territory belonging to the United States within the States, as beyond them. It comprehends all the public domain, wherever it may be. The argument is, that the power to make "ALL needful rules and regulations" "is a power of legislation," "a full legislative power;" "that it includes all subjects of legislation in the territory," and is without any limitations, except the positive prohibitions which affect all the powers of congress. Congress may then regulate or prohibit slavery upon the public domain within the new States, and such a prohibition would permanently affect the capacity of a slave, whose master might carry him to it. And why not? Because no power has been conferred on congress. This is a conclusion universally admitted. But the power to "make rules and regulations respecting the territory" is not restrained by State lines, nor are there any constitutional prohibitions upon its exercise in the domain of the United States within the States; and whatever rules and regulations respecting territory congress may constitutionally make are supreme, and are not dependent on the *situs* [status] of "the territory."

The author of the Farmer's Letters, so famous in the ante-revolutionary history, thus states the argument made by the American loyalists in favor of the claim of the British parliament to legislate in all cases whatever over the colonies: "It has been urged with great vehemence against us," he says, "and it seems to be thought their FORT by our adversaries, that a power of regulation is a power of legislation; and a power of legislation, if constitutional, must be universal and supreme, in the utmost sense of the word. It is therefore concluded that the colonies, by acknowledging the power of regulation, acknowledged every other power."

This sophism imposed upon a portion of the patriots of that day. Chief Justice Marshall, in his life of Washington, says "that many of the best-informed men in Massachusetts had perhaps adopted the opinion of the parliamentary right of internal government over the colonies;" "that the English statute book furnishes many instances of its exercise;" "that in no case recollected, was their authority openly controverted;" and "that the general court of Massachusetts, on a late occasion, openly recognized the principle." (Marsh. Wash. v. 2, p. 75, 76.)

But the more eminent men of Massachusetts rejected it; and another patriot of the time employs the instance to warn us of "the stealth with which oppression approaches," and "the enormities towards which precedents travel." And the people of the United States, as we have seen, appealed to the last argument, rather than acquiesce in their authority. Could it have been the purpose of Washington and his illustrious associates, by the use of ambiguous, equivocal, and expansive words, such as "rules," "regulations," "territory," to re-establish in the constitution of their country that *fort* which had been prostrated amid the toils and with the sufferings and sacrifices of seven years of war? Are these words to be understood as the Norths, the Grenvilles, Hillsboroughs, Hutchinsons, and Dunmores—in a word, as George III would have understood them—or are we to look for their interpretation to Patrick Henry or Samuel Adams, to Jefferson, and Jay, and Dickinson; to the sage Franklin, or to Hamilton, who from his early manhood was engaged in combating British constructions of such words? We know that the resolution of congress of 1780 contemplated that the new States to be formed under their recommendation were to have the same rights of sovereignty, freedom, and independence, as the old. That every resolution, cession, compact, and ordinance, of the States, observed the same liberal principle. That the Union of the constitution is a union formed of equal States; and that new States, when admitted, were to enter "this Union." Had another union been proposed in "any pointed manner," it would have encountered not only "strong" but successful opposition. The disunion between Great Britain and her colonies originated in the antipathy of the latter to "rules and regulations" made by a remote power respecting their internal policy. In forming the constitution, this fact was ever present in the minds of its authors. The people were assured by their most trusted statesmen "that the jurisdiction of the federal government is limited to certain enumerated objects, which concern all members of the republic," and "that the local or municipal authorities form distinct portions of supremacy, no more subject within their respective spheres to the general authority, than the general authority is subject to them within its own sphere." Still, this did not content them. Under the lead of Hancock and Samuel Adams, of Patrick Henry and George Mason, they demanded an explicit declaration that no more power was to be exercised than they had delegated. And the ninth and tenth amendments to the constitution were designed to include the reserved rights of the States, and the people, within all the sanctions of that instrument, and to bind the authorities, State and federal, by the judicial oath it prescribes, to their recognition and observance. Is it probable, therefore, that the supreme and irresponsible power, which is now claimed for congress over boundless territories, the use of which cannot fail to react upon the political system of the States, to its subversion, was ever within the contemplation of the statesmen who conducted the counsels of the people in the formation of this constitution? When the questions that came to the surface upon the acquisition of Louisiana were presented to the mind of Jefferson, he wrote: "I had rather ask an enlargement of power from the nation, where it is found necessary, than to assume it by a construction which would make our powers boundless. Our peculiar security is in the possession of a written constitution. Let us not make it blank paper by construction. I say the same as to the opinion of those who consider the grant of the treaty-making power as boundless. If it is, then we have no constitution. If it has bounds, they can be no others than the definitions of the powers which that instrument gives. It specifies and delineates the operations permitted to the federal government, and gives the powers necessary to carry them into execution." The publication of the journals of the federal convention in 1819, of the debates reported by Mr. Madison in 1840, and the mass of private correspondence of the early statesmen before and since, enable us to approach the discussion of the aims of those who made the constitution, with some insight and confidence.

I have endeavored, with the assistance of these, to find a solution for the grave and difficult question involved in this inquiry. My opinion is, that the claim for congress of supreme power in the territories, under the grant to "dispose of and make all needful rules and regulations respecting *territory*," is not supported by the historical evidence drawn from the revolution, the confederation, or the deliberations which preceded the ratification of the federal constitution. The ordinance of 1787 depended upon the action of the congress of the confederation, the assent of the State of Virginia, and the acquiescence of the people who recognized the validity of that plea of necessity which supported so many of the acts of the governments of that time; and the federal government accepted the ordinance as a recognized and valid engagement of the confederation.

In referring to the precedents of 1798 and 1800, I find the constitution was plainly violated by the invasion of the rights of a sovereign State, both of soil and jurisdiction; and in reference to that of 1804, the wisest statesmen protested against it, and the President more than doubted its policy and the power of the government.

Mr. John Quincy Adams, at a later period, says of the last act, "that the president found congress mounted to the pitch of passing those acts, without inquiring where they acquired the authority, and he conquered his own scruples as they had done theirs." But this court cannot undertake for themselves the same conquest. They acknowledge that our peculiar security is in the possession of a written constitution, and they cannot make it blank paper by construction.

They look to its delineation of the operations of the federal government, and they must not exceed the limits it marks out, in their administration. The court have said "that congress cannot exercise municipal jurisdiction, sovereignty, or eminent domain, within the limits of a State or elsewhere, beyond what has been delegated." We are then to find the authority for supreme power in the territories in the constitution. What are the limits upon the operations of a government invested with legislative, executive, and judiciary powers, and charged with the power to dispose of and to make all needful rules and regulations respecting a vast public domain? The feudal system would have recognized the claim made on behalf of the federal government for supreme power over persons and things in the territories, as an incident to this title—that is, the title to dispose of and make rules and regulations respecting it.

The Norman lawyers of William the Conqueror would have yielded an implicit assent to the doctrine, that a supreme sovereignty is an inseparable incident to a grant to dispose of and to make all needful rules and regulations respecting the public domain. But an American patriot, in contrasting the European and American systems, may affirm, "that European sovereigns give lands to their colonists, but reserve to themselves a power to control their property, liberty, and privileges; but the American government sells the lands belonging to the people of the several States (i. e., United States) to their citizens, who are already in the possession of personal and political rights, which the government did not give, and cannot take away." And the advocates for government sovereignty in the territories have been compelled to abate a portion of the pretensions originally made in its behalf, and to admit that the constitutional prohibitions upon congress operate in the territories. But a constitutional prohibition is not requisite to ascertain a limitation upon the authority of the several departments of the federal government. Nor are the States or people restrained by any enumeration or definition of their rights or liberties.

To impair or diminish either, the department must produce an authority from the people themselves, in their constitution; and, as we have seen, a power to make rules and regulations respecting the public domain does not confer a municipal sovereignty over persons and things upon it. But as this is "thought their fort" by our adversaries, I propose a more definite examination of it. We have seen, congress does not dispose of or make rules and regulations respecting domain belonging to themselves, but belonging to the United States.

These conferred on their mandatory, congress, [sic] authority to dispose of the territory which belonged to them in common; and to accomplish that object beneficially and effectually, they gave an authority to make suitable rules and regulations respecting it. When the power of disposition is fulfilled, the authority to make rules and regulations terminates, for it attaches only upon territory "belonging to the United States."

Consequently, the power to make rules and regulations, from the nature of the subject, is restricted to such administrative and conservatory acts as are needful for the preservation of the public domain, and its preparation for sale or disposition. The system of land surveys; the reservations for schools, internal improvements, military sites, and public buildings; the preemption claims of settlers; the establishment of land offices, and boards of inquiry, to determine the validity of land titles; the modes of entry, and sale, and of conferring titles; the protection of the lands from trespass and waste; the partition of the public domain into municipal subdivisions, having reference to the erection of territorial governments and States; and perhaps the selection, under their authority, of suitable laws for the protection of the settlers, until there may be a sufficient number of them to form a self-sustaining municipal government—these important rules and regulations will sufficiently illustrate the scope and operation of the 3d section of the 4th article of the constitution. But this clause in the constitution does not exhaust the powers of congress within the territorial subdivisions, or over the persons who inhabit them. Congress may exercise there all the powers of government which belong to them as the legislature of the United States, of which these territories make a part. (Loughborough *v.* Blake, 5 Wheat. 317.) Thus the laws of taxation, for the regulation of foreign, federal, and Indian commerce, and so for the abolition of the slave trade, for the protection of copyrights and inventions, for the establishment of postal communication and courts of justice, and for the punishment of crimes, are as operative there as within the States. I admit that to mark the bounds for the jurisdiction of the government of the United States within the territory, and of its power in respect to persons and things within the municipal subdivisions it has created, is a work of delicacy and difficulty, and, in a great measure, is beyond the cognizance of the judiciary department of that government. How much municipal power may be exercised by the people of the territory, before their admission to the Union, the courts of justice cannot decide. This must depend, for the most part, on political considerations, which cannot enter into the determination of a case of law or equity. I do not feel called upon to define the jurisdiction of congress. It is sufficient for the decision of this case to ascertain whether the residuary sovereignty of the States or people has been invaded by the 8th section of the act of 6th March, 1820, I have cited, in so far as it concerns the capacity and *status* of persons in the condition and circumstances of the plaintiff and his family.

These States, at the adoption of the federal constitution, were organized communities, having distinct systems of municipal law, which, though derived from a common source, and recognising in the main similar principles, yet in some respects had become unlike, and on a particular subject promised to be antagonistic.

Their systems provided protection for life, liberty, and property, among their citizens, and for the determination of the condition and capacity of the persons domiciled within their limits. These institutions, for the most part, were placed beyond the control of the federal government. The constitution allows congress to coin money, and regulate its value; to regulate foreign and Federal commerce; to secure, for a limited period, to authors and inventors, a property in their writings and discoveries; and to make rules concerning captures in war; and, within the limits of these powers, it has exercised, rightly, to a greater or less extent, the power to determine what shall and what shall not be property.

But the great powers of war and negotiation, finance, postal communication, and commerce, in general, when employed in respect to the property of a citizen, refer to, and depend upon, the municipal laws of the States, to ascertain and determine what is property, and the rights of the owner, and the tenure by which it is held.

Whatever these constitutions and laws validly determine to be property, it is the duty of the federal government, through the domain of jurisdiction merely federal, to recognize to be property.

And this principle follows from the structure of the respective governments, State and federal, and their reciprocal relations. They are different agents and trustees of the people of the several States, appointed with different powers and with distinct purposes, but whose acts, within the scope of their respective jurisdictions, are mutually obligatory. They are respectively the depositories of such powers of legislation as the people were willing to surrender, and their duty is to co-operate within their several jurisdictions to maintain the rights of the same citizens under both governments unimpaired. A proscription, therefore, of the constitution and laws of one or more States, determining property, on the part of the federal government, by which the stability of its social system may be endangered, is plainly repugnant to the conditions on which the federal constitution was adopted, or which that government was designed to accomplish. Each of the States surrendered its powers of war and negotiation, to raise armies and to support a navy, and all of these powers are sometimes required to preserve a State from disaster and ruin. The federal government was constituted to exercise these powers for the preservation of the States, respectively, and to secure to all their citizens the enjoyment of the rights which were not surrendered to the federal government. The provident care of the statesmen who projected the constitution was signalized by such a distribution of the powers of government as to exclude many of the motives and opportunities for promoting provocations and spreading discord among the States, and for guarding against those partial combinations, so destructive of the community of interest, sentiment, and feeling, which are so essential to the support of the Union. The distinguishing features of their system consist in the exclusion of the federal government from the local and internal concerns of, and in the establishment of an independent internal government within, the States. And it is a significant fact in the history of the United States, that those controversies which have been productive of the greatest animosity, and have occasioned most peril to the peace of the Union, have had their origin in the well-sustained opinion of a minority among the people, that the federal government had overstepped its constitutional limits to grant some exclusive privilege, or to disturb the legitimate distribution of property or power among the States or individuals. Nor can a more signal instance of this be found than is furnished by the act before us. No candid or rational man can hesitate to believe, that if the subject of the eighth section of the act of March, 1820, had never been introduced into congress and made the basis of legislation, no interest common to the Union would have been seriously affected. And, certainly, the creation, within this Union, of large confederacies of unfriendly and frowning States, which has been the tendency, and, to an alarming extent, the result, produced by the agitation arising from it, does not commend it to the patriot or statesman. This court have determined that the intermigration of slaves was not committed to the jurisdiction or control of congress. Wherever a master is entitled to go within the United States, his slave may accompany him, without any impediment from, or fear of, congressional legislation or interference. The question then arises, whether congress, which can exercise no jurisdiction over the relations of master and slave within the limits of the Union, and is bound to recognize and respect the rights and relations that validly exist under the constitutions and laws of the States, can deny the exercise of those rights, and prohibit the continuance of those relations, within the territories.

And the citation of State statutes prohibiting the immigration of slaves, and of the decisions of State courts enforcing the forfeiture of the master's title in accordance with their rule, only darkens the discussion. For the question is, have congress the municipal sovereignty in the territories which the State legislatures have derived from the authority of the people, and exercise in the States?

And this depends upon the construction of the article in the constitution before referred to.

And, in my opinion, that clause confers no power upon congress to dissolve the relations of the master and slave on the domain of the United States, either within or without any of the States.

The eighth section of the act of congress of the 6th of March, 1820, did not, in my opinion, operate to determine the domestic condition and *status* of the plaintiff and his family during their sojourn in Minnesota territory, or after their return to Missouri.

The question occurs as to the judgment to be given in this case. It appeared upon the trial that the plaintiff, in 1834, was in a state of slavery in Missouri, and he had been in Missouri for near fifteen years in that condition when this suit was brought. Nor does it appear that he at any time possessed another state or condition, *de facto*. His claim to freedom depends upon his temporary relocation, from the domicile of his origin, in company with his master, to communities where the law of slavery did not prevail. My examination is confined to the case, as it was submitted upon uncontested evidence, upon appropriate issues to the jury, and upon the instructions given and refused by the court upon that evidence. My opinion is, that the opinion of the circuit court was correct upon all the claims involved in those issues, and that the verdict of the jury was justified by the evidence and instructions.

The jury have returned that the plaintiff and his family are slaves.

Upon this record, it is apparent that this is not a controversy between citizens of different States; and that the plaintiff, at no period of the life which has been submitted to the view of the court, has had a capacity to maintain a suit in the courts of the United States. And in so far as the argument of the chief justice upon the plea in abatement has a reference to the plaintiff or his family, in any of the conditions or circumstances of their lives, as presented in the evidence, I concur in that portion of his opinion. I concur in the judgment which expresses the conclusion that the Circuit Court should not have rendered a general judgment.

The capacity of the plaintiff to sue is involved in the pleas in bar, and the verdict of the jury discloses an incapacity under the constitution. Under the constitution of the United States, his is an incapacity to sue in their courts, while, by the laws of Missouri, the operation of the verdict would be more extensive. I think it a safe conclusion to enforce the lesser disability imposed by the constitution of the United States, and leave to the plaintiff all his rights in Missouri. I think the judgment should be affirmed, on the ground that the circuit court had no jurisdiction, or that the case should be reversed and remanded, that the suit may be dismissed.

Mr. Justice CATRON.

The defendant pleaded to the jurisdiction of the circuit court, that the plaintiff was a negro of African blood; the descendant of Africans, who had been imported and sold in this country as slaves, and thus had no capacity as a citizen of Missouri to maintain a suit in the circuit court. The court sustained a demurrer to this plea, and a trial was had upon the pleas, of the general issue, and also that the plaintiff and his family were slaves, belonging to the defendant. In this trial, a verdict was given for the defendant.

The judgment of the circuit court upon the plea in abatement is not open, in my opinion, to examination in this court upon the plaintiff's writ.

The judgment was given for him conformably to the prayer of his demurrer. He cannot assign an error in such a judgment. (Tidd's Pr. 1163; 2 Williams's Saund. 46 *a;* 2 Iredell N. C. 87; 2 W. and S. 391.) Nor does the fact that the judgment was given on a plea to the jurisdiction, avoid the application of this rule. (Capron *v.* Van Noorden, 2 Cr. 126; 6 Wend. 465; 7 Met. 598; 5 Pike, 1005.)

The declaration discloses a case within the jurisdiction of the court—a controversy between citizens of different States. The plea in abatement, impugning these jurisdictional averments, was waived when the defendant answered to the declaration by pleas to the merits. The proceedings on that plea remain a part of the technical record, to show the history of the case, but are not open to the review of this court by a writ of error. The authorities are very conclusive on this point. Shepherd *v.* Graves, 14 How. 505; Bailey *v.* Dozier, 6 How. 23; 1 Stewart, (Alabama,) 46; 10 Ben. Monroe, (Kentucky,) 555; 2 Stewart, (Alabama,) 370, 443; 2 Scammon, (Illinois,) 78. Nor can the court assume, as admitted facts, the averments of the plea from the confession of the demurrer. That confession was for a single object, and cannot be used for any other purpose than to test the validity of the plea. Tompkins *v.* Ashley, 1 Moody and Mackin, 32; 33 Maine, 96, 100.

There being nothing in controversy here but the merits, I will proceed to discuss them.

The plaintiff claims to have acquired property in himself, and became free, by being kept in Illinois during two years.

The constitution, laws, and policy, of Illinois, are somewhat peculiar respecting slavery. Unless the master becomes an inhabitant of that State, the slaves he takes there do not acquire their freedom; and if they return with their master to the slave State of his domicile, they cannot assert their freedom after their return. For the reasons and authorities on this point, I refer to the opinion of my brother Nelson, with which I not only concur, but think his opinion is the most conclusive argument on the subject within my knowledge.

It is next insisted for the plaintiff, that his freedom (and that of his wife and eldest child) was obtained by force of the act of congress of 1820, usually known as the Missouri compromise act, which declares: "That in all that territory ceded by France to the United States, which lies north of thirty-six degrees thirty minutes north latitude, slavery and involuntary servitude shall be, and are hereby, *forever prohibited.*"

From this prohibition, the territory now constituting the State of Missouri was excepted; which exception to the stipulation gave it the designation of a compromise.

The first question presented on this act is, whether congress had power to make such compromise. For, if power was wanting, then no freedom could be acquired by the defendant under the act.

That congress has no authority to pass laws and bind men's rights beyond the powers conferred by the constitution, is not open to controversy. But it is insisted that, by the constitution, congress has power to legislate for and govern the territories of the United States, and that by force of the power to govern, laws could be enacted, prohibiting slavery in any portion of the Louisiana territory; and, of course, to abolish slavery *in all* parts of it, whilst it was, or is, governed as a territory.

My opinion is, that congress is vested with power to govern the territories of the United States by force of the third section of the fourth article of the constitution. And I will state my reasons for this opinion.

Almost every provision in that instrument has a history that must be understood, before the brief and sententious language employed can be comprehended in the relations its authors intended. We must bring before us the state of things presented to the convention, and in regard to which it acted, when the compound provision was made, declaring: 1st. That "new States may be admitted by the congress into this Union." 2d. "The congress shall have power to dispose of and make all needful rules and regulations respecting the territory or other property belonging to the United States. And nothing in this constitution shall be so construed as to prejudice any claims of the United States, or any particular State."

Having ascertained the historical facts giving rise to these provisions, the difficulty of arriving at the true meaning of the language employed will be greatly lessened.

The history of these facts is substantially as follows:

The king of Great Britain, by his proclamation of 1763, virtually claimed that the country west of the mountains had been conquered from France, and ceded to the crown of Great Britain by the treaty of Paris of that year, and he says: "We reserve it under our sovereignty, protection, and dominion, for the use of the Indians."

This country was conquered from the crown of Great Britain, and surrendered to the United States by the treaty of peace of 1783. The colonial charters of Virginia, North Carolina, and Georgia, included it. Other States set up pretensions of claim to some portions of the territory north of the Ohio, but they were of no value, as I suppose. (5 Wheat. 375.)

As this vacant country had been won by the blood and treasure of all the States, those whose charters did not reach it, insisted that the country belonged to the States united, and that the lands should be disposed of for the benefit of the whole; and to which end, the western territory should be ceded to the States united. The contest was stringent and angry, long before the convention convened, and deeply agitated that body. As a matter of justice, and to quiet the controversy, Virginia consented to cede the country north of the Ohio as early as 1783; and in 1784 the deed of cession was executed, by her delegates in the congress of the confederation, conveying to the United States in congress assembled, for the benefit of said States, "all right, title, and claim, as well of soil as of jurisdiction, which this commonwealth hath to the *territory* or tract of country within the limits of the Virginia charter, situate, lying, and being to the northwest of the river Ohio." In 1787, (July 13,) the ordinance was passed by the old congress to govern the territory.

Massachusetts had ceded her pretension of claim to western territory in 1785, Connecticut hers in 1786, and New York had ceded hers. In August, 1787, South Carolina ceded to the confederation her pretension of claim to territory west of that State. And North Carolina was expected to cede hers, which she did do, in April, 1790. And so Georgia was confidently expected to cede her large domain, now constituting the territory of the States of Alabama and Mississippi.

At the time the constitution was under consideration, there had been ceded to the United States, or was shortly expected to be ceded, all the western country, from the British Canada line to Florida, and from the head of the Mississippi almost to its mouth, except that portion which now constitutes the State of Kentucky.

Although Virginia had conferred on the congress of the confederation power to govern the territory north of the Ohio, still, it cannot be denied, as I think, that power was wanting to admit a new State under the articles of confederation.

With these facts prominently before the convention, they proposed to accomplish these ends:

1st. To give power to admit new States.

2d. To dispose of the public lands in the territories, and such as might remain undisposed of in the new States after they were admitted.

And, thirdly, to give power to govern the different territories as incipient States, not of the Union, and fit them for admission. No one in the convention seems to have doubted that these powers were necessary. As early as the third day of its session, (May 29th,) Edmund Randolph brought forward a set of resolutions containing nearly all the germs of the constitution, the tenth of which is as follows:

"*Resolved*, That provision ought to be made for the admission of States lawfully arising within the limits of the United States, whether from a voluntary junction of government and territory or otherwise, with the consent of a number of voices in the national legislature less than the whole."

August 18th, Mr. Madison submitted, in order to be referred to the committee of detail, the following powers as proper to be added to those of the general legislature:

"To dispose of the unappropriated lands of the United States." "To institute temporary governments for new States arising therein." (3 Madison Papers, 1353.)

These, with the resolution, that a district for the location of the seat of government should be provided, and some others, were referred, without a dissent, to the committee of detail, to arrange and put them into satisfactory language.

Gouverneur Morris constructed the clauses, and combined the views of a majority on the two provisions, to admit new States; and secondly, to dispose of the public lands, and to govern the territories, in the mean time, between the cessions of the States and the admission into the Union of new States arising in the ceded territory. (3 Madison Papers, 1456 to 1466.)

It was hardly possible to separate the power "to make all needful rules and regulations" respecting the government of the territory and the disposition of the public lands.

North of the Ohio, Virginia conveyed the lands, and vested the jurisdiction in the thirteen original States, before the constitution was formed. She had the sole title and sole sovereignty, and the same power to cede, on any terms she saw proper, that the king of England had to grant the Virginia colonial charter of 1609, or to grant the charter of Pennsylvania to William Penn. The thirteen States, through their representatives and deputed ministers in the old congress, had the same right to govern that Virginia had before the cession. (Baldwin's Constitutional Views, 90.) And the sixth article of the constitution adopted all engagements entered into by the congress of the confederation, as valid against the United States; and that the laws, made in pursuance of the new constitution, to carry out this engagement, should be the supreme law of the land, and the judges bound thereby. To give the compact, and the ordinance, which was part of it, full effect under the new government, the act of August 7th, 1789, was passed, which declares, "Whereas, in order that the ordinance of the United States in congress assembled, for the government of the territory northwest of the river Ohio, may have full effect, it is requisite that certain provisions should be made, so as to adapt the same to the present constitution of the United States." It is then provided that the governor and other officers should be appointed by the president, with the consent of the Senate; and be subject to removal, &c., in like manner that they were by the old congress, whose functions had ceased.

By the powers to govern, given by the constitution, those amendments to the ordinance could be made, but congress guardedly abstained from touching the compact of Virginia, further than to adapt it to the new constitution.

It is due to myself to say, that it is asking much of a judge, who has for nearly twenty years been exercising jurisdiction, from the western Missouri line to the Rocky Mountains, and, on this understanding of the constitution, inflicting the extreme penalty of death for crimes committed where the direct legislation of congress was the only rule, to agree that he had been all the while acting in mistake, and as an usurper.

More than sixty years have passed away since congress has exercised power to govern the territories, by its legislation directly, or by territorial charters, subject to repeal at all times, and it is now too late to call that power into question, if this court could disregard its own decisions; which it cannot do, as I think. It was held in the case of Cross *v.* Harrison, (16 How. 193–'4,) that the sovereignty of California was in the United States, in virtue of the constitution, by which power had been given to congress to dispose of and make all needful rules and regulations respecting the territory or other property belonging to the United States, with the power to admit new States into the Union. That decision followed preceding ones, there cited. The question was then presented, how it was possible for the judicial mind to conceive that the United States government, created solely by the constitution, could, by a lawful treaty, acquire territory over which the acquiring power had no jurisdiction to hold and govern it, by force of the instrument under whose authority the country was acquired; and the foregoing was the conclusion of this court on the proposition. What was there announced, was most deliberately done, and with a purpose. The only question here is, as I think, how far the power of congress is limited.

As to the northwest territory, Virginia had the right to abolish slavery there; and she did so agree in 1787, with the other States in the congress of the confederation, by assenting to and adopting the ordinance of 1787, for the government of the northwest territory. She did this also by an act of her legislature, passed afterwards, which was a treaty in fact.

Before the new constitution was adopted, she had as much right to treat and agree as any European government had. And, having excluded slavery, the new government was bound by that engagement by article six of the new constitution. This only meant that slavery should not exist whilst the United States exercised the power of government, in the territorial form; for, when a new State came in, it might do so, with or without slavery.

My opinion is, that congress had no power, in face of the compact between Virginia and the twelve other States, to *force* slavery into the northwest territory, because there, it was bound to that "engagement," and could not break it.

In 1790, North Carolina ceded her western territory, now the State of Tennessee, and stipulated that the inhabitants thereof should enjoy all the privileges and advantages of the ordinance for governing the territory north of the Ohio river, and that congress should assume the government, and accept the cession, under the express conditions contained in the ordinance: *Provided,* "That no regulation made, or to be made, by congress, shall tend to emancipate slaves."

In 1802, Georgia ceded her western territory to the United States, with the provision that the ordinance of 1787 should in all its parts extend to the territory ceded, "that article only excepted which forbids slavery." Congress had no more power to legislate slavery *out* from the North Carolina and Georgia cessions, than it had power to legislate slavery in, north of the Ohio. No power existed in congress to legislate at all, affecting slavery, in either case. The inhabitants, as respected this description of property, stood protected whilst they were governed by congress, in like manner that they were protected before the cession was made, and when they were, respectively, parts of North Carolina and Georgia.

And how does the power of congress stand west of the Mississippi river? The country there was acquired from France, by treaty, in 1803. It declares, that the first consul, in the name of the French republic, doth hereby cede to the United States, in full sovereignty, the colony or province of Louisiana, with all the rights and appurtenances of the said territory. And, by article third, that "the inhabitants of the ceded territory shall be incorporated in the Union of the United States, and admitted as soon as possible, according to the principles of the federal constitution, to the enjoyment of all the rights, advantages, and immunities, of citizens of the United States; and, in the mean time, they shall be maintained and protected in the free enjoyment of their liberty, property, and the religion which they profess."

Louisiana was a province where slavery was not only lawful, but where property in slaves was the most valuable of all personal property. The province was ceded as a unit, with an equal right pertaining to all its inhabitants, in every part thereof, to own slaves. It was, to a great extent, a vacant country, having in it few civilized inhabitants. No one portion of the colony, of a proper size for a State of the Union had a sufficient number of inhabitants to claim admission into the Union. To enable the United States to fulfil the treaty, additional population was indispensable, and obviously desired with anxiety by both sides, so that the whole country should, as soon as possible, become States of the Union. And for this contemplated future population, the treaty [w]as expressly provided as it did for the inhabitants residing in the province when the treaty was made. All these were to be protected *"in the mean time;"* that is to say, at all times, between the date of the treaty and the time when the portion of the territory where the inhabitants resided was admitted into the Union as a State.

At the date of the treaty, each inhabitant had the right to the *free* enjoyment of his property, alike with his liberty and his religion, in every part of Louisiana; the province then being one country, he might go everywhere in it, and carry his liberty, property, and religion, with him, and in which he was to be maintained and protected, until he became a citizen of a State of the Union of the United States. This cannot be denied to the original inhabitants and their descendants. And, if it be true that immigrants were equally protected, it must follow that they can also stand on the treaty.

The settled doctrine in the State courts of Louisiana is, that a French subject coming to the Orleans territory, after the treaty of 1803 was made, and before Louisiana was admitted into the Union, and being an inhabitant at the time of the admission, became a citizen of the United States by that act; that he was one of the inhabitants contemplated by the third article of the treaty, which referred to all the inhabitants embraced within the new State on its admission.

That this is the true construction, I have no doubt.

If power existed to draw a line at thirty-six degrees thirty minutes north, so congress had equal power to draw the line on the thirtieth degree—that is, due west from the city of New Orleans—and to declare that north of *that line* slavery should never exist. Suppose this had been done before 1812, when Louisiana came into the Union, and the question of infraction of the treaty had then been presented on the present assumption of power to prohibit slavery, who doubts what the decision of this court would have been on such an act of congress; yet, the difference between the supposed line, and that on thirty-six degrees thirty minutes north, is only in the degree of grossness presented by the lower line.

The Missouri Compromise line of 1820 was very aggressive; it declared that slavery was abolished forever throughout a country reaching from the Mississippi river to the Pacific ocean, stretching over thirty-two degrees of longitude, and twelve and a half degrees of latitude on its eastern side, sweeping over four-fifths, to say no more, of the original province of Louisiana.

That the United States government stipulated in favor of the inhabitants to the extent here contended for, has not been seriously denied, as far as I know; but the argument is, that congress had authority to *repeal* the third article of the treaty of 1803, in so far as it secured the right to hold slave property, in a portion of the ceded territory, leaving the right to exist in other parts. In other words, that congress could repeal the third article entirely, at its pleasure. This I deny.

The compacts with North Carolina and Georgia were treaties also, and stood on the same footing of the Louisiana treaty; on the assumption of power to repeal the one, it must have extended to all, and congress could have excluded the slaveholder of North Carolina from the enjoyment of his lands in the territory now the State of Tennessee, where the citizens of the mother State were the principal proprietors.

And so in the case of Georgia. Her citizens could have been refused the right to emigrate to the Mississippi or Alabama territory, unless they left their most valuable and cherished property behind them.

The constitution was framed in reference to facts then existing or likely to arise: the instrument looked to no theories of government. In the vigorous debates in the convention, as reported by Mr. Madison and others, surrounding facts, and the condition and necessities of the country, gave rise to almost every provision; and among those facts, it was prominently true, that congress dare not be intrusted with power to provide that, if North Carolina or Georgia ceded her western territory, the citizens of the State (in either case) could be prohibited, at the pleasure of congress, from removing to their lands, then granted to a large extent, in the country likely to be ceded, unless they left their slaves behind. That such an attempt, in the face of a population fresh from the war of the revolution, and then engaged in war with the great confederacy of Indians, extending from the mouth of the Ohio to the Gulf of Mexico, would end in open revolt, all intelligent men knew.

In view of these facts, let us inquire how the question stands by the terms of the constitution, aside from the treaty? How it stood in public opinion when the Georgia cession was made, in 1802, is apparent from the fact that no guaranty was required by Georgia of the United States, for the protection of slave property. The federal constitution was relied on, to secure the rights of Georgia and her citizens during the territorial condition of the country. She relied on the indisputable truths, that the States were by the constitution made equals in political rights, and equals in the right to participate in the common property of all the States united, and held in trust for them. The constitution having provided that "The citizens of each State shall be entitled to all privileges and immunities of citizens of the several States," the right to enjoy the territory as equals was reserved to the States, and to the citizens of the States, respectively. The cited clause is not that citizens of the United States shall have equal privileges in the territories, but the citizen of each State shall come there in right of his State, and enjoy the common property. He secures his equality through the equality of his State, by virtue of that great fundamental condition of the Union—the equality of the States.

Congress cannot do indirectly what the constitution prohibits directly. If the slaveholder is prohibited from going to the territory with his slaves, who are parts of his family in name and in fact, it will follow that men owning lawful property in their own States, carrying with them the equality of their State to enjoy the common property, may be told, you cannot come here with your slaves, and he will be held out at the border. By this subterfuge, owners of slave property, to the amount of thousand[s] of millions, might be almost as effectually excluded from removing into the territory of Louisiana north of thirty-six degrees thirty minutes, as if the law declared that owners of slaves, as a class, should be excluded, even if their slaves were left behind.

Just as well might congress have said to those of the north, you shall not introduce into the territory south of said line your cattle or horses, as the country is already overstocked; nor can you introduce your tools of trade, or machines, as the policy of congress is to encourage the culture of sugar and cotton south of the line, and so to provide that the northern people shall manufacture for those of the south, and barter for the staple articles slave labor produces. And thus the northern farmer and mechanic would be held out, as the slaveholder was for thirty years, by the Missouri restriction.

If congress could prohibit one species of property, lawful throughout Louisiana when it was acquired, and lawful in the State from whence it was brought, so congress might exclude any or all property.

The case before us will illustrate the construction contended for. Dr. Emerson was a citizen of Missouri; he had an equal right to go to the territory with every citizen of other States. This is undeniable, as I suppose. Scott was Dr. Emerson's lawful property in Missouri; he carried his Missouri title with him; and the precise question here is, whether congress had the power to annul that title. It is idle to say, that if congress could not defeat the title *directly,* that it might be done indirectly, by drawing a narrow circle around the slave population of upper Louisiana, and declaring that if the slave went beyond it he should be free. Such assumption is mere evasion, and entitled to no consideration. And it is equally idle to contend, that because congress has express power to regulate commerce among the Indian tribes, and to prohibit intercourse with the Indians, that therefore Dr. Emerson's title might be defeated within the country ceded by the Indians to the United States as early as 1805, and which embraces Fort Snelling. (Am. State Papers, vol. 1, p. 734.) We *must* meet the question, whether congress had the power to declare that a citizen of a State, carrying with him his equal rights, secured to him through his State, could be stripped of his goods and slaves, and be deprived of any participation in the common property? If this be the true meaning of the constitution, equality of rights to enjoy a common country (equal to a thousand miles square) may be cut off by a geographical line, and a great portion of our citizens excluded from it.

Ingenious, indirect evasions of the constitution have been attempted and defeated heretofore. In the passenger cases, (7 How. R.) the attempt was made to impose a tax on the masters, crews, and passengers of vessels, the constitution having prohibited a tax on the vessel itself; but this court held the attempt to be a mere evasion, and pronounced the tax illegal.

I admit that Virginia could, and lawfully did, prohibit slavery northwest of the Ohio, by her charter of cession, and that the territory was taken by the United States with this condition imposed. I also admit that France could, by the treaty of 1803, have prohibited slavery in any part of the ceded territory, and imposed it on the United States as a fundamental condition of the cession, in the mean time, till new States were admitted in the Union.

I concur with Judge Baldwin, that federal power is exercised over all the territory within the United States, pursuant to the constitution; *and,* the conditions of the cession, whether it was a part of the original territory of a State of the Union, or of a foreign State, ceded by deed or treaty; the right of the United States in or over it depends on the contract of cession, which operates to incorporate as well the territory as its inhabitants into the Union. (Baldwin's Constitutional Views, 84.)

My opinion is, that the third article of the treaty of 1803, ceding Louisiana to the United States, stands protected by the constitution, and cannot be repealed by congress.

And, secondly, that the act of 1820, known as the Missouri compromise, violates the most leading feature of the constitution—a feature on which the Union depends, and which secures to the respective States and their citizens and entire EQUALITY of rights, privileges, and immunities.

On these grounds, I hold the compromise act to have been void; and, consequently, that the plaintiff, Scott, can claim no benefit under it.

For the reasons above stated, I concur with my brother, judges that the plaintiff, Scott, is a slave, and was so when this suit was brought.

> Mr. Justice MCLEAN and Mr. Justice CURTIS dissented.
>
> Mr. Justice MCLEAN dissenting.

This case is before us on a writ of error from the circuit court for the district of Missouri.

An action of trespass was brought, which charges the defendant with an assault and imprisonment of the plaintiff, and also of Harriet Scott, his wife, Eliza and Lizzie, his two children, on the ground that they were his slaves, which was without right on his part, and against law.

The defendant filed a plea in abatement, "that said causes of action, and each and every of them, if any such accrued to the said Dred Scott, accrued out of the jurisdiction of this court, and exclusively within the jurisdiction of the courts of the State of Missouri, for that to wit, said plaintiff, Dred Scott, is not a citizen of the State of Missouri, as alleged in his declaration, because he is a negro of African descent, his ancestors were of pure African blood, and were brought into this country and sold as negro slaves; and this the said Sandford is ready to verify; wherefore he prays judgment whether the court can or will take further cognizance of the action aforesaid."

To this a demurrer was filed, which, on argument, was sustained by the court, the plea in abatement being held insufficient; the defendant was ruled to plead over. Under this rule he pleaded: 1. Not guilty; 2. That Dred Scott was a negro slave, the property of the defendant; and 3. That Harriet, the wife, and Eliza and Lizzie, the daughters of the plaintiff, were the lawful slaves of the defendant.

Issue was joined on the first plea, and replications of *de injuria* were filed to the other pleas.

The parties agreed to the following facts: In the year 1834, the plaintiff was a negro slave belonging to Dr. Emerson, who was a surgeon in the army of the United States. In that year, Dr. Emerson took the plaintiff from the State of Missouri to the post of Rock Island, in the State of Illinois, and held him there as a slave until the month of April or May, 1836. At the time last mentioned, Dr. Emerson removed the plaintiff from Rock Island to the military post at Fort Snelling, situate on the west bank of the Mississippi river, in the territory Known as Upper Louisiana, acquired by the United States of France, and situate north of latitude thirty-six degrees thirty minutes north, and north of the State of Missouri. Dr. Emerson held the plaintiff in slavery, at Fort Snelling, from the last-mentioned date until the year 1838.

In the year 1835, Harriet, who is named in the second count of the plaintiff's declaration, was the negro slave of Major Taliaferro, who belonged to the army of the United States. In that year, Major Taliaferro took Harriet to Fort Snelling, a military post situated as hereinbefore stated, and kept her there as a slave until the year 1836, and then sold and delivered her as a slave, at Fort Snelling, unto Dr. Emerson, who held her in slavery, at that place, until the year 1838.

In the year 1836, the plaintiff and Harriet were married at Fort Snelling, with the consent of Dr. Emerson, who claimed to be their master and owner. Eliza and Lizzie, named in the third count of the plaintiff's declaration, are the fruit of that marriage. Eliza is about fourteen years old, and was born on board the steamboat Gipsey, north of the north line of the State of Missouri, and upon the river Mississippi. Lizzie is about seven years old, and was born in the State of Missouri, at the military post called Jefferson Barracks.

In the year 1838, Dr. Emerson removed the plaintiff and said Harriet and their daughter Eliza from Fort Snelling to the State of Missouri, where they have ever since resided.

Before the commencement of the suit, Dr. Emerson sold and conveyed the plaintiff, Harriet, Eliza, and Lizzie, to the defendant, as slaves, and he has ever since claimed to hold them as slaves.

At the times mentioned in the plaintiff's declaration, the defendant, claiming to be the owner, laid his hands upon said plaintiff, Harriet, Eliza, and Lizzie, and imprisoned them; doing in this respect, however, no more than he might lawfully do, if they were of right his slaves at such times.

In the first place, the plea to the jurisdiction is not before us, on this writ of error. A demurrer to the plea was sustained, which ruled the plea bad, and the defendant, on leave, pleaded over.

The decision on the demurrer was in favor of the plaintiff; and as the plaintiff prosecutes this writ of error, he does not complain of the decision on the demurrer. The defendant might have complained of this decision, as against him, and have prosecuted a writ of error, to reverse it. But as the case, under the instruction of the court to the jury, was decided in his favor, of course he had no ground of complaint.

But it is said, if the court, on looking at the record, shall clearly perceive that the circuit court had no jurisdiction, it is a ground for the dismissal of the case. This may be characterized as rather a sharp practice, and one which seldom, if ever, occurs. No case was cited in the argument as authority, and not a single case precisely in point is recollected in our reports. The pleadings do not show a want of jurisdiction. This want of jurisdiction can only be ascertained by a judgment on the demurrer to the special plea. No such case, it is believed, can be cited. But if this rule of practice is to be applied in this case, and the plaintiff in error is required to answer and maintain as well the points ruled in his favor, as to show the error of those ruled against him, he has more than an ordinary duty to perform. Under such circumstances, the want of jurisdiction in the circuit court must be so clear as not to admit of doubt. Now, the plea which raises the question of jurisdiction, in my judgment, is radically defective. The gravamen of the plea is this: "That the plaintiff is a negro of African descent, his ancestors being of pure African blood, and were brought into this country, and sold as negro slaves."

There is no averment in this plea which shows or conduces to show an inability in the plaintiff to sue in the circuit court. It does not allege that the plaintiff had his domicile in any other State, nor that he is not a free man in Missouri. He is averred to have had a negro ancestry, but this does not show that he is not a citizen of Missouri, within the meaning of the act of congress authorizing him to sue in the circuit court. It has never been held necessary, to constitute a citizen within the act, that he should have the qualifications of an elector. Females and minors may sue in the federal courts, and so may any individual who has a permanent domicile in the State under whose laws his rights are protected, and to which he owes allegiance.

Being born under our constitution and laws, no naturalization is required, as one of foreign birth, to make him a citizen. The most general and appropriate definition of the term citizen is "a freeman." Being a freeman, and having his domicile in a State different from that of the defendant, he is a citizen within the act of congress, and the courts of the Union are open to him.

It has often been held, that the jurisdiction, as regards parties, can only be exercised between citizens of different States, and that a mere residence is not sufficient; but this has been said to distinguish a temporary from a permanent residence.

To constitute a good plea to the jurisdiction, it must negative those qualities and rights which enable an individual to sue in the Federal courts. This has not been done; and on this ground the plea was defective, and the demurrer was properly sustained. No implication can aid a plea in abatement or in bar; it must be complete in itself; the facts stated, if true, must abate or bar the right of the plaintiff to sue. This is not the character of the above plea. The facts stated, if admitted, are not inconsistent with other facts, which may be presumed, and which bring the plaintiff within the act of congress.

The pleader has not the boldness to allege that the plaintiff is a slave, as that would assume against him the matter in controversy, and embrace the entire merits of the case in a plea to the jurisdiction. But beyond the facts set out in the plea, the court, to sustain it, must assume the plaintiff to be a slave, which is decisive on the merits. This is a short and an effectual mode of deciding the cause; but I am yet to learn that it is sanctioned by any known rule of pleading.

The defendant's counsel complain, that if the court take jurisdiction on the ground that the plaintiff is free, the assumption is against the right of the master. This argument is easily answered. In the first place, the plea does not show him to be a slave; it does not follow that a man is not free whose ancestors were slaves. The reports of the supreme court of Missouri show that this assumption has many exceptions; and there is no averment in the plea that the plaintiff is not within them.

By all the rules of pleading, this is a fatal defect in the plea. If there be doubt, what rule of construction has been established in the slave States? In Jacob *v.* Sharp, (Meigs's Rep. Tennessee, 114,) the court held, when there was doubt as to the construction of a will which emancipated a slave, "it must be construed to be subordinate to the higher and more important right of freedom."

No injustice can result to the master, from an exercise of jurisdiction in this cause. Such a decision does not in any degree affect the merits of the case; it only enables the plaintiff to assert his claims to freedom before this tribunal. If the jurisdiction be ruled against him, on the ground that he is a slave, it is decisive of his fate.

It has been argued that, if a colored person be made a citizen of a State, he cannot sue in the federal court. The constitution declares that Federal jurisdiction "may be exercised between citizens of different States," and the same is provided in the act of 1789. The above argument is properly met by saying that "the constitution was intended to be a practical instrument; and where its language is too plain to be misunderstood, the argument ends."

In Chirae *v.* Charae, (2 Wheat. 261; 4 Curtis, 99,) this court says: "That the power of naturalization is exclusively in congress does not seem to be, and certainly ought not to be, controverted." No person can legally be made a citizen of a State, and consequently a citizen of the United States, of foreign birth, unless he be naturalized under the acts of congress. Congress has power "to establish a uniform rule of naturalization."

It is a power which belongs exclusively to congress, as intimately connected with our federal relations. A State may authorize foreigners to hold real estate within its jurisdiction, but it has no power to naturalize foreigners, and give them the rights of citizens. Such a right is opposed to the acts of congress on the subject of naturalization, and subversive of the federal powers. I regret that any countenance should be given from this bench to a practice like this in some of the States, which has no warrant in the constitution.

In the argument, it was said that a colored citizen would not be an agreeable member of society. This is more a matter of taste than of law. Several of the States have admitted persons of color to the right of suffrage, and in this view have recognized them as citizens; and this has been done in the slave as well as the free States. On the question of citizenship, it must be admitted that we have not been very fastidious. Under the late treaty with Mexico, we have made citizens of all grades, combinations, and colors. The same was done in the admission of Louisiana and Florida. No one ever doubted, and no court ever held, that the people of these territories did not become citizens under the treaty. They have exercised all the rights of citizens, without being naturalized under the acts of congress.

There are several important principles involved in this case, which have been argued, and which may be considered under the following heads:

1. The locality of slavery, as settled by this court and the courts of the States.

2. The relation which the federal government bears to slavery in the States.
3. The power of congress to establish territorial governments, and to prohibit the introduction of slavery therein.
4. The effect of taking slaves into a new State or territory, and so holding them, where slavery is prohibited.
5. Whether the return of a slave under the control of his master, after being entitled to his freedom, reduces him to his former condition.
6. Are the decisions of the supreme court of Missouri, on the questions before us, binding on this court, within the rule adopted.

In the course of my judicial duties, I have had occasion to consider and decide several of the above points.

1. As to the locality of slavery. The civil law throughout the continent of Europe, it is believed, without an exception, is, that slavery can exist only within the territory where it is established; and that, if a slave escapes, or is carried beyond such territory, his master cannot reclaim him, unless by virtue of some express stipulation. (Grotius, lib. 2, chap. 15, 5, 1; lib. 10, chap. 10, 2, 1; Wicqueposts Ambassador, lib. 1, p. 418; 4 Martin, 385; Case of the Creole in the House of Lords, 1842; 1 Phillimore on International Law, 316, 335.)

There is no nation in Europe which considers itself bound to return to his master a fugitive slave, under the civil law or the law of nations. On the contrary, the slave is held to be free where there is no treaty obligation, or compact in some other form, to return him to his master. The Roman law did now allow freedom to be sold. An ambassador or any other public functionary could not take a slave to France, Spain, or any other country of Europe, without emancipating him. A number of slaves escaped from a Florida plantation, and were received on board of ship by Admiral Cochrane; by the king's bench, they were held to be free. (2 Barn. and Cres. 440.)

In the great and leading case of Prigg v. The State of Pennsylvania, (16 Peters, 594; 14 Curtis, 421,) this court say that, by the general law of nations, no nation is bound to recognize the state of slavery, as found within its territorial dominions, where it is in opposition to its own policy and institutions, in favor of the subjects of other nations where slavery is organized. If it does it, it is as a matter of comity, and not as a matter of international right. The state of slavery is deemed to be a mere municipal regulation, founded upon and limited to the range of the territorial laws. This was fully recognized in Somersett's case, (Lafft's Rep. 1; 20 Howell's State Trials, 79,) which was decided before the American revolution.

There was some contrariety of opinion among the judges on certain points ruled in Prigg's case, but there was none in regard to the great principle, that slavery is limited to the range of the laws under which it is sanctioned.

No case in England appears to have been more thoroughly examined than that of Somersett. The judgment pronounced by Lord Mansfield was the judgment of the court of king's bench. The cause was argued at great length, and with great ability, by Hargrave and others, who stood among the most eminent counsel in England. It was held under advisement from term to term, and a due sense of its importance was felt and expressed by the bench.

In giving the opinion of the court, Lord Mansfield said: "The state of slavery is of such a nature that it is incapable of being introduced on any reasons, moral or political, but only by positive law, which preserves its force long after the reasons, occasion, and time itself, from whence it was created, is erased from the memory; it is of a nature that nothing can be suffered to support it but positive law."

He referred to the contrary opinion of Lord Hardwicke, in October, 1749, as chancellor: "That he and Lord Talbot, when attorney and solicitor general, were of opinion that no such claim, as here presented, for freedom, was valid."

The weight of this decision is sought [thought] to be impaired, from the terms in which it was described by the exuberant imagination of Curran. The words of Lord Mansfield, in giving the opinion of the court, were such as were fit to be used by a great judge, in a most important case. It is a sufficient answer to all objections to that judgment, that it was pronounced before the revolution, and that it was considered by this court as the highest authority. For near a century, the decision in Somersett's case has remained the law of England. The case of the slave Grace, decided by Lord Stowell in 1827, does not, as has been supposed, overrule the judgment of Lord Mansfield. Lord Stowell held that, during the residence of the slave in England, "No dominion, authority, or coercion, can be exercised over him." Under another head, I shall have occasion to examine the opinion in the case of Grace.

To the position, that slavery can only exist except under the authority of law, it is objected, that in few if in any instances has it been established by statutory enactment. This is no answer to the doctrine laid down by the court. Almost all the principles of the common law had their foundation in usage. Slavery was introduced into the colonies of this country by Great Britain at an early period of their history, and it was protected and cherished, until it became incorporated into the colonial policy. It is immaterial whether a system of slavery was introduced by express law, or otherwise, if it have the authority of law. There is no slave State where the institution is not recognized and protected by statutory enactments and judicial decisions. Slaves are made property by the laws of the slave States, and as such are liable to the claims of creditors; they descend to heirs, are taxed, and in the south they are a subject of commerce.

In the case of Rankin v. Lydia, (2 A. K. Marshall's Rep.) Judge Mills, speaking for the court of appeals of Kentucky, says: "In deciding the question, (of slavery,) we disclaim the influence of the general principles of liberty, which we all admire, and conceive it ought to be decided by the law as it is, and not as it ought to be. Slavery is sanctioned by the laws of this State, and the right to hold slaves under our municipal regulations is unquestionable. But we view this as a right existing by positive law of a municipal character, without foundation in the law of nature, or the unwritten and common law."

I will now consider the relation which the federal government bears to slavery in the States:

Slavery is emphatically a State institution. In the ninth section of the first article of the constitution, it is provided "that the migration or importation of such persons as any of the States now existing shall think proper to admit, shall not be prohibited by the congress prior to the year 1808, but a tax or duty may be imposed on such importation, not exceeding ten dollars for each person."

In the convention, it was proposed by a committee of eleven to limit the importation of slaves to the year 1800, when Mr. Pinckney moved to extend the time to the year 1808. This motion was carried—New Hampshire, Massachusetts, Connecticut, Maryland, North Carolina, South Carolina, and Georgia, voting in the affirmative; and New Jersey, Pennsylvania, and Virginia, in the negative. In opposition to the motion, Mr. Madison said: "Twenty years will produce all the mischief that can be apprehended from the liberty to import slaves; so long a term will be more dishonorable to the American character than to say nothing about it in the constitution." (Madison Papers.)

The provision in regard to the slave trade shows clearly that congress considered slavery a State institution, to be continued and regulated by its individual sovereignty; and to conciliate that interest, the slave trade was continued twenty years, not as a general measure, but for the "benefit of such States as shall think proper to encourage it."

In the case of Groves *v.* Slaughter, (15 Peters, 499; 14 Curtis, 137,) Messrs. Clay and Webster contended that, under the commercial power, congress had a right to regulate the slave trade among the several States; but the court held that congress had no power to interfere with slavery as it exists in the States, or to regulate what is called the slave trade among them. If this trade were subject to the commercial power, it would follow that congress could abolish or establish slavery in every State of the Union.

The only connection which the federal government holds with slaves in a State, arises from that provision of the constitution which declares that "No person held to service or labor in one State, under the laws thereof, escaping into another, shall, in consequence of any law or regulation therein, be discharged from such service or labor, but shall be delivered up, on claim of the party to whom such service or labor may be due."

This being a fundamental law of the federal government, it rests mainly for its execution, as has been held, on the judicial power of the Union; and so far as the rendition of fugitives from labor has become a subject of judicial action, the federal obligation has been faithfully discharged.

In the formation of the federal constitution, care was taken to confer no power on the federal government to interfere with this institution in the States. In the provision respecting the slave trade, in fixing the ratio of representation, and providing for the reclamation of fugitives from labor, slaves were referred to as persons, and in no other respect are they considered in the constitution.

We need not refer to the mercenary spirit which introduced the infamous traffic in slaves, to show the degradation of negro slavery in our country. This system was imposed upon our colonial settlements by the mother country, and it is due to truth to say that the commercial colonies and States were chiefly engaged in the traffic. But we know as a historical fact, that James Madison, that great and good man, a leading member in the federal convention, was solicitous to guard the language of that instrument so as not to convey the idea that there could be property in man.

I prefer the lights of Madison, Hamilton, and Jay, as a means of construing the constitution in all its bearings, rather than to look behind that period, into a traffic which is now declared to be piracy, and punished with death by Christian nations. I do not like to draw the sources of our domestic relations from so dark a ground. Our independence was a great epoch in the history of freedom; and while I admit the government was not made expecially for the colored race, yet many of them were citizens of the New England States, and exercised, the rights of suffrage when the constitution was adopted, and it was not doubted by any intelligent person that its tendencies would greatly ameliorate their condition.

Many of the States, on the adoption of the constitution, or shortly afterward, took measures to abolish slavery within their respective jurisdictions; and it is a well-known fact that a belief was cherished by the leading men, south as well as north, that the institution of slavery would gradually decline, until it would become extinct. The increased value of slave labor, in the culture of cotton and sugar, prevented the realization of this expectation. Like all other communities and States, the south were influenced by what they considered to be their own interests.

But if we are to turn our attention to the dark ages of the world, why confine our view to colored slavery? On the same principles, white men were made slaves. All slavery has its origin in power, and is against right.

The power of congress to establish territorial governments, and to prohibit the introduction of slavery therein, is the next point to be considered.

After the cession of western territory by Virginia and other States, to the United States, the public attention was directed to the best mode of disposing of it for the general benefit. While in attendence on the federal convention, Mr. Madison, in a letter to Edmund Randolph, dated the 22d April, 1787, says: "Congress are deliberating on the plan most eligible for disposing of the western territory not yet surveyed. Some alteration will probably be made in the ordinance on that subject." And in the same letter he says: "The inhabitants of the Illinois complain of the land jobbers, &c., who are purchasing titles among them. Those of St. Vincent's complain of the defective criminal and civil justice among them, as well as of military protection." And on the next day he writes to Mr. Jefferson: "The government of the settlements on the Illinois and Wabash is a subject very perplexing in itself, and rendered more so by our ignorance of the many circumstances on which a right judgment depends. The inhabitants at those places claim protection against the savages, and some provision for both civil and criminal justice."

In May, 1787, Mr. Edmund Randolph submitted to the federal convention certain propositions, as the basis of a federal government, among which was the following:

"*Resolved*, That provision ought to be made for the admission of States lawfully arising within the limits of the United States, whether from a voluntary junction of government and territory or otherwise, with the consent of a number of voices in the national legislature less than the whole."

Afterward, Mr. Madison submitted to the convention, in order to be referred to the committee of detail, the following powers, as proper to be added to those of general legislation:

"To dispose of the unappropriated lands of the United States. To institute temporary governments for new States arising therein. To regulate affairs with the Indians, as well within as without the limits of the United States."

Other propositions were made in reference to the same subjects, which it would be tedious to enumerate. Mr. Gouverneur Morris proposed the following:

"The legislature shall have power to dispose of and make all needful rules and regulations respecting the territory or other property belonging to the United States; and nothing in this constitution contained shall be so construed as to prejudice any claims either of the United States or of any particular State."

This was adopted as a part of the constitution, with two verbal alterations—congress was substituted for legislature, and the word *either* was stricken out.

In the organization of the new government, but little revenue for a series of years was expected from commerce. The public lands were considered as the principal resource of the country for the payment of the revolutionary debt. Direct taxation was the means relied on to pay the current expenses of the government. The short period that occurred between the cession of western lands to the Federal government by Virginia and other States, and the adoption of the constitution, was sufficient to show the necessity of a proper land system and a temporary government. This was clearly seen by propositions and remarks in the federal convention, some of which are above cited, by the passage of the ordinance of 1787, and the adoption of that instrument by congress, under the constitution, which gave to it validity.

It will be recollected that the deed of cession of western territory was made to the United States by Virginia in 1784, and that it required the territory ceded to be laid out into States, that the land should be disposed of for the common benefit of the States, and that all right, title, and claim, as well of soil as of jurisdiction, were ceded; and this was the form of cession from other States.

On the 13th of July, the ordinance of 1787 was passed, "for the government of the United States territory northwest of the river Ohio," with but one dissenting vote. This instrument provided there should be organized in the territory not less than three nor more than five States, designating their boundaries. It passed while the federal convention was in session, about two months before the constitution was adopted by the convention. The members of the convention must therefore have been well acquainted with the provisions of the ordinance. It provided for a temporary government, as initiatory to the formation of State governments. Slavery was prohibited in the territory.

Can any one suppose that the eminent men of the federal convention could have overlooked or neglected a matter so vitally important to the country, in the organization of temporary governments for the vast territory northwest of the river Ohio? In the 3d section of the 4th article of the constitution, they did make provision for the admission of new States, the sale of the public lands, and the temporary government of the territory. Without a temporary government, new States could not have been formed, nor could the public lands have been sold.

If the third section were before us now for consideration for the first time, under the facts stated, I could not hesitate to say there was adequate legislative power given in it. The power to make all needful rules and regulations is a power to legislate. This no one will controvert, as congress cannot make "rules and regulations," except by legislation. But it is argued that the word territory is used as synonymous with the word land; and that the rules and regulations of congress are limited to the disposition of lands and other property belonging to the United States. That this is not the true construction of the section appears from the fact that in the first line of the section "the power to dispose of the public lands" is given expressly, and, in addition, to make all needful rules and regulations. The power to dispose of is complete in itself, and requires nothing more. It authorizes congress to use the proper means within its discretion, and any further provision for this purpose would be a useless verbiage. As a composition, the constitution is remarkably free from such a charge.

In the discussion of the power of congress to govern a territory, in the case of the Atlantic Insurance Company *v.* Canter, (1 Peters, 511; 7 Curtis, 685,) Chief Justice Marshall, speaking for the court, said, in regard to the people of Florida, "they do not, however, participate in political power; they do not share in the government till Florida shall become a State; in the mean time, Florida continues to be a territory of the United States, governed by virtue of that clause in the constitution which empowers congress "to make all needful rules and regulations respecting the territory or other property belonging to the United States."

And he adds, "perhaps the power of governing a territory belonging to the United States, which has not, by becoming a State, acquired the means of self-government, may result necessarily from the fact that it is not within the jurisdiction of any particular State, and is within the power and jurisdiction of the United States. The right to govern may be the inevitable consequence of the right to acquire territory; whichever may be the source whence the power is derived, the possession of it is unquestioned." And in the close of the opinion, the court say, "in legislating for them [the territories,] congress exercises the combined powers of the general and State governments."

Some consider the opinion to be loose and inconclusive; others, that it is *obiter dicta;* and the last sentence is objected to as recognizing absolute power in congress over territories. The learned and eloquent Wirt, who, in the argument of a cause before the court, had occasion to cite a few sentences from an opinion of the chief justice, observed, "no one can mistake the style, the words so completely match the thought."

I can see no want of precision in the language of the chief justice; his meaning cannot be mistaken. He states, first, the third section as giving power to congress to govern the territories, and two other grounds from which the power may also be implied. The objection seems to be, that the chief justice did not say which of the grounds stated he considered the source of the power. He did not specifically state this, but he did say, "whichever may be the source whence the power is derived, the possession of it is unquestioned." No opinion of the court could have been expressed with a stronger emphasis; the power in congress is unquestioned. But those who have undertaken to criticise the opinion, consider it without authority, because the chief justice did not designate specially the power. This is a singular objection. If the power be unquestioned, it can be a matter of no importance on which ground it is exercised.

The opinion clearly was not *obiter dicta*. The turning point in the case was, whether congress had power to authorize the territorial legislature of Florida to pass the law under which the territorial court was established, whose decree was brought before this court for revision. The power of congress, therefore, was the point in issue.

The word "territory," according to Worcester, "means land, country, a district of country under a temporary government." The words "territory or other property," as used, do imply, from the use of the pronoun other, that territory was used as descriptive of land; but does it follow that it was not used also as descriptive of a district of country? In both of these senses it belonged to the United States—as land, for the purpose of sale; as territory, for the purpose of government.

But, if it be admitted that the word territory as used means land, and nothing but land, the power of congress to organize a temporary government is clear. It has power to make all needful regulations respecting the public lands, and the extent of those "needful regulations" depends upon the direction of congress, where the means are appropriate to the end, and do not conflict with any of the prohibitions of the constitution. If a temporary government be deemed needful, necessary, requisite, or is wanted, congress has power to establish it. This court says, in McCulloch v. The State of Maryland, (4 Wheat. 316,) "If a certain means to carry into effect any of the powers expressly given by the constitution to the government of the Union be an appropriate measure, not prohibited by the constitution, the degree of its necessity is a question of legislative discretion, not of judicial cognizance."

The power to establish post offices and post roads gives power to congress to make contracts for the transportation of the mail, and to punish all who commit depredations upon it in its transit, or at its places of distribution. Congress has power to regulate commerce, and, in the exercise of its discretion, to lay an embargo, which suspends commerce; so, under the same power, harbors, lighthouses, breakwaters, &c., are constructed.

Did Chief Justice Marshall, in saying that congress governed a territory, by exercising the combined powers of the federal and State governments, refer to unlimited discretion? A government which can make white men slaves? Surely, such a remark in the argument must have been inadvertently uttered. On the contrary, there is no power in the constitution by which congress can make either white or black men slaves. In organizing the government of a territory, congress is limited to means appropriate to the attainment of the constitutional object. No powers can be exercised which are prohibited by the constitution, or which are contrary to its spirit; so that, whether the object may be the protection of the persons and property of purchasers of the public lands, or of communities who have been annexed to the Union by conquest or purchase, they are initiatory to the establishment of State governments, and no more power can be claimed or exercised than is necessary to the attainment of the end. This is the limitation of all the federal powers.

But congress has no power to regulate the internal concerns of a State, as of a territory; consequently, in providing for the government of a territory, to some extent, the combined powers of the federal and State governments are necessarily exercised.

If congress should deem slaves or free colored persons injurious to the population of a free territory, as conducing to lessen the value of the public lands, or on any other ground connected with the public interest, they have the power to prohibit them from becoming settlers in it. This can be sustained on the ground of a sound national policy, which is so clearly shown in our history by practical results, that it would seem no considerate individual can question it. And, as regards any unfairness of such a policy to our southern brethren, as urged in the argument, it is only necessary to say that, with one-fourth of the federal population of the Union, they have in the slave States a larger extent of fertile territory than is included in the free States; and it is submitted, if masters of slaves be restricted from bringing them into free territory, that the restriction on the free citizens of non-slaveholding States, by bringing slaves into free territory, is four times greater than that complained of by the south. But, not only so; some three or four hundred thousand holders of slaves, by bringing them into free territory, impose a restriction on twenty millions of the free States. The repugnancy to slavery would probably prevent fifty or a hundred freemen from settling in a slave territory, where one slaveholder would be prevented from settling in a free territory.

This remark is made in answer to the argument urged, that a prohibition of slavery in the free territories is inconsistent with the continuance of the Union.

Where a territorial government is established in a slave territory, it has uniformly remained in that condition until the people form a State constitution; the same course where the territory is free, both parties acting in good faith, would be attended with satisfactory results.

The sovereignty of the federal government extends to the entire limits of our territory. Should any foreign power invade our jurisdiction, it would be repelled. There is a law of congress to punish our citizens for crimes committed in districts of country where there is no organized government. Criminals are brought to certain territories or States, designated in the law, for punishment. Death has been inflicted in Arkansas and in Missouri, on individuals, for murders committed beyond the limit of any organized territory or State; and no one doubts that such a jurisdiction was rightfully exercised. If there be a right to acquire territory, there necessarily must be an implied power to govern it. When the military force of the Union shall conquer a country, may not congress provide for the government of such country? This would be an implied power essential to the acquisition of new territory. This power has been exercised, without doubt of its constitutionality, over territory acquired by conquest and purchase.

And when there is a large district of country within the United States, and not within any State government, if it be necessary to establish a temporary government to carry out a power expressly vested in congress—as the disposition of the public lands—may not such government be instituted by congress? How do we read the constitution? Is it not a practical instrument?

In such cases, no implication of a power can arise which is inhibited by the constitution, or which may be against the theory of its construction. As my opinion rests on the third section, these remarks are made as an intimation that the power to establish a temporary government may arise, also, on the other two grounds stated in the opinion of the court in the insurance case, without weakening the third section.

I would here simply remark, that the constitution was formed for our whole country. An expansion or contraction of our territory required no change in the fundamental law. When we consider the men who laid the foundation of our government and carried it into operation, the men who occupied the bench, who filled the halls of legislation and the chief magistracy, it would seem, if any question could be settled clear of all doubt, it was the power of congress to establish territorial governments. Slavery was prohibited in the entire northwestern territory, with the approbation of leading men, south and north; but this prohibition was not retained when this ordinance was adopted for the government of southern territories, where slavery existed. In a late republication of a letter of Mr. Madison, dated November 27, 1819, speaking of this power of congress to prohibit slavery in a territory, he infers there is no such power, from the fact that it has not been exercised. This is not a very satisfactory argument against any power, as there are but few, if any, subjects on which the constitutional powers of congress are exhausted. It is true, as Mr. Madison states, that congress, in the act to establish a government in the Mississippi territory, prohibited the importation of slaves into it from foreign parts; but it is equally true, that in the act erecting Louisiana into two territories, congress declared, "it shall not be lawful for any person to bring into Orleans territory, from any port or place within the limits of the United States, any slave which shall have been imported since 1798, or which may hereafter be imported, except by a citizen of the United States who settles in the territory, under the penalty of the freedom of such slave."

The inference of Mr. Madison, therefore, against the power of congress, is of no force, as it was founded on a fact supposed, which did not exist.

It is refreshing to turn to the early incidents of our history, and learn wisdom from the acts of the great men who have gone to their account. I refer to a report in the house of representatives, by John Randolph, of Roanoke, as chairman of a committee, in March, 1803—fifty-four years ago. From the convention held at Vincennes, in Indiana, by their president, and from the people of the territory, a petition was presented to congress, praying the suspension of the provision which prohibited slavery in that territory. The report stated "that the rapid population of the State of Ohio sufficiently evinces, in the opinion of your committee, that the labor of slaves is not necessary to promote the growth and settlement of colonies in that region. That this labor, demonstrably the dearest of any, can only be employed to advantage in the cultivation of products more valuable than any known to that quarter of the United States; that the committee deem it highly dangerous and inexpedient to impair a provision wisely calculated to promote the happiness and prosperity of the northwestern country, and to give strength and security to that extensive frontier. In the salutary operation of this sagacious and benevolent restraint, it is believed that the inhabitants will, at no very distant day, find ample remuneration for a temporary privation of labor and of emigration." (1 vol. State Papers, Public Lands, 160.)

The judicial mind of this country, State and federal, has agreed on no subject, within its legitimate action, with equal unanimity, as on the power of congress to establish territorial governments. No court, State or federal, no judge or statesman, is known to have had any doubts on this question for nearly sixty years after the power was exercised. Such governments have been established from the sources of the Ohio to the Gulf of Mexico, extending to the lakes on the north and the Pacific Ocean on the west, and from the lines of Georgia to Texas.

Great interests have grown up under the territorial laws over a country more than five times greater in extent than the original thirteen States; and these interests, corporate or otherwise, have been cherished and consolidated by a benign policy, without any one supposing the law-making power had united with the judiciary, under the universal sanction of the whole country, to usurp a jurisdiction which did not belong to them. Such a discovery at this late date is more extraordinary than anything which has occurred in the judicial history of this or any other country. Texas, under a previous organization, was admitted as a State; but no State can be admitted into the Union which has not been organized under some form of government. Without temporary governments, our public lands could not have been sold, nor our wildernesses reduced to cultivation, and the population protected; nor could our flourishing States, west and south, have been formed.

What do the lessons of wisdom and experience teach, under such circumstances, if the new light, which has so suddenly and unexpectedly burst upon us, be true? Acquiescence; acquiescence under a settled construction of the constitution for sixty years, though it may be erroneous; which has secured to the country an advancement and prosperity beyond the power of computation.

An act of James Madison, when president, forcibly illustrates this policy. He had made up his opinion that congress had no power under the constitution to establish a national bank. In 1815, congress passed a bill to establish a bank. He vetoed the bill, on objections other than constitutional. In his message, he speaks as a wise statesman and chief magistrate, as follows:

"Waiving the question of the constitutional authority of the legislature to establish an incorporated bank, as being precluded, in my judgment, by the repeated recognitions under varied circumstances of the validity of such an institution, in acts of the legislative, executive, and judicial branches of the government, accompanied by indications, in different modes, of a concurrence of the general will of the nation."

Has this impressive lesson of practical wisdom become lost to the present generation?

If the great and fundamental principles of our government are never to be settled, there can be no lasting prosperity. The constitution will become a floating waif on the billows of popular excitement.

The prohibition of slavery north of thirty-six degrees thirty minutes, and of the State of Missouri, contained in the act admitting that State into the Union, was passed by a vote of 134, in the house of representatives, to 42. Before Mr. Monroe signed the act, it was submitted by him to his cabinet, and they held the restriction of slavery in a territory to be within the constitutional powers of congress. It would be singular, if in 1804 congress had power to prohibit the introduction of slaves in Orleans territory from any other part of the Union, under the penalty of freedom to the slave, if the same power, embodied in the Missouri compromise, could not be exercised in 1820.

But this law of congress, which prohibits slavery north of Missouri and of thirty-six degrees thirty minutes, is declared to have been null and void by my brethren. And this opinion is founded mainly, as I understand, on the distinction drawn between the ordinance of 1787 and the Missouri compromise line. In what does the distinction consist? The ordinance, it is said, was a compact entered into by the confederated States before the adoption of the constitution; and that in the cession of territory authority was given to establish a territorial government.

It is clear that the ordinance did not go into operation by virtue of the authority of the confederation, but by reason of its modification and adoption by congress under the constitution. It seems to be supposed, in the opinion of the court, that the articles of cession placed it on a different footing from territories subsequently acquired. I am unable to perceive the force of this distinction. That the ordinance was intended for the government of the northwestern territory, and was limited to such territory, is admitted. It was extended to southern territories, with modifications, by acts of congress, and to some northern territories. But the ordinance was made valid by the act of congress, and without such act could have been of no force. It rested for its validity on the act of congress, the same, in my opinion, as the Missouri compromise line.

If congress may establish a territorial government in the exercise of its discretion, it is a clear principle that a court cannot control that discretion. This being the case, I do not see on what ground the act is held to be void. It did not purport to forfeit property, or take it for public purposes. It only prohibited slavery; in doing which, it followed the ordinance of 1787.

I will now consider the fourth head, which is: "The effect of taking slaves into a State or territory, and so holding them, where slavery is prohibited."

If the principle laid down in the case of Prigg v. The State of Pennsylvania is to be maintained, and it is certainly to be maintained until overruled, as the law of this court, there can be no difficulty on this point. In that case, the court says: "The state of slavery is deemed to be a mere municipal regulation, founded upon and limited to the range of the territorial laws." If this be so, slavery can exist nowhere except under the authority of law, founded on usage having the force of law, or by statutory recognition. And the court further says: "It is manifest, from this consideration, that if the constitution had not contained the clause requiring the rendition of fugitives from labor, every non-slaveholding State in the Union would have been at liberty to have declared free all runaway slaves coming within its limits, and to have given them entire immunity and protection against the claims of their masters."

Now, if a slave abscond, he may be reclaimed; but if he accompany his master into a State or territory where slavery is prohibited, such slave cannot be said to have left the service of his master where his services were legalized. And if slavery be limited to the range of the territorial laws, how can the slave be coerced to serve in a State or territory, not only without the authority of law, but against its express provisions? What gives the master the right to control the will of his slave? The local law, which exists in some form. But where there is no such law, can the master control the will of the slave by force? Where no slavery exists, the presumption, without regard to color, is in favor of freedom. Under such a jurisdiction, may the colored man be levied on as the property of his master by a creditor? On the decease of the master, does the slave descend to his heirs as property? Can the master sell him? Any one or all of these acts may be done to the slave, where he is legally held to service. But where the law does not confer this power, it cannot be exercised.

Lord Mansfield held that a slave brought into England was free. Lord Stowell agreed with Lord Mansfield in this respect, and that the slave could not be coerced in England; but on her voluntary return to Antigua, the place of her slave domicile, her former status attached. The law of England did not prohibit slavery, but did not authorize it. The jurisdiction which prohibits slavery is much stronger in behalf of the slave within it, than where it only does not authorize it.

By virtue of what law is it, that a master may take his slave into free territory, and exact from him the duties of a slave? The law of the territory does not sanction it. No authority can be claimed under the constitution of the United States, or any law of congress. Will it be said that the slave is taken as property, the same as other property which the master may own? To this I answer, that colored persons are made property by the law of the State, and no such power has been given to congress. Does the master carry with him the law of the State from which he removes into the territory? And does that enable him to coerce his slave in the territory? Let us test this theory. If this may be done by a master from one slave State, it may be done by a master from every other slave State. This right is supposed to be connected with the person of the master, by virtue of the local law. Is it transferable? May it be negotiated, as a promissory note or bill of exchange? If it be assigned to a man from a free State, may he coerce the slave by virtue of it? What shall this thing be denominated? Is it personal or real property? Or is it an indefinable fragment of sovereignty, which every person carries with him from his late domicile? One thing is certain, that its origin has been very recent, and it is unknown to the laws of any civilized country.

A slave is brought to England from one of its islands, where slavery was introduced and maintained by the mother country. Although there is no law prohibiting slavery in England, yet there is no law authorizing it; and, for near a century, its courts have declared that the slave there is free from the coercion of the master. Lords Mansfield and Stowell agree upon this point, and there is no dissenting authority.

There is no other description of property which was not protected in England, brought from one of its slave islands. Does not this show that property in a human being does not arise from nature or from the common law, but, in the language of this court, "it is a mere municipal regulation, founded upon and limited to the range of the territorial laws?" This decision is not a mere argument, but it is the end of the law, in regard to the extent of slavery. Until it shall be overturned, it is not a point for argument; it is obligatory on myself and my brethren, and on all judicial tribunals over which this court exercises an appellate power.

It is said the territories are common property of the States, and that every man has a right to go there with his property. This is not controverted. But the court say a slave is not property beyond the operation of the local law which makes him such. Never was a truth more authoritatively and justly uttered by man. Suppose a master of a slave in a British island owned a million of property in England; would that authorize him to take his slaves with him to England? The constitution, in express terms, recognizes the *status* of slavery as founded on the municipal law: "No person held to service or labor in one State, *under the laws thereof,* escaping into another, shall," &c. Now, unless the fugitive escape from a place where, by the municipal law, he is held to labor, this provision affords no remedy to the master. What can be more conclusive than this? Suppose a slave escape from a territory where slavery is not authorized by law, can he be reclaimed?

In this case, a majority of the court have said that a slave may be taken by his master into a territory of the United States, the same as a horse, or any other kind of property. It is true, this was said by the court, as also many other things, which are of no authority. Nothing that has been said by them, which has not a direct bearing on the jurisdiction of the court, against which they decided, can be considered am authority. I shall certainly not regard it as such. The question of jurisdiction, being before the court, was decided by them authoritatively, but nothing beyond that question. A slave is not a mere chattel. He bears the impress of his Maker, and is amenable to the laws of God and man; and he is destined to an endless existence.

Under this head I shall chiefly rely on the decisions of the supreme courts of the southern States, and especially of the State of Missouri.

In the first and second sections of the sixth article of the constitution of Illinois, it is declared that neither slavery nor involuntary servitude shall hereafter be introduced into this State, otherwise than for the punishment of crimes whereof the party shall have been duly convicted; and in the second section it is declared that any violation of this article shall effect the emancipation of such person from his obligation to service. In Illinois, a right of transit through the State is given the master with his slaves. This is a matter which, as I suppose, belongs exclusively to the State.

The supreme court of Illinois, in the case of Jarrot *v.* Jarrot, (2 Gilmer, 7,) said:

> After the conquest of this territory by Virginia, she ceded it to the United States, and stipulated that the titles and possessions, rights and liberties, of the French settlers, should be guaranteed to them. This, it has been contended, secured them in the possession of those negroes as slaves which they held before that time, and that neither congress nor the convention had power to deprive them of it; or, in other words, that the ordinance and constitution should not be so interpreted and understood as applying to such slaves, when it is therein declared that there shall be neither slavery nor involuntary servitude in the northwest territory, nor in the State of Illinois, otherwise than in the punishment of crimes. But it was held that

those rights could not be thus protected, but must yield to the ordinance and Constitution.

The first slave case decided by the supreme court of Missouri, contained in the reports, was Winny *v.* Whitesides, (1 Missouri Rep. 473,) at October term, 1824. It appeared that, more than twenty-five years before, the defendant, with her husband, had removed from Carolina to Illinois, and brought with them the plaintiff; that they continued to reside in Illinois three or four years, retaining the plaintiff as a slave; after which, they removed to Missouri, taking her with them.

The court held, that if a slave be detained in Illinois until he be entitled to freedom, the right of the owner does not revive when he finds the negro in a slave State.

That when a slave is taken to Illinois by his owner, who takes up his residence there, the slave is entitled to freedom.

In the case of Lagrange *v.* Chouteau, (2 Missouri Rep. 20, at May term, 1828,) it was decided that the ordinance of 1787 was intended as a fundamental law for those who may choose to live under it, rather than as a penal statute.

That any sort of residence contrived or permitted by the legal owner of the slave, upon the faith of secret trusts or contracts, in order to defeat or evade the ordinance, and thereby introduce slavery *de facto,* would entitle such slave to freedom.

In Julia *v.* McKinney, (3 Missouri Rep. 279,) it was held, where a slave was settled in the State of Illinois, but with an intention on the part of the owner to be removed at some future day, that hiring said slave to a person to labor for one or two days, and receiving the pay for the hire, the slave is entitled to her freedom, under the second section of the sixth article of the constitution of Illinois.

Rachel *v.* Walker, (4 Missouri Rep. 350, June term, 1836) is a case involving, in every particular, the principles of the case before us. Rachel sued for her freedom; and it appeared that she had been bought as a slave in Missouri, by Stockton, an officer of the army, taken to Fort Snelling, where he was stationed, and she was retained there as a slave a year; and then Stockton removed to Prairie du Chien, taking Rachel with him as a slave, where he continued to hold her three years, and then he took her to the State of Missouri, and sold her as a slave.

"Fort Snelling was admitted to be on the west side of the Mississippi river, and north of the State of Missouri, in the territory of the United States. That Prairie du Chien was in the Michigan territory, on the east side of the Mississippi river. Walker, the defendant, held Rachel under Stockton."

The court said, in this case:

> The officer lived in Missouri territory, at the time he bought the slave; he sent to a slaveholding country and procured her; this was his voluntary act, done without any other reason than that of his convenience; and he and

those claiming under him must be holden to abide the consequences of introducing slavery both in Missouri territory and Michigan, contrary to law; and on that ground Rachel was declared to be entitled to freedom.

In answer to the argument that, as an officer of the army, the master had a right to take his slave into free territory, the court said no authority of law or the government compelled him to keep the plaintiff there as a slave.

"Shall it be said, that because an officer of the army owns slaves in Virginia, that when, as officer and soldier, he is required to take the command of a fort in the non-slaveholding States or territories, he thereby has a right to take with him as many slaves as will suit his interests or convenience? It surely cannot be law. If this be true, the court say, then it is also true that the convenience or supposed convenience of the officer repeals, as to him and others who have the same character, the ordinance and the act of 1821, admitting Missouri into the Union, and also the prohibition of the several laws and constitutions of the non-slaveholding States."

In Wilson *v.* Melvin, (4 Missouri R. 592,) it appeared the defendant left Tennessee with an intention of residing in Illinois, taking his negroes with him. After a month's stay in Illinois, he took his negroes to St. Louis, and hired them, then returned to Illinois. On these facts, the inferior court instructed the jury that the defendant was a sojourner in Illinois. This the supreme court held was error, and the judgment was reversed.

The case of Dred Scott *v.* Emerson (15 Missouri R. 682, March term, 1852) will now be stated. This case involved the identical question before us, Emerson having, since the hearing, sold the plaintiff to Sandford, the defendant.

Two of the judges ruled the case, the chief justice dissenting. It cannot be improper to state the grounds of the opinion of the court, and of the dissent.

The court say: "Cases of this kind are not strangers in our court. Persons have been frequently here adjudged to be entitled to their freedom, on the ground that their masters held them in slavery in territories or States in which that institution is prohibited. From the first case decided in our court, it might be inferred that this result was brought about by a presumed assent of the master, from the fact of having voluntarily taken his slave to a place where the relation of master and slave did not exist. But subsequent cases base the right to 'exact the forfeiture of emancipation,' as they term it, on the ground, it would seem, that it was the duty of the courts of this State to carry into effect the constitution and laws of other States and territories, regardless of the rights, the policy, or the institutions, of the people of this State."

And the court say that the States of the Union, in their municipal concerns, are regarded as foreign to each other; that the courts of one State do not take notice of the laws of other States, unless proved as facts, and that every State has the right to determine how far its comity to other States shall extend; and it is laid down, that when there is no act of manumission decreed to the free State, the courts of the slave States cannot be called to give effect to the law of the free State. Comity, it alleges, between States, depends upon the discretion of both, which may be varied by circumstances. And it is declared by the court, "that times are not as they were when the former decisions on this subject were made." Since then, not only individuals but States have been possessed with a dark and fell spirit in relation to slavery, whose gratification is sought in the pursuit of measures whose inevitable consequence must be the overthrow and destruction of our government. Under such circumstances, it does not behoove the State of Missouri to show the least countenance to any measure which might gratify this spirit. She is willing to assume her full responsibility for the existence of slavery within her limits, nor does she seek to share or divide it with others.

Chief Justice Gamble dissented from the other two judges. He says:

In every slaveholding State in the Union, the subject of emancipation is regulated by statute; and the forms are prescribed in which it shall be effected. Whenever the forms required by the laws of the State in which the master and slave are resident are complied with, the emancipation is complete, and the slave is free. If the right of the person thus emancipated is subsequently drawn in question in another State, it will be ascertained and determined by the law of the State in which the slave and his former master resided; and when it appears that such law has been complied with, the right to freedom will be fully sustained in the courts of all the slaveholding States, although the act of emancipation may not be in the form required by law in which the court sits.

In all such cases, courts continually administer the law of the country where the right was acquired; and when that law becomes known to the court, it is just as much a matter of course to decide the rights of the parties according to its requirements, as it is to settle the title of real estate situated in our State by its own laws.

This appears to me a most satisfactory answer to the argument of the court. Chief Justice continues: "The perfect equality of the different States lies at the foundation of the Union. As the institution of slavery in the States is one over which the constitution of the United States gives no power to the general government, it is left to be adopted or rejected by the several States, as they think best; nor can any one State, or number of States, claim the right to interfere with any other State upon the question of admitting or excluding this institution.

"A citizen of Missouri, who removes with his slave to Illinois, has no right to complain that the fundamental law of that State to which he removes, and in which he makes his residence, dissolves the relation between him and his slave. It is as much his own voluntary act, as if he had executed a deed of emancipation. No one can pretend ignorance of this constitutional provision, and," he says, "the decisions which have heretofore been made in this State, and in many other slaveholding States, give effect to this and other similar provisions, on the ground that the master, by making the free State the residence of his slave, has submitted his right to the operation of the law of such State; and this," he says, "is the same in law as a regular deed of emancipation."

He adds: "I regard the question as conclusively settled by repeated adjudications of this court, and, if I doubted or denied the propriety of those decisions, I would not feel myself any more at liberty to overturn them, than I would any other series of decisions by which the law of any other question was settled. There is with me," he says, "nothing in the law relating to slavery which distinguishes it from the law on any other subject, or allows any more accommodation to the temporary public excitements which are gathered around it."

"In this State," he says, "it has been recognized from the beginning of the government as a correct position in law, that a master who takes his slave to reside in a State or territory where slavery is prohibited, thereby emancipates his slave." These decisions, which come down to the year 1837, seemed to have so fully settled the question, that since that time there has been no case bringing it before the court for any reconsideration, until the present. In the case of Winny v. Whitesides, the question was made in the argument, "whether one nation would execute the penal laws of another," and the court replied in this language, (Huberus, quoted in 4 Dallas,) which says, "personal rights or disabilities obtained or communicated by the laws of any particular place are of a nature which accompany the person wherever he goes;" and the chief justice observed, in the case of Rachel v. Walker, the act of congress called the Missouri compromise was held as operative as the ordinance of 1787.

When Dred Scott, his wife and children, were removed from Fort Snelling to Missouri, in 1838, they were free, as the law was then settled, and continued for fourteen years afterwards, up to 1852, when the above decision was made. Prior to this, for nearly thirty years, as Chief Justice Gamble declares, the residence of a master with his slave in the State of Illinois, or in the territory north of Missouri, where slavery was prohibited by the act called the Missouri compromise, would manumit the slave as effectually as if he had executed a deed of emancipation; and that an officer of the army who takes his slave into that State or territory, and holds him there as a slave, liberates him the same as any other citizen—and down to the above time it was settled by numerous and uniform decisions, and that on the return of the slave to Missouri, his former condition of slavery did not attach. Such was the settled law of Missouri until the decision of Scott and Emerson.

In the case of Sylvia v. Kirby, (17 Misso. Rep. 434,) the court followed the above decision, observing it was similar in all respects to the case of Scott and Emerson.

This court follows the established construction of the statutes of a State by its supreme court. Such a construction is considered as a part of the statute, and we follow it to avoid two rules of property in the same State. But we do not follow the decisions of the supreme court of a State beyond a statutory construction as a rule of decision for this court. State decisions are always viewed with respect and treated as authority; but we follow the settled construction of the statutes, not because it is of binding authority, but in pursuance of a rule of judicial policy.

But there is no pretence that the case of Dred Scott *v.* Emerson turned upon the construction of a Missouri statute; nor was there any established rule of property which could have rightfully influenced the decision. On the contrary, the decision overruled the settled law for near thirty years.

This is said by my brethren to be a Missouri question; but there is nothing which gives it this character, except that it involves the right to persons claimed as slaves who reside in Missouri, and the decision was made by the supreme court of that State. It involves a right claimed under an act of congress and the constitution of Illinois, and which cannot be decided without the consideration and construction of those laws. But the supreme court of Missouri held, in this case, that it will not regard either of those laws, without which there was no case before it; and Dred Scott, having been a slave, remains a slave. In this respect it is admitted this is a Missouri question—a case which has but one side, if the act of congress and the constitution of Illinois are not recognized.

And does such a case constitute a rule of decision for this court—a case to be followed by this court? The course of decision so long and so uniformly maintained established a comity or law between Missouri and the free States and territories where slavery was prohibited, which must be somewhat regarded in this case. Rights sanctioned for twenty-eight years ought not and cannot be repudiated, with any semblance of justice, by one or two decisions, influenced, as declared, by a determination to counteract the excitement against slavery in the free States.

The courts of Louisiana having held, for a series of years, that where a master took his slave to France, or any free State, he was entitled to freedom, and that on bringing him back the status of slavery did not attach, the legislature of Louisiana declared by an act that the slave should not be made free under such circumstances. This regulated the rights of the master from the time the act took effect. But the decision of the Missouri court, reversing a former decision, affects all previous decisions, technically, made on the same principles, unless such decisions are protected by the lapse of time or the statute of limitations. Dred Scott and his family, beyond all controversy, were free under the decisions made for twenty-eight years, before the case of Scott *v.* Emerson. This was the undoubted law of Missouri for fourteen years after Scott and his family were brought back to that State. And the grave question arises, whether this law may be so disregarded as to enslave free persons. I am strongly inclined to think that a rule of decision so well settled as not to be questioned, cannot be annulled by a single decision of the court. Such rights may be inoperative under the decision in future; but I cannot well perceive how it can have the same effect in prior cases.

It is admitted, that when a former decision is reversed, the technical effect of the judgment is to make all previous adjudications on the same question erroneous. But the case before us was not that the law had been erroneously construed, but that, under the circumstances which then existed, that law would not be recognized; and the reason for this is declared to be the excitement against the institution of slavery in the free States. While I lament this excitement as much as any one, I cannot assent that it shall be made a basis of judicial action.

In 1816, the common law, by statute, was made a part of the law of Missouri; and that includes the great principles of international law. These principles cannot be abrogated by judicial decisions. It will require the same exercise of power to abolish the common law, as to introduce it. International law is founded in the opinions generally received and acted on by civilized nations, and enforced by moral sanctions. It becomes a more authoritative system when it results from special compacts, founded on modified rules, adapted to the exigencies of human society; it is in fact an international morality, adapted to the best interests of nations. And in regard to the States of this Union, on the subject of slavery, it is eminently fitted for a rule of action, subject to the federal constitution. "The laws of nations are but the natural rights of man applied to nations." (Vattel.)

If the common law have the force of a statutory enactment in Missouri, it is clear, as it seems to me, that a slave who, by a residence in Illinois in the service of his master, becomes entitled to his freedom, cannot again be reduced to slavery by returning to his former domicile in a slave State. It is unnecessary to say what legislative power might do by a general act in such a case, but it would be singular if a freeman could be made a slave by the exercise of a judicial discretion. And it would be still more extraordinary if this could be done, not only in the absence of special legislation, but in a State where the common law is in force.

It is supposed by some, that the third article in the treaty of cession of Louisiana to this country, by France, in 1803, may have some bearing on this question. The article referred to provides, "that the inhabitants of the ceded territory shall be incorporated into the Union, and enjoy all the advantages of citizens of the United States, and in the mean time they shall be maintained and protected in the free enjoyment of their liberty, property, and the religion they profess."

As slavery existed in Louisiana at the time of the cession, it is supposed this is a guaranty that there should be no change in its condition.

The answer to this is, in the first place, that such a subject does not belong to the treaty-making power; and any such arrangement would have been nugatory. And, in the second place, by no admissible construction can the guaranty be carried further than the protection of property in slaves at that time in the ceded territory. And this has been complied with. The organization of the slave States of Louisiana, Missouri, and Arkansas, embraced every slave in Louisiana at the time of the cession. This removes every ground of objection under the treaty. There is therefore no pretence, growing out of the treaty, that any part of the territory of Louisiana, as ceded, beyond the organized States, is slave territory.

Under the fifth head, we were to consider whether the status of slavery attached to the plaintiff and wife, on their return to Missouri.

This doctrine is not asserted in the late opinion of the supreme court of Missouri, and up to 1852 the contrary doctrine was uniformly maintained by that court.

In its late decision, the court say that it will not give effect in Missouri to the laws of Illinois, or the law of congress called the Missouri compromise. This was the effect of the decision, though its terms were, that the court would not take notice, judicially, of those laws.

In 1851, the court of appeals of South Carolina recognized the principle, that a slave, being taken to a free State, became free. (Commonwealth *v.* Pleasants, 10 Leigh Rep. 697.) In Betty *v.* Horton, the court of appeals held that the freedom of the slave was acquired by the action of the laws of Massachusetts, by the said slave being taken there. (5 Leigh Rep. 615.)

The slave States have generally adopted the rule, that where the master, by a residence with his slave in a State or territory where slavery is prohibited, the slave was entitled to his freedom everywhere. This was the settled doctrine of the supreme court of Missouri. It has been so held in Mississippi, in Virginia, in Louisiana, formerly in Kentucky, Maryland, and in other States.

The law, where a contract is made and is to be executed, governs it. This does not depend upon comity, but upon the law of the contract. And if, in the language of the supreme court of Missouri, the master, by taking his slave to Illinois, and employing him there as a slave, emancipates him as effectually as by a deed of emancipation, is it possible that such an act is not matter for adjudication in any slave State where the master may take him? Does not the master assent to the law, when he places himself under it in a free State?

The States of Missouri and Illinois are bounded by a common line. The one prohibits slavery, the other admits it. This has been done by the exercise of that sovereign power which appertains to each. We are bound to respect the institutions of each, as emanating from the voluntary action of the people. Have the people of either any right to disturb the relations of the other? Each State rests upon the basis of its own sovereignty, protected by the constitution. Our Union has been the foundation of our prosperity and national glory. Shall we not cherish and maintain it? This can only be done by respecting the legal rights of each State.

If a citizen of a free State shall entice or enable a slave to escape from the service of his master, the law holds him responsible, not only for the loss of the slave, but he is liable to be indicted and fined for the misdemeanor. And I am bound here to say, that I have never found a jury in the four States which constitute my circuit, which have not sustained this law, where the evidence required them to sustain it. And it is proper that I should also say, that more cases have arisen in my circuit, by reason of its extent and locality, than in all other parts of the Union. This has been done to vindicate the sovereign rights of the southern States, and protect the legal interests of our brethren of the south.

Let these facts be contrasted with the case now before the court. Illinois has declared in the most solemn and impressive form that there shall be neither slavery nor involuntary servitude in that State, and that any slave brought into it, with a view of becoming a resident, shall be emancipated. And effect has been given to this provision of the constitution by the decision of the supreme court of that State. With a full knowledge of these facts, a slave is brought from Missouri to Rock Island, in the State of Illinois, and is retained there as a slave for two years, and then taken to Fort Snelling, where slavery is prohibited by the Missouri compromise act, and there he is detained two years longer in a state of slavery. Harriet, his wife, was also kept at the same place four years as a slave, having been purchased in Missouri. They were then removed to the State of Missouri, and sold as slaves, and in the action before us they are not only claimed as slaves, but a majority of my brethren have held that on their being returned to Missouri the status of slavery attached to them.

I am not able to reconcile this result with the respect due to the State of Illinois. Having the same rights of sovereignty as the State of Missouri in adopting a constitution, I can perceive no reason why the institutions of Illinois should not receive the same consideration as those of Missouri. Allowing to my brethren the same right of judgment that I exercise myself, I must be permitted to say that it seems to me the principle laid down will enable the people of a slave State to introduce slavery into a free State, for a longer or shorter time, as may suit their convenience; and by returning the slave to the State whence he was brought, by force or otherwise, the status of slavery attaches, and protects the rights of the master, and defies the sovereignty of the free State. There is no evidence before us that Dred Scott and his family returned to Missouri voluntarily. The contrary is inferable from the agreed case: "In the year 1838, Dr. Emerson removed the plaintiff and said Harriet, and their daughter Eliza, from Fort Snelling to the State of Missouri, where they have ever since resided." This is the agreed case; and can it be inferred from this that Scott and family returned to Missouri voluntarily? He was removed; which shows that he was passive, as a slave, having exercised no volition on the subject. He did not resist the master by absconding or force. But that was not sufficient to bring him within Lord Stowell's decision; he must have acted voluntarily. It would be a mockery of law and an outrage on his rights to coerce his return, and then claim that it was voluntary, and on that ground that his former status of slavery attached.

If the decision be placed on this ground, it is a fact for a jury to decide, whether the return was voluntary, or else the fact should be distinctly admitted. A presumption against the plaintiff in this respect, I say with confidence, is not authorized from the facts admitted.

In coming to the conclusion that a voluntary return by Grace to her former domicile, slavery attached, Lord Stowell took great pains to show that England forced slavery upon her colonies, and that it was maintained by numerous acts of parliament and public policy, and, in short, that the system of slavery was not only established by Great Britain in her West Indian colonies, but that it was popular and profitable to many of the wealthy and influential people of England, who were engaged in trade, or owned and cultivated plantations in the colonies. No one can read his elaborate views, and not be struck with the great difference between England and her colonies, and the free and slave States of this Union. While slavery in the colonies of England is subject to the power of the mother country, our States, especially in regard to slavery, are independent, resting upon their own sovereignties, and subject only to international laws, which apply to independent States.

In the case of Williams, who was a slave in Granada, having run away, came to England, Lord Stowell said: "The four judges all concur in this—that he was a slave in Granada, though a free man in England, and he would have continued a free man in all other parts of the world except Granada."

Strader v. Graham (10 Howard, 82, and 18 Curtis, 305) has been cited as having a direct bearing in the case before us. In that case the court say: "It was exclusively in the power of Kentucky to determine, for itself, whether the employment of slaves in another State should or should not make them free on their return." No question was before the court in that case, except that of jurisdiction. And any opinion given on any other point is *obiter dictum,* and of no authority. In the conclusion of his opinion, the chief justice said: "In every view of the subject, therefore, this court has no jurisdiction of the case, and the writ of error must on that ground be dismissed."

In the case of Spencer v. Negro Dennis, (8 Gill's Rep. 321,) the court say: "Once free, and always free, is the maxim of Maryland law upon the subject. Freedom having once vested, by no compact between the master and the liberated slave, nor by any condition subsequent, attached by the master to the gift of freedom, can a state of slavery be reproduced."

In Hunter v. Bulcher, (1 Leigh, 172:)

"By a statute of Maryland of 1796, all slaves brought into that State to reside are declared free; a Virginian-born slave is carried by his master to Maryland; the master settled there, and keeps the slave there in bondage for twelve years, the statute in force all the time; then he brings him as a slave to Virginia, and sells him there. Adjudged, in an action brought by the man against the purchaser, that he is free."

Judge Kerr, in the case, says:

"Agreeing, as I do, with the general view taken in this case by my brother Green, I would not add a word, but to mark the exact extent to which I mean to go. The law of Maryland having enacted that slaves carried into that State for sale or to reside shall be free, and the owner of the slave here having carried him to Maryland, and voluntarily submitting himself and the slave to that law, it governs the case."

In every decision of a slave case prior to that of Dred Scott *v.* Emerson, the supreme court of Missouri considered it as turning upon the constitution of Illinois, the ordinance of 1787, or the Missouri compromise act of 1820. The court treated these acts as in force, and held itself bound to execute them, by declaring the slave to be free who had acquired a domicile under them with the consent of his master.

The late decision reversed this whole line of adjudication, and held that neither the constitution and laws of the States, nor acts of congress in relation to territories, could be judicially noticed by the supreme court of Missouri. This is believed to be in conflict with the decisions of all the courts in the southern States, with some exceptions of recent cases.

In Marie Louise *v.* Morat *et al.* (9 Louisiana Rep. 475,) it was held, where a slave having been taken to the kingdom of France or other country by the owner, where slavery is not tolerated, operates on the condition of the slave, and produces immediate emancipation; and that, where a slave thus becomes free, the master cannot reduce him again to slavery.

Josephine *v.* Poultney, (Louisiana Annual Rep. 329,) "where the owner removes with a slave into a State in which slavery is prohibited, with the intention of residing there, the slave will be thereby emancipated, and their subsequent return to the State of Louisiana cannot restore the relation of master and slave." To the same import are the cases of Smith *v.* Smith, (13 Louisiana Rep. 441; Thomas *v.* Generis, Louisiana Rep. 483; Harry et al. *v.* Decker and Hopkins, Walker's Mississippi Rep. 36.) It was held that, "slaves within the jurisdiction of the northwestern territory became freemen by virtue of the ordinance of 1787, and can assert their claim to freedom in the courts of Mississippi." (Griffith *v.* Fanny, 1 Virginia Rep. 143.) It was decided that a negro held in servitude in Ohio, under a deed executed in Virginia, is entitled to freedom by the constitution of Ohio.

The case of Rhodes *v.* Bell (2 Howard, 307; 15 Curtis, 152) involved the main principle in the case before us. A person residing in Washington city purchased a slave in Alexandria, and brought him to Washington. Washington continued under the law of Maryland, Alexandria under the law of Virginia. The act of Maryland of November, 1796, (2 Maxcy's Laws, 351,) declared any one who shall bring any negro, mulatto, or other slave, into Maryland, such slave should be free. The above slave, by reason of his being brought into Washington city, was declared by this court to be free. This, it appears to me, is a much stronger case against the slave than the facts in the case of Scott.

In Bush *v.* White, (3 Monroe, 104,) the court say:

"That the ordinance was paramount to the territorial laws, and restrained the legislative power there as effectually as a constitution in an organized State. It was a public act of the legislature of the Union, and a part of the supreme law of the land; and, as such, this court is as much bound to take notice of it as it can be of any other law."

In the case of Rankin *v.* Lydia, before cited, Judge Mills, speaking for the court of appeals of Kentucky, says:

"If, by the positive provision in our code, we can and must hold our slaves in the one case, and statutory provisions equally positive decide against that right in the other, and liberate the slave, he must, by an authority equally imperious, be declared free. Every argument which supports the right of the master on one side, based upon the force of written law, must be equally conclusive in favor of the slave, when he can point out in the statute the clause which secures his freedom."

And he further said:

"Free people of color in all the States are, it is believed, quasi citizens, or, at least, denizens. Although none of the States may allow them the privilege of office and suffrage, yet all other civil and conventional rights are secured to them; at least, such rights were evidently secured to them by the ordinance in question for the government of Indiana. If these rights are vested in that or any other portion of the United States, can it be compatible with the spirit of our confederated government to deny their existence in any other part? Is there less comity existing between State and State, or State and territory, than exists between the despotic governments of Europe?"

These are the words of a learned and great judge, born and educated in a slave State.

I now come to inquire, under the sixth and last head, "whether the decisions of the supreme court of Missouri, on the question before us, are binding on this court."

While we respect the learning and high intelligence of the State courts, and consider their decisions, with others, as authority, we follow them only where they give a construction to the State statutes. On this head, I consider myself fortunate in being able to turn to the decision of this court, given by Mr. Justice Grier, in Pease *v.* Peck, a case from the State of Michigan, (18 Howard, 589,) decided in December term, 1855. Speaking for the court, Judge Grier said:

"We entertain the highest respect for that learned court, (the supreme court of Michigan,) and in any question affecting the construction of their own laws, where we entertain any doubt, would be glad to be relieved from doubt and responsibility by reposing on their decision. There are, it is true, many dicta to be found in our decisions, averring that the courts of the United States are bound to follow the decisions of the State courts on the construction of their own laws. But although this may be correct, yet a rather strong expression of a general rule, it cannot be received as the annunciation of a maxim of universal application. Accordingly, our reports furnish many cases of exceptions to it. In all cases where there is a settled construction of the laws of a State, by its highest judicature established by admitted precedent, it is the practice of the courts of the United States to receive and adopt it, without criticism or further inquiry. When the decisions of the State court are not consistent, we do not feel bound to follow the last, if it is contrary to our own convictions; and much more is this the case where, after a long course of consistent decisions, some new light suddenly springs up, or an excited public opinion has elicited new doctrines subversive of former safe precedent."

These words, it appears to me, have a stronger application to the case before us than they had to the cause in which they were spoken as the opinion of this court; and I regret that they do not seem to be as fresh in the recollection of some of my brethren as in my own. For twenty-eight years, the decisions of the supreme court of Missouri were consistent on all the points made in this case. But this consistent course was suddenly terminated, whether by some new light suddenly springing up, or an excited public opinion, or both, it is not necessary to say. In the case of Scott *v.* Emerson, in 1852, they were overturned and repudiated.

This, then, is the very case in which seven of my brethren declared they would not follow the last decision. On this authority I may well repose. I can desire no other or better basis.

But there is another ground which I deem conclusive, and which I will restate.

The supreme court of Missouri refused to notice the act of congress or the constitution of Illinois, under which Dred Scott, his wife and children, claimed that they are entitled to freedom.

This being rejected by the Missouri court, there was no case before it, or least it was a case with only one side. And this is the case which, in the opinion of this court, we are bound to follow. The Missouri court disregards the express provisions of an act of congress and the constitution of a sovereign State, both of which laws for twenty-eight years it had not only regarded, but carried into effect.

If a State court may do this, on a question involving the liberty of a human being, what protection do the laws afford? So far from this being a Missouri question, it is a question, as it would seem, within the twenty-fifth section of the judiciary act, where a right to freedom being set up under the act of congress, and the decision being against such right, it may be brought for revision before this court, from the supreme court of Missouri.

I think the judgment of the court below should be reversed.

Mr. Justice CURTIS dissenting.

I dissent from the opinion pronounced by the chief justice, and from the judgment which the majority of the court think it proper to render in this case. The plaintiff alleged, in his declaration, that he was a citizen of the State of Missouri, and that the defendant was a citizen of the State of New York. It is not doubted that it was necessary to make each of these allegations, to sustain the jurisdiction of the circuit court. The defendant denied, by a plea to the jurisdiction, either sufficient or insufficient, that the plaintiff was a citizen of the State of Missouri. The plaintiff demurred to that plea. The circuit court adjudged the plea insufficient, and the first question for our consideration is, whether the sufficiency of that plea is before this court for judgment, upon this writ of error. The part of the judicial power of the United States, conferred by congress on the circuit courts, being limited to certain described cases and controversies, the question whether a particular case is within the cognizance of a circuit court, may be raised by a plea to the jurisdiction of such court. When that question has been raised, the circuit court must, in the first instance, pass upon and determine it. Whether its determination be final, or subject to review by this appellate court, must depend upon the will of congress; upon which body the constitution has conferred the power, with certain restrictions, to establish inferior courts, to determine their jurisdiction, and to regulate the appellate power of this court. The twenty-second section of the judiciary act of 1789, which allows a writ of error from final judgments of circuit courts, provides that there shall be no reversal in this court, on such writ of error, for error in ruling any plea in abatement, *other than a plea to the jurisdiction of the court*. Accordingly it has been held, from the origin of the court to the present day, that circuit courts have not been made by congress the final judges of their own jurisdiction in civil cases. And that when a record comes here upon a writ of error or appeal, and, on its inspection, it appears to this court that the circuit court had not jurisdiction, its judgment must be reversed, and the cause remanded, to be dismissed for want of jurisdiction.

It is alleged by the defendant in error, in this case, that the plea to the jurisdiction was a sufficient plea; that it shows, on inspection of its allegations, confessed by the demurrer, that the plaintiff was not a citizen of the State of Missouri; that upon this record, it must appear to this court that the case was not within the judicial power of the United States, as defined and granted by the constitution, because it was not a suit by a citizen of one State against a citizen of another State.

To this it is answered, first, that the defendant, by pleading over, after the plea to the jurisdiction was adjudged insufficient, finally waived all benefit of that plea.

When that plea was adjudged insufficient, the defendant was obliged to answer over. He held no alternative. He could not stop the further progress of the case in the circuit court by a writ of error, on which the sufficiency of his plea to the jurisdiction could be tried in this court, because the judgment on that plea was not final, and no writ of error would lie. He was forced to plead to the merits. It cannot be true, then, that he waived the benefit of his plea to the jurisdiction by answering over. Waiver includes consent. Here, there was no consent. And if the benefit of the plea was finally lost, it must be, not by any waiver, but because the laws of the United States have not provided any mode of reviewing the decision of the circuit court on such a plea, when that decision is against the defendant. This is not the law. Whether the decision of the circuit court on a plea to the jurisdiction be against the plaintiff, or against the defendant, the losing party may have any alleged error in law, in ruling such a plea, examined in this court on a writ of error, when the matter in controversy exceeds the sum or value of two thousand dollars. If the decision be against the plaintiff, and his suit dismissed for want of jurisdiction, the judgment is technically final, and he may at once sue out his writ of error. (Mollan *v.* Torrance, 9 Wheat. 537.) If the decision be against the defendant, though he must answer over, and wait for a final judgment in the cause, he may then have his writ of error, and upon it obtain the judgment of this court on any question of law apparent on the record, touching the jurisdiction. The fact that he pleaded over to the merits, under compulsion, can have no effect on his right to object to the jurisdiction. If this were not so, the condition of the two parties would be grossly unequal. For if a plea to the jurisdiction were ruled against the plaintiff, he could at once take his writ of error, and have the ruling reviewed here; while, if the same plea were ruled against the defendant, he must not only wait for a final judgment, but could in no event have the ruling of the circuit court upon the plea reviewed by this court. I know of no ground for saying that the laws of the United States have thus discriminated between the parties to a suit in its courts.

It is further objected, that as the judgment of the circuit court was in favor of the defendant, and the writ of error in this cause was sued out by the plaintiff, the defendant is not in a condition to assign any error in the record, and therefore this court is precluded from considering the question whether the circuit court had jurisdiction.

The practice of this court does not require a technical assignment of errors. (See the rule.) Upon a writ of error, the whole record is open for inspection; and if any error be found in it, the judgment is reversed. (Bank of U. S. *v.* Smith, 11 Wheat. 171.)

It is true, as a general rule, that the court will not allow a party to rely on anything as cause for reversing a judgment, which was for his advantage. In this, we follow an ancient rule of the common law. But so careful was that law of the preservation of the course of its courts, that it made an exception out of that general rule, and allowed a party to assign for error that which was for his advantage, if it were a departure by the court itself from its settled course of procedure. The cases on this subject are collected in Bac. Ab. Error H. 4. And this court followed this practice in Capron *v.* Van Noorden, (2 Cranch, 126,) where the plaintiff below procured the reversal of a judgment for the defendant, on the ground that the plaintiff's allegations of citizenship had not shown jurisdiction.

But it is not necessary to determine whether the defendant can be allowed to assign want of jurisdiction as an error in a judgment in his own favor. The true question is, not what either of the parties may be allowed to do, but whether this court will affirm or reverse a judgment of the circuit court on the merits, when it appears on the record, by a plea to the jurisdiction, that it is a case to which the judicial power of the United States does not extend. The course of the court is, where no motion is made by either party, on its own motion, to reverse such a judgment for want of jurisdiction, not only in cases where it is shown, negatively, by a plea to the jurisdiction, that jurisdiction does not exist, but even where it does not appear, affirmatively, that it does exist. (Pequignot *v.* The Pennsylvania R. R. Co. 16 How. 104.) It acts upon the principle that the judicial power of the United States must not be exerted in a case to which it does not extend, even if both parties desire to have it exerted. (Cutler *v.* Rae, 7 How. 729.) I consider, therefore, that when there was a plea to the jurisdiction of the circuit court in a case brought here by a writ of error, the first duty of this court is, *sua sponte,* if not moved to it by either party, to examine the sufficiency of that plea; and thus to take care that neither the circuit court nor this court shall use the judicial power of the United States in a case to which the constitution and laws of the United States have not extended that power.

I proceed, therefore, to examine the plea to the jurisdiction.

I do not perceive any sound reason why it is not to be judged by the rules of the common law applicable to such pleas. It is true, where the jurisdiction of the circuit court depends on the citizenship of the parties, it is incumbent on the plaintiff to allege on the record the necessary citizenship; but when he has done so, the defendant must interpose a plea in abatement, the allegations whereof show that the court has not jurisdiction; and it is incumbent on him to prove the truth of his plea.

In Sheppard *v.* Graves, (17 How. 27,) the rules on this subject are thus stated in the opinion of the court: "That although, in the courts of the United States, it is necessary to set forth the grounds of their cognizance as courts of limited jurisdiction, yet wherever jurisdiction shall be averred in the pleadings, in conformity with the laws creating those courts, it must be taken, *prima facie,* as existing; and it is incumbent on him who would impeach that jurisdiction for causes dehors the pleading, to allege and prove such causes; that the necessity for the allegation, and the burden of sustaining it by proof, both rest upon the party taking the exception." These positions are sustained by the authorities there cited, as well as by Wickliffe *v.* Owings, (17 How. 47.)

When, therefore, as in this case, the necessary averments as to citizenship are made on the record, and jurisdiction is assumed to exist, and the defendant comes by a plea to the jurisdiction to displace that presumption, he occupies, in my judgment, precisely the position described in Bacon Ab. Abatement: "Abatement, in the general acceptation of the word, signifies a plea, put in by the defendant, in which he shows cause to the court why he should not be impleaded; or, if at all, not in the manner and form he now is."

This being, then, a plea in abatement, to the jurisdiction of the court, I must judge of its sufficiency by those rules of the common law applicable to such pleas.

The plea was as follows: "And the said John F. A. Sandford, in his own proper person, comes and says that this court ought not to have or take further cognizance of the action aforesaid, because he says that said cause of action, and each and every of them, (if any such have accrued to the said Dred Scott,) accrued to the said Dred Scott out of the jurisdiction of this court, and exclusively within the jurisdiction of the courts of the State of Missouri; for that, to wit, the said plaintiff, Dred Scott, is not a citizen of the State of Missouri, as alleged in his declaration, because he is a negro of African descent; his ancestors were of pure African blood, and were brought into this country and sold as negro slaves, and this the said Sandford is ready to verify. Wherefore, he prays judgment whether this court can or will take further cognizance of the action aforesaid."

The plaintiff demurred, and the judgment of the circuit court was, that the plea was insufficient.

I cannot treat this plea as a general traverse of the citizenship alleged by the plaintiff. Indeed, if it were so treated, the plea was clearly bad, for it concludes with a verification, and not to the country, as a general traverse should. And though this defect in a plea in bar must be pointed out by a special demurrer, it is never necessary to demur specially to a plea in abatement; all matters, though of form only, may be taken advantage of upon a general demurrer to such a plea. (Chitty on Pl. 465.)

The truth is, that though not drawn with the utmost technical accuracy, it is a special traverse of the plaintiff's allegation of citizenship, and was a suitable and proper mode of traverse under the circumstances. By reference to Mr. Stephen's description of the uses of such a traverse, contained in his excellent analysis of pleadings, (Steph. on Pl. 176,) it will be seen how precisely this plea meets one of his descriptions. No doubt the defendant might have traversed, by a common or general traverse, the plaintiff's allegation that he was a citizen of the State of Missouri, concluding to the country. The issue thus presented being joined, would have involved matter of law, on which the jury must have passed, under the direction of the court. But by traversing the plaintiff's citizenship specially—that is, averring those facts on which the defendant relied to show that in point of law the plaintiff was not a citizen, and basing the traverse on those facts as a deduction therefrom—opportunity was given to do, what was done; that is, to present directly to the court, by a demurrer, the sufficiency of those facts to negative, in point of law, the plaintiff's allegation of citizenship. This, then, being a special, and not a general or common traverse, the rule is settled, that the facts thus set out in the plea, as the reason or ground of the traverse, must of themselves constitute, in point of law, a negative of the allegation thus traversed. (Stephen on Pl. 183; Ch. on Pl. 620.) And upon a demurrer to this plea, the question which arises is, whether the facts, that the plaintiff is a negro, of African descent, whose ancestors were of pure African blood, and were brought into this country and sold as negro slaves, *may all be true, and yet* the plaintiff be a citizen of the State of Missouri, within the meaning of the constitution and laws of the United States, which confer on citizens of one State the right to sue citizens of another State in the circuit courts. Undoubtedly, if these facts, taken together, amount to an allegation that, at the time of action brought, the plaintiff was himself a slave, the plea is sufficient. It has been suggested that the plea, in legal effect, does so aver, because, if his ancestors were sold as slaves, the presumption is they continued slaves; and if so, the presumption is, the plaintiff was born a slave; and if so, the presumption is, he continued to be a slave to the time of action brought.

I cannot think such presumptions can be resorted to, to help out defective averments in pleading; especially, in pleading in abatement, where the utmost certainty and precision are required. (Chitty on Pl. 457.) That the plaintiff himself was a slave at the time of action brought, is a substantive fact, having no necessary connection with the fact that his parents were sold as slaves. For they might have been sold after he was born; or the plaintiff himself, if once a slave, might have become a freeman before action brought. To aver that his ancestors were sold as slaves, is not equivalent, in point of law, to an averment that he was a slave. If it were, he could not even confess and avoid the averment of the slavery of his ancestors, which would be monstrous; and if it be not equivalent in point of law, it cannot be treated as amounting thereto when demurred to; for a demurrer confesses only those substantive facts which are well pleaded, and not other distinct substantive facts which might be inferred therefrom by a jury. To treat an averment that the plaintiff's ancestors were Africans, brought to this country and sold as slaves, as amounting to an averment on the record that he was a slave, because it may lay some foundation for presuming so, is to hold that the facts actually alleged may be treated as intended as evidence of another distinct facts not alleged. But it is a cardinal rule of pleading, laid down in Dowman's case, (9 Rep. 9 *b*,) and in even earlier authorities therein referred to, "that evidence shall never be pleaded, for it only tends to prove matter of fact; and therefore the matter of fact shall be pleaded." Or, as the rule is sometimes stated, pleadings must not be argumentative. (Stephen on Pleading, 384, and authorities cited by him.) In Com. Dig. Pleader E. 3, and Bac. Abridgement, Pleas I, 5, and Stephen on Pl. many decisions under this rule are collected. In trover, for an indenture whereby A granted a manor, it is no plea that A did not grant the manor, for it does not answer the declaration except by argument. (Yelv. 223.)

So in trespass for taking and carrying away the plaintiff's goods, the defendant pleaded that the plaintiff never had any goods. The court said, "this is an infallible argument that the defendant is not guilty, but it is no plea." (Dyer, *a* 43.)

In ejectment, the defendant pleaded a surrender of a copyhold by the hand of Fosset, the steward. The plaintiff replied, that Fosset was not steward. The court held this no issue, for it traversed the surrender only argumentatively. (Cro. Elis. 260.)

In these cases, and many others reported in the books, the inferences from the facts stated were irresistible. But the court held they did not, when demurred to, amount to such inferable facts. In the case at bar, the inference that the defendant was a slave at the time of action brought, even if it can be made at all, from the fact that his parents were slaves, is certainly not a necessary inference. This case, therefore, is like that of Digby *v.* Alexander. (8 Bing. 116.) In that case, the defendant pleaded many facts strongly tending to show that he was once Earl of Stirling; but as there was no positive allegation that he was so at the time of action brought, and as every fact averred might be true, and yet the defendant not have been Earl of Stirling at the time of action brought, the plea was held to be insufficient.

A lawful seizing of land is presumed to continue. But if, in an action of trespass *quare clausum,* the defendant were to plead that he was lawfully seized of the *locus in quo,* one month before the time of the alleged trespass, I should have no doubt it would be a bad plea. (See Mollan *v.* Torrance, 9 Wheat, 537.) So if a plea to the jurisdiction, instead of alleging that the plaintiff was a citizen of the same State as the defendant, were to allege that the plaintiff's ancestors were citizens of that State, I think the plea could not be supported. My judgment would be, as it is in this case, that if the defendant meant to aver a particular substantive fact, as existing at the time of action brought, he must do it directly and explicitly, and not by way of inference from certain other averments, which are quite consistent with the contrary hypothesis. I cannot, therefore, treat this plea as containing an averment that the plaintiff himself was a slave at the time of action brought; and the inquiry recurs, whether the facts, that he is of African descent, and that his parents were once slaves, are necessarily inconsistent with his own citizenship in the State of Missouri, within the meaning of the constitution and laws of the United States.

In Gassies *v.* Ballon, (6 Pet. 761,) the defendant was described on the record as a naturalized citizen of the United States, residing in Louisiana. The court held this equivalent to an averment that the defendant was a citizen of Louisiana; because a citizen of the United States, residing in any State of the Union, is, for purposes of jurisdiction, a citizen of that State. Now, the plea to the jurisdiction in this case does not controvert the fact that the plaintiff resided in Missouri at the date of the writ. If he did then reside there, and was also a citizen of the United States, no provisions contained in the constitution or laws of Missouri can deprive the plaintiff of his right to sue citizens of States other than Missouri, in the courts of the United States.

So that, under the allegations contained in this plea, and admitted by the demurrer, the question is, whether any person of African descent, whose ancestors were sold as slaves in the United States, can be a citizen of the United States. If any such person can be a citizen, this plaintiff has the right to the judgment of the court that he is so; for no cause is shown by the plea why he is not so, except his descent and the slavery of his ancestors.

The first section of the second article of the constitution uses the language, "a citizen of the United States at the time of the adoption of the constitution." One mode of approaching this question is, to inquire who were citizens of the United States at the time of the adoption of the constitution.

Citizens of the United States at the time of the adoption of the constitution can have been no other than citizens of the United States under the confederation. By the articles of confederation, a government was organized, the style whereof was, "The United States of America." This government was in existence when the constitution was framed and proposed for adoption, and was to be superseded by the new government of the United States of America, organized under the constitution. When, therefore, the constitution speaks of citizenship of the United States, existing at the time of the adoption of the constitution, it must necessarily refer to citizenship under the government which existed prior to and at the time of such adoption.

Without going into any question concerning the powers of the confederation to govern the territory of the United States out of the limits of the States, and consequently to sustain the relation of government and citizen in respect to the inhabitants of such territory, it may safely be said that the citizens of the several States were citizens of the United States under the confederation.

That government was simply a confederacy of the several States, possessing a few defined powers over subjects of general concern, each State retaining every power, jurisdiction, and right, not expressly delegated to the United States in congress assembled. And no power was thus delegated to the government of the confederation, to act on any question of citizenship, or to make any rules in respect thereto. The whole matter was left to stand upon the action of the several States, and to the natural consequence of such action, that the citizens of each State should be citizens of that confederacy into which that State had entered, the style whereof was, "The United States of America."

To determine whether any free persons, descended from Africans held in slavery, were citizens of the United States under the confederation, and consequently at the time of the adoption of the constitution of the United States, it is only necessary to know whether any such persons were citizens of either of the States under the confederation, at the time of the adoption of the constitution.

Of this there can be no doubt. At the time of the ratification of the articles of confederation, all free native-born inhabitants of the States of New Hampshire, Massachusetts, New York, New Jersey, and North Carolina, though descended from African slaves, were not only citizens of those States, but such of them as had the other necessary qualifications possessed the franchise of electors, on equal terms with other citizens.

The supreme court of North Carolina, in the case of the State *v.* Manuel, (4 Dev. and Bat. 20,) has declared the law of that State on this subject, in terms which I believe to be as sound law in the other States I have enumerated, as it was in North Carolina.

"According to the laws of this State," says Judge Gaston, in delivering the opinion of the court, "all human beings within it, who are not slaves, fall within one of two classes. Whatever distinctions may have existed in the Roman laws between citizens and free inhabitants, they are unknown to our institutions. Before our revolution, all free persons born within the dominions of the king of Great Britain, whatever their color or complexion, were native-born British subjects—those born out of his allegiance were aliens. Slavery did not exist in England, but it did in the British colonies. Slaves were not in legal parlance persons, but property. The moment the incapacity, the disqualification of slavery, was removed, they became persons, and were then either British subjects, or not British subjects, according as they were or were not born within the allegiance of the British king. Upon the revolution, no other change took place in the laws of North Carolina than was consequent on the transition from a colony dependent on a European king, to a free and sovereign State. Slaves remained slaves. British subjects in North Carolina became North Carolina freemen. Foreigners, until made members of the State, remained aliens. Slaves, manumitted here, became freemen, and therefore, if born within North Carolina, are citizens of North Carolina, and all free persons born within the State are born citizens of the State. The constitution extended the elective franchise to every freeman who had arrived at the age of twenty-one, and paid a public tax; and it is a matter of universal notoriety, that, under it, free persons, without regard to color, claimed and exercised the franchise, until it was taken from free men of color a few years since by our amended constitution."

In the State *v.* Newcomb, (5 Iredell's R. 253,) decided in 1844, the same court referred to this case of the State *v.* Manuel, and said: "That case underwent a very laborious investigation, both by the bar and the bench. The case was brought here by appeal, and was felt to be one of great importance in principle. It was considered with an anxiety and care worthy of the principle involved, and which give it a controlling influence and authority on all questions of a similar character."

An argument from speculative premises, however well chosen, that the then state of opinion in the commonwealth of Massachusetts was not consistent with the natural rights of people of color who were born on that soil, and that they were not, by the constitution of 1780 of that State, admitted to the condition of citizens, would be received with surprise by the people of that State, who know their own political history. It is true, beyond all controversy, that persons of color, descended from African slaves, were by that constitution made citizens of the State; and such of them as have had the necessary qualifications, have held and exercised the elective franchise, as citizens, from that time to the present. (See Com. *v.* Aves, 18 Pick. R. 210.)

The constitution of New Hampshire conferred the elective franchise upon "every inhabitant of the State having the necessary qualifications," of which color or descent was not one.

The constitution of New York gave the right to vote to "every male inhabitant, who shall have resided," &c.; making no discrimination between free colored persons and others. (See Con. of N. Y. Art. 2, Rev. Stats. of N. Y. vol. 1, p. 126.)

That of New Jersey, to "all inhabitants of this colony, of full age, who are worth £50 proclamation money, clear estate."

New York, by its constitution of 1820, required colored persons to have some qualifications as prerequisites for voting, which white persons need not possess. And New Jersey, by its present constitution, restricts the right to vote to white male citizens. But these changes can have no other effect upon the present inquiry, except to show, that before they were made, no such restrictions existed; and colored in common with white persons, were not only citizens of those States, but entitled to the elective franchise on the same qualifications as white persons, as they now are in New Hampshire and Massachusetts. I shall not enter into an examination of the existing opinions of that period respecting the African race, nor into any discussion concerning the meaning of those who asserted, in the declaration of independence, that all men are created equal; that they are endowed by their Creator with certain inalienable rights; that among these are life, liberty, and the pursuit of happiness. My own opinion is, that a calm comparison of these assertions of universal abstract truths, and of their own individual opinions and acts, would not leave these men under any reproach of inconsistency; that the great truths they asserted on that solemn occasion, they were ready and anxious to make effectual, wherever a necessary regard to circumstances, which no statesman can disregard without producing more evil than good, would allow; and that it would not be just to them, nor true in itself, to allege that they intended to say that the Creator of all men had endowed the white race, exclusively, with the great natural rights which the declaration of independence asserts. But this is not the place of vindicate their memory. As I conceive, we should deal here, not with such disputes, if there can be a dispute concerning this subject, but with those substantial facts evinced by the written constitutions of States, and by the notorious practice under them. And they show, in a manner which no argument can obscure, that in some of the original thirteen States, free colored persons, before and at the time of the formation of the constitution, were citizens of those States.

The fourth of the fundamental articles of the confederation was as follows: "The free inhabitants of each of these States, paupers, vagabonds, and fugitives from justice, excepted, shall be entitled to all the privileges and immunities of free citizens in the several States."

The fact that free persons of color were citizens of some of the several States, and the consequence, that this fourth article of the confederation would have the effect to confer on such persons the privileges and immunities of general citizenship, were not only known to those who framed and adopted those articles, but the evidence is decisive, that the fourth article was intended to have that effect, and that more restricted language, which would have excluded such persons, was deliberately and purposely rejected.

On the 25th of June, 1778, the articles of confederation being under consideration by the congress, the delegates from South Carolina moved to amend this fourth article, by inserting after the word "free," and before the word "inhabitants," the word "white," so that the privileges and immunities of general citizenship would be secured only to white persons. Two States voted for the amendment, eight States against it, and the vote of one State was divided. The language of the article stood unchanged, and both by its terms of inclusion, "free inhabitants," and the strong implication from its terms of exclusion, "paupers, vagabonds, and fugitives from justice," who alone were excepted, it is clear, that under the confederation, and at the time of the adoption of the constitution, free colored persons of African descent might be, and, by reason of their citizenship in certain States, were entitled to the privileges and immunities of general citizenship of the United States.

Did the constitution of the United States deprive them or their descendants of citizenship?

That constitution was ordained and established by the people of the United States, through the action, in each State, or those persons who were qualified by its laws to act thereon, in behalf of themselves and all other citizens of that State. In some of the States, as we have seen, colored persons were among those qualified by law to act on this subject. These colored persons were not only included in the body of "the people of the United States," by whom the constitution was ordained and established, but in at least five of the States they had the power to act, and doubtless did act, by their suffrages, upon the question of its adoption. It would be strange, if we were to find in that instrument anything which deprived of their citizenship any part of the people of the United States who were among those by whom it was established.

I can find nothing in the constitution which, *proprio vigore*, deprives of their citizenship any class of persons who were citizens of the United States at the time of its adoption, or who should be native-born citizens of any State after its adoption; nor any power enabling congress to disfranchise persons born on the soil of any State, and entitled to citizenship of such State by its constitution and laws. And my opinion is, that, under the constitution of the United States, every free person born on the soil of a State, who is a citizen of that State by force of its constitution or laws, is also a citizen of the United States.

I will proceed to state the grounds of that opinion.

The first section of the second article of the constitution uses the language, "a natural-born citizen." It thus assumes that citizenship may be acquired by birth. Undoubtedly, this language of the constitution was used in reference to that principle of public law, well understood in this country at the time of the adoption of the constitution, which referred citizenship to the place of birth. At the declaration of independence, and ever since, the received general doctrine has been, in conformity with the common law, that free persons born within either of the colonies were subjects of the king; that by the declaration of independence, and the consequent acquisition of sovereignty by the several States, all such persons ceased to be subjects, and became citizens of the several States, except so far as some of them were disfranchised by the legislative power of the States, or availed themselves, seasonably [reasonably], of the right to adhere to the British crown in the civil contest, and thus to continue British subjects. (McIlvain *v.* Coxe's Lessee, 4 Cranch, 209; Inglis *v.* Sailor's Snug Harbor, 3 Peters, p. 99; Shanks *v.* Dupont, Ibid., p. 242.)

The constitution having recognized the rule that persons born within the several States are citizens of the United States, one of four things must be true:

First. That the constitution itself has described what native-born persons shall or shall not be citizens of the United States; or,

Second. That it has empowered congress to do so; or,

Third. That all free persons, born within the several States, are citizens of the United States; or,

Fourth. That it is left to each State to determine what free persons, born within its limits, shall be citizens of such State, and *thereby* be citizens of the United States.

If there be such a thing as citizenship of the United States acquired by birth within the States, which the constitution expressly recognizes, and no one denies, then these four alternatives embrace the entire subject, and it only remains to select that one which is true.

That the constitution itself has defined citizenship of the United States by declaring what persons, born within the several States, shall or shall not be citizens of the United States, will not be pretended. It contains no such declaration. We may dismiss the first alternative, as without doubt unfounded.

Has it empowered congress to enact what free persons, born within the several States, shall or shall not be citizens of the United States?

Before examining the various provisions of the constitution which may relate to this question, it is important to consider for a moment the substantial nature of this inquiry. It is, in effect, whether the constitution has empowered congress to create privileged classes within the States, who alone can be entitled to the franchises and powers of citizenship of the United States. If it be admitted that the constitution has enabled congress to declare what free persons, born within the several States, shall be citizens of the United States, it must at the same time be admitted that it is an unlimited power. If this subject is within the control of congress, it must depend wholly on its discretion. For, certainly, no limits of that discretion can be found in the constitution, which is wholly silent concerning it; and the necessary consequence is, that the federal government may select classes of persons within the several States who alone can be entitled to the political privileges of citizenship of the United States. If this power exists, what persons born within the States may be president or vice president of the United States, or members of either house of congress, or hold any office or enjoy any privilege whereof citizenship of the United States is a necessary qualification, must depend solely on the will of congress. By virtue of it, though congress can grant no title of nobility, they may create an oligarchy, in whose hands would be concentrated the entire power of the federal government.

It is a substantive power, distinct in its nature from all others; capable of affecting not only the relations of the States to the general government, but of controlling the political condition of the people of the United States. Certainly we ought to find this power granted by the constitution, at least by some necessary inference, before we can say it does not remain to the States or the people. I proceed therefore to examine all the provisions of the constitution which may have some bearing on this subject.

Among the powers expressly granted to congress is "the power to establish a uniform rule of naturalization." It is not doubted that this is a power to prescribe a rule for the removal of the disabilities consequent on foreign birth. To hold that it extends further than this, would do violence to the meaning of the term naturalization, fixed in the common law, (Co. Lit. 8 a, 129 a; 2 Ves. sen. 286; 2 Bl. Com. 293,) and in the minds of those who concurred in framing and adopting the constitution. It was in this sense of conferring on an alien and his issue the rights and powers of a native-born citizen, that it was employed in the declaration of independence. It was in this sense it was expounded in the federalist, (No. 42,) has been understood by congress, by the judiciary, (2 Wheat. 259, 269; 3 Wash. R. 313, 322; 12 Wheat. 277,) and by commentators on the constitution. (3 Story's Com. on Con. 1–3; 1 Rawle on Con. 84–88; 1 Tucker's Bl. Com. App. 255–259.)

It appears, then, that the only power expressly granted to congress to legislate concerning citizenship, is confined to the removal of the disabilities of foreign birth.

Whether there be anything in the constitution from which a broader power may be implied, will best be seen when we come to examine the two other alternatives, which are, whether all free persons, born on the soil of the several States, or only such of them as may be citizens of each State, respectively, are thereby citizens of the United States. The last of these alternatives, in my judgment, contains the truth.

Undoubtedly, as has already been said, it is a principle of public law, recognized by the constitution itself, that birth on the soil of a country both creates the duties and confers the rights of citizenship. But it must be remembered, that though the constitution was to form a government, and under it the United States of America were to be one united sovereign nation, to which loyalty and obedience on the one side, and from which protection and privileges on the other, would be due, yet the several sovereign States, whose people were then citizens, were not only to continue in existence, but with powers unimpaired, except so far as they were granted by the people to the national government.

Among the powers unquestionably possessed by the several States, was that of determining what persons should and what persons should not be citizens. It was practicable to confer on the Government of the Union this entire power. It embraced what may, well enough for the purpose now in view, be divided into three parts. *First:* The power to remove the disabilities of alienage, either by special acts in reference to each individual case, or by establishing a rule of naturalization to be administered and applied by the courts. *Second:* Determining what persons should enjoy the privileges of citizenship, in respect to the internal affairs of the several States. *Third:* What native-born persons should be citizens of the United States.

The first-named power, that of establishing a uniform rule of naturalization, was granted; and here the grant, according to its terms, stopped. Construing a constitution containing only limited and defined powers of government, the argument derived from this definite and restricted power to establish a rule of naturalization, must be admitted to be exceedingly strong. I do not say it is necessarily decisive. It might be controlled by other parts of the constitution. But when this particular subject of citizenship was under consideration, and, in the clause specially intended to define the extent of power concerning it, we find a particular part of this entire power separated from the residue, and conferred on the general government, there arises a strong presumption that this is all which is granted, and that the residue is left to the States and to the people. And this presumption is, in my opinion, converted into a certainty, by an examination of all such other clauses of the constitution as touch this subject.

I will examine each which can have any possible bearing on this question.

The first clause of the second section of the third article of the constitution is, "The judicial power shall extend to controversies between a State and citizens of another State; between citizens of different States; between citizens of the same State, claiming lands under grants of different States; and between States, or the citizens thereof, and foreign States, citizens, or subjects." I do not think this clause has any considerable bearing upon the particular inquiry now under consideration. Its purpose was, to extend the judicial power to those controversies into which local feelings or interests might so enter as to disturb the course of justice, or give rise to suspicions that they had done so, and thus possibly give occasion to jealousy or ill will between different States, or a particular State and a foreign nation. At the same time, I would remark, in passing, that it has never been held, I do not know that it has ever been supposed, that any citizen of a State could bring himself under this clause and the eleventh and twelfth sections of the judiciary act of 1789, passed in pursuance of it, who was not a citizen of the United States. But I have referred to the clause, only because it is one of the places where citizenship is mentioned by the constitution. Whether it is entitled to any weight in this inquiry or not, it refers only to citizenship of the several States; it recognizes that; but it does not recognize citizenship of the United States as something distinct therefrom.

As has been said, the purpose of this clause did not necessarily connect it with citizenship of the United States, even if that were something distinct from citizenship of the several States, in the contemplation of the constitution. This cannot be said of other clauses of the constitution, which I now proceed to refer to.

"The citizens of each State shall be entitled to all the privileges and immunities of citizens of the several States." Nowhere else in the constitution is there anything concerning a general citizenship; but here, privileges and immunities to be enjoyed throughout the United States, under and by force of the national compact, are granted and secured. In selecting those who are to enjoy these national rights of citizenship, how are they described? As citizens of each State. It is to them these national rights are secured. The qualification for them is not to be looked for in any provision of the constitution or laws of the United States. They are to be citizens of the several States, and, as such, the privileges and immunities of general citizenship, derived from and guarantied by the constitution, are to be enjoyed by them. It would seem that if it had been intended to constitute a class of native-born persons within the States, who should derive their citizenship of the United States from the action of the federal government, this was an occasion for referring to them. It cannot be supposed that it was the purpose of this article to confer the privileges and immunities of citizens in all the States upon persons not citizens of the United States.

And if it was intended to secure these rights only to citizens of the United States, how has the constitution here described such persons? Simply as citizens of each State.

But, further: though, as I shall presently more fully state, I do not think the enjoyment of the elective franchise essential to citizenship, there can be no doubt it is one of the chiefest attributes of citizenship under the American constitution[s]; and the just and constitutional possession of this right is decisive evidence of citizenship. The provisions made by a constitution on this subject must therefore be looked to as bearing directly on the question what persons are citizens under that constitution; and as being decisive, to this extent, that all such persons as are allowed by the constitution to exercise the elective franchise, and thus to participate in the government of the United States, must be deemed citizens of the United States.

Here, again, the consideration presses itself upon us, that if there was designed to be a particular class of native-born persons within the States, deriving their citizenship from the constitution and laws of the United States, they should at least have been referred to as those by whom the president and house of representatives were to be elected, and to whom they should be responsible.

Instead of that, we again find this subject referred to the laws of the several States. The electors of president are to be appointed in such manner as the legislature of each State may direct, and the qualifications of electors of members of the house of representatives shall be the same as for electors of the most numerous branch of the State legislature.

Laying aside, then, the case of aliens, concerning which the constitution of the United States has provided, and confining our view to free persons born within the several States, we find that the constitution has recognized the general principle of public law, that allegiance and citizenship depend on the place of birth; that it has not attempted practically to apply this principle by designating the particular classes of persons who should or should not come under it; that when we turn to the constitution for an answer to the question, what free persons, born within the several States, are citizens of the United States, the only answer we can receive from any of its express provisions is, the citizens of the several States are to enjoy the privileges and immunities of citizens in every State, and their franchise as electors under the constitution depends on their citizenship in the several States. Add to this, that the constitution was ordained by the citizens of the several States; that they were "the people of the United States," for whom and whose posterity the government was declared in the preamble of the constitution to be made; that each of them was "a citizen of the United States at the time of the adoption of the constitution," within the meaning of those words in that instrument; that by them the government was to be and was in fact organized; and that no power is conferred on the government of the Union to discriminate between them, or to disfranchise any of them—the necessary conclusion is, that those persons born within the several States, who, by force of their respective constitutions and laws, are citizens of the State, are thereby citizens of the United States.

It may be proper here to notice some supposed objections to this view of the subject.

It has been often asserted that the constitution was made exclusively by and for the white race. It has already been shown that in five of the thirteen original States, colored persons then possessed the elective franchise, and were among those by whom the constitution was ordained and established. If so, it is not true, in point of fact, that the constitution was made exclusively by the white race. And that it was made exclusively for the white race is, in my opinion, not only an assumption not warranted by anything in the constitution, but contradicted by its opening declaration, that it was ordained and established by the people of the United States, for themselves and their posterity. And as free colored persons were then citizens of at least five States, and so in every sense part of the people of the United States, they were among those for whom and whose posterity the constitution was ordained and established.

Again, it has been objected, that if the constitution has left to the several States the rightful power to determine who of their inhabitants shall be citizens of the United States, the States may make aliens citizens.

The answer is obvious. The constitution has left to the States the determination what persons, born within their respective limits, shall acquire by birth citizenship of the United States; it has not left to them any power to prescribe any rule for the removal of the disabilities of alienage. This power is exclusively in congress.

It has been further objected, that if free colored persons, born within a particular State, and made citizens of that State by its constitution and laws, are thereby made citizens of the United States, then, under the second section of the fourth article of the constitution, such persons would be entitled to all the privileges and immunities of citizens in the several States; and if so, then colored persons could vote, and be eligible to not only federal offices, but offices even in those States whose constitution and laws disqualify colored persons from voting or being elected to office.

But this position rests upon an assumption which I deem untenable. Its basis is, that no one can be deemed a citizen of the United States who is not entitled to enjoy all the privileges and franchises which are conferred on any citizen. (See 1 Lit. Kentucky R. 326.) That this is not true, under the constitution of the United States, seems to me clear.

A naturalized citizen cannot be president of the United States, nor a senator till after the lapse of nine years, nor a representative till after the lapse of seven years, from his naturalization. Yet, as soon as naturalized, he is certainly a citizen of the United States. Nor is any inhabitant of the district of Columbia, or of either of the territories, eligible to the office of senator or representative in congress, though they may be citizens of the United States. So, in all the States, numerous persons, though citizens, cannot vote, or cannot hold office, either on account of their age, or sex, or the want of the necessary legal qualifications. The truth is, that citizenship, under the constitution of the United States, is not dependent on the possession of any particular political or even of all civil rights; and any attempt so to define it must lead to error. To what citizens the elective franchise shall be confided, is a question to be determined by each State, in accordance with its own views of the necessities or expediencies of its condition. What civil rights shall be enjoyed by its citizens, and whether all shall enjoy the same, or how they may be gained or lost, are to be determined in the same way.

One may confine the right of suffrage to white male citizens; another may extend it to colored persons and females; one may allow all persons above a prescribed age to convey property and transact business; another may exclude married women. But whether native-born women, or persons under age, or under guardianship because insane or spendthrifts, be excluded from voting or holding office, or allowed to do so, I apprehend no one will deny that they are citizens of the United States. Besides, this clause of the constitution does not confer on the citizens of one State, in all other States, specific and enumerated privileges and immunities. They are entitled to such as belong to citizenship, but not to such as belong to particular citizens attended by other qualifications. Privileges and immunities which belong to certain citizens of a State, by reason of the operation of causes other than mere citizenship, are not conferred. Thus, if the laws of a State require, in addition to citizenship of the State, some qualification for office, or the exercise of the elective franchise, citizens of all other States, coming thither to reside, and not possessing those qualifications, cannot enjoy those privileges, not because they are not to be deemed entitled to the privileges of citizens of the State in which they reside, but because they, in common with the native-born citizens of that State, must have the qualifications prescribed by law for the enjoyment of such privileges, under its constitution and laws. It rests with the States themselves so to frame their constitutions and laws as not to attach a particular privilege or immunity to mere naked citizenship. If one of the States will not deny to any of its own citizens a particular privilege or immunity, if it confer it on all of them by reason of mere naked citizenship, then it may be claimed by every citizen of each State by force of the constitution; and it must be borne in mind, that the difficulties which attend the allowance of the claims of colored persons to be citizens of the United States are not avoided by saying that, though each State may make them its citizens, they are not thereby made citizens of the United States, because the privileges of general citizenship are secured to the citizens of each State. The language of the constitution is, "The citizens of each State shall be entitled to all privileges and immunities of citizens in the several States." If each State may make such persons its citizens, they became, as such, entitled to the benefits of this article, if there be a native-born citizenship of the United States distinct from a native-born citizenship of the several States.

There is one view of this article entitled to consideration in this connection. It is manifestly copied from the fourth of the articles of confederation, with only slight changes of phraseology, which render its meaning more precise, and dropping the clause which excluded paupers, vagabonds, and fugitives from justice, probably because these cases, could be dealt with under the police powers of the States, and a special provision therefor was not necessary. It has been suggested, that in adopting it into the constitution, the words "free inhabitants" were changed for the word "citizens." An examination of the forms of expression commonly used in the State papers of that day, and an attention to the substance of this article of the confederation, will show that the words "free inhabitants," as then used, were synonymous with citizens. When the articles of confederation were adopted, we were in the midst of the war of the revolution, and there were very few persons then embraced in the words "free inhabitants," who were not born on our soil. It was not a time when many, save the children of the soil, were willing to embark their fortunes in our cause; and though there might be an inaccuracy in the uses of words to call free inhabitants citizens, it was then a technical rather than a substantial difference. If we look into the constitutions and State papers of that period, we find the inhabitants or people of these colonies, or the inhabitants of this State, or commonwealth, employed to designate those whom we should now denominate citizens. The substance and purpose of the article prove it was in this sense it used these words: it secures to the free inhabitants of each State the privileges and immunities of free citizens in every State. It is not conceivable that the States should have agreed to extend the privileges of citizenship to persons not entitled to enjoy the privileges of citizens in the States where they dwelt; that under this article there was a class of persons in some of the States, not citizens, to whom were secured all the privileges and immunities of citizens when they went into other States; and the just conclusion is, that though the constitution cured an inaccuracy of language, it left the substance of this article in the national constitution the same as it was in the articles of confederation.

The history of this fourth article, respecting the attempt to exclude free persons of color from its operation, has been already stated. It is reasonable to conclude that this history was known to those who framed and adopted the constitution. That under this fourth article of the confederation, free persons of color might be entitled to the privileges of general citizenship, if otherwise entitled thereto, is clear. When this article was, in substance, placed in and made part of the constitution of the United States, with no change in its language calculated to exclude free colored persons from the benefit of its provisions, the presumption is, to say the least, strong, that the practical effect which it was designed to have, and did have, under the former government, it was designed to have, and should have, under the new government.

It may be further objected, that if free colored persons may be citizens of the United States, it depends only on the will of a master whether he will emancipate his slave, and thereby make him a citizen. Not so. The master is subject to the will of the State. Whether he shall be allowed to emancipate his slave at all; if so, on what conditions; and what is to be the political *status* of the freed man, depend, not on the will of the master, but on the will of the State, upon which the political *status* of all its native-born inhabitants depends. Under the constitution of the United States, each State has retained this power of determining the political *status* of its native-born inhabitants, and no exception thereto can be found in the constitution. And if a master in a slaveholding State should carry his slave into a free State, and there emancipate him, he would not thereby make him a native-born citizen of that State, and consequently no privileges could be claimed by such emancipated slave as a citizen of the United States. For, whatever powers the States may exercise to confer privileges of citizenship on persons not born on their soil, the constitution of the United States does not recognize such citizens. As has already been said, it recognizes the great principle of public law, that allegiance and citizenship spring from the place of birth. It leaves to the States the application of that principle to individual cases. It secured to the citizens of each State the privileges and immunities of citizens in every other State. But it does not allow to the States the power to make aliens citizens, or permit one State to take persons born on the soil of another State, and, contrary to the laws and policy of the State where they were born, make them its citizens, and so citizens of the United States. No such deviation from the great rule of public law was contemplated by the constitution; and when any such attempt shall be actually made, it is to be met by applying to it those rules of law and those principles of good faith which will be sufficient to decide it, and not, in my judgment, by denying that all the free native-born inhabitants of a State, who are its citizens under its constitution and laws, are also citizens of the United States.

It has sometimes been urged that colored persons are shown not to be citizens of the United States by the fact that the naturalization laws apply only to white persons. But whether a person born in the United States be or be not a citizen, cannot depend on laws which refer only to aliens, and do not affect the *status* of persons born in the United States. The utmost effect which can be attributed to them is, to show that congress has not deemed it expedient generally to apply the rule to colored aliens. That they might do so, if though fit, is clear. The constitution has not excluded them. And since that has conferred the power on congress to naturalize colored aliens, it certainly shows color is not a necessary qualification for citizenship under the constitution of the United States. It may be added, that the power to make colored persons citizens of the United States, under the constitution, has been actually exercised in repeated and important instances. (See the Treaties with the Choctaws, of September 27, 1830, art. 14; with the Cherokees, of May 23, 1836, art. 12 Treaty of Guadalupe Hidalgo, February 2, 1848, art. 8.)

I do not deem it necessary to review at length the legislation of congress having more or less bearing on the citizenship of colored persons. It does not seem to me to have any considerable tendency to prove that it has been considered by the legislative department of the government, that no such persons are citizens of the United States. Undoubtedly they have been debarred from the exercise of particular rights or privileges extended to white persons, but, I believe, always in terms which, by implication, admit they may be citizens. Thus the act of May 17, 1792, for the organization of the militia, directs the enrolment of "every free, able-bodied, white male citizen." An assumption that none but white persons are citizens, would be as inconsistent with the just import of this language, as that all citizens are able-bodied, or males.

So the act of February 28, 1803, (2 Stat. at Large, 205,) to prevent the importation of certain persons into States, when by the laws thereof their admission is prohibited, in its first section forbids all masters of vessels to import or bring "any negro, mulatto, or other person of color, not being a native, *a citizen,* or registered seaman of the United States," &c.

The acts of March 3, 1813, section 1, (2 Stat. at Large, 809,) and March 1, 1817, section 3, (3 Stat. at Large, 351,) concerning seamen, certainly imply there may be persons of color, natives of the United States, who are not citizens of the United States. This implication is undoubtedly in accordance with the fact. For not only slaves, but free persons of color, born in some of the States, are not citizens. But there is nothing in these laws inconsistent with the citizenship of persons of color in others of the States, nor with their being citizens of the United States.

Whether much or little weight should be attached to the particular phraseology of these and other laws, which were not passed with any direct reference to this subject, I consider their tendency to be, as already indicated, to show that, in the apprehension of their framers, color was not a necessary qualification of citizenship. It would be strange, if laws were found on our statute book to that effect, when, by solemn treaties, large bodies of Mexican and North American Indians as well as free colored inhabitants of Louisiana have been admitted to citizenship of the United States.

In the legislative debates which preceded the admission of the State of Missouri into the Union, this question was agitated. Its result is found in the resolution of congress, of March 5, 1821, for the admission of that State into the Union. The constitution of Missouri, under which that State applied for admission into the Union, provided, that it should be the duty of the Legislature "to pass laws to prevent free negroes and mulattoes from coming to and settling in the State, under any pretext whatever." One ground of objection to the admission of the State under this constitution was, that it would require the legislature to exclude free persons of color, who would be entitled, under the second section of the fourth article of the constitution, not only to come within the State, but to enjoy there the privileges and immunities of citizens. The resolution of congress admitting the State was upon the fundamental condition, "that the constitution of Missouri shall never be construed to authorize the passage of any law, and that no law shall be passed in conformity thereto, by which any citizen of either of the States of this Union shall be excluded from the enjoyment of any of the privileges and immunities to which such citizen is entitled under the constitution of the United States." It is true, that neither this legislative declaration, nor anything in the constitution or laws of Missouri, could confer or take away any privilege or immunity granted by the constitution. But it is also true, that it expresses the then conviction of the legislative power of the United States, that free negroes, as citizens of some of the States, might be entitled to the privileges and immunities of citizens in all the States.

The conclusions at which I have arrived on this part of the case are:

First. That the free native-born citizens of each State are citizens of the United States.

Second. That as free colored persons born within some of the States are citizens of those States, such persons are also citizens of the United States.

Third. That every such citizen, residing in any State, has the right to sue and is liable to be sued in the Federal courts, as a citizen of that State in which he resides.

Fourth. That as the plea to the jurisdiction in this case shows no facts, except that the plaintiff was of African descent, and his ancestors were sold as slaves, and as these facts are not inconsistent with his citizenship of the United States, and his residence in the State of Missouri, the plea to the jurisdiction was bad, and the judgment of the circuit court overruling it was correct.

I dissent, therefore, from that part of the opinion of the majority of the court, in which it is held that a person of African descent cannot be a citizen of the United States; and I regret I must go further, and dissent both from what I deem their assumption of authority to examine the constitutionality of the act of congress commonly called the Missouri compromise act, and the grounds and conclusions announced in their opinion.

Having first decided that they were bound to consider the sufficiency of the plea to the jurisdiction of the circuit court, and having decided that this plea showed that the circuit court had not jurisdiction, and consequently that this is a case to which the judicial power of the United States does not extend, they have gone on to examine the merits of the case as they appeared on the trial before the court and jury, on the issues joined on the pleas in bar, and so have reached the question of the power of congress to pass the act of 1820. On so grave a subject as this, I feel obliged to say that, in my opinion, such an exertion of judicial power transcends the limits of the authority of the court, as described by its repeated decisions, and, as I understand, acknowledged in this opinion of the majority of the court.

In the course of that opinion, it became necessary to comment on the case of Legrand *v.* Darnall, (reported in 2 Peters's R. 664.) In that case, a bill was filed, by one alleged to be a citizen of Maryland, against one alleged to be a citizen of Pennsylvania. The bill stated that the defendant was the son of a white man by one of his slaves; and that the defendant's father devised to him certain lands, the title to which was put in controversy by the bill. These facts were admitted in the answer, and upon these and other facts the court made its decree, founded on the principle that a devise of land by a master to a slave was by implication also a bequest of his freedom. The facts that the defendant was of African descent, and was born a slave, were not only before the court, but entered into the entire substance of its inquiries. The opinion of the majority of my brethren in this case disposes of the case of Legrand *v.* Darnall, by saying, among other things, that as the fact that the defendant was born a slave only came before this court on the bill and answer, it was then too late to raise the question of the personal disability of the party, and therefore that decision is altogether inapplicable in this case.

In this I concur. Since the decision of this court in Livingston *v.* Story, (11 Pet. 351,) the law has been settled, that when the declaration or bill contains the necessary averments of citizenship, this court cannot look at the record, to see whether those averments are true, except so far as they are put in issue by a plea to the jurisdiction. In that case, the defendant denied by his answer that Mr. Livingston was a citizen of New York, as he had alleged in the bill. Both parties went into proofs. The court refused to examine those proofs, with reference to the personal disability of the plaintiff. This is the settled law of the court, affirmed so lately as Shepherd *v.* Graves, (14 How. 27,) and Wickliff *v.* Owings, (17 How. 51.) (See also De Wolf *v.* Rabaud, 1 Pet. 476.) But I do not understand this to be a rule which the court may depart from at its pleasure. If it be a rule, it is as binding on the court as on the suitors. If it removes from the latter the power to take any objection to the personal disability of a party alleged by the record to be competent, which is not shown by a plea to the jurisdiction, it is because the court are forbidden by law to consider and decide on objections so taken. I do not consider it to be within the scope of the judicial power of the majority of the court to pass upon any question respecting the plaintiff's citizenship in Missouri, save that raised by the plea to the jurisdiction; and I do not hold any opinion of this court, or any court, binding, when expressed on a question not legitimately before it. (Carroll *v.* Carroll, 16 How. 275.) The judgment of this court is, that the case is to be dismissed for want of jurisdiction, because the plaintiff was not a citizen of Missouri, as he alleged in his declaration. Into that judgment, according to the settled course of this court, nothing appearing after a plea to the merits can enter. A great question of constitutional law, deeply affecting the peace and welfare of the country, is not, in my opinion, a fit subject to be thus reached.

But as, in my opinion, the circuit court had jurisdiction, I am obliged to consider the question whether its judgment on the merits of the case should stand or be reversed.

The residence of the plaintiff in the State of Illinois, and the residence of himself and his wife in the territory acquired from France lying north of latitude thirty-six degrees thirty minutes, and north of the State of Missouri, are each relied on by the plaintiff in error. As the residence in the territory affects the plaintiff's wife and children as well as himself, I must inquire what was its effect.

The general question may be stated to be, whether the plaintiff's *status*, as a slave, was so changed by his residence within that territory, that he was not a slave in the State of Missouri, at the time this action was brought.

In such cases, two inquiries arise, which may be confounded, but should be kept distinct.

The first is, what was the law of the territory into which the master and slave went, respecting the relation between them?

The second is, whether the State of Missouri recognizes and allows the effect of that law of the territory, on the *status* of the slave, on his return within its jurisdiction.

As to the first of these questions, the will of States and nations, by whose municipal law slavery is not recognized, has been manifested in three different ways.

One is, absolutely to dissolve the relation, and terminate the rights of the master existing under the law of the country whence the parties came. This is said by Lord Stowell, in the case of the slave Grace, (2 Hag. Ad. R. 94,) and by the supreme court of Louisiana in the case of Maria Louise *v.* Marot, (9 Louis. R. 473,) to be the law of France; and it has been the law of several States of this Union, in respect to slaves introduced under certain conditions. (Wilson *v.* Isabel, 5 Call's R. 430; Hunter *v.* Hulcher, 1 Leigh, 172; Stewart *v.* Oaks, 5 Har. and John. 107.)

The second is, where the municipal law of a country not recognising slavery, it is the will of the State to refuse the master all aid to exercise any control over his slave; and if he attempt to do so, in a manner justifiable only by that relation, to prevent the exercise of that control. But no law exists, designed to operate directly on the relation of master and slave, and put an end to that relation. This is said by Lord Stowell, in the case above mentioned, to be the law of England, and by Mr. Chief Justice Shaw, in the case of the Commonwealth *v.* Aves, (18 Pick. 193,) to be the law of Massachusetts.

The third is, to make a distinction between the case of a master and his slave only temporarily in the country, *animo non manendi*, and those who are there to reside for permanent or indefinite purposes. This is said by Mr. Wheaton to be the law of Prussia, and was formerly the statute law of several States of our Union. It is necessary in this case to keep in view this distinction between those countries whose laws are designed to act directly on the *status* of a slave, and make him a freeman, and those where his master can obtain no aid from the laws to enforce his rights.

It is to the last case only that the authorities, out of Missouri, relied on by defendant, apply, when the residence in the nonslaveholding Territory was permanent. In the Commonwealth *v.* Aves, (18 Pick. 218,) Mr. Chief Justice Shaw said: "From the principle above stated, on which a slave brought here becomes free, to wit: that he becomes entitled to the protection of our laws, it would seem to follow, as a necessary conclusion, that if the slave waives the protection of those laws, and returns to the State where he is held as a slave, his condition is not changed." It was upon this ground, as is apparent from his whole reasoning, that Sir William Scott rests his opinion in the case of the slave Grace. To use one of his expressions, the effect of the law of England was to put the liberty of the slave into a parenthesis. If there had been an act of parliament declaring that a slave coming to England with his master should thereby be deemed no longer to be a slave, it is easy to see that the learned judge could not have arrived at the same conclusion. This distinction is very clearly stated and shown by President Tucker, in his opinion in the case of Betty *v.* Horton. (5 Leigh's Virginia R. 615.) (See also Hunter *v.* Fletcher, 1 Leigh's Va. R. 172; Maria Louise *v.* Marot, 9 Louisiana R.; Smith *v.* Smith, 13 Ib. 441; Thomas *v.* Genevieve, 16 Ib. 483; Rankin *v.* Lydia, 2 A. K. Marshall, 467; Davies *v.* Tingle, 8 B. Munroe, 539; Griffeth *v.* Fanny, Gilm. Va. R. 143; Lumford *v.* Coquillon, 14 Martin's La. R. 405; Josephine *v.* Poultney, 1 Louis. Ann. R. 329.)

But if the acts of congress on this subject are valid, the law of the territory of Wisconsin, within whose limits the residence of the plaintiff and his wife, and their marriage and the birth of one or both of their children, took place, falls under the first category, and is a law operating directly on the *status* of the slave. By the eighth section of the act of March 6, 1820, (3 Stat. at Large, 548,) it was enacted that, within this territory, "slavery and involuntary servitude, otherwise than in the punishment of crimes, whereof the parties shall have been duly convicted, shall be, and is hereby, forever prohibited: *Provided, always,* that any person escaping into the same, from whom labor or service is lawfully claimed in any State or Territory of the United States, such fugitive may be lawfully reclaimed, and conveyed to the person claiming his or her labor or service, as aforesaid."

By the act of April 20, 1836, (4 Stat. at Large, 10,) passed in the same month and year of the removal of the plaintiff to Fort Snelling, this part of the territory ceded by France, where Fort Snelling is, together with so much of the territory of the United States east of the Mississippi as now constitutes the State of Wisconsin, was brought under a territorial government, under the name of the territory of Wisconsin. By the eighteenth section of this act, it was enacted, "That the inhabitants of this territory shall be entitled to and enjoy all and singular the rights, privileges, and advantages, granted and secured to the people of the territory of the United States northwest of the river Ohio, by the articles of compact contained in the ordinance for the government of said territory, passed on the 13th day of July, 1787; and shall be subject to all the restrictions and prohibitions in said articles of compact imposed upon the people of the said territory." The sixth article of that compact is, "there shall be neither slavery nor involuntary servitude in the said territory, otherwise than in the punishment of crimes, whereof the party shall have been duly convicted. *Provided, always,* that any person escaping into the same, from whom labor or service is lawfully claimed in any one of the original States, such fugitive may be lawfully reclaimed, and conveyed to the person claiming his or her labor or service, as aforesaid." By other provisions of this act establishing the territory of Wisconsin, the laws of the United States, and the then existing laws of the State of Michigan, are extended over the territory; the latter being subject to alteration and repeal by the legislative power of the territory created by the act.

Fort Snelling was within the territory of Wisconsin, and these laws were extended over it. The Indian title to that site for a military post had been acquired from the Sioux nation as early as September 23, 1805, (Am. State Papers, Indian Affairs, vol. 1, p. 744,) and until the erection of the territorial government, the persons at that post were governed by the rules and articles of war, and such laws of the United States, including the eighth section of the act of March 6, 1820, prohibiting slavery, as were applicable to their condition; but after the erection of the territory, and the extension of the laws of the United States and the laws of Michigan over the whole of the territory, including this military post, the persons residing there were under the dominion of those laws in all particulars to which the rules and articles of war did not apply.

It thus appears that, by these acts of congress, not only was a general system of municipal law borrowed from the State of Michigan, which did not tolerate slavery, but it was positively enacted that slavery and involuntary servitude, with only one exception, specifically described, should not exist there. It is not simply that slavery is not recognized and cannot be aided by the municipal law. It is recognized for the purpose of being absolutely prohibited, and declared incapable of existing within the territory, save in the instance of a fugitive slave.

It would not be easy for the legislature to employ more explicit language to signify its will that the *status* of slavery should not exist within the territory, than the words found in the act of 1820, and in the ordinance of 1787; and if any doubt could exist concerning their application to cases of masters coming into the territory with their slaves to reside, that doubt must yield to the inference required by the words of exception. That exception is, of cases of fugitive slaves. An exception from a prohibition marks the extent of the prohibition; for it would be absurd, as well as useless, to except from a prohibition a case not contained within it. (9 Wheat. 200.) I must conclude, therefore, that it was the will of congress that the state of involuntary servitude of a slave, coming into the territory with his master, should cease to exist. The supreme court of Missouri so held in Rachel *v.* Walker, (4 Misso. R. 350,) which was the case of a military officer going into the territory with two slaves.

But it is a distinct question, whether the law of Missouri recognized and allowed effect to the change wrought in the *status* of the plaintiff, by force of the laws of the territory of Wisconsin.

I say the law of Missouri, because a judicial tribunal, in one State or nation, can recognize personal rights acquired by force of the law of any other State or nation, only so far as it is the law of the former State that those rights should be recognized. But, in the absence of positive law to the contrary, the will of every civilized State must be presumed to be to allow such effect to foreign laws as is in accordance with the settled rules of international law. And legal tribunals are bound to act on this presumption. It may be assumed that the motive of the State in allowing such operation to foreign laws is what has been termed comity. But, as has justly been said, (per Chief Justice Taney, 13 Pet. 589,) it is the comity of the State, not of the court. The judges have nothing to do with the motive of the State. Their duty is simply to ascertain and give effect to its will. And when it is found by them that its will to depart from a rule of international law has not been manifested by the State, they are bound to assume that its will is to give effect to it. Undoubtedly, every sovereign State may refuse to recognize a change, wrought by the law of a foreign State, on the *status* of a person, while within such foreign State, even in cases where the rules of international law require that recognition. Its will to refuse such recognition may be manifested by what we term statute law, or by the customary law of the State. It is within the province of its judicial tribunals to inquire and adjudge whether it appears, from the statute or customary law of the State, to be the will of the State to refuse to recognize such changes of *status* by force of foreign law, as the rules of the law of nations require to be recognized. But, in my opinion, it is not within the province of any judicial tribunal to refuse such recognition from any political considerations, or any view it may take of the exterior political relations between the State and one or more foreign States, or any impressions it may have that a change of foreign opinion and action on the subject of slavery may afford a reason why the State should change its own action. To understand and give just effect to such considerations, and to change the action of the State in consequence of them, are functions of diplomatists and legislators, not of judges.

The inquiry to be made on this part of the case is, therefore, whether the State of Missouri has, by its statute, or its customary law, manifested its will to displace any rule of international law, applicable to a change of the *status* of a slave, by foreign law.

I have not heard it suggested that there was any statute of the State of Missouri bearing on this question. The customary law of Missouri is the common law, introduced by statute in 1816. (1 Ter. Laws, 436.) And the common law, as Blackstone says, (4 Com. 67,) adopts, in its full extent, the law of nations, and holds it to be a part of the law of the land.

I know of no sufficient warrant for declaring that any rule of international law, concerning the recognition, in that State, of a change of *status*, wrought by an extra-territorial law, has been displaced or varied by the will of the State of Missouri.

I proceed then to inquire what the rules of international law prescribe concerning the change of *status* of the plaintiff wrought by the law of the territory of Wisconsin.

It is generally agreed by writers upon international law, and the rule has been judicially applied in a great number of cases, that wherever any question may arise concerning the *status* of a person, it must be determined according to that law which has next previously rightfully operated on and fixed that *status*. And, further, that the laws of a country do not rightfully operate upon and fix the *status* of persons who are within its limits *in itinere*, or who are abiding there for definite temporary purposes, as for health, curiosity, or occasional business; that these laws, known to writers on public and private international law as personal statutes, operate only on the inhabitants of the country. Not that it is or can be denied that each independent nation may, if it thinks fit, apply them to all persons within their limits. But when this is done, not in conformity with the principles of international law, other States are not understood to be willing to recognize or allow effect to such applications of personal statutes.

It becomes necessary, therefore, to inquire whether the operation of the laws of the territory of Wisconsin upon the *status* of the plaintiff was or was not such an operation as these principles of international law require other States to recognize and allow effect to.

And this renders it needful to attend to the particular facts and circumstances of this case.

It appears that this case came on for trial before the circuit court and a jury, upon an issue, in substance, whether the plaintiff, together with his wife and children, were the slaves of the defendant.

The court instructed the jury that, "upon the facts in this case, the law is with the defendant." This withdrew from the jury the consideration and decision of every matter of fact. The evidence in the case consisted of written admissions, signed by the counsel of the parties. If the case had been submitted to the judgment of the court, upon an agreed statement of facts, entered of record, in place of a special verdict, it would have been necessary for the court below, and for this court, to pronounce its judgment solely on those facts, thus agreed, without inferring any other facts therefrom. By the rules of the common law applicable to such a case, and by force of the seventh article of the amendments of the constitution, this court is precluded from finding any fact not agreed to by the parties on the record. No submission to the court on a statement of facts was made. It was a trial by jury, in which certain admissions, made by the parties, were the evidence. The jury were not only competent, but were bound to draw from that evidence every inference which, in their judgment, exercised according to the rules of law, it would warrant. The circuit court took from the jury the power to draw any inferences from the admissions made by the parties, and decided the case for the defendant. This course can be justified here, if at all, only by its appearing that upon the facts agreed, and all such inferences of fact favorable to the plaintiff's case, as the jury might have been warranted in drawing from those admissions, the law was with the defendant. Otherwise, the plaintiff would be deprived of the benefit of his trial by jury, by whom, for aught we can know, those inferences favorable to his case would have been drawn.

The material facts agreed, bearing on this part of the case, are, that Dr. Emerson, the plaintiff's master, resided about two years at the military post of Fort Snelling, being a surgeon in the army of the United States, his domicile of origin being unknown; and what, if anything, he had done, to preserve or change his domicile prior to his residence at Rock Island, being also unknown.

Now, it is true, that under some circumstances the residence of a military officer at a particular place, in the discharge of his official duties, does not amount to the acquisition of a technical domicile. But it cannot be affirmed, with correctness, that it never does. There being actual residence, and this being presumptive evidence of domicile, all the circumstances of the case must be considered, before a legal conclusion can be reached, that his place of residence is not his domicile. If a military officer stationed at a particular post should entertain an expectation that his residence there would be indefinitely protracted, and in consequence should remove his family to the place where his duties were to be discharged, form a permanent domestic establishment there, exercise there the civil rights and discharge the civil duties of an inhabitant, while he did no act and manifested no intent to have a domicile elsewhere, I think no one would say that the mere fact that he was himself liable to be called away by the orders of the government would prevent his acquisition of a technical domicile at the place of the residence of himself and his family. In other words, I do not think a military officer incapable of acquiring a domicile. (Bruce *v.* Bruce, 2 Bos. and Pul. 230; Munroe *v.* Douglass, 5 Mad. Ch. R. 232.) This being so, this case stands thus: there was evidence before the jury that Emerson resided about two years at Fort Snelling, in the territory of Wisconsin. This may or may not have been with such intent as to make it his technical domicile. The presumption is that it was. It is so laid down by this court, in Ennis *v.* Smith, (14 How.) and the authorities in support of the position are there referred to. His intent was a question of fact for the jury. (Fitchburg *v.* Winchendon, 4 Cush. 190.)

The case was taken from the jury. If they had power to find that the presumption of the necessary intent had not been rebutted, we cannot say, on this record, that Emerson had not his technical domicile at Fort Snelling. But, for reasons which I shall now proceed to give, I do not deem it necessary in this case to determine the question of the technical domicile of Dr. Emerson.

It must be admitted that the inquiry whether the law of a particular country has rightfully fixed the *status* of a person, so that in accordance with the principles of international law that *status* should be recognized in other jurisdictions, ordinarily depends on the question whether the person was domiciled in the country whose laws are asserted to have fixed his *status*. But, in the United States, questions of this kind may arise, where an attempt to decide solely with reference to technical domicile, tested by the rules which are applicable to changes of places of abode from one country to another, would not be consistent with sound principles. And, in my judgment, this is one of those cases.

The residence of the plaintiff, who was taken by his master, Dr. Emerson, as a slave, from Missouri to the State of Illinois, and thence to the territory of Wisconsin, must be deemed to have been for the time being, and until he asserted his own separate intention, the same as the residence of his master; and the inquiry, whether the personal statutes of the territory were rightfully extended over the plaintiff, and ought, in accordance with the rules of international law, to be allowed to fix his *status,* must depend upon the circumstances under which Dr. Emerson went into that territory, and remained there; and upon the further question, whether anything was there rightfully done by the plaintiff to cause those personal statutes to operate on him.

Dr. Emerson was an officer in the army of the United States. He went into the territory to discharge his duty to the United States. The place was out of the jurisdiction of any particular State, and within the exclusive jurisdiction of the United States. It does not appear where the domicile of origin of Dr. Emerson was, nor whether or not he had lost it, and gained another domicile, nor of what particular State, if any, he was a citizen.

On what ground can it be denied that all valid laws of the United States, constitutionally enacted by congress for the government of the territory, rightfully extended over an officer of the United States and his servant who went into the territory to remain there for an indefinite length of time, to take part in its civil or military affairs? They were not foreigners, coming from abroad. Dr. Emerson was a citizen of the country which had exclusive jurisdiction over the territory; and not only a citizen, but he went there in a public capacity, in the service of the same sovereignty which made the laws. Whatever those laws might be, whether of the kind denominated personal statutes, or not, so far as they were intended by the legislative will, constitutionally expressed, to operate on him and his servant, and on the relations between them, they had a rightful operation, and no other State or country can refuse to allow that those laws might rightfully operate on the plaintiff and his servant, because such a refusal would be a denial that the United States could, by laws constitutionally enacted, govern their own servants, residing on their own territory, over which the United States had the exclusive control, and in respect to which they are an independent sovereign power. Whether the laws now in question were constitutionally enacted, I repeat once more, is a separate question. But, assuming that they were, and that they operated directly on the *status* of the plaintiff, I consider that no other State or country could question the rightful power of the United States so to legislate, or, consistently with the settled rules of international law, could refuse to recognize the effects of such legislation upon the *status* of their officers and servants, as valid everywhere.

This alone would, in my apprehension, be sufficient to decide this question.

But there are other facts stated on the record which should not be passed over. It is agreed that, in the year 1836, the plaintiff, while residing in the territory, was married, with the consent of Dr. Emerson, to Harriet, named in the declaration as his wife, and that Eliza and Lizzie were the children of that marriage, the first named having been born on the Mississippi river, north of the line of Missouri, and the other having been born after their return to Missouri. And the inquiry is, whether, after the marriage of the plaintiff in the territory, with the consent of Dr. Emerson, any other State or country can, consistently with the settled rules of international law, refuse to recognize and treat him as a free man, when suing for the liberty of himself, his wife, and the children of the marriage. It is in reference to his *status*, as viewed in other States and countries, that the contract of marriage and the birth of children becomes strictly material. At the same time, it is proper to observe that the female to whom he was married having been taken to the same military post of Fort Snelling as a slave, and Dr. Emerson claiming also to be her master at the time of her marriage, her *status*, and that of the children of the marriage, are also affected by the same considerations.

If the laws of congress governing the territory of Wisconsin were constitutional and valid laws, there can be no doubt these parties were capable of contracting a lawful marriage, attended with all the usual civil rights and obligations of that condition. In that territory they were absolutely free persons, having full capacity to enter into the civil contract of marriage.

It is a principle of international law, settled beyond controversy in England and America, that a marriage, valid by the law of the place where it was contracted, and not in fraud of the law of any other place, is valid everywhere; and that no technical domicile at the place of the contract is necessary to make it so. (See Bishop on Mar. and Div. 125–129, where the cases are collected.)

If, in Missouri, the plaintiff were held to be a slave, the validity and operation of his contract of marriage must be denied. He can have no legal rights; of course, not those of a husband and father. And the same is true of his wife and children. The denial of his rights is the denial of theirs. So that, though lawfully married in the territory, when they came out of it, into the State of Missouri, they were no longer husband and wife; and a child of that lawful marriage, though born under the same dominion where its parents contracted a lawful marriage, is not the fruit of that marriage, nor the child of its father, but subject to the maxim, *partus sequitur ventrem.*

It must be borne in mind that in this case there is no ground for the inquiry, whether it be the will of the State of Missouri not to recognize the validity of the marriage of a fugitive slave, who escapes into a State or country where slavery is not allowed, and there contracts a marriage; or the validity of such a marriage, where the master, being a citizen of the State of Missouri, voluntarily goes with his slave, *in itinere,* into a State or country which does not permit slavery to exist, and the slave there contracts marriage without the consent of his master; for in this case, it is agreed, Dr. Emerson did consent; and no further question can arise concerning his rights, so far as their assertion is inconsistent with the validity of the marriage. Nor do I know of any ground for the assertion that this marriage was in fraud of any law of Missouri. It has been held by this court, that a bequest of property by a master to his slave, by necessary implication entitles the slave to his freedom; because, only as a freeman could he take and hold the bequest. (Legrand *v.* Darnall, 2 Pet. R. 664.) It has also been held, that when a master goes with his slave to reside for an indefinite period in a State where slavery is not tolerated, this operates as an act of manumission; because it is sufficiently expressive of the consent of the master that the slave should be free. (2 Marshall's Ken. R. 470; 14 Martin's Louis. R. 401.)

What, then, shall we say of the consent of the master, that the slave may contract a lawful marriage, attended with all the civil rights and duties which belong to that relation; that he may enter into a relation which none but a free man can assume—a relation which involves not only the rights and duties of the slave, but those of the other party to the contract, and of their descendants to the remotest generation? In my judgment, there can be no more effectual abandonment of the legal rights of a master over his slave, than by the consent of the master that the slave should enter into a contract of marriage, in a free State, attended by all the civil rights and obligations which belong to that condition.

And any claim by Dr. Emerson, or any one claiming under him, the effect of which is to deny the validity of this marriage, and the lawful paternity of the children born from it, wherever asserted, is, in my judgment, a claim inconsistent with good faith and sound reason, as well as with the rules of international law. And I go further: in my opinion, a law of the State of Missouri, which should thus annul a marriage, lawfully contracted by these parties while resident in Wisconsin, not in fraud of any law of Missouri, or of any right of Dr. Emerson, who consented thereto, would be a law impairing the obligation of a contract, and within the prohibition of the Constitution of the United States. (See 4 Wheat. 629, 695, 696.)

To avoid misapprehension on this important and difficult subject, I will state, distinctly, the conclusions at which I have arrived. They are:

First. The rules of international law respecting the emancipation of slaves, by the rightful operation of the laws of another State or country upon the *status* of the slave, while resident in such foreign State or country, are part of the common law of Missouri, and have not been abrogated by any statute law of that State.

Second. The laws of the United States, constitutionally enacted, which operated directly on and changed the *status* of a slave coming into the territory of Wisconsin with his master, who went thither to reside for an indefinite length of time, in the performance of his duties as an officer of the United States, had a rightful operation on the *status* of the slave, and it is in conformity with the rules of international law that this change of *status* should be recognized everywhere.

Third. The laws of the United States, in operation in the territory of Wisconsin at the time of the plaintiff's residence there, did act directly on the *status* of the plaintiff, and change his *status* to that of a free man.

Fourth. The plaintiff and his wife were capable of contracting, and, with the consent of Dr. Emerson, did contract a marriage in that territory, valid under its laws; and the validity of this marriage cannot be questioned in Missouri, save by showing that it was in fraud of the laws of that State, or of some right derived from them; which cannot be shown in this case, because the master consented to it.

Fifth. That the consent of the master that his slave, residing in a country which does not tolerate slavery, may enter into a lawful contract of marriage, attended with the civil rights and duties which being to that condition, is an effectual act of emancipation. And the law does not enable Dr. Emerson, or any one claiming under him, to assert a title to the married persons as slaves, and thus destroy the obligation of the contract of marriage, and bastardize their issue, and reduce them to slavery.

But it is insisted that the supreme court of Missouri has settled this case by its decision in Scott *v.* Emerson, (15 Missouri Reports, 576,) and that this decision is in conformity with the weight of authority elsewhere, and with sound principles. If the supreme court of Missouri had placed its decision on the ground that it appeared Dr. Emerson never became domiciled in the territory, and so its laws could not rightfully operate on him and his slave; and the facts that he went there to reside indefinitely, as an officer of the United States, and that the plaintiff was lawfully married there, with Dr. Emerson's consent, were left out of view, the decision would find support in other cases, and I might not be prepared to deny its correctness. But the decision is not rested on this ground. The domicile of Dr. Emerson in that territory is not questioned in that decision; and it is placed on a broad denial of the operation, in Missouri, of the law of any foreign State or country upon the *status* of a slave, going with his master from Missouri into such foreign State or country, even though they went thither to become, and actually became, permanent inhabitants of such foreign State or country, the laws whereof acted directly on the *status* of the slave, and changed his *status* to that of a freeman.

To the correctness of such a decision I cannot assent. In my judgment, the opinion of the majority of the court in that case is in conflict with its previous decisions, with a great weight of judicial authority in other slaveholding States, and with fundamental principles of private international law. Mr. Chief Justice Gamble, in his dissenting opinion in that case, said:

"I regard the question as conclusively settled by repeated adjudications of this court; and if I doubted or denied the propriety of those decisions, I would not feel myself any more at liberty to overturn them, than I would any other series of decisions by which the law upon any other question had been settled. There is with me nothing in the law of slavery which distinguishes it from the law on any other subject, or allows any more accommodation to the temporary excitements which have gathered around it. * * * * * * But in the midst of all such excitement, it is proper that the judicial mind, calm and self-balanced, should adhere to principles established when there was no feeling to disturb the view of the legal questions upon which the rights of parties depend."

"In this State, it has been recognized from the beginning of the government as a correct position in law, that the master who takes his slave to reside in a State or territory where slavery is prohibited, thereby emancipates his slave." (Winney *v.* Whitesides, 1 Mo. 473; Le Grange *v.* Chouteau, 2 Mo. 20; Milley *v.* Smith, Ib. 36; Ralph *v.* Duncan, 3 Mo. 194; Julia *v.* McKinney, Ib. 270; Nat *v.* Ruddle, Ib. 400; Rachel *v.* Walker, 4 Mo. 350; Wilson *v.* Melvin, 592.)

Chief Justice Gamble has also examined the decisions of the courts of other States in which slavery is established, and finds them in accordance with these preceding decisions of the supreme court of Missouri to which he refers.

It would be a useless parade of learning for me to go over the ground which he has so fully and ably occupied.

But it is further insisted we are bound to follow this decision. I do not think so. In this case, it is to be determined what laws of the United States were in operation in the territory of Wisconsin, and what was their effect on the *status* of the plaintiff. Could the plaintiff contract a lawful marriage there? Does any law of the State of Missouri impair the obligation of that contract of marriage, destroy his rights as a husband, bastardize the issue of the marriage, and reduce them to a state of slavery?

These questions, which arise exclusively under the constitution and laws of the United States, this court, under the constitution and laws of the United States, has the rightful authority finally to decide. And if we look beyond these questions, we come to the consideration whether the rules of international law, which are part of the laws of Missouri until displaced by some statute not alleged to exist, do or do not require the *status* of the plaintiff, as fixed by the laws of the territory of Wisconsin, to be recognized in Missouri. Upon such a question, not depending on any statute or local usage, but on principles of universal jurisprudence, this court has repeatedly asserted it could not hold itself bound by the decisions of State courts, however great respect might be felt for their learning, ability, and impartiality. (See Swift *v.* Tyson, 16 Peters's R. 1; Carpenter *v.* The Providence Ins. Co. Ib. 495; Foxcroft *v.* Mallet, 4 How. 353; Rowan *v.* Runnels, 5 How. 134.)

Some reliance has been placed on the fact that the decision in the supreme court of Missouri was between these parties, and the suit there was abandoned to obtain another trial in the courts of the United States.

In Homer *v.* Brown, (16 How. 354,) this court made a decision upon the construction of a devise of lands, in direct opposition to the unanimous opinion of the supreme court of Massachusetts, between the same parties, respecting the same subject-matter—the claimant having become nonsuit in the State court, in order to bring his action in the circuit court of the United States. I did not sit in that case, having been of counsel for one of the parties while at the bar; but, on examining the report of the argument of the counsel for the plaintiff in error, I find they made the point, that this court ought to give effect to the construction put upon the will by the State court, to the end that rights respecting lands may be governed by one law, and that the law of the place where the lands are situated; that they referred to the State decision of the case, reported in 3 Cushing, 390, and to many decisions of this court. But this court does not seem to have considered the point of sufficient importance to notice it in their opinions. In Millar *v.* Austin, (13 How. 218,) an action was brought by the endorsee of a written promise. The question was, whether it was negotiable under a statute of Ohio. The supreme court of that State having decided it was not negotiable, the plaintiff became nonsuit, and brought his action in the circuit court of the United States. The decision of the supreme court of the State, reported in 4 Ves. L. J. 527, was relied on. This court unanimously held the paper to be negotiable.

When the decisions of the highest court of a State are directly in conflict with each other, it has been repeatedly held, here, that the last decision is not necessarily to be taken as the rule. (State Bank *v.* Knoop, 16 How. 369; Pease *v.* Peck, 18 How. 599.)

To these considerations I desire to add, that it was not made known to the supreme court of Missouri, so far as appears, that the plaintiff was married in Wisconsin with the consent of Dr. Emerson, and it is not made known to us that

Dr. Emerson was a citizen of Missouri, a fact to which that court seem to have attached much importance.

Sitting here to administer the law between these parties, I do not feel at liberty to surrender my own convictions of what the law requires, to the authority of the decision in 15 Missouri Reports.

I have thus far assumed, merely for the purpose of the argument, that the laws of the United States, respecting slavery in this territory, were constitutionally enacted by congress. It remains to inquire whether they are constitutional and binding laws.

In the argument of this part of the case at bar, it was justly considered by all the counsel to be necessary to ascertain the source of the power of congress over the territory belonging to the United States. Until this is ascertained, it is not possible to determine the extent of that power. On the one side it was maintained that the constitution contains no express grant of power to organize and govern what is now known to the laws of the United States as a territory. That whatever power of this kind exists, is derived by implication from the capacity of the United States to hold and acquire territory out of the limits of any State, and the necessity for its having some government.

On the other side, it was insisted that the constitution has not failed to make an express provision for this end, and that it is found in the third section of the fourth article of the constitution.

To determine which of these is the correct view, it is needful to advert to some facts respecting this subject, which existed when the constitution was framed and adopted. It will be found that these facts not only shed much light on the question, whether the framers of the constitution omitted to make a provision concerning the power of congress to organize and govern Territories, but they will also aid in the construction of any provision which may have been made respecting this subject.

Under the confederation, the unsettled territory within the limits of the United States had been a subject of deep interest. Some of the States insisted that these lands were within their chartered boundaries, and that they had succeeded to the title of the crown to the soil. On the other hand, it was argued that the vacant lands had been acquired by the United States, by the war carried on by them under a common government and for the common interest.

This dispute was further complicated by unsettled questions of boundary among several States. It not only delayed the accession of Maryland to the confederation, but at one time seriously threatened its existence. (5 Jour. of Cong. 208, 442.) Under the pressure of these circumstances, congress earnestly recommended to the several States a cession of their claims and rights to the United States. (5 Jour. of Cong. 442.) And before the constitution was framed, it had been begun. That by New York had been made on the 1st day of March, 1781;

that of Virginia on the 1st day of March, 1784; that of Massachusetts on the 19th day of April, 1785; that of Connecticut on the 14th day of September, 1786; that of South Carolina on the 8th day of August, 1787, while the convention for framing the constitution was in session.

It is very material to observe, in this connection, that each of these acts cedes, in terms, to the United States, as well the jurisdiction as [to] the soil.

It is also equally important to note that, when the constitution was framed and adopted, this plan of vesting in the United States, for the common good, the great tracts of ungranted lands claimed by the several States, in which so deep an interest was felt, was yet incomplete. It remained for North Carolina and Georgia to cede their extensive and valuable claims. These were made, by North Carolina on the 25th day of February, 1790, and by Georgia on the 24th day of April, 1802. The terms of these last-mentioned cessions will hereafter be noticed in another connection; but I observe here that each of them distinctly shows, upon its face, that they were not only in execution of the general plan proposed by the congress of the confederation, but of a formed purpose of each of these States, existing when the assent of their respective people was given to the constitution of the United States.

It appears, then, that when the federal constitution was framed, and presented to the people of the several States for their consideration, the unsettled territory was viewed as justly applicable to the common benefit, so far as it then had or might attain thereafter a pecuniary value; and so far as it might become the seat of new States, to be admitted into the Union upon an equal footing with the original States. And also that the relations of the United States to that unsettled territory were of different kinds. The titles of the States of New York, Virginia, Massachusetts, Connecticut, and South Carolina, as well of soil as of jurisdiction, had been transferred to the United States. North Carolina and Georgia had not actually made transfers, but a confident expectation, founded on their appreciation of the justice of the general claim, and fully justified by the results, was entertained, that these cessions would be made. The ordinance of 1787 had made provision for the temporary government of so much of the territory actually ceded as lay northwest of the river Ohio.

But it must have been apparent, both to the framers of the constitution and the people of the several States who were to act upon it, that the government thus provided for could not continue, unless the constitution should confer on the United States the necessary powers to continue it. That temporary government, under the ordinance, was to consist of certain officers, to be appointed by and responsible to the congress of the confederation; their powers had been conferred and defined by the ordinance. So far as it provided for the temporary government of the territory, it was an ordinary act of legislation, deriving its force from the legislative power of congress, and depending for its vitality upon the continuance of that legislative power. But the officers to be appointed for the northwestern territory, after the adoption of the constitution, must necessarily be officers of the

United States, and not of the congress of the confederation; appointed and commissioned by the president, and exercising powers derived from the United States under the constitution.

Such was the relation between the United States and the northwestern territory, which all reflecting men must have foreseen would exist, when the government created by the constitution should supersede that of the confederation. That if the new government should be without power to govern this territory, it could not appoint and commission officers, and send them into the territory, to exercise there [sic] legislative, judicial, and executive power; and that this territory, which was even then foreseen to be so important, both politically and financially, to all the existing States, must be left not only without the control of the general government, in respect to its future political relations to the rest of the States, but absolutely without any government, save what its inhabitants, acting in their primary capacity, might from time to time create for themselves.

But this northwestern territory was not the only territory, the soil and jurisdiction whereof were then understood to have been ceded to the United States. The cession by South Carolina, made in August, 1787, was of "all the territory included within the river Mississippi, and a line beginning at that part of the said river which is intersected by the southern boundary of North Carolina, and continuing along the said boundary line until it intersects the ridge or chain of mountains which divides the eastern from the western waters; then to be continued along the top of the said ridge of mountains, until it intersects a line to be drawn due west from the head of the southern branch of the Tugaloo river, to the said mountains; and thence to run a due west course to the river Mississippi."

It is true that by subsequent explorations it was ascertained that the source of the Tugaloo river, upon which the title of South Carolina depended, was so far to the northward, that the transfer conveyed only a narrow slip of land, about twelve miles wide, lying on the top of the ridge of mountains, and extending from the northern boundary of Georgia to the southern boundary of North Carolina. But this was a discovery made long after the cession, and there can be no doubt that the State of South Carolina, in making the cession, and the congress in accepting it, viewed it as a transfer to the United States of the soil and jurisdiction of an extensive and important part of the unsettled territory ceded by the crown of Great Britain by the treaty of peace, though its quantity or extent then remained to be ascertained.[5]

It must be remembered also, as has been already stated, that not only was there a confident expectation entertained by the other States, that North Carolina and Georgia would complete the plan already so far executed by New York, Virginia, Massachusetts, Connecticut, and South Carolina, but that the opinion was in no small degree prevalent, that the just title to this "back country," as it was termed, had vested in the United States by the treaty of peace, and could not rightfully be claimed by any individual State.

There is another consideration applicable to this part of the subject, and entitled, in my judgment, to great weight.

The congress of the confederation had assumed the power not only to dispose of the lands ceded, but to institute governments and make laws for their inhabitants. In other words, they had proceeded to act under the cession, which, as we have seen, was as well of the jurisdiction as of the soil. This ordinance was passed on the 13th of July, 1787. The convention for framing the constitution was then in session at Philadelphia. The proof is direct and decisive, that it was known to the convention.[6] It is equally clear that it was admitted and understood not to be within the legitimate powers of the confederation to pass this ordinance. (Jefferson's Works, vol. 9, pp. 251, 276; Federalist, Nos. 38, 43.)

The importance of conferring on the new government regular powers commensurate with the objects to be attained, and thus avoiding the alternative of a failure to execute the trust assumed by the acceptance of the cessions made and expected, or its execution by usurpation, could scarcely fail to be perceived. That it was in fact perceived, is clearly shown by the Federalist, (No. 38,) where this very argument is made use of in commendation of the constitution.

Keeping these facts in view, it may confidently be asserted that there is very strong reason to believe, before we examine the constitution itself, that the necessity for a competent grant of power to hold, dispose of, and govern territory, ceded and expected to be ceded, could not have escaped the attention of those who framed or adopted the constitution; and that if it did not escape their attention, it could not fail to be adequately provided for.

Any other conclusion would involve the assumption that a subject of the gravest national concern, respecting which the small States felt so much jealousy that it had been almost an insurmountable obstacle to the formation of the confederation, and as to which all the States had deep pecuniary and political interests, and which had been so recently and constantly agitated, was nevertheless overlooked; or that such a subject was not overlooked, but designedly left unprovided for, though it was manifestly a subject of common concern, which belonged to the care of the general government, and adequate provision for which could not fail to be deemed necessary and proper.

The admission of new States, to be framed out of the ceded territory, early attracted the attention of the convention. Among the resolutions introduced by Mr. Randolph, on the 29th of May, was one on this subject, (Res. No. 10, 5 Elliot, 128,) which, having been affirmed in committee of the whole, on the 5th of June, (5 Elliot, 156,) and reported to the convention on the 13th of June, (5 Elliot, 190,) was referred to the committee of detail, to prepare the constitution, on the 26th of July. (5 Elliot, 376.) This committee reported an article for the admission of new States "lawfully constituted or established." Nothing was said concerning the power of congress to prepare or form such States. This omission struck Mr. Madison, who, on the 18th of August, (5 Elliot, 439,) moved for the insertion of power to dispose of the unappropriated lands of the United States, and to institute temporary governments for new States arising therein.

On the 29th of August, (5 Elliot, 492,) the report of the committee was taken up, and after debate, which exhibited great diversity of views concerning the proper mode of providing for the subject, arising out of the supposed diversity of interests of the large and small States, and between those which had and those which had not unsettled territory, but no difference of opinion respecting the propriety and necessity of some adequate provision for the subject, Gouverneur Morris moved the clause as it stands in the constitution. This met with general approbation, and was at once adopted. The whole section is as follows:

"New States may be admitted by the congress into this Union; but no new State shall be formed or erected within the jurisdiction of any other State, nor any State be formed by the junction of two or more States, or parts of States, without the consent of the legislatures of the States concerned, as well as of congress.

"The congress shall have power to dispose of and make all needful rules and regulations respecting the territory or other property belonging to the United States; and nothing in this constitution shall be so construed as to prejudice any claims of the United States or any particular State."

That congress has some power to institute temporary governments over the territory, I believe all agree; and, if it be admitted that the necessity of some power to govern the territory of the United States could not and did not escape the attention of the convention and the people, and that the necessity is so great, that, in the absence of any express grant, it is strong enough to raise an implication of the existence of that power, it would seem to follow that it is also strong enough to afford material aid in construing an express grant of power respecting that territory; and that they who maintain the existence of the power, without finding any words at all in which it is conveyed, should be willing to receive a reasonable interpretation of language of the constitution, manifestly intended to relate to the territory, and to convey to congress some authority concerning it.

It would seem, also, that when we find the subject-matter of the growth and formation and admission of new States, and the disposal of the territory for these ends, were under consideration, and that some provision therefor was expressly made, it is improbable that it would be, in its terms, a grossly inadequate provision; and that an indispensably necessary power to institute temporary governments, and to legislate for the inhabitants of the territory, was passed silently by, and left to be deduced from the necessity of the case.

In the argument at the bar, great attention has been paid to the meaning of the word "territory."

Ordinarily, when the territory of a sovereign power is spoken of, it refers to that tract of country which is under the political jurisdiction of that sovereign power. Thus Chief Justice Marshall (in United States *v.* Bevans, 3 Wheat. 386) says: "What, then, is the extent of jurisdiction which a State possesses? We answer, without hesitation, the jurisdiction of a State is coextensive with its territory." Examples might easily be multiplied of this use of the word, but they are unnecessary, because it is familiar. But the word "territory" is not used in this broad and general sense in this clause of the constitution.

At the time of the adoption of the constitution, the United States held a great tract of country northwest of the Ohio; another tract, then of unknown extent, ceded by South Carolina; and a confident expectation was then entertained, and afterwards realized, that they then were or would become the owners of other great tracts, claimed by North Carolina and Georgia. These ceded tracts lay within the limits of the United States, and out of the limits of any particular State; and the cessions embraced the civil and political jurisdiction, and so much of the soil as had not previously been granted to individuals.

These words, "territory belonging to the United States," were not used in the constitution to describe an abstraction, but to identify and apply to these actual subjects matter then existing and belonging to the United States, and other similar subjects which might afterwards be acquired; and this being so, all the essential qualities and incidents attending such actual subjects are embraced within the words "territory belonging to the United States," as fully as if each of those essential qualities and incidents had been specifically described.

I say, the essential qualities and incidents. But in determining what were the essential qualities and incidents of the subject with which they were dealing, we must take into consideration not only all the particular facts which were immediately before them, but the great consideration, ever present to the minds of those who framed and adopted the constitution, that they were making a frame of government for the people of the United States and their posterity, under which they hoped the United States might be, what they have now become, a great and powerful nation, possessing the power to make war and to conclude treaties, and thus to acquire territory. (See Cerre *v.* Pitot, 6 Cr. 336; Am. Ins. Co. *v.* Canter, 1 Pet. 542.) With these in view, I turn to examine the clause of the article now in question.

It is said this provision has no application to any territory save that then belonging to the United States. I have already shown that, when the constitution was framed, a confident expectation was entertained, which was speedily realized, that North Carolina and Georgia would cede their claims to that great territory which lay west of those States. No doubt has been suggested that the first clause of this same article, which enabled congress to admit new States, refers to and includes new States to be formed out of this territory, expected to be thereafter ceded by North Carolina and Georgia, as well as new States to be formed out of territory northwest of the Ohio, which then had been ceded by Virginia. It must have been seen, therefore, that the same necessity would exist for an authority to dispose of and make all needful regulations respecting this territory, when ceded, as existed for a like authority respecting territory which had been ceded.

No reason has been suggested why any reluctance should have been felt, by the framers of the constitution, to apply this provision to all the territory which might belong to the United States, or why any distinction should have been made, founded on the accidental circumstance of the dates of the cessions; a circumstance in no way material as respects the necessity for rules and regulations, or the propriety of conferring on the congress power to make them. And if we look at the course of the debates in the convention on this article, we shall find that the then unceded lands, so far from having been left out of view in adopting this article, constituted, in the minds of members, a subject of even paramount importance.

Again, in what an extraordinary position would the limitation of this clause to territory then belonging to the United States, place the territory which lay within the chartered limits of North Carolina and Georgia. The title to that territory was then claimed by those States, and by the United States; their respective claims are purposely left unsettled by the express words of this clause; and when cessions were made by those States, they were merely of their claims to this territory, the United States neither admitting nor denying the validity of those claims; so that it was impossible then, and has ever since remained impossible, to know whether this territory did or did not then belong to the United States; and, consequently, to know whether it was within or without the authority conferred by this clause, to dispose of and make rules and regulations respecting the territory of the United States. This attributes to the eminent men who acted on this subject a want of ability and forecast, or a want of attention to the known facts upon which they were acting, in which I cannot concur.

There is not, in my judgment, anything in the language, the history, or the subject-matter of this article, which restricts its operation to territory owned by the United States when the Constitution was adopted.

But it is also insisted that provisions of the constitution respecting territory belonging to the United States do not apply to territory acquired by treaty from a foreign nation. This objection must rest upon the position that the constitution did not authorize the federal government to acquire foreign territory, and consequently has made no provision for its government when acquired; or, that though the acquisition of foreign territory was contemplated by the constitution, its provisions concerning the admission of new States, and the making of all needful rules and regulations respecting territory belonging to the United States, were not designed to be applicable to territory acquired from foreign nations.

It is undoubtedly true, that at the date of the treaty of 1803, between the United States and France, for the cession of Louisiana, it was made a question, whether the constitution had conferred on the executive department of the government of the United States power to acquire foreign territory by a treaty.

There is evidence that very grave doubts were then entertained concerning the existence of this power. But that there was then a settled opinion in the executive and legislative branches of the government, that this power did not exist, cannot be admitted, without at the same time imputing to those who negotiated and ratified the treaty, and passed the laws necessary to carry it into execution, a deliberate and known violation of their oaths to support the constitution; and whatever doubts may them [then] have existed, the question must now be taken to have been settled. Four distinct acquisitions of foreign territory have been made by as many different treaties, under as many different administrations. Six States, formed on such territory, are now in the Union. Every branch of this government, during a period of more than fifty years, has participated in these transactions. To question their validity now, is vain. As was said by Mr. Chief Justice Marshall, in the American Insurance Company *v.* Canter, (1 Peters, 542,) "the constitution confers absolutely on the government of the Union the powers of making war and of making treaties; consequently, sequently, that government possesses the power of acquiring territory, either by conquest or treaty." (See Cerré *v.* Pitot, 6 Cr. 336.) And I add, it also possesses the power of governing it, when acquired, not by resorting to supposititious powers, nowhere found described in the constitution, but expressly granted in the authority to make all needful rules and regulations respecting the territory of the United States.

There was to be established by the constitution a frame of government, under which the people of the United States and their posterity were to continue indefinitely. To take one of its provisions, the language of which is broad enough to extend throughout the existence of the government, and embrace all territory belonging to the United States throughout all time, and the purposes and objects of which apply to all territory of the United States, and narrow it down to territory belonging to the United States when the constitution was framed, while at the same time it is admitted that the constitution contemplated and authorized the acquisition, from time to time, of other and foreign territory, seems to me to be an interpretation as inconsistent with the nature and purposes of the instrument, as it is with its language, and I can have no hesitation in rejecting it.

I construe this clause, therefore, as if it had read, congress shall have power to make all needful rules and regulations respecting those tracts of country, out of the limits of the several States, which the United States have acquired, or may hereafter acquire, by cessions, as well of the jurisdiction as of the soil, so far as the soil may be the property of the party making the cession, at the time of making it.

It has been urged that the words "rules and regulations" are not appropriate terms in which to convey authority to make laws for the government of the territory.

But it must be remembered that this is a grant of power to the congress—that it is therefore necessarily a grant of power to legislate—and, certainly, rules and regulations respecting a particular subject, made by the legislative power of a country, can be nothing but laws. Nor do the particular terms employed, in my judgment, tend in any degree to restrict this legislative power. Power granted to a legislature to make all needful rules and regulations respecting the territory, is a power to pass all needful laws respecting it.

The word regulate, or regulation, is several times used in the constitution. It is used in the fourth section of the first article to describe those laws of the States which prescribe the times, places, and manner, of choosing senators and representatives; in the second section of the fourth article, to designate the legislative action of a State on the subject of fugitives from service, having a very close relation to the matter of our present inquiry; in the second section of the third article, to empower congress to fix the extent of the appellate jurisdiction of this court; and, finally, in the eighth section of the first article are the words, "Congress shall have power to regulate commerce."

It is unnecessary to describe the body of legislation which has been enacted under this grant of power; its variety and extent are well known. But it may be mentioned, in passing, that under this power to regulate commerce, congress has enacted a great system of municipal laws, and extended it over the vessels and crews of the United States on the high seas and in foreign ports, and even over citizens of the United States resident in China; and has established judicatures, with power to inflict even capital punishment within that country.

If, then, this clause does contain a power to legislate respecting the territory, what are the limits of that power?

To this I answer, that, in common with all the other legislative powers of congress, it finds limits in the express prohibitions on congress not to do certain things; that, in the exercise of the legislative power, congress cannot pass an ex post facto law or bill of attainder; and so in respect to each of the other prohibitions contained in the constitution.

Besides this, the rules and regulations must be needful. But undoubtedly the question whether a particular rule or regulation be needful, must be finally determined by congress itself. Whether a law be needful, is a legislative or political, not a judicial, question. Whatever congress deems needful is so, under the grant of power.

Nor am I aware that it has ever been questioned that laws providing for the temporary government of the settlers on the public lands are needful, not only to prepare them for admission to the Union as States, but even to enable the United States to dispose of the lands.

Without government and social order, there can be no property; for without law, its ownership, its use, and the power of disposing of it, cease to exist, in the sense in which those words are used and understood in all civilized States.

Since, then, this power was manifestly conferred to enable the United States to dispose of its public lands to settlers, and to admit them into the Union as States, when in the judgment of congress they should be fitted therefor, since these were the needs provided for, since it is confessed that government is indispensable to provide for those needs, and the power is, to make *all needful* rules and regulations respecting the territory, I cannot doubt that this is a power to govern the inhabitants of the territory, by such laws as congress deems needful, until they obtain admission as States.

Whether they should be thus governed solely by laws enacted by congress, or partly by laws enacted by legislative power conferred by congress, is one of those questions which depend on the judgment of congress—a question which of these is needful.

But it is insisted, that whatever other powers congress may have respecting the territory of the United States, the subject of negro slavery forms an exception.

The constitution declares that congress shall have power to make "*all* needful rules and regulations" respecting the territory belonging to the United States.

The assertion is, though the constitution says all, it does not mean all—though it says all, without qualification, it means all except such as allow or prohibit slavery. It cannot be doubted that it is incumbent on those who would thus introduce an exception not found in the language of the instrument, to exhibit some solid and satisfactory reason, drawn from the subject-matter or the purposes and objects of the clause, the context, or from other provisions of the constitution, showing that the words employed in this clause are not to be understood according to their clear, plain, and natural signification.

The subject-matter is the territory of the United States out of the limits of every State, and consequently under the exclusive power of the people of the United States. Their will respecting it, manifested in the constitution, can be subject to no restriction. The purposes and objects of the clause were the enactment of laws concerning the disposal of the public lands, and the temporary government of the settlers thereon until new States should be formed. It will not be questioned that, when the constitution of the United States was framed and adopted, the allowance and the prohibition of negro slavery were recognized subjects of municipal legislation; every State had in some measure acted thereon; and the only legislative act concerning the territory—the ordinance of 1787, which had then so recently been passed—contained a prohibition of slavery. The purpose and object of the clause being to enable congress to provide a body of municipal law for the government of the settlers, the allowance or the prohibition of slavery comes within the known and recognized scope of that purpose and object.

There is nothing in the context which qualifies the grant of power. The regulations must be "respecting the territory." An enactment that slavery may or may not exist there, is a regulation respecting the territory. Regulations must be needful; but it is necessarily left to the legislative discretion to determine whether a law be needful. No other clause of the constitution has been referred to at the bar, or has been seen by me, which imposes any restriction or makes any exception concerning the power of congress to allow or prohibit slavery in the territory belonging to the United States.

A practical construction, nearly contemporaneous with the adoption of the constitution, and continued by repeated instances through a long series of years, may always influence, and in doubtful cases should determine, the judicial mind, on a question of the interpretation of the constitution. (Stuart *v.* Laird, 1 Cranch, 269; Martin *v.* Hunter, 1 Wheat. 304; Cohens *v.* Virginia, 6 Wheat. 264; Prigg *v.* Pennsylvania, 16 Pet. 621; Cooley *v.* Port Wardens, 12 How. 315.)

In this view, I proceed briefly to examine the practical construction placed on the clause now in question, so far as it respects the inclusion therein of power to permit or prohibit slavery in the territories.

It has already been stated, that after the government of the United States was organized under the constitution, the temporary government of the territory northwest of the river Ohio could no longer exist, save under the powers conferred on congress by the constitution. Whatever legislative, judicial, or executive authority should be exercised therein could be derived only from the people of the United States under the constitution. And, accordingly, an act was passed on the 7th day of August, 1789, (1 Stat. at Large, 50,) which recites: "Whereas, in order that the ordinance of the United States in congress assembled, for the government of the territory northwest of the river Ohio, *may continue to have full effect,* it is required that certain provisions should be made, so as to adapt the same to the present constitution of the United States." It then provides for the appointment by the president of all officers, who, by force of the ordinance, were to have been appointed by the congress of the confederation, and their commission in the manner required by the constitution; and empowers the secretary of the territory to exercise the powers of the governor in case of the death or necessary absence of the latter.

Here is an explicit declaration of the will of the first congress, of which fourteen members, including Mr. Madison, had been members of the convention which framed the constitution, that the ordinance, one article of which prohibited slavery, "should continue to have full effect." Gen. Washington, who signed this bill, as president, was the president of that convention.

It does not appear to me to be important, in this connection, that that clause in the ordinance which prohibited slavery was one of a series of articles of what is therein termed a compact. The congress of the confederation had no power to make such a compact, nor to act at all on the subject; and after what had been so recently said by Mr. Madison on this subject, in the thirty-eighth number of the *Federalist,* I cannot suppose that he, or any others who voted for this bill, attributed any intrinsic effect to what was denominated in the ordinance a compact between "the original States and the people and States in the new territory;" there being no new States then in existence in the territory, with whom a compact could be made, and the few scattered inhabitants, unorganized into a political body, not being capable of becoming a party to a treaty, even if the congress of the confederation had had power to make one touching the government of that territory.

I consider the passage of this law to have been an assertion by the first congress of the power of the United States to prohibit slavery within this part of the territory of the United States; for it clearly shows that slavery was thereafter to be prohibited there, and it could be prohibited only by an exertion of the power of the United States, under the constitution; no other power being capable of operating within that territory after the constitution took effect.

On the 2d of April, 1790, (1 Stat. at Large, 106,) the first congress passed an act accepting a deed of cession by North Carolina of that territory afterwards erected into the State of Tennessee. The fourth express condition contained in this deed of cession, after providing that the inhabitants of the territory shall be temporarily governed in the same manner as those beyond the Ohio, is followed by these words: "*Provided, always,* that no regulations made or to be made by congress shall tend to emancipate slaves."

This provision shows that it was then understood congress might make a regulation prohibiting slavery, and that congress might also allow it to continue to exist in the territory; and accordingly, when, a few days later, congress passed the act of May 20th, 1790, (1 Stat. at Large, 123,) for the government of the territory south of the river Ohio, it provided, "and the government of the territory south of the Ohio shall be similar to that now exercised in the territory northwest of the Ohio, except so far as is otherwise provided in the conditions expressed in an act of congress of the present session, entitled, [']An act to accept a cession of the claims of the State of North Carolina to a certain district of western territory.[']" Under the government thus established, slavery existed until the territory became the State of Tennessee.

On the 7th of April, 1798, (1 Stat. at Large, 649,) an act was passed to establish a government in the Mississippi territory in all respects like that exercised in the territory northwest of the Ohio, "excepting and excluding the last article of the ordinance made for the government thereof by the late congress, on the 13th day of July, 1787." When the limits of this territory had been amicably settled with Georgia, and the latter ceded all its claim thereto, it was one stipulation in the compact of cession, that the ordinance of July 13th, 1787, "shall in all its parts extend to the territory contained in the present act of cession, that article only excepted which forbids slavery." The government of this territory was subsequently established and organized under the act of May 10th, 1800; but so much of the ordinance as prohibited slavery was not put in operation there.

Without going minutely into the details of each case, I will now give reference to two classes of acts, in one of which congress has extended the ordinance of 1787, including the article prohibiting slavery, over different territories, and thus exerted its power to prohibit it; in the other, congress has erected governments over territories acquired from France and Spain, in which slavery already existed, but refused to apply to them that part of the government under the ordinance which excluded slavery.

Of the first class are the act of May 7th, 1800, (2 Stat. at Large, 58,) for the government of the Indiana territory; the act of January 11th, 1805, (2 Stat. at Large, 309,) for the government of Michigan territory; the act of May 3d, 1809,

(2 Stat. at Large, 514,) for the government of the Illinois territory; the act of April 20th, 1836, (5 Stat. at Large, 10,) for the government of the territory of Wisconsin; the act of June 12th, 1838, for the government of the territory of Iowa; the act of August 14th, 1848, for the government of the territory of Oregon. To these instances should be added the act of March 6th, 1820, (3 Stat. at Large, 548,) prohibiting slavery in the territory acquired from France, being northwest of Missouri, and north of thirty-six degrees thirty minutes north latitude.

Of the second class, in which congress refused to interfere with slavery already existing under the municipal law of France or Spain, and established governments by which slavery was recognized and allowed, are: the act of March 26th, 1804, (2 Stat. at Large, 283,) for the government of Louisiana; the act of March 2d, 1805, (2 Stat. at Large, 322,) for the government of the territory of Orleans; the act of June 4th, 1812, (2 Stat. at Large, 743,) for the government of the Missouri territory; the act of March 30th, 1822, (3 Stat. at Large, 654,) for the government of the territory of Florida. Here are eight distinct instances, beginning with the first congress, and coming down to the year 1848, in which congress has excluded slavery from the territory of the United States; and six distinct instances in which congress organized governments of territories by which slavery was recognized and continued, beginning also with the first congress, and coming down to the year 1822. These acts were severally signed by seven presidents of the United States, beginning with General Washington, and coming regularly down as far as Mr. John Quincy Adams, thus including all who were in public life when the constitution was adopted.

If the practical construction of the constitution contemporaneously with its going into effect, by men intimately acquainted with its history from their personal participation in framing and adopting it, and continued by them through a long series of acts of the gravest importance, be entitled to weight in the judicial mind on a question of construction, it would seem to be difficult to resist the force of the acts above adverted to.

It appears, however, from what has taken place at the bar, that notwithstanding the language of the constitution, and the long line of legislative and executive precedents under it, three different and opposite views are taken of the power of congress respecting slavery in the territories.

One is, that though congress can make a regulation prohibiting slavery in a territory, they cannot make a regulation allowing it; another is, that it can neither be established nor prohibited by congress, but that the people of a territory, when organized by congress, can establish or prohibit slavery; while the third is, that the constitution itself secures to every citizen who holds slaves, under the laws of any State, the indefeasible right to carry them into any territory, and there hold them as property.

No particular clause of the constitution has been referred to at the bar in support of either of these views. The first seems to be rested upon general considerations concerning the social and moral evils of slavery, its relations to republican governments, its inconsistency with the declaration of independence and with natural right.

The second is drawn from consideration equally general, concerning the right of self-government, and the nature of the political institutions which have been established by the people of the United States.

While the third is said to rest upon the equal right of all citizens to go with their property upon the public domain, and the inequality of a regulation which would admit the property of some and exclude the property of other citizens; and, inasmuch as slaves are chiefly held by citizens of those particular States where slavery is established, it is insisted that a regulation excluding slavery from a territory operates, practically, to make an unjust discrimination between citizens of different States, in respect to their use and enjoyment of the territory of the United States.

With the weight of either of these considerations, when presented to congress to influence its action, this court has no concern. One or the other may be justly entitled to guide or control the legislative judgment upon what is a needful regulation. The question here is, whether they are sufficient to authorize this court to insert into this clause of the constitution an exception of the exclusion or allowance of slavery, not found therein, nor in any other part of that instrument. To engraft on any instrument a substantive exception not found in it, must be admitted to be a matter attended with great difficulty. And the difficulty increases with the importance of the instrument, and the magnitude and complexity of the interests involved in its construction. To allow this to be done with the constitution, upon reasons purely political, renders its judicial interpretation impossible—because judicial tribunals, as such, cannot decide upon political considerations. Political reasons have not the requisite certainty to afford rules of juridical interpretation. They are different in different men. They are different in the same men at different times. And when a strict interpretation of the constitution, according to the fixed rules which govern the interpretation of laws, is abandoned, and the theoretical opinions of individuals are allowed to control its meaning, we have no longer a constitution; we are under the government of individual men, who for the time being have power to declare what the constitution is, according to their own views of what it ought to mean. When such a method of interpretation of the constitution obtains, in place of a republican government, with limited and defined powers, we have a government which is merely an exponent of the will of congress; or what, in my opinion, would not be preferable, an exponent of the individual political opinions of the members of this court.

If it can be shown, by anything in the constitution itself, that when it confers on congress the power to make *all* needful rules and regulations respecting the territory belonging to the United States, the exclusion or the allowance of slavery was excepted; or if anything in the history of this provision tends to show that such an exception was intended by those who framed and adopted the constitution to be introduced into it, I hold it to be my duty carefully to consider, and to allow just weight to such considerations in interpreting the positive text of the constitution. But where the constitution has said *all* needful rules and regulations, I must find something more than theoretical reasoning to induce me to say it did not mean all.

There have been eminent instances in this court closely analogous to this one, in which such an attempt to introduce an exception, not found in the constitution itself, has failed of success.

By the eighth section of the first article, congress has the power of exclusive legislation in all cases whatsoever within this district.

In the case of Loughborough *v.* Blake, (5 Wheat. 324,) the question arose, whether congress has power to impose direct taxes on persons and property in this district. It was insisted, that though the grant of power was in its terms broad enough to include direct taxation, it must be limited by the principle, that taxation and representation are inseparable. It would not be easy to fix on any political truth, better established or more fully admitted in our country, than that taxation and representation must exist together. We went into the war of the revolution to assert it, and it is incorporated as fundamental into all American governments. But however true and important this maxim may be, it is not necessarily of universal application. It was for the people of the United States, who ordained the constitution, to decide whether it should or should not be permitted to operate within this district. Their decision was embodied in the words of the constitution; and as that contained no such exception as would permit the maxim to operate in this district, this court, interpreting that language, held that the exception did not exist.

Again, the constitution confers on congress power to regulate commerce with foreign nations. Under this, congress passed an act on the 22d of December, 1807, unlimited in duration, laying an embargo on all ships and vessels in the ports or within the limits and jurisdiction of the United States. No law of the United States ever pressed so severely upon particular States. Though the constitutionality of the law was contested with an earnestness and zeal proportioned to the ruinous effects which were felt from it, and though, as Mr. Chief Justice Marshall has said, (9 Wheat. 192,) "a want of acuteness in discovering objections to a measure to which they felt the most deep-rooted hostility will not be imputed to those who were arrayed in opposition to this," I am not aware that the fact that it prohibited the use of a particular species of property, belonging almost exclusively to citizens of a few States, and this indefinitely, was ever supposed to show that it was unconstitutional. Something much more stringent, as a ground of legal judgment, was relied on—that the power to regulate commerce did not include the power to annihilate commerce.

But the decision was, that under the power to regulate commerce, the power of congress over the subject was restricted only by those exceptions and limitations contained in the constitution; and as neither the clause in question, which was a general grant of power to regulate commerce, nor any other clause of the constitution, imposed any restrictions as to the duration of an embargo, an unlimited prohibition of the use of the shipping of the country was within the power of congress. On this subject, Mr. Justice Daniel, speaking for the court in the case of United States *v.* Marigold, (9 How. 560,) says: "Congress are, by the constitution, vested with the power to regulate commerce with foreign nations; and however, at periods of high excitement, an application of the terms 'to regulate commerce,' such as would embrace absolute prohibition, may have been questioned, yet, since the passage of the embargo and non-intercourse laws, and the repeated judicial sanctions these statutes have received, it can scarcely at this day be open to doubt, that every subject falling legitimately within the sphere of commercial regulation may be partially or wholly excluded, when either measure shall be demanded by the safety or the important interests of the entire nation. The power once conceded, it may operate on any and every subject of commerce to which the legislative discretion may apply it."

If power to regulate commerce extends to an indefinite prohibition of the use of all vessels belonging to citizens of the several States, and may operate, without exception, upon every subject of commerce to which the legislative discretion may apply it, upon what grounds can I say that power to make all needful rules and regulations respecting the territory of the United States is subject to an exception of the allowance or prohibition of slavery therein?

While the regulation is one "respecting the territory," while it is, in the judgment of congress, "a needful regulation," and is thus completely within the words of the grant, while no other clause of the constitution can be shown, which requires the insertion of an exception respecting slavery, and while the practical construction for a period of upwards of fifty years forbids such an exception, it would, in my opinion, violate every sound rule of interpretation to force that exception into the constitution upon the strength of abstract political reasoning, which we are bound to believe the people of the United States thought insufficient to induce them to limit the power of congress, because what they have said contains no such limitation.

Before I proceed further to notice some other grounds of supposed objection to this power of congress, I desire to say, that if it were not for my anxiety to insist upon what I deem a correct exposition of the constitution, if I looked only to the purposes of the argument, the source of the power of congress asserted in the opinion of the majority of the court would answer those purposes equally well. For they admit that congress has power to organize and govern the territories until they arrive at a suitable condition for admission to the Union; they admit, also, that the kind of government which shall thus exist should be regulated by the condition and wants of each territory, and that it is necessarily committed to the discretion of congress to enact such laws for that purpose as that discretion may dictate; and no limit to that discretion has been shown, or even suggested, save those positive prohibitions to legislate, which are found in the constitution.

I confess myself unable to perceive any difference whatever between my own opinion of the general extent of the power of congress and the opinion of the majority of the court, save that I consider it derivable from the express language of the constitution, while they hold it to be silently implied from the power to acquire territory. Looking at the power of congress over the territories as of the extent just described, what positive prohibition exists in the constitution, which restrained congress from enacting a law in 1820 to prohibit slavery north of thirty-six degrees thirty minutes north latitude?

The only one suggested is that clause in the fifth article of the amendments of the constitution which declares that no person shall be deprived of his life, liberty, or property, without due process of law. I will now proceed to examine the question, whether this clause is entitled to the effect thus attributed to it. It is necessary, first, to have a clear view of the nature and incidents of that particular species of property which is now in question.

Slavery, being contrary to natural right, is created only by municipal law. This is not only plain in itself, and agreed by all writers on the subject, but is inferable from the constitution, and has been explicitly declared by this court. The constitution refers to slaves as "persons held to service in one State, under the laws thereof." Nothing can more clearly describe a *status* created by municipal law. In Prigg *v*. Pennsylvania, (10 Pet. 611,) this court said: "The state of slavery is deemed to be a mere municipal regulation, founded on and limited to the range of territorial laws." In Rankin *v*. Lydia, (2 Marsh. 12, 470,) the supreme court of appeals of Kentucky said: "Slavery is sanctioned by the laws of this State, and the right to hold them under our municipal regulations is unquestionable. But we view this as a right existing by positive law of a municipal character, without foundation in the law of nature or the unwritten common law." I am not acquainted with any case or writer questioning the correctness of this doctrine. (See also 1 Burge, Col. and For. Laws, 738–741, where the authorities are collected.)

The *status* of slavery is not necessarily always attended with the same powers on the part of the master. The master is subject to the supreme power of the State, whose will controls his action towards his slave, and this control must be defined and regulated by the municipal law. In one State, as at one period of the Roman law, it may put the life of the slave into the hand of the master; others, as those of the United States, which tolerate slavery, may treat the slave as a person, when the master takes his life; while in others, the law may recognize a right of the slave to be protected from cruel treatment. In other words, the *status* of slavery embraces every condition, from that in which the slave is known to the law simply as a chattel, with no civil rights, to that in which he is recognized as a person for all purposes, save the compulsory power of directing and receiving the fruits of his labor. Which of these conditions shall attend the *status* of slavery, must depend on the municipal law which creates and upholds it.

And not only must the *status* of slavery be created and measured by municipal law, but the rights, powers, and obligations, which grow out of that *status*, must be defined, protected, and enforced, by such laws. The liability of the master for the torts and crimes of his slave, and of third persons for assaulting or injuring or harboring or kidnapping him, the forms and modes of emancipation and sale, their subjection to the debts of the master, succession by death of the master, suits for freedom, the capacity of the slave to be party to a suit, or to be a witness, with such police regulations as have existed in all civilized States where slavery has been tolerated, are among the subjects upon which municipal legislation becomes necessary when slavery is introduced.

Is it conceivable that the constitution has conferred the right on every citizen to become a resident on the territory of the United States with his slaves, and there to hold them as such, but has neither made nor provided for any municipal regulations which are essential to the existence of slavery?

Is it not more rational to conclude that they who framed and adopted the constitution were aware that persons held to service under the laws of a State are property only to the extent and under the conditions fixed by those laws; that they must cease to be available as property, when their owners voluntarily place them permanently within another jurisdiction, where no municipal laws on the subject of slavery exist; and that, being aware of these principles, and having said nothing to interfere with or displace them, or to compel congress to legislate in any particular manner on the subject, and having empowered congress to make all needful rules and regulations respecting the territory of the United States, it was their intention to leave to the discretion of congress what regulations, if any, should be made concerning slavery therein? Moreover, if the right exists, what are its limits, and what are its conditions? If citizens of the United States have the right to take their slaves to a territory, and hold them there as slaves, without regard to the laws of the territory, I suppose this right is not to be restricted to the citizens of slaveholding States. A citizen of a State which does not tolerate slavery can hardly be denied the power of doing the same thing. And what law of slavery does either take with him to the territory? If it be said to be those laws respecting slavery which existed in the particular State from which each slave last came, what an anomaly is this? Where else can we find, under the law of any civilized country, the power to introduce and permanently continue diverse systems of foreign municipal law, for holding persons in slavery? I say, not merely to introduce, but permanently to continue, these anomalies. For the offspring of the female must be governed by the foreign municipal laws to which the mother was subject; and when any slave is sold or passes by succession on the death of the owner, there must pass with him, by a species of subrogation, and as a kind of unknown *jus in re,* the foreign municipal laws which constituted, regulated, and preserved, the *status* of the slave before his exportation. Whatever theoretical importance may be now supposed to belong to the maintenance of such a right, I feel a perfect conviction that it would, if ever tried, prove to be as impracticable in fact, as it is, in my judgment, monstrous in theory.

I consider the assumption which lies at the basis of this theory to be unsound; not in its just sense, and when properly understood, but in the sense which has been attached to it. That assumption is, that the territory ceded by France was acquired for the equal benefit of all the citizens of the United States. I agree to the position. But it was acquired for their benefit in their collective, not their individual, capacities. It was acquired for their benefit, as an organized political society, subsisting as "the people of the United States," under the constitution of the United States; to be administered justly and impartially, and as nearly as possible for the equal benefit of every individual citizen, according to the best judgment and discretion of the congress; to whose power, as the legislature of the nation which acquired it, the people of the United States have committed its administration. Whatever individual claims may be founded on local circumstances, or sectional differences of condition, cannot, in my opinion, be recognized in this court, without arrogating to the judicial branch of the government powers not committed to it; and which, with all the unaffected respect I feel for it, when acting in its proper sphere. I do not think it fitted to wield.

Nor, in my judgment, will the position, that a prohibition to bring slaves into a territory deprives any one of his property without due process of law, bear examination.

It must be remembered that this restriction on the legislative power is not peculiar to the constitution of the United States; it was borrowed from *Magna Charta;* was brought to America by our ancestors, as part of their inherited liberties, and has existed in all the States, usually in the very words of the great charter. It existed in every political community in America in 1787, when the ordinance prohibiting slavery north and west of the Ohio was passed.

And if a prohibition of slavery in a territory in 1820 violated this principle of *Magna Charta,* the ordinance of 1787 also violated it; and what power had, I do not say the congress of the confederation alone, but the legislature of Virginia, of the legislature of any or all the States of the confederacy, to consent to such a violation? The people of the States had conferred no such power. I think I may at least say, if the congress did then violate *Magna Charta* by the ordinance, no one discovered that violation. Besides, if the prohibition upon all persons, citizens as well as others, to bring slaves into a Territory, and a declaration that if brought they shall be free, deprives citizens of their property without due process of law, what shall we say of the legislation of many of the slaveholding States which have enacted the same prohibition? As early as October, 1778, a law was passed in Virginia, that thereafter no slave should be imported into that commonwealth by sea or by land, and that every slave who should be imported should become free.

A citizen of Virginia purchased in Maryland a slave who belonged to another citizen of Virginia, and removed with the slave to Virginia. The slave sued for her freedom, and recovered it; as may be seen in Wilson *v.* Isabel, (5 Call's R. 425.) See also Hunter *v.* Hulsher, (1 Leigh, 172;) and a similar law has been recognized as valid in Maryland, in Stewart *v.* Oaks, (5 Har. and John. 107.) I am not aware that such laws, though they exist in many States, were ever supposed to be in conflict with the principle of *Magna Charta* incorporated into the State constitutions. It was certainly understood by the convention which framed the constitution, and has been so understood ever since, that, under the power to regulate commerce, congress could prohibit the importation of slaves; and the exercise of the power was restrained till 1808. A citizen of the United States owns slaves in Cuba, and brings them to the United States, where they are set free by the legislation of congress. Does this legislation deprive him of his property without due process of law? If so, what becomes of the laws prohibiting the slave trade? If not, how can similar regulation respecting a territory violate the fifth amendment of the constitution?

Some reliance was placed by the defendant's counsel upon the fact that the prohibition of slavery in this territory was in the words, "that slavery, & c., shall be and is hereby *forever* prohibited." But the insertion of the word *forever* can have no legal effect. Every enactment not expressly limited in its duration continues in force until repealed or abrogated by some competent power, and the use of the word "forever" can give to the law no more durable operation. The argument is, that congress cannot so legislate as to bind the future States formed out of the territory, and that in this instance it has attempted to do so. Of the political reasons which may have induced the congress to use these words, and which caused them to expect that subsequent legislatures would conform their action to the then general opinion of the country that it ought to be permanent, this court can take no cognizance.

However fit such considerations are to control the action of congress, and however reluctant a statesman may be to disturb what has been settled, every law made by congress may be repealed, and, saving private rights, and public rights gained by States, its repeal is subject to the absolute will of the same power which enacted it. If congress had enacted that the crime of murder, committed in this Indian territory, north of thirty-six degrees thirty minutes, by or on any white man, should *forever* be punishable with death, it would seem to me an insufficient objection to an indictment, found while it was a territory, that at some future day States might exist there, and so the law was invalid, because, by its terms, it was to continue in force forever. Such an objection rests upon a misapprehension of the province and power of courts respecting the constitutionality of laws enacted by the legislature.

If the constitution prescribe one rule, and the law another and different rule, it is the duty of courts to declare that the constitution, and not the law, governs the case before them for judgment. If the law include no case save those for which the constitution has furnished a different rule, or no case which the legislature has the power to govern, then the law can have no operation. If it includes cases which the legislature has power to govern, and concerning which the constitution does not prescribe a different rule, the law governs those cases, though it may, in its terms, attempt to include others, on which it cannot operate. In other words, this court cannot declare void an act of congress which constitutionally embraces some cases, though other cases, within its terms, are beyond the control of congress, or beyond the reach of that particular law. If, therefore, congress had power to make a law excluding slavery from this territory while under the exclusive power of the United States, the use of the word "forever" does not invalidate the law, so long as congress has the exclusive legislative power in the territory.

But it is further insisted that the treaty of 1803, between the United States and France, by which this territory was acquired, has so restrained the constitutional powers of congress, that it cannot, by law, prohibit the introduction of slavery into that part of this territory north and west of Missouri, and north of thirty-six degrees thirty minutes north latitude.

By a treaty with a foreign nation, the United States may rightfully stipulate that the congress will or will not exercise its legislative power in some particular manner, on some particular subject. Such promises, when made, should be voluntarily kept, with the most scrupulous good faith. But that a treaty with a foreign nation can deprive the congress of any part of the legislative power conferred by the people, so that it no longer can legislate as it was empowered by the constitution to do, I more than doubt.

The powers of the government do and must remain unimpaired. The responsibility of the government to a foreign nation, for the exercise of those powers, is quite another matter. That responsibility is to be met, and justified to the foreign nation, according to the requirements of the rules of public law; but never upon the assumption that the United States had parted with or restricted any power of acting according to its own free will, governed solely by its own appreciation of its duty.

The second section of the fourth article is, "This constitution, and the laws of the United States which shall be made in pursuance thereof, and all treaties made or which shall be made under the authority of the United States, shall be the supreme law of the land." This has made treaties part of our municipal law; but it has not assigned to them any particular degree of authority, nor declared that laws so enacted shall be irreparable. No supremacy is assigned to treaties over acts of congress. That they are not perpetual, and must be in some way repealable, all will agree.

If the president and the senate alone possess the power to repeal or modify a law found in a treaty, inasmuch as they can change or abrogate one treaty only by making another inconsistent with the first, the government of the United States could not act at all, to that effect, without the consent of some foreign government. I do not consider, I am not aware it has ever been considered, that the constitution has placed our country in this helpless condition. The action of congress in repealing the treaties with France by the act of July 7th, 1798, (1 Stat. at Large, 578,) was in conformity with these views. In the case of Taylor *et al. v.* Morton, (2 Curtis's Cir. Ct. R. 454,) I had occasion to consider this subject, and I adhere to the views there expressed.

If, therefore, it were admitted that the treaty between the United States and France did contain an express stipulation that the United States would not exclude slavery from so much of the ceded territory as is now in question, this court could not declare that an act of congress excluding it was void by force of the treaty. Whether or not a case existed sufficient to justify a refusal to execute such a stipulation, would not be a judicial, but a political and legislative question, wholly beyond the authority of this court to try and determine. It would belong to diplomacy and legislation, and not to the administration of existing laws. Such a stipulation in a treaty, to legislate or not to legislate in a particular way, has been repeatedly held in this court to address itself to the political or the legislative power, by whose action thereon this court is bound. (Foster *v.* Nicolson, 2 Peters, 314; Garcia *v.* Lee, 12 Peters, 519.)

But, in my judgment, this treaty contains no stipulation in any manner affecting the action of the United States respecting the territory in question. Before examining the language of the treaty, it is material to bear in mind that the part of the ceded territory lying north of thirty-six degrees thirty minutes, and west and north of the present State of Missouri, was then a wilderness, uninhabited save by savages, whose possessory title had not then been extinguished.

It is impossible for me to conceive on what ground France could have advanced a claim, or could have desired to advance a claim, to restrain the United States from making any rules and regulations respecting this territory, which the United States might think fit to make; and still less can I conceive of any reason which would have induced the United States to yield to such a claim. It was to be expected that France would desire to make the change of sovereignty and jurisdiction as little burdensome as possible to the then inhabitants of Louisiana, and might well exhibit even an anxious solicitude to protect their property and persons, and secure to them and their posterity their religious and political rights; and the United States, as a just government, might readily accede to all proper stipulations respecting those who were about to have their allegiance transferred. But what interest France could have in uninhabited territory, which, in the language of the treaty, was to be transferred "forever, and in full sovereignty," to the United States, or how the United States could consent to allow a foreign nation to interfere in its purely internal affairs, in which that foreign nation had no concern whatever, is difficult for me to conjecture. In my judgment, this treaty contains nothing of the kind.

The third article is supposed to have a bearing on the question. It is as follows: "The inhabitants of the ceded territory shall be incorporated in the Union of the United States, and admitted as soon as possible, according to the principles of the federal constitution, to the enjoyment of all the rights, advantages, and immunities, of citizens of the United States; and in the mean time they shall be maintained and protected in the enjoyment of their liberty, property, and the religion they profess."

There are two views of this article, each of which, I think, decisively shows that it was not intended to restrain the congress from excluding slavery from that part of the ceded territory then uninhabited. The first is, that, manifestly, its sole object was to protect individual rights of the then inhabitants of the territory. They are to be "maintained and protected in the free enjoyment of their liberty, property, and the religion they profess." But this article does not secure to them the right to go upon the public domain ceded by the treaty, either with or without their slaves. The right or power of doing this did not exist before or at the time the treaty was made. The French and Spanish governments while they held the country, as well as the United States when they acquired it, always exercised the undoubted right of excluding inhabitants from the Indian country, and of determining when and on what conditions it should be opened to settlers. And a stipulation, that the then inhabitants of Louisiana should be protected in their property, can have no reference to their use of that property, where they had no right, under the treaty, to go with it, save at the will of the United States. If one who was an inhabitant of Louisiana at the time of the treaty had afterwards taken property then owned by him, consisting of fire-arms, ammunition, and spirits, and had gone into the Indian country north of thirty-six degrees thirty minutes, to sell them to the Indians, all must agree the third article of the treaty would not have protected him from indictment under the act of congress of March 30, 1802, (2 Stat. at Large, 139,) adopted and extended to this territory by the act of March 26, 1804. (2 Stat. at Large, 283.)

Besides, whatever rights were secured were individual rights. If congress should pass any law which violated such rights of any individual, and those rights were of such a character as not to be within the lawful control of congress under the constitution, that individual could complain, and the act of congress, as to such rights of his, would be inoperative; but it would be valid and operative as to all other persons, whose individual rights did not come under the protection of the treaty. And inasmuch as it does not appear that any inhabitant of Louisiana, whose rights were secured by treaty, had been injured, it would be wholly inadmissible for this court to assume, first, that one or more such cases may have existed; and, second, that if any did exist, the entire law was void—not only as to those cases, if any, in which it could not rightfully operate, but as to all others, wholly unconnected with the treaty, in which such law could rightfully operate.

But it is quite unnecessary, in my opinion, to pursue this inquiry further, because it clearly appears from the language of the article, and it has been decided by this court, that the stipulation was temporary, and ceased to have any effect when the then inhabitants of the territory of Louisiana, in whose behalf the stipulation was made, were incorporated into the Union.

In the cases of New Orleans *v.* De Armas *et al.*, (9 Peters, 223,) the question was, whether a title to property, which existed at the date of the treaty, continued to be protected by the treaty after the State of Louisiana was admitted to the Union. The third article of the treaty was relied on. Mr. Chief Justice Marshall said: "This article obviously contemplates two objects. One, that Louisiana shall be admitted into the Union as soon as possible, on an equal footing with the other States; and the other, that, till such admission, the inhabitants of the ceded territory shall be protected in the free enjoyment of their liberty, property, and religion. Had any one of these rights been violated while these stipulations continued in force, the individual supposing himself to be injured might have brought his case into this court," under the twenty-fifth section of the judicial act. But this stipulation ceased to operate when Louisiana became a member of the Union, and its inhabitants were "admitted to the enjoyment of all the rights, advantages, and immunities, of citizens of the United States."

The cases of Chouteau *v.* Marguerita, (12 Peters, 507,) and Permoli *v.* New Orleans, (3 How. 589,) are in conformity with this view of the treaty.

To convert this temporary stipulation of the treaty, in behalf of French subjects who then inhabited a small portion of Louisiana, into a permanent restriction upon the power of congress to regulate territory then uninhabited, and to assert that it not only restrains congress from affecting the rights of property of the then inhabitants, but enabled them and all other citizens of the United States to go into any part of the ceded territory with their slaves, and hold them there, is a construction of this treaty so opposed to its natural meaning, and so far beyond its subject-matter and the evident design of the parties, that I cannot assent to it. In my opinion, this treaty has no bearing on the present question.

For these reasons, I am of opinion that so much of the several acts of congress as prohibited slavery and involuntary servitude within that part of the territory of Wisconsin lying north of thirty-six degrees thirty minutes north latitude, and west of the river Mississippi, were constitutional and valid laws.

I have expressed my opinion, and the reasons therefor, at far greater length than I could have wished, upon the different questions on which I have found it necessary to pass, to arrive at a judgment on the case at bar. These questions are numerous, and the grave importance of some of them required me to exhibit fully the grounds of my opinion. I have touched no question which, in the view I have taken, it was not absolutely necessary for me to pass upon, to ascertain whether the judgment of the circuit court should stand or be reversed. I have avoided no question on which the validity of that judgment depends. To have done either more or less, would have been inconsistent with my views of my duty.

In my opinion, the judgment of the circuit court should be reversed, and the cause remanded for a new trial.

Notes

1. Vide Gibbons's Decline and Fall of the Roman Empire. London edition of 1825, vol. 3d, chap. 44, p. 183.

2. Letter from James Madison to Robert Walsh, November 27th, 1819, on the subject of the Missouri Compromise.

3. Mr. Varnum said: "The bill provided such a government as had never been known in the United States." Mr. Eustis: "The government laid down in this bill is certainly a new thing in the United States." Mr. Lucas: "It has been remarked, that this bill establishes elementary principles never previously introduced in the government of any territory of the United States. Granting the truth of this observation," &c., &c. Mr. Macon: "My first objection to the principle contained in this section is, that it establishes a species of government unknown to the United States." Mr. Boyle: "Were the president an angel instead of a man, I would not clothe him with this power." Mr. G. W. Campbell: "On examining the section, it will appear that it really establishes a complete despotism." Mr. Sloan: "Can anything be more repugnant to the principles of just government? Can anything be more despotic?"—*Annals of Congress*, 1803–'4.

4. Mr. Jefferson wrote: "The Missouri question is the most portentous one that ever threatened our Union. In the gloomiest moments of the revolutionary war, I never had any apprehension equal to that I feel from this source."

5. *Note by Mr. Justice Curtis.* This statement that *some* territory did actually pass by this cession, is taken from the opinion of the court, delivered by Mr. Justice Wayne, in the case of Howard v. Ingersoll, reported in 13 How. 405. It is an obscure matter, and, on some examination of it, I have been led to doubt whether any territory actually passed by this cession. But as the fact is not important to the argument, I have not thought it necessary further to investigate it.

6. It was published in a newspaper at Philadelphia, in May, and a copy of it was sent by R. H. Lee to Gen. Washington, on the 15th of July. (See p. 261, Cor. of Am. Rev. vol. 4, and Writings of Washington, vol. 9, p. 174.)

STEPHEN V. R. ABLEMAN, PLAINTIFF IN ERROR, V. SHERMAN M. BOOTH; AND THE UNITED STATES, PLAINTIFF IN ERROR, V. SHERMAN M. BOOTH

Supreme Court of the United States
March 7, 1859
21 Howard (62 U.S.) 506 (1859); and, 22 Howard (63 U.S.) 130 (1859)

This case arose from an 1854 fugitive slave recapture in Wisconsin. A slave owner, Benjamin S. Garland, located his runaway slave, Joshua Glover, working at a mill outside Racine. Glover applied to the United States commissioner in Milwaukee for a writ of rendition as authorized under the Fugitive Slave Act of 1850. With the writ granted, Garland and a deputy marshal went to Glover's cabin, forcibly subdued him, and took him to a Milwaukee jail. Outraged at this action, a mob formed, broke into the jail, removed Glover, and allowed him to escape. At the same time, the local editor of an abolitionist newspaper, Sherman M. Booth, had obtained a *state* writ of habeas corpus (a judicial inquiry into why a person was being held, and known as "the Great Writ" because of its defense of individual liberty) ordering the federal marshal, Stephen V. R. Ableman, to turn over the prisoner. Ableman refused the writ and by doing so set up this federalism problem: could a state court compel an action from a federal court or federal officer? After a long and protracted series of legal appeals by both parties, during which federal and state authorities could not cooperate on this flash-point issue on the return of fugitive slaves and the extent of federal power over the state, the litigation reached the United States Supreme Court. For a unanimous court, Chief Justice Roger B. Taney issued a decision with broad nationalist language denying that a state could obstruct a valid national statute such as the Fugitive Slave Act of 1850. Wisconsin's Supreme Court still split on whether they could issue a habeas corpus in the case even after Taney's decision arguing the state's right to control its own affairs. Taney's nationalism in this case is balanced by the localism of Wisconsin's reaction; ironically, these positions constitute a reversal of the political and legal positions that Taney and a northern state might be expected to take in this historical context.

1. The act of congress of September 18, 1850, usually called the fugitive slave law, is constitutional and valid.
2. The exclusive jurisdiction for offenses against the law in the State of Wisconsin is vested in the district court of the United States for that district, and from its judgment no appeal or writ of error lies to any other court, State or federal.
3. The commissioner of the United States has authority to examine and commit, for the action of the district court and its grand jury, a prisoner charged with an offense against that act; and no State court has jurisdiction or authority to release a prisoner so committed.
4. State courts have no power to review or reverse the judgment of the courts of the United States; and an attempt to do this, by virtue of a writ of *habeas corpus*, is without jurisdiction, and a violation of the law and constitution of the United States.
5. From any such judgment or order of the supreme court of the State a writ of error lies to this court under the 25th section of the judiciary act.
6. When a State court is informed that a person is unlawfully imprisoned, it is its duty, by reason of its general power to release persons so situated, to issue the writ; and when it is made known to the court that the person is held by virtue of order of a court of the United States, the writ should be discharged.
7. So, when the officer who holds the prisoner under such authority is served with the writ, he should make return of the cause of the commitment and his authority for holding him, but should not deliver the prisoner to the court or part with custody.

THESE two cases were brought by writ of error to the supreme court of Wisconsin. The facts are stated in the opinion.

Mr. Black, attorney general, appeared for plaintiff.

Mr. Booth furnished pamphlet and arguments, and the opinions of the supreme court of Wisconsin were also produced.

Mr. Chief Justice TANEY delivered the opinion of the court.

The plaintiff in error in the first of these cases is the marshal of the United States for the district of Wisconsin, and the two cases have arisen out of the same transaction, and depend, to some extent, upon the same principles. On that account, they have been argued and considered together; and the following are the facts as they appear in the transcripts before us:

Sherman M. Booth was charged before Winfield Smith, a commissioner duly appointed by the district court of the United States for the district of Wisconsin, with having, on the 11th day of March, 1854, aided and abetted, at Milwaukee, in the said district, the escape of a fugitive slave from the deputy marshal, who had him in custody under a warrant issued by the district judge of the United States for that district, under the act of congress of September 18, 1850.

Upon the examination before the commissioner, he was satisfied that an offence had been committed as charged, and that there was probable cause to believe that Booth had been guilty of it; and thereupon held him to bail to appear and answer before the district court of the United States for the district of Wisconsin, on the first Monday in July then next ensuing. But on the 26th of May his bail or surety in the recognizance delivered him to the marshal, in the presence of the commissioner, and requested the commissioner to recommit Booth to the custody of the marshal; and he having failed to recognize again for his appearance before the district court, the commissioner committed him to the custody of the marshal, to be delivered to the keeper of the jail until he should be discharged by due course of law.

Booth made application on the next day, the 27th of May, to A. D. Smith, one of the justices of the supreme court of the State of Wisconsin, for a writ of *habeas corpus*, stating that he was restrained of his liberty by Stephen V. R. Ableman, marshal of the United States for that district, under the warrant of commitment hereinbefore mentioned; and alleging that his imprisonment was illegal, because the act of congress of September 18, 1850, was unconstitutional and void; and also that the warrant was defective, and did not describe the offense created by that act, even if the act were valid.

Upon this application, the justice, on the same day, issued the writ of *habeas corpus*, directed to the marshal, requiring him forthwith to have the body of Booth before him, (the said justice,) together with the time and cause of his imprisonment. The marshal thereupon, on the day above mentioned, produced Booth, and made his return, stating that he was received into his custody as marshal on the day before, and held in custody by virtue of the warrant of the commissioner above mentioned, a copy of which he annexed to and returned with the writ.

To this return Booth demurred, as not sufficient in law to justify his detention. And upon the hearing the justice decided that his detention was illegal, and ordered the marshal to discharge him and set him at liberty, which was accordingly done.

Afterwards, on the 9th of June, in the same year, the marshal applied to the supreme court of the State for a *certiorari*, setting forth in his application the proceedings hereinbefore mentioned, and charging that the release of Booth by the justice was erroneous and unlawful, and praying that his proceedings might be brought before the supreme court of the State for revision.

The *certiorari* was allowed on the same day; and the writ was accordingly issued on the 12th of the same month, and returnable on the third Tuesday of the month; and on the 20th the return was made by the justice, stating the proceedings, as hereinbefore mentioned.

The case was argued before the supreme court of the State, and on the 19th of July it pronounced its judgment, affirming the decision of the associate justice discharging Booth from imprisonment, with costs against Ableman, the marshal.

Afterwards, on the 26th of October, the marshal sued out a writ of error, returnable to this court on the first Monday of December, 1854, in order to bring the judgment here for revision; and the defendant in error was regularly cited to appear on that day; and the record and proceedings were certified to this court by the clerk of the State court in the usual form, in obedience to the writ of error. And on the 4th of December, Booth, the defendant in error, filed a memorandum in writing in this court, stating that he had been cited to appear here in this case, and that he submitted it to the judgment of this court on the reasoning in the argument and opinions in the printed pamphlets therewith sent.

After the judgment was entered in the supreme court of Wisconsin, and before the writ of error was sued out, the State court entered on its record, that, in the final judgment it had rendered, the validity of the act of congress of September 18, 1850, and of February 12, 1793, and the authority of the marshal to hold the defendant in his custody, under the process mentioned in his return to the writ of *habeas corpus,* were respectively drawn in question, and the decision of the court in the final judgment was against their validity, respectively.

This certificate was not necessary to give this court jurisdiction, because the proceedings upon their face show that these questions arose, and how they were decided; but it shows that at that time the supreme court of Wisconsin did not question their obligation to obey the writ of error, nor the authority of this court to re-examine their judgment in the cases specified. And the certificate is given for the purpose of placing distinctly on the record the points that were raised and decided in that court, in order that this court might have no difficulty in exercising its appellate power, and pronouncing its judgment upon all of them.

We come now to the second case. At the January term of the district court of the United States for the district of Wisconsin, after Booth had been set at liberty, and after the transcript of the proceedings in the case above mentioned had been returned to and filed in this court, the grand jury found a bill of indictment against Booth for the offence with which he was charged before the commissioner, and from which the State court had discharged him. The indictment was found on the 4th of January, 1855. On the 9th a motion was made, by counsel on behalf of the accused, to quash the indictment, which was overruled by the court; and he thereupon pleaded not guilty, upon which issue was joined. On the 10th a jury was called and appeared in court, when he challenged the array; but the challenge was overruled and the jury empanelled. The trial, it appears, continued from day to day, until the 13th, when the jury found him guilty in the manner and form in which he stood indicted in the fourth and fifth counts. On the 16th he moved for a new trial and in arrest of judgment, which motions were argued on the 20th, and on the 23d the court overruled the motions, and sentenced the prisoner to be imprisoned for one month, and to pay a fine of $1,000 and the costs of prosecution; and that he remain in custody until the sentence was complied with.

We have stated more particularly these proceedings, from a sense of justice to the district court, as they show that every opportunity of making his defense was afforded him, and that his case was fully heard and considered.

On the 26th of January, three days after the sentence was passed, the prisoner by his counsel filed his petition in the supreme court of the State, and with his petition filed a copy of the proceedings in the district court, and also affidavits from the foreman and one other member of the jury who tried him, stating that their verdict was, guilty on the fourth and fifth counts, and not guilty on the other three; and stated in his petition that his imprisonment was illegal, because the fugitive slave law was unconstitutional; that the district court had no jurisdiction to try or punish him for the matter charged against him, and that the proceedings and sentence of that court were absolute nullities in law. Various other objections to the proceedings are alleged, which are unimportant in the questions now before the court, and need not, therefore, be particularly stated. On the next day, the 27th, the court directed two writs of *habeas corpus* to be issued—one to the marshal, and one to the sheriff of Milwaukee, to whose actual keeping the prisoner was committed by the marshal, by order of the district court. The *habeas corpus* directed each of them to produce the body of the prisoner, and make known the cause of his imprisonment, immediately after the receipt of the writ.

On the 30th of January the marshal made his return, not acknowledging the jurisdiction, but stating the sentence of the district court as his authority; that the prisoner was delivered to, and was then in the actual keeping of the sheriff of Milwaukee county, by order of the court, and he therefore had no control of the body of the prisoner; and if the sheriff had not received him, he should have so reported to the district court, and should have conveyed him to some other place or prison, as the court should command.

On the same day the sheriff produced the body of Booth before the State court, and returned that he had been committed to his custody by the marshal, by virtue of a transcript, a true copy of which was annexed to his return, and which was the only process or authority by which he detained him.

This transcript was a full copy of the proceedings and sentence in the district court of the United States, as hereinbefore stated. To this return the accused, by his counsel, filed a general demurrer.

The court ordered the hearing to be postponed until the 2d of February, and notice to be given to the district attorney of the United States. It was accordingly heard on that day, and on the next, (February 3d,) the court decided that the imprisonment was illegal, and ordered and adjudged that Booth be, and he was by that judgment, forever discharged from that imprisonment and restraint, and he was accordingly set at liberty.

On the 21st of April next following, the attorney general of the United States presented a petition to the chief justice of the supreme court, stating briefly the facts in the case, and at the same time presenting an exemplification of the proceedings hereinbefore stated, duly certified by the clerk of the State court, and averring in his petition that the State court had no jurisdiction in the case, and praying that a writ of error might issue to bring its judgment before this court to correct the error. The writ of error was allowed and issued, and, according to the rules and practice of the court, was returnable on the first Monday of December, 1855, and a citation for the defendant in error to appear on that day was issued by the chief justice at the same time.

No return having been made to this writ, the attorney general, on the 1st of February, 1856, filed affidavits, showing that the writ of error had been duly served on the clerk of the supreme court of Wisconsin, at his office, on the 30th of May, 1855, and the citation served on the defendant in error on the 28th of June, in the same year. And also the affidavit of the district attorney of the United States for the district of Wisconsin, setting forth that when he served the writ of error upon the clerk, as above mentioned, he was informed by the clerk, and has also been informed by one of the justices of the supreme court, which released Booth, *"that the court had directed the clerk to make no return to the writ of error, and to enter no order upon the journals or records of the court concerning the same."* And, upon these proofs, the attorney general moved the court for an order upon the clerk to make return to the writ of error, on or before the first day of the next ensuing term of this court. The rule was accordingly laid, and on the 22d of July, 1856, the attorney general filed with the clerk of this court the affidavit of the marshal of the district of Wisconsin, that he had served the rule on the clerk on the 7th of the month above mentioned; and no return having been made, the attorney general, on the 27th of February, 1857, moved for leave to file the certified copy of the record of the supreme court of Wisconsin, which he had produced with his application for the writ of error, and to docket the case in this court, in conformity with a motion to that effect made at the last term. And the court thereupon, on the 6th of March, 1857, ordered the copy of the record filed by the attorney general to be received and entered on the docket of this court, to have the same effect and legal operation as if returned by the clerk with the writ of error, and that the case stand for argument at the next ensuing term, without further notice to either party.

The case was accordingly docketed, but was not reached for argument in the regular order and practice of the court until the present term.

This detailed statement of the proceedings in the different courts has appeared to be necessary in order to form a just estimate of the action of the different tribunals in which it has been heard, and to account for the delay in the final decision of a case, which, from its character, would seem to have demanded prompt action. The first case, indeed, was reached for trial two terms ago. But as the two cases are different portions of the same prosecution for the same offence, they unavoidably, to some extent, involve the same principles of law, and it would hardly have been proper to hear and decide the first before the other was ready for hearing and decision. They have accordingly been argued together, by the attorney general of the United States, at the present term. No counsel has in either case appeared for the defendant in error. But we have the pamphlet arguments filed and referred to by Booth in the first case, as hereinbefore mentioned, also the opinions and arguments of the supreme court of Wisconsin, and of the judges who compose it, in full, and are enabled, therefore, to see the grounds on which they rely to support their decisions.

It will be seen, from the foregoing statement of facts, that a judge of the supreme court of the State of Wisconsin in the first of these cases, claimed and exercised the right to supervise and annul the proceedings of a commissioner of the United States, and to discharge a prisoner, who had been committed by the commissioner for an offence against the laws of this Government, and that this exercise of power by the judge was afterwards sanctioned and affirmed by the supreme court of the State.

In the second case, the State court has gone a step further, and claimed and exercised jurisdiction over the proceedings and judgment of a district court of the United States, and upon a summary and collateral proceeding, by *habeas corpus,* has set aside and annulled its judgment, and discharged a prisoner who had been tried and found guilty of an offence against the laws of the United States, and sentenced to imprisonment by the district court.

And it further appears that the State court have not only claimed and exercised this jurisdiction, but have also determined that their decision is final and conclusive upon all the courts of the United States, and ordered their clerk to disregard and refuse obedience to the writ of error issued by this court, pursuant to the act of congress of 1789, to bring here for examination and revision the judgment of the State court.

These propositions are new in the jurisprudence of the United States, as well as of the States; and the supremacy of the State courts over the courts of the United States, in cases arising under the constitution and laws of the United States, is now for the first time asserted and acted upon in the supreme court of a State.

The supremacy is not, indeed, set forth distinctly and broadly, in so many words, in the printed opinions of the judges. It is intermixed with elaborate discussions of different provisions in the fugitive slave law, and of the privileges and power of the writ of *habeas corpus.* But the paramount power of the State court lies at the foundation of these decisions; for their commentaries upon the provisions of that law, and upon the privileges and power of the writ of *habeas corpus,* were out of place, and their judicial action upon them without authority of law, unless they had the power to revise and control the proceedings in the criminal case of which they were speaking; and their judgments, releasing the prisoner, and disregarding the writ of error from this court, can rest upon no other foundation.

If the judicial power exercised in this instance has been reserved to the States, no offence against the laws of the United States can be punished by their own courts, without the permission and according to the judgment of the courts of the State in which the party happens to be imprisoned; for, if the supreme court of Wisconsin possessed the power it has exercised in relation to offences against the act of congress in question, it necessarily follows that they must have the same judicial authority in relation to any other law of the United States; and, consequently, their supervising and controlling power would embrace the whole criminal code of the United States, and extend to offences against our revenue laws, or any other law intended to guard the different departments of the general government from fraud or violence. And it would embrace all crimes, from the highest to the lowest; including felonies, which are punished with death, as well as misdemeanors, which are punished by imprisonment. And, moreover, if the power is possessed by the supreme court of the State of Wisconsin, it must belong equally to every other State in the Union, when the prisoner is within its territorial limits; and it is very certain that the State courts would not always agree in opinion; and it would often happen, that an act which was admitted to be an offence, and justly punished, in one State, would be regarded as innocent, and indeed as praiseworthy, in another.

It would seem to be hardly necessary to do more than state the result to which these decisions of the State courts must inevitably lead. It is, of itself, a sufficient and conclusive answer; for no one will suppose that a government which has now lasted nearly seventy years, enforcing its laws by its own tribunals, and preserving the union of the States, could have lasted a single year, or fulfilled the high trusts committed to it, if offences against its laws could not have been punished without the consent of the State in which the culprit was found.

The judges of the supreme court of Wisconsin do not distinctly state from what source they suppose they have derived this judicial power. There can be no such thing as judicial authority, unless it is conferred by a government or sovereignty; and if the judges and courts of Wisconsin possess the jurisdiction they claim, they must derive it either from the United States or the State. It certainly has not been conferred on them by the United States; and it is equally clear it was not in the power of the State to confer it, even if it had attempted to do so; for no State can authorize one of its judges or courts to exercise judicial power, by *habeas corpus* or otherwise, within the jurisdiction of another and independent government. And although the State of Wisconsin is sovereign within its territorial limits to a certain extent, yet that sovereignty is limited and restricted by the constitution of the United States. And the powers of the general government, and of the State, although both exist and are exercised within the same territorial limits, are yet separate and distinct sovereignties, acting separately and independently of each other, within their respective spheres. And the sphere of action appropriated to the United States is as far beyond the reach of the judicial process issued by a State judge or a State court, as if the line of division was traced by landmarks and monuments visible to the eye. And the State of Wisconsin had no more power to authorize these proceedings of its judges and courts, than it would have had if the prisoner had been confined in Michigan, or in any other State of the Union, for an offence against the laws of the State in which he was imprisoned.

It is, however, due to the State to say, that we do not find this claim of paramount jurisdiction in the State courts over the courts of the United States asserted or countenanced by the constitution or laws of the State. We find it only in the decisions of the judges of the supreme court. Indeed, at the very time these decisions were made, there was a statute of the State which declares that a person brought up on a *habeas corpus* shall be remanded, if it appears that he is confined:

1st. By virtue of process, by any court or judge of the United States, in a case where such court or judge has exclusive jurisdiction; or,

2d. By virtue of the final judgment or decree of any competent court of civil or criminal jurisdiction. (Revised Statutes of the State of Wisconsin, 1849, ch. 124, page 629.)

Even, therefore, if these cases depended upon the laws of Wisconsin, it would be difficult to find in these provisions such a grant of judicial power as the supreme court claims to have derived from the State.

But, as we have already said, questions of this kind must always depend upon the constitution and laws of the United States, and not of a State. The constitution was not formed merely to guard the States against danger from foreign nations, but mainly to secure union and harmony at home; for if this object could be attained, there would be but little danger from abroad; and to accomplish this purpose, it was felt by the statesmen who framed the constitution, and by the people who adopted it, that it was necessary that many of the rights of sovereignty which the States then possessed should be ceded to the general government; and that, in the sphere of action assigned to it, it should be supreme, and strong enough to execute its own laws by its own tribunals, without interruption from a State or from State authorities. And it was evident that anything short of this would be inadequate to the main objects for which the government was established; and that local interests, local passions or prejudices, incited and fostered by individuals for sinister purposes, would lead to acts of aggression and injustice by one State upon the rights of another, which would ultimately terminate in violence and force, unless there was a common arbiter between them, armed with power enough to protect and guard the rights of all, by appropriate laws, to be carried into execution peacefully by its judicial tribunals.

The language of the constitution, by which this power is granted, is too plain to admit of doubt or to need comment. It declares that "this constitution, and the laws of the United States which shall be passed in pursuance thereof, and all treaties made, or which shall be made, under the authority of the United States, shall be the supreme law of the land, and the judges in every State shall be bound thereby, anything in the constitution or laws of any State to the contrary notwithstanding."

But the supremacy thus conferred on this government could not peacefully be maintained, unless it was clothed with judicial power, equally paramount in authority to carry it into execution; for if left to the courts of justice of the several States, conflicting decisions would unavoidably take place, and the local tribunals could hardly be expected to be always free from the local influences of which we have spoken. And the constitution and laws and treaties of the United States, and the powers granted to the federal government, would soon receive different interpretations in different States, and the government of the United States would soon become one thing in one State and another thing in another. It was essential, therefore, to its very existence as a government, that it should have the power of establishing courts of justice, altogether independent of State power, to carry into effect its own laws; and that a tribunal should be established in which all cases which might arise under the constitution and laws and treaties of the United States, whether in a State court or a court of the United States, should be finally and conclusively decided. Without such a tribunal, it is obvious that there would be no uniformity of judicial decision; and that the supremacy, (which is but another name for independence,) so carefully provided in the clause of the constitution above referred to, could not possibly be maintained peacefully, unless it was associated with this paramount judicial authority.

Accordingly, it was conferred on the general government, in clear, precise, and comprehensive terms. It is declared that its judicial power shall (among other subjects enumerated) extend to all cases in law and equity arising under the constitution and laws of the United States, and that in such cases, as well as the others there enumerated, this court shall have appellate jurisdiction both as to law and fact, with such exceptions and under such regulations as congress shall make. The appellate power, it will be observed, is conferred on this court in all cases or suits in which such a question shall arise. It is not confined to suits in the inferior courts of the United States, but extends to all cases where such a question arises, whether it be in a judicial tribunal of a State or of the United States. And it is manifest that this ultimate appellate power in a tribunal created by the constitution itself was deemed essential to secure the independence and supremacy of the general government in the sphere of action assigned to it; to make the constitution and laws of the United States uniform, and the same in every State; and to guard against evils which would inevitably arise from conflicting opinions between the courts of a State and of the United States, if there was no common arbiter authorized to decide between them.

The importance which the framers of the constitution attached to such a tribunal, for the purpose of preserving internal tranquility, is strikingly manifested by the clause which gives this court jurisdiction over the sovereign States which compose this Union, when a controversy arises between them. Instead of reserving the right to seek redress for injustice from another State by their sovereign powers, they have bound themselves to submit to the decision of this court, and to abide by its judgment. And it is not out of place to say, here, that experience has demonstrated that this power was not unwisely surrendered by the States; for in the time that has already elapsed since this government came into existence, several irritating and angry controversies have taken place between adjoining States, in relation to their respective boundaries, and which have sometimes threatened to end in force and violence, but for the power vested in this court to hear them and decide between them.

The same purposes are clearly indicated by the different language employed when conferring supremacy upon the laws of the United States, and jurisdiction upon its courts. In the first case, it provides that "this constitution, and the laws of the United States *which shall be made in pursuance thereof,* shall be the supreme law of the land, and obligatory upon the judges in every State." The words in italics show the precision and foresight which marks every clause in the instrument. The sovereignty to be created was to be limited in its powers of legislation, and if it passed a law not authorized by its enumerated powers, it was not to be regarded as the supreme law of the land, nor were the State judges bound to carry it into execution. And as the courts of a State, and the courts of the United States, might, and indeed certainly would, often differ as to the extent of the powers conferred by the general government, it was manifest that serious controversies would arise between the authorities of the United States and of the States, which must be settled by force of arms, unless some tribunal was created to decide between them finally and with out appeal.

The constitution has accordingly provided, as far as human foresight could provide, against this danger. And in conferring judicial power upon the federal government, it declares that the jurisdiction of its courts shall extend to all cases arising under "this constitution" and the laws of the United States—leaving out the words of restriction contained in the grant of legislative power which we have above noticed. The judicial power covers every legislative act of congress, whether it be made within the limits of its delegated powers, or be an assumption of power beyond the grants in the constitution.

This judicial power was justly regarded as indispensable, not merely to maintain the supremacy of the laws of the United States, but also to guard the States from any encroachment upon their reserved rights by the general government. And as the constitution is the fundamental and supreme law, if it appears that an act of congress is not pursuant to and within the limits of the power assigned to the federal government, it is the duty of the courts of the United States to declare it unconstitutional and void. The grant of judicial power is not confined to the administration of laws passed in pursuance to the provisions of the constitution, nor confined to the interpretation of such laws; but, by the very terms of the grant, the constitution is under their view when any act of congress is brought before them, and it is their duty to declare the law void, and refuse to execute it, if it is not pursuant to the legislative powers conferred upon congress. And as the final appellate power in all such questions is given to this court, controversies as to the respective powers of the United States and the States, instead of being determined by military and physical force, are heard, investigated, and finally settled, with the calmness and deliberation of judicial inquiry. And no one can fail to see, that if such an arbiter had not been provided, in our complicated system of government, internal tranquility could not have been preserved; and if such controversies were left to arbitrament of physical force, our government, State and national, would soon cease to be governments of laws, and revolutions by force of arms would take the place of courts of justice and judicial decisions.

In organizing such a tribunal, it is evident that every precaution was taken, which human wisdom could devise, to fit it for the high duty with which it was intrusted. It was not left to congress to create it by law; for the States could hardly be expected to confide in the impartiality of a tribunal created exclusively by the general government, without any participation on their part. And as the performance of its duty would sometimes come in conflict with individual ambition or interests, and powerful political combinations, an act of congress establishing such a tribunal might be repealed in order to establish another more subservient to the predominant political influences or excited passions of the day. This tribunal, therefore, was erected, and the powers of which we have spoken conferred upon it, not by the federal government, but by the people of the States, who formed and adopted that government, and conferred upon it all the powers, legislative, executive, and judicial, which it now possesses. And in order to secure its independence, and enable it faithfully and firmly to perform its duty, it engrafted it upon the constitution itself, and declared that this court should have appellate power in all cases arising under the constitution and laws of the United States. So long, therefore, as this constitution shall endure, this tribunal must exist with it, deciding in the peaceful forms of judicial proceeding the angry and irritating controversies between sovereignties, which in other countries have been determined by the arbitrament of force.

These principles of constitutional law are confirmed and illustrated by the clause which confers legislative power upon congress. That power is specifically given in article 1, section 8, paragraph 18, in the following words;

> To make all laws which shall be necessary and proper to carry into execution the foregoing powers, and all other powers vested by this constitution in the government of the United States, or in any department or officer thereof.

Under this clause of the constitution, it became the duty of congress to pass such laws as were necessary and proper to carry into execution the powers vested in the judicial department. And in the performance of this duty, the first congress, at its first session, passed the act of 1789, ch. 20, entitled *"An act to establish the judicial courts of the United States."* It will be remembered that many of the members of the convention were also members of this congress, and it cannot be supposed that they did not understand the meaning and intention of the great instrument which they had so anxiously and deliberately considered, clause by clause, and assisted to frame. And the law they passed to carry into execution the powers vested in the judicial department of the government proves, past doubt, that their interpretation of the appellate powers conferred on this court was the same with that which we have now given; for by the 25th section of the act of 1789, congress authorized writs of error to be issued from this court to a State court, whenever a right had been claimed under the constitution or laws of the United States, and the decision of the State court was against it. And to make this appellate power effectual, and altogether independent of the action of State tribunals, this act further provides, that upon writs of error to a State court, instead of remanding the cause for a final decision in the State court, this court may at their discretion, if the cause shall have been once remanded before, proceed to a final decision of the same, and award execution.

These provisions in the act of 1789 tell us, in language not to be mistaken, the great importance which the patriots and statement of the first congress attached to this appellate power, and the foresight and care with which they guarded its free and independent exercise against interference or obstruction by States or State tribunals.

In the case before the supreme court of Wisconsin, a right was claimed under the constitution and laws of the United States, and the decision was against the right claimed; and it refuses obedience to the writ of error, and regards its own judgment as final. It has not only reversed and annulled the judgment of the district court of the United States, but it has reversed and annulled the provisions of the constitution itself, and the act of congress of 1789, and made the superior and appellate tribunal the inferior and subordinate one.

We do not question the authority of State court, or judge, who is authorized by the laws of the State to issue the writ of *habeas corpus,* to issue it in any case where the party is imprisoned within its territorial limits, provided it does not appear, when the application is made, that the person imprisoned is in custody under the authority of the United States. The court or judge has a right to inquire, in this mode of proceeding, for what cause and by what authority the prisoner is confined within the territorial limits of the State sovereignty. And it is the duty of the marshal, or other person having the custody of the prisoner, to make known to the judge or court, by a proper return, the authority by which he holds him in custody. This right to inquire by process of *habeas corpus,* and the duty of the officer to make a return, a grows, necessarily, out of the complex character of our government, and the existence of two distinct and separate sovereignties within the same territorial space, each of them restricted in its powers, and each within its sphere of action, prescribed by the constitution of the United States, independent of the other. But, after the return is made, and the State judge or court judicially apprized that the party is in custody under the authority of the United States, they can proceed no further. They then know that the prisoner is within the dominion and jurisdiction of another government, and that neither the writ of *habeas corpus,* nor any other process issued under State authority, can pass over the line of division between the two sovereignties. He is then within the dominion and exclusive jurisdiction of the United States. If he has committed an offence against their laws, their tribunals alone can punish him. If he is wrongfully imprisoned, their judicial tribunals can release him and afford him redress. And although, as we have said, it is the duty of the marshal, or other person holding him, to make known, by a proper return, the authority under which he detains him, it is at the same time imperatively his duty to obey the process of the United States, to hold the prisoner in custody under it, and to refuse obedience to the mandate or process of any other government. And consequently it is his duty not to take the prisoner, nor suffer him to be taken, before a State judge or court upon a *habeas corpus* issued under State authority. No State judge or court, after they are judicially informed that the party is imprisoned under the authority of the United States, has any right to interfere with him, or to require him to be brought before them. And if the authority of a State, in the form of judicial process or otherwise, should attempt to control the marshal or other authorized officer or agent of the United States, in any respect, in the custody of his prisoner, it would be his duty to resist it, and to call to his aid any force that might be necessary to maintain the authority of law against illegal interference. No judicial process, whatever form it may assume, can have any lawful authority outside of the limits of the jurisdiction of the court or judge by whom it is issued; and an attempt to enforce it beyond these boundaries is nothing less than lawless violence.

Nor is there anything in this supremacy of the general government, or the jurisdiction of its judicial tribunals, to awaken the jealousy or offend the natural and just pride of State sovereignty. Neither this government, nor the powers of which we are speaking, were forced upon the States. The constitution of the United States, with all the powers conferred by it on the general government, and surrendered by the States, was the voluntary act of the people of the several States, deliberately done, for their own protection and safety against injustice from one another. And their anxiety to preserve it in full force, in all its powers, and to guard against resistance to or evasion of its authority, on the part of a State, is proved by the clause which requires that the members of the State legislatures, and all executive and judicial officers of the several States, (as well as those of the general government,) shall be bound, by oath or affirmation, to support this constitution. This is the last and closing clause of the constitution, and inserted when the whole frame of government, with the powers hereinbefore specified, had been adopted by the convention; and it was in that form, and with these powers, that the constitution was submitted to the people of the several States, for their consideration and decision.

Now, it certainly can be no humiliation to the citizen of a republic to yield a ready obedience to the laws as administered by the constituted authorities. On the contrary, it is among his first and highest duties as a citizen, because free government cannot exist without it. Nor can it be inconsistent with the dignity of a sovereign State to observe faithfully, and in the spirit of sincerity and truth, the compact into which it voluntarily entered when it became a State of this Union. On the contrary, the highest honor of sovereignty is untarnished faith. And certainly no faith could be more deliberately and solemnly pledged than that which every State has plighted [pledged] to the other States to support the constitution as it is, in all its provisions, until they shall be altered in the manner which the constitution itself prescribes. In the emphatic language of the pledge required, it is *to support this constitution.* And no power is more clearly conferred by the constitution and laws of the United States, than the power of this court to decide, ultimately and finally, all cases arising under such constitution and laws; and for that purpose to bring here for revision, by writ of error, the judgment of a State court, where such questions have arisen, and the right claimed under them denied by the highest judicial tribunal in the State.

We are sensible that we have extended the examination of these decisions beyond the limits required by any intrinsic difficulty in the questions. But the decisions in question were made by the supreme judicial tribunal of the State; and when a court so elevated in its position has pronounced a judgment which, if it could be maintained, would subvert the very foundations of this government, it seemed to be the duty of this court, when exercising its appellate power, to show plainly the grave errors into which the State court has fallen, and the consequences to which they would inevitably lead. But it can hardly be necessary to point out the errors which followed their mistaken view of the jurisdiction they might lawfully exercise; because, if there was any defect of power in the commissioner, or in his mode of proceeding, it was for the tribunals of the United States to revise and correct it, and not for a State court. And as regards the decision of the district court, it had exclusive and final jurisdiction by the laws of the United States; and neither the regularity of its proceedings nor the validity of its sentence could be called in question in any other court, either of a State or the United States, by *habeas corpus* or any other process.

But although we think it unnecessary to discuss these questions, yet, as they have been decided by the State court, and are before us on the record, and we are not willing to be misunderstood, it is proper to say that, in the judgment of this court, the act of congress commonly called the fugitive slave law is, in all of its provisions, fully authorized by the constitution of the United States; that the commissioner had lawful authority to issue the warrant and commit the party, and that his proceedings were regular and conformable to law. We have already stated the opinion and judgment of the court as to the exclusive jurisdiction of the district court, and the appellate powers which this court is authorized and required to exercise. And if any argument was needed to show the wisdom and necessity of this appellate power, the cases before us sufficiently prove it, and at the same time emphatically call for its exercise.

The judgment of the supreme court of Wisconsin must therefore be reversed in each of the cases now before the court.

GRAND JURY INDICTMENT OF JOHN BROWN

October 26, 1859
Jefferson County, Virginia
[Robert M. De Witt], *The Life, Trial, and Execution of Capt. John Brown, known as "Old Brown of Ossawatomie," with a full account of the attempted insurrection at Harper's Ferry. Compiled from official and authentic sources. Including Cooke's confession, and all of the incidents of the execution* (New York: Robert M. De Witt, Publisher, [1859]), 59–61.

On October 16, 1859, John Brown and his followers (sixteen whites including John Brown, three free blacks, one freed slave, and one fugitive slave) began their raid on the United States Arsenal at Harper's Ferry, Virginia (now West Virginia). They succeeded in capturing the arsenal but failed in their efforts to spark a general slave rebellion in the Upper South and, as they had hoped, throughout the South. Instead, the local population resisted Brown's efforts, and the area's slave population failed to rise up and support his actions. The raid's failure can be blamed on Brown and his plan, which proved so poorly developed that he had not even tried to inform the local slave population of his intentions. Ironically, the first person killed in Brown's raid was Haywood Sheppard, the baggage master of a train stopped by the raiders and a free black. After a day's stand-off, on the morning of October 18, in a three- to four-minute operation, and after the rejection of an offer to surrender immediately, the Virginia state militia and a detachment of United States Marines stormed the arsenal, subdued the remaining raiders, and captured the injured John Brown. Ten of Brown's raiders had been killed in the retaking of the arsenal, while the raiders killed three civilians and one of the Marines and wounded nine others.

On October 26, the local grand jury handed down the following seldom-seen indictment of John Brown and others, charging them with murder, conspiracy, and treason against the Commonwealth of Virginia. Their trial started the next day and lasted until

November 2, when the jury found Brown and his associates guilty of all charges. On December 2, 1859, at 11:15 A.M., John Brown hanged; the coroner declared him dead at 11:50, and he is buried on his farm at North Elba, New York. In life and death, Brown proved a polarizing person and a symbol of abolitionism. This indictment is interesting for the legalese of the era and also for its allegations of the crimes committed by Brown.

Judicial Circuit of Virginia, Jefferson County, to wit.—The Jurors of the Commonwealth of Virginia, in and for the body of the County of Jefferson, duly impaneled, and attending upon the Circuit Court of said county, upon their oaths do present that John Brown, Aaron C. Stephen, alias Aaron D. Stephens, and Edwin Coppie, white men, and Shields Green and John Copland, free negroes, together with divers other evil-minded and traitorous persons to the Jurors unknown, not having the fear of God before their eyes, but being moved and seduced by the false and malignant counsel of other evil and traitorous persons and the instigations of the devil, did, severally, on the sixteenth, seventeenth, and eighteenth days of the month of October, in the year of our Lord eighteen hundred and fifty-nine, and on divers other days before and after that time, within the Commonwealth of Virginia, and the County of Jefferson aforesaid, and within the jurisdiction of this Court, with other confederates to the Jurors unknown, feloniously and traitorously make rebellion and levy war against the said Commonwealth of Virginia, and to effect, carry out, and fulfill their said wicked and treasonable ends and purposes did, then and there, as a band of organized soldiers, attack, seize, and hold a certain part and place within the county and State aforesaid, and within the jurisdiction aforesaid, known and called by the name Harper's Ferry, and then and there did forcibly capture, make prisoners of, and detain divers good and loyal citizens of said Commonwealth, to wit: Lewis W. Washington, John M. Allstadt, Archibald M. Kitzmiller, Benjamin J. Mills, John E. P. Dangerfield, Armstead Ball, John Donoho, and did then and there slay and murder, by shooting with firearms, called Sharpe's rifles, divers good and loyal citizens of said Commonwealth, to wit: Thomas Boerly, George W. Turner, Fontaine Beckham, together with Luke Quinn, a soldier of the United States, and Hayward Sheppard, a free negro, and did then and there, in manner aforesaid, wound divers other good and loyal citizens of said Commonwealth, and did then and there feloniously and traitorously establish and set up, without authority of the Legislature of the Commonwealth of Virginia, A Government, separate from, and hostile to, the existing Government of said Commonwealth; and did then and there hold and exercise divers offices under said usurped Government, to wit: the said John brown as Commander-in-Chief of the military forces, the said Aaron C. Stephens alias Aaron D. Stephens, as Captain, the said Edwin Coppie, as Lieutenant, and the said Shields Green and John Copland as soldiers; and did then and there require and compel obedience to said officers; and then there did hold and profess alliance and fidelity to said usurped Government; and under color of the usurped authority aforesaid, did then and there resist forcibly and with warlike arms, the execution of the laws of the Commonwealth of Virginia, and with firearms did wound and maim divers other good and loyal citizens of said Commonwealth, to the Jurors unknown, when attempting, with lawful authority, to uphold and maintain said Constitution and Laws of the Commonwealth of Virginia, and for the purpose end, and aim of overthrowing and abolishing the Constitution and laws of said Commonwealth, and establishing in the place thereof, another and different government, and constitution and laws hostile thereto, did then and there feloniously and traitorously, and in military array join in open battle and deadly warfare with the civil officers and soldiers in the lawful service of the said Commonwealth of Virginia, and did then and there shoot and discharge divers guns and pistols, charged with gunpowder and leaden balls, against and upon divers parties of the militia and volunteers embodied and acting under the command of Colonel Robert W. Baylor, and Colonel John Thomas Gibson, and other officers of said Commonwealth, with lawful authority to quell and subdue the said John Brown, Aaron C. Stephens, alias Aaron D. Stephens, Edwin Coppie, Shields Green, and John Copland, and other rebels and traitors assembled, organized, and acting with them, as aforesaid, to the evil example of all others in like case offending, and against the peace and dignity of the Commonwealth.

Second Count.—And the Jurors aforesaid, upon their oath aforesaid, do further present that the said John Brown, Aaron C. Stephens, alias Aaron D. Stephens, and Edwin Coppie, Shields Green, and John Copland, severally, on the sixteenth, seventeenth, and eighteenth days of October, in the year of our Lord eighteen hundred and fifty-nine, in the said County of Jefferson, and Commonwealth of Virginia, and within the jurisdiction of this Court, not having the fear of God before their eyes, but moved and seduced by the false and malignant counsel of others, and the instigations of the devil, did each severally, maliciously, and feloniously conspire with each other, and with a certain John E. Cook, John Kagi, Charles Tidd, and others to the jurors unknown, to induce certain slaves, to wit:—Jim, Sam, Mason, Catesby, ... the slaves and property of Lewis W. Washington, and Henry, Levi, Ben Jerry, Phil, George, and Bill, the slaves and property of John H. Allstadt, and other slaves to the Jurors unknown, to rebel and make insurrection against their masters and owners, and against the Government and the Constitution and laws of the Commonwealth of Virginia: and then and there did maliciously and feloniously advise said slaves, and other slaves to the Jurors unknown, to rebel and make insurrection against their masters and owners, and against the Government, the Constitution and laws of the Commonwealth of Virginia to the evil example of all others in like cases offending and against the peace and dignity of the Commonwealth.

Third Count.—And the Jurors aforesaid, upon their oath aforesaid, further present that the said John Brown, Aaron C. Stephens, alias Aaron D. Stephens, and Edwin Coppie, Shields Green, and John Copland, severally, on the sixteenth, seventeenth, and eighteenth days of October, in the year of our Lord eighteen hundred and fifty-nine, in the said County of Jefferson, and Commonwealth of Virginia, aforesaid, and within the jurisdiction aforesaid, in and upon the bodies of Thomas Boerly, George W. Turner, Fontaine Beckman, Luke Quinn, white persons, and Hayward Sheppard, a free negro, in the peace of the Commonwealth then and there being, feloniously, willfully, and of their malice aforethought, did make an assault, with firearms, called Sharpe's rifles, and other deadly weapons to the Jurors unknown, then and there, charged with gunpowder and leaden bullets, did then and there feloniously, willfully, and of their malice aforethought, shoot and discharge the same against the bodies severally and respectively of the said Thomas Boerly, George W. Turner, Fontaine Beckham, Luke Quinn, and Hayward Sheppard; and that the said John Brown, Aaron C. Stephens, alias Aaron D. Stephens, and Edwin Coppie, Shields Green, and John Copland, with leaden bullets aforesaid, out of the firearms called Sharpe's rifles, aforesaid, shot and discharged as aforesaid, and with the other deadly weapons to the jurors unknown, as aforesaid, then and there feloniously, willfully, and of their malice aforethought did strike, penetrate, and wound the said Thomas Boerly, George W. Turner, Fontaine Beckham, Luke Quinn, and Hayward Sheppard, each severally; to wit: the said Thomas Boerly in and upon the left side; the said George W. Turner in and upon the left shoulder; the said Fontaine Beckham in and upon the right breast; the said Like Quinn in and upon the abdomen, and the said Hayward Sheppard in and upon the back and side, giving to the said Thomas Boerly, George W. Turner, Fontaine Beckham, Luke Quinn, and Hayward Sheppard, then and there with the leaden bullets, so as aforesaid shot and discharged by them, severally and respectively out of the Sharpe's rifles aforesaid, and with the other deadly weapons to the Jurors unknown, as aforesaid, each one mortal wound, of which said mortal wounds they the said Thomas Boerly, George W. Turner, Fontaine Beckham, Luke Quinn, and Hayward Sheppard each died; and so the Jurors aforesaid upon their oaths aforesaid, do say that the said John Brown, Aaron C. Stephens, alias Aaron D. Stephens, and Edwin Coppie, Shields Green, and John Copland, then and there, them the said Thomas Boerly, George W. Turner, Fontaine Beckham, Luke Quinn, and Hayward Sheppard, in the manner aforesaid, and by the means aforesaid, feloniously, willfully, and of their, and each of their malice aforethought, did kill and murder, against the peace and dignity of the Commonwealth.

Fourth Count. —And the Jurors aforesaid, upon their oath aforesaid, further present that the said John Brown, Aaron C. Stephens, alias Aaron D. Stephens, and Edwin Coppie, Shields Green, and John Copland, severally, on the sixteenth, seventeenth, and eighteenth days of October, in the year of our Lord eighteen hundred and fifty-nine, in the said County of Jefferson, and Commonwealth of Virginia, aforesaid, and within the jurisdiction of this Court, in and upon the bodies of Thomas Boerly, George W. Turner, and Fontaine Beckham, in the peace of the Commonwealth, then and there being feloniously, willfully, and of their malice aforethought, did make an assault, and with their guns called Sharpe's rifles, then and there charged with gunpowder and leaden bullets, did then and there feloniously, willfully, and of their, and each of their malice aforethought, shoot and discharge the same against the bodies of the said Thomas Boerly, George W. Turner, and Fontaine Beckham and that the said John Brown, Aaron C. Stephens, alias Aaron D. Stephens, and Edwin Coppie, Shields Green, with leaden bullets aforesaid, shot out of the Sharpe's rifles aforesaid, then and there, feloniously, willfully, and of their malice aforethought, did strike, penetrate, and wound the said Thomas Boerly, George W. Turner, and Fontaine Beckham, each severally, viz.: The said Thomas Boerly in and upon the left side; the said George W. Turner, in and upon the left shoulder and breast; and the said Fontaine Beckham in and upon the right breast, giving to the said Thomas Boerly, George W. Turner, and Fontaine Beckham, then and there, with leaden bullets aforesaid, shot by them severally out of Sharpe's rifles aforesaid, each one mortal wound, of which said mortal wounds they the said Thomas Boerly, George W. Turner, and Fontaine Beckham then and there died; and that the said John Copland, then and there, feloniously, willfully, and of his malice aforethought, was present, aiding, helping, abetting, comforting and assisting the said John Brown, Aaron C. Stephens, alias Aaron D. Stephens, and Edwin Coppie, Shields Green in the felony and murder aforesaid, in manner aforesaid to commit. And so the Jurors aforesaid, upon their oaths, do say that the said John Brown, Aaron C. Stephens, alias Aaron D. Stephens, and Edwin Coppie, Shields Green, and John Copland, then and there them, the said Thomas Boerly, George W. Turner, and Fontaine Beckham, in the manner aforesaid and by the means aforesaid, feloniously, willfully, and of their and each of their malice aforethought, did kill, and murder against the peace and dignity of the Commonwealth of Virginia.

Lewis W. Washington, John H. Allstadt, John E. P. Dangerfield, Alexander Kelly, Emanuel Spangler, Armstead M. Ball, Joseph A. Brus, William Johnson, Lewis P. Starry, Archibald H. Kitzmiller, were sworn in open Court this 26th day of October, 1859, to given evidence to the Grand Jury upon this bill of indictment.

                    Teste: Robert T. Brown, Clerk

                    A true copy of said indictment

                    Teste: Robert T. Brown

                    Clerk of the Circuit Court of Jefferson
                    County, in the State of Virginia.

Which bill of indictment the Grand Jury returned this 26th day of October.

A true bill. Thomas Rutherford, Foreman
October 26, 1859.

LEMMON V. PEOPLE

Court of Appeals of New York
March 1860
20 N.Y. 562 (1860)

Few issues so strained the bonds of friendship and judicial comity (the respect by one state or jurisdiction shown to another state or jurisdiction of the formal paper, status, and property of another state) than the issue of sojourning slaves. Defined as property under the laws and traditions of border and southern states, by the 1850s northern and midwestern states no longer recognized property in persons and sought to avoid the presence of slavery on their soil. Yet, southern businessmen and travelers, commuting with their baggage and their property (their personal slaves) occasionally had to transit through free states during the course of their business trips or personal voyages. As a result, slave owners found themselves in free states, not seeking permanent residence or for the purpose of selling their slave property but to change ships or trains to reach their final destination. In this case, Juliette Lemmon, traveling with eight of her slaves and her husband, Jonathan, left Richmond, Virginia (a slave jurisdiction) bound for Texas (another slave jurisdiction). But, to match up with a ship bound for the Texas coast, the Lemmons traveled to New York City (a non-slave jurisdiction). Once there, the presence of the slaves on Manhattan Island became known to a local antislavery activist, who swore out a writ of habeas corpus petitioning the local court to free the eight blacks, arguing that they were being unlawfully confined. At first instance, the judge heard the issues and freed the eight individuals. The Lemmons then appealed to the Supreme Court (a district court in New York state), and that court upheld the first judge's decision to free them. After that loss, the Lemmons appealed to the highest appellate court in New York state, the Court of Appeals, which handed down this ruling in March 1860.

This case is important both for what it reveals about the growing problem of comity between the states and the increasing sectionalism in law in the turbulent decade of the 1850s. It is also important because observers at the time feared that if appealed to the United States Supreme Court, with Chief Justice Roger B. Taney presiding, and in light of his 1857 decision in *Dred Scott v. Sandford*, a majority of the justices might decide slavery existed nationally and that free states (not just free territories, as decided in *Dred Scott*) may not prohibit slavery from their soil in any manner. A "second *Dred Scott*" decision might result in "slavery national" versus "freedom national," as supported by the new Republican Party and most clearly articulated by Salmon P. Chase of Ohio. Though this case never reached the United States Supreme Court, this decision suggests just how strained were the legal ties that bound the Union in 1860.

PRIOR HISTORY: Appeal from the Supreme Court. On the 6th day of November, 1852, Louis Napoleon, a colored citizen of this State, made application upon a sufficient petition and affidavit to Mr. Justice Paine of the Superior Court of the city of New York, for a writ of habeas corpus to be directed to one Jonathan Lemmon and the keeper of house No. 3 Carlisle street, New York, requiring them to bring before said justice the bodies of eight colored persons, one man, two women and five children, who on the day preceding were confined and restrained of their liberty on board the steamer City of Richmond, in the harbor of New York, and were taken there from on the night of that day to No. 3 Carlisle street, and there detained under the pretence that they were slaves.

The writ accordingly issued, and on the same day one of the constables of the city of New York brought up the eight colored persons, who appeared to be known only by their christian names as Emeline, Robert, Lewis, Amanda, Nancy, Ann, Lewis and Edward. Lemmon made a return to the writ under oath, in which he averred that the eight persons named were the slaves and property of Juliet Lemmon his wife, who had been the owner of such persons as slaves for several years, she being a resident and citizen of the State of Virginia: that service and labor as slaves was due by them under the Constitution and laws of Virginia: "that the said Juliet, with her said slaves, persons or property, is now in transitu or transit from the State of Virginia aforesaid to the State of Texas, the ultimate place of destination and another slaveholding State of the United States of America, and that she was so on her way in transitu or transit when the aforesaid eight persons or slaves were taken from her custody or possession under the writ of habeas corpus:" "that the said Juliet never had any intention of bringing the said slaves or persons into the State of New York to remain therein, and that she did not bring them into said State in any manner nor for any purpose whatever, except transitu or transit from the State of Virginia aforesaid through the port or harbor of New York, on board of steamship for their place of destination, the State of Texas aforesaid: that the said Juliet, as such owner of the aforesaid slaves or persons, was at the time they were taken from her as aforesaid, on the writ of habeas corpus, and she thereby deprived of the possession of them, passing with them through the said harbor of New York, where she was compelled by necessity to touch or land, without, on her part, remaining or intending to remain longer than necessary:" "that the said slaves, sailing from the port of Norfolk in the said State of Virginia, on board the steamship City of Richmond, never touched, landed nor came into the harbor or State of New York except for the mere purpose of passage and transit from the State of Virginia, aforesaid, to the State of Texas, aforesaid, and for no other purpose, intention, object or design whatever: that the said Juliet with her said slaves was compelled by necessity or accident to take passage in the steamship City of Richmond, before named, from the aforesaid port of Norfolk and State of Virginia for the State of Texas aforesaid, the ultimate place of destination." The return also denied any intention, on the part of Mrs. Lemmon or her husband, of selling the negroes.

To this return the relator orally interposed a general demurrer. Mr. Justice Paine held the case under advisement until the 13th of November, 1852, when he discharged the colored Virginians.

Lemmon sued out a writ of certiorari from the Supreme Court, where the proceedings were reviewed at general term in the first district, and the order of Mr. Justice Paine was affirmed in December, 1857. Lemmon appealed to this court.

DISPOSITION: Judgment affirmed.

COUNSEL: Charles O'Conor, for the appellant.
I. Except so far as the State of New York could rightfully, and without transcending restraints imposed upon her sovereignty by the Constitution of the United States, forbid the status of slavery to exist within her borders in the person of an African negro, and except so far as she has, in fact, expressly or impliedly forbidden it by actual legislation, an African negro may be lawfully held in that condition in this State
1. The ancient general or common law of this State authorized the holding of negroes as slaves therein. The judiciary never had any constitutional power to annul, repeal or set aside this law; and, consequently, it is only by force of some positive enactment of the legislative authority that one coming into our territory with slaves in his lawful possession could suffer any loss or diminution of his title to them as his property. (1.) In every known judgment, argument or opinion of court, judge or counsel relating to the subject, it is admitted in some form, that at an early period negro slavery existed under the municipal law in each one of the thirteen original States

which formed this Republic, by declaring its independence in 1776, and adopting its Constitution in 1789. By what means it had its first reception and establishment in any of them as an institution sanctioned by law, may not be historically traceable; but in most, if not all of them, and certainly in New York, it was expressly recognized by statute prior to the time when the States themselves asserted their independence. (28 October, 1806, Van Schaick's Laws, 69; 29 October, 1733, id., 157; Colonial Slave Act of N.Y. March 8, 1773; Jack v. Martin, 12 Wend., 328; Jackson v. Bulloch, 12 Conn., 42; id., 61; Commonwealth v. Aves, 18 Pick., 208, 209; Scott v. Sandford, 19 How., 407, 408; Hargrave's Argt., point 5th, 20 State Trials, 60; Per McLean, J., 16 Pet., 660; 15 id., 507.) (2.) Negro slavery never was a part of the municipal law of England, and consequently it was not imported thence by the first colonists. Nor did they adopt any system of villenage or other permanent domestic slavery of any kind which had ever existed in England or been known to or regulated by the laws or usages of that kingdom. They were a homogeneous race of the free white men; and in a society composed of such persons, the slavery of its own members, endowed by nature with mental and physical equality, must ever be repugnant to an enlightened sense of justice. Of course, the colonists abhorred it, saw that it was not suited to their condition and left it behind them when they emigrated. (Doctor and Student Dialogue, 2 Ch., 18, 19; Wheaton v. Donaldson, 8 Pet., 659; Van Ness v. Pacard, 2 Pet., 444; 1 Kent Com., 373; Const. N.Y. art. 1, § 17; Neal v. Farmer, 9 Cobb's Geo. R., 562, 578.) (3.) As neither the political bondage nor the domestic slavery which the European by fraud and violence imposed upon his white brethren ever had a legal foothold in the territory now occupied by these States, the inflated speeches of French and British judges and orators touching the purity of the air and soil of their respective countries, whatever other purpose they may serve, are altogether irrelevant to the inquiry what was or is the law of any State in this Union on the subject of negro slavery. (Frence Eloq., A. D., 1738, 20 State Trials, 11, note; English Eloq., A. D., 1762, 2 Eden, 117, Ld. Northington; Id., 1765, 1 Bl. Com., 127, 124; Id., 1771, 20 State Trials, 1 Ld. Mansfield; Scotch Eloq., 1778, id., 6, note; Irish Eloq., 1793, Rowa's Trial, Curran; Judge McLean's criticism in Dred Scott, 19 How., 535; Lord Stowell's criticism, 2 Hagg. Ad., 109.) (a.) The only argument against negro slavery found in the English cases at all suitable for a judicial forum rests on the historical fact that it was unknown to the English law. Mr. Hargrave, in Somerset's case, showed that white Englishmen were alone subject to the municipal slave laws of that country at any time; that negro slavery was a new institution which it required the legislative power to introduce. (20 State Trials, 55; Com. v. Aves, 18 Pick., 214.) (b.) Lord Holt and Mr. Justice Powell were Mr. Hargrave's high authority for the proposition that whilst the common law of England recognized white English slaves or villeins and the right of property in them; yet it "took no notice of a negro." That a white man might "be a villein in England," but "that as soon as a negro comes into England he became free." It was only negro liberty that the know-nothingism of English and French law established. English and French air had not its true enfranchising purity till drawn through the nostrils of a negro. White slaves had long respired it without their status being at all affected. (Smith v. Brown, 2 Salk., 666; 20 State Trials, 55, note.) (c.) Lord Mansfield said in Somerset's case, "The state of slavery is of such a nature that it is incapable of being introduced on any reason, moral or political, but only by positive law," and negrophilism has been in raptures with him ever since. Nevertheless it was a bald inconsequential truism. It might be equally well said of any other new thing not recognized in any known existing law. (Per Ashhurst, J., 3 J.R., 63.) (4.) The judiciary never had power to annul, repeal or set aside the slave law of this State which we have shown existed with the sanction of the Legislature prior to the Revolution. (a.) Judicial tribunals in this country are a part of the government, but by the genius of our institutions, and the very words of our fundamental charters, they are restrained from any exercise of the law-making power. That governmental function is assigned to a separate department. (b.) By this strict separation of governmental powers, we have given form and permanency to a maxim of politico-legal science always acknowledged by the sages of the English law in theory, though often violated in practice. (c.) For proofs of this Acknowledgment we refer to the habitual definition of judicial power—jus dare et non jus facere. Again, the wise and learned Sir Jonathan Eardley Wilmot says "Statute law and common law originally flowed from the same fountain—the Legislature. Statute law is the will of the Legislature; the common law is nothing else but statutes worn out by time; all our law begun by consent of the Legislature; and whether it is now law by usage or by writing it is the same thing." (Collins v. Blantern, 2 Wils., 348; 1 Kent, 472.) This is sound doctrine; but it has often been departed from in practice. (d.) In some instances the departure has been very striking. The legislative authority of Great Britain, in 1285, sought by the celebrated statute de donis to make entailed lands absolutely inalienable. As far as the plain and direct expression of its sovereign will by the supreme law-making power could have that effect, they were rendered inalienable. The judges, without a shadow of constitutional right, contrived the absurd and irrational fiction of a common recovery, and thereby virtually repealed the statute. (2 Bl. Com., 116, Per Mansfield; 1 Burr., 115, Ld. Ch. J. Willes; Willes, 452.) The English legislature was governed by what we, with our present lights, may deem a pernicious policy, tending to restrain commerce in land, to tie it up in few hands, and to draw into operation numerous social evils. The unfettering of estates by the English judges, through the devices to which they resorted, had its origin in a wise regard for the interests of the people; but in them, it was mere trick and rank usurpation. So Lord Eldon, from his place as President of the House of Lords, at a period when constitutional law was better understood in England, in pronouncing the judgment upon the case of the Queensberry leases (1 Bligh's P. Rep., 1st series, 435, A. D. 1819), says: "The power of judges in this respect may be doubted. Upon that subject, as it applies to English law, I have formed an opinion that the judges of this age in England would not have been permitted to get rid of the statute of English entails as judges of that age did soon after the passing of the statute de donis. (38 Eng. L. and Eq., 444.) (e.) Those lawyers who have failed to perceive, as Lord Eldon did, the necessity of keeping separate the great departments of the government, whose professional pride was greater than their knowledge of constitutional jurisprudence, have frequently boasted of a tendency amongst the English juris-consults and judges to defeat what to them seemed impolitic and unjust resolutions of the legislative department. They erred. Far better that supposed mischiefs should exist for a time by the ill-advised sanction of the Legislature than that, by usurping powers not granted, the high priest of justice should defile himself and the temple in which he officiates by the sin of willfully violating the fundamental law. Error should not be combated by error, by crime, or by ingeniously conceived fraudulent devices and evasions, but by fair argument and open remonstrance addressed to those whom the Constitution has invested with the sole power of orderly and legitimate correction. An instance of this ill-considered self-gratulation may be found in the otherwise admirably written argument of Mr. Hargrave, as counsel for the negro Somerset before Lord Mansfield. The last sentence of that argument, vaguely to be sure, and, perhaps, somewhat covertly, commends the astuteness of the English judges in circumventing the lord under the system of English villenage, by which they gradually undermined that part of the ancient law of England. (20 Howell's State Trials, 67; Id., 27.) Negro slavery in the West Indies was sanctioned by numerous English statutes. This afforded an argument certainly of much force in favor of permitting an English subject, who lawfully held slaves in that part of the British dominions, temporarily to visit England with his bondman. The argument was opposed by this appeal to judicial pride; it was overruled by the dictum of a judge much more renowned for his tendencies to usurp the power of making law than for any inclination to diminish prerogative or to defend the liberty of his white fellow subjects. The pride of office, the pride of learning and an ostentatious vanity, rather than any tenderness for the rights and enjoyments of the lowly, dictated the loose declamation by which he installed himself as the champion of negro emancipation. 2. The judicial department has no right to declare negro slavery to be contrary to the law of nature, or immoral, or unjust, or to take any measures or introduce any policy for its suppression founded on any such ideas. Courts are only authorized to administer the municipal law. Judges have no commission to promulgate or enforce their notions of general justice, natural right or morality, but only that which is the known law of the land. (1 Kent's Com., 448; Doctor and Student Dialogue, 1 ch., 18, 19; per Maule, J., 13 Ad. & Ell., N. S., 387, note.) 3. In the forensic sense of the word law, there is no such thing as a law of nature bearing upon the lawfulness of slavery, or indeed upon any other question in jurisprudence. The law of nature is in every juridical sense, a mere figure of speech. In a state of nature, if the existence of human beings in such a state may be supposed, there is no law. The prudential resolves of an individual for his own government, do not come under the denomination of law. Law, in the forensic sense, is wholly of social origin. It is a restraint imposed by society upon itself and its members. (Rutherforth's Inst., B. 1, ch. 1, § 6, 7; 1 Bl. Com., 43; 1 Kent, 2; Wheaton's Elements of Int. Law, 2, 19; Cooper's Justinian, notes, 405; Bowyer on Public Law, 47, and onward.) (1.) If there was any such thing as a law of nature, in the forensic sense of the word law, it must be of absolute and paramount obligation in all climes, ages, courts and places. Inborn with the moral constitution of man, it must control him everywhere, and overrule as vicious, corrupt and void every opposing decree or resolution of courts or legislatures. And accordingly Blackstone, repeating the idle speech of others upon the subject, tells us that the law of nature is binding all over the globe; and that no human laws are of any validity if contrary to it. (1 Wendell's Blackstone, 40, 41, 42, and notes.) Yet, as the judiciary of England have at all times acknowledged negro slavery to be a valid basis of legal rights, it follows either that such slavery, in the practical judgment of the common law, is not contrary to the law of nature, or if it be, that such law of nature is of no force in any English court. (Acc. Bouvier's Inst., § 9; Brougham Ed. Rev., Apl. 1858, 235.) (2.) The common law judges of England, whilst they broke the fetters of any negro slave who came into that country, held themselves bound to enforce contracts for the purchase and sale of such slaves, and to give redress for damages done to the right of property in them. This involves the proposition that there was no paramount law of nature which courts could act upon prohibiting negro slavery. (Madrazo v. Willes, 3 B. & Ald., 353; 18 Pick., 215; Smith v. Brown, Salk., 666; Cases cited in note, 20 State Trials, 51; The Slave Grace, 2 Hagg. Adm., 104.) (3.) The highest courts of England and of this country having jurisdiction over questions of public or international law, have decided that holding negroes in bondage as slaves is not contrary to the law of nations. (The Antelope, 10 Wheat., 66; 18 Pick., 211; The Slave Grace, 2 Hagg. Adm., 104, 122.) (4.) When Justinian says in his Institutes (book 1, tit. 2, § 2), and elsewhere, that slavery is contrary to the law of nature, he means no more than that it does not exist by nature but is introduced by human law, which is true of most if not all other rights and obligations. His definition of the law of nature (book 1, tit. 2) de jure naturali proves this; his full sanctions of slavery in book 1 (tit. 3, § 2, tit. 8, § 1) confirm it. (Cushing's Domat., § 97; Bowyer on Public Law, 48.) (5.) All perfect rights, cognizable or enforceable as such in judicial tribunals, exist only by virtue of the law of that State or country in which they are claimed or asserted. The whole idea of property arose from compact. It has no origin in any law of nature as supposed in the court below. (5 Sandf., 711; Rutherforth's Inst., book 1, ch. 3, §§ 6, 7.) (6.) The law of nature spoken of by law writers, if the phrase has any practical import, means that morality which its notions of policy leads each nation to recognize as of universal obligation, which it therefore observes itself and, so far as it may, enforces upon others. It cannot be pretended that there ever was in England, or that there now is in any State of this Union, a law, by any name, thus outlawing negro slavery. The common law of all these countries has always regarded it as the basis of individual rights; and statute laws in all of them recognized and enforced it. (The Slave Grace, 2 Hagg. Adm., 104; Per Shaw, Ch. J., 18 Pick., 215; 1 Kent, 2, 3; 3 id., 2; 2 Wood's Civil Law, 2.) (a.) No civilized state on earth can maintain this absolute outlawry of negro slavery; for in some of its forms slavery has existed in all ages; and no lawgiver of paramount authority has ever condemned it. (Cooper's Justinian, notes, 410, Inst., book 1, tit. 3; Per Bartley, Ch. J., 6 Ohio N.S., 724; Senator Benjamin, 1858.) (b.) It has never been determined by the judicial tribunals of any country that any right, otherwise perfect, loses its claim to protection by the mere fact of its being founded on the ownership of a negro slave. (7.) The proposition that freedom is the general rule and slavery the local exception, has no foundation in any just view of the law as a science. Equally groundless is the distinction taken by Judge Paine between slave property and other movables. (a.)

Property in movables does not exist by nature, neither is there any common law of nations touching its acquisition or transfer. (Bowyer on Universal Public Law, 50.) (b.) Every title to movables must have an origin in some law. That origin is always in and by the municipal law of the place where it is acquired, and such law never has per se any extraterritorial operation. (c.) When the movables, with or without the presence of their owner, come within any other country than that under whose laws the title to them was acquired, it depends on the will of such latter State how far it will take notice of and recognize, quoad such property and its owner, the foreign law. (Bank of Augusta v. Earle, 13 Pet., 589.) (d.) It has become a universal practice among civilized nations to recognize such foreign law except so far as it may be specially proscribed. This usage amounts to an agreement between the nations, and hence the idea of property by the so-called law of nations. (e.) Hence it will be seen that property in African negroes is not an exception to any general rule. Upon rational principles, it is no more local or peculiar than other property. And there is so much of universality about it that in no civilized State or country could it be absolutely denied all legal protection. 4. In fact there is no violation of the principles of enlightened justice nor any departure from the dictates of pure benevolence in holding negroes in a state of slavery. (1.) Men, whether black or white, cannot exist with ordinary comfort and in reasonable safety otherwise than in the social state. (2.) Negroes, alone and unaided by the guardianship of another race, cannot sustain a civilized social state. (a.) This proposition does not require for its support an assertion or denial of the unity of the human race, the application of Noah's malediction (9 Geo., 582), or the possibility that time has changed and may again change the Ethiopian's physical and moral nature. (b.) It is only necessary to view the negro as he is, and to credit the palpable and undeniable truth, that the latter phenomenon cannot happen within thousands of years. For all the ends of jurisprudence this is a perpetuity. (Facciolati's Latin Lexicon Aethiops.) (c.) The negro never has sustained a civilized social organization, and that he never can is sufficiently manifest from history. It is proven by the rapid though gradual retrogression of Hayti toward the profoundest depths of destitution, ignorance and barbarism. (McCulloch's Geo., Hayti, 693, 694; De Bow's Rev., vol. 24, 203.) (d.) That, alone and unaided, he never can sustain a civilized social organization is proven to all reasonable minds by the fact that one single member of his race has never attained proficiency in any art or science requiring the employment of high intellectual capacity. A mediocrity below the standard of qualification for the important duties of government, for guiding the affairs of society, or for progress in the abstract sciences, may be common in individuals of other races; but it is universal amongst negroes. Not one single negro has ever risen above it. (Malte Brun's Geo., book 59, 8; Gregoire's Literature of the Negroes; Biog. Univ. Supt., vol. 56, 83, Gregoire.) (e.) It follows that in order to obtain the measure of reasonable personal enjoyment and of usefulness to himself and others for which he is adapted by nature, the negro must remain in a state of pupilage under the government of some other race. (f.)

He is a child of the sun. In cold climates he perishes; in the territories adapted to his labors, and in which alone his race can be perpetuated, he will not toil save on compulsion, and the white man cannot; but each can perform his appointed task—the negro can labor, the white man can govern. (3.) Morality, or those dictates of enlightened reason which have sometimes been called the law of nature, do not oblige any man to serve another without an equivalent reward for the service rendered. (a.) The obligations of charity form no exception to this rule. Charity enjoins gratuitous service to those who are unable to repay; it is not due to sturdy indolence. (Doctor and Student Dialogue, 1, ch. 6.) (b.) The universal voice of mankind concedes to the parent a right to the profit and pleasure which may be derived by him from the services of his minor child as a due return for guardianship and nurture. (c.) Who shall deny the claim of the intellectual white race to its compensation for the mental toil of governing and guiding the negro laborer? The learned and skillful statesman, soldier, physician, preacher or other expert in any great department of human exertion where mind holds dominion over matter, is clothed with power, and surrounded with materials for the enjoyment of mental and physical luxuries, in proportion to the measure of his capacity and attainments. And all this is at the cost of the mechanical and agricultural laborer, to whom such enjoyments are denied. If the social order, founded in the different natural capacities of individuals in the same family, which produces these inequalities, is not unjust, who can rightfully say of the like inequality in condition between races differing in capacity, that it is contrary to a law of nature, or that the governing race who conform to it are guilty of fraud and rapine, or that they commit a violence to right reason which is forbidden by morality? (4.) "Honeste vivere, alterum non laedere et suum cuique tribuere," are all the precepts of the moral law. The honorable slaveholder keeps them as perfectly as any other member of human society. (Inst., book 1, tit. 1, § 3; 1 Bl. Com., 40; 9 Georgia, 582.) (a.) The cruelties of vicious slave owners and the horrors of the slave trade are topics quite irrelevant. It is universal experience that wealth and power afford occasion for the development of man's evil propensities; but as they are also the necessary means of his improvement, they cannot be called evils in their own nature. (b.) The tone of mind, which, arrogating to itself superior purity of life and a higher moral tone than in the then existing state of knowledge could be supposed to have existed among the guests at the marriage in Cana of Galilee (John, ch. ii), enjoins, as a duty, total abstinence from wine, is well kept up in the assumption of a political and moral excellence beyond the mental reach of our sires, and the consequent demand for an immediate abolition of negro slavery. (c.) Certain assumptions of anti-slavery agitators have been too much indulged by the moderate, peaceful, and conservative. Ch. J. Marshall let pass uncondemned their irrelevant triviality about the law of nature (6 Pet. Cond., 36; 10 Wheat., 114), and Ch. J. Taney concedes to them that the negro race, merely because denied political rights, is to be regarded as "unfortunate" (19 How., 407), and "unhappy" (id., 409). The fathers of the Republic, when forming a temporary league, in the face of the foe and on the eve of battle (7 Cush., 295), declined to peril all by delay and discord upon a scruple about inserting in the compact an unnecessary word (19 How., 575); but when those to whom for peace sake "an inch" has been thus conceded, proceeding on the "take an ell" principle, demand, as a consequence of the precedent, the power to destroy, we must withdraw all such concessions and go back to principles.

II. The unconstitutional and revolutionary anti-slavery resolution n1 of April, 1857, cannot retroact so as to affect this case. (Vol. 2, 797; Westminster Review, vol. 45, 76–98, article Manifest Destiny.) Prior to that time, no legislative act of this State had ever declared that to breathe our air or touch our soil should work emancipation ipso facto; nor had any statute been enacted which, by its true interpretation, denied to our fellow citizens of other States an uninterrupted transitus through our territory with their negro slaves. 1. The special injunctions and guarantees of the Federal Constitution secure to citizens of the several States free intercourse with all parts of the Republic. 2. Even inter-state comity, in its simplest form, awards a free transit to members of a friendly State with their families and rights of property, without disturbance of their domestic relations. (Curtis Arg., 18 Pick., 195, and cases cited; Paine, J., 5 Sand., 710; McDougall Arg., 4 Scam., 467, 468.) 3. Whatever others may do, no American judge can pronounce slave property an exception to this rule upon the general ground that slavery is immoral or unjust. Every American citizen is bound by the Constitution of the United States to regard it as being free from any moral taint which could affect its claims to legal recognition and protection, so long as any State in the Union shall uphold it. (1.) The provisions of the Federal Constitution for its protection cannot otherwise be kept in candor and good faith. (2.) In this spirit, faithful Christians and even honorable unbelievers keep all lawful contracts. (3.) Portia's mode of keeping promises (Merchant of Venice, act 4, scene 1), is allowable only in respect to pacts having the form of contracts, but which are of no binding force or obligation in law or morals. (4.) The American citizen, who, applying Shakspeare's doctrine, carries in his bosom a chapel illuminated by the "higher law," and devoted to those infernal deities, Evasion and Circumvention, may be justified if the constitutional compact be void; but if it be valid, he violates honor and conscience. It may be, however, that his devices are too subtle and ingenious to be reached by ordinary legal sanctions. (Last sentence in re Kirk, 1 Park. Cr. Cases, 95; Commonwealth v. Fitzgerald, 7 L. R., 379; Sim's Case, 7 Cush., 298; 1 R. S., 657, §§ 1, 16.)

N1 The People of this State will not allow Slavery within her borders in any form or under any pretence, or for any time, however short. Joint Resolution of April 16, 1857.

III. The act of March 31st, 1817, as revised in 1830, even with the modification of its effect wrought by the repeal of its exceptions in 1841, rightly understood, does not deny such right of passage. (Laws of 1817, 138, §§ 9, 15, 16, 17; 1 R. S., 656, §§ 1–16; Laws of 1841, 227, § 1.) 1. The words "imported, introduced, or brought into this State," unless extended by construction far beyond their import, do not apply to the mere transitus of a slave, in custody of a citizen of a slaveholding State being his owner, when quietly passing through this State on lawful occasion and without unnecessary delay. (Laws of 1817, 136, § 9; Laws of 1841, 227; Opinion in this case, 5 Sand., 716.) (1.) The repeal by the act of 1841 of the special privileges given by sections 3–7 inclusive of the act of 1817, in the view most adverse to the slave owner, merely left the words "imported, introduced or brought into" to be applied according to their natural import without those sections. So construed they would not extend to a mere carrying through the State. The word "Into" differs in meaning from the word "WITHIN" as used in the legislation of 1857, and marks the characteristic difference between it and that of 1817. (2.) It is impossible to give to the legislation of 1817 the comprehensive effect which was designed by the treasonable resolution of 1857. All will admit that a fugitive from slavery in Virginia, found in Vermont, may be carried back through New York under an extradition certificate. This would seem to prove that carrying through the State was not, in the judgment of the Legislature, a bringing into the State within the meaning of the act of 1817. (Curia by Story, J., 16 Pet., 624; Curia by Shaw, J., 18 Pick., 224.)

IV. The State of New York cannot, without violating the Constitution of the United States, restrain a citizen of a sister State from peaceably passing through her territory with his slaves or other property on a lawful visit to a State where slavery is allowed by law. (1.) Congress has power "to regulate commerce with foreign nations, and among the several States and with the Indian tribes." (Const. U. S., art. 1, § 8, subd. 3.) (2.) This power is absolutely exclusive in Congress, so that no State can constitutionally enact any regulation of commerce between the States whether Congress has exercised the same power over the matter in question or left it free. (Passenger Cases, 7 How. U. S. R., 572; per McLean, J., 7 How., 400; per Wayne, J., and the Court, 7 How., 410, 411; per McKinley, J., 7 How., 455; per Story, J., City of N. Y. v. Miln, 11 Pet., 158, 159, 156; Per Shaw, Ch. J., Sim's Case, 7 Cush., 299, 317.) (1.) At all events, the States have not reserved the right to prohibit and thus destroy commerce or any portion of it. (2.) The judgment below asserts that a citizen of Virginia, in possession of his slave property, cannot pass through the navigable waters of a non-slaveholding State on board of a coasting steamer enrolled and licensed under the laws of Congress, without risk of having his vessel arrested under State law and his property torn from him by force of Lord Mansfield's obiter dictum in Somerset's case. (2 Hagg., 107; Gibbons v. Ogden, 9 Wheat., 1; Com. v. Fitzgerald, 7 L. R., 381; In re Kirk., 1 Park. Cr. Cas., 69, cannot be sustained.) (3.) That proposition cannot be maintained. Each State is required to give full faith and credit to the public acts of every other (art. 4, § 1) to surrender to every other fugitives [sic] from its justice, or from any personal duty (art. 4, § 2, sub. 2, 3). No citizen can be deprived of his privileges and immunities by the action of a State other than his own. (Id., § 1.) Commerce between the States is placed under the exclusive control of Congress. (Art. 1, § 8, subd. 3.) And Congress itself is forbidden to impose any burden on the external trade of a particular State, or to burden or prefer it in any way. (Const., art. 1, § 8, subd. 2; § 9, subd. 5.) (4.) Until the present case, it seems to have been universally conceded, and, at all events, it is clear in law, that a citizen of any State in the Union may freely pass through an intermediate State to the territory of a third without sacrificing any of his rights. (Per Shaw, Ch. J., 18 Pick., 224, 225; per Curren, Willard v. People, 4 Scam., 468; Sewell's Slaves, 3 Am. Juris., 406, 407; 7 How. U. S. R., 461, Passenger cases.) 3. The word "commerce," as it is used in this constitutional grant of exclusive power to Congress, includes the transportation of persons and the whole subject of intercourse between our citizens of different States as well as between them and foreigners. Consequently, no State can impose duties, imposts or burdens of any kind, much less penal forfeitures, upon the citizens of other States for passing through her territories with their property, nor can any State interrupt or disturb them in such passage. (Passenger Cases, 7 How. U. S. R., 572; per McLean, J., 7 How., 401, 405, 407; per Wayne, J., and the court, 7 How., 412, 413, 430, 352; per Wayne, J., 7 How., 433, 435; per Catron, J., 7 How., 450, 451; per McKinley, J., 7 How., 453; per Grier, J.,

7 How., 461, 463, fourth point, 464; per Baldwin, J., Groves v. Slaughter, 15 Pet., 510, 511, 513, 515, 516, in point as to slaves; Argt. of Mr. Clay, 15 Pet., 489, Mr. Webster,495; R. J. Walker, contra, app., 48 and onward; Curia per Marshall, J., Gibbons v. Ogden, 5 Pet., Cond., 567.) 4. This doctrine does not preclude a State from exercising absolute control over all trading of any kind within her borders; nor from any precautionary regulations for the preservation of her citizens or their property from contact with any person or thing which might be dangerous or injurious to their health, morals or safety. (Per McLean, J., 7 How., 402, 403, 406, 408; per Wayne, J., 7 How., 417, 424, 426, 428; per Grier, J., 7 How., 457; per Baldwin, J., 14 Pet., 615; per Story, J., 16 Pet., 625; 5 How., 569, 570, 571; Gibbons v. Ogden, 9 Wheat., 1; 5 Pet., Cond., 578.)

V. The constitutional guaranty to "the citizens of each State," that they "shall be entitled to all privileges and immunities of citizens in the several States" (art. 4, § 2, subd. 1) affords the citizen of any State, peacefully passing through another, a right to immunity from such disturbance as the plaintiff suffered from the order now under review. 1. This section would lose much of its force and beneficial effect if it were construed to secure to the non-resident citizen in traveling through a State only such "rights" as such State may allow to its own citizens. Its object was to exempt him from State power, not to subject him to it. (1.) Class legislation is deemed perfectly legitimate. A State may impose grievous burdens on its own citizens of particular classes, say those of foreign birth, of German origin, over or under a particular age, owning slaves any where, or pursuing a particular occupation, &c. It may establish an agrarian law. Perhaps Utah might visit heavy penalties upon any of its male citizens for breathing its pure air or touching its pure soil without having at least six wives; an Amazonia may arise among our new States, and exhibit such a rule in the feminine gender. (Frost v. Brisbin, 19 Wend., 15; Brown v. Maryland, 6 Pet., Cond., 562.) (2.) Under a construction and policy of this kind, the non-slaveholding States could pen up all slaveholders within their own States as effectually as the slave is himself confined by the rule applied in this case. This power cannot be conceded. (per Grier, J., 7 How., 461, 464.) 2. The section is not to be thus narrowed. The Constitution recognizes the legal character "citizen of the United States" as well as citizen of a particular State. (Art. 1, § 3, subd 3; art. 2, § 1, subd. 5.) The latter term refers only to domicil; for every citizen of a particular State is a citizen of the United States. And the object of this section is to secure to the citizen, when within a State in which he is not domiciled, the general privileges and immunities which, in the very nature of citizenship, as recognized and established by the Federal Constitution, belonged to that status; so that by no partial and adverse legislation of a State into which he might go as a stranger or a sojourner can he be deprived of them. It is a curb set upon State legislation harmonizing with the provision which extends the aegis of the federal judiciary to the non-resident citizen in all controversies between him and the citizens of the State in which he may be temporarily sojourning. (Art. 3,

§ 2; per Curtis, J., 19 How., 580.) 3. This section, like its brother in the judicial article, applies only to the stranger. The moment a citizen of Virginia, ceasing from his journey, sits down in the State of New York without the intent of leaving, or makes, in fact, any stay beyond the reasonable halt of a wayfarer, he becomes a citizen of New York, and relinquishes all benefit from these important guaranties of the Federal Constitution. 4. By the comity of civilized nations, the stranger is allowed to pass through a friendly territory without molestation. Even belligerents are allowed to pass their armies over a friendly neutral territory. (Vattel, book 3, ch. 7, §§ 119, 127; Vattel, book 2, ch. 8, §§ 108, 109, 110; ch. 10, §§ 132, 133, 134.) This comity, before existing between the States, was converted by the Constitution into an absolute right of the citizen. By the section quoted the citizen of each State is secured in all the general privileges and immunities of a citizen of the United States whilst temporarily and necessarily within a State other than that of his domicil. One of these is to be free from all burdens and taxation whatever; for, upon general principles, taxation is only imposed on residents or on dealings; another is to be free from local class legislation, for as a wayfarer he cannot be a member of any body of persons organized, governed or defined as a class under the State law. The words "privileges and immunities" are here used essentially, though perhaps not exclusively, in a passive sense. The object is not to compel States to give strangers the same "rights" which they award to their own citizens; but to exempt the stranger from burdens, or obstructions of any kind. To stop his vessel or his carriage in transitu and carry off his negro servant—recognized as his property by the laws of his own State and the Federal Constitution—is a manifest invasion of his just "privileges and immunities." 5. Comity, as understood in speaking of the practice of friendly nations towards each other, which has been denominated international law, has no place in the relation between the States of this Union, except occasionally, in particular cases, to illustrate, by a somewhat remote analogy, the duty of a State toward the citizens of another State, or in giving due effect to rights arising under its laws. That duty is imposed, not by comity, as a rule of action, but by the Federal Constitution. (Bowyer's Public Law, 161, 162.) (1.) Comity, like municipal law, has its foundation in compact, express or implied. The social or international compact between the States, as such, was fixed by the Federal Constitution. (Const. U. S., art. 1, § 10.) (2.) A State might enact that all obligations arising from the relation of parent and child during the minority of the latter are abolished within this State, and any child hereafter "imported, introduced or brought into this State," shall thenceforth from all such obligations be free. A State might enact that the relation of husband and wife was fraught with mischievous consequences, and in fact a cover for gross tyranny and oppression; "that the said relation shall no longer exist within this State; and that any wife hereafter imported, introduced or brought into this State shall, thenceforth, from all obligations of that condition, be free." Young America might hurrah for the first law, and the class known as "strong minded women" might applaud the enactment of the latter. On that occasion, one of the latter class upon a rostrum proclaiming "liberty to all women" might well adopt the anti-slavery speech of Judge Swan (6 Ohio, 671), giving it a new application, "The positive prohibition becomes an active, operating, ruling principle, and not a parenthesis. It strikes down and destroys." What is there to protect this Union from the ruin and desolation of such laws except the guaranties of the Federal Constitution now relied upon? Unless they are enforced, in the form and to the extent which we demand, the unbridled sovereignty of our smallest State, so long as our present Union lasts, will hold in its hand the power of dissolving our whole social system. Evil passions or some new fanaticism might at any moment set that power in motion.

VI. The general doctrines of the court in Dred Scott's case must be maintained, their alleged novelty notwithstanding. 1. That admiralty jurisdiction could exist without either tides or salt, was an idea too novel even for the great mind of Chief Justice Marshall; but, at last, judicial wisdom, sharpened and impelled by strong necessity, cast aside these immaterial incidents and looking to the substance of the thing, found in the Constitution a government for our great rivers and inland seas. (Genesee Chief v. Fitzhugh, 12 How. U. S. R., 443; Judge Daniel's Dissent, 464.) 2. Whilst, in actual administration, some words used in our great political charters must thus be taken to comprehend more than was in the contemplation or intent of their framers; others, if we would preserve the Republic, must be carefully limited to the sphere covered by their mental vision at the time. (1.) If Utah should make its peculiar institution a religious duty, as Thugs regard murder, and should conduct its rites with all the decency and external purity of patriarchal times, Congress, within its sphere, and the several States, within theirs, might still legislate against it to any extent without violating constitutional restraints. Our Republic was founded by a civilization, with the existence of which this practice is incompatible. Self-preservation, if not a law of nature, is an invariable practice among men. If a State should fall into Thugism and respect the assassination of travelers as a religious ceremony, could not Congress and the federal judiciary, or the national executive by its military force repress the practice? (Edinb. Rev. for July, 1858, 120.) (2.) The "men" who made the Declaration of Independence in 1776; the "free inhabitants" spoken of in the Articles of Confederation (art. 4), in November, 1777, and the "inhabitants" and "male inhabitants" mentioned in the State Constitutions of that day (19 How., 574), did not include all to whom these terms were lexicographically applicable. Indians living in their tribes were not included (20 Johns., 710, 734; 19 How., 404.) The negroes were not included (19 How.; Curtis, J., Contra, 19 How., 582.) When at the close of our revolutionary struggle the same great family of States sat down to frame the laws for a more perfect and a perpetual union, the "citizens" whom they recognized as the supreme original source of all political power were the same class who acted together at the outset. If, in such rare instances and to such limited extent as to escape notice (18 Pick., 209), negroes had been permitted in particular places, by an overstrained liberality in the interpretation of laws, or by ignorance of them, to glide noiselessly into a partial exercise of political power, an inference fatal to the Republic should not thence be drawn. De minimis non curat lex. (3.) The negro was forever excluded from social union by an indubitable law of nature; what folly it would have been to endow him with political equality. Indeed, it was impossible. It never has been done; it cannot be done. (4.) Whenever the judiciary of the Union shall declare in respect to the emancipated negroes of the North that they are "citizens" of the State in which they dwell, and therefore under the Constitution (Art. 4, § 2, subd. 1), "entitled in the several (other) States to all privileges and immunities of citizens," the law of nature, to which negro-philism so frequently appeals, will irresistibly demand the dissolution of our Union. We maintain that the negro was not permitted during the storm of battle to steal into a place in the fundamental institutions of our country, where, with full power to accomplish the fell purpose, he may lurk until the hour when it shall be his pleasure to apply the torch and explode our Republic forever.

VII. "It is highly fit that the court below should be corrected in the view which it has taken of this matter, since the doctrine laid down by it in this sentence is inconsistent with the peace of this country and the rights of other States." (Per Lord Stowell, 1 Dod., 99.)

Joseph Blunt, for The People, respondents.

I. The state of slavery is contrary to natural right, and is not regarded with favor in any system of jurisprudence. All legal intendment is against it, and in favor of freedom. Slavery is the ownership of a man under the local laws of a State where slavery exists. It is not derived from any compact or consent of the slave. It originates in force, and its continuance is maintained by force. According to the law of slavery, the children of the slave become slaves. His labor and all the products of his labor belong to his master, and that labor may be coerced, at the discretion of the master, by stripes, or any other punishment short of death. Slavery requires a peculiar system of laws to enforce the rules of the master, which are irreconcilable with the jurisprudence of States where it does not exist.

The Roman law did not allow freedom to be sold. (Edict. Theod., §§ 94, 95.) Slavery is contra naturam. (Just. Inst., lib. 1, tit. 3; Aristotle Politic., lib. 1, ch. 3.) Fortescue, in his discourse to Henry VI, on the laws of England, says: Ab homine et pro vitio introducta est servitus. Sed libertas a Deo hominis est. indita naturoe. (Cap. 42.) The right to a slave is different from the right to other property. (Vide Esclavage in Code de l'Humanite; 18 Pick., 216; 2 McLean, 596; 16 Pet., 11; Forbes v. Cochrane, 2 Barn. & Cress., 448.)

II. The law of slavery is local, and does not operate beyond the territory of the State where it is established. When the slave is carried, or escapes beyond its jurisdiction, he becomes free, and the State to which he resorts is under no obligation to restore him, except by virtue of express stipulation. (Grotius, lib. 2, ch. 15, 5,

1; id., chap. 10, 2, 1; Wicquefort's Embassador, lib. 1, p. 418; Bodin de Rep., lib. 1, cap. 5; 4 Martin, 385.) Case of the Creole and opinion in the House of Lords, 1842. (1 Phillimore on International Law, 316–345.)

In 1531, the Supreme Court at Mechlin rejected an application for surrendering a fugitive slave from Spain. (Gudelin de Jure Noviss, lib. 1, ch. 5.)

In 1738, Jean Borcaut, a slave from St. Domingo, was landed in France, and some formalities required by the edict of 1716 having been omitted, he was declared free. (15 vol., Causes Celebres, 3.) Before 1716, slaves from the colonies became free as soon as they landed in France. (Id.)

In 1758, Francisque, a negro slave from Hindostan, was brought into France, and although the formalities of the edicts of 1716 and 1738 had been complied with, he was declared free, because those edicts had not been extended to slaves from the East Indies. (3d Denissart Decisions Nouvelles, 406.)

In [missing year], a Pole went into Russia, and sold himself into slavery; having been taken into Holland he claimed his freedom, and was declared free. (Wiquefort's Ambassador et Ses Fonctions, lib. 1, p. 418; Phill. on International Law, 342.)

Bodinus, in De Republica, cites two cases of the same character in France. One where a Spanish Ambassador brought a slave in his retinue, and in spite of all remonstrance he was declared free. The other, a Spanish merchant, touching at Toulon, on his way to Genoa by sea, with a slave on board, and the slave was declared free. (Bodin. de Rep., lib. 1, 41.)

In 1762, Stanley v. Harvey (2 Eden. Ch. Rep., 126), Lord Northington held that a slave becomes free as soon as he lands in England. In the case of Knight, the negro, the Sessions Court, in Scotland, in 1770, held the same principle (Fergusson's Rep. on Divorce, App., 396.) In the Somerset case, Lord Mansfield held, a negro who had been bought in Virginia and brought to England, to be free. (20 Howell S. T., 82.) In 1824, the doctrine was applied to thirty-eight slaves who came on board of a British man-of-war off Florida, having escaped from a Florida plantation. Admiral Cockburn held them to be free, and the owner, Forbes, sued him in the King's Bench for their value. Judgment for defendant, on the ground that they became free by coming on board a British ship, it being neutral territory. (2 Barn. & Cres., 448; 3 Dowl. & Ryl., 697.)

In 1820, the Court of Appeals in Kentucky held, that where a slave born in Kentucky had been taken into Indiana under territorial laws, allowing the introduction of slaves without their becoming free, and afterwards was brought back to Kentucky, she became free.

The court said, that "in deciding this question, we disclaim the influence of the general principles of liberty which we all admire, and conceive it ought to be decided by the law as it is, and not as it ought to be. Slavery is sanctioned by the laws of this State, and the right to hold them under our municipal regulations, is unquestionable. But we view this as a right existing by positive law of a municipal character, without foundation in the law of nature, or the unwritten and common law." (Rankin v. Lydia, 2 A. K. Marsh. R., 470.) Again, "it is the right of another to the labor of a slave, whether exercised or not, which constitutes slavery, or involuntary servitude. The right, then, during the seven years' residence of Lydia in Indiana, was not only suspended, but ceased to exist; and we are not aware of any law of this State which can or does bring into operation the right of slavery when once destroyed. It would be a construction without language to be construed—implication without any scrap of law, written or unwritten, statutory or common, from which the inference could be drawn—to revive the right to a slave, when that right had passed over to the slave himself, and he had become free." (Id., 472.)

In 1805, the Court of Appeals of Virginia held, that a Virginia slave, taken by its owner into Maryland, and kept there more than a year, became free upon being brought back to Virginia—that State having prohibited the importation of slaves. (Wilson v. Isbell, 5 Call's R., 430; Hunter v. Fulcher, 1 Leigh., 172.)

In 1813, a slave, occasionally taken by his owner from Maryland, to work his quarry in Virginia, in all twelve months, was held to have become free—the law of Virginia having prohibited the importation of slaves. (Stewart v. Oakes, 5 Farr. & Johns., 107.)

In 1824, the Supreme Court of Louisiana held, that a slave taken from Kentucky into Ohio to reside, became free; and that having become free, removal into a slave State with her master did not make her a slave again. (14 Martin's R., 401.) In 1835 it held that a slave taken into France, and afterwards brought back to Louisiana, became free. (Marie Louise v. Marot, 8 Louis. R., 475.) In 1816 the same court held that a person claimed as a slave by a bill of sale executed in a free State or territory, must be deemed free, unless the right of conveying him out of that State could be justified, by proving him to be a fugitive slave. (Forsyth v. Nash, 4 Martin, 390.) Before the act of 1846, the courts of Louisiana always held that a slave taken into a free State became free; and that he did not become a slave upon being brought back. (Eugenie v. Preval, 2 Louis. Annual R., 180; Smith v. Smith, 13 Louis. R., 444; Virginia v. Himel, 10 Louis. Ann. R., 185; Josephine v. Poultney, 1 id., 328; 14 Martin Louis. R., 401.)

The Supreme Court of Missouri held, that the actual residence of a slave in Illinois is sufficient evidence of freedom. (Milly v. Smith, 2 Mo. Rep., 36, in 1829.) Also, that a slave taken into Illinois on his route to Missouri, but hired by a resident while there, became free. (Julia v. McKinney, 3 id., 270, in 1833.) The same, where the slave on his journey was detained four weeks in Illinois. (Wilson v. Melvin, 4 id., 592, in 1837.) And where an army officer took his slave to his post in the northwestern territory, the slave was held free. (Rachel v. Walker, 4 id., 350, in 1836.)

In 1851, the Court of Appeals in South Carolina, in an action for the value of a slave, recognized the principle that a slave landing in a free State became free. (Ellis v. Welch, 4 Rich., 468.)

In 1840, the General Court of Virginia held that a slave taken by her master into Massachusetts and brought back into Virginia, was entitled to her freedom. (Commonwealth v. Pleasant, 10 Leigh., 697; Betty v. Horton, 5 id., 615.) In this case the court held that this freedom was acquired by the action of the law of Massachusetts upon the slaves coming there.

In 1833, Chief Justice Shaw held that a slave temporarily brought by his owner into Massachusetts, became free. (Commonwealth v. Aves, 18 Pick. R., 193.)

III. The provision in the Federal Constitution relating to fugitive slaves, recognizes this principle of universal jurisprudence, and imposes on the free States an obligation which is limited to fugitive slaves. If slaves were recognized as property under the Constitution, this provision would be unnecessary. When this provision was under discussion it was amended by striking out the word "legally" before "held to service;" because some thought slavery could not be legal in a moral point of view, and substituting "under the laws thereof." (Journal of Federal Constitution, 1787, pages 306, 365, 384.) It was then deemed improper to admit in the Constitution the idea that there could be property in men. (Madison's Works, 1429.) C. C. Pinckney, in speaking of this provision, says: "We have obtained a right to recover our slaves, in whatever part of America they may take refuge—which is a right we had not before." (16 Peters, 648.)

IV. The persons here claimed as slaves, are free by the express enactment of the Legislature of this State. (1 R. S., 656, part 1, tit. 7, § 1.) "No person held as a slave shall be imported, introduced, or brought into this State, on any pretence whatever. Every such person shall be free." "Every person brought into this State as a slave shall be free." The exception originally made in favor of persons in transitu with their slaves, was repealed in 1841. (Ch. 247.)

The right to declare and control the condition of its citizens is a right belonging to the States, and has not been conferred on the Federal Government. Otherwise the whole power over slavery must be deemed within the control of Congress.

V. They cannot be held by virtue of any provision of the Constitution of the United States. The provisions cited on the argument before Mr. Justice Paine are: That relating to fugitives from justice. (Art. 4, § 2.) That full faith and credit shall be given in each State to each State, to the public acts of every other State. (Art. 4, § 1.) That the citizens of each State shall be entitled to all privileges and immunities of citizens in the several States. (Art. 4, § 2.) That no citizen shall be deprived of life, liberty, or property, without due process of law. (Art. 5 of Amendments.) None of these provisions have any reference to this case. They are not fugitives escaping into this State from another State. We give full faith and credit to the act of Virginia, that made these persons slaves there. We allow the appellant all the privileges and immunities of a citizen of this State. He has not been deprived of property by these proceedings. The appellant had no property in these persons. It ceased to be property when he brought them into the State of New York.

The Constitution of the United States is a grant of powers to the General Government. It follows, by necessary consequence, that what is not granted is reserved. If there is no grant of power to enforce upon New York the obligation to allow a citizen of a slave State to bring his slaves here and retain them here as slaves, while sojourning or passing through this State, the General Government has not the power; and the right to do so does not exist. New York having prohibited the act, no jurisdiction can declare her law unconstitutional. She has the right to reiterate the law of nature—to purge her soil of an evil that exists only in violation of natural right—to maintain, in practice as well as theory, the sacred rights of persons and personal liberty. Even in consenting to the reclamation of fugitives from service, she does not acknowledge the law of slavery. She agrees to ignore that question; and not to inquire into the nature of the duty of service on the part of the fugitive, whether a slave or an apprentice; but to remit him to the courts of the State from which he fled. But this is the extent of her duty, her bond extends no further than to the fugitive. As to all other persons, her laws protect their personal liberty against all claimants.

It was not contemplated, at the formation of the Constitution, that slavery was to be a permanent institution of the United States. It is inconsistent with the principle that lies at the foundation of our government. It is in contradiction to the Declaration of Independence, and to the preamble to the Constitution. All the provisions of that instrument and contemporaneous history look to its ultimate extinction by the legislation and action of the State governments. (Emancipation acts of Vermont in 1777; New Hampshire, 1783; Rhode Island, 1784; Connecticut, 1784; New York, 1799; New Jersey, 1804; and Pennsylvania, 1780; Bill of Rights of Massachusetts, and decision in James v. Lechmere, in 1770, that slavery was illegal in that State; 2d vol. Franklin's Works, 517; Madison's Works, 1429; Jefferson's Notes, 152; Washington's Will, 1 vol., 569; Helper's Crisis, 193–224.)

In incorporating the fugitive slave provision into the Constitution, the Convention was careful not to do anything which should imply their sanction of slavery as legal. The provision reported by the committee, September 12, 1787, read, "legally held to service;" and it was amended September 15, by striking out "legally," so as to read "held to service under the laws thereof." (Journal, 384, and Madison, pp. 1558 and 1589.) The word "service" was substituted for "servitude," on motion of Edmund Randolph; the latter being descriptive of slaves, and the former of free persons. (3 Mad., 1569.)

VI. These persons are not to be held as slaves, under any implied covenants between the States of the Union, nor by any rule of comity.
1. There is no implied obligation on the part of New York, to allow a slave within her borders, in any form or under any circumstances. The provision

relating to the surrender of fugitives from service, is the only possible case where such an obligation can arise. And by incorporating this provision in the Constitution, every other case is excluded. Expressio unius, exclusion alterius. If the general right existed, and it was admitted that a slave of a slave State might still be held if escaping into or taken into a free State in transitu, the constitutional provision as to fugitives would be superfluous.

2. No comity of States requires us to admit slavery into our State in any form.

In extending comity towards the laws of other States, it is the State and not the Court that establishes the rule. (Chief Justice Taney, in Augusta v. Earle, 13 Pet., 589; Grotius, L. ii, ch. xxii, § 16.)

There can be no such comity here, because the State has made an express statute declaring these persons to be free. Comity is not an obligation to be enforced by a superior, but a courtesy allowed by the party assuming the duty. In deciding whether comity requires any act, we look to our own laws and adjudication for authority. And it can never be exercised in violation of our laws. (Story, Conflict of Laws, §§ 23, 24, 36, 37; Willard v. The People, 4 Scam., 461; Commonwealth v. Aves, 18 Pick. R., 221; 3 Am. Jurist, 404.)

No comity requires us to allow an act here, by citizens of another State, that if done by our own citizens would be a felony.

The comity of nations is based upon principles that destroy all right to hold these persons as slaves. The laws of moral right, the recognition of personal liberty by the law of nations forbid it. A state prisoner, escaping from Austria or Italy (a slave to the law), cannot be reclaimed. A serf from Russia, or a Barbary slave, brought hither by his master, in transitu, could not be here restrained from liberty by any law or comity. To discover (says Vattel, in his Preliminary Discourse) the rights and duties of nations, we must investigate the natural rights and duties of individuals. The laws of nations are, in their origin, only natural rights of men applied to nations. (§ 6, Montes. Spirit of Laws, b. 15, ch. v, § 5.) If the sanctity of personal liberty was as much regarded in practice as it is in the theories of government, and law and morals—if courts and legislatures declared in this particular case the admitted general law, a cogent argument may be drawn in favor of the liberty of these persons, from the maxims and principles of the laws of nations, as developed by the highest authority. Says Vattel (Le Droit des Gens., lib. 3, ch. 8, § 152), after remarking briefly upon the question, whether or not prisoners of war can be enslaved, "This topic has been enough discussed. I shall not pursue it. Fortunately this disgrace to humanity has been banished from Europe." (Grot., L. ii, ch. x, § 1.)

VII. These persons cannot be restrained of their liberty, whatever may have been their state in Virginia. If restrained of liberty here, it must be either under and by virtue of our laws, or under the laws of Virginia. The allegation of the writ is, that they were held and confined in a certain house in this city, against their will. The answer is, they are slaves. Our laws prohibit any such holding.

They furnish no remedy if the person claimed refuse to be detained. The question here is, can they be detained? Certainly not by our laws; and our courts can only administer our own laws. The laws of Virginia are not in force here. If the slave resists, how can he be compelled to subjection? If the master has not the power to enforce obedience, he cannot invoke the aid of law, for no law exists for such a case. It follows, that our laws, in this respect, if they remain neutral, leave the parties to their natural rights. This being so, the slave is free.

VIII. They are free by the common law. (Co. Litt., 124, b; Somerset's Case, 20 Howell's State Trial, 79; Knight v. Wedderburn, id., p. 2; Forbes v. Cochrane, 2 Barn. & Cress., 448; Greenwood v. Curtis, 6 Mass. R., 366; Case of the Antelope, 10 Wheat., 420; Jones v. Van Zandt, 2 McLean, 596.)

William M. Evarts, for the respondents.

I. The writ of habeas corpus belongs of right to every person restrained of liberty within this State, under any pretence whatsoever, unless by certain judicial process of Federal or State authority. (2 R. S., 563, § 21.) This right is absolute (1) against legislative invasion, and (2) against judicial discretion. (Const. art. 1, § 4; 1 R. S., 565, § 31.)

In behalf of a human being, restrained of liberty within this State, the writ, by a legal necessity, must issue. The office of the writ is to enlarge the person in whose behalf it issues, unless legal cause be shown for the restraint of liberty or its continuation; and enlargement of liberty, unless such cause to the contrary be shown, flows from the writ by the same legal necessity that required the writ to be issued. (2 R. S., 567, § 39.)

II. The whole question of the case, then, is, does the relation of slave owner and slave, which subsisted in Virginia between Mrs. Lemmon and these persons while there, attend upon them while commorant within this State, in the course of travel from Virginia to Texas, so as to furnish "legal cause" for the restraint of liberty complained of, and so as to compel the authority and power of this State to sanction and maintain such restraint of liberty.

1. Legal cause of restraint can be none other than an authority to maintain the restraint which has the force of law within this State. Nothing has or can claim the authority of law within this State, unless it proceeds—
    a. From the sovereignty of the State, and is found in the Constitution or Statutes of the State, or in its unwritten common (or customary) law; or—
    b From the Federal Government, whose Constitution and Statutes have the force of law within this State. So far as the law of nations has force within this State, and so far as, "by comity," the laws of other sovereignties have force within this State, they derive their efficacy, not from their own vigor, but by administration as a part of the law of this State. (Story Confl. Laws, §§ 18, 20, 23, 25, 29, 33, 35, 37, 38; Bank of

Augusta v. Earle, 13 Pet., 519, 589; Dalrymple v. Dalrymple, 2 Hagg. Consist. R., 59; Dred Scott v. Sandford, 19 How., 460, 461, 486, 487.)

2. The Constitution of the United States and the federal statutes give no law on the subject. The Federal Constitution and legislation under it have, in principle and theory, no concern with the domestic institutions, the social basis, the social relations, the civil conditions, which obtain within the several States. The actual exceptions are special and limited, and prove the rule. They are—

   a. A reference to the civil conditions obtaining within the States to furnish an artificial enumeration of persons as the basis of federal representation and direct taxation distributively between the States.
   b. A reference to the political rights of suffrage within the States as, respectively, supplying the basis of the federal suffrage therein.
   c. A provision securing to the citizens of every State within every other the privileges and immunities (whatever they may be) accorded in each to its own citizens.
   d. A provision preventing the laws or regulations of any State governing the civil condition of persons within it, from operating upon the condition of persons "held to service or labor in one State, under the laws thereof, escaping into another." (Const. U. S., art. 1, § 2, subd. 1 and 3; art. 4, § 2, subd. 1 and 3; Laws of Slave States and of Free States on Slavery; Ex parte Simmons, 4 Wash. C. C. R., 396; Jones v. Van Zandt, 2 McLean, 597; Groves v. Slaughter, 15 Peters, 506, 508–510; Prigg v. Pennsylvania, 16 Pet., 611, 612, 622, 623, 625; Strader v. Graham, 10 How., 82, 93; New York v. Miln, 11 Pet., 136; Dred Scott v. Sandford; Ch. J., 452; Nelson, J., 459, 461; Campbell, J., 508, 509, 516, 517.)

   None of these provisions, in terms or by any intendment, support the right of the slave owner in his own State or in any other State, except the last. This, by its terms, is limited to its special case, and necessarily excludes federal intervention in every other.

3. The common law of this State permits the existence of slavery in no case within its limits. (Const., art. 1, § 17; Sommersett's case, 20 How. St. Trials, 79; Knight v. Wedderburn, id., 2; Forbes v. Cochrane, 2 Barn. & Cress., 448; Shanley v. Harvey, 2 Eden, 126; The Slave Grace, 2 Hagg. Adm., 118, 104; Story Confl. Laws, § 96; Co. Litt., 124 b.)

4. The statute law of this State effects a universal proscription and prohibition of the condition of slavery within the limits of the State. (1 R. S., 656, § 1; id., 659, § 16; 2 R. S., 664, § 28; Dred Scott v. Sandford, 19 How., 591, 595; Laws of 1857, 797.)

III. It remains only to be considered whether, under the principles of the law of nations, as governing the intercourse of friendly States, and as adopted and incorporated into the administration of our municipal law, comity requires the recognition and support of the relation of slave owner and slave between strangers passing through our territory, notwithstanding the absolute policy and comprehensive legislation which prohibit that relation and render the civil condition of slavery impossible in our own society.

The comity, it is to be observed, under inquiry, is (1) of the State and not of the Court, which latter has no authority to exercise comity in behalf of the State, but only a judicial power of determining whether the main policy and actual legislation of the State exhibit the comity inquired of; and (2) whether the comity extends to yielding the affirmative aid of the State to maintain the mastery of the slave owner and the subjection of the slave. (Story Confl. Laws, § 38; Bank of Augusta v. Earle, 13 Pet., 589; Dred Scott v. Sandford, 19 How., 591.)

1. The principles, policy, sentiments, public reason and conscience, and authoritative will of the State sovereignty, as such, have been expressed in the most authentic form, and with the most distinct meaning, that slavery, whencesoever it comes, and by whatsoever casual access, or for whatsoever transient stay, shall not be tolerated upon our soil.

That the particular case of slavery during transit has not escaped the intent or effect of the legislation on the subject, appears in the express permission once accorded to it, and the subsequent abrogation of such permission. (1 R. S., part 1, ch. 20, tit. 7, §§ 6, 7; Repealing act, Laws 1841, ch. 247.) Upon such a declaration of the principles and sentiments of the State, through its Legislature, there is no opportunity or scope for judicial doubt or determination. (Story Confl. Laws, §§ 36, 37, 23, 24; Vattel, 1, §§ 1, 2.)

2. But, were such manifest enactment of the sovereign will in the premises wanting, as matter of general reason and universal authority, the status of slavery is never upheld in the case of strangers, resident or in transit, when the domestic laws reject and suppress such status as a civil condition or social relation.
    a. The same reasons of justice and policy which forbid the sanction of law and the aid of public force to the proscribed status among our own population, forbid them in the case of strangers within our territory.
    b. The status of slavery is not a natural relation, but contrary to nature, and at every moment it subsists, it is an ever new and active violation of the law of nature. (Const. Va., Bill of Rights, §§ 1, 14, 15; Taylor's Elements of Civil Law, 429; 2 Dev., 263; 9 Geo., 580; Henning's Statutes at Large, vol. 10, 129; id., 11, 322, 324.)

It originates in mere predominance of physical force, and is continued by mere predominance of social force or municipal law.

Whenever and wherever the physical force in the one stage, or the social force or municipal law in the other stage, fails, the status falls, for it has nothing to rest upon.

To continue and defend the status, then, within our territory, the stranger must appeal to some municipal law. He has brought with him no system of municipal law to be a weapon and a shield to this status; he finds no such system here. His appeal to force against nature, to law against justice, is vain, and his captive is free.

    c. The law of nations, built upon the law of nature, has adopted this same view of the status of slavery, as resting on force against right, and finding no support outside of the jurisdiction of the municipal law which establishes it.
    d. A State proscribing the status of slavery in its domestic system, has no apparatus, either of law or of force, to maintain the relation between strangers.

It has no code of the slave owner's rights or of the slave's submission, no processes for the enforcement of either, no rules of evidence or adjudication in the premises, no guard-houses, prisons or whipping-posts to uphold the slave owner's power and crush the slave's resistance.

But a comity which should recognize a status that can subsist only by force, and yet refuse the force to sustain it, is illusory. If we recognize the fragment of slavery imported by a stranger, we must adopt the fabric of which it is a fragment and from which it derives its vitality.

If the slave be eloigned by fraud or force, the owner must have replevin for him or trover for his value.

If a creditor obtain a foreign attachment against the slave owner, the sheriff must seize and sell the slaves.

If the owner die, the surrogate must administer the slave as assets.

If the slave give birth to offspring, we have a native-born slave.

If the owner, enforcing obedience to his caprices, maim or slay his slave, we must admit the status as a plea in bar to the public justice.

If the slave be tried for crime, upon his owner's complaint, the testimony of his fellow slaves must be excluded.

If the slave be imprisoned or executed for crime, the value taken by the State must be made good to the owner, as for "private property taken for public use."

Everything or nothing, is the demand from our comity; everything or nothing, must be our answer.

    e. The rule of the law of nations which permits the transit of strangers and their property through a friendly State does not require our laws to uphold the relation of slave owner and slave between strangers.

By the law of nations, men are not the subject of property.

By the law of nations, the municipal law which makes men the subject of property, is limited with the power to enforce itself, that is by its territorial jurisdiction.

By the law of nations, then, the strangers stand upon our soil in their natural relations as men, their artificial relation being absolutely terminated. (The Antelope, 10 Wheat., 120, 121, and cases ut supra.)

> f. The principle of the law of nations which attributes to the law of the domicil the power to fix the civil status of persons, does not require our laws to uphold, within our own territory, the relation of slave owner and slave between strangers.

This principle only requires us (1) to recognise the consequences, in reference to subjects within our own jurisdiction (so far as may be done without prejudice to domestic interests), of the status existing abroad; and (2) where the status itself is brought within our limits and is here permissible as a domestic status, to recognize the foreign law as an authentic origin and support of the actual status.

It is thus that marriage contracted in a foreign domicil, according to the municipal law there, will be maintained as a continuing marriage here, with such traits as belong to that relation here; yet, incestuous marriage or polygamy, lawful in the foreign domicil, cannot be held as a lawful continuing relation here. (Story Confl. Laws, §§ 51, 51 a., 89, 113, 114, 96, 104, 620, 624.)

> g. This free and sovereign State, in determining to which of two external laws it will by comity add the vigor of its adoption and administration within its territory, viz., a foreign municipal law of force against right, or the law of nations conformed to its own domestic policy under the same impulse which has purged its own system of the odious and violent injustice of slavery, will prefer the law of nations to the law of Virginia, and set the slave free.

Impius et crudelis judicandus est, qui libertati non favet. Nostra jura in omni casu libertati dant favorem. (Co. Litt., ut supra.)

JUDGES: Denio, J., Wright, J. Davies, Bacon and Welles, Js., concurred. Clerke, J. (Dissenting.) Comstock, Ch. J., observed in substance. Selden, J.

OPINION BY: Denio, Wright

OPINION:

Denio, J. The petition upon which the writ of habeas corpus was issued, states that the colored persons sought to be discharged from imprisonment were, on the preceding night, taken from the steamer City of Richmond, in the harbor of New York, and at the time of presenting the petition, were confined in a certain house in Carlisle street in that city. The writ is directed to the appellant by the name of "Lemmings," as the person having in charge "eight colored persons lately taken from the steamer City of Richmond, and to the man in whose house in Carlisle street they were confined." The return is made by Lemmon, the appellant, and it speaks of the colored persons who are therein alleged to be slaves, and the property of Juliet Lemmon, as "the eight slaves or persons named in the said writ of habeas corpus." It alleges that they were taken out of the possession of Mrs. Lemmon, while in transitu between Norfolk, in Virginia, and the State of Texas, and that both Virginia and Texas are slaveholding States; that she had no intention of bringing the slaves into this State to remain therein, or in any manner except on their transit as aforesaid through the port of New York; that she was compelled by necessity to touch or land, but did not intend to remain longer than necessary, and that such landing was for the purpose of passage and transit and not otherwise, and that she did not intend to sell the slaves. It is also stated that she was compelled by "necessity or accident" to take passage from Norfolk in the above mentioned steamship, and that Texas was her ultimate place of destination.

I understand the effect of these statements to be that Mrs. Lemmon, being the owner of these slaves, desired to take them from her residence in Norfolk to the State of Texas; and, as a means of effecting that purpose, she embarked, in the steamship mentioned, for New York, with a view to secure a passage from thence to her place of destination. As nothing is said of any stress of weather, and no marine casualty is mentioned, the necessity of landing, which is spoken of, refers, no doubt, to the exigency of that mode of prosecuting her journey. If the ship in which she arrived was not bound for the Gulf of Mexico, she would be under the necessity of landing at New York to reembark in some other vessel sailing for that part of the United States; and this, I suppose, is what it was intended to state. The necessity or accident which is mentioned as having compelled her to embark at Norfolk in the City of Richmond, is understood to refer to some circumstance which prevented her making a direct voyage from Virginia to Texas. The question to be decided is whether the bringing the slaves into this State under these circumstances entitled them to their freedom.

The intention, and the effect, of the statutes of this State bearing upon the point are very plain and unequivocal. By an act passed in 1817, it was declared that no person held as a slave should be imported, introduced or brought into this State on any pretence whatever, except in the cases afterwards mentioned in the act, and any slave brought here contrary to the act was declared to be free. Among the excepted cases was that of a person, not an inhabitant of the State, passing through it, who was allowed to bring his slaves with him; but they were not to remain in the State longer than nine months. (Laws of 1817, ch. 137, §§ 9, 15.) The portions of this act which concern the present question were reenacted at the revision of the laws in 1830. The first and last sections of the title are in the following language:

§ 1. No person held as a slave shall be imported, introduced or brought into this State on any pretence whatsoever, except in the cases hereinafter specified. Every such person shall be free. Every person held as a slave who hath been introduced or brought in this State contrary to the laws in force at the time, shall be free.

§ 16. Every person born in this State, whether white or colored, is free. Every person who shall hereafter be born within this State shall be free; and every person brought into this State as a slave, except as authorized by this title, shall be free. (R. S., part 1, ch 20, tit. 7.)

The intermediate sections, three to seven inclusive, contain the exceptions. Section 6 is as follows: "Any person, not being an inhabitant of this State, who shall be traveling to or from, or passing through this State, may bring with him any person lawfully held in slavery, and may take such person with him from this State; but the person so held in slavery shall not reside or continue in this State more than nine months; if such residence be continued beyond that time such person shall be free." In the year 1841, the Legislature repealed this section, together with the four containing other exceptions to the general provisions above mentioned. (Ch. 247.) The effect of this repeal was to render the 1st and 16th sections absolute and unqualified. If any doubt of this could be entertained upon the perusal of the part of the title left unrepealed, the rules of construction would oblige us to look at the repealed portions in order to ascertain the sense of the residue. (Bussey v. Story, 4 Barn. & Adolph., 98.) Thus examined, the meaning of the statute is as plain as though the Legislature had declared in terms that if any person should introduce a slave into this State, in the course of a journey to or from it, or in passing through it, the slave shall be free.

If, therefore, the Legislature had the constitutional power to enact this statute, the law of the State precisely meets the case of the persons who were brought before the judge on the writ of habeas corpus, and his order discharging them from constraint was unquestionably correct. Every sovereign State has a right to determine by its laws the condition of all persons who may at any time be within its jurisdiction; to exclude therefrom those whose introduction would contravene its policy, or to declare the conditions upon which they may be received, and what subordination or restraint may lawfully be allowed by one class or description of persons over another. Each State has, moreover, the right to enact such rules as it may see fit respecting the title to property, and to declare what subjects shall, within the State, possess the attributes of property, and what shall be incapable of a proprietary right. These powers may of course be variously limited or modified by its own constitutional or fundamental laws; but independently of such restraints (and none are alleged to exist affecting this case) the legislative authority of the State over these subjects is without limit or control, except so far as the State has voluntarily abridged her jurisdiction by arrangements with other States.

There are, it is true, many cases where the conditions impressed upon persons and property by the laws of other friendly States may and ought to be recognized within our own jurisdiction. These are defined, in the absence of express legislation, by the general assent and by the practice and usage of civilized countries, and being considered as incorporated into the municipal law, are freely administered by the courts. They are not, however, thus allowed on account of any supposed power residing in another State to enact laws which should be binding on our tribunals, but from the presumed assent of the law-making power to abide by the usages of other civilized States. Hence it follows that where the Legislature of the State, in which a right or privilege is claimed on the ground of comity, has by its laws spoken upon the subject of the alleged right, the tribunals are not at liberty to search for the rule of decision among the doctrines of international comity, but are bound to adopt the directions laid down by the political government of their own State. We have not, therefore, considered it necessary to inquire whether by the law of nations, a country where negro slavery is established has generally a right to claim of a neighboring State, in which it is not allowed, the right to have that species of property recognized and protected in the course of a lawful journey taken by the owner through the last mentioned country, as would undoubtedly be the case with a subject recognized as property everywhere; and it is proper to say that the counsel for the appellant has not urged that principle in support of the claim of Mrs. Lemmon.

What has been said as to the right of a sovereign State to determine the status of persons within its jurisdiction applies to the States of this Union, except as it has been modified or restrained by the Constitution of the United States (Groves v. Slaughter, 15 Pet., 419; Moore v. The People of Illinois, 14 How. 13; City of New York v. Miln, 11 Pet., 131, 139.) There are undoubtedly reasons, independently of the provisions of the Federal Constitution, for conciliatory legislation on the part of the several States, towards the polity, institutions and interests of each other, of a much more persuasive character than those which prevail even between the most friendly States unconnected by any political union; but these are addressed exclusively to the political power of the respective States; so that whatever opinion we might entertain as to the reasonableness, or policy, or even of the moral obligation of the non–slave-holding States to establish provisions similar to those which have been stricken out of the Revised Statutes, it is not in our power, while administering the laws of this State in one of its tribunals of justice, to act at all upon those sentiments, when we see, as we cannot fail to do, that the Legislature has deliberately repudiated them.

The power which has been mentioned as residing in the States is assumed by the Constitution itself to extend to persons held as slaves by such of the States as allow the condition of slavery, and to apply also to a slave in the territory of another State, which did not allow slavery, even unaccompanied with an intention on the part of the owner to hold him in a state of slavery in such other State. The provision respecting the return of fugitives from service contains a very strong implication to that effect. It declares that no person held to service or labor in one State, under the laws thereof, escaping into another, shall in consequence of any law or regulation therein, be discharged from such service or labor, &c. There was at least one State which at the adoption of the Constitution did not tolerate slavery; and in several of the other States the number of slaves was so small and the prevailing sentiment in favor of emancipation so strong, that it was morally certain that slavery would be speedily abolished. It was assumed by the authors of the Constitution, that the fact of a Federative Union would not of itself create a duty on the part of the States which should abolish slavery to respect the rights of the owners of slaves escaping thence from the States where it continued to exist. The apprehension was not that any of the States would establish rules or regulations looking primarily to the emancipation of fugitives from labor, but that the abolition of slavery in any State would draw after it the principle that a person held in slavery would immediately become free on arriving, in any manner, within the limits of such State. That principle had then recently been acted upon in England in a case of great notoriety, which could not fail to be well known to the cultivated and intelligent men who were the principal actors in framing the Federal Constitution. A Virginia gentleman of the name of Stewart had occasion to make a voyage from his home in that Colony to England, on his own affairs, with the intention of returning as soon as they were transacted; and he took with him as his personal servant his negro slave, Somerset, whom he had purchased in Virginia and was entitled to hold in a state of slavery by the laws prevailing there. While they were in London, the negro absconded from the service of his master, but was re-taken and put on board a vessel lying in the Thames bound to Jamaica, where slavery also prevailed, for the purpose of being there sold as a slave. On application to Lord Mansfield, Chief Justice of the King's Bench, a writ of habeas corpus was issued to Knowles as master of the vessel, whose return to the writ disclosed the foregoing facts. Lord Mansfield referred the case to the decision of the Court of King's Bench, where it was held, by the unanimous opinion of the judges, that the restraint was illegal, and the negro was discharged. (The Negro Case, 11 Harg. S. T., 340; Somerset v. Stewart, Lofft, 1.) It was the opinion of the court that a state of slavery could not exist except by force of positive law, and it being considered that there was no law to uphold it in England, the principles of the law respecting the writ of habeas corpus immediately applied themselves to the case, and it became impossible to continue the imprisonment of the negro. The case was decided in 1772, and from that time it became a maxim that slaves could not exist in England. The idea was reiterated in the popular literature of the language, and fixed in the public mind by a striking metaphor which attributed to the atmosphere of the British Islands a quality which caused the shackles of the slave to fall off. The laws of England respecting personal rights were in general the laws of the Colonies, and they continued the same system after the Revolution by provisions in their Constitutions, adopting the common law subject to alterations by their own statutes. The literature of the Colonies was that of the mother country.

The aspect in which the case of fugitive slaves was presented to the authors of the Constitution therefore was this: A number of the States had very little interest in continuing the institution of slavery, and were likely soon to abolish it within their limits. When they should do so, the principle of the laws of England as to personal rights and the remedies for illegal imprisonment, would immediately prevail in such States. The judgment in Somerset's case and the principles announced by Lord Mansfield, were standing admonitions that even a temporary restraint of personal liberty by virtue of a title derived under the laws of slavery, could not be sustained where that institution did not exist by positive law, and where the remedy by habeas corpus, which was a cherished institution of this country as well as in England, was established. Reading the provision for the rendition of fugitive slaves, in the light which these considerations afford, it is impossible not to perceive that the Convention assumed the general principle to be that the escape of a slave from a State in which he was lawfully held to service into one which had abolished slavery would ipso facto transform him into a free man. This was recognized as the legal consequence of a slave going into a State where slavery did not exist, even though it were without the consent and against the will of the owner. A fortiori he would be free if the master voluntarily brought him into a free State for any purpose of his own. But the provision in the Constitution extended no further than the case of fugitives. As to such cases, the admitted general consequence of the presence of a slave in a free State was not to prevail, but he was by an express provision in the federal compact to be returned to the party to whom the service was due. Other cases were left to be governed by the general laws applicable to them. This was not unreasonable, as the owner was free to determine whether he would voluntarily permit his slave to go within a jurisdiction which did not allow him to be held in bondage. That was within his own power, but he could not always prevent his slaves from escaping out of the State in which their servile condition was recognized. The provision was precisely suited to the exigency of the case, and it went no further.

In examining other arrangements of the Constitution, apparently inserted for purposes having no reference to slavery, we ought to bear in mind that when passing the fugitive slave provision the Convention was contemplating the future existence of States which should have abolished slavery, in a political union with other States where the institution would still remain in force. It would naturally be supposed that if there were other cases in which the rights of slave owners ought to be protected in the States which should abolish slavery, they would be adjusted in connection with the provision looking specially to that case, instead of being left to be deduced by construction from clauses intended primarily for cases to which slavery had no necessary relation. It has been decided that the fugitive clause does not extend beyond the case of the actual escape of a slave from one State to another. (Ex parte Simmons, 4 Wash. C. C. 396.) But the provision is plainly so limited by its own language.

The Constitution declares that the citizens of each State shall be entitled to all privileges and immunities of citizens in the several States. (Art. 4, § 2.) No provision in that instrument has so strongly tended to constitute the citizens of the United States one people as this. Its influence in that direction cannot be fully estimated without a consideration of what would have been the condition of the people if it or some similar provision had not been inserted. Prior to the adoption of the Articles of Confederation, the British colonies on this continent had no political connection, except that they were severally dependencies of the British crown. Their relation to each other was the same which they respectively bore to the other English colonies, whether on this continent or in Europe or Asia. When, in consequence of the Revolution, they severally became independent and sovereign States, the citizens of each State would have been under all the disabilities of alienage in every other, but for a provision in the compacts into which they entered whereby that consequence was avoided. The articles adopted during the Revolution formed essentially a league for mutual protection against external force; but in passing them it was felt to be necessary to secure a community of intercourse which would not necessarily obtain even among closely allied States. This was effected by the fourth article of that instrument, which declared that the free inhabitants of each of the States (paupers, vagabonds, and fugitives from justice excepted) should be entitled to all privileges and immunities of free citizens in the several States, and that the people of each State should have free ingress and egress to and from any other State, and should enjoy therein all the privileges of trade and commerce, subject to the same duties, impositions and restrictions as the inhabitants thereof, respectively. The Constitution organized a still more intimate Union, constituting the States, for all external purposes and for certain enumerated domestic objects, a single nation; but still the principle of State sovereignty was retained as to all subjects, except such as were embraced in the delegations of power to the General Government or prohibited to the States. The social status of the people, and their personal and relative rights as respects each other, the definition and arrangements of property, were among the reserved powers of the States. The provision conferring rights of citizenship upon the citizens of every State in every other State, was inserted substantially as it stood in the Articles of Confederation. The question now to be considered is, how far the State jurisdiction over the subjects just mentioned is restricted by the provision we are considering; or, to come at once to the precise point in controversy, whether it obliges the State governments to recognize, in any way, within their own jurisdiction, the property in slaves which the citizens of States in which slavery prevails may lawfully claim within their own States—beyond the case of fugitive slaves. The language is that they shall have the privileges and immunities of citizens in the several States. In my opinion the meaning is, that in a given State, every citizen of every other State shall have the same privileges and immunities—that is, the same rights—which the citizens of that State possess. In the first place, they are not to be subjected to any of the disabilities of alienage. They can hold property by the same titles by which every other citizen may hold it, and by no other. Again, any discriminating legislation which should place them in a worse situation than a proper citizen of the particular State would be unlawful. But the clause has nothing to do with the distinctions founded on domicil. A citizen of Virginia, having his home in that State, and never having been within the State of New York, has the same rights under our laws which a native born citizen, domiciled elsewhere, would have, and no other rights. Either can be the proprietor of property here, but neither can claim any rights which under our laws belong only to residents of the State. But where the laws of the several States differ, a citizen of one State asserting rights in another, must claim them according to the laws of the last mentioned State, not according to those which obtain in his own.

The position that a citizen carries with him, into every State into which he may go, the legal institutions of the one in which he was born, cannot be supported. A very little reflection will show the fallacy of the idea. Our laws declare contracts depending upon games of chance or skill, lotteries, wagering policies of insurance, bargains for more than 7 per cent per annum of interest, and many others, void. In other States such contracts, or some of them, may be lawful. But no one would contend that if made within this State by a citizen of another State where they would have been lawful, they would be enforced in our courts. Certain of them, if made in another State and in conformity with the laws there, would be executed by our tribunals upon the principles of comity; and the case would be the same if they were made in Europe or in any other foreign country. The clause has nothing to do with the doctrine of international comity. That doctrine, as has been remarked, depends upon the usage of civilized nations and the presumed assent of the legislative authority of the particular State in which the right is claimed; and an express denial of the right by that authority is decisive against the claim. How then, is the case of the appellant aided by the provision under consideration?

The Legislature has declared, in effect, that no person shall bring a slave into this State, even in the course of a journey between two slaveholding States, and that if he does, the slave shall be free. Our own citizens are of course bound by this regulation. If the owner of these slaves is not in like manner bound it is because, in her quality of citizen of another State, she has rights superior to those of any citizen of New York, and because, in coming here, or sending her slaves here for a temporary purpose, she has brought with her, or sent with them, the laws of Virginia, and is entitled to have those laws enforced in the courts, notwithstanding the mandate of our own laws to the contrary. But the position of the appellant proves too much. The privileges and immunities secured to the citizens of each

State by the Constitution are not limited by time, or by the purpose for which, in a particular case, they may be desired, but are permanent and absolute in their character. Hence, if the appellant can claim exemption from the operation of the statute on which the respondent relies, on the ground that she is a citizen of a State where slavery is allowed, and that our courts are obliged to respect the title which those laws confer, she may retain slaves here during her pleasure; and, as one of the chief attributes of property is the power to use it, and to sell or dispose of it, I do not see how she could be debarred of these rights within our jurisdiction as long as she may choose to exercise them. She could not, perhaps, sell them to a citizen of New York, who would at all events be bound by our laws, but any other citizen of a slave State—who would equally bring with him the immunities and privileges of his own State—might lawfully traffic in the slave property. But my opinion is that she has no more right to the protection of this property than one of the citizens of this State would have upon bringing them here under the same circumstances, and that the clause of the Constitution referred to has no application to the case. I concede that this clause gives to citizens of each State entire freedom of intercourse with every other State, and that any law which should attempt to deny them free ingress or egress would be void. But it is citizens only who possess these rights, and slaves certainly are not citizens. Even free negroes, as is well known, have been alleged not to possess that quality. In Moore v. The State of Illinois, already referred to, the Supreme Court of the United States, in its published opinion, declared that the States retained the power to forbid the introduction into their territory of paupers, criminals or fugitive slaves. The case was a conviction under a statute of Illinois, making it penal to harbor or secrete any negro, mulatto or person of color being a slave or servant owing service or labor to any other person. The indictment was for secreting a fugitive slave who had fled from his owner in Missouri. The owner had not intervened to reclaim him so as to bring the fugitive law into operation, and the case was placed by the court on the ground that it was within the legitimate power of State legislation, in the promotion of its policy, to exclude an unacceptable population. I do not at all doubt the right to exclude a slave as I do not consider him embraced under the provision securing a common citizenship; but it does not seem to me clear that one who is truly a citizen of another State can be thus excluded, though he may be a pauper or a criminal, unless he be a fugitive from justice. The fourth article of confederation contained an exception to the provision for a common citizenship, excluding from its benefits paupers and vagabonds as well as fugitives from justice; but this exception was omitted in the corresponding provision of the Constitution. If a slave attempting to come into a State of his own accord can be excluded on the ground mentioned, namely, because as a slave he is an unacceptable inhabitant, as it is very clear he may be, it would seem to follow that he might be expelled if accompanied by his master. It might, it is true, be less mischievous to permit the residence of such a person when under the restraint of his owner; but of this the

Legislature must judge. But it is not the right of the slave but of the master which is supposed to be protected under the clause respecting citizenship. The answer to the claim in that aspect has been already given. It is that the owner cannot lawfully do anything which our laws do not permit to be done by one of our own citizens, and as a citizen of this State cannot bring a slave within its limits except under the condition that he shall immediately become free, the owner of these slaves could not do it without involving herself in the same consequences.

It remains to consider the effect upon this case of the provision by which power is given to Congress to regulate commerce among the several States. (Art. 1, § 8, P 3.) If the slaves had been passing through the navigable waters of this State in a vessel having a coasting license granted under the act of Congress regulating the coasting trade, in the course of a voyage between two slave States, and in that situation had been interrupted by the operation of the writ of habeas corpus, I am not prepared to say that they could have been discharged under the provision of the statute. So if in the course of such a voyage they had been landed on the territory of the State in consequence of a marine accident or by stress of weather. In either case they would, in strictness of language, have been introduced and brought into the State. In the latter case, their being here being involuntary, as regards the owner, they would not have been "brought here" within the meaning of the statute. (Case of the brig Enterprize, in the decisions of the Commission of Claims, under the Convention of 1853, p. 187.) But the case does not present either of these features. Its actual circumstances are these: Mrs. Lemmon being the owner of these slaves, at her residence in Norfolk, chose to take them to the State of Texas for a purpose not disclosed, further than that it was not in order to sell them. Geographically, New York is not on the route of such a voyage, but we can readily see that it would be convenient to bring them to that city from which vessels sail to most of the ports in the Union, to be embarked from thence in a ship bound to a port in the extreme southern part of the Union. This was what was actually done. She came with the negroes to New York by sea, in order to embark from thence to Texas; and when the writ of habeas corpus was served they were staying at a house in the city, ready to set out when a vessel should sail, and not intending to remain longer than should be necessary.

The act under consideration is not in any just sense a regulation of commerce. It does not suggest to me the idea that it has any connection with that subject. It would have an extensive operation altogether independent of commerce. It is not therefore within the scope of the decision of the Supreme Court in the passenger cases. (7 How. 283.) In those cases the States of New York and Massachusetts had imposed taxes upon passengers arriving by sea at the ports of those States. The court considering the carrying of passengers coming here from foreign countries or being transported by sea between ports in different States, to be an operation of foreign and inter-state commerce, and holding moreover that the power to regulate commerce was exclusively vested in Congress, declared those acts to be a violation of the Constitution of the United States. It may be considered as settled by those judgments that an act of State legislation acting directly upon the subject of foreign or inter-state commerce, and being in substance a regulation of that subject, would be unwarranted, whether its provisions were hostile to any particular act of Congress or not. But there is a class of cases which may incidentally affect the subject of commerce, but in respect to which the States are free to act until the ground has been covered by an act of Congress. State legislation upon these subjects is not hostile to the power residing in Congress to regulate commerce; but if Congress in execution of that power shall have enacted special regulations touching the particular subject, such regulations then become exclusive of all interference on the part of the States. This is shown by the case of Wilson v. The Black Bird Creek Swamp Company (2 Pet., 250). The State of Delaware had authorized a corporation to erect a dam across a creek below tide-water, in order to drain a marsh. The validity of the act was drawn in question, on the ground that it was in conflict with the power of Congress to regulate commerce. The object of the work authorized by the State law was to improve the health of the neighborhood. In giving the opinion of the court, Chief Justice Marshall observed that "means to produce these objects (that is, health and the like), provided they do not come in collision with the powers of the General Government, are undoubtedly within those which are reserved to the States. But the measure authorized by this act stops a navigable creek, and must be supposed to abridge the rights of those who have been accustomed to use it. But this abridgment, unless it comes in conflict with the Constitution or a law of the United States, is an affair between the government of Delaware and its citizens, of which this court can take no cognizance." "If Congress had passed any act which bore upon the case—any act in execution of the powers to regulate commerce, the object of which was to control State legislation over these small navigable creeks into which the tide flows—we should feel not much difficulty in saying that a State law being in conflict with such act would be void. But Congress has passed no such act. The repugnancy of the law of Delaware with the Constitution is placed entirely on its repugnancy with the power to regulate commerce with foreign nations and among the several States—a power which has not been exercised so as to affect the question." The same principle has been affirmed in Sturges v. Crowninshield (4 Wheat. 122), and in Moore v. Houston (5 Wheat. 1); and since the Passenger cases, it has been reiterated in the Pilot case (Cooley v. The Board of Wardens of Philadelphia, 12 How. 299). The application of the rule to the present case is plain. We will concede, for the purpose of the argument, that the transportation of slaves from one slaveholding State to another is an act of inter-state commerce, which may be legally protected and regulated by federal legislation. Acts have been passed to regulate the coasting trade, so that if these slaves had been in transitu between Virginia and Texas, in a coasting vessel, at the time the habeas corpus was served, they could not have been interfered with while passing through the navigable waters of a free State by the authority of a law of such State. But they were not thus in transit at that time. Congress has not passed any act to regulate commerce between the State when carried on by land, or otherwise than in coasting vessels. But conceding that, in order to facilitate commerce among the States, Congress has power to provide for precisely such a case as the present—the case of persons, whose transportation is the subject of commercial intercourse, being carried by a coasting vessel to a convenient port in another State, with a view of being there landed, for the purpose of being again embarked on a fresh coasting voyage to a third port, which was to be their final destination—the unexercised power to enact such a law, to regulate such a transit, would not affect the power of the States to deal with the status of all persons within their territory in the meantime, and before the existence of such a law. It would be a law to regulate commerce carried on partly by land and partly by water—a subject upon which Congress has not thought proper to act at all. Should it do so hereafter, it might limit and curtail the authority of the States to execute such an act as the present in a case in which it should interfere with such paramount legislation of Congress. I repeat the remark, that the law of the State under consideration has no aspect which refers directly to commerce among the States. It would have a large and important operation upon cases falling within its provisions, and having no connection with any commercial enterprise. It is then, so far as the commercial clause is concerned, generally valid; but in the case of supposable federal legislation, under the power conferred upon Congress to regulate commerce, circumstances might arise where its execution, by freeing a slave cargo landed on our shores, in the course of an inter-state voyage, would interfere with the provisions of an act of Congress. The present state of federal legislation however, does not, in my opinion, raise any conflict between it and the laws of this State under consideration. Upon the whole case, I have come to the conclusion that there is nothing in the National Constitution or the laws of Congress to preclude the State judicial authorities from declaring these slaves thus introduced into the territory of this State, free, and setting them at liberty, according to the direction of the statute referred to. For the foregoing reasons, I am in favor of affirming the judgment of the Supreme Court.

Wright, J. No person can be restrained of his liberty within this State, unless legal cause be shown for such restraint. The habeas corpus act operates to remove the subject from private force into the public forum: and enlargement of liberty, unless some cause in law be shown to the contrary, flows from the writ by a legal necessity. (Const., art. 1, § 4; 2 R. S., 563, § 21; id., 565, § 39.) The restraint cannot be continued for any moment of time, unless the authority to maintain it have the force of law within the State.

In November, 1852, a writ of habeas corpus on behalf of eight colored persons, was issued by a Justice of the Superior Court in the city of New York, to inquire into the cause of their detention. The appellant showed for cause that they were slaves of his wife in Virginia, of which State before that time he and his wife had been citizens and there domiciled, and that she held them as such in New York, in transit from Virginia through New York to Texas, where they intended to establish a new domicil. The return to the writ stated substantially that the route and mode of travel was by steamer from Norfolk, in Virginia, to the port of New York, and thence by a new voyage to Texas. In execution of this plan of travel, they and their slaves had reached the city of New York, and were awaiting the opportunity of a voyage to Texas, with no mention on their part that they or the eight colored persons should remain in New York for any other time, or for any other purpose, than until opportunity should present to take passage for all to Texas. The whole question, therefore, on these facts is, whether the cause shown was a legal one. If the relation of slave owner and slave which subsisted in Virginia between Mrs. Lemmon and these colored persons while there, by force of law attend upon them while commorant within this State in the course of travel from Virginia to Texas, and New York, though a sovereign State, be compelled to sanction and maintain the condition of slavery for any purpose, and cannot effect a universal proscription and prohibition of it within her territorial limits, then is legal cause of restraint shown: otherwise not.

The question is one affecting the State in her sovereignty. As a sovereign State she may determine and regulate the status or social and civil condition of her citizens, and every description of persons within her territory. This power she possesses exclusively; and when she has declared or expressed her will in this respect, no authority or power from without can rightly interfere, except in the single instance of a slave escaping from a State of the Union into her territory; and in this, only because she has, by compact, yielded her right of sovereignty. (U. S. Const., art. 4, § 2.) She has the undoubted right to forbid the status of slavery to exist in any form, or for any time, or for any purpose, within her borders, and declare that a slave brought into her territory from a foreign State, under any pretence whatever, shall be free. If she has done this, then neither an African negro nor any other person, white or black, can be held within her limits, for any moment of time, in a condition of bondage. It cannot affect the question, that at some time in her history as a colony or State she has tolerated slavery on her soil, or that the status has ever had a legal cognition: for without regard to time or circumstances, the State may, at her will, change the civil condition of her inhabitants and her domestic policy, and proscribe and prohibit that which before had existed. I do not say that she may convert any description of her free inhabitants or citizens into slaves; for slavery is repugnant to natural justice and right, has no support in any principle of international law, and is antagonistic to the genius and spirit of republican government. Besides, liberty is the natural condition of men, and is world-wide: whilst slavery is local, and beginning in physical force, can only be supported and sustained by positive law. "Slavery," says Montesquieu, "not only violates the laws of nature and of civil society; it also wounds the best forms of government; in a democracy where all men are equal slavery is contrary to the spirit of the Constitution."

It is not denied that New York has effectually exerted her sovereignty to the extent that the relation of slave owner and slave cannot be maintained by her citizens, or persons or citizens of any other State or nation domiciled within her territory, or who make any stay beyond the reasonable halt of wayfarers, and that this she might rightfully do. It will not stop here to inquire whether this is not virtually conceding the whole question in the case. It is urged that this is as far as the State had gone when the present case arose; and if I comprehend the argument rightly, as far as she can ever go without transcending restraints imposed upon her sovereignty by the Constitution of the United States, or violating the principles of the law of nations as governing the intercourse of friendly States. I shall show that neither of these propositions are maintainable, and that in the legislation of the State on the subject of slavery, the case of the status during transit has not escaped its intent and effect; but that if it were otherwise, when the domestic laws reject and suppress the status as a civil condition or social relation, as matter of reason and authority it is never upheld in the case of strangers resident or in transit.

1st. How far has the State gone in the expression of her sovereign will, that slavery, by whatsoever casual access, or for whatsoever transient stay, shall not be tolerated upon her soil? When negro slavery was first introduced and established as an institution in the Colony of New York, is not easily traceable. It never had any foundation in the law of nature, and was not recognized by the common law. (Somerset's case, Lofft's R., 1; S. C., 20; Howell's State Trials, 2.) Yet it existed in the Colony by force of local law, and was continued by the same sanction in a mild form in the eastern part of the State, after New York became an independent sovereignty. The public sentiment, reason and conscience, however, continued to frown on it until, in 1817, steps were taken by the legislative department of the government to effect its total abolition before 1830. As indicative of the public sentiment, in 1820 the Legislature, with unanimity, adopted a resolution requesting our Representatives in Congress to oppose the admission of any State into the Union, without making the prohibition of slavery therein an indispensable condition of admission; and in the preamble to the resolution, recited that they considered slavery to be an evil much to be deplored. The statute of 1817, provided against importing, introducing, or bringing into the State, on any pretence whatever, except in certain cases therein specified, persons held as slaves under the laws of other States. Amongst these cases, was that of a person, not being an inhabitant of our State, who should be traveling to or from, or passing through the State. He might bring with him any person held by him in slavery under the laws of the State from which he came, and might take such person with him from the State of New York; but the person held in slavery should not reside or continue in our State more than nine months, and if such residence were continued beyond that time, such person should be free. These provisions against introducing or bringing foreign slaves into the State, except in the case of an inhabitant of another State, temporarily sojourning in or passing through this State, were re-enacted in the revision of the Statutes in 1830, with this additional section: "Every person born within this State, whether white or colored, is free; every person who shall hereafter be born within this State shall be free, and every person brought into this State as a slave, except as authorized by this title, shall be free." (1 R. S., 656, 657, § 6; id., 659, § 16.) Here was an authoritative and emphatic declaration of the sovereign will, that freedom should be the only condition of all descriptions of persons, resident or domiciled within the State, and that no slave should be brought therein, under any pretence whatever, except by his master, an inhabitant of another State, who was traveling to or from, or passing through this State. Thus slavery was left without the support of even the municipal law, except in the instance of sojourners, and then only for a period of nine months, and slave owners of other States passing with their slaves through our own. But in 1841, the sanction of the municipal law even in these cases was taken away. The Legislature, in 1841, repealed all the sections of the Revised Statutes allowing slaves to be brought voluntarily into the State, under any circumstances, leaving the provisions still in operation, that no person held as a slave should be imported, introduced or brought into the State on any pretence whatever; and if brought in, should be free. (Laws of 1841, ch. 247.) That this legislation was intended to reach the case of the transitus of a slave in custody of an inhabitant of a slaveholding State claiming to be his owner, and to leave no legal basis for the status of slavery in any form or for any purpose to rest upon, within the limits of the State, is evident. By the law of 1830, the privilege was secured to the foreign slaveholder of temporarily sojourning in or passing through the State with his slaves. In 1841 this privilege is taken away by the affirmative action of the law-making power. So, also, by the law of 1830, any person who, or whose family, resided part of the year in this State, and part of the year in any other State, might remove or bring with him or them, from time to time, any person lawfully held by him in slavery, into this State, and might carry such person with him or them out of it. This was denied by the Legislature in 1841. The obvious intent and effect of the repealing act of 1841 was to declare every person upon the soil of this State, even though he may have been held as a slave by the laws of another State, to be free, except in the single instance of a person held in slavery in any State of the United States under the laws thereof, who should escape into this State. With the courtesy of this legislation, so far as it might operate to affect friendly intercourse with citizens of slaveholding States, as a judicial tribunal, we have nothing to do. We are only to determine the intent and effect of the legislation. It is but just, however, to the political power of the State, to remark, that it was not conceived in any spirit of irrational propagandism or partizanship, but to effectuate a policy based upon principle, and in accordance with public sentiment. The fact that it has been the law of the State for nearly twenty years, and through successive changes of the political power, is cogent proof that it rests upon the foundation of a public sentiment not limited in extent to any party or faction. The effect of the legislation was to render the civil condition of slavery impossible in our own society. Liberty and slavery, as civil conditions, mean no more than the establishment of law, and the means to enforce or protect the one or the other. As the status of slavery is sustained and supported exclusively by positive law (and this has been so held as to the status in Virginia by her courts), if we have no law to uphold it, but on the contrary, proscribe and prohibit it, it cannot exist for an instant of time within our jurisdiction. (4 Munford's R., 209; 2 Hen. & Munford, 149.) Of course I mean with this qualification, that there is no duty or obligation in respect thereto, imposed on the sovereignty of the State by the Federal Constitution, or the rules of international law.

2d. Is there anything in the Federal Constitution to hinder the State from pursuing her own policy in regulating the social and civil condition of every description of persons that are or may come within her jurisdictional limits, or that enjoins on her the duty of maintaining the status of slavery in the case of slaves from another State of the Union voluntarily brought into her territory? It ought not to be necessary at this day to affirm the doctrine, that the Federal Constitution has no concern, nor was it designed to have, with the social basis and relations and civil conditions which obtain within the several States. The Federal Constitution is but the compact of the people of separate and independent sovereignties, yielding none of the rights pertaining to those sovereignties within their respective territorial limits, except in a few special cases. This was the nature of the compact as explained by its framers and contemporaneous expounders, and since by the Federal Courts, although it has become common of late to strive to find something in this bond of Federal Union to sustain and uphold a particular social relation and condition outside of the range of the laws which give it vitality. (Ex parte Simmons, 4 Wash. C. C. 396; Groves v. Slaughter, 15 Pet., 508; Prigg v. Commonwealth of Penn., 16 Pet., 611, 625; Strader v. Graham 10 How. R., 82, 93.) Although the status of African slavery had at some time been recognized in all of the original States, at the period of the formation of the Federal Constitution some of them had abolished the institution, and others were on the eve of abolishing it; whilst others were maintaining it with increasing vigor. There are but three sections in the whole instrument that allude to the existence of slavery under the laws of any of the States, and then not in terms but as explained by the light of contemporaneous history, and in such a way as to stamp the institution as local. There are the provisions apportioning federal representation and direct taxation (U. S. Const., art. 1, § 2, subd. 3) in relation to "persons held to labor in one State, under the laws thereof, escaping into another" (Const., art. 4, § 2) and restraining Congress, prior to 1808, from prohibiting "the migration or importation of such persons as any of the States now existing shall think proper to admit." (Const., art. 1, § 9.) The latter provision, it is known, was urged with much earnestness by the delegates from two or three of the Southern States, with the view to restrain Congress from prohibiting the foreign slave trade before 1808. In Groves v. Slaughter (15 Pet., 506), Judge McLean thought the provision recognized the power to be in the State to admit or prohibit, at the discretion of each State, the introduction of slaves into her territory. He says: "The importation of certain persons, meaning slaves, which was not to be prohibited before 1808, was limited to such States then existing as shall think proper to admit them. Some of the States at that time prohibited the admission of slaves, and their right to do so was as strongly implied by this provision as the right of other States that admitted them." But the provision has long ceased to have any practical operation. Congress has prohibited the importation of slaves into any of the States of the Union, and the slave trade is declared to be piracy. The provision has no importance now, except it be to show, that in the view of the framers of the Constitution, slavery was local in its character; that the power over it belonged to the States respectively, and that it was not to be recognized or receive any aid from the federal authority; but on the contrary, by all the means it possessed, federal power, after 1808, was to be exerted to suppress it. The provision in respect to apportioning representation in Congress, alludes remotely and only impliedly to the fact that slavery existed in any of the States. The representative population was to be "determined by adding to the whole number of free persons including those bound to service for a term of years, and excluding Indians not taxed, three-fifths of all other persons." No duty or obligation was imposed on the States; nor is there the remotest sanction or recognition of slaves as property outside of the range of the territorial laws which treat them as such. The third provision is simply a consent of the State as parties to the federal compact to the reclamation of fugitives from service. In speaking of this clause, Judge Story said, in delivering the opinion of the Supreme Court of the United States in Prigg v. Commonwealth of Pennsylvania: "By the general laws of nations, no nation is bound to recognize the state of slavery as to foreign slaves found within its territorial dominions, when it is in opposition to its own policy and institutions, in favor of the subjects of other nations where slavery is recognized. If it does it, it is as a matter of comity and not as a matter of international right. The state of slavery is deemed to be a municipal regulation, founded upon and limited to the range of the territorial laws. This was fully recognized in Somerset's case, which was decided before the American Revolution. It is manifest, from this consideration, that if the Constitution had not contained this clause, every non-slaveholding State in the Union would have been at liberty to have declared free all runaway slaves coming within its limits, and to have given them entire immunity and protection against the claims of their masters; a course which would have created the most bitter animosities, and engendered perpetual strife between the different States. The clause was accordingly adopted into the Constitution by the unanimous consent of the framers of it; a proof at once of its intrinsic and practical necessity." The learned judge was right in saying that the clause, as it stands in the instrument, was adopted with entire unanimity; but it was not adopted as originally reported.

There were many eminent and patriotic men in and out of the Convention, both north and south, that did not contemplate that slavery was to be perpetual in any of the States of the Union, and amongst these was the illustrious presiding officer of the Convention, from Virginia. It was certainly inconsistent with the principle that lies at the foundation of our government. In incorporating the fugitive slave provision in the Constitution, the Convention was careful not to do anything which should imply its sanction of slavery as legal. The provision, as originally reported, read, "legally held to service," and it was amended by striking out the word "legally" and made to read "held to service or labor in one State, under the laws thereof." (See Journal, 384; Madison's Works, 1558, 1589.)

So, also, the word "service" was substituted for "servitude," on motion of a delegate from Virginia; the latter being descriptive of slaves. (3 Madison's Works, 1569.) The term "slave" is not used in the Constitution, and if the phrase, "a person held to service or labor in one State under the laws thereof," is to be construed as meaning slaves, then the Federal Constitution treats slaves as persons and not as property, and it acts upon them as persons and not as property, though the latter character may be given to them by the laws of the States in which slavery is tolerated. It is entirely clear that the Convention was averse to giving any sanction to the law of slavery, by an express or implied acknowledgment that human beings could be made the subject of property; and it is moreover manifest from all the provisions of the Constitution, and from contemporaneous history, that the ultimate extinction of slavery in the United States, by the legislation and action of the State governments (instead of adopting or devising any means or legal machinery for perpetuating it), was contemplated by many of the eminent statesmen and patriots who framed the Federal Constitution, and their contemporaries both north and south. The provision in relation to fugitives from service, is the only one in the Constitution that, by an intendment, supports the right of a slave owner in his own State, or in any other State. This, by its terms, is limited to its special case, and necessarily excludes federal intervention in every other. This has been always so regarded by the federal courts and the cases uniformly recognize the doctrine, that both the Constitution and laws of the United States apply only to fugitives escaping from one State and fleeing to another; that beyond this the power over the subject of slavery is exclusively with the several States, and that their action cannot be controlled by the Federal Government. Indeed, the exclusive right of the State of Missouri to determine and regulate the status of persons within her territory, was the only point in judgment in the Dred Scott case, and all beyond this was obiter. (Ex parte Simmons, 4 Wash. C. C. 396; Groves v. Slaughter, 15 Pet., 508; Strader v. Graham, 10 Howard, 92.) Any other doctrine might prove more disastrous to the status of slavery than to that of liberty in the States, for, from the moment that it is conceded that, by the exercise of any powers granted in the Constitution to the Federal Government, it may rightly interfere in the regulation of the social and civil condition of any description of persons within the territorial limits of the respective States of the Union, it is not difficult to foresee the ultimate result.

The provision of the Federal Constitution conferring on Congress the power to regulate commerce among the several States, is now invoked as a restraint upon State action. It is difficult to perceive how this provision can have any application to the case under consideration. It is not pretended that the persons claimed to be held as slaves were in transit to Texas as articles of commerce; nor that, being with their alleged owner, on board a coasting vessel, enrolled and licensed under the laws of Congress, such vessel was driven, by stress of weather or otherwise, into the navigable waters of this State. Indeed, the case showed that their owner had voluntarily brought them into the State; that taking passage from Norfolk to New York, his and their voyage in the coasting steamer had terminated, and he was sojourning in the city with them, awaiting the opportunity to start on a new voyage to Texas. It is certainly not the case of the owner of slaves, passing from one slave State to another, being compelled, by accident or distress, to touch or land in this State. In such case, probably, our law would not act upon the status of the slave, not being within its spirit and intention; but as Congress has not yet undertaken to regulate the internal slave trade, even if it has authority to do so, in no just sense could even such a case be said to raise the question of the right of federal intervention. But in no view can the provision empowering Congress to regulate commerce among the States affect the power of the respective States over the subject of slavery. Even those who have contended for the right in Congress, under the commercial power, as it is called, to regulate the traffic in slaves, among the several States, admit that it is competent for a State, with the view of effectuating its system of policy in the abolition of slavery, to entirely prohibit the importation of slaves, for any purpose, into her territory. But apart from effectuating any object of police or promoting any rule of policy, the power over the whole subject is with the States respectively; and this was so declared by the Supreme Federal Court, in Groves v. Slaughter (15 Pet., 508), a case in which it was attempted to be urged that a provision in the Constitution of Mississippi, prohibiting the importation of slaves into that State for sale, was in conflict with the commercial power of the Federal Government. As was said by Chief Justice Taney, in that case, "each of the States has a right to determine for itself whether it will or will not allow persons of this description (slaves) to be brought within its limits from another State, either for sale or for any other purpose, and also to prescribe the manner and mode in which they may be introduced, and to determine their condition and treatment within their respective territories; and the action of the several States upon this subject cannot be controlled by Congress, either by virtue of its power to regulate commerce, or by virtue of any other power conferred by the Constitution of the United States." The case of Groves v. Slaughter was deemed at the time to have settled the question against the right in Congress, under the commercial claim, to regulate the internal slave trade, or to interfere in any way with the power of the States to severally protect themselves, under any and all circumstances, against an external evil.

The constitutional provision that "the citizens of each State shall be entitled to all the privileges and immunities of citizens in the several States" (U. S. Const., art. 4, § 2, subd. 1), is also invoked as having some bearing on the question of the appellant's right. I think this is the first occasion in the juridical history of the country that an attempt has been made to torture this provision into a guaranty of the right of a slave owner to bring his slaves into, and hold them for any purpose in, a non-slaveholding State. The provision was always understood as having but one design and meaning, viz., to secure to the citizens of every State, within every other, the privileges and immunities (whatever they might be) accorded in each to its own citizens. It was intended to guard against a State discriminating in favor of its own citizens. A citizen of Virginia coming into New York was to be entitled to all the privileges and immunities accorded to the citizens of New York. He was not to be received or treated as an alien or enemy in the particular sovereignty.

Prior to the adoption of the Federal Constitution, and even under the Confederation, the only kind of citizenship was that which prevailed in the respective States. The Articles of Confederation provided "that the free inhabitants of each of the States (paupers, vagabonds and fugitives from justice excepted), should be entitled to all privileges and immunities of free citizens in the several States; and the people of each State should have free ingress and egress to and from any other State, and should enjoy therein all the privileges of trade and commerce, subject to the same duties, impositions and restrictions as the inhabitants thereof, respectively." (Art. 4.) This article limited the right to the free inhabitants of the States, implying that there were inhabitants of the States in the Confederacy that were not free, and to whom the privileges and immunities were not extended. But when the framers of the Constitution came to re-model this clause, having conferred exclusive power upon the Federal Government to regulate commercial intercourse, and imposed the obligation upon the States, respectively, to deliver up fugitives escaping from service, and being unwilling, even impliedly, to sanction, by federal authority, the legality of the state of slavery, they omitted the provisions of the article in relation to commercial intercourse, and substituted for the words, "the free inhabitants of each State," the words, "the citizens of each State," and made the provision to read as it now stands in the Constitution. If the provision can be construed to confer upon a citizen of Virginia the privilege of holding slaves in New York, when there is no law to uphold the status, and the privilege is denied to our own citizens, then Judge Story and the Federal Court fell into a grave error in the opinion, that if it were not for the fugitive slave provision, New York would have been at liberty to have declared free all slaves coming within her limits, and have given them entire immunity and protection; and so, also, did Chief Justice Taney mistake the character of the instrument, when declaring that there was nothing in the Constitution to control the action of a State in relation to slavery within her limits. But it seems a work of supererogation to pursue this inquiry. It never yet has been doubted that the sovereign powers vested in the State governments remain intact and unimpaired, except so far as they are granted to the government of the United States; and that the latter government can claim no powers which are not granted to it by the Constitution, either expressly or by necessary implication. There is no grant of power to the Federal Government, and no provision of the Constitution from which any can be implied, over the subject of slavery in the States, except in the single case of a fugitive from service. The general power is with the States, except as it has been specially limited by the Federal Constitution; and this special limitation has been rightly considered as a forcible implication in proof of the existence of the general power in the States. So it was considered in Lunsford v. Coquillon (14 Martin's R., 403), a case arising in a slaveholding State, in which the authority of States was fully recognized to make laws dissolving the relation of master and slave. Such a construction of the Constitution and law of the United States, say that court, can work injury to no one, for the principle acts only on the willing, and volenti non fit injuria.

3d. Is the State, upon principles of comity, or any rule of public law, having force within the State, required to recognize and support the relation of master and slave, between strangers sojourning in or passing through her territory? The relation exists, if at all, under the laws of Virginia, and it is not claimed that there is any paramount obligation resting on this State to recognize and administer the laws of Virginia within her territory, if they be contrary or repugnant to her policy or prejudicial to her interests. She may voluntarily concede that the foreign law shall operate within her jurisdiction, and to the extent of such concession, it becomes a part of her municipal law. Comity, however, never can be exercised in violation of our own laws; and in deciding whether comity requires any act, we look to our own laws for authority. There can be no application of the principles of comity, when the State absolutely refuses to recognize or give effect to the foreign law, or the relation it establishes, as being inconsistent with her own laws, and contrary to her policy. The policy and will of the State in respect to the toleration of slavery, in any form, or however transient the stay, within her territory, has been distinctly and unmistakably expressed. Before the repealing act of 1841, our statutes operated to absolutely dissolve the relation of master and slave, and make the latter a freeman, except in the case of a master and slave, inhabitants of another State, temporarily in or passing through the State. In the latter cases, though the master could obtain no affirmative aid from the municipal law to enforce restraint of the liberty of the slave, yet the State, exercising comity, expressly permitted the relation to exist for the space of nine months. To this extent the State consented that the foreign law of slavery should have effect within her limits, and the relation of master and slave was not to be dissolved by force of the municipal law, unless the stay was continued beyond nine months. There can be no doubt that without this express exception, the statute of 1830 would have acted directly upon the status of any slave brought voluntarily into the State, and made him a freeman. As a matter of comity, however, the will of the State then was, that in the case of an inhabitant of another State passing through our territory with his slaves, the status of the latter should not be affected by our laws. But, in 1841, the State, by actual legislation, abrogated the permission accorded to slavery during transit, and declared it to be her will, that, under all circumstances, a slave voluntarily brought into the State should be free, and that the status should not be tolerated within her borders. It is for the State to establish the rule, and exercise comity, and not the courts in her behalf, and she may or may not, as she chooses, exercise it. The courts have but the power of determining whether the comity inquired of be indicated by her policy and actual legislation. The State has declared, through her Legislature, that the status of African slavery shall not exist, and her laws transform the slave into a freeman the instant he is brought voluntarily upon her soil. Her will is that neither upon principles of comity to strangers passing through her territory, nor in any other way, shall the relation of slave owner and slave be held or supported. Instead, therefore, of recognizing or extending any law of comity towards a slaveholder passing through her territory with his slaves, she refuses to recognize or extend such comity, or allow the law of the sovereignty which sustains the relation of master and slave to be administered as a part of the law of the State. She says, in effect, to the foreign slave owner, if you bring your slaves within the State, on any pretence whatever, neither by comity nor in any other way shall the municipal law let in and give place to the foreign law; but the relation established and sustained only by the foreign municipal law shall terminate, and the persons before held as slaves shall stand upon her soil in their natural relations as men and as freemen. It is conceded that she may go to this extent if there be no restraint on her action by the Federal Constitution; and to this extent, I think, her policy and actual legislation clearly indicate that she has gone. But if there were no actual legislation reaching the case of slavery in transit, the policy of the State would forbid the sanction of law, and the aid of public force, to the proscribed status in the case of strangers within our territory. It is the status, the unjust and unnatural relation, which the policy of the State aims to suppress, and her policy fails, at least in part, if the status be upheld at all. Upon the same rule that she would permit the Virginia lady in this case to pass through her territory with slaves, she would be constrained to allow the slave trader, with his gang, to pass, even at the risk of public disorder which would inevitably attend such a transit. The State deems that the public peace, her internal safety and domestic interests, require the total suppression of a social condition that violates the law of nature (Virginia Bill of Rights, §§ 1, 15); a status, declared by Lord Mansfield, in Sommerset's case, to be "of such a nature that it is incapable of being introduced on any reasons, moral or political;" that originates in the predominance of physical force, and is continued by the mere predominance of social force, the subject knowing or obedient to no law but the will of the master, and all of whose issue is involved in the misfortune of the parent; a status which the law of nations treats as resting on force against right, and finding no support outside of the municipal law which establishes it. (Taylor's Elements of Civil Law, 429; Sommerset's case, 20 Howell's State Trials, 2; 2 Devereaux's R., 263.) Why should not the State be able to utterly suppress it within her jurisdiction? She is not required by the rule of the law of nations, which permits the transit of strangers and their property through a friendly State, to uphold it. Men are not the subject of property by such law, nor by any law, except that of the State in which the status exists; not even by the Federal Constitution, which is supposed by some to have been made only to guard and protect the rights of a particular race; for in that human beings, without regard to color or country, are treated as persons and not as property. The public law exacts no obligation from this State to enforce the municipal law which makes men the subject of property; but by that law the strangers stand upon our soil in their natural condition as men. Nor can it be justly pretended that by the principle which attributes to the law of the domicil the power to fix the civil status of persons, any obligation rests on the State to recognize and uphold within her territory the relation of slave owner and slave between strangers. So far as it may be done without prejudice to her domestic interests, she may be required to recognize the consequences of the status existing abroad in reference to subjects within her own jurisdiction; and when it is brought within her limits, and is there permissible as a domestic regulation, to recognize the foreign law as an authentic origin and support of the actual status. (Story's Confl. Of Laws , §§ 51, 89, 96, 113, 114, 104, 620, 624.) But no further than they are consistent with her own laws, and not repugnant or prejudicial to her domestic policy and interests, is the State required to give effect to these laws of the domicil.

My conclusions are, that legal cause was not shown for restraining the colored persons, in whose behalf the writ of habeas corpus was issued, of their liberty; and that they were rightly discharged. I have aimed to examine the question involved in a legal, and not in a political aspect; the only view, in my judgment, becoming a judicial tribunal to take. Our laws declare these persons to be free; and there is nothing which can claim the authority of law within this State, by which they may be held as slaves. Neither the law of nature or nations, nor the Federal Constitution, impose any duty or obligation on the State to maintain the state of slavery within her territory, in any form or under any circumstances, or to recognize and give effect to the law of Virginia, by which alone the relation exists, nor does it find any support or recognition in the common law.

The judgment of the Supreme Court should be affirmed.

Davies, Bacon and Welles, Js., concurred.

DISSENT BY: Clerke; Comstock; Selden

DISSENT:

Clerke, J. (Dissenting.) A considerable proportion of the discussion in this case was occupied by observations, not at all necessary to a proper disposition of it; nor were they calculated, in the slightest degree, in my opinion, to aid the court in solving the questions presented for its determination. Whether slavery is agreeable or in opposition to the law of nature; whether it is morally right or wrong; whether it is expedient or inexpedient; whether the African race are adapted, by their physical and moral organization, only to this condition; whether they can be induced to labor only by compulsion; whether the fairest and most fertile portions of the earth—those lying near and within the tropical zones—can alone be cultivated to any extent by that race, and whether, if without their labor, therefore, this large portion of the globe will, contrary to the manifest design of the Creator, continue or become a sterile waste, are questions very interesting within the domain of theology, or ethics, or political economy, but totally inappropriate to the discussion of the purely legal questions now presented for our consideration. Those questions are, 1st, whether the Legislature of this State has declared that all slaves brought by their masters into this State, under any circumstances whatever, even for a moment, shall be free; and 2d, if it has so declared, had it the constitutional power to do so.

1. The act passed in 1817, and re-enacted in 1830, declares that no person held as a slave shall be imported, introduced, or brought into this State, on any pretence whatsoever, except in the cases therein specified, and that every such person shall be free. One of the excepted cases allows a person, not an inhabitant of this State, traveling to or from, or passing through this State, to bring his slave here and take him away again; but if the slave continues here more than nine months, he shall be free. These exceptions were repealed by an act passed May 25, 1841, amending the Revised Statutes in relation to persons held in slavery. Although there appears to be no ambiguity in the language of those acts, I am not surprised that some incredulity has been expressed in relation to their entire meaning. What, it may be plausibly asked, could be the object of the Legislature in interfering with persons passing through our territory? It is not to be supposed a priori, that any one member of the brotherhood of States would adopt any legislation for the purpose of affecting persons with whom, as a social or political community, it has no possible concern. If the slave were to remain here for any time, legislators may, indeed, fear some detriment, some demoralization from his presence; but what could the most nervous or fastidious guardians of the public interests apprehend from persons passing through the State. Neither could it add one jot or title to the sum of slavery in the world. To suppose, therefore, it may be said, that the acts referred to aimed at such persons, would be imputing a spirit of the most wanton aggression to the legislators who passed them. It would be mere propagandism, of which we should not suppose any community capable, who were not in a condition of revolutionary excitement, and fanatical exaltation, like that of the French people during their first revolution, when they undertook to force their

theories of spurious democracy on the other nations of Europe, disturbing its peace for more than twenty years, and causing wide-spread slaughter and desolation. But, notwithstanding all these reasons, which may be plausibly suggested in considering the intent of the Legislature, the language of the acts referred to is too plain to admit of any doubt of that intent. It evidently intended to declare that all slaves voluntarily brought into this State, under any circumstances whatever, should become instantly free.

2. But it is a question of much greater difficulty, whether the Legislature had the constitutional power to do so.

New York is a member of a confederacy of free and sovereign States, united for certain specific and limited purposes, under a solemn written covenant. And this covenant not only establishes a confederacy of States, but also, in regard to its most material functions, it gives this confederacy the character of a homogeneous national government. The Constitution is not alone federal or alone national; but, by the almost divine wisdom which presided over its formation, while its framers desired to preserve the independence and sovereignty of each State within the sphere of ordinary domestic legislation, yet they evidently designed to incorporate this people into one nation, not only in its character as a member of the great family of nations, but also in the internal, moral, social and political effect of the Union upon the people themselves. It was essential to this grand design that there should be as free and as uninterrupted an intercommunication between the inhabitants and citizens of the different States, as between the inhabitants and citizens of the same State. The people of the United States, therefore, "in order to form a more perfect union" than had existed under the old Confederacy, declare and provide, among other things in the Constitution under which we have now the privilege of living, that Congress (alone) shall have power to regulate commerce among the several States; to establish a uniform rule of naturalization, and uniform laws on the subject of bankruptcies; to coin money as the genuine national circulating medium; to regulate its value; to fix the standard of weights and measures; to establish post-offices and post-roads; to promote the progress of science and the useful arts, by securing for limited times to authors and inventors the exclusive right to their respective writings and discoveries. It also provides that no tax or duties shall be laid on articles exported from any State, and that no preference shall be given, by any regulation of commerce or revenue, to the ports of one State over another; that vessels bound to or from one State, shall not be obliged to enter, clear or pay duties in another; that full faith or credit shall be given in each State to the public acts, records and judicial proceedings of every other State, and that citizens of each State shall be entitled to all the privileges and immunities of citizens in the several States. The people, in adopting this Constitution, declare in its very preamble that they intended to form a more perfect union than had bound them under the old Articles of Confederation, the fourth article of which declared that the better to secure and perpetuate mutual friendship and intercourse among the people of the different States, the free inhabitants of each State should be entitled to all the privileges and immunities of free citizens in the several States: that the people of each State should have free ingress to and from any other State, and should enjoy therein all the privileges of trade and commerce, as the inhabitants thereof respectively, subject to the same duties, impositions and restrictions; provided that those restrictions shall not extend so far as to prevent the removal of property, imported into any State, to any other State of which the owner is an inhabitant. Most assuredly, the people who adopted the present Constitution did not intend that the intercourse between the people of the different States should be more limited or restricted than the States, in their corporate capacity, provided in the Articles of Confederation. On the contrary, they contemplated, as we have seen, a more perfect union, and a more perfect and unrestricted intercourse; and they amply secured it by the provisions to which I have referred.

Is it consistent with this purpose of perfect union, and perfect and unrestricted intercourse, that property which the citizen of one State brings into another State, for the purpose of passing through it to a State where he intends to take up his residence, shall be confiscated in the State through which he is passing, or shall be declared to be no property, and liberated from his control? If he, indeed, brings his property voluntarily, with the design of taking up his residence in another State, or sojourning there for any purpose of business, even for a brief period, he subjects himself to the legislation of that State, with regard to his personal rights and the rights relating to property.

By the law of nations, the citizens of one government have a right of passage through the territory of another, peaceably, for business or pleasure; and the latter acquires no right over such person or his property. This privilege is yielded between foreign nations towards each other without any express compact. It is a principle of the unwritten law of nations.

Of course this principle is much more imperative on the several States than between foreign nations in their relations towards each other. For it can be clearly deduced, as we have seen, from the compact on which their union is based. Therefore, making this principle of the law of nations applicable to the compact which exists between the several States, we say, that the citizens of any one State have a right of passage through the territory of another, peaceably, for business or pleasure; and the latter acquires no right over such person or his property. But the judge who decided this case in the first instance (by whose reasoning, I may be permitted here to say, I was erroneously influenced in voting at the general term of the Supreme Court in the first district), while admitting the principle of the law of nations, which I have quoted, says that the property, which the writers on the law of nations speak of, is merchandise or inanimate things, and that the principle, therefore, is not applicable to the slaves, who, by the law of nature and of nations, he contends, cannot be property. Foreign nations, undoubtedly, between whom no express compact exists, are at liberty to make this exception. But can any of the States of this confederacy, under the compact which unites them, do the same? Can they make this distinction? In other words, can any one State insist, under the federal compact, in reference to the rights of the citizens of any other State, that there is no such thing as the right of such citizens, in their own States, to the service and labor of any person. This is property; and whether the person is held to service and labor for a limited period, or for life, it matters not; it is still property—recognized as an existing institution by the people who framed the present Constitution, and binding upon their posterity forever, unless that Constitution should be modified or dissolved by common consent.

The learned judge who rendered the decision in the first instance in this case, would, of course, admit, on his own reasoning, that, if by the law of nations the right was recognized to property in slaves, the principle would apply to that species of property as well as to any other, and its inviolability would be upheld whenever its owner was passing with it through any territory of the family of nations. Can it be disputed that the obligations of the States of this Union towards each other are less imperative than those of the family of nations would be towards each other, if a right to this species of property was recognized by the implied compact by which their conduct is regulated. The position, therefore, of the learned judge, and of the general term, can only be maintained on the supposition that the compact which binds the States together does not recognize the right to the labor and service of slaves as property; and that each State is at liberty to act towards other States, in this matter, according to its own particular opinions in relation to the justice or expediency of holding such property. It may be, therefore, necessary more particularly, though briefly, to inquire what were and what had been the circumstances of the original States, in relation to this subject, at the time of the adoption of the present Constitution; what was the common understanding in relation to it, as pointed out by the debates in the Convention, and what does the Constitution itself, by express provisions or necessary implication, indicate on this ever-important subject.

When this Constitution was adopted by the deliberate consent of the States and the people, slavery existed in every State, except Massachusetts and New Hampshire. It had existed in all the New England colonies from a very early period. The four colonies of Massachusetts Bay, Plymouth, Connecticut and New Haven, had formed a confederation, in which, among other things, they had stipulated with each other for the restoration of runaway servants, "and," to employ the language of Mr. Curtis (History of the Constitution of the United States, 2d vol., 453, 454), "there is undoubted evidence that African slaves, as other persons in servitude, were included in this provision. Slavery in Massachusetts had not been confined to Africans, but included Indians captured in war, and persons of our race condemned for crimes. The early colonists of Massachusetts held and practised the law of Moses." "They regarded it," said the same writer in a note, "as lawful to buy and sell slaves taken in lawful war, or reduced to servitude by judicial sentence, and placed them under the same privileges as those given by the Mosaic law."

Slavery had not only existed for a long period in all the colonies, but at the time of the formation of the Constitution it was likely to continue to exist for a long time in the greater number of the States. In five of them the slave population, composed of the African race, was very numerous, while in the other States they were comparatively few. It was in this condition of things that the representatives of the States assembled to frame a Constitution for their more perfect union, and for the common preservation of their rights, not only from external attacks, but from internal aggression. Their deliberations began with the conviction and acknowledgment that property in slaves existed to a great extent in nearly all the States; and soon it became necessary to consider whether the slave population should be included in the ratio of representation. They must be regarded, in order to make a satisfactory provision on this subject, indispensable to the completion of the Constitution, either as persons or as chattels, or as both. "In framing the new Union, it was equally necessary, as soon as the equality of the representation by States should give place to a proportional and unequal representation, to regard the inhabitants in one or the other capacity, or in both capacities, or leave the States in which they were found, and to which their position was a matter of grave importance, out of the Union["] (Curtis' Hist. Const. U. S., 20, 22.) And what was the result of those convictions and deliberations? Undoubtedly, that while slavery should be deemed a local institution, depending upon the power of each State to determine what persons should share in the civil and political rights of the community the right is fully recognized in the Constitution, that any of the States may continue and allow the right of property in the labor and service of slaves.

The portions of the Constitution more directly bearing on this subject are the 3d subdivision of the 2d section of the 1st article, and the 3d subdivision of the 2d section of the 4th article. The former relates to the apportionment of representatives and direct taxes, necessarily compelling a discrimination between the different classes of inhabitants. It was contended, on behalf of some of the northern States, that slaves ought not to be included in the numerical rule of representation. Slaves, it was contended, are considered as property, and not as persons, and, therefore, ought to be comprehended in estimates of taxation, which are founded on property, and to be excluded from representation, which is regulated by a census of persons. The representatives of the southern States, on the other hand, contended that slaves were not considered merely as property, but that they were also considered as persons; and Mr. Jay, in his paper on this subject in the Federalist, which, recollect, was published before the submission of the Constitution for ratification by the States, says "the true state of the case is, that they partake of both these qualities; being considered by our laws in some respects as persons, and in other respects as property." "The Federal Constitution," he adds, "therefore decides with great propriety on the case of our slaves, when it views them in the mixed character of persons and property."

But in addition to this, if anything can be necessary, it has been adjudicated in the celebrated Dred Scott case, in a court whose decisions on this subject are controlling, that the Constitution of the United States recognizes slaves as property, and this is an essential element of the decision. Chief Justice Taney, who delivered the opinion of the court, says:

> The only two provisions which point to them and include them, treat them as property, and make it the duty of the government to protect it; no other power, in relation to this race, is to be found in the Constitution; and as it is a government of special, delegated powers, no authority beyond these two provisions can be constitutionally exercised. The government of the United States had no right to interfere for any other purpose but that of protecting the rights of the owner, leaving it altogether with the several States to deal with this race, whether emancipated or not, as each State may think justice, humanity, and the interests and safety of society may require. The States evidently intended to reserve this power exclusively to themselves.
>
> No one, we presume, supposes that any change in public opinion or feeling, in relation to this unfortunate race, in the civilized nations of Europe or in this country, should induce the court to give to the words of the Constitution a more liberal construction in their favor than they were intended to bear when the instrument was framed and adopted. Such an argument would be altogether inadmissible in any tribunal called on to interpret it. If any of its provisions are deemed unjust, there is a mode prescribed in the instrument itself, by which it may be amended; but while it remains unaltered, it must be construed now as it was understood at the time of its adoption. It is not only the same in words, but the same in meaning, and delegates the same powers to the government, and reserves and secures the same rights and privileges to the citizen; and as long as it continues to exist in its present form, it speaks not only in the same words, but with the same meaning and intent with which it spoke when it came from the hands of its framers, and was voted on and adopted by the people of the United States. Any other rule of construction would abrogate the judicial character of this court, and make it the mere reflex of the popular opinion or passion of the day. This court was not created by the Constitution for such purposes. Higher and graver trusts have been confided to it, and it must not falter in the path of duty.

Moreover, besides the necessary implication from the avowed purpose of the 3d subdivision of the 2d section, article 1st, of the National Constitution, the language itself recognizes the condition of slavery. It says: "Representatives and direct taxes shall be apportioned among the several States, which shall be included within this Union, according to their respective numbers, which shall be determined by adding to the whole number of free persons, including those bound to service for a term of years, and excluding Indians not taxed, three-fifths of all other persons." What other persons? The words are employed in direct contrast to free persons, and indisputably mean persons not free. It has been asserted, with an air of triumph, that the word "slave" is not employed in the Constitution. This was a matter of taste, I suppose, about which the members of the Convention did not think it worth while to contend. They had a higher and more practical purpose than to indulge any strife about a word; they were dealing with things— with realities; and, instead of calling those "slaves," who, in the apportionment of representatives and direct taxes, were to be added to free persons, they called them "other persons"—of course persons not free.

If, then, by the law of nations, the citizen of one government has a right of passage with what is recognized as property by that law, through the territory of another, peaceably, and that too without the latter's acquiring any right of control over the person or property, is not a citizen of any State of this confederacy entitled, under the compact upon which it is founded, to a right of passage through the territory of any other State, with what that compact recognizes as property, without the latter's acquiring any right of control over that property.

Surely, this compact of sovereignties is not less obligatory on the parties to it, than is the law of nations on those who are subject to it. Is the one in derogation of the other? Or does it not rather magnify and render more precise and tangible, and greatly extend, the duties and obligations imported by the law of nations? This inviolability of the slave property of the citizens of other States, while passing through the territory of free States, in analogy to the principle of the law of nations, to which I have adverted, clearly in no way interferes with the supreme authority of each State over those persons and things that come within the range of its dominion. By universal law, every sovereign and independent community has complete and supreme dominion over every person and thing within its territory, not there for the purpose of passing through it, or not there in the capacity of ambassadors from foreign nations, or their servants.

But, it is asserted, that the privilege accorded to the citizens of one foreign nation to pass unmolested with their property through the territory of any other, is founded merely on comity. If by this is meant that the nation within whose territory the property of a stranger is confiscated, is not responsible for its acts in that respect, the idea is incorrect. Such an act would be a valid cause for a resort to the only method by which nations can obtain redress after remonstrance or negotiation fails; but if it is meant that these words import that the judicial tribunals can only administer the law as declared by the law-making power of their own particular nation, and the injured nation can only seek peaceable redress by appealing to the executive, and through it to the law-making power, the proposition is correct. But, as I have shown, the relations of the different States of this Union towards each other are of a much closer and more positive nature than those between foreign nations towards each other. For many purposes they are one nation; war between them is legally impossible; and this comity, impliedly recognized by the law of nations, ripens, in the compact cementing these States, into an express conventional obligation, which is not to be enforced by an appeal to arms, but to be recognized and enforced by the judicial tribunals.

The error into which the judge who decided this case in the first instance fell, consisted in supposing, because the law of nations refused to recognize slaves as property, the several States of this Union were at liberty to do the same; forgetting that the compact, by which the latter are governed in their relation towards each other, modifies the law of nations in this respect; and while each particular State is at liberty to abolish or Retain slavery in reference to its own inhabitants and within its own borders, as its sense of right or expediency may dictate, it is not permitted in its dealings or intercourse with other States or their inhabitants to ignore the right to property in the labor and service of persons in transitu from those States. The Supreme Court having fallen into the same error, their order should be reversed.

To avoid the possibility of misapprehension, I will briefly recapitulate the positions which I hold in the foregoing opinion:

Every State is at liberty, in reference to all who come within its territory, with the intent of taking up their abode in it for any length of time, to declare what can or cannot be held as property. As, however, by the law or implied agreement which regulates the intercourse of separate and independent nations towards each other, all things belonging to the citizen of anyone nation, recognized as property by that law, are exempt in their passage through the territory of any other, from all interference and control of the latter; so, a fortiori, by the positive compact which regulates the dealings and intercourse of these States towards each other, things belonging to the citizen of any one State, recognized as property by that compact, are exempt, in their passage through the territory of any other State, from all interference and control of the latter. The right to the labor and service of persons held in slavery, is incontestably recognized as property in the Constitution of the United States. The right yielded by what is termed comity under the law of nations, ripens, in necessary accordance with the declared purpose and tenor of the Constitution of the United States, into a conventional obligation, essential to its contemplated and thorough operation as an instrument of federative and national government. While the violation of the right yielded by what is termed comity under the law of nations, would, under certain circumstances, be a just cause of war, the rights growing out of this conventional obligation are properly within the cognizance of the judicial tribunals, which they are bound to recognize and enforce.

That portion of the act of the Legislature of this State which declares that a slave brought into it belonging to a person not an inhabitant of it shall be free, is unconstitutional and void, so far as it applies to a citizen of any other State of this Union, where the right to property in the service and labor of slaves exists, who is passing through this State, and who has no intention of remaining here a moment longer than the exigencies of his journey require.

Comstock, Ch. J., observed in substance, that since the last term of the court, his time had been wholly occupied in an examination of other causes argued at that term. To this case, therefore, he had not yet been able to give the attention which its importance might justify. He had no hesitation in declaring it to be his opinion that the legislation of this State, on which the question in the case depends, is directly opposed to the rules of comity and justice which ought to regulate intercourse between the States of this Union; and he was not prepared to hold that such legislation does not violate the obligations imposed on all the States by the Federal Constitution. Without, however, wishing to delay the decision which a majority of his brethren were prepared to make, he contented himself with dissenting from the judgment.

Selden, J. I have been prevented, by want of time and the pressure of other duties, from giving to this case that careful examination which is due to its importance, and to the elaborate and able arguments of the counsel, and am not prepared, therefore, definitely to determine whether the act of 1841 is or is not in conflict with any express provisions of the United States Constitution. But however this may be, I cannot but regard it as a gross violation of those principles of justice and comity which should at all times pervade our inter-state legislation, as well as wholly inconsistent with the general spirit of our national compact. While, therefore, I am not prepared at this time to give such reasons as would justify me in holding the law to be void, I am equally unprepared to concur in the conclusion to which the majority of my associates have arrived.

Judgment affirmed.

In the Matter of the Commonwealth of Kentucky, One of the United States of America, by Beriah Magoffin, Governor, and the Executive Authority Thereof, Petitioner v. William Dennison, Governor and Executive Authority of the State of Ohio

Supreme Court of the United States
March 14, 1861
24 How. (65 U.S. 10) 66 (1861)

On October 4, 1859, a free African American from Ohio, Willis Lago, allegedly enticed an African American slave woman, Charlotte, to leave her Kentucky owner, cross the Ohio River, and reside with him in Ohio. When this theft of slave property was discovered, the Woodword County, Kentucky, grand jury indicted Lago for the crime of assisting a slave to escape. Kentucky asked Ohio to return Lago to stand trial for the charge, but Ohio's governor and attorney general refused. Kentucky then asked the United States Supreme Court for a judicial order, a writ of mandamus, to force Ohio to return Lago.

Several issues are at work in this decision. The first issue to notice is its timing, its historical context. This case reached the U.S. Supreme Court in 1861, just as the crisis of the Union was peaking. Parties delivered their oral arguments on February 28, 1861, (during the secession winter of 1860–1861) and Chief Justice Roger B. Taney for a unanimous Court handed down this decision on March 14, ten days after President Abraham Lincoln took office. Thus, because of its timing, any Supreme Court decision that involved whether the Court (a branch of the federal government) could force or coerce a state to do anything was sure to be controversial, political, and debated.

Next at issue was whether the federal government, through its judicial branch, could command a state to act in a manner not prescribed by that state's own laws. Because slave stealing was not a crime in Ohio, was Ohio (through the legal principle of comity, the voluntary recognition by courts of one jurisdiction of the laws and the judicial decisions of another) bound to recognize Kentucky's slave laws and return Lago for trial? Could the Supreme Court force such recognition of comity? Though one might expect a decision written by the southern sympathizer and the author of the 1857 *Dred Scott* decision to answer in the affirmative, Taney held that the states could decide for themselves whether to comply (whether they had a "duty") to honor such requests. Taney held that federal law did not require state compliance but "leave it to the States to exercise it or not, as might best comport with their own sense of justice, and their own interest and convenience." Therefore, "if the Governor of Ohio refuses to discharge this duty, there is no power delegated to the General Government, either through the Judicial Department or any other department, to use any coercive means to compel him." In this instance, Ohio could and did resist properly the intrusion of slave law into its borders; Taney's defense of state power trumped his defense of slave law.

Reprinted here are the briefs and arguments for both states, followed by the decision of the Supreme Court. Although political and military events overshadowed the ruling, this decision suggests just how fluid the legal and political arguments were about what states could and could not do in regard to the divisive and corrosive issue of slave law.

A MOTION was made in behalf of the State of Kentucky, by the direction and in the name of the Governor of the State, for a rule on the Governor of Ohio to show cause why a mandamus should not be issued by this court, commanding him to cause Willis Lago, a fugitive from justice, to be delivered up, to be removed to the State of Kentucky, having jurisdiction of the crime with which he is charged.

The facts on which this motion was made are as follows:

The grand jury of Woodford Circuit Court, in the State of Kentucky, at October term, 1859, returned to the court the following indictment against the said Lago:

1. In a suit between two States, this court has original jurisdiction, without any further act of Congress regulating the mode and form in which it shall be exercised.
2. A suit by or against the Governor of a State, as such, in his official character, is a suit by or against the State.
3. A writ of mandamus does not issue in virtue of any prerogative power, and, in modern practice, is nothing more than an ordinary action at law in cases where it is the appropriate remedy.

4. The words "treason, felony, or other crime," in the second clause of the second section of the fourth article of the Constitution of the United States, include every offence forbidden and made punishable by the laws of the State where the offence is committed.
5. It was the duty of the Executive authority of Ohio, upon the demand made by the Governor of Kentucky, and the production of the indictment, duly certified, to cause Lago to be delivered up to the agent of the Governor of Kentucky who was appointed to demand and receive him.
6. The duty of the Governor of Ohio was merely ministerial, and he had no right to exercise and discretionary power as to the nature of character of the crime charged in the indictment.
7. The word "duty," in the act of 1793, means the moral obligation of the State to perform the compact in the Constitution, when Congress had, by that act, regulated the mode in which the duty was to be performed.
8. But Congress cannot coerce a State officer, as such, to perform any duty by act of Congress. The State officer may perform it if he thinks proper, and it may be a moral duty to perform it. But if he refuses, no law of Congress can compel him.
9. The Governor of Ohio cannot, through the Judiciary or any other Department of the General Government, be compelled to deliver up Lago; and, upon that ground only, this motion for a mandamus was overruled.

WOODFORD CIRCUIT COURT.

The Commonwealth of Kentucky against Willis Lago, free man of color.

The grand jury of Woodford county, in the name and by the authority of the Commonwealth of Kentucky, accuse Willis Lago, free man of color, of the crime of assisting a slave to escape, &c., committed as follows, namely: the said Willis Lago, free man of color, on the fourth day of October 1859, in the county aforesaid, not having lawful claim, and not having any color of claim thereto, did seduce and entice Charlotte, a slave, the property of C. W. Nuckols, to leave her owner and possessor, and did aid and assist said slave in an attempt to make her escape from her said owner and possessor, against the peace and dignity of the Commonwealth of Kentucky.

w. s. downey, Com. Attorney.

On the back of said indictment is the following endorsement: "A true bill; L. A. Berry, foreman. Returned by grand jury, October term, 1859."

A copy of this indictment, certified and authenticated, according to the act of Congress of 1793, was presented to the Governor of Ohio by the authorized agent of the Governor of Kentucky, and the arrest and delivery of the fugitive demanded.

The Governor of Ohio referred the matter to the Attorney General of the State of Ohio, for his opinion and advice, and received from him a written opinion, upon which he acted, and refused to arrest or deliver up the fugitive, and, with his refusal, communicated to the Governor of Kentucky the opinion of the Attorney General, to show the grounds on which he refused. The written opinion of the Attorney General is as follows:

OFFICE OF THE ATTORNEY GENERAL,
Columbus, Ohio, April 14, 1860.

SIR: The requisition, with its accompanying documents, made upon you by the Governor of Kentucky, for the surrender of Willis Lago, described to be a "fugitive from the justice of the laws of" that State, may, for all present purpose, be regarded as sufficiently complying with the provisions of the Federal Constitution and the act of Congress touching the extradition of fugitives from justice, if the alleged offence charged against Lago can be considered as either "treason, felony, or other crime," within the fair scope of these provisions.

Attached to the requisition is an authenticated copy of the indictment on which the demand is predicated; and this, omitting merely the title of the case and the venue, is in the words and figures following:

"The grand jury of Woodford county, in the name and by the authority of the Commonwealth of Kentucky, accuse Willis Lago, free man of color, of the crime of assisting a slave to escape, &c., committed as follows, viz: the said Willis Lago, free man of color, on the fourth day of October, 1859, in the county aforesaid, not having lawful claim, and not having any color of claim thereto, did seduce and entice Charlotte, a slave, the property of C. W. Nuckols, to leave her owner and possessor, and did aid and assist said slave in an attempt to make her escape from her said owner and possessor, against the peace and dignity of the Commonwealth of Kentucky."

This indictment, it must be admitted, is quite inartificially framed, and it might be found difficult to vindicate its validity according to the rules of criminal pleading which obtain in our own courts, or wheresoever else the common law prevails. This objection, however, if it have any force, loses its importance in the presence of other considerations, which, in my judgment, must control the fate of the application.

The act of which Lago is thus accused by the grand jury of Woodford county certainly is not "treason," according to any code of any country, and just as certainly is not "felony," or any other crime, under the laws of this State, or by the common law. On the other hand, the laws of Kentucky do denounce this act as a "crime," and the question is thus presented whether, under the Federal Constitution, one State is under an obligation to surrender its citizens or residents to any other State, on the charge that they have committed an offence not known to the laws of the former, nor affecting the public safety, nor regarded as malum in se by the general judgment and conscience of civilized nations.

This question must, in my opinion, be resolved against the existence of any such obligation. There are many acts—such as the creation of nuisances, selling vinous or spirituous liquors, horse racing, trespassing on public lands, keeping tavern without license, permitting dogs to run at large—declared by the laws of most of the States to be crimes, for the commission of which the offender is visited with fine or imprisonment, or with both; and yet it will not be insisted that the power of extradition, as defined by the Constitution, applies to these or the like offences. Obviously a line must be somewhere drawn, distinguishing offences which do from offences which do not fall within the scope of this power. The right rule, in my opinion, is that which holds the power to be limited to such acts as constitute either treason or felony by the common law, as that stood when the Constitution was adopted, or which are regarded as crimes by the usages and laws of all civilized nations. This rule is sufficiently vindicated by the consideration that no other has ever been suggested, at once so easy of application to all cases, so just to the several States, and so consistent in its operation with the rights and security of the citizen.

The application of this rule is decisive against the demand now urged for the surrender of Lago. The offence charged against him does not rank among those upon which the constitutional provision was intended to operate, and you have, therefore, no authority to comply with the requisition made upon you by the Governor of Kentucky.

Entertaining no doubt as to the rightfulness of this conclusion, I am highly gratified in being able to fortify it by the authority of my learned and eminent predecessor, who first filled this office, and who officially advised the Governor of that day, that in a case substantially similar to the one now presented, he ought not to issue his warrant of extradition. Other authority, if needed, may be found in the fact that this rule is conformable to the ancient and settled usage of the State.

To guard against possible misapprehension, let me add that the power of extradition is not to be exercised, as of course, in every case which may apparently fall within the rule here asserted. While it is limited to these cases, the very nature of the power is such, that its exercise, even under this limitation, must always be guided by a sound legal discretion, applying itself to the particular circumstances of each case as it shall be presented.

The communication, in a formal manner, of the preceding opinion, has been long but unavoidably deferred by causes of which you are fully apprised. Though this delay is greatly to be regretted, it can have had no prejudicial effect, as the agent appointed by the Governor of Kentucky to receive Lago was long since officially, though informally, advised that no case had been presented which would warrant his extradition.

Very respectfully, your obedient servant,
C. P. WOLCOTT.
To the GOVERNOR.

Some further correspondence took place between the Governors, which it is not necessary to state; and the Governor of Ohio, having finally refused to cause the arrest and delivery of the fugitive, this motion was made on the part of Kentucky.

Upon the motion being made, the court ordered notice of it to be served on the Governor and Attorney General of Ohio, to appear on a day mentioned in the notice. The Attorney General of Ohio appeared, but under a protest, made by order of the Governor of Ohio, against the jurisdiction of the court to issue the mandamus moved for.

The case was fully argued by Mr. Stevenson and Mr. Marshall on behalf of the State of Kentucky, and by Mr. Wolcott, the Attorney General of Ohio, on the part of that State.

The great importance of the principles involved in this case has induced the reporter to allow a large space to the arguments of the respective counsel.

That of Messrs. Cooper and Marshall and Mr. Stevenson, for the State of Kentucky, was as follows:

The State of Kentucky, interested in the preservation of the integrity of her own laws, and in the punishment of such as offend against them on her own soil, comes, as a party plaintiff in this proceeding, before the Supreme Court of the United States, as a court of original jurisdiction, to ask for a mandamus against Mr. Dennison, who is the Governor of Ohio, and as such, exercises the Executive authority of said State.

The second paragraph of section 2, article 4, of the Constitution of the United States, reads thus; "A person charged in any State with treason, felony, or other crime, who shall flee from justice and be found in another State, shall, on demand of the Executive authority of the State from which he fled, be delivered up, to be removed to the State having jurisdiction of the crime."

To execute this obligation of the Constitution the act of Congress of 1793 was passed, (Statutes at L., 302, sec. 1,) in which, by the first section, the duty to be performed, and the person by whom to be performed, in the event of a demand under the Constitution, are prescribed. That duty is simple, and is stated thus: "It shall be the duty of the Executive authority of the State or Territory to which such person shall have fled, to cause him or her to be arrested and secured, and notice of the arrest to be given to the Executive authority making such demands, or to the agent of such authority appointed to receive the fugitive, and to cause the fugitive to be delivered to such agent when he shall appear."

One Lago, who was indicted for an act denounced as a crime by the law of Kentucky, fled, and was found in Ohio, and was demanded by Governor Magoffin, the Executive authority of the State of Kentucky, of Governor Dennison, the Governor of Ohio, and at the time Executive authority thereof. All the conditions were observed to complete a proper demand, according to the act of Congress. It is further shown that, for reasons set forth in the official reply of Governor Dennison, as Executive authority of Ohio, the demand was not complied with, and that he refused to arrest Lago at all. Upon that refusal this proceeding is taken.

The Commonwealth of Kentucky is properly the plaintiff in this case.

"Where an application is made, the object of which is to obtain the benefit of certain provisions of an act of Parliament, &c., those for whose benefit such provisions were inserted in the act, &c., should be the applicants for the rule, although they may be neither specially nor nominally mentioned."

>Tapping on Mandamus, 289.

The duty prescribed by the Constitution and law was to have been performed by the defendant, Dennison, as the officer wielding the Executive authority of the State of Ohio. He is, therefore, the proper person against whom to institute the proceeding.

Is mandamus the proper remedy? We will not extend this brief by reciting what is said of the authority of the Court of B. R. over mandamus. It has been used since the days of Edward II, in England, and has been the suppletory police power of the kingdom.

>Tapping on Mandamus, 5–30.
>
>Cowp., 378; 2 B. and C., 198.
>
>Burrows, 1265–'68.
>
>15 East., 135.
>
>3 Blacks. Com., 110.

In this court it is acknowledged as an action, a case, rather than as a "prerogative writ."

The proceeding on mandamus is a case within the meaning of the act of Congress. It is an action or suit brought in a court of justice, asserting a right, and is presented according to the forms of judicial proceeding.

>12 Peters, 614; 2 Peters, 450.

It is not by the office of the person to whom the writ is directed, but the nature of the thing to be done, that the propriety or impropriety of issuing a mandamus is to be determined.

>1 Cranch, 170.

This court (in 3 Howard, 99) treats the mandamus as "an action," and that "a party is entitled to it when there is no other adequate remedy." This court refuses to entertain the action of assumpsit for matter which might have been proved on a former action of mandamus.

There is no remedy for the grievance inflicted on the State of Kentucky by the refusal of Governor Dennison, unless the mandamus applied for will lie. If mandamus will lie in any case where the Supreme Court exercises original jurisdiction, all considerations and conditions concur to point it out as the proper remedy in this case; for—

1. The duty to be performed is single, simple, only ministerial and public in its nature and office.

2. The party directed to perform it is certainly named.
3. No other adequate remedy exists or is prescribed by law.
4. The duty is distinctly prescribed by the Constitution and the act of 1793.
5. The office held by Mr. Dennison does not shield him from the performance; "it is the nature of the duty which determines the propriety of mandamus as a remedy."

The Supreme Court of the United States has never adjudicated the question of this remedy as now it is presented.

In the case of the United States v. Lawrence, 3 Dallas, 53, (A. D. 1795,) this court was applied to as a court of original jurisdiction, and it entertained the jurisdiction. The case was disposed of on the point, that the duty of Judge Lawrence involved the exercise of a discretion in the execution of his office which this court could not control.

In the case of Marbury v. Madison, 1 Cranch, 175, a careful reading of the opinion will show that the mandamus was refused because the act of 1789 was unconstitutional, in so far as it disturbed the constitutional distribution of the judicial power of this court. The application was to this court, in its original jurisdiction, whereas the case belonged to it only under its appellate jurisdiction, and therefore the rule was discharged.

In McIntyre v. Wood, 7 Cranch, 504, the point was as to the power of the Circuit Court of the United States; and the same remark applies to the case of McCluney v. Silliman, 6 Wheat., 600. The reasoning of those cases is sufficiently satisfactory, but it has no application in this case.

Ex parte Roberts, 6 Peters, 216, and Ex parte Davenport, 6 Peters, 664, were applications to control the judge of an inferior court by mandamus, which were refused because of the discretion the inferior officer had the right to exercise. Ex parte Bradstreet, 8 Peters, 634, and Ex parte Story, 12 Peters, 339, were cases addressed to this court, in the exercise of its appellate jurisdiction; so was the case of Kendall v. United States, which was very elaborately argued, 12 Peters, 525 to 655. Ex parte Guthrie, and all the rest of the cases of the applications for mandamus, have been to this court as an appellate court. This is the first case in our judicial history in which a mandamus has been asked for in a case falling properly within the original jurisdiction of the Supreme Court.

The judicial power of the United States is vested, by the Constitution, in the Supreme Court, and in such inferior courts as Congress may from time to time establish. This power "shall extend" to a number of classes of cases, among which are "all cases in law or equity arising under this Constitution, the laws of the United States," &c., &c., and, within the enumerated classes, ["]in all cases in which a State shall be a party, the Supreme Court shall have original jurisdiction.["]

It is respectfully submitted that, under these constitutional grants of power and jurisdiction, this court may, debito justitiae, entertain the application for mandamus where a State is a party, and this without resort to the act of Congress distributing the means of enforcing the jurisdiction. The judicial power, so far as this jurisdiction of the court is concerned, is vested by the Constitution; it would neither remain dormant, nor would it expire, though the Legislative power had never passed a law to authorize certain processes to assert such jurisdiction. We adopt the view taken by the counsel in the case of the United States v. Peters, 3 Dallas, 126: "The judicial power is abstract or relative; in the former character, the court, for itself, declares the law and distributes justice; in the latter, it superintends and controls the conduct of other tribunals by a prohibitory or mandatory interposition. This superintending authority has been deposited in the Supreme Court by the Federal Constitution, and it becomes a duty to exercise it upon every proper occasion." "It is certain the Constitution fixes no limitation to the exercise of this power by this court upon the subject; nor does the law, but by the implication in the 14th section of the act of 1789, that the writs issued shall be allowable by principle and usage," and necessary to the exercise of the jurisdiction belonging to the court. If mandamus would then be granted by the Court of King's Bench, debito justitiae, it can be issued in a case of original jurisdiction, upon a proper showing, by this court; and the express power is extended by the 14th section of the judiciary act of 1789, if the writ is necessary to the exercise of the jurisdiction belonging to the court.

If mandamus should not be regarded as a "prerogative writ," but as an action, a case, it falls, in this matter, directly within the vested power and original jurisdiction of the court, and can be entertained independently of the judiciary act, as a constitutional "power" of this court.

Where is the great conservative power which is to regulate State sovereignties in the execution of their constitutional obligations, if this court renounces, or shrinks from, the legitimate exercise of the functions with which it is invested by the Constitution?

The original jurisdiction of this court is limited to those cases in which foreign ambassadors, ministers, consuls, and American States, are interested; but in this range it has no limit. There is no judge who can interpose to exercise power over them but this court, in its original jurisdiction. From the very nature of the Constitution, the great police power of the mandamus, as between the States, is a necessity to the exercise of the jurisdiction conferred on this court. Therefore, Kentucky approaches this tribunal with the violated obligation of Ohio in one hand, and with the Constitution in the other, conferring full jurisdiction on this court, as a court of original jurisdiction in all cases in law or equity in which a State is a party, and shows that, for the grievance she suffers, there is no legal remedy but mandamus.

"It is the case which gives the jurisdiction, not the court." 1 Wheat., Martin v. Hunter's Lessee.

Under the precepts of the law of nations, the obligation to deliver fugitives from justice touched only a few classes of criminals—those whose crimes "touched the State," or were so enormous as to make them hostes humani generis—positioners, assassins, &c. These were delivered up, when convicted or tried, and sometimes before. This was done for comity. Vattel, Book 1, c. 19; B. 2, 6.

The character of this obligation was more frequently rendered certain by treaty, as in our treaties with Great Britain and France. But the Constitution of the United States has, among the States of the Union, extended and enlarged the rule of the publicists. Whereas they obeyed the demand in cases of criminals "convicted or tried," our States obey the demand where a person is charged with treason, felony, or other crime; whereas they only obeyed the demand in cases of heinous crimes, our States enter into the obligation for "other crime," making their obligation as broad as the word crime can be extended. Crime can be extended in its signification. Crime is synonymous with misdemeanor, (4 Black. Com., 5,) and includes every offence below felony punished by indictment as an offence against the public, (9 Wendell, 222.) We know that, in the first draft of this clause of the Constitution, the words "high misdemeanor" were used. They were stricken out, and "other crime" inserted, because "high misdemeanor" might be technical and too limited. The framers wanted "to comprehend all proper cases." (5 Elliott, 487.) To use the language of a learned judge, "there is a dependence that justice will be done; and the Constitution rests on this confidence for the vindication of the compact for [']a more perfect Union.[']"

The Constitution reposes in the Federal Government the discretion of conducting the foreign intercourse of these States with foreign Powers. This is manifest by the power given to the Executive "to receive ambassadors, public ministers, and consuls, and, by and with the consent of the Senate, to appoint ambassadors and other public ministers, and consuls," and, by and with the consent of the Senate, to make treaties. The correlative inhibitions to the States are expressed in the same instrument: "No State shall enter into any treaty, alliance, or confederation."Article 1, section 10: "No State shall enter into any agreement with a foreign Power," &c. This court has coincided with the view here expressed, in the opinion rendered in the case of Holmes v. Jennison, 14 Pet., 575. A Governor of one of these United States cannot surrender a fugitive from justice from a foreign country to the agents of that Power. This is exclusively within the sphere of the Federal Power. Ib.

The Constitution is harmonious in its complicated structure. As the Federal Government is the repository of the power over foreign intercourse, so the inter-State intercourse is established upon a fixed and stable basis, by dispensing with comity and the rule of the publicists, and making the obligation to render criminals to the jurisdiction they have offended a perfect obligation, in express constitutional compact. The States have left themselves no discretion on this subject. They cannot enlarge, diminish, abridge, or modify, the constitutional arrangement: "No State shall, without the consent of Congress, enter into any agreement or compact with another State," &c.

Congress cannot waive an express and mandatory provision of the Constitution. A person charged with treason, felony, or other crime, &c., shall be delivered up, &c. Can two of these States negotiate with each other a modification of this obligation? Certainly not. Can they with the consent of Congress? Certainly not. It is a fixed, well-defined, and perfect obligation, which furnishes all the essentials for its own execution, if properly considered, as an inter-State obligation, subject to the Judicial branch of the Government to enforce its due and proper execution. It expresses plainly what is to be done, upon whose demand it is to be done, the circumstances under which it is to be done, and the purpose for which it is to be done. By whom it is to be done, the Constitution did not prescribe; for, it may be, that was a matter in which the State might have a choice. Congress acted; yet the Executive of the State was left to be guided by his State authority or his own responsibility as to the mode in which he would cause the arrest and delivery of the fugitive; but, beyond this simple and single ministerial performance, the Constitution and the law have left him no discretion whatever. He is a mere instrument of the Constitution, pointed out by the law, because he holds the Executive authority of his State, and is a sworn officer of the Constitution of the United States, bound by his oath to observe its mandates, and the laws of the United States made in pursuance thereof, as the supreme law of the land, even in preference to those of his own State. The Executive authority of the State was indicated, because the duty to be performed was of a very delicate nature, and a discourteous exhibition of power within the demesnes of a State was to be avoided, such as arresting one, without regular process, who might be within the protection of the State.

It would not be within the right or competency of the State of Ohio to refuse this delivery. All her departments could not make a law effective to prevent it. Can her Executive alone avoid it? If he can, why may not any one else, no matter how appointed or in what way qualified? Another could not be qualified by a stronger oath to support the Constitution, and the laws of the United States made in pursuance of it; for the Constitution requires this Executive to take that oath, and qualifies his right to the gubernatorial chair of his State by the fact of his taking or refusing to take that oath. Were he to refuse, as Governor of Ohio, to take the oath to support the Constitution of the United States, and to maintain the laws made in pursuance thereof, is there no power, by mandamus, in the Judicial Department of this Government, to compel obedience to a duty expressed on the face of the Constitution?

The State of Ohio must be considered as yet willing to abide by her constitutional obligation, for this refusal is not the act of the Government of the State; it is only the act of her Executive, of one department of her Government. The State is bound so strongly by the terms of the Constitution, she cannot refuse. If, then, she is consenting, and Kentucky is demanding, and only Mr. Dennison refusing, it remains to be seen whether there resides in the Judicial Department of the

Federal Government power to compel him to the performance of a ministerial duty assigned to him by law, in order to execute the inter-State covenants inscribed in the Constitution. In that memorable case of Prigg v. Pennsylvania, (16 Pet., 539,) several leading principles of construction were asserted, to the observance of which we now invite the attention of this court.

1. When the end is required, the means are given; when the duty is enjoined, the ability to perform it is contemplated to exist on the part of the functionaries to whom it is intrusted.

2. The General Government is bound, through its own departments, Legislative, Judicial, or Executive, as the case may be, to carry into effect all the rights and duties imposed upon it by the Constitution.

We are perfectly aware that reliance may be placed on the very case from which these principles are extracted, to prove that the obligation to deliver the fugitive from justice is "exclusively Federal," and that, therefore, it may be insisted that Congress cannot direct a State Executive authority to execute it, but must impose this duty on some person who will be amenable, as belonging to one of the departments of the Federal Government. The court says the obligation is "exclusively Federal"—that "the States cannot be compelled to enforce it." From this dictum the inference is drawn that, if the person indicated to perform the duty, (though it be only ministerial,) holds any office under the State Government, this court cannot or will not compel him to perform the duty, but will wait for Congress to remodel the legislation of 1793, so as to make the person exclusively a Federal officer. We resist the propriety of such inference from the points decided by the court in Prigg's case. The court alluded to the resort which the claimant of a fugitive from service must have to the Judiciary to ascertain a fact, in order to support a right upon the finding of the fact, and did intimate that the action of the State magistracy was voluntary, though valid, unless prohibited by the State. In the case of a fugitive from justice, however, there is no fact to be ascertained, no question to be adjudicated, no necessity to appeal to any one to support a right, but simply to deliver upon a demand. Will it be replied that, to afford even this facility, Congress must, by law, indicate who is to perform the duty? We rejoin, that Congress has so indicated by the act of 1793. As well might the defendant plead his citizenship or inhabitancy in Ohio to relieve him, as that he is relieved by being Governor, or holding an office by authority of the State. The power of this Government extends so far that the performance of a public duty may be demanded, and the incumbent of a particular office may be required to perform it, especially where the duty is only ministerial, though at the same time he may be in office in the State. We think it is eminently proper that the Executive authority of the State should be the power indicated for the performance of this duty; because that officer is, at the same time, sworn to support the Constitution of the United States, and the laws of Congress made in pursuance thereof; and because he represents the State on which the demand is made, and is bound by the constitutional compact on which the demand is founded.

The obligation is said to be "exclusively Federal." Does it not bind the State of Ohio? Is it not from her power the compact subtracts? We think the State has peculiarly come under the obligation expressed in the clause in question. Her hands are tied by the clause. Without the clause she might have been guided by her own discretion or by comity; now she is obliged, by the terms of the covenant to which she has consented. It may be she cannot be compelled to enforce the delivery of the fugitive; it may be the General Government is compelled, through its own departments, "to carry this into effect;" but that necessity does not shift the obligation. The citizen owes obedience to the law, and is under obligation to perform the duties the law enjoins; but, if he fails, the court enforces the law, and secures the right which was infringed by the violation of the duty. Nothing can be more familiar than an obligation resting upon one party, and the right and power to enforce its execution vested in another. We submit, very respectfully, that this is just the case under our Constitution. The obligation to surrender the fugitive from justice rests upon the State; the power and duty to enforce the obligation reside in the General Government. The State of Virginia failing in 1790 to deliver certain fugitives upon the demand of Governor Mifflin, of Pennsylvania, he brought the facts before the President, and the act of 1793 was the consequence, whereby the Executive of the State was directed to perform the duty answering such demand. Every condition has been met. They who would escape the conclusion at which we wish to arrive must take the position not only that, in our system, the States may prohibit the use of their State agencies to the General Government in carrying the supreme law into effect within their boundaries, but this further position, that it is not in the power of the Federal Government to demand of any one in a State to perform a duty essential to the execution of the obligations inscribed in the Constitution.

We may well ask the Supreme Court to pause before ruling to this extent. When we remember that all Executive, Legislative, and Judicial officers, in the several States, are required, by the express letter of the Constitution of the United States, to be sworn "to support the Constitution," and that "the laws of Congress made in pursuance thereof are the supreme law of the land," overriding all State laws coming into conflict with them—that this body of State officers is bound solemnly to render obedience primarily to this supreme law, even in their respective jurisdictions, and though opposed to their State laws—it is difficult to comprehend the wisdom of that policy which teaches that those States can prohibit the use of these agencies in carrying into effect those very laws which the State has consented to observe as the supreme law, and its agents have been sworn to support as paramount. It seems to us that the policy leads to a multiplication of officers, thus increasing the burdens of the people, and to conflicts between State and Federal agencies, by inculcating the idea that there is an incompatibility in the exercise of official fidelity to the State and Federal jurisdictions at the same time. Under our system of government, administered in its true spirit, there never can be a conflict. It is pernicious to the best interests to build on this foundation, for "a house divided against itself will fall." The State functionary owes allegiance and obedience to the Constitution of the United States, and the laws made in pursuance thereof, before everything else. The State owes the same obedience and observance to the same power. The Constitution enters and pervades our system everywhere. It surrounds the States and the people like an atmosphere vital to them, and ever in contact with them. To the officials of States, in every department of State Government, it is ever present with the oath to be rendered for its support, to remind them that, while they perform the functions of a limited jurisdiction, they are at the same time the conservative sentinels of that larger system, whose forces control the course and destiny of their State and of their fellow-citizens. The planet of the heavens revolves upon its own axis, and pursues its peculiar orbit; but it, and all who inhabit it, are at the same time particles of an infinite system, whose balanced and regulated forces acting upon it assure its safety, and preserve it from destructive collision with the spheres that surround it. The planet and its inhabitants are not taught that they cannot obey the laws of the Great Architect and Ruler.

The Constitution of the United States engages three articles in asserting the construction of its departments of Government, defining their powers, and prohibiting the exercise of these to the States. So precise is it, that no restraint is laid upon a State but that an examination will prove it is because the same power vested in the new Government. With the 4th article a new class is entered upon; they are not powers, but obligations and compacts, in which it is impossible to understand anything else (as it seems to us) than that the States are bound inter se, and are understood to be actors. They are a class of cases to be rendered effective by the action of the States, and by the action of the General Government—concurrent powers. The rule is well settled that in such cases, when Congress acts, the rule it establishes obtains.

We submit to the court that the case of Prigg v. Pennsylvania has been modified by the subsequent decision of Moore v. the People of Illinois, (14 Howard,) so far at least as to authorize State legislation, which is ancillary to the effectuation of the obligation to be "carried into effect" by the Federal power. We hope the court will not carry the exclusive action of the Federal power so far as to say that it cannot indicate "the Executive authority of a State" as the instrument to perform the purely ministerial act required by the 2d section, 4th article, of the Constitution.

We refer, especially, to the opinion of Justice McLean in Prigg's case, because it is directly in line with the views we now present, and seems to us to be conclusive.

The duty required of the Governor of Ohio, in arresting a fugitive from justice, results from an express obligation of his State, which he, as the Executive authority of that State, is directed by the act of seventeen hundred and ninety-three to carry out. He has no judgment to exercise touching the point of arrest. He cannot even hear a question on the point of identity of person, that a judge might hear on habeas corpus. He cannot consider the question of guilt or innocence.

9 Wendell, 221.

We refer to Clark's case because it is a strong case, adjudicated in the better days of the Republic by a patriotic public officer, who strove only to perform his duty under the law.

May every State Executive at pleasure violate the Constitution in its most direct mandates, and most express obligations? Has the Judicial power an arm not strong enough to reach him? If so, the obligations of the Constitution may at any time and under any pretext be avoided; the instrument is a myth.

Governor Dennison has mistaken his power in this matter, by assuming the discretion to judge in regard to the alleged crime. The words of the Constitution are unambiguous. That the crime is to be judged by the law of the State through whose Executive the demand is made, appears from the Constitution itself, for the object of the delivery of the fugitive is, "that he may be removed to the State having jurisdiction of the crime." To say that the authority on whom the demand is made shall judge of the guilt of the party, or of the fact of the crime, or whether the alleged act is a crime, is to nullify the sense, object, and intent, of the framers of the Constitution, and to assume a supervisory power by the Executive of a State over the law-making and police powers of another State. The police power of the States was reserved, and has never been surrendered to the Federal Government.

Moore v. the People of Illinois, 14 Howard, 18.

11 Pet., 139.

The Governor of Ohio, in refusing the demand, has not denied his general responsibility, under the Constitution and law of the United States, to make delivery of a fugitive from justice. His refusal was based upon the allegation that the offence charged in the Kentucky indictment was not crime, according to the signification of that word in the Constitution, and that therefore there was no obligation to deliver arising under the compact, nor springing from comity, because the offence was not known to civilized nations generally, to the common law, or to the statutes or polity of Ohio. In the views we have submitted already as to the duty of Governor Dennison, these positions are controverted. To confine the term to such offence as was denominated crime at the date of the Constitution, would give a restricted operation to the instrument, which would vastly impair its adaptation to the progress and wants of society. It would, in effect, destroy the force of this clause of the Constitution at its inception, and, instead of placing the States in bonds of mutual obligation to vindicate the jurisdiction of each other through future years, would make each a supervisor of the police power of the others, and, by reason of conflicting policies in their progress, would inevitably lead to alienation, confusion, and ultimate discord. "The instrument was not intended to provide merely for the exigencies of a few years, but was to endure through a lapse of ages, the events of which were locked up in the inscrutable purposes of Providence. Hence its powers are expressed in general terms," &c.

1 Wheat., 305, 326.

The instrument was intended not only for those who framed it, but for posterity; not merely for the society of 1787, but for American society in all future time, and embraced in the word "crime" not merely what was punishable by indictment at the date of the instrument, but whatever each State in its progress might so declare. If this be not true, this family of American States are not connected by links stronger than a rope of sand. We will not elaborate this point further in this place, but may, if deemed proper, dwell upon it hereafter, together with reference to such works as will justify the views we suggest.

It only remains for the counsel for the demandant to say that the State of Kentucky, in bringing this case before the Supreme Court, pursues the law as it exists, and asks its enforcement, if the law can be enforced. If the act of Congress has exceeded the power vested in Congress by the Constitution, and we have been, since 1793, acting through instruments over which the Government has no control, Kentucky desires, through the Supreme Court, to know the fact, so that Congress may, without delay, so treat this important subject as hereafter to assure the faithful and prompt execution of this clause of the Constitution. To her it is a vital question; as to all the other States, in fact, whose institutions are similar to hers.

The argument of Mr. Wolcott, on behalf of the State of Ohio, was as follows:

I. The Government of the United States is one of limited and enumerated powers, derived primarily from the specific grants of the Constitution, which is at once the source and the law of all its being. It is a necessary correlative of this proposition, and one declared by the fundamental law itself, that each State still retains complete, exclusive, and supreme power, over all persons and things within its limits, where that power has not been specially granted or restrained by the Constitution; and that, in respect to all this mass of undelegated and unprohibited power, the States stand to each other and to the General Government as absolutely foreign nations.

> Gibbons v. Ogden, 9 Wheat., 203–208.
>
> Brown v. Marland, 12 Wheat., 419, 443.
>
> Wilson v. Blackbird Creek Co., 2 Peters, 251, 252.
>
> Buckner v. Finley, 2 Peters, 586, 590.
>
> New York v. Miln, 11 Peters, 102, 139.
>
> United States Bank v. Daniel, 12 Peters, 32, 34.

> Rhode Island v. Massachusetts, 12 Peters, 720.
>
> License Cases, 5 How., 504, 588.

II. The Judicial Department of the Federal Government, sharing of necessity the intrinsic quality which marks that Government in its unity, is also one of limited and specific powers, and, in its tribunals of every grade, is subject to three conditions of universal application:

1. Ex vi termini, it is confined to the discharge of functions purely judicial in their nature.

> Hayburn's Case, in notis, 2 Dall., 409.

2. These functions can be exerted only in the precise cases enumerated by the Constitution as subject to the judicial authority, and which, it has been said, range themselves in two general classes:
   a. Cases in which the authority depends on the nature of the controversy, without respect to the character of the parties; and—
   b. Cases in which the authority depends on the character of the parties, without regard to the nature of the controversy.

> Cohens v. Virginia, 6 Wheat., 264, 293.

But this is evidently to be taken as subject to another qualfication; for—

3. The judicial power exercised in these specific cases must be the "judicial power of the United States." In other words, the authority of the Judicial Department is restrained not only by the limitations specially affixed to it, but also by those more general considerations which grow out of the very nature and purpose of a Federal Government. Thus the judicial power of the United States cannot extend to a controversy in which a State may, even by a purely civil action, pursue a citizen of another State for his violation of its municipal laws. Though in that instance the controversy would, as to its subject-matter, be one proper for judicial cognizance, in the general sense of that term, and would also, in respect of its parties, fall within the enumerated cases, yet no tribunal of the United States could entertain it, because all matters of merely internal concern have been kept by the States for their own original, exclusive, and sovereign control.

> New York City v. Miln, 11 Pet., 139.
>
> License Cases, 5 How., 588.

III. The Supreme Court of the United States, while fettered by each of the conditions so attaching to the whole Judicial Department—of which it is simply the highest organ—has been otherwise so narrowly confined as to permit it to wield, in an original form, only a very scant degree of the scant power confided to the range of the Judicial Department. The Constitution assumed the existence of, but did not create this tribunal, and it delineated the outlines of the judicial authority with which it might or should be endowed. Of necessity, all judicial power must be exerted in an original or appellate form, and the Constitution has declared the precise cases in which, under either of these forms, the judicial power of the United States may be imparted to the Supreme Court.

The original jurisdiction, (and the present inquiry concerns that alone,) thus permitted to it, is expressly limited to—

1. Cases "affecting ambassadors, other public ministers, or consuls;" and—
2. Cases "in which a State shall be a party," and, since the adoption of the eleventh amendment, in which a State shall be the plaintiff, or other pursuing party. This means, that a State, in its sole corporate capacity, shall be the "entire prosecuting party on the record," with a persona standi in judicio of its own—a direct legal or equitable right pertaining to it, as a distinct unity. It is not enough that it may be "consequentially affected or indirectly interested."

> Fowler v. Lindsay, 3 Dall., 411.
> United States v. Peters, 5 Cranch, 115, 139.
> Osborne v. United States Bank, 9 Wheat., 738, 850–857.
> United States Bank v. Planters' Bank, 9 Wheat., 904, 906.
> Wheeling Bridge Case, 13 How., 518, 559.

IV. The Constitution does not, of itself, vest any power of action in the Supreme Court. It simply enables the court, under the regulating control of Congress, to exert judicial authority in the prescribed cases; but the existence in the court of the power itself, and the methods and instruments of its exercise, depend on the affirmative legislative action of Congress. The Supreme Court, in respect of both forms of its jurisdiction, is the organ of the Constitution and the law.

> Chisholm v. Georgia, 2 Dall., 419, 432, 452.
> Marbury v. Madison, 1 Cranch, 137, 173.
> Bollman's Case, Ex parte, 4 Cranch, 75, 93, 94.
> Wayman v. Southard, 10 Wheat., 1, 21, 22.
> New York v. New Jersey, 5 Pet., 284, 290.
> Crane's Case, Ex parte, 5 Pet., 190, 193.
> Rhode Island v. Massachusetts, 12 Pet., 657, 721, 722.

Kendall v. United States, 12 Pet., 524, 622.
Christie's Case, Ex parte, 3 How., 293, 322.

The Congress, exercising its power in this behalf, has regulated the jurisdiction of this court, and its forms and mode of proceeding. These regulations, so far as they bear upon the present purpose, are substantially as follows:

1. The original cognizance of this court, as to cases in which a State is a party, has been limited to "controversies of a civil nature"—a limitation not expressed by the Constitution, and yet certainly effectual.

Judiciary Act, sec. 13.

2. Power has been given to the Supreme Court to issue two named writs: the writ of prohibition to a named court, for a named purpose; and the "writ of mandamus, in cases warranted by the principles and usages of law, to any courts appointed, or persons holding office, under the authority of the United States."

Judiciary Act, sec. 13.

The general authority to regulate its modes of proceeding conferred on this court by the "process act," (sec. 2,) and to issue "other writs," ancillary to the exercise of its jurisdiction, conferred by the judiciary act, (sec. 14,) does not enable the court to enlarge the uses of the writ of mandamus. The process act expressly shuts out from its operation "the forms of proceeding," which "are provided for by the judiciary act;" and the judiciary act, in terms, limits the court to the issue of "such other writs" as are "not specially provided for by statute." Moreover, on settled and necessary principles, the express grant of this writ, as against a specific class of functionaries—otherwise within the scope of its most ordinary uses, and to whom, as of course, it would ren [run], without distinct grant, if the court had a general authority to employ it—is a clear exclusion of any such authority, and an emphatic prohibition against the use of the writ in any other case, for any other purpose.

Christie, Ex parte, 3 How., 293, 322.

V. Arranging, in continuous order, the ascertained general conditions which limit the existence and exercise of the original jurisdiction of the Supreme Court in all possible cases, except only those "affecting ambassadors, other public ministers, and consuls," of whom there is now no question, it will be seen that no controversy can gain a foothold here, unless it be—

1. Appropriate for the action of judicial, as distinguished from political power.
2. Within the scope of "the judicial power of the United States," as distinguished from the general mass of judicial power reserved by and to the several States for their own exclusive exercise.
3. Instituted by a State, as the "entire party" plaintiff on record, in virtue of such direct legal or equitable interest in the subject-matter as, according to

the ordinary rules applied to other parties, entitles it to "move" a case at law, or in equity, against a party subject to the control of the court.
4. Of a "civil" as opposed to one of a criminal "nature;" and—
5. Conducted in a form of proceeding consistent with its subject-matter, with the character of its parties, and with the regulations prescribed by Congress for the use of that form of proceeding.

But the controversy, if a writ of mandamus can be so called, moved for by the present application, has no one of all these vital characteristics; for—

VI. The subject-matter of the controversy excludes it from discussion or adjudication by any judicial tribunal.
1. It is not appropriate for the action of judicial power, since it only concerns the execution of a compact between States—independent as to each other—for the extradition of fugitive offenders. Affecting the States at large as to their exterior relations, and their reciprocal national rights and duties, it is, in essence, a political question. Without express provision, committing them, under specific regulations, to the judicial authority, the performance of national engagements addresses itself to the department wielding the political power, and able to weigh political considerations. No such valid provision has been made in respect of this compact.

>Marbury v. Madison, 1 Cranch, 137, 170.
>
>United States v. Palmer, 3 Wheat., 610, 634, 670.
>
>The Divina Pastora, 4 Wheat., 52, 63.
>
>Foster v. Neilson, 2 Peters, 253, 307, 314.
>
>Cherokee Nation v. Georgia, 5 Peters, 1, 20.
>
>United States v. Arredondo, 6 Peters, 691, 735.

2. If fit for judicial cognizance under any circumstances, or by any tribunal, the subject of the proceeding is, nevertheless, not within the scope of the judicial power of the United States.
   a. The Constitution has not granted any power to any department of the Federal Government concerning the reclamation of fugitives from justice, as between the States. The provision which it contains in this behalf is a simple engagement made by the States with each other, regulating matters of purely State concern, and addressed to the States alone. If, as an original question, this

Interpretation could be doubted, it has become the fixed one by long usage and acquiescence. Since the foundation of the Government, each State has habitually determined for itself the extent of this obligation; many of them (and Kentucky is one, 1 Stanton's Rev. Stat., 557) have regulated its discharge by express enactment; but never, until now, has the authority of the Federal Government been invoked to constrain its fulfilment. This practical exposition, acted upon for nearly eighty years, is too strong and obstinate to be shaken or controlled.

Note.—Upon this ground, as well as another, yet to be noticed, the act of Congress relating to fugitives from justice is clearly void. No inference of power in the Federal Government over this subject can be drawn from acquiescence in its provisions, for the act, in defining the cases to which it extends, follows the precise language of the stipulation itself, and, in terms, leaves its execution wholly to the authorities of the States themselves. The States, doubtless, have generally observed the rules it declares for the mere manner of surrender; not, however, as having the force of law, but by reason of their inherent fitness and convenience.

VII. The proceeding is not one in which a State is the pursuing party on the record; nor is any State so interested in its subject-matter as to be entitled to pursue here any form of controversy in respect to it; nor is the adversary party one over whom this court can, under any circumstances, or by any mode, exercise any control.

1. The writ of mandamus—as will hereafter more distinctly appear—is a prerogative writ, issued by the Government, in its own name, to its own functionaries, to redress or prevent a wrong done or threatened to itself as a Government. Awarded upon this ground and for this purpose, the Government is, of necessity, the prosecutor on the record. The relator is no "party" to the writ, and the writ constitutes the whole "case," or "controversy." If granted in this case, it will be a proceeding instituted by "The United States of America" against "The Governor of Ohio." Though the State of Kentucky may be interested in the performance of that duty, yet the writ will issue upon reasons of public policy, simply to constrain the discharge of a public duty, imposed by the authority of the General Government, and essential to its own peculiar welfare. But if the applicant for the writ can be deemed the prosecuting party of record, still—
2. The Commonwealth of Kentucky has not such an interest in the discharge of the asserted duty as entitles her to set the writ in motion. The ground on which it must base its interest in the extradition of Lago is simply one phase of that general obligation, springing out of the social compact itself, which binds every organized political community to avenge all injuries aimed at the being or welfare of its society. Certainly, this is the first and highest of all governmental duties; but nevertheless it is, in juridical language, a "duty of imperfect obligation," incapable in its essence of precise exposition or admeasurement, and its fulfilment depends on moral and social considerations, accosting the community at large, which a judicial tribunal can neither weigh, define, nor enforce. But if there by any such right in this behalf as may constitute a foundation for legal proceedings to enforce it, then—

3. The claim made for the surrender of Lago must be prosecuted by the Executive authority, eo nomine, of the Commonwealth of Kentucky. That "authority" alone is empowered by the Constitution to demand the extradition, and, by parity of reason, can alone institute proceedings for its enforcement. But a suit by or against a State functionary, as such, is not a suit by or against the State itself.

> 19 Osborne v. United States Bank, 9 Wheat., 852, 859.
>
> United States Bank v. Planters' Bank, 6 Wheat., 904.

4. The official personage against whom the writ is prayed is not subject, in any form or degree, to the jurisdiction of this court. The proceeding is against him in his official character and respects his official duty; so that if from any cause the present incumbent of the office should, prior to the execution of the writ, be divested of his official position, the writ itself would, in the same instant and ex necessitate rei, fall impotent—a mere brutum fulmen. The proceeding, then, is aimed at the supreme Executive of the State of Ohio, to "coerce" the exercise of one of its imagined functions. But no power has been confided to any Department of the Federal Government to impose a duty upon any functionaries of a State, or to constrain the discharge of their official concerns.

> Martin v. Hunter's Lessee, 1 Wheat., 304, 336.
>
> Houston v. Moore, 5 Wheat., 1, 21, 22.
>
> Prigg v. Pennsylvania, 16 Peters, 539.

Note.—Upon this ground, also, the act of Congress relating to fugitives from justice, which speaks only to State authorities, is void.

VIII. The controversy raised by the motion is not of a civil nature. It involves no question of the rights of person or the rights of property. The power of the court is invoked simply in aid of the administration of the criminal code of Kentucky, to the end that she may be able to try Lago for an imputed offence against her laws, and, if guilty, to imprison him in her penitentiary.

IX. The original jurisdiction of this court cannot be exercised through the method of the writ of mandamus; and this disability springs as well from the inherent nature of the writ itself as from the regulations prescribed for its use by the Legislative power.

1. The nature and functions of the writ are so peculiar as to forbid its employment, save for a single purpose, by any of the courts of the United States. The writ comes to us from the common law; and this court has judicially

determined that the common-law remedies in the Federal tribunals are to be according to the principles of that law as settled in England, (Campbell v. Robinson, 3 Wheat., 221,) subject, of course, to the modifications made by Congress, or under its authority, and also to such limitations as result from the constitution of the court and the nature of the Federal Government. According to these principles, this writ, as tersely defined by Lord Mansfield, is "a high prerogative one, flowing from the King himself, sitting in the Court of King's Bench, superintending the police, and preserving the peace of the country."

Rex v. Barker, 1 Bl. Rep., 300, 352.

Stated in a different form, the writ at common law is issued by a tribunal in which not only the judicial sovereignty, but the prerogative of general superintendency resides, and it is employed extra-judicially (Audley v. Jay, Popham, 176) as well as judicially. Its judicial use is to supervise the administration of the King's justice by his inferior judicatures; and its extra-judicial function is "to preserve peace, order, and good government," by constraining the prompt and rightful performance of every public duty confided to any public functionary or tribunal by "Parliament or the King's Charter."

Tapping on Mandamus, S. 6, 11, 12.

Bacon's Ab. Tit. Mandamus, A.

Butler's Nisi Prius, 195.

Rex v. Baker, 3 Burr, 1266.

Rex v. Bank of England, 2 Barn. and Ald., 622.

Rex v. Fowey, 2 Barn. and Cr., 596.

Rex v. North Riding, 2 Barn. and Cr., 290.

Rex v. E. C. Railway, 10 Ad. and El., 557.

Kendall v. United States, 12 Peters, 621.

But this court is one of very special and limited jurisdiction. The judicial sovereignty, in its general sense, does not reside here; and it has no prerogative power, no police power, no power to superintend the conduct of public affairs. All its attributes are purely judicial; and from its very constitution, the power to issue this writ, in the large sense of the common law, cannot be given to this court. Of necessity, it can employ the writ only in its judicial operation, and as a revisionary process directed to some inferior judicature charged with the administration of the justice of the Federal Government. Otherwise stated, the court cannot, under the Constitution, be empowered to issue the writ of mandamus, save to the inferior judicatures of the United States, in the exercise of its appellate jurisdiction.

Marbury v. Madison, 1 Cranch, 137, 176.

Kendall v. United States, 12 Peters, 524, 621.

2. The judicial act, as already noticed, in regulating the conditions under which the great common-law writs may be issued by this court, has interdicted the employment of this writ, except as it may, agreeably to "the principles and usages of law," be directed against "courts appointed, or persons holding office, under the authority of the United States." (Sec. 13.) In effect, however, the power to issue the writ is not co-extensive with even the narrow boundaries so prescribed. For the court, considering the validity of this provision, and recognising the incompatibility of any of the common-law functions of the writ with the limited and peculiar nature of its original power, has solemnly determined that the Constitution prohibits it from issuing the writ, except to the courts of the Federal Government, in the exercise of its appellate jurisdiction.

Marbury v. Madison, 1 Cranch, 137, 176.

Kendall v. United States, 12 Peters, 524, 621.

But the party against whom the writ is now invoked does not come within either of the categories prescribed by the judicial act. The Governor of Ohio is not a "court appointed, or a person holding office, under the authority of the United States."

X. The results now attained demonstrate that the controversy which the present application seeks to inaugurate is, in its form and in its essence, in its whole and in its every part and element, beyond the utmost sweep of the jurisdiction of this court. The power to compose this national and political strife does not reside in this tribunal; the pursuing party cannot cross its threshold; the party pursued is without the reach of its arm; the subject of the difference has been excluded from its action; and the writ which it is solicited to grant has been denied to it as a method for the exercise of its original jurisdiction.

Mr. Chief Justice TANEY delivered the opinion of the court.

The court is sensible of the importance of this case, and of the great interest and gravity of the questions involved in it, and which have been raised and fully argued at the bar.

Some of them, however, are not now for the first time brought to the attention of this court; and the objections made to the jurisdiction, and the form and nature of the process to be issued, and upon whom it is to be served, have all been heretofore considered and decided, and cannot now be regarded as open to further dispute.

As early as 1792, in the case of Georgia v. Brailsford, the court exercised the original jurisdiction conferred by the Constitution, without any further legislation by Congress, to regulate it, than the act of 1789. And no question was then made, nor any doubt then expressed, as to the authority of the court. The same power was again exercised without objection in the case of Oswold v. the State of Georgia, in which the court regulated the form and nature of the process against the State, and directed it to be served on the Governor and Attorney General. But in the case of Chisholm's Executors v. the State of Georgia, at February term, 1793, reported in 2 Dall., 419, the authority of the court in this respect was questioned, and brought to its attention in the argument of counsel; and the report shows how carefully and thoroughly the subject was considered. Each of the judges delivered a separate opinion, in which these questions, as to the jurisdiction of the court, and the mode of exercising it, are elaborately examined.

Mr. Chief Justice Jay, Mr. Justice Cushing, Mr. Justice Wilson, and Mr. Justice Blair, decided in favor of the jurisdiction, and held that process served on the Governor and Attorney General was sufficient. Mr. Justice Iredell differed, and thought that further legislation by Congress was necessary to give the jurisdiction, and regulate the manner in which it should be exercised. But the opinion of the majority of the court upon these points has always been since followed. And in the case of New Jersey v. New York, in 1831, 5 Pet., 284, Chief Justice Marshall, in delivering the opinion of the court, refers to the case of Chisholm v. the State of Georgia, and to the opinions then delivered, and the judgment pronounced, in terms of high respect, and after enumerating the various cases in which that decision had been acted on, reaffirms it in the following words:

> It has been settled by our predecessors, on great deliberation, that this court may exercise its original jurisdiction in suits against a State, under the authority conferred by the Constitution and existing acts of Congress. The rule respecting the process, the persons on whom it is to be served, and the time of service, are fixed. The course of the court, on the failure of the State to appear after due service of process, has been also prescribed.

And in the same case, page 289, he states in full the process which had been established by the court as a rule of practice in the case of Grayson v. the State of Virginia, 3 Dall., 320, and ever since followed. This rule directs, "that when process at common law, or in equity, shall issue against a State, the same shall be served upon the Governor or chief Executive magistrate and the Attorney General of such State."

It is equally well settled, that a mandamus in modern practice is nothing more than an action at law between the parties, and is not now regarded as a prerogative writ. It undoubtedly came into use by virtue of the prerogative power of the English Crown, and was subject to regulations and rules which have long since been disused. But the right to the writ, and the power to issue it, has ceased to depend upon any prerogative power, and it is now regarded as an ordinary process in cases to which it is applicable. It was so held by this court in the cases of Kendall v. United States, 12 Pet., 615; Kendall v. Stokes and others, 3 How., 100.

So, also, as to the process in the name of the Governor, in his official capacity, in behalf of the State.

In the case of Madraso v. the Governor of Georgia, 1 Pet., 110, it was decided, that in a case where the chief magistrate of a State is sued, not by his name as an individual, but by his style of office, and the claim made upon him is entirely in his official character, the State itself may be considered a party on the record. This was a case where the State was the defendant; the practice, where it is plaintiff, has been frequently adopted of suing in the name of the Governor in behalf of the State, and was indeed the form originally used, and always recognised as the suit of the State.

Thus, in the first case to be found in our reports, in which a suit was brought by a State, it was entitled, and set forth in the bill, as the suit of "the State of Georgia, by Edward Tellfair, Governor of the said State, complainant, against Samuel Brailsford and others;" and the second case, which was as early as 1793, was entitled and set forth in the pleadings as the suit of "His Excellency Edward Tellfair, Esquire, Governor and Commander-in-chief in and over the State of Georgia, in behalf of the said State, complainant, against Samuel Brailsford and others, defendants."

The cases referred to leave no question open to controversy, as to the jurisdiction of the court. They show that it has been the established doctrine upon this subject ever since the act of 1789, that in all cases where original jurisdiction is given by the Constitution, this court has authority to exercise it without any further act of Congress to regulate its process or confer jurisdiction, and that the court may regulate and mould the process it uses in such manner as in its judgment will best promote the purposes of justice. And that it has also been settled, that where the State is a party, party, plaintiff or defendant, the Governor represents the State, and the suit may be, in form, a suit by him as Governor in behalf of the State, where the State is plaintiff, and he must be summoned or notified as the officer representing the State, where the State is defendant. And further, that the writ of mandamus does not issue from or by any prerogative power, and is nothing more than the ordinary process of a court of justice, to which every one is entitled, where it is the appropriate process for asserting the right he claims.

We may therefore dismiss the question of jurisdiction without further comment, as it is very clear, that if the right claimed by Kentucky can be enforced by judicial process, the proceeding by mandamus is the only mode in which the object can be accomplished.

This brings us to the examination of the clause of the Constitution which has given rise to this controversy. It is in the following words: "A person charged in any State with treason, felony, or other crime, who shall flee from justice, and be found in another State, shall, on demand of the Executive authority of the State from which he fled, be delivered up, to be removed to the State having jurisdiction of the crime."

Looking to the language of the clause, it is difficult to comprehend how any doubt could have arisen as to its meaning and construction. The words, "treason, felony, or other crime," in their plain and obvious import, as well as in their legal and technical sense, embrace every act forbidden and made punishable to a law of the State. The word "crime" of itself includes every offence, from the highest to the lowest in the grade of offences, and includes what are called "misdemeanors," as well as treason and felony.

>4 Bl. Com., 5, 6, and note 3, Wendall's edition.

But as the word crime would have included treason and felony, without specially mentioning those offences, it seems to be supposed that the natural and legal import of the word, by associating it with those offences, must be restricted and confined to offences already known to the common law and to the usage of nations, and regarded as offences in every civilized community, and that they do not extend to acts made offences by local statutes growing out of local circumstances, nor to offences against ordinary police regulations. This is one of the grounds upon which the Governor of Ohio refused to deliver Lago, under the advice of the Attorney General of that State.

But this inference is founded upon an obvious mistake as to the purposes for which the words "treason and felony" were introduced. They were introduced for the purpose of guarding against any restriction of the word "crime," and to prevent this provision from being construed by the rules and usages of independent nations in compacts for delivering up fugitives from justice. According to these usages, even where they admitted the obligation to deliver the fugitive, persons who fled on account of political offences were almost always excepted, and the nation upon which the demand is made also uniformly claims and exercises a discretion in weighing the evidence of the crime, and the character of the offence. The policy of different nations, in this respect, with the opinions of eminent writers upon public law, are collected in Wheaton on the Law of Nations, 171; Foelix, 312; and Martin, Vere's edition, 182. And the English Government, from which we have borrowed our general system of law and jurisprudence, has always refused to deliver up political offenders who had sought an asylum within its dominions. And as the States of this Union, although united as one nation for certain specified purposes, are yet, so far as concerns their internal government, separate sovereignties, independent of each other, it was obviously deemed necessary to show, by the terms used, that this compact was not to be regarded or construed as an ordinary treaty for extradition between nations altogether independent of each other, but was intended to embrace political offences against the sovereignty of the State, as well as all other crimes. And as treason was also a "felony," (4 Bl.Com., 94,) it was necessary to insert those words, to show, in language that could not be mistaken, that political offenders were included in it. For this was not a compact of peace and comity between separate nations who had no claim on each other for mutual support, but a compact binding them to give aid and assistance to each other in executing their laws, and to support each other in preserving order and law within its confines, whenever such aid was needed and required; for it is manifest that the statesmen who framed the Constitution were fully sensible, that from the complex character of the Government, it must fail unless the States mutually supported each other and the General Government; and that nothing would be more likely to disturb its peace, and end in discord, than permitting an offender against the laws of a State, by passing over a mathematical line which divides it from another, to defy its process, and stand ready, under the protection of the State, to repeat the offence as soon as another opportunity offered.

Indeed, the necessity of this policy of mutual support, in bringing offenders to justice, without any exception as to the character and nature of the crime, seems to have been first recognised and acted on by the American colonies; for we find, by Winthrop's History of Massachusetts, vol. 2, pages 121 and 126, that as early as 1643, by "articles of Confederation between the plantations under the Government of Massachusetts, the plantation under the Government of New Plymouth, the plantations under the Government of Connecticut, and the Government of New Haven, with the plantations in combination therewith,"[close up] these plantations pledged themselves to each other, that, upon the escape of any prisoner or fugitive for any criminal cause, whether by breaking prison, or getting from the officer, or otherwise escaping, upon the certificate of two magistrates of the jurisdiction out of which the escape was made that he was a prisoner or such an offender at the time of the escape, the magistrate, or some of them, of the jurisdiction where, for the present, the said prisoner or fugitive abideth, shall forthwith grant such a warrant as the case will bear, for the apprehending of any such person, and the delivery of him into the hands of the officer or other person who pursueth him; and if there be help required for the safe returning of any such offender, then it shall be granted unto him that craves the same, he paying the charges thereof.["] It will be seen that this agreement gave no discretion to the magistrate of the Government where the offender was found; but he was bound to arrest and deliver, upon the production of the certificate under which he was demanded.

When the thirteen colonies formed a Confederation for mutual support, a similar provision was introduced, most probably suggested by the advantages which the plantations had derived from their compact with one another. But, as these colonies had then, by the Declaration of Independence, become separate and independent sovereignties, against which treason might be committed, their compact is carefully worded, so as to include treason and felony—that is, political offences—as well as crimes of an inferior grade. It is in the following words: "If any person, guilty of or charged with treason, felony, or other high misdemeanor, in any State, shall flee from justice, and be found in any other of the United States, he shall, upon demand of the Governor or Executive power of the State from which he fled, be delivered up and removed to the State having jurisdiction of his offence."

And when these colonies were about to form a still closer union by the present Constitution, but yet preserving their sovereignty, they had learned from experience the necessity of this provision for the internal safety of each of them, and to promote concord and harmony among all their members; and it is introduced in the Constitution substantially in the same words, but substituting the word "crime" for the words "high misdemeanor," and thereby showing the deliberate purpose to include every offence known to the law of the State from which the party charged had fled.

The argument on behalf of the Governor of Ohio, which insists upon excluding from this clause new offences created by a statute of the State, and growing out of its local institutions, and which are not admitted to be offences in the State where the fugitive is found, nor so regarded by the general usage of civilized nations, would render the clause useless for any practical purpose. For where can the line of division be drawn with anything like certainty? Who is to mark it? The Governor of the demanding State would probably draw one line, and the Governor of the other State another. And, if they differed, who is to decide between them? Under such a vague and indefinite construction, the article would not be a bond of peace and union, but a constant source of controversy and irritating discussion. It would have been far better to omit it altogether, and to have left it to the comity of the States, and their own sense of their respective interests, than to have inserted it so conferring a right, and yet defining that right so loosely as to make it a never-failing subject of dispute and ill-will.

The clause in question, like the clause in the Confederation, authorizes the demand to be made by the Executive authority of the State where the crime was committed, but does not in so many words specify the officer of the State upon whom the demand is to be made, and whose duty it is to have the fugitive delivered and removed to the State having jurisdiction of the crime. But, under the Confederation, it is plain that the demand was to be made on the Governor or Executive authority of the State, and could be made on no other department or officer; for the Confederation was only a league of separate sovereignties, in which each State, within its own limits, held and exercised all the powers of sovereignty; and the Confederation had no officer, either executive, judicial, or ministerial, through whom it could exercise an authority within the limits of a State. In the present Constitution, however, these powers, to a limited extent, have been conferred on the General Government within the territories of the several States. But the part of the clause in relation to the mode of demanding and surrendering the fugitive is, (with the exception of an unimportant word or two,) a literal copy of the article of the Confederation, and it is plain that the mode of the demand and the official authority by and to whom it was addressed, under the Confederation, must have been in the minds of the members of the Convention when this article was introduced, and that, in adopting the same words, they manifestly intended to sanction the mode of proceeding practiced under the Confederation—that is, of demanding the fugitive from the Executive authority, and making it his duty to cause him to be delivered up.

Looking, therefore, to the words of the Constitution—to the obvious policy and necessity of this provision to preserve harmony between States, and order and law within their respective borders, and to its early adoption by the colonies, and then by the Confederated States, whose mutual interest it was to give each other aid and support whenever it was needed—the conclusion is irresistible, that this compact engrafted in the Constitution included, and was intended to include, every offence made punishable by the law of the State in which it was committed, and that it gives the right to the Executive authority of the State to demand the fugitive from the Executive authority of the State in which he is found; that the right given to "demand" implies that it is an absolute right; and it follows that there must be a correlative obligation to deliver, without any reference to the character of the crime charged, or to the policy or laws of the State to which the fugitive has fled.

This is evidently the construction put upon this article in the act of Congress of 1793, under which the proceedings now before us are instituted. It is therefore the construction put upon it almost co[n]temporaneously with the commencement of the Government itself, and when Washington was still at its head, and many of those who had assisted in framing it were members of the Congress which enacted the law.

The Constitution having established the right on one part and the obligation on the other, it became necessary to provide by law the mode of carrying it into execution. The Governor of the State could not, upon a charge made before him, demand the fugitive; for, according to the principles upon which all of our institutions are founded, the Executive Department can act only in subordination of the Judicial Department, where rights of person or property are concerned, and its duty in those cases consists only in aiding to support the judicial process and enforcing its authority, when its interposition for that purpose becomes necessary, and is called for by the Judicial Department. The Executive authority of the State, therefore, was not authorized by this article to make the demand unless the party was charged in the regular course of judicial proceedings. And it was equally necessary that the Executive authority of the State upon which the demand was made, when called on to render his aid, should be satisfied by competent proof that the party was so charged. This proceeding, when duly authenticated, is his authority for arresting the offender.

This duty of providing by law the regulations necessary to carry this compact into execution, from the nature of the duty and the object in view, was manifestly devolved upon Congress; for if it was left to the States, each State might require different proof to authenticate the judicial proceeding upon which the demand was founded; and as the duty of the Governor of the State where the fugitive was found is, in such cases, merely ministerial, without the right to exercise either executive or judicial discretion, he could not lawfully issue a warrant to arrest an individual without a law of the State or of Congress to authorize it. These difficulties presented themselves as early as 1791, in a demand made by the Governor of Pennsylvania upon the Governor of Virginia, and both of them admitted the propriety of bringing the subject before the President, who immediately submitted the matter to the consideration of Congress. And this led to the act of 1793, of which we are now speaking. All difficulty as to the mode of authenticating the judicial proceeding was removed by the article in the Constitution, which declares, "that full faith and credit shall be given in each State to the public acts, records, and judicial proceedings, of every other State; and the Congress may by general laws prescribe the manner in which acts, records, and proceedings, shall be proved, and the effect thereof." And without doubt the provision of which we are now speaking—that is, for the delivery of a fugitive, which requires official communications between States, and the authentication of official documents—was in the minds of the framers of the Constitution, and had its influence in inducing them to give this power to Congress. And acting upon this authority, and the clause of the Constitution which is the subject of the present controversy, Congress passed the act of 1793, February 12th, which, as far as relates to this subject, is in the following words:

> Section 1. That whenever the Executive authority of any State in the Union, or of either of the Territories northwest or south of the river Ohio, shall demand any person as a fugitive from justice of the Executive authority of any such State or Territory to which such person shall have fled, and shall, moreover, produce the copy of an indictment found, or an affidavit made before a magistrate of any State or Territory as aforesaid, charging the person so demanded with having committed treason, felony, or other crime, certified as authentic by the Governor or chief Magistrate of the State or Territory from whence the person so charged fled, it shall be the duty of the Executive authority of the State or Territory to which such person shall have fled to cause him or her to be arrested and secured, and notice of the arrest to be given to the Executive authority making such demand, or to the agent of such authority appointed to receive the fugitive, and to cause the fugitive to be delivered to such agent when he shall appear; but if no such agent shall appear within six months from the time of the arrest, the prisoner may be discharged. And all costs or expenses incurred in the apprehending, securing,

and transmitting such fugitive to the State or Territory making such demand shall be paid by such State or Territory.

Section 2. And be it further enacted, That any agent, appointed as aforesaid, who shall receive the fugitive into his custody, shall be empowered to transport him or her to the State or Territory from which he or she shall have fled; and if any person or persons shall by force set at liberty or rescue the fugitive from such agent while transporting as aforesaid, the person or persons so offending shall, on conviction, be fined not exceeding five hundred dollars, and be imprisoned not exceeding one year.

It will be observed, that the judicial acts which are necessary to authorize the demand are plainly specified in the act of Congress; and the certificate of the Executive authority is made conclusive as to their verity when presented to the Executive of the State where the fugitive is found. He has no right to look behind them, or to question them, or to look into the character of the crime specified in this judicial proceeding. The duty which he is to perform is, as we have already said, merely ministerial—that is, to cause the party to be arrested, and delivered to the agent or authority of the State where the crime was committed. It is said in the argument, that the Executive officer upon whom this demand is made must have a discretionary executive power, because he must inquire and decide who is the person demanded. But this certainly is not a discretionary duty upon which he is to exercise any judgment, but is a mere ministerial duty—that, is, to do the act required to be done by him, and such as every marshal and sheriff must perform when process, either criminal or civil, is placed in his hands to be served on the person named in it. And it never has been supposed that this duty involved and [any] discretionary power, or made him anything more than a mere ministerial officer; and such is the position and character of the Executive of the State under this law, when the demand is made upon him and the requisite evidence produced. The Governor has only to issue his warrant to an agent or officer to arrest the party named in the demand.

The question which remains to be examined is a grave and important one. When the demand was made, the proofs required by the act of 1793 to support it were exhibited to the Governor of Ohio, duly certified and authenticated; and the objection made to the validity of the indictment is altogether untenable. Kentucky has an undoubted right to regulate the forms of pleading and process in her own courts, in criminal as well as civil cases, and is not bound to conform to those of any other State. And whether the charge against Lago is legally and sufficiently laid in this indictment according to the laws of Kentucky, is a judicial question to be decided by the courts of the State, and not by the Executive authority of the State of Ohio.

The demand being thus made, the act of Congress declares, that "it shall be the duty of the Executive authority of the State" to cause the fugitive to be arrested and secured, and delivered to the agent of the demanding State. The words, "it shall be the duty," in ordinary legislation, imply the assertion of the power to command and to coerce obedience. But looking to the subject-matter of this law, and the relations which the United States and the several States bear to each other, the court is of opinion, the words "it shall be the duty" were not used as mandatory and compulsory, but as declaratory of the moral duty which this compact created, when Congress had provided the mode of carrying it into execution. The act does not provide any means to compel the execution of this duty, nor inflict any punishment for neglect or refusal on the part of the Executive of the State; nor is there any clause or provision in the Constitution which arms the Government of the United States with this power. Indeed, such a power would place every State under the control and dominion of the General Government, even in the administration of its internal concerns and reserved rights. And we think it clear, that the Federal Government, under the Constitution, has no power to impose on a State officer, as such, any duty whatever, and compel him to perform it; for if it possessed this power, it might overload the officer with duties which would fill up all his time, and disable him from performing his obligations to the State, and might impose on him duties of a character incompatible with the rank and dignity to which he was elevated by the State.

It is true that Congress may authorize a particular State officer to perform a particular duty; but if he declines to do so, it does not follow that he may be coerced, or punished for his refusal. And we are very far from supposing, that in using this word "duty," the statesmen who framed and passed the law, or the President who approved and signed it, intended to exercise a coercive power over State officers not warranted by the Constitution. But the General Government having in that law fulfilled the duty devolved upon it, by prescribing the proof and mode of authentication upon which the State authorities were bound to deliver the fugitive, the word "duty" in the law points to the obligation on the State to carry it into execution.

It is true that in the early days of the Government, Congress relied with confidence upon the co-operation and support of the States, when exercising the legitimate powers of the General Government, and were accustomed to receive it, upon principles of comity, and from a sense of mutual and common interest, where no such duty was imposed by the Constitution. And laws were passed authorizing State courts to entertain jurisdiction in proceedings by the United States to recover penalties and forfeitures incurred by breaches of their revenue laws, and giving to the State courts the same authority with the District Court of the United States to enforce such penalties and forfeitures, and also the power to hear the allegations of parties, and to take proofs, if an application for a remission of the penalty or forfeiture should be made, according to the provisions of the acts of Congress. And these powers were for some years exercised by State tribunals, readily, and without objection, until in some of the States it was declined because it interfered with and retarded the performance of duties which properly belonged to them, as State courts; and in other States, doubts appear to have arisen as to the power of the courts, acting under the authority of the State, to inflict these penalties and forfeitures for offences against the General Government, unless especially authorized to do so by the State.

And in these cases the co-operation of the States was a matter of comity, which the several sovereignties extended to one another for their mutual benefit. It was not regarded by either party as an obligation imposed by the Constitution. And the acts of Congress conferring the jurisdiction merely give the power to the State tribunals, but do not purport to regard it as a duty, and they leave it to the States to exercise it or not, as might best comport with their own sense of justice, and their own interest and convenience.

But the language of the act of 1793 is very different. It does not purport to give authority to the State Executive to arrest and deliver the fugitive, but requires it to be done, and the language of the law implies an absolute obligation which the State authority is bound to perform. And when it speaks of the duty of the Governor, it evidently points to the duty imposed by the Constitution in the clause we are now considering. The performance of this duty, however, is left to depend on the fidelity of the State Executive to the compact entered into with the other States when it adopted the Constitution of the United States, and became a member of the Union. It was so left by the Constitution, and necessarily so left by the act of 1793.

And it would seem that when the Constitution was framed, and when this law was passed, it was confidently believed that a sense of justice and of mutual interest would insure a faithful execution of this constitutional provision by the Executive of every State, for every State had an equal interest in the execution of a compact absolutely essential to their peace and well being in their internal concerns, as well as members of the Union. Hence, the use of the words ordinarily employed when an undoubted obligation is required to be performed, "it shall be his duty."

But if the Governor of Ohio refuses to discharge this duty, there is no power delegated to the General Government, either through the Judicial Department or any other department, to use any coercive means to compel him.

And upon this ground the motion for the mandamus must be overruled.

Ex parte Merryman

Circuit Court, D. Maryland
April Term, 1861
17 Fed. Cas. 144, Case #9,487

In response to the April 14, 1861, firing on Fort Sumter by South Carolina forces of the Confederacy, President Abraham Lincoln issued a proclamation calling 75,000 militiamen into federal service for ninety days to deal with the southern insurrection. On April 19, Union troops trying to reach Washington, D.C., had been attacked in Baltimore by crowds of rowdies and civilians, and that attack led to deaths among both the troops and the civilians. On April 27, in an attempt to deal with the secessionist threat in Maryland, Lincoln suspended the writ of habeas corpus that allowed the military to arrest and hold persons without appeal to the normal civilian courts. Among those arrested and held in Fort McHenry by the military was John Merryman, a Marylander of wealth who served as a lieutenant in a secessionist cavalry unit and who had participated in burning bridges and tearing down telegraph lines. Merryman's attorney petitioned the federal Circuit Court in Baltimore for a writ of habeas corpus. Sitting on that circuit was the southern sympathizer Chief Justice Roger B. Taney of the United States Supreme Court, who heard the petition. He granted the writ, but the officer in charge of Ft. McHenry refused the writ on the grounds that the President had suspended it. Taney then produced this review of the facts of the case, held that the Constitution authorized only Congress to suspend the writ, not the president, and therefore concluded that Merryman ought to be released. The Lincoln administration ignored Taney's holding and, in time, this legal dispute became buried among the other legal and constitutional developments of the Civil War. Yet, the fundamental civil liberties and constitutional question remained—the powers of the president in war time to ensure loyalty and deal with internal security challenges.

Habeas corpus—Power to Suspend in Time of War—President—Military Authority—Suspension by Congress

1. On the 25th May 1861, the petitioner, a citizen of Baltimore county, in the state of Maryland, was arrested by a military force, acting under orders of a major-general of the United States army, commanding in the state of Pennsylvania, and committed to the custody of the general commanding Fort McHenry, within the district of Maryland; on the 26th May 1861, a writ of habeas corpus was issued by the chief justice of the United States, sitting at chambers, directed to the commandant of the fort, commanding him to produce the body of the petitioner before the chief justice, in Baltimore city, on the 27th day of May 1861; on the last-mentioned day, the writ was returned served, and the officer to whom it was directed declined to produce the petitioner, giving as his excuse the following reasons: 1. That the petitioner was arrested by the orders of the major-general commanding in Pennsylvania, upon the charge of treason, in being "publicly associated with and holding a commission as lieutenant in a company having in their possession arms belonging to the United States, and avowing his purpose of armed hostility against the government." 2. That he (the officer having the petitioner in custody) was duly authorized by the president of the United States, in such cases, to suspend the writ of habeas corpus for the public safety. *Held*, that the petitioner was entitled to be set at liberty and discharged immediately from confinement, upon the grounds following: 1. That the president, under the constitution of the United States, cannot suspend the privilege of the writ of habeas corpus, nor authorize a military officer to do it. 2. That a military officer has no right to arrest and detain a person not subject to the rules and articles of war, for an offence against the law of the United States, except in aid of the judicial authority, and subject to its control; and if the party be arrested by the military, it is the duty of the officer to deliver over immediately to the civil authority, to be dealt with according to law.

2. Under the constitution of the United States, congress is the only power which can authorize the suspension of the privilege of the writ.

On the 26th May 1861, the following sworn petition was presented to the chief justice of the United States, on behalf of John Merryman, then in confinement in Fort McHenry:

> To the Hon. Roger B. Taney, Chief Justice of the Supreme Court of the United States: The petition of John Merryman, of Baltimore county and state of Maryland, respectfully shows, that being at home, in his own domicile, he was, about the hour of two o'clock a. m., on the 25th day of May, A. D. 1861, aroused from his bed by an armed force pretending to act under military orders from some person to your petitioner unknown. That he was by said armed force, deprived of his liberty, by being taken into custody, and removed from his said home to Fort McHenry, near to the city of Balti-

more, and in the district aforesaid, and where your petitioner now is in close custody. That he has been so imprisoned without any process or color of law whatsoever, and that none such is pretended by those who are thus detaining him; and that no warrant from any court, magistrate or other person having legal authority to issue the same exists to justify such arrest; but to the contrary, the same, as above stated, hath been done without color of law and in violation of constitution and laws of the United States, of which he is a citizen. That since his arrest, he has been informed, that some order, purporting to come from one General Keim, of Pennsylvania, to this petitioner unknown, directing the arrest of the captain of some company in Baltimore county, of which company the petitioner never was and is not captain, was the pretended ground of his arrest, and is the sole ground, as he believes, on which he is now detained. That the person now so detaining him at said fort is Brigadier-General George Cadwalader, the military commander of said post, professing to act in the premises under or by color of the authority of the United States. Your petitioner, therefore, prays that the writ of habeas corpus may issue, to be directed to the said George Cadwalader, commanding him to produce your petitioner before you, judge as aforesaid, with the cause, if any, for his arrest and detention, to the end that your petitioner be discharged and restored to liberty, and as in duty, &c. John Merryman. Fort McKenry, 25th May 1861.

United States of America, District of Maryland, to wit: Before the subscriber, a commissioner appointed by the circuit court of the United States, in and for the Fourth circuit and district of Maryland, to take affidavits, & c., personally appeared the 25th day of May, A. D. 1861, Geo. H. Williams, of the city of Baltimore and district aforesaid, and made oath on the Holy Evangely of Almighty God, that the matters and facts stated in the foregoing petition are true, to the best of his knowledge, information and belief; and that the said petition was signed in his presence by the petitioner, and would have been sworn to by him, said petitioner, but that he was, at the time, and still is, in close custody, and all access to him denied, except to his counsel and his brother-in-law this deponent being one of said counsel. Sworn to before me, the 25th day of May, A. D. 1861. John Hanan, U. S. Commissioner.

United States of America, District of Maryland, to wit: Before the subscriber, a commissioner appointed by the circuit court of the United States, in and for the Fourth circuit and district of Maryland, to take affidavits, & c., personally appeared this 26th day of May, 1861, George H. Williams, of the city of Baltimore and district aforesaid, and made oath on the Holy Evangely of Almighty God, that on the 26th day of May, he went to Fort McHenry, in the preceding affidavit mentioned, and obtained an interview with Gen. Geo. Cadwalader, then and there in command, and deponent, one of the counsel of said John Merryman, in the foregoing petition named, and at his request, and declaring himself to be such counsel, requested and demanded that he might be permitted to see the written papers, and to be permitted to make copies thereof, under and by which he, the said general, detained the said Merryman in custody, and that to said demand the said Gen. Cadwalader replied, that he would neither permit the deponent, though officially requesting and demanding, as such counsel, to read the said papers, nor to have or make copies thereof. Sworn to this 26th day of May, A. D. 1861, before me. John Hanan, U. S. Commissioner for Maryland.

Upon this petition the chief justice passed the following order:

In the matter of the petition of John Merryman, for a writ of habeas corpus: Ordered, this 26th day of May, A. D. 1861, that the writ of habeas corpus issue in this case, as prayed, and that the same be directed to General George Cadwalader, and be issued in the usual form, by Thomas Spicer, clerk of the circuit court of the United States in and for the district of Maryland, and that the said writ of habeas corpus be returnable at eleven o'clock, on Monday, the 27th of May 1861, at the circuit court room, in the Masonic Hall, in the city of Baltimore, before me, chief justice of the supreme court of United States. R. B. Taney.

In obedience to this order, Mr. Spicer issued the following writ:

District of Maryland, to wit: The United States of America, to General George Cadwalader, Greeting: You are hereby commanded to be and appear before the Honorable Roger B. Taney, chief justice of the supreme court of the United States, at the United States court-room, in the Masonic Hall, in the city of Baltimore, on Monday, the 27th day of May 1861, at eleven o'clock in the morning, and that you have with you the body of John Merryman, of Baltimore county, and now in your custody, and that you certify and make known the day and cause of the caption and detention of the said John Merryman, and that you then and there, do, submit to, and receive whatsoever the said chief justice shall determine upon concerning you on this behalf, according to law, and have you then and there this writ. Witness, the Honorable R. B. Taney, chief justice of our supreme court, &c. Thomas Spicer, Clerk. Issued 26th May 1861.

The marshal made return that he had served the writ on General Cadwalader, on the same day on which it issued; and filed that return on the 27th May 1861, on which day, at eleven o'clock precisely, the chief justice took his seat on the bench. In a few minutes, Colonel Lee, a military officer, appeared with General Cadwalader's return to the writ, which is as follows:

> Headquarters, Department of Annapolis, Fort McHenry, May 26 1861. To the Hon. Roger B. Taney, Chief Justice of the Supreme Court of the United States, Baltimore, Md.—Sir: The undersigned, to whom the annexed writ, of this date, signed by Thomas Spicer, clerk of the supreme court of the United States, is directed, most respectfully states, that the arrest of Mr. John Merryman, in the said writ named, was not made with his knowledge, or by his order or direction, but was made by Col. Samuel Yohe, acting under the orders of Major-General William H. Keim, both of said officers being in the military service of the United States, but not within the limits of his command. The prisoner was brought to this post on the 20th inst., by Adjutant James Wittimore and Lieut. Wm. H. Abel, by order of Col. Yohe, and is charged with various acts of treason, and with being publicly associated with and holding a commission as lieutenant in a company having in their possession arms belonging to the United States, and avowing his purpose of armed hostility against the government. He is also informed that it can be clearly established, that the prisoner has made often and unreserved declarations of his association with this organized force, as being in avowed hostility to the government, and in readiness to co-operate with those engaged in the present rebellion against the government of the United States. He has further to inform you, that he is duly authorized by the president of the United States, in such cases, to suspend the writ of habeas corpus, for the public safety. This is a high and delicate trust, and it has been enjoined upon him that it should be executed with judgment and discretion, but he is nevertheless also instructed that in times of civil strife, errors, if any, should be on the side of the safety of the country. He most respectfully submits for your consideration, that those who should co-operate in the present trying and painful position in which our country is placed, should not, by any unnecessary want of confidence in each other, increase our embarrassments. He, therefore, respectfully requests that you will postpone further action upon this case, until he can receive instructions from the president of the United States, when you shall hear further from him. I have the honor to be, with high respect, your obedient servant, George Cadwalader, Brevet Major-General U. S. A. Commanding.

The chief justice then inquired of the officer whether he had brought with him the body of John Merryman, and on being answered that he had no instructions but to deliver the return, the chief justice said: "General Cadwalader was commanded to produce the body of Mr. Merryman before me this morning, that the case might be heard, and the petitioner be either remanded to custody, or set at liberty, if held on insufficient grounds; but he has acted in disobedience to the writ, and I therefore direct that an attachment be at once issued against him, returnable before me here, at twelve o'clock to-morrow." The order was then passed as follows:

> Ordered, that an attachment forthwith issue against General George Cadwalader for a contempt, in refusing to produce the body of John Merryman, according to the command of the writ of habeas corpus, returnable and returned before me to-day, and that said attachment be returned before me at twelve o'clock to-morrow, at the room of the circuit court. R. B. Taney. Monday, May 27 1861.

The clerk issued the writ of attachment as directed. At twelve o'clock, on the 28th May 1861, the chief justice again took his seat on the bench, and called for the marshal's return to the writ of attachment. It was as follows:

> I hereby certify to the Honorable Roger B. Taney, chief justice of the supreme court of the United States, that by virtue of the within writ of attachment, to me directed, on the 27th day of May 1861, I proceeded, on this 28th day of May 1861, to Fort McHenry, for the purpose of serving the said writ. I sent in my name at the outer gate; the messenger returned with the reply, "that there was no answer to my card," and therefore, I could not serve the writ, as I was commanded. I was not permitted to enter the gate. So answers Washington Bonifant, U. S. Marshal for the District of Maryland.

After it was read, the chief justice said, that the marshal had the power to summon the posse comitatus to aid him in seizing and bringing before the court, the party named in the attachment, who would, when so brought in, be liable to punishment by fine and imprisonment; but where, as in this case, the power refusing obedience was so notoriously superior to any the marshal could command, he held that officer excused from doing anything more than he had done. The chief justice then proceeded as follows:

> I ordered this attachment yesterday, because, upon the face of the return, the detention of the prisoner was unlawful, upon the grounds: 1. That the president, under the constitution of the United States, cannot suspend the privilege of the writ of habeas corpus, nor authorize a military officer to do it. 2. A military officer has no right to arrest and detain a person not subject to the rules and articles of war, for an offence against the laws of the United States, except in aid of the judicial authority, and subject to its control; and if the party be arrested by the military, it is the duty of the officer to deliver him over immediately to the civil authority, to be dealt with according to

law. It is, therefore, very clear that John Merryman, the petitioner, is entitled to be set at liberty and discharged immediately from imprisonment. I forbore yesterday to state orally the provisions of the constitution of the United States, which make those principles the fundamental law of the Union, because an oral statement might be misunderstood in some portions of it, and I shall therefore put my opinion in writing, and file it in the office of the clerk of the circuit court, in the course of this week.

He concluded by saying, that he should cause his opinion, when filed, and all the proceedings, to be laid before the president, in order that he might perform his constitutional duty, to enforce the laws, by securing obedience to the process of the United States.

TANEY, Circuit Justice.

The application in this case for a writ of habeas corpus is made to me under the 14th section of the judiciary act of 1789 [1 Stat. 81], which renders effectual for the citizen the constitutional privilege of the writ of habeas corpus. That act gives to the courts of the United States, as well as to each justice of the supreme court, and to every district judge, power to grant writs of habeas corpus for the purpose of an inquiry into the cause of commitment. The petition was presented to me, at Washington, under the impression that I would order the prisoner to be brought before me there, but as he was confined in Fort McHenry, in the city of Baltimore, which is in my circuit, I resolved to hear it in the latter city, as obedience to the writ, under such circumstances, would not withdraw General Cadwalader, who had him in charge, from the limits of his military command.

The petition presents the following case: The petitioner resides in Maryland, in Baltimore county; while peaceably in his own house, with his family, it was at two o'clock on the morning of the 25th of May 1861, entered by an armed force, professing to act under military orders; he was then compelled to rise from his bed, taken into custody, and conveyed to Fort McHenry, where he is imprisoned by the commanding officer, without warrant from any lawful authority.

The commander of the fort, General George Cadwalader, by whom he is detained in confinement, in his return to the writ, does not deny any of the facts alleged in the petition. He states that the prisoner was arrested by order of General Keim, of Pennsylvania, and conducted as aforesaid to Fort McHenry, by his order, and placed in his (General Cadwalader's) custody, to be there detained by him as a prisoner.

A copy of the warrant or order under which the prisoner was arrested was demanded by his counsel, and refused: and it is not alleged in the return, that any specific act, constituting any offence against the laws of the United States, has been charged against him upon oath, but he appears to have been arrested upon general charges of treason and rebellion, without proof, and without giving the names of the witnesses, or specifying the acts which, in the judgment of the military officer, constituted these crimes. Having the prisoner thus in custody upon these vague and unsupported accusations, he refuses to obey the writ of habeas corpus, upon the ground that he is duly authorized by the president to suspend it.

The case, then, is simply this: a military officer, residing in Pennsylvania, issues an order to arrest a citizen of Maryland, upon vague and indefinite charges, without any proof, so far as appears; under this order, his house is entered in the night, he is seized as a prisoner, and conveyed to Fort McHenry, and there kept in close confinement; and when a habeas corpus is served on the commanding officer, requiring him to produce the prisoner before a justice of the supreme court, in order that he may examine into the legality of the imprisonment, the answer of the officer, is that he is authorized by the president to suspend the writ of habeas corpus at his discretion, and in the exercise of that discretion, suspends it in this case, and on that ground refuses obedience to the writ.

As the case comes before me, therefore, I understand that the president not only claims the right to suspend the writ of habeas corpus himself, at his discretion, but to delegate that discretionary power to a military officer, and to leave it to him to determine whether he will or will not obey judicial process that may be served upon him. No official notice has been given to the courts of justice, or to the public, by proclamation or otherwise, that the president claimed this power, and had exercised it in the manner stated in the return. And I certainly listened to it with some surprise, for I had supposed it to be one of those points of constitutional law upon which there was no difference of opinion, and that it was admitted on all hands, that the privilege of the writ could not be suspended, except by act of congress.

When the conspiracy of which Aaron Burr was the head, became so formidable, and was so extensively ramified, as to justify, in Mr. Jefferson's opinion, the suspension of the writ, he claimed, on his part, no power to suspend it, but communicated his opinion to congress, with all the proofs in his possession, in order that congress might exercise its discretion upon the subject, and determine whether the public safety required it. And in the debate which took place upon the subject, no one suggested that Mr. Jefferson might exercise the power himself, if, in his opinion, the public safety demanded it.

Having, therefore, regarded the question as too plain and too well settled to be open to dispute, if the commanding officer had stated that, upon his own responsibility, and in the exercise of his own discretion, he refused obedience to the writ, I should have contented myself with referring to the clause in the constitution, and to the construction it received from every jurist and statesman of that day, when the case of Burr was before them. But being thus officially notified that the privilege of the writ has been suspended, under the orders, and by the authority of the president, and believing, as I do, that the president has exercised a power which he does not possess under the constitution, a proper respect for the high office he fills, requires me to state plainly and fully the grounds of my opinion, in order to show that I have not ventured to question the legality of his act, without a careful and deliberate examination of the whole subject.

The clause of the constitution, which authorizes the suspension of the privilege of the writ of habeas corpus, is in the 9th section of the first article. This article is devoted to the legislative department of the United States, and has not the slightest reference to the executive department. It begins by providing "that all legislative powers therein granted, shall be vested in a congress of the United States, which shall consist of a senate and house of representatives." And after prescribing the manner in which these two branches of the legislative department shall be chosen, it proceeds to enumerate specifically the legislative powers which it thereby grants [and legislative powers which it expressly prohibits]; and at the conclusion of this specification, a clause is inserted giving congress "the power to make all laws which shall be necessary and proper for carrying into execution the foregoing powers, and all other powers vested by this constitution in the government of the United States, or in any department or officer thereof."

The power of legislation granted by this latter clause is, by its words, carefully confined to the specific objects before enumerated. But as this limitation was unavoidably somewhat indefinite, it was deemed necessary to guard more effectually certain great cardinal principles, essential to the liberty of the citizen, and to the rights and equality of the states, by denying to congress, in express terms, any power of legislation over them. It was apprehended, it seems, that such legislation might be attempted, under the pretext that it was necessary and proper to carry into execution the powers granted; and it was determined, that there should be no room to doubt, where rights of such vital importance were concerned; and accordingly, this clause is immediately followed by an enumeration of certain subjects, to which the powers of legislation shall not extend. The great importance which the framers of the constitution attached to the privilege of the writ of habeas corpus, to protect the liberty of the citizen, is proved by the fact, that its suspension, except in cases of invasion or rebellion, is first in the list of prohibited powers; and even in these cases the power is denied, and its exercise prohibited, unless the public safety shall require it.

It is true, that in the cases mentioned, congress is, of necessity, the judge of whether the public safety does or does not require it; and their judgment is conclusive. But the introduction of these words is a standing admonition to the legislative body of the danger of suspending it, and of the extreme caution they should exercise, before they give the government of the United States such power over the liberty of a citizen.

It is the second article of the constitution that provides for the organization of the executive department, enumerates the powers conferred on it, and prescribes its duties. And if the high power over the liberty of the citizen now claimed, was intended to be conferred on the president, it would undoubtedly be found in plain words in this article; but there is not a word in it that can furnish the slightest ground to justify the exercise of the power.

The article begins by declaring that the executive power shall be vested in a president of the United States of America, to hold his office during the term of four years; and then proceeds to prescribe the mode of election, and to specify, in precise and plain words, the powers delegated to him, and the duties imposed upon him. The short term for which he is elected, and the narrow limits to which his power is confined, show the jealousy and apprehension of future danger which the framers of the constitution felt in relation to that department of the government, and how carefully they withheld from it many of the powers belonging to the executive branch of the English government which were considered as dangerous to the liberty of the subject; and conferred (and that in clear and specific terms) those powers only which were deemed essential to secure the successful operation of the government.

He is elected, as I have already said, for the brief term of four years, and is made personally responsible, by impeachment, for malfeasance in office; he is, from necessity, and the nature of his duties, the commander-in-chief of the army and navy, and of the militia, when called into actual service; but no appropriation for the support of the army can be made by congress for a longer term than two years, so that it is in the power of the succeeding house of representatives to withhold the appropriation for its support, and thus disband it, if, in their judgment, the president used, or designed to use it for improper purposes. And although the militia, when in actual service, is under his command, yet the appointment of the officers is reserved to the states, as a security against the use of the military power for purposes dangerous to the liberties of the people, or the rights of the states.

So too, his powers in relation to the civil duties and authority necessarily conferred on him are carefully restricted, as well as those belonging to his military character. He cannot appoint the ordinary officers of government, nor make a treaty with a foreign nation or Indian tribe, without the advice and consent of the senate, and cannot appoint even inferior officers, unless he is authorized by an act of congress to do so. He is not empowered to arrest any one charged with an offence against the United States, and whom he may, from the evidence before him, believe to be guilty; nor can he authorize any officer, civil or military, to exercise this power, for the fifth article of the amendments to the constitution expressly provides that no person "shall be deprived of life, liberty or property, without due process of law"—that is, judicial process.

Even if the privilege of the writ of habeas corpus were suspended by act of congress, and a party not subject to the rules and articles of war were afterwards arrested and imprisoned by regular judicial process, he could not be detained in prison, or brought to trial before a military tribunal, for the article in the amendments to the constitution immediately following the one above referred to (that is, the sixth article) provides, that "in all criminal prosecutions, the accused shall enjoy the right to a speedy and public trial by an impartial jury of the state and district wherein the crime shall have been committed, which district shall have been previously ascertained by law; and to be informed of the nature and cause of the accusation; to be confronted with the witnesses against him; to have compulsory process for obtaining witnesses in his favor; and to have the assistance of counsel for his defence."

The only power, therefore, which the president possesses, where the "life, liberty or property" of a private citizen is concerned, is the power and duty prescribed in the third section of the second article, which requires "that he shall take care that the laws shall be faithfully executed." He is not authorized to execute them himself, or through agents or officers, civil or military, appointed by himself, but he is to take care that they be faithfully carried into execution, as they are expounded and adjudged by the co-ordinate branch of the government to which that duty is assigned by the constitution. It is thus made his duty to come in aid of the judicial authority, if it shall be resisted by a force too strong to be overcome without the assistance of the executive arm; but in exercising this power he acts in subordination to judicial authority, assisting it to execute its process and enforce its judgments.

With such provisions in the constitution, expressed in language too clear to be misunderstood by any one, I can see no ground whatever for supposing that the president, in any emergency, or in any state of things, can authorize the suspension of the privileges of the writ of habeas corpus, or the arrest of a citizen, except in aid of the judicial power. He certainly does not faithfully execute the laws, if he takes upon himself legislative power, by suspending the writ of habeas corpus, and the judicial power also, by arresting and imprisoning a person without due process of law.

Nor can any argument be drawn from the nature of sovereignty, or the necessity of government, for self-defence in times of tumult and danger. The government of the United States is one of delegated and limited powers; it derives its existence and authority altogether from the constitution, and neither of its branches, executive, legislative or judicial, can exercise any of the powers of government beyond those specified and granted; for the tenth article of the amendments to the constitution, in express terms, provides that "the powers not delegated to the United States by the constitution, nor prohibited by it to the states, are reserved to the states, respectively, or to the people."

Indeed, the security against imprisonment by executive authority, provided for in the fifth article of the amendments to the constitution, which I have before quoted, is nothing more than a copy of a like provision in the English constitution, which had been firmly established before the declaration of independence. Blackstone states it in the following words: "To make imprisonment lawful, it must be either by process of law from the courts of judicature, or by warrant from some legal officer having authority to commit to prison." 1 Bl[ackstone's]. Comm[entary]. 137.

The people of the United Colonies, who had themselves lived under its protection, while they were British subjects, were well aware of the necessity of this safeguard for their personal liberty. And no one can believe that, in framing a government intended to guard still more efficiently the rights and liberties of the citizen, against executive encroachment and oppression, they would have conferred on the president a power which the history of England had proved to be dangerous and oppressive in the hands of the crown; and which the people of England had compelled it to surrender, after a long and obstinate struggle on the part of the English executive to usurp and retain it.

The right of the subject to the benefit of the writ of habeas corpus, it must be recollected, was one of the great points in controversy, during the long struggle in England between arbitrary government and free institutions, and must therefore have strongly attracted the attention of the statesmen engaged in framing a new and, as they supposed, a freer government than the one which they had thrown off by the revolution. From the earliest history of the common law, if a person were imprisoned, no matter by what authority, he had a right to the writ of habeas corpus, to bring his case before the king's bench; if no specific offence were charged against him in the warrant of commitment, he was entitled to be forthwith discharged; and if an offence were charged which was bailable in its character, the court was bound to set him at liberty on bail. The most exciting contests between the crown and the people of England, from the time of Magna Charta, were in relation to the privilege of this writ, and they continued until the passage of the statute of 31 Car. II., commonly known as the great habeas corpus act.

This statute put an end to the struggle, and finally and firmly secured the liberty of the subject against the usurpation and oppression of the executive branch of the government. It nevertheless conferred no new right upon the subject, but only secured a right already existing; for, although the right could not justly be denied, there was often no effectual remedy against its violation. Until the statute of 13 Wm. III., the judges held their offices at the pleasure of the king, and the influence which he exercised over timid, time-serving and partisan judges, often induced them, upon some pretext or other, to refuse to discharge the party, although entitled by law to his discharge, or delayed their decision, from time to time, so as to prolong the imprisonment of persons who were obnoxious to the king for their political opinions, or had incurred his resentment in any other way.

The great and inestimable value of the habeas corpus act of the 31 Car. II. is, that it contains provisions which compel courts and judges, and all parties concerned, to perform their duties promptly, in the manner specified in the statute.

A passage in Blackstone's Commentaries, showing the ancient state of the law on this subject, and the abuses which were practised through the power and influence of the crown, and a short extract from Hallam's Constitutional History, stating the circumstances which gave rise to the passage of this statute, explain briefly, but fully, all that is material to this subject.

Blackstone says: "To assert an absolute exemption from imprisonment in all cases is inconsistent with every idea of law and political society, and in the end would destroy all civil liberty by rendering its protection impossible. But the glory of the English law consists in clearly defining the times, the causes and the extent, when, wherefore and to what degree, the imprisonment of the subject may be lawful. This it is which induces the absolute necessity of expressing upon every commitment the reason for which it is made, that the court, upon a habeas corpus, may examine into its validity, and according to the circumstances of the case, may discharge, admit to bail or remand the prisoner. And yet early in the reign of Charles I, the court of kings bench, relying on some arbitrary precedents (and those perhaps misunderstood) determined that they would not, upon a habeas corpus, either bail or deliver a prisoner, though committed without any cause assigned, in case he was committed by the special command of the king or by the lords of the privy council. This drew on a parliamentary inquiry, and produced the "Petition of Right" (3 Car. I.) which recites this illegal judgment, and enacts that no freeman hereafter shall be so imprisoned or detained. But when, in the following year, Mr. Selden and others were committed by the lords of the council, in pursuance of his majesty's special command, under a general charge of "notable contempts, and stirring up sedition against the king and government," the judges delayed for two terms (including also the long vacation) to deliver an opinion how far such a charge was bailable; and when at length they agreed that it was, they however annexed a condition of finding sureties for their good behavior, which still protracted their imprisonment, the chief justice, Sir Nicholas Hyde, at the same time, declaring that "if they were again remanded for that cause, perhaps the court would not afterwards grant a habeas corpus, being already made acquainted with the cause of the imprisonment." But this was heard with indignation and astonishment by every lawyer present, according to Mr. Selden's own account of the matter, whose resentment was not cooled at the distance of four and twenty years." 3 Bl. Comm. 133, 134.

It is worthy of remark, that the offences charged against the prisoner in this case, and relied on as a justification for his arrest and imprisonment, in their nature and character, and in the loose and vague manner in which they are stated, bear a striking resemblance to those assigned in the warrant for the arrest of Mr. Selden. And yet, even at that day, the warrant was regarded as such a flagrant violation of the rights of the subject that the delay of the time-serving judges to set him at liberty, upon the habeas corpus issued in his behalf, excited the universal indignation of the bar.

The extract from Hallam's Constitutional History is equally impressive and equally in point: "It is a very common mistake, and that not only among foreigners, but many from whom some knowledge of our constitutional laws might be expected, to suppose that this statute of Car. II. enlarged in a great degree our liberties, and forms a sort of epoch in their history. But though a very beneficial enactment, and eminently remedial in many cases of illegal imprisonment, it introduced no new principle, nor conferred any right upon the subject. From the earliest records of the English law, no freeman could be detained in prison, except upon a criminal charge or conviction, or for a civil debt. In the former case it was always in his power to demand of the court of king's bench a writ of habeas corpus ad subjiciendum, directed to the person detaining him in custody, by which he was enjoined to bring up the body of the prisoner, with the warrant of commitment, that the court might judge of its sufficiency, and remand the party, admit him to bail, or discharge him, according to the nature of the charge. This writ issued of right, and could not be refused by the court. It was not to bestow an immunity from arbitrary imprisonment, which is abundantly provided for in Magna Charta (if indeed it is not more ancient), that the statute of Car. II. was enacted, but to cut off the abuses by which the government's lust of power, and the servile subtlety of the crown lawyers, had impaired so fundamental a privilege."

While the value set upon this writ in England has been so great, that the removal of the abuses which embarrassed its employment has been looked upon as almost a new grant of liberty to the subject, it is not to be wondered at, that the continuance of the writ thus made effective should have been the object of the most jealous care. Accordingly, no power in England short of that of parliament can suspend or authorize the suspension of the writ of habeas corpus. I quote again from Blackstone (1 Bl. Comm. 136): "But the happiness of our constitution is, that it is not left to the executive power to determine when the danger of the state is so great as to render this measure expedient. It is the parliament only or legislative power that, whenever it sees proper, can authorize the crown by suspending the habeas corpus for a short and limited time, to imprison suspected persons without giving any reason for so doing." If the president of the United States may suspend the writ, then the constitution of the United States has conferred upon him more regal and absolute power over the liberty of the citizen, than the people of England have thought it safe to entrust to the crown; a power which the queen of England cannot exercise at this day, and which could not have been lawfully exercised by the sovereign even in the reign of Charles the First.

But I am not left to form my judgment upon this great question, from analogies between the English government and our own, or the commentaries of English jurists, or the decisions of English courts, although upon this subject they are entitled to the highest respect, and are justly regarded and received as authoritative by our courts of justice. To guide me to a right conclusion, I have the Commentaries on the Constitution of the United States of the late Mr. Justice Story, not only one of the most eminent jurists of the age, but for a long time one of the brightest ornaments of the supreme court of the United States; and also the clear and authoritative decision of that court itself, given more than half a century since, and conclusively establishing the principles I have above stated.

Mr. Justice Story, speaking, in his Commentaries, of the habeas corpus clause in the constitution, says: "It is obvious that cases of a peculiar emergency may arise, which may justify, nay, even require, the temporary suspension of any right to the writ. But as it has frequently happened in foreign countries, and even in England, that the writ has, upon various pretexts and occasions, been suspended, whereby persons apprehended upon suspicion have suffered a long imprisonment, sometimes from design, and sometimes because they were forgotten, the right to suspend it is expressly confined to cases of rebellion or invasion, where the public safety may require it. A very just and wholesome restraint, which cuts down at a blow a fruitful means of oppression, capable of being abused, in bad times, to the worst of purposes. Hitherto, no suspension of the writ has ever been authorized by congress, since the establishment of the constitution. It would seem, as the power is given to congress to suspend the writ of habeas corpus, in cases of rebellion or invasion, that the right to judge whether the exigency had arisen must exclusively belong to that body." 3 Story, Comm. Const. § 1336.

And Chief Justice Marshall, in delivering the opinion of the supreme court in the case of Ex parte Bollman and Swartwout, uses this decisive language: "It may be worthy of remark, that this act (speaking of the one under which I am proceeding) was passed by the first congress of the United States, sitting under a constitution which had declared "that the privilege of the writ of habeas corpus should not be suspended, unless when, in cases of rebellion or invasion, the public safety may require it." Acting under the immediate influence of this injunction, they must have felt, with peculiar force, the obligation of providing efficient means, by which this great constitutional privilege should receive life and activity; for if the means be not in existence, the privilege itself would be lost, although no law for its suspension should be enacted. ["]Under the impression of this obligation, they give to all the courts the power of awarding writs of habeas corpus." And again on page 101: "If at any time, the public safety should require the suspension of the powers vested by this act in the courts of the United States, it is for the legislature to say so. That question depends on political considerations, on which the legislature is to decide; until the legislative will be expressed, this court can only see its duty, and must obey the laws." I can add nothing to these clear and emphatic words of my great predecessor.

But the documents before me show, that the military authority in this case has gone far beyond the mere suspension of the privilege of the writ of habeas corpus. It has, by force of arms, thrust aside the judicial authorities and officers to whom the constitution has confided the power and duty of interpreting and administering the laws, and substituted a military government in its place, to be administered and executed by military officers. For, at the time these proceedings were had against John Merryman, the district judge of Maryland, the commissioner appointed under the act of congress, the district attorney and the marshal, all resided in the city of Baltimore, a few miles only from the home of the prisoner. Up to that time, there had never been the slightest resistance or obstruction to the process of any court or judicial officer of the United States, in Maryland, except by the military authority. And if a military officer, or any other person, had reason to believe that the prisoner had committed any offence against the laws of the United States, it was his duty to give information of the fact and the evidence to support it, to the district attorney; it would then have become the duty of that officer to bring the matter before the district judge or commissioner, and if there was sufficient legal evidence to justify his arrest, the judge or commissioner would have issued his warrant to the marshal to arrest him; and upon the hearing of the case, would have held him to bail, or committed him for trial, according to the character of the offence, as it appeared in the testimony, or would have discharged him immediately, if there was not sufficient evidence to support the accusation. There was no danger of any obstruction or resistance to the action of the civil authorities, and therefore no reason whatever for the interposition of the military.

Yet, under these circumstances, a military officer, stationed in Pennsylvania, without giving any information to the district attorney, and without any application to the judicial authorities, assumes to himself the judicial power in the district of Maryland; undertakes to decide what constitutes the crime of treason or rebellion; what evidence (if indeed he required any) is sufficient to support the accusation and justify the commitment; and commits the party, without a hearing, even before himself, to close custody, in a strongly garrisoned fort, to be there held, it would seem, during the pleasure of those who committed him.

The constitution provides, as I have before said, that "no person shall be deprived of life, liberty or property, without due process of law." It declares that "the right of the people to be secure in their persons, houses, papers and effects, against unreasonable searches and seizures, shall not be violated; and no warrant shall issue, but upon probable cause, supported by oath or affirmation, and particularly describing the place to be searched, and the persons or things to be seized." It provides that the party accused shall be entitled to a speedy trial in a court of justice.

These great and fundamental laws, which congress itself could not suspend, have been disregarded and suspended, like the writ of habeas corpus, by a military order, supported by force of arms. Such is the case now before me, and I can only say that if the authority which the constitution has confided to the judiciary department and judicial officers, may thus, upon any pretext or under any circumstances, be usurped by the military power, at its discretion, the people of the United States are no longer living under a government of laws, but every citizen holds life, liberty and property at the will and pleasure of the army officer in whose military district he may happen to be found.

In such a case, my duty was too plain to be mistaken. I have exercised all the power which the constitution and laws confer upon me, but that power has been resisted by a force too strong for me to overcome. It is possible that the officer who has incurred this grave responsibility may have misunderstood his instructions, and exceeded the authority intended to be given him; I shall, therefore, order all the proceedings in this case, with my opinion, to be filed and recorded in the circuit court of the United States for the district of Maryland, and direct the clerk to transmit a copy, under seal, to the president of the United States. It will then remain for that high officer, in fulfillment of his constitutional obligation to "take care that the laws be faithfully executed," to determine what measures he will take to cause the civil process of the United States to be respected and enforced.

The Prize Cases

The Brig *Amy Warwick*

The Barque *Hiawatha*

The Schooner *Brilliante*

The Schooner *Crenshaw*

Supreme Court of the United States
March 10, 1863
2 Black (67 U.S.) 635 (1863)

By a 5–4 vote, a majority of the justices of the United States Supreme Court voted to uphold President Abraham Lincoln's April 19, 1861, declaration of a blockade around the seceded states, even though Congress had not authorized the blockade. In July 1861, Congress did authorize the move, but a number of ships had been captured and held as blockade runners *before* Congress acted, and this litigation arose from those seizures by federal authorities. Associate Justice Robert C. Grier wrote the majority opinion supporting Lincoln's theory of the war as a "domestic insurrection," and as such, the president could take action to deal with the insurrection, including establishing a naval blockade. In this fashion, the United States could fight the war without granting the so-called Confederacy existence as a country. For the four-justice minority, Associate Justice Samuel Nelson argued more narrowly that the Constitution allowed only Congress to declare war, not the president. As a result, the president could not take such emergency actions, including declaring the blockade, and thus the seizure of blockade runners was illegal and unconstitutional. For Nelson, all crews, cargoes, and ships ought to be released. But, by the implication of the majority's decision, if the president has the power as commander and chief to declare a blockade, then other presidential proclamations in times of emergency also had the force of law and were constitutional, such as the suspension of habeas corpus and, later in the war, the Emancipation Proclamation.

These were cases in which the vessels named, together with their cargoes, were severally captured and brought in as prizes by public ships of the United States. The libels were filed by the proper District Attorneys, on behalf of the United States and on behalf of the officers and crews of the ships, by which the captures were respectively made. In each case the District Court pronounced a decree of condemnation, from which the claimants took an appeal.

The *Amy Warwick* was a merchant vessel, and belonged to Richmond. Her registered owners were David and William Currie, Abraham Warwick and George W. Allen, who resided at that place. Previous to her capture she had made a voyage from New York to Richmond, and thence to Rio de Janeiro, Brazil. At the last named port she shipped a cargo of coffee, 5,100 bags, to be delivered at New York, Philadelphia, Baltimore or Richmond, according to the orders which the master would receive at Hampton Roads. She was on her voyage from Rio to Hampton Roads and off Cape Henry when she was captured (July 10th, 1861) by the Quaker City. At the time of the capture the barque was sailing under American colors, and her commander was ignorant of the war. The Quaker City carried her into Boston, where she was labeled as enemy's property. The claimants of the vessel were the persons already named as owners. James Dunlap, Robert Edmonds, John L. Phipps, and Charles Brown claimed the cargo. The claimants in their several answers denied any hostility on their part to the Government or Laws of the United States, averred that the master was ignorant of any blockade, embargo or other interdiction of commerce with the ports of Virginia, and asserted generally that the capture was unlawful.

The *Crenshaw* was captured by the United States Steamer *Star*, at the mouth of James River, on the 17th of May, 1861. She was bound for Liverpool with a cargo of tobacco from Richmond, and was owned by David and William Currie, who admitted the existence of an insurrection in Virginia against the Laws and Government of the United States, but averred that they were innocent of it. The claimants of the cargo made similar answers, and all the claimants asserted that they had no such notice of the blockade as rendered the vessel or cargo liable to seizure for leaving the port of Richmond at the time when the voyage was commenced. She was condemned as prize on the ground that she had broken, or was attempting to break, the blockade at the time of her capture.

The *Hiawatha* was a British barque, and was on her voyage from Richmond to Liverpool with a cargo of tobacco. She left Richmond on the 17th of May, 1861, and was captured in Hampton Roads on the 20th by the Minnesota, and taken to New York. Her owners were Miller, Massman & Co., of Liverpool, who denied her liability to capture and condemnation on the ground that no sufficient notice had been given of the blockade. The claimants of the cargo put their right to restoration upon a similar basis.

The *Brilliante* was a Mexican schooner, owned by Rafael Preciat and Julian Gual, residents of Campeche. She had on board a cargo of flour, part of which was owned by the owners of the vessel, and part by the Señores Ybana & Donde, who were also Mexican citizens. She had a regular clearance at Campeche for New Orleans, and had made the voyage between those ports. At New Orleans she took in her cargo of flour, part to be delivered at Sisal and part at Campeche, and took a clearance for both those places. On her homeward voyage she anchored in Biloxi Bay, intending to communicate with some vessel of the blockading fleet and get a permit to go to sea, and while so at anchor she was taken by two boats sent off from the Massachusetts. She was carried into Key West, where the legal proceedings against her were prosecuted in the District Court of the United States for the District of Florida.

The minuter circumstances of each case, and the points of fact, as well as law, on which all the cases turned, in this Court and in the Court below, are set forth with such precision in the opinions of both Mr. Justice Grier and Mr. Justice Nelson, that more than the brief narrative above given does not seem to be necessary.

The case of the *Amy Warwick* was argued by *Mr. Dana*, of Massachusetts, for Libellants, and by *Mr. Bangs*, of Massachusetts, for Claimants.

The *Crenshaw*, by *Mr. Eames*, of Washington City, for Libellants, and by *Messrs. Lord, Edwards*, and *Donohue*, of New York, for Claimants.

The *Hiawatha*, by *Mr. Evarts* and *Mr. Sedgwick*, of New York, for Libellants, and by *Mr. Edwards*, of New York, for Claimants.

The *Brilliante*, by *Mr. Eames*, of Washington City, for Libellants, and by *Mr. Carlisle*, of Washington City, for Claimants.

One argument on each side is all that can be given. Those of Mr. Dana and Mr. Carlisle have been selected, not for any reason which implies that the Reporter has presumed to pronounce judgment upon their merits as compared with those of the other distinguished counsel, but because they came to his hands in a form which relieved him of the labor which the others would have cost to re-write and condense them.

Mr. Carlisle. The Brilliante is a regularly registered Mexican ship. Her principal owner, although a Mexican citizen by birth, had been naturalized in the United States. He was, before and at the time of the seizure, the United States Consul at the port of Campeche, a port on the coast of Mexico. The vessel was seized by the United States ship Massachusetts, in Biloxi Bay, north of Ship Island, between *Pas Crétien* and Pascagoula Bay, on the 23d of June, 1861.

She had sailed from New Orleans, with a cargo of six hundred barrels of flour, put on board there about the 16th of that month, four hundred barrels for the house of the claimant, (American Consul at Campeche,) and the residue for the Mexican house of Ybana & Donde, at Sisal, also a port on the coast of

Mexico; to which houses it was respectively consigned, they being owners of the same, in these proportions.

I. There was no actual breach. The question is of intent.

At the time of the seizure, the Brilliante was lying at anchor in Biloxi Bay, and had so lain at anchor twenty-four hours or more. "She came out from New Orleans and anchored in Biloxi Bay, so as to be able to communicate with one of the blockading vessels, but did not see any vessel of war. On the next day, on which the vessel was seized, the sea was too rough to go on board the Massachusetts, which was lying in sight."

Mr. Preciat, the claimant, "wished to go on board one of the blockading vessels, to see if he could get a permit to go out to sea; otherwise he intended to have returned with the vessel to New Orleans." (Deposition of the said Preciat, taken *in preparatorio,* Record, p. 11.) He was returning to Campeche, "to attend to the duties of his office *(U. S. Consul,)* and business generally." On going to New Orleans, he had a letter from the Commander of the Brooklyn, one of the blockading squadron, to the Commander of the Niagara, another of them, forwarding him to Mobile, where his son was at school, and whom he desired to take home. The passengers and crew mutinied, and refused to go to Mobile. The mate, taking control, steered for New Orleans, where the vessel arrived and the crew were discharged. These facts appear from the declarations *in preparatorio.* The libel and decree are exclusively founded on the alleged attempt to leave New Orleans. The claimant had a right to except that his application to return, although sailing from New Orleans, would have been granted; or, if not granted, that he would have been allowed the option of going back to New Orleans; which he declares, on his examination, was his intention, if not permitted to return to Campeche. He swears that he had no intention to violate the blockade. There is nothing to contradict him, but everything corroborates his declaration. He was at anchor twenty-four hours, and a considerable portion of that time in sight of one of the blockading vessels, which the evidence shows he could not safely attempt to reach in consequence of the state of the weather. Before that period there is nothing to show that he might not have run the blockade safely; nor is there any reason suggested or supposable why he cast anchor, except that he had no intent to violate the blockade. His public character as United States Consul, and the facts before referred to, go in confirmation of this.

But chiefly, the terms of the President's proclamation instituting this so-called blockade, are important to be considered upon this question of intent. The condition of things was unprecedented. From the nature and structure of our peculiar system of government, it *could have had* no precedent. The co-existence of Federal and State sovereignties, and the double allegiance of the people of the States, which no statesman or lawyer has doubted till now, and which this Court has repeatedly recognized as lying at the foundation of some of its most important decisions; the delegation of special and limited powers to the Federal Government, with the express reservation of all other powers "to the States and the people thereof" who created the Union and established the Constitution; the powers proposed to be granted and which were refused, and the general course of the debates on the constitution; all concurred in presenting this to the President as a case of the first impression. Assuming the power to close the ports of the seceded States, he evidently did so with doubt and hesitation. If the power be conceded to him, it cannot be denied that he might modify the strict law of blockade, and impose a qualified interruption of commerce. He might well have doubted whether, under the Constitution which he had sworn to support, a state of *war* could exist between a State, or States, and the Federal Union; whether, when it ceased to be insurrection, and became the formal and deliberate act of State sovereignty, his executive powers extended to such an exigency. Certainly, the words of the Acts of Congress authorizing him to use the navy did not embrace such a case. It was not quite certain that it had assumed this imposing shape. The President, so late as his message of July, was confident that it had not. He believed that the State sovereignties had been usurped by discontented leaders and a factious and inconsiderable minority. With the information laid before him, he declared that these seceded States were full of people devoted to the Union. Well, therefore, might he hesitate to exercise, even if he supposed himself to possess, the power of declaring or "recognizing" a state of *war*. His powers in cases of insurrection or invasion were clear and undoubted. He had the army, the navy, and the militia of the States (the United States having no militia except in the federal territories) confided to his command, *sub modo*.

But insurrection is not war; and invasion is not war. The Constitution expressly distinguishes them, and treats them as wholly different subjects. But this belongs to a subsequent question in the argument. It is now referred to as bearing upon the construction of the proclamation, and consequently upon the question of *intent* to break *a blockade*. It is true that the proclamation calls it a blockade. But the message speaks of it as proceedings *"in the nature of a blockade."* And the proclamation itself, by its terms and provisions, substantially conforms to the latter description. It founds itself upon the existence of *"an insurrection."* It pronounces the disturbance to be by *"a combination of persons."* It proceeds upon the Acts of Congress provided for *"insurrections"* by *"combinations of persons."* It declares that the executive measures are provisional and temporary only, *"until Congress shall have assembled and deliberated upon the said unlawful proceedings."* It requires the seceded States to disperse, and return peaceably "to their respective place of abode in twenty days."

"These "combinations of persons," and these "unlawful proceedings," are not at all recognized as presenting a case for belligerent rights and obligations. Naturally and prudently, the President did not assume to proclaim a strict blockade, with the extreme rights which obtain between belligerents, and with the corresponding rights of neutrals. He first called out the *militia of the States,* as such.

He then used the army and the navy, under the Act of 1807. But he knew that this was not war. It was the suppression of insurrection. Consequently, in this use of the navy, he did not contemplate capture *jure belli*. Long after the period involved in this case, he maintained to all the civilized world, (see Mr. Seward's diplomatic correspondence, 1861,) that to attribute anything of belligerent right to these *"combinations of persons"* and these *"unlawful proceedings,"* was an outrage and an offence to the United States. In effect, his position was that it was purely a *municipal* question; and, of course, there could be no blockade, in the international sense, and no capture *jure belli*.

Accordingly, the proclamation threatens not the regular proceedings of a prize Court, but *"such proceedings as may be deemed advisable."* And these proceedings are to follow upon a seizure to be made in the precise and only case where a vessel shall have attempted to enter or leave a port, and shall have been "duly warned by the commander of one of the blockading vessels, who will endorse on her register the fact and date of such warning; *and if the same vessel shall again* attempt to enter or to leave," &c., then these undescribed proceeding shall take place.

Under these circumstances, upon the question of intent, it is submitted that the case is with the claimant.

But II. The terms of the proclamation, assuming it to have intended a *blockade*, (*jure belli*,) excuse this vessel and cargo. The only authority necessary to be referred to here is the case of *Md. Ins. Co.* vs. *Woods*, (6 Cr., 49,) decided by this Court. It is to be argued from, *a fortiori*. The qualified blockade, by a belligerent, was recognized. Notoriety of blockade in fact, and perhaps actual knowledge, are admitted in that case. But because a special warning off was provided for in this notice of the blockade, restoration was decreed. This Court said there, that they could not perceive the reasons for this modification. Nevertheless, they held it imperative. Here, the reasons are apparent.

III. This seizure took place before Congress had convened to act in the premises. It was made during that period when the President, casting about among doubtful expedients, had used the navy, under the Acts of Congress for suppressing insurrection and repelling invasion, and had used this force "*in the nature* of a blockade." It is denied that during this period there was WAR, or that the rights and obligations of war, either under the municipal or international law, had arisen. Of consequence, blockade and the prize jurisdiction could not have existed. The question here is, how can the United States, under the Constitution, be involved in war? And, to admit for a moment a modern question, who has the power to accept, recognize, or admit a state of *war*, so that such a *status* will affect the people of the States, and foreign nations and their subjects, with the consequences of war, municipally and internationally? How are treaties suspended or abrogated? When are citizens residing in the several States placed in the condition of alien enemies, or of persons *(nolens volens)* identified with the Territory of a public enemy, in a state of public war, whether foreign or civil?

And, again, if this was not *war*, in any legal sense, who has the power of closing a port of entry of the United States against the trade of a foreign nation, to whom all ports of entry are open by treaty? This vessel and her cargo were wholly Mexican. The Port of New Orleans was a port of entry, open to her, for ingress and egress, and for all lawful commerce. How was it closed? It is clear that it was not closed by legislation. Nor was the Treaty with Mexico, which might have been suspended or abrogated by Act of Congress, (being only the "supreme law of the land," in the same sense with such acts,) in any degree disturbed by the National Legislature.

Now, this decree of condemnation could only be founded upon one of two alternatives: *seizure* under the municipal law, or *capture* under the international law, for violation, or attempt at violation, of a blockade.

It is plain that there was no municipal law by which it could be justified. The President cannot make, alter, or suspend "the supreme law of the land;" and this condemnation rests solely upon his authority.

IV. Was it capture? Blockade is a belligerent right. There must be war, before there can be blockade in the international sense, giving jurisdiction in prize. There may be an interruption of commerce, *"in the nature of a blockade."* But this is the exercise of the legislative power, and is purely municipal. The distinction is plainly shown in *Rose* vs. *Himely*, (4 Cr., 272). But this legislative power does not reside in the President. The Constitution, in its first section, lays the corner-stone of the edifice it was erecting, declaring that *"all* legislative powers herein *granted* shall be vested in a Congress of the United States, which shall consist," &c. Therefore, it only remains to inquire, was there *war?*

But it has been objected that this question is not open here to this foreign claimant. This is a mistake. It is a principle of the law of nations that "the *sovereign* power of the State has alone the authority to make war." Wheat. on Captures, 40; Wildman, vol. 2, chap. 1. And Vattel (Lib. III, cap. 1, sec. 4) says: "The *sovereign* power has alone the authority to make war. But as the different rights which constitute this power, originally resident in the body of the nation, may be separated or limited, according to the will of the nation, *we are to seek the power of making war in the particular Constitution of each State."* And Bacon (Ab. Tit. Prerogative) says: "It is *intex jura summi imperii,* and in England is lodged in the King; though, as my Lord Hale says, it ever succeeds best when done by parliamentary advice."

The counsel for the United States, speaking for the President, take very bold and very alarming positions upon this question. One of them testifies, in well-considered rhetoric, his amazement that a judicial tribunal should be called upon to determine whether the political power was authorized to do what it has done. He is astounded that he should be required to "ask permission of your Honors for the whole political power of the Government to exercise the ordinary right of self-defence." He pictures to himself how the world will be appalled when it finds that *"one of our Courts"* has decided that "the war is at an end." He tells us that this is merely a Prize Court, and that the Prize Court sits "by commission of the sovereign," merely as "an inquest to ascertain whether the capture has been made according to the will and intent of the sovereign." That, all the world over, the Courts merely *construe* the acts of the political power. That *war* is only "a state of things." It is the conflict of opposing forces, with guns and swords and bayonets, in large numbers; and the Executive power being actually engaged in such conflict, war exists conclusively for this "one of our Courts," sitting by "commission of the sovereign."

Another of the learned counsel tells us that "the sovereign has assumed the responsibility. *His* Prize Court has no commission to thwart his purpose, or overrule his construction of the law of nations." And he added a significant admonition—that if "the pure and simple function of the Prize Court be transcended, then the Court is no longer a Court of the sovereign, but an ally of the enemy."

What place is this, where such thoughts are uttered? If the question were asked literally, and the dull walls of this old Senate Hall could comprehend and answer, they would give back in echoes the voices of departed patriots and statesmen—"this place is sacred to the Constitution of the United States."

But what tribunal is this? Is it "one of our Courts?" Does it sit "by commission of the sovereign?" Who is its sovereign? and what is its commission? It acknowledges the same sovereign, and none other, that is sovereign of the President and of Congress—the "respective States," and "the people" thereof. It has the same commission, and none other, which gives authority to the President and to Congress—the Constitution. It arose at the creation of this Government, coeval and co-ordinate with the Executive and Legislature, independent of either or both. More, it was charged with the sublime trust and duty of sitting in judgment upon their acts, for the protection of the rights of individuals and of States, whenever "a case" should come before it, as this has come, challenging the Constitutional authority of such acts.

This is a Government created, defined, and limited by a *written* Constitution, every article, clause, and expression in which was pondered and criticised, as probably no document in the affairs of men was ever before tested, refined, and ascertained. It is the office of this Court, as an organic element of the Government, to construe this *Magna Charta*, and to bring all cases which come before it to this test. So that, as well by the peculiar quality of this Court, as by the clear doctrine of the law of nations, the question is here to be put and answered, *was there war?* Not, was there *"a state of things"* involving in point of fact all the deadly machinery, and all "the pomp and circumstance" of war; but, had "the sovereign power of the State" declared war; declared that it should exist, or that, by the act of an enemy, it *did already* exist; war with its legal incidents municipal and international?

In this first great experiment of a written Constitution, of course it was explicitly and exclusively declared, in words as plain as language affords, where this tremendous power should reside. *To Congress* is entrusted the power "to declare war, grant letters of marque and reprisal, and make rules concerning captures on land and water." Art. I., sec. 8, par. 11.

It is not pretended that at the time of this so-called capture, Congress had declared that there should be war, or that war existed, or had in any manner dealt with the question of war. The "state of things" which the counsel for the Government call "war," had arisen in vacation. But the Constitution had expressly provided for this case, and plainly distinguished it from "war." This necessity for national defence or offence, by military force, might arise by *"insurrection or invasion."* The former is domestic, the latter foreign violence. But even in this latter case, namely, an invasion by a foreign nation, in itself an act of war by that nation, the Constitution did not depart from its inexorable rule that the country could only be involved in the legal consequences of war by Act of Congress. It contemplated temporary measures by the Executive. It authorized Congress *"to provide for calling forth the militia to execute the laws of the Union, suppress insurrections, and* REPEL INVASIONS." Art. I., sec. 8, par. 15. So that, side by side, the two cases are distinctly provided for; the power to suppress insurrections and repel invasions, which Congress might delegate to the President by a general law (as it did); and the power to put the country in the state of war, which was limited to Congress alone, acting upon the particular case.

But it has been maintained that the Acts of Congress passed subsequently to these seizures, have by retroaction recognized and validated a previous state of war. This is utterly inconsistent with the idea of a Government created by written Constitution. To affirm that when a careful and scrupulous distribution of powers has been made between the three great departments of free Government, either one may exercise the powers of the other, and that a subsequent cession or approval by the competent power will validate the act, is to convert the Constitution into a mere shadow. The maxim between private principal and agent, *"omnis ratihibitio,"* &c., cannot apply. The supposed *"ratihibitio"* is not by the principal who speaks in the Constitution, but by another agent of the principal having no right to delegate the special power. The matter then comes back necessarily to the pure question of the power of the President under the Constitution. And this is, perhaps, the most extraordinary part of the argument for the United States. It is founded upon a figure of speech, which is repugnant to the genius of republican institutions, and, above all, to our written Constitution. It makes the President, in some sort, the impersonation of the country, and invokes for him the power and right to use all the force he can command, to *"save the life of the nation."* The principle of self-defense is asserted; and all power is claimed for the President. This is to assert that the Constitution contemplated and tacitly provided that the President should be dictator, and all Constitutional Government be at an end, whenever he should think that "the life of the nation" is in danger. To suppose that this Court would desire argument against such a notion, would be offensive.

It comes to the plea of necessity. The Constitution knows no such word. When it pronounced its purpose "to form a perfect Union, establish justice, secure domestic tranquillity, provide for the common defense, promote the general welfare, and secure the blessings of liberty to ourselves and our posterity," it declared that to these ends the people did *"ordain and establish this Constitution."* In this form, and by these means, and by this distribution of powers, and not otherwise, did they provide for these ends; and they excluded all others. Any other means and powers are not Constitutional, but revolutionary.

The whole matter comes, then, to a few propositions. To justify this condemnation, there must have been *war* at the time of this so-called capture; not war as the old essayists describe it, beginning with the war between Cain and Abel; not a fight between two, or between thousands; not a conflict carried on with these or those weapons, or by these or those numbers of men; but war as known to international law—war carrying with it the mutual recognition of the opponents as *belligerents;* giving rise to the right of blockade of *the enemy's* ports, and affecting all other nations with the character of neutrals, until they shall have mixed themselves in the contest. War, in this, the only sense important to this question, is matter of law, and not merely matter of fact.

But the Constitution, providing specially not only for armed opposition to the law, and for insurrection, (embracing its largest proportions,) but also for *invasion by a foreign enemy,* treats as totally distinct the question of *war.* It contemplates all these contingencies. For the execution of the law, for insurrection, and for *invasion,* (an act of war,) Congress provided by the Acts of 1792, 1795, and 1807.

For the case of *war,* that is, to put the country in a state of war, with the municipal and international incidents of war, Congress did not provide; because the Constitution confided that case to Congress, as exclusively and without power of delegation, as it granted the judicial power to this Court and such inferior tribunals as Congress might create. Congress had not declared war to begin, or to exist already, at the date in question. Therefore, war did not exist; blockade did not exist; and there could be no capture for breach of blockade, or intent to break it.

The power of the Executive in respect of insurrection and invasion is derived from the Constitution, and cannot transcend the limits and provisions imposed by that instrument. The President is Commander-in-Chief of the Army and Navy. He may use these forces in case of opposition to the laws, insurrection, or invasion, as Congress has provided. But when he has thus used the whole force of the nation, he has only used a power which Congress is authorized to confer upon him in the special cases enumerated in the Constitution. *War* is reserved to the judgment of Congress itself, upon the actual case arisen.

The idea of retroaction, validating the usurpation of authority, is incompatible with the theory of this Government, founded upon a written Constitution distributing with exactness the powers which it confers.

Mr. Dana. The case of the Amy Warwick presents a single question, which may be stated thus: At the time of the capture, was it competent for the President to treat as prize of war property found on the high seas, for the sole reason that it belonged to persons residing and doing business in Richmond, Virginia?

There are certain propositions applicable to war with acknowledged foreign nations, which must first be established. An examination of the reasons on which those propositions rest will aid in determining whether the propositions are also applicable to internal wars. The general rule may be stated thus:

Property found on the high seas, subject to the ownership and control of persons who themselves reside in the territory of the enemy, and thus subject to the jurisdiction and control of the enemy, is liable to capture as prize of war.

The above cases will be found to sustain the following propositions which I suppose will not be controverted, as applicable to cases of war with a recognized foreign power, and therefore are not elaborated.

First. It is immaterial in such case, whether the owner of the property has or has not taken part in the war, or given aid or comfort to the enemy, under whose power he resides.

Second. It is immaterial whether he be or be not, by birth or naturalization, a citizen or subject of the enemy; and if he be, whether he be loyal to his sovereign, or in sympathy with and actually aiding the capturing power.

Third. He may be a subject of a neutral sovereign. He may even be a special and privileged resident, as consul of a neutral power. Still, if property subject to his ownership and control, while he so resides, is found at sea, engaged in commerce, though it be lawful commerce with neutrals, it comes under the rule. Its capture is one of the justifiable modes of coercing the enemy with whom he resides.

Fourth. The owner may even be a citizen of the country making the capture; and there may be no evidence that he is disloyal to his own country, or that his residence with the enemy is not accidental or forcible. These are immaterial inquiries. The loss to him is immaterial, in the judicial point of view. The recognized right to coerce the enemy power affects the property, as it was situated when captured. The Court can look no farther. It is a political question whether the exercise of the right shall be insisted on.

Fifth. It is not necessary to show that the property in the particular case, if not captured, or if restored, would in fact have benefitted the enemy, and that its capture would tend to the injury of the enemy. The laws of war go by general rules. Property *in a certain predicament* is condemned, the general rule being founded on the experience and concession that property so situated is or may be useful to the enemy in the war, and that the rights of neutrals and the dictates of humanity do not forbid its capture.

Sixth. It is not necessary that the property shall be at the time on a voyage to or from the enemy's country. The reason for the rule ordinarily seems stronger where the voyage is directly to the enemy's country, so that but for the capture it would have been actually subject to his control. But the rule is the same, wherever the vessel is bound. We have a right to prevent commerce and its gains on the part of persons residing in the territory of the enemy. And if the owner is friendly to the power under which he lives, the proceeds, subject to order in a foreign port, may be especially useful to that power.

I will now proceed to an examination of the reasons on which the preceding propositions rest, and afterwards consider whether those reasons are not equally applicable to an internal war.

WAR is simply the exercise of force by bodies politic, or bodies assuming to be bodies politic, against each other, for the purpose of coercion. The means and modes of doing this are called belligerent powers. The customs and opinions of modern civilization have recognized certain modes of coercing the power you are acting against as justifiable. Injury to private persons or their property is avoided as far as it reasonably can be. Wherever private property is taken or destroyed, it is because it is of such a character, or so situated, as to make its capture a justifiable means of coercing the power with which you are at war. For war is not upon the theory of punishing individuals for offences, on the contrary (except for violations of rules of war), it ignores jurisdiction, penalties and crimes, and is only a system of coercion of the power you are acting against.

If, then, the hostile power has title or direct interest in the property, as if it is public property, it is, of course, liable to capture.

If the property is of a character ordinarily used in war, and in the possession of that power, or on its way to his possession, it is liable to capture. In such case it is immaterial in whom is the title.

The hostile power has an interest in the private property of all persons living within its limits or control; for such property is a subject of taxation, contribution, confiscation and use, with or without compensation. But the humanity of modern times has abstained from the taking of private property not liable to use in war, when on land. Some of the reasons for this, are, the infinite varieties of its character, the difficulty of discriminating among these varieties, the need of much of it to support the life of non-combatant persons and animals, and, above all, the moral dangers attending searches and captures in households. But on the high seas, these reasons do not apply. Strictly personal effects are not taken. Merchandise sent to sea, is sent voluntarily, embarked by merchants on an enterprise of profit, taking the risks, is in the custody of men trained and paid for the business, and its value is usually capable of compensation in money. The sea is *res omnium*. It is the common field of war, as well as of commerce. The object of maritime commerce is the enriching of the owner by the transit over the common field, and it is the most usual object of revenue to the power under whose government the owner resides.

For these and other reasons, the rule of coercion by capture is applied to private property at sea. *If the power with which you are at war has such an interest in its transit, arrival or existence, as to make its capture one of the fair modes of coercion, you may take it. The reason why you may capture it is that it is a justifiable mode of coercing the power with which you are at war. The fact which makes it a justifiable mode of coercing that power, is that the owner is residing under his jurisdiction and control.*

It is therefore evident, from this course of reasoning, that the capture in case *of enemy property does not rest at all on any actual or constructive criminality or hostility of the owner.* Suppose him to be a neutral, he has a right to reside with your enemy, and trade to and from thence, as against all your laws and the laws of war. If he is a loyal subject of your own, and is accidentally or forcibly detained in your enemy's country, and even is struggling to get away, his property is liable to capture, on this general principle. It is for the political power alone to say whether it will forego the condemnation. The Courts must adjudicate it to be a lawful prize. If he be a born and willing subject of your enemy, your right to capture is none the greater, nor is the legal reason for the capture different, though the reason may be more gratifying to the moral sense, and the capture more satisfactory. If the trader residing there is suspected of disaffection to that power, and of affection for you, his property is all the more likely to be subjected to contributions, if not actual confiscation by your enemy. He is not his own master, still less the master of his property. He and it are under your enemy's jurisdiction and control. You may capture it and refuse to restore it to the claimant, while he so resides and the war lasts, even if you compensate or remunerate him afterwards. But that is a political question. The Courts can only condemn it, if the political power asks for its condemnation.

Such being the rules applicable to external wars, and such the reasons on which the rules rest, we come to the question whether they are not equally applicable to internal wars?

But, first, the following general rule is established on authority.

In internal wars, it is competent for the sovereign to exercise belligerent powers generally.

None of the above cited cases make any distinction among belligerent powers, but treat them all as equally open to the sovereign in case of internal war.

The reasons on which the rules respecting belligerent powers rest, are applicable to internal wars as well as to external wars.

1. The object of the sovereign is to coerce the power which is organized against him, and making war upon him.
2. This power exercises jurisdiction and control *de facto,* and claims it *de jure* over the territory. It compels obedience, and exacts allegiance from all inhabitants of the territory, without respect to their wishes. It compels each inhabitant to pay taxes and imposts upon his property, to aid in the war, and makes his property liable to contribution or confiscation. This power therefore has the same interest in the merchandise of an inhabitant of the territory at sea, for the purposes of the war, as if it were an acknowledged

sovereign. And the parent state has the same interest in the capture of the property, for the purpose of coercing the rebel power.
3. The right of the sovereign to capture it *jure belli, is not derived from any actual or presumed disloyalty or criminality of the owner*. It is equally immaterial, as in a foreign war, whether the owner is a citizen alien or friend. Whether in other respects he has taken part in the war, or on which side. Whether the rebel power considers him faithful to them, or suspects him, or has him in prison as a traitor. The test and the reason is *the predicament of the property*.
4. If the owner was hostile to the *de facto* government under which he lives, and they had actually declared the property in question to be confiscated, before its capture, it would not be doubted that it was subject to capture. But their laws and rules respecting allegiance, obedience, contribution, confiscation and taxation, govern and affect this property, *in fact* (although, the sovereign will not admit *de jure*), so long as it is out of the actual custody and control of the parent sovereign.
5. It does not follow from his residence that the owner of the property in civil wars, owes general allegiance to the sovereign. He may be an alien, or even a mercenary soldier, or a political agent of some power that has recognized the rebels as a nation.
6. Suppose a part of a sovereign's dominions are wrested from him in public war, and his enemy establishes a civil as well as military government over it, and claims it as his own, and the local authorities and a majority of the inhabitants acquiesce in the new dynasty, and it is established *de facto*, can it be doubted that it is *competent* for the sovereign to capture property of its inhabitants, at sea, as a means of coercion of the power possessing it?

It is still a political question with the sovereign, whether he will capture such property, and if condemned, whether, after a peace, he will compensate the owner, on proof of merit.

I will now consider certain objections made to the application to internal wars of the doctrine of *enemy's property*.

1. It is objected that the exercise of this power is inconsistent with the claim to civil jurisdiction over the owner.

Not more so than in foreign war. There the property of a subject is liable to capture, if it is in a certain predicament, *e. g.* if it is the peculiar product of enemy territory, and exported thence, or if the owner resides (however unwillingly) in the enemy's territory and under his jurisdiction.

2. It is objected that so the property of a loyal citizen may be condemned.

Not more so, than in foreign war. The property in the given predicament may belong to a loyal friend and subject, or an indifferent neutral. It is a political question whether the right shall be exerted over all such property, on reasons of general policy, or whether exceptions shall be made in case the owner so resident is loyal to us, or sympathizes with us.

It is worthy of remark that the sovereign can exercise these belligerent powers at first, if ever. The lapse of time gives him no new rights of war. The recognition of the rebel state as belligerent by foreign powers, confers no right on the sovereign. It only recognizes an existing right. The recognition of rebel States as sovereign by foreign powers, confers on the sovereign no new war power. The moment he ceases to claim jurisdiction over the rebel territory, the war ceases to be a civil war, and becomes an international war.

The objections really amount to this, that *war powers can never be exercised in civil wars, at any stage, except by the rebels.*

According to this theory, if the civil war is one in which each party claims to be the state, neither can exercise belligerent powers. If neither makes that claim, both may exercise them. If one claims to be the state, and the other does not, (as in this case,) the latter only can exercise them.

3. It is contended that if the owner is a traitor, his property is exempt from confiscation by the Constitution. Art. 3, sec. 3, and the Act 1790, ch. 9, sec. 24.

But there is no allegation or evidence that the claimants of this property are traitors. The Government has never treated or proceeded against them as such. And if they be traitors, they cannot compel the Government to proceed against them by indictment as traitors, and bring them within the clause of the Constitution. It cannot be admitted that the clause of the Constitution would exempt their personal property from confiscation, by proof on their part, of the commission of treason by them, if they were not proceeded against as traitors.

4. If it is objected that a traitor cannot personally be treated as a belligerent, or as levying war, I answer that the Constitution not only contemplates that treason may take the form of war, but confines treason, under our laws, to acts of such character and magnitude as amount to "*levying war* against the United States," or aiding those who are so levying war. Constitution, art. 3, sec. 3.

Having then established the position that in internal wars the sovereign may exercise belligerent powers, and that captures on the high seas on the ground of enemy's property from [form] no exception to the rule, and are equally open to him with other powers, we come to consider what must be the condition of territory on which the owner resides to make his property enemy's property within the meaning of the law of prizes.

First. What is the rule in the case of external wars?

It is not necessary that the residence should be within the regular dominions of the enemy, as they were when the war began, or as they shall have since been established by treaty or public law.

It is sufficient if the territory is in the permanent occupation of the enemy, who has established himself there, not avowedly for temporary purposes, but to hold so long as war shall enable him to hold it. If the enemy has established a civil and military government over it, and claims and exacts allegiance from all inhabitants, levies taxes, &c., the case admits of no doubt. . . .

The reason of the rule is this: The property must either be condemned or restored to the claimant. If restored, it goes under his legal control. He is a resident of the enemy's country, and this property, so restored, would go into the control of the enemy and add to his resources. The object of maritime capture is to straiten and reduce the enemy's means and resources. *Ex. gr.* if this ship had been permitted to go to Richmond, she and her cargo would have paid duties to the rebel government. They could have taken the vessel for military purposes. They could have taken the cargo for military necessities, with or without compensation as they should see fit. If they regarded the owner as an enemy, they could take it as a prize of war, or by way of confiscation.

(The law of prize of war, which condemns property that even by misfortune of a friendly owner, is impressed with a hostile character, or is going, when captured, into enemy's control, or will so go if restored, must not be confounded with municipal forfeiture or confiscation, which is usually penal or punitive for some offence of the owner.)

These reasons show that they are equally applicable to internal wars. The test is whether *the residence of the owner is under the established de facto jurisdiction and control of the enemy.*

In the Castine case, there can be no doubt that it was *competent* for our Government to capture a vessel bound into that port in that state of things, and belonging to a person residing there, without reference to whether he was, as to his general political allegiance, a citizen of the United States, or a neutral alien, or a British subject.

It is not necessary to draw a fine line as to what is to be deemed enemy's territory, for the purpose of deciding this case,—if the above principles are applicable to internal war. I suppose it will be conceded that the nature and character of the occupation of Richmond, Va., was more than sufficient to constitute it enemy's territory, within the meaning of the rule.

We are now brought to another branch of the question before the Court. Conceding that the Sovereign may exercise belligerent powers in internal wars, and that capture on the ground of enemy's property is among those powers, and that Richmond was enemy's territory—it is still contended that under our Constitution, the exercise of these powers was not made by the proper authorities, and in the proper state of things.

It is contended that the President cannot exercise war powers until Congress shall first have "declared war," or, at least, done some act recognizing that a case exists for the exercise of war powers, and of what war powers.

There is nothing in the distribution of powers under our Constitution which makes the exercise of this war power illegal, by reason of the authority under which this capture was made.

I. It is not necessary to the exercise of war powers by the President, in a case of foreign war, that there should be a preceding act of Congress declaring war.

The Constitution gives to Congress the power to "declare war."

But there are two parties to a war. War is *a state of things,* and not an act of legislative will. If a foreign power springs a war upon us by sea and land, during a recess of Congress, exercising all belligerent rights of capture, the question is, whether the President can repel war with war, and make prisoners and prizes by the army, navy and militia which he has called into service and employed to repel the invasion, in pursuance of general acts of Congress, before Congress can meet? or whether that would be illegal?

In the case of the Mexican war, there was only a subsequent recognition of a state of war by Congress; yet all the prior acts of the President were lawful acts of war.

It is enough to state the proposition. If it be not so, there is no protection to the State.

The question is not what would be the result of a conflict between the Executive and Legislature, during an actual invasion by a foreign enemy, the Legislature refusing to declare war. But it is as to the power of the President before Congress shall have acted, in case of a war actually existing. It is not as to the right *to initiate a war, as a voluntary act of sovereignty.* That is vested only in Congress.

II. In case of civil war, the President may, in the absence of any Act of Congress on the subject, meet the war by the exercise of belligerent maritime capture.

The same overwhelming reasons of necessity govern this position, as the preceding.

This position has been recognized by every Court into which the prize causes have been brought in this country, by Judge Dunlop, the District of Columbia; Judge Giles, in Maryland; Judge Marvin, in Florida; Judge Betts, in New York; Judge Sprague, in Massachusetts; Judge Cadwalader, in Pennsylvania.

There are general Acts of Congress clothing the President with power to use the army and navy to suppress insurrections. Act 1795, ch. 36, sec. 2; Act 1807, ch. 39.

And it must be admitted that the function of using the army and navy for that purpose is an Executive function. But it is contended that before they are used as belligerent powers, before captures can be made, on grounds of blockade and enemy property, Congress must pass upon the case, and determine whether the powers shall be exerted.

Now, if Congress must so adjudge in the first instance, why not throughout the war? Civil wars change their character, from day to day and place to place. Congress should be a council of war in perpetual session, to determine when, how long, and how far this or that belligerent right shall be exerted.

The function to use the army and navy being in the President, the mode of using them, within the rules of civilized warfare, and subject to established laws of Congress, must be subject to his discretion as a necessary incident to the use, in the absence of any Act of Congress controlling him.

III. There were no Acts of Congress at the time of this capture (July 10, 1861,) in any way controlling this discretion of the President.

IV. Since the capture, Congress has recognized the validity of these acts of the President.

The Act Aug. 6, 1861, ch. 63, sec. 3, legalizes, among other things, the proclamations, acts and orders of the President respecting the navy. This includes the blockades, and the orders respecting captures.

The Act March 25, 1862, ch. 50, regulating prize proceedings, in sec. 5, recognizes prize causes as "now pending" in the Courts.

The proclamations make the blockades belligerent acts, and not municipal surveillance. They are declared to be "in pursuance of the law of nations," and guaranteed to be made effective and actual, and provision is made for warning.

They had been always treated as blockades under the laws of war, by the Executive, by the Courts and by neutral powers, before the passage of this Act.

Act July 17, 1862, ch. 204, sec. 12, recognizes prize causes as *now pending*, and regulates them; and recognizes decrees of condemnation in pending cases.

The Resolution of July 17, 1862 (No. 65) regulates the custody of prize money now in the Registry of the Courts.

When these acts were passed, Congress knew that great numbers of captures had been made, solely on the ground of "enemy property;" that the President had, through the several U. S. Attorneys, asked for their condemnation; that they had been condemned, solely on that ground, in all the chief districts; that condemnation on that ground had been refused in none; and that the proceeds of prizes condemned as enemy property were in the Treasury awaiting distribution.

All the acts for the increase of the army and navy, and for raising volunteers, speak of this state of things as a "war."

It is contended that the Act of July, 1861, ch. 3, secs. 5 and 6, is an action by Congress on the subject, inconsistent with condemnation of this property.

To this, I reply:

I. The capture, in this case, was before the passage of the act. The statute does not retroact.

It is an established rule to interpret statutory law as taking effect from its passage, not as varying the law or its administration by retroactive operations.

The statute does not in its terms contemplate a retroactive effect, but rather the reverse. Congress at the time of passing it knew that the President had exercised, as of right, full belligerent power to capture at sea on all the recognized grounds of war,— contraband, breach of blockade, and enemy property; and that the Courts were entertaining prize jurisdiction on those grounds.

Under such circumstances, if Congress intended to make void all those acts, it should be expressed in terms, unless it were necessarily and unavoidably the result of the statute, construed with all the established presumptions against retroaction.

All the Courts of the United States which have acted on prize causes since the passage of the act, have construed it as not retroactive.

II. There is no inconsistency in Congress, declining to act on the exercise of war powers by the President in the past, and at the same time making new and special provisions, qualifying or altering the mode of exercising those powers after a future event.

III. To give it a retroactive effect, would render this statute inconsistent with the Act of August 6th, 1861, ch. 63, sec. 3.

IV. The Act of 13th of August, 1861, does not relate to belligerent captures and prizes. It provides for civil forfeitures and confiscations, in the exercise of civil jurisdiction.

1. The terms "captures" and "prize" are not used. The terms are "seizure," "forfeiture," and "confiscation." The former are terms of war, the latter, of civil proceedings.
2. The Secretary of the Treasury has full powers of remission of the "forfeitures," as in revenue cases, under Act of 1797, ch. 13, vol. 1, p. 506. This he may do, by general regulations of the Treasury Department. This is unknown to prize or belligerent proceedings, and inapplicable to them.
3. Sec. 9 gives jurisdiction over the "forfeitures," to certain Courts, which would be unnecessary if these were cases of prize.
4. The prize laws give an interest to the captors. Under this statute, the title rests in the United States by "forfeiture."
5. Sec. 6 introduces a principle unknown to prize law, to wit: That the whole vessel is condemned, on the sole ground that the owner of a part resided in enemy's territory. Congress can hardly have intended that.

That such is the true construction of the section, appears from the debates at the time of its passage.

This construction has been put upon it by the Courts, and the Treasury has adopted it, and authorized a remission of the forfeiture of the shares owned by residents in loyal States, under certain circumstances.

The true construction of the act, I respectfully submit to be this:

It is not an act specially providing for the present rebellion, or, in terms, alluding to it. It is a general act, applicable to all times, and to rebellions or civil wars, of every possible character. The President might or might not, at his option, apply it to the present rebellion by issuing or not his proclamation. The act is applicable, at the option of any President, to a rebellion which is carried on under State authority, and it is applicable to no other.

Property may often be so situated as to become the subject both of condemnation as prize of war, and forfeiture by civil law. In that case, the prize law has the precedence. The cases of the *Rapid, St. Lawrence, Alexander,* and *Joseph,* in [missing portion] (1 Gallison's Rep.)

In further proof that this statute was not intended to establish or regulate or modify or affect the law of prize, it is observable that it touches small portions of entire matters over which the President had been exercising the right of belligerent capture, and has exercised them still without objection by Congress.

Sec. 6 does not forfeit vessels of persons residing in the rebel States, if found in the ports of those States. A rebel man-of-war could not be forfeited under that act if found in their own ports, nor if found elsewhere, if the title was in a neutral or a citizen of a loyal State. (Nor could it be condemned under the Act of August 6th, 1861, unless the owner of the vessel knowingly allowed it to be used in the war.)

Sec. 5 forfeits no property unless passing between the designated States and the other States. If found in the rebel States, or passing between rebel States, it is not forfeited, even if it be contraband of war. (Nor would it be forfeited if found there, under the Act of August 6th, 1861, unless the owner had knowingly allowed it to be used in the war.) If found at sea, passing between two rebel States, or between a rebel State and a neutral port, it would escape. Under this statute, no property could be seized for breach of blockade, unless passing between a rebel and a loyal State; no vessel could be seized for breach of blockade unless it was not only passing between a rebel and a loyal State, but carrying cargo; and the fact that the property was contraband would not forfeit it or the vessel carrying it, if it was bound from a neutral port.

That the rebellion had come to a state requiring the exercise by us of the war powers of blockade and capture, has been passed upon by the political department of the Government,—by both the Executive and Legislative branches. That is conclusive on the Courts. President's proclamations of April 15, April 19, 1861, and April 27, May 3, 1861; Acts of Congress, Aug. 6, 1861, ch. 63, sec. 3; March 25, 1862, ch. 50; and July 17, 1862, ch. 234, sec. 12.

Whether a particular place, which the owner of the vessel inhabits, is enemy's territory, is for the Court to decide. The *Gerasimo,* (11 Moore, Pr. C., 101).

If the political department of the Government has decided that question, that is, of course, conclusive on the Courts.

If it has not been passed upon by the political department, the Court must decide it as a question of fact.

In this case, the political department decided that Richmond was in enemy territory, on the 10th of July, 1861. Proclamation of April 27, 1861, and Aug. 16, 1861; Act of Congress of Aug. 6, 1861, ch. 63, sec. 3.

We are brought, then, to three propositions:—

I. The right to capture, on the high seas, the property of persons residing in the enemy's territory, may be exercised in internal war.

II. In the present war, that right has been exercised by an authority which this Court must deem competent.

III. Richmond, Virginia, was enemy's territory, within the meaning of the law of prize, *jure belli,* at the time of this capture.

1. Neutrals may question the existence of a blockade, and challenge the legal authority of the party which has undertaken to establish it.
2. One belligerent, engaged in actual war, has a right to blockade the ports of the other, and neutrals are bound to respect that right.

3. To justify the exercise of this right, and legalize the capture of a neutral vessel for violating it, a state of actual war must exist, and the neutral must have knowledge or notice that it is the intention of one belligerent to blockade the ports of the other.
4. To create this and other belligerent rights, as against neutrals, it is not necessary that the party claiming them should be at war with a separate and independent power: the parties to a civil war are in the same predicament as two nations who engage in a contest and have recourse to arms.
5. A state of actual war may exist without any formal declaration of it by either party; and this is true of both a civil and a foreign war.
6. A civil war exists, and may be prosecuted on the same footing as if those opposing the Government were foreign invaders, whenever the regular course of justice is interrupted by revolt, rebellion, or insurrection, so that the Courts cannot be kept open.
7. The present civil war between the United States and the so called Confederate States, has such character and magnitude as to give the United States the same rights and powers which they might exercise in the case of a national or foreign war; and they have, therefore, the right *jure bello* to institute a blockade of any ports in possession of the rebellious States.
8. The proclamation of blockade by the President is of itself conclusive evidence that a state of war existed, which demanded and authorized recourse to such a measure.
9. All persons residing within the territory occupied by the hostile party in this contest, are liable to be treated as enemies, though not foreigners.
10. It is a settled rule, that a vessel in a blockaded port is presumed to have notice of a blockade as soon as it commences.
11. The proclamation of blockade having allowed fifteen days for neutrals to leave, a vessel which overstays the time is liable to capture although she was prevented by accident from getting out sooner.
12. To make a capture lawful, it is not necessary that a warning of the blockade should have been previously endorsed on the register of the captured vessel.

Mr. Justice GRIER.

There are certain propositions of law which must necessarily affect the ultimate decision of these cases, and many others, which it will be proper to discuss and decide before we notice the special facts peculiar to each.

They are, 1st. Had the President a right to institute a blockade of ports in possession of persons in armed rebellion against the Government, on the principles of international law, as known and acknowledged among civilized States?

2d. Was the property of persons domiciled or residing within those States a proper subject of capture on the sea as "enemies' property?"

I. Neutrals have a right to challenge the existence of a blockade *de facto,* and also the authority of the party exercising the right to institute it. They have a right to enter the ports of a friendly nation for the purposes of trade and commerce, but are bound to recognize the rights of a belligerent engaged in actual war, to use this mode of coercion, for the purpose of subduing the enemy.

That a blockade *de facto* actually existed, and was formally declared and notified by the President on the 27th and 30th of April, 1861, is an admitted fact in these cases.

That the President, as the Executive Chief of the Government and Commander-in-chief of the Army and Navy, was the proper person to make such notification, has not been, and cannot be disputed.

The right of prize and capture has its origin in the *"jus belli,"* and is governed and adjudged under the law of nations. To legitimate the capture of a neutral vessel or property on the high seas, a war must exist *de facto,* and the neutral must have a knowledge or notice of the intention of one of the parties belligerent to use this mode of coercion against a port, city, or territory, in possession of the other.

Let us enquire whether, at the time this blockade was instituted, a state of war existed which would justify a resort to these means of subduing the hostile force.

War has been well defined to be, "That state in which a nation prosecutes its right by force."

The parties belligerent in a public war are independent nations. But it is not necessary to constitute war, that both parties should be acknowledged as independent nations or sovereign States. A war may exist where one of the belligerents, claims sovereign rights as against the other.

Insurrection against a government may or may not culminate in an organized rebellion, but a civil war always begins by insurrection against the lawful authority of the Government. A civil war is never solemnly declared; it becomes such by its accidents—the number, power, and organization of the persons who originate and carry it on. When the party in rebellion occupy and hold in a hostile manner a certain portion of territory; have declared their independence; have cast off their allegiance; have organized armies; have commenced hostilities against their former sovereign, the world acknowledges them as belligerents, and the contest a *war.* They claim to be in arms to establish their liberty and independence, in order to become a sovereign State, while the sovereign party treats them as insurgents and rebels who owe allegiance, and who should be punished with death for their treason.

The laws of war, as established among nations, have their foundation in reason, and all tend to mitigate the cruelties and misery produced by the scourge of war. Hence the parties to a civil war usually concede to each other belligerent rights. They exchange prisoners, and adopt the other courtesies and rules common to public or national wars.

"A civil war," says Vattel, "breaks the bands of society and government, or at least suspends their force and effect; it produces in the nation two independent parties, who consider each other as enemies, and acknowledge no common judge. Those two parties, therefore, must necessarily be considered as constituting, at least for a time, two separate bodies, two distinct societies. Having no common superior to judge between them, they stand in precisely the same predicament as two nations who engage in a contest and have recourse to arms.["]

"This being the case, it is very evident that the common laws of war—those maxims of humanity, moderation, and honor—ought to be observed by both parties in every civil war. Should the sovereign conceive he has a right to hang up his prisoners as rebels, the opposite party will make reprisals, &c., &c.; the war will become cruel, horrible, and every day more destructive to the nation."

As a civil war is never publicly proclaimed, *eo nomine*, against insurgents, its actual existence is a fact in our domestic history which the Court is bound to notice and to know.

The true test of its existence, as found in the writings of the sages of the common law, may be thus summarily stated: "When the regular course of justice is interrupted by revolt, rebellion, or insurrection, so that the Courts of Justice cannot be kept open, *civil war exists* and hostilities may be prosecuted on the same footing as if those opposing the Government were foreign enemies invading the land."

By the Constitution, Congress alone has the power to declare a national or foreign war. It cannot declare war against a State, or any number of States, by virtue of any clause in the Constitution. The Constitution confers on the President the whole Executive power. He is bound to take care that the laws be faithfully executed. He is Commander-in-chief of the Army and Navy of the United States, and of the militia of the several States when called into the actual service of the United States. He has no power to initiate or declare a war either against a foreign nation or a domestic State. But by the Acts of Congress of February 28th, 1795, and 3d of March, 1807, he is authorized to called out the militia and use the military and naval forces of the United States in case of invasion by foreign nations, and to suppress insurrection against the government of a State or of the United States.

If a war be made by invasion of a foreign nation, the President is not only authorized but bound to resist force by force. He does not initiate the war, but is bound to accept the challenge without waiting for any special legislative authority. And whether the hostile party be a foreign invader, or States organized in rebellion, it is none the less a war, although the declaration of it be *"unilateral."* Lord Stowell (1 Dodson, 247) observes, "It is not the less a war on *that account*, for war may exist without a declaration on either side. It is so laid down by the best writers on the law of nations. A declaration of war by one country only, is not a mere challenge to be accepted or refused at pleasure by the other.

The battles of Palo Alto and Resaca de la Palma had been fought before the passage of the Act of Congress of May 13th, 1846, which recognized *"a state of war as existing by the act of the Republic of Mexico."* This act not only provided for the future prosecution of the war, but was itself a vindication and ratification of the Act of the President in accepting the challenge without a previous formal declaration of war by Congress.

This greatest of civil wars was not gradually developed by popular commotion, tumultuous assemblies, or local unorganized insurrections. However long may have been its previous conception, it nevertheless sprung forth suddenly from the parent brain, a Minerva in the full panoply of *war*. The President was bound to meet it in the shape it presented itself, without waiting for Congress to baptize it with a name; and no name given to it by him or them could change the fact.

It is not the less a civil war, with belligerent parties in hostile array, because it may be called an "insurrection" by one side, and the insurgents be considered as rebels or traitors. It is not necessary that the independence of the revolted province or State be acknowledged in order to constitute it a party belligerent in a war according to the law of nations. Foreign nations acknowledge it as war by a declaration of neutrality. The condition of neutrality cannot exist unless there be two belligerent parties. In the case of the *Santissma Trinidad*, (7 Wheaton, 337,) this Court say: "The Government of the United States has recognized the existence of a civil war between Spain and her colonies, and has avowed her determination to remain neutral between the parties. Each party is therefore deemed by us a belligerent nation, having, so far as concerns us, the sovereign rights of war." (See also 3 Binn., 252.)

As soon as the news of the attack on Fort Sumter, and the organization of a government by the seceding States, assuming to act as belligerents, could become known in Europe, to wit, on the 13th of May, 1861, the Queen of England issued her proclamation of neutrality, "recognizing hostilities as existing between the Government of the United States of American and *certain States* styling themselves the Confederate States of America." This was immediately followed by similar declarations or silent acquiescence by other nations.

After such an official recognition by the sovereign, a citizen of a foreign State is estopped to deny the existence of a war with all its consequences as regards neutrals. They cannot ask a Court to affect a technical ignorance of the existence of a war, which all the world acknowledges to be the greatest civil war known in the history of the human race, and thus cripple the arm of the Government and paralyze its power by subtle definitions and ingenious sophisms.

The law of nations is also called the law of nature; it is founded on the common consent as well as the common sense of the world. It contains no such anomalous doctrine as that which this Court are now for the first time desired to pronounce, to wit: That insurgents who have risen in rebellion against their sovereign, expelled her Courts, established a revolutionary government, organized armies, and commenced hostilities, are not *enemies* because they are *traitors;* and a war levied on the Government by traitors, in order to dismember and destroy it, is not a *war* because it is an "insurrection."

Whether the President in fulfilling his duties, as Commander-in-chief, in suppressing an insurrection, has met with such armed hostile resistance, and a civil war of such alarming proportions as will compel him to accord to them the character of belligerents, is a question to be decided *by him*, and this Court must be governed by the decisions and acts of the political department of the Government to which this power was entrusted. "He must determine what degree of force the crisis demands." The proclamation of blockade is itself official and conclusive evidence to the Court that a state of war existed which demanded and authorized a recourse to such a measure, under the circumstances peculiar to the case.

The correspondence of Lord Lyons with the Secretary of State admits the fact and concludes the question.

If it were necessary to the technical existence of a war, that it should have a legislative sanction, we find it in almost every act passed at the extraordinary session of the Legislature of 1861, which was wholly employed in enacting laws to enable the Government to prosecute the war with vigor and efficiency. And finally, in 1861, we find Congress *"ex majore cautela"* and in anticipation of such astute objections, passing an act "approving, legalizing, and making valid all the acts, proclamations, and orders of the President, &c., as if they had been *issued and done under the previous express authority* and direction of the Congress of the United States."

Without admitting that such an act was necessary under the circumstances, it is plain that if the President had in any manner assumed powers which it was necessary should have the authority or sanction of Congress, that on the well known principle of law, *"omnis ratihabitio retrotrahitur et mandato equiparatur,"* this ratification has operated to perfectly cure the defect. In the case of *Brown vs. United States*, (8 Cr., 131, 132, 133,) Mr. Justice Story treats of this subject, and cites numerous authorities to which we may refer to prove this position, and concludes, "I am perfectly satisfied that no subject can commence hostilities or capture property of an enemy, when the sovereign has prohibited it. But suppose he did, I would ask if the sovereign may not ratify his proceedings, and thus by a retroactive operation give validity to them?"

Although Mr. Justice Story dissented from the majority of the Court on the whole case, the doctrine stated by him on this point is correct and fully substantiated by authority.

The objection made to this act of ratification, that it is *ex post facto*, and therefore unconstitutional and void, might possibly have some weight on the trial of an indictment in a criminal Court. But precedents from that source cannot be received as authoritative in a tribunal administering public and international law.

On this first question therefore we are of the opinion that the President had a right, *jure belli*, to institute a blockade of ports in possession of the States in rebellion, which neutrals are bound to regard.

II. We come now to the consideration of the second question. What is included in the term *"enemies' property?"*

Is the property of all persons residing within the territory of the States now in rebellion, captured on the high seas, to be treated as "enemies' property" whether the owner be in arms against the Government or not

The right of one belligerent not only to coerce the other by direct force, but also to cripple his resources by the seizure or destruction of his property, is a necessary result of a state of war. Money and wealth, the products of agriculture and commerce, are said to be the sinews of war, and as necessary in its conduct as numbers and physical force. Hence it is, that the laws of war recognize the right of a belligerent to cut these sinews of the power of the enemy, by capturing his property on the high seas.

The appellants contend that the term "enemy" is properly applicable to those only who are subjects or citizens of a foreign State at war with our own. They quote from the pages of the common law, which say, "that persons who wage war against the King may be of two kinds, subjects or citizens. The former are not proper enemies, but rebels and traitors; the latter are those that come properly under the name of enemies."

They insist, moreover, that the President himself, in his proclamation, admits that great numbers of the persons residing within the territories in possession of the insurgent government, are loyal in their feelings, and forced by compulsion and the violence of the rebellious and revolutionary party and its "*de facto* government" to submit to their laws and assist in their scheme of revolution; that the acts of the usurping government cannot legally sever the bond of their allegiance; they have, therefore, a co-relative right to claim the protection of the government for their persons and property, and to be treated as loyal citizens, till legally convicted of having renounced their allegiance and made war against the Government by treasonably resisting its laws.

They contend, also, that insurrection is the act of individuals and not of a government or sovereignty; that the individuals engaged are subjects of law. That confiscation of their property can be effected only under a municipal law. That by the law of the land such confiscation cannot take place without the conviction of the owner of some offence, and finally that the secession ordinances are nullities and ineffectual to release any citizen from his allegiance to the national Government, and consequently that the Constitution and Laws of the United States are still operative over persons in all the States for punishment as well as protection.

This argument rests on the assumption of two propositions, each of which is without foundation on the established law of nations. It assumes that where a civil war exists, the party belligerent claiming to be sovereign, cannot, for some unknown reason, exercise the rights of belligerents, although the revolutionary party may. Being sovereign, he can exercise only sovereign rights over the other party. The insurgent may be killed on the battle-field or by the executioner; his property on land may be confiscated under the municipal law; but the commerce on the ocean, which supplies the rebels with means to support the war, cannot be made the subject of capture under the laws of war, because it is "*unconstitu-*

tional!!!" Now, it is a proposition never doubted, that the belligerent party who claims to be sovereign, may exercise both belligerent and sovereign rights[.] (see 4 Cr., 272.) Treating the other party as a belligerent and using only the milder modes of coercion which the law of nations has introduced to mitigate the rigors of war, cannot be a subject of complaint by the party to whom it is accorded as a grace or granted as a necessity. We have shown that a civil war such as that now waged between the Northern and Southern States is properly conducted according to the humane regulations of public law as regards capture on the ocean.

Under the very peculiar Constitution of this Government, although the citizens owe supreme allegiance to the Federal Government, they owe also a qualified allegiance to the State in which they are domiciled. Their persons and property are subject to its laws.

Hence, in organizing this rebellion, they have *acted as States* claiming to be sovereign over all persons and property within their respective limits, and asserting a right to absolve their citizens from their allegiance to the Federal Government. Several of these States have combined to form a new confederacy, claiming to be acknowledged by the world as a sovereign State. Their right to do so is now being decided by wager of battle. The ports and territory of each of these States are held in hostility to the General Government. It is no loose, unorganized insurrection, having no defined boundary or possession. It has a boundary marked by lines of bayonets, and which can be crossed only by force—south of this line is enemies' territory, because it is claimed and held in possession by an organized, hostile and belligerent power.

All persons residing within this territory whose property may be used to increase the revenues of the hostile power are, in this contest, liable to be treated as enemies, though not foreigners. They have cast off their allegiance and made war on their Government, and are none the less enemies because they are traitors.

But in defining the meaning of the term "enemies' property," we will be led into error if we refer to Fleta and Lord Coke for their definition of the word "enemy." It is a technical phrase peculiar to prize courts, and depends upon principles of public policy as distinguished from the common law.

Whether property be liable to capture as "enemies' property" does not in any manner depend on the personal allegiance of the owner. "It is the illegal traffic that stamps it as "enemies' property." It is of no consequence whether it belongs to an ally or a citizen. 8 Cr., 384. ["]The owner, *pro hac vice,* is an enemy." 3 Wash. C. C. R., 183.

The produce of the soil of the hostile territory, as well as other property engaged in the commerce of the hostile power, as the source of its wealth and strength, are always regarded as legitimate prize, without regard to the domicile of the owner, and much more so if he reside and trade within their territory.

III. We now proceed to notice the facts peculiar to the several cases submitted for our consideration. The principles which have just been stated apply alike to all of them.

I. The case of the brig *Amy Warwick*.

This vessel was captured upon the high seas by the United States gunboat Quaker City, and with her cargo was sent into the district of Massachusetts for condemnation. The brig was claimed by David Currie and others. The cargo consisted of coffee, and was claimed, four hundred bags by Edmund Davenport & Co., and four thousand seven hundred bags by Dunlap, Moncure & Co. The title of these parties as respectively claimed was conceded. All the claimants at the time of the capture, and for a long time before, were residents of Richmond, Va., and were engaged in business there. Consequently, their property was justly condemned as "enemies' property."

The claim of Phipps & Co. for their advance was allowed by the Court below. That part of the decree was not appealed from and is not before us. The case presents no question but that of enemies' property.

The decree below is affirmed with costs.

II. The case of the *Hiawatha*.

The Court below in decreeing against the claimants proceeded upon the ground that the cargo was shipped after notice of the blockade.

The fact is clearly established, and if there were no qualifying circumstances, would well warrant the decree. But after a careful examination of the correspondence of the State and Navy Departments, found in the record, we are not satisfied that the British Minister erred in the construction he put upon it, which was that a license was given to all vessels in the blockaded ports to depart with their cargoes within fifteen days after the blockade was established, whether the cargoes were taken on board before or after the notice of the blockade. All reasonable doubts should be resolved in favor of the claimants. Any other course would be inconsistent with the right administration of the law and the character of a just Government. But the record discloses another ground upon which the decree must be sustained. On the 19th of April the President issued a proclamation announcing his intention to blockade the ports of the several States therein named.

On the 27th of April he issued a further proclamation announcing his intention to blockade the ports of Virginia and North Carolina in addition to those of the States named in the previous one. On the 30th of April Commodore Pendergrast issued his proclamation announcing the blockade as established. These proclamations were communicated to the British Minister as soon as they were issued. On the 5th of May the British Consul at Richmond wrote to Lord Lyons that he had advised those representing the owners of the Hiawatha that there would be no difficulty in her leaving in ballast. He added, *"but to this they will not consent."* On the 8th of May Lord Lyons made an application to the Secretary of State relative to this vessel. The matter was referred to the Navy Department. On the same day the Secretary of the Navy replied: "Fifteen days have been specified as a limit for neutrals to leave the ports *after actual blockade has commenced*, with or without cargo, and there are yet five or six days for neutrals to leave: with proper diligence on the part of persons interested *I see no reason for exemption to any."* Here was a distinct warning that the vessel must leave within the time limited, *after the commencement of the blockade.* On the 10th of May she completed the discharge of her cargo.

On the next day she commenced lading for her outer voyage, and by working night and day, on the 15th of May she had taken in a full cargo of cotton and tobacco. On that day the British Consul gave her a certificate, wherein he referred to the proclamation of the 27th of April, "in which it was announced that a blockade would be enforced of the ports of Virginia," and added, that "the best information attainable" "pointed to the 2d of May as the day when an efficient blockade was supposed to have been established."

On the 16th of May she was ready for sea, but there was no steam-tug in port to tow her down the river. At six o'clock, P. M., on the 17th she was taken in tow by the steam-tug David Currie. The tug had not sufficient power and the Hiawatha came to anchor again. On the 18th, at six o'clock, A. M., she was taken in tow by the steam-tug William Allison and towed out to sea. On the 20th of May she was captured in Hampton Roads, off Fortress Monroe, and taken with her cargo into the Southern District of New York for condemnation.

The energy with which the labor of lading her was pressed evinces the consciousness of those concerned of the peril of delay beyond the time limited by the proclamation for her departure. The time was fifteen days *from the establishment of the blockade.* The blockade was effectual on the 30th of April.

There is no controversy upon the subject. The fifteen days expired on the 15th of May—the day she completed her lading. A vessel being in a blockaded port is presumed to have notice of the blockade as soon as it commences. This is a settled rule in the law of nations.

The certificate of the Consul states, that according to his information the blockade commenced on the 2d of May. It is not easy to imagine how he could have arrived at this conclusion. The James river is a great commercial thoroughfare. It would seem that news of so important an event must have swept up its waters to Richmond, as news of interest spreads along the streets of a city. Such circumstances must have immediately become known to the parties as were sufficient to put them upon inquiry, and were therefore equivalent to full notice. But, conceding the 2d of May to be the day from which the computation is to be made, then, the fifteen days expired on the 17th of May. Her voyage down the river was not effectively begun until the 18th of May. This was after the expiration of the time allowed. In either view she became delinquent, and was guilty of a breach of the blockade. The proclamation allowed fifteen days—not fifteen days, *and until a steam-tug could be procured.* The difficulty of procuring a tug was one of the accidents which must have been foreseen and should have been provided for. Those concerned, notwithstanding the warnings they received, in their eagerness to realize the profits of a full cargo, took the hazards of the adventure and must now bear the consequences. If she could overstay the time limited for a short period she could for a long one. Whatever the excess of time, the principle involved is the same.

It is insisted for the claimants that according to the President's proclamation on the 19th of April, the Hiawatha was not liable to capture, until "the commander of one of the blockading vessels" had "duly warned" her, endorsed "on her register the date and fact of such warning," and she had again attempted "to leave the blockaded port." To this proposition there are several answers:

1st. There is no such provision in the proclamation of the 27th of April touching *the ports of Virginia*.

It simply announces that a blockade of those ports would be established.

2d. The proclamation of Commodore Pendergrast limits the warning to those who should approach the line of the blockade in ignorance of its existence. This action of the naval commander has not been disavowed by his Government, and is conclusive in a Prize Court. The warning proposed by this proclamation is according to the law of nations, and it is all that the law requires.

3d. If the provision referred to in the Proclamation of the 19th of April be applicable to the ports of Virginia, it must be considered in the light of the surrounding circumstances.

It was intended for the benefit of the innocent, not of the guilty. It would be absurd to warn parties who had full previous knowledge. According to the construction contended for, a vessel seeking to evade the blockade might approach and retreat any number of times, and when caught her captors could do nothing but warn her and endorse the warning upon her registry. The same process might be repeated at every port on the blockaded coast. Indeed, according to the literal terms of the proclamation, the Alabama might approach, and if captured, insist upon the warning and endorsement of her registry, and then upon her discharge. A construction drawing after it consequences so absurb [sic], is a "*felo de se.*"

The cargo must share the fate of the vessel.

The decree below is affirmed with costs.

III. The case of the Brilliante, No. 134, presents but little difficulty. This was a Mexican vessel, with a cargo belonging to Mexican citizens, seized on the 23d of June, 1861, in Biloxi Bay, in an attempt to escape from New Orleans by running the blockade, which had been established there by an efficient force on the 15th of May preceding. She was carried by the captors to Key West, where she was libelled in the District Court of the United States for the Southern District of Florida, and condemned with her cargo as prize of war.

From the deposition of Don Rafael Preciat, who was part owner of the vessel and partner in the ownership of the cargo, and also was on board from the time she left her home port at Campeche until her capture, the following facts may be gathered.

In approaching New Orleans with a cargo from Sisal, she found the United States ship-of-war Brooklyn blockading the mouth of the Mississippi River at

Pass a Loutre, and was by the officer of that vessel informed of the blockade and forbid to enter. The witness had a son at Spring Hill College, near Mobile, whom he desired to get away; and the Commander of the Brooklyn gave him a letter to the Commander of the Niagara, recommending that he should be permitted to land and get his son. On leaving the Brooklyn she started along the coast in the direction of the Niagara, but instead of seeking that vessel, she evaded her, and went to New Orleans by way of Lake Ponchartrain. At New Orleans she discharged her cargo and took in another, and in attempting to escape by the way she intended, was captured as already stated.

Some attempt has been made to excuse her entrance to New Orleans by showing that the crew refused to proceed towards Mobile; but this is immaterial, as her condemnation is not for her successful entrance, but for her unsuccessful attempt to escape.

It is also urged that she was entitled to warning at the time of her capture, by virtue of the provision in the President's proclamation establishing the blockade. But whatever may be the sound construction of that provision in reference to warning vessels in its application to vessels which had notice of the blockade, the question does not arise in this case; because, from the statement of the owner of the vessel himself, she was warned by the officer of the Brooklyn.

The fact that the vessel's register was not produced by either party to show a warning endorsed on it, can make no difference. It cannot be supposed that such endorsement on the ship's register is to be the only evidence of warning; for if this were admitted, the vessel would only have to destroy her register, and with it the only evidence in which she could be condemned, or she would only need to keep several registers and destroy the one having the endorsement.

We entertain no doubt that this vessel and cargo were justly condemned as neutral property for running the blockade, of which she had been fairly warned, and which she had once successfully violated.

The judgment is therefore affirmed.

The case of the Crenshaw, No. 163, on the other hand, presents the question of "enemies' property," pure and simple. This vessel was seized in Hampton Roads on the 17th of May, 1861, by the blockading force at that point under flag-officer Stringham, and was carried as a prize of war into New York. The vessel and the larger part of the cargo were, at the time of the capture, owned by citizens of the State of Virginia, residing in Richmond; and the vessel had on board, among her papers, a clearance signed on the 14th of May by R. H. Lortin, Collector of the Port of Richmond, of the Confederate States of America.

Upon the principles already settled, the vessel and such parts of her cargo as came within the description of enemies' property, were rightfully condemned. It is however claimed that ten tierces of tobacco strips shipped by Ludlam & Watson at Richmond, to be delivered to shipper's order at Liverpool, and thirty tierces of tobacco strips shipped by W. O. Clark at Richmond, to order of Messrs. Sam'l

Irven or assigns, Liverpool, are not enemies' property, and should be restored to claimants.

The claim for the ten tierces, as interposed by Henry Ludlam in behalf of himself and others, and the statement of the claimant's petition, are sworn to by Gustave Henikin, who holds the bill of lading, which is endorsed—"deliver to Ludlam & Henikin, for Chas. Lear & Sons, Liverpool. Ludlam & Watson."

Mr. Henikin states that his partner, Henry Ludlam, was in Europe, that Watson, (the partner of Ludlam & Watson, resident in Richmond,) was out of the jurisdiction of the Court, and that his knowledge of the facts embraced in the petition is derived from his connections with it as partner of Ludlam, and from correspondence and business relations with the shippers. The extent of his knowledge thus set forth is not very satisfactory nor is the claim stated in a manner to relieve it of any embarrassment growing out of this fact. He sets forth substantially that Ludlam & Watson, the shippers, was a firm composed of Henry Ludlam, a citizen and resident of Rhode Island, and G. F. Watson, a citizen and resident of Richmond, Va., doing business in Richmond; and that Henry Ludlam was also doing business in New York in partnership with Gustave Henikin, under the style of Ludlam & Henikin, and that Lear & Sons were a mercantile partnership, composed of British subjects, residing in Liverpool. Then, speaking in behalf of all these parties, the petitioner says, they are owners of the ten tierces of tobacco, and *bona fide* owners of the bill of lading for the same, and that said tobacco was from the time of the shipment on board of the Crenshaw in the Port of Richmond, and still is the property of the claimants.

It will be seen at once, that the statement does not profess to set out what are the distinct interests of each individual in this property, nor the separate interests of the three partnership firms thus claiming it. Nor is there any attempt to show how any person beside Ludlam & Watson of Richmond, who were the shippers, acquired any interest in it. It is a joint claim on the part of all the persons mentioned, all of whom are asserted to be *bona fide* holders of the bill of lading. It is perfectly consistent with all that was stated, that Ludlam & Watson were the real owners of the property. The bill of lading, which is to shipper's order or assigns, throws no light on the subject, and there is not a particle of other testimony in reference to the claim in the record. The Court decreed that the interest of Lear & Sons in the ten tierces of tobacco be restored to them and that they pay costs, unless they furnished further proof that the property was *bona fide* neutral. They failed to furnish better proof and appealed on account of the costs.

We are of the opinion that the decree does them no injustice, and in the doubtful circumstances in which this claim stands, on their own statement, should have had great hesitation in giving them the property if the captors had appealed.

In reference to the claim of Ludlam, we are not sufficiently advised of what it is by his pleading or by the proof, to set apart for him, if it were just. But we are of the opinion that the firm of Ludlam & Watson, doing business in Richmond, where Watson, the active member of the firm, resided, must be ruled by his status in reference to the property of the firm under his control in the enemy country.

The property was, through his residence in that country, subjected to the power of the enemy, and comes within the category of "enemies' property."

There is more difficulty in reference to the claim of Irvin & Co. to the thirty tierces of tobacco strips.

It very clearly appears that Irvin & Co., claimants, purchased this tobacco before the war broke out, with their own means, which were then in Richmond, and that they are citizens and residents of New York.

It is claimed that the property should be condemned on the ground that the transaction constitutes an illegal traffic with the enemy. This certainly cannot be held to apply to the purchase of the tobacco, which was bought and paid for before hostilities commenced. If it is intended to apply the principle of illegal traffic to the attempt to withdraw the property from the enemy country, it would seem that the order of the Secretary of the Navy allowing fifteen days for all vessels to withdraw from the blockaded ports, with or without cargo, should be held to apply to the property of one of our own citizens, residing in New York, already bought and paid for, as well as to any neutral cargo. If this be correct, it would seem that the property of Irvin & Co. should be restored to them as that of Laurie, Son & Co. was.

The right of Scott & Clarke to commissions on profits really constituted no interest in the property, and presents no cognizable feature in the case.

This property will therefore be restored to the claimants.

Mr. Justice NELSON, dissenting.

The property in this case, vessel and cargo, was seized by a Government vessel on the 20th of May, 1861, in Hampton Roads, for an alleged violation of the blockade of the ports of the State of Virginia. The Hiawatha was British vessel and the cargo belonged to British subjects. The vessel had entered the James River before the blockade, on her way to City Point, upwards of one hundred miles from the mouth, where she took in her cargo. She finished loading on the 15th of May, but was delayed from departing on her outward voyage till the 17th for want of a tug to tow her down the river. She arrived at Hampton Roads on the 20th, where, the blockade in the meantime having been established, she was met by one of the ships and the boarding officer endorsed on her register, "ordered not to enter any port in Virginia, or south of it." This occurred some three miles above the place where the flag ship was stationed, and the boarding officer directed the master to heave his ship to when he came abreast of the flag ship, which was done, when she was taken in charge as prize.

On the 30th April, flag officer Pendergrast, U. S. ship Cumberland, off Fortress Monroe, in Hampton Roads, gave the following notice: "All vessels passing the capes of Virginia, coming from a distances and ignorant of the proclamation, (the proclamation of the President of the 27th of April that a blockade would be established,) will be warned off; and those passing Fortress Monroe will be required to anchor under the guns of the fort and subject themselves to an examination."

The Hiawatha, while engaged in putting on board her cargo at City Point, became the subject of correspondence between the British Minister and the Secretary of State, under date of the 8th and 9th of May, which drew from the Secretary of the Navy a letter of the 9th, in which, after referring to the above notice of the flag officer Pendergrast, and stating that it had been sent to the Baltimore and Norfolk papers, and by one or more published, advised the Minister that fifteen days had been fixed as a limit for neutrals to leave the ports after an actual blockade had commenced, with or without cargo. The inquiry of the British Minister had referred not only to the time that a vessel would be allowed to depart, but whether it might be laden within the time. This vessel, according to the advice of the Secretary, would be entitled to the whole of the 15th of May to leave City Point, her port of lading. As we have seen, her cargo was on board within the time, but the vessel was delayed in her departure for want of a tug to tow her down the river.

We think it very clear upon all the evidence that there was no intention on the part of the master to break the blockade, that the seizure under the circumstances was not warranted, and upon the merits that the ship and cargo should have been restored.

Another ground of objection to this seizure is, that the vessel was entitled to a warning endorsed on her papers by an officer of the blockading force, according to the terms of the proclamation of the President; and that she was not liable to capture except for the second attempt to leave the port.

The proclamation, after certain recitals, not material in this branch of the case, provides as follows: the President has "deemed it advisable to set on foot a blockade of the ports within the States aforesaid, (the States referred to in the recitals,) in pursuance of the laws of the United States and of the law of nations, in such case made and provided." "If, therefore, with a view to violate such blockade, a vessel shall approach or shall attempt to leave either of said ports, she will be duly warned by the commander of one of the blockading vessels, who will endorse on her register the fact and date of such warning, and if the same vessel shall again attempt to enter or leave the blockaded port, she will be captured and sent to the nearest convenient port for such proceedings against her and her cargo, as prize, as may be deemed advisable."

The proclamation of the President of the 27th of April extended that of the 19th to the States of Virginia and North Carolina.

It will be observed that this warning applies to vessels attempting to enter or leave the port, and is therefore applicable to the Hiawatha.

We must confess that we have not heard any satisfactory answer to the objection founded upon the terms of this proclamation.

It has been said that the proclamation, among other grounds, as stated on its face, is founded on the "law of nations," and hence draws after it the law of blockade as found in that code, and that a warning is dispensed with in all cases where the vessel is chargeable with previous notice or knowledge that the port is blockaded. But the obvious answer to the suggestion is, that there is no necessary connection between the authority upon which the proclamation is issued and the terms prescribed as the condition of its penalties or enforcement, and, besides, if founded upon the law of nations, surely it was competent for the President to mitigate the rigors of that code and apply to neutrals the more lenient and friendly principles of international law. We do not doubt but that considerations of this character influenced the President in prescribing these favorable terms in respect to neutrals; for, in his message a few months later to Congress, (4th of July,) he observes: "a proclamation was issued for closing the ports of the insurrectionary districts" (not by blockade, but) "by proceedings *in the nature of a blockade.*"

This view of the proclamation seems to have been entertained by the Secretary of the Navy, under whose orders it was carried into execution. In his report to the President, 4th July, the observes, after referring to the necessity of interdicting commerce at those ports where the Government were not permitted to collect the revenue, that "in the performance of this domestic municipal duty the property and interests of foreigners became, to some extent, involved in our home questions, and with a view of extending to them every comity that circumstances would justify, the rules of blockade were adopted, and, as far as practicable, made applicable to the cases that occurred under this embargo or non-intercourse of the insurgent States. The commanders, he observes, were directed to permit the vessels of foreigners to depart within fifteen days as in case of actual effective blockade, and their vessels were not to be seized unless they attempted, after having been once warned off, to enter an interdicted port in disregard of such warning."

The question is not a new one in this Court. The British Government had notified the United States of the blockade of certain ports in the West Indies, but "not to consider blockades as existing, unless in respect to particular ports which may be actually invested, and, then, not to capture vessels bound to such ports, unless they shall have been previously warned not to enter them."

The question arose upon this blockade in *Mar. In. Co. vs. Woods, (6 Cranch, 29.)*

Chief Justice Marshall, in delivering the opinion of the Court, observed, "The words of the order are not satisfied by any previous notice which the vessel may have obtained, otherwise than by her being warned off. This is a technical term which is well understood. It is not satisfied by notice received in any other manner. The effect of this order is, that a vessel cannot be placed in the situation of one having notice of the blockade until she is warned off. It gives her a right to inquire of the blockading squadron, if she shall not receive this warning from one capable of giving it, and, consequently, dispenses with her making that inquiry elsewhere. While this order was in force a neutral vessel might lawfully sail for a blockaded port, knowing it to be blockaded, and being found sailing towards such port, would not constitute an attempt to break the blockade until she should be warned off."

We are of opinion, therefore, that, according to the very terms of the proclamation, neutral ships were entitled to a warning by one of the blockading squadron and could be lawfully seized only on the second attempt to enter or leave the port.

It is remarkable, also, that both the President and the Secretary, in referring to the blockade, treat the measure, not as a blockade under the law of nations, but as a restraint upon commerce at the interdicted ports under the municipal laws of the Government.

Another objection taken to the seizure of this vessel and cargo is, that there was no existing war between the United States and the States in insurrection within the meaning of the law of nations, which drew after it the consequences of a public or civil war. A contest by force between independent sovereign States is called a public war; and, when duly commenced by proclamation or otherwise, it entitles both of the belligerent parties to all the rights of war against each other, and as respects neutral nations. Chancellor Kent observes, "Though a solemn declaration, or previous notice to the enemy, be now laid aside, it is essential that some formal public act, proceeding directly from the competent source, should announce to the people at home their new relations and duties growing out of a state of war, and which should equally apprize neutral nations of the fact, to enable them to conform their conduct to the rights belonging to the new state of things." "Such an official act operates from its date to legalize all hostile acts, in like manner as a treaty of peace operates from its date to annul them." He further observes, "as war cannot lawfully be commenced on the part of the United States without an act of Congress, such act is, of course, a formal notice to all the world, and equivalent to the most solemn declaration."

The legal consequences resulting from a state of war between two countries at this day are well understood, and will be found described in every approved work on the subject of international law. The people of the two countries become immediately the enemies of each other—all intercourse commercial or otherwise between them unlawful—all contracts existing at the commencement of the war suspended, and all made during its existence utterly void. The insurance of enemies' property, the drawing of bills of exchange or purchase on the enemies' country, the remission of bills or money to it are illegal and void. Existing partnerships between citizens or subjects of the two countries are dissolved, and, in fine, interdiction of trade and intercourse direct or indirect is absolute and complete by the mere force and effect of war itself. All the property of the people of the two countries on land or sea are subject to capture and confiscation by the adverse party as enemies' property, with certain qualifications as it respects property on land, all treaties between the belligerent parties are annulled. The ports of the respective countries may be blockaded, and letters of marque and reprisal granted as rights of war, and the law of prizes as defined by the law of nations comes into full and complete operation, resulting from maritime captures, *jure belli*. War also effects a change in the mutual relations of all States or countries, not directly, as in the case of the belligerents, but immediately and indirectly, though they take no part in the contest, but remain neutral.

This great and pervading change in the existing condition of a country, and in the relations of all her citizens or subjects, external and internal, from a state of peace, is the immediate effect and result of a state of war: and hence the same code which has annexed to the existence of a war all these disturbing consequences has declared that the right of making war belongs exclusively to the supreme or sovereign power of the State.

This power in all civilized nations is regulated by the fundamental laws or municipal constitution of the country.

By our constitution this power is lodged in Congress. Congress shall have power "to declare war, grant letters of marque and reprisal, and make rules concerning captures on land and water."

We have thus far been considering the status of the citizens or subjects of a country at the breaking out of a public war when recognized or declared by the competent power.

In the case of a rebellion or resistance of a portion of the people of a country against the established government, there is no doubt, if in its progress and enlargement the government thus sought to be overthrown sees fit, it may by the competent power recognize or declare the existence of a state of civil war, which will draw after it all the consequences and rights of war between the contending parties as in the case of a public war. Mr. Wheaton observes, speaking of civil war, "But the general usage of nations regards such a war as entitling both the contending parties to all the rights of war as against each other, and even as respects neutral nations." It is not to be denied, therefore, that if a civil war existed between that portion of the people in organized insurrection to overthrow this Government at the time this vessel and cargo were seized, and if she was guilty of a violation of the blockade, she would be lawful prize of war. But before this insurrection against the established Government can be dealt with on the footing of a civil war, within the meaning of the law of nations and the Constitution of the United States, and which will draw after it belligerent rights, it must be recognized or declared by the war-making power of the Government. No power short of this can change the legal status of the Government or the relations of its citizens from that of peace to a state of war, or bring into existence all those duties and obligations of neutral third parties growing out of a state of war. The war power of the Government must be exercised before this changed condition of the Government and people and of neutral third parties can be admitted. There is no difference in this respect between a civil or a public war.

We have been more particular upon this branch of the case that would seem to be required, on account of any doubt or difficulties attending the subject in view of the approved works upon the law of nations or from the adjudication of the courts, but, because some confusion existed on the argument as to the definition of a war that drew after it all the rights of prize of war. Indeed, a great portion of the argument proceeded upon the ground that these rights could be called into operation—enemies' property captured—blockades set on foot and all the rights of war enforced in prize courts—by a species of war unknown to the law of nations and to the Constitution of the United States.

An idea seemed to be entertained that all that was necessary to constitute a war was organized hostility in the district of country in a state of rebellion—that conflicts on land and on sea—the taking of towns and capture of fleets—in fine, the magnitude and dimensions of the resistance against the Government—constituted war with all the belligerent rights belonging to civil war. With a view to enforce this idea, we had, during the argument, an imposing historical detail of the several measures adopted by the Confederate States to enable them to resist the authority of the general Government, and of many bold and daring acts of resistance and of conflict. It was said that war was to be ascertained by looking at the armies and navies or public force of the contending parties, and the battles lost and won—that in the language of one of the learned counsel, "Whenever the situation of opposing hostilities has assumed the proportions and pursued the methods of war, then peace is driven out, the ordinary authority and administration of law are suspended, and war in fact and by necessity is the *status* of the nation until peace is restored and the laws resumed their dominion."

Now, in one sense, no doubt this is war, and may be a war of the most extensive and threatening dimensions and effects, but it is a statement simply of its existence in a material sense, and has no relevancy or weight when the question is what constitutes war in a legal sense, in the sense of the law of nations, and of the Constitution of the United States? For it must be a war in this sense to attach to it all the consequences that belong to belligerent rights. Instead, therefore, of inquiring after armies and navies, and victories lost and won, or organized rebellion against the general Government, the inquiry should be into the law of nations and into the municipal fundamental laws of the Government. For we find there that to constitute a civil war in the sense in which we are speaking, before it can exist, in contemplation of law, it must be recognized or declared by the sovereign power of the State, and which sovereign power by our Constitution is lodged in the Congress of the United States—civil war, therefore, under our system of government, can exist only by an act of Congress, which requires the assent of two of the great departments of the Government, the Executive and Legislative.

We have thus far been speaking of the war power under the Constitution of the United States, and as known and recognized by the law of nations. But we are asked, what would become of the peace and integrity of the Union in case of an insurrection at home or invasion from abroad if this power could not be exercised by the President in the recess of Congress, and until that body could be assembled?

The framers of the Constitution fully comprehended this question, and provided for the contingency. Indeed, it would have been surprising if they had not, as a rebellion had occurred in the State of Massachusetts while the Convention was in session, and which had become so general that it was quelled only by calling upon the military power of the State. The Constitution declares that Congress shall have power "to provide for calling forth the militia to execute the laws of the Union, suppress insurrections, and repel invasions." Another clause, "that the President shall be Commander-in-chief of the Army and Navy of the United States, and of the militia of the several States when called into the actual service of United States;" and, again, "He shall take care that the laws shall be faithfully executed." Congress passed laws on this subject in 1792 and 1795. 1 United States Laws, pp. 264, 424.

The last Act provided that whenever the United States shall be invaded or be in imminent danger of invasion from a foreign nation, it shall be lawful for the President to call forth such number of the militia most convenient to the place of danger, and in case of insurrection in any State against the Government thereof, it shall be lawful for the President, on the application of the Legislature of such State, if in session, or if not, of the Executive of the State, to call forth such number of militia of any other State or States as he may judge sufficient to suppress such insurrection.

The 2d section provides, that when the laws of the United States shall be opposed, or the execution obstructed in any State by combinations too powerful to be suppressed by the course of judicial proceedings, it shall be lawful for the President to call forth the militia of such State, or of any other State or States as may be necessary to suppress such combinations; and by the Act 3 March, 1807, (2 U. S. Laws, 443,) it is provided that in case of insurrection or obstruction of the laws, either in the United States or of any State of Territory, where it is lawful for the President to call forth the militia for the purpose of suppressing such insurrection, and causing the laws to be executed, it shall be lawful to employ for the same purpose such part of the land and naval forces of the United States as shall be judged necessary.

It will be seen, therefore, that ample provision has been made under the Constitution and laws against any sudden and unexpected disturbance of the public peace from insurrection at home or invasion from abroad. The whole military and naval power of the country is put under the control of the President to meet the emergency. He may call out a force in proportion to its necessities, one regiment or fifty, one ship-of-war or any number at his discretion. If, like the insurrection in the State of Pennsylvania in 1793, the disturbance is confined to a small district of country, a few regiments of the militia may be sufficient to suppress it. If of the dimension of the present, when it first broke out, a much larger force would be required. But whatever its numbers, whether great or small, that may be required, ample provision is here made; and whether great or small, the nature of the power is the same. It is the exercise of a power under the municipal laws of the country and not under the law of nations; and, as we see, furnishes the most ample means of repelling attacks from abroad or suppressing disturbances at home until the assembling of Congress, who can, if it be deemed necessary, bring into operation the war power, and thus change the nature and character of the contest. Then, instead of being carried on under the municipal law of 1795, it would be under the law of nations, and the Acts of Congress as war measures with all the rights of war.

It has been argued that the authority conferred on the President by the Act of 1795 invests him with the war power. But the obvious answer is, that it proceeds from a different clause in the Constitution and which is given for different purposes and objects, namely, to execute the laws and preserve the public order and tranquillity of the country in a time of peace by preventing or suppressing any public disorder or disturbance by foreign or domestic enemies. Certainly, if there is any force in this argument, then we are in a state of war with all the rights of war, and all the penal consequences attending it every time this power is exercised by calling out a military force to execute the laws or to suppress insurrection or rebellion; for the nature of the power cannot depend upon the numbers called out. If so, what numbers will constitute war and what numbers will not? It has also been argued that this power of the President from necessity should be construed as vesting him with the war power, or the Republic might greatly suffer or be in danger from the attacks of the hostile party before the assembling to Congress. But we have seen that the whole military and naval force are in his hands under the municipal laws of the country. He can meet the adversary upon land and water with all the forces of the Government. The truth is, this idea of the existence of any necessity for clothing the President with the war power, under the Act of 1795, is simply a monstrous exaggeration; for, besides having the command of the whole of the army and navy, Congress can be assembled within any thirty days, if the safety of the country requires that the war power shall be brought into operation.

The Acts of 1795 and 1805 did not, and could not under the Constitution, confer on the President the power of declaring war against a State of this Union, or of deciding that war existed, and upon that ground authorize the capture and confiscation of the property of every citizen of the State whenever it was found on the waters. The laws of war, whether the war be civil or *inter gents*, as we have seen, convert every citizen of the hostile State into a public enemy, and treat him accordingly, whatever may have been his previous conduct. This great power over the business and property of the citizen is reserved to the legislative department by the express words of the Constitution. It cannot be delegated or surrendered to the Executive. Congress alone can determine whether war exists or should be declared; and until they have acted, no citizen of the State can be punished in his person or property, unless he has committed some offence against a law of Congress passed before the act was committed, which made it a crime, and defined the punishment. The penalty of confiscation for the acts of others with which he had no concern cannot lawfully be inflicted.

In the breaking out of a rebellion against the established Government, the usage in all civilized countries, in its first stages, is to suppress it by confining the public forces and the operations of the Government against those in rebellion, and at the same time extending encouragement and support to the loyal people with a view to their co-operation in putting down the insurgents. This course is not only the dictate of wisdom, but of justice. This was the practice of England in Monmouth's rebellion in the reign of James the Second, and in the rebellions of 1715 and 1745, by the Pretender and his son, and also in the beginning of the rebellion of the Thirteen Colonies of 1776. It is a personal war against the individuals engaged in resisting the authority of the Government. This was the character of the war of our Revolution till the passage of the Act of the Parliament of Great Britain of the 16th of George Third, 1776. By that act all trade and commerce with the Thirteen Colonies was interdicted and all ships and cargoes belonging to the inhabitants subjected to forfeiture as if the same were the ships and effects of open enemies. From this time the war became a territorial civil war between the contending parties, with all the rights of war known to the law of nations. Down to this period the war was personal against the rebels, and encouragement and support constantly extended to the loyal subjects who adhered to their allegiance, and although the power to make war existed exclusively in the King, and of course this personal war carried on under his authority, and a partial exercise of the war power, no captures of the ships or cargo of the rebels as enemies' property on the sea, or confiscation in Prize Courts as rights of war, took place until after the passage of the Act of Parliament. Until the passage of the act the American subjects were not regarded as enemies in the sense of the law of nations. The distinction between the loyal and rebel subjects was constantly observed. That act provided for the capture and confiscation as prize of their property as if the same were the proper[ty] "of open enemies." For the first time the distinction was obliterated.

So the war carried on by the President against the insurrectionary districts in the Southern States, as in the case of the King of Great Britain in the American Revolution, was a personal war against those in rebellion, and with encouragement and support of loyal citizens with a view to their co-operation and aid in suppressing the insurgents, with this difference, as the war-making power belonged to the King, he might have recognized or declared the war at the beginning to be a civil war, which would draw after it all the rights of a belligerent, but in the case of the President no such power existed: the war therefore from necessity was a personal war, until Congress assembled and acted upon this state of things.

Down to this period the only enemy recognized by the Government was the persons engaged in the rebellion, all others were peaceful citizens, entitled to all the privileges of citizens under the Constitution. Certainly it cannot rightfully be said that the President has the power to convert a loyal citizen into a belligerent enemy or confiscate his property as enemy's property.

Congress assembled on the call for an extra session the 4th of July, 1861, and among the first acts passed was one in which the President was authorized by proclamation to interdict all trade and intercourse between all the inhabitants of States in insurrection and the rest of the United States, subjecting vessel and cargo to capture and condemnation as prize, and also to direct the capture of any ship or vessel belonging in whole or in part to any inhabitant of a State whose inhabitants are declared by the proclamation to be in a state of insurrection, found at sea or in any part of the rest of the United States. Act of Congress of 13th of July, 1861, secs. 5, 6. The 4th section also authorized the President to close any port in a Collection District obstructed so that the revenue could not be collected, and provided for the capture and condemnation of any vessel attempting to enter.

The President's Proclamation was issued on the 16th of August following, and embraced Georgia, North and South Carolina, part of Virginia, Tennessee, Alabama, Louisiana, Texas, Arkansas, Mississippi and Florida.

This Act of Congress, we think, recognized a state of civil war between the Government and the Confederate States, and made it territorial. The Act of Parliament of 1776, which converted the rebellion of the Colonies into a civil territorial war, resembles, in its leading features, the act to which we have referred. Government in recognizing or declaring the existence of a civil war between itself and a portion of the people in insurrection usually modifies its effects with a view as far as practicable to favor the innocent and loyal citizens or subjects involved in the war. It is only the urgent necessities of the Government, arising from the magnitude of the resistance, that can excuse the conversion of the personal into a territorial war, and thus confound all distinction between guilt and innocence; hence the modification in the Act of Parliament declaring the territorial war.

It is found in the 44th section of the Act, which for the encouragement of well affected persons, and to afford speedy protection to those desirous of returning to their allegiance, provided for declaring such inhabitants of any colony, county, town, port, or place, at peace with his majesty, and after such notice by proclamation there should be no further captures. The Act of 13th of July provides that the President may, in his discretion, permit commercial intercourse with any such part of a State or section, the inhabitants of which are declared to be in a state of insurrection (§ 5), obviously intending to favor loyal citizens and encourage others to return to their loyalty. And the 8th section provides that the Secretary of the Treasury may mitigate or remit the forfeitures and penalties incurred under the act. The Act of 31st July is also one of a kindred character. That appropriates $2,000,000 to be expended under the authority of the President in supplying and delivering arms and munitions of war to loyal citizens residing in any of the States of which the inhabitants are in rebellion, or in which it may be threatened. We agree, therefore, that the Act 13th July, 1861, recognized a state of civil war between the Government and the people of the State described in that proclamation.

The cases of the *United States* vs. *Palmer*, (3 Wh., 610); *Divina Pastora*, and 4 Ibid., 52, and that class of cases to be found in the reports are referred to as furnishing authority for the exercise of the war power claimed for the President in the present case. These cases hold that when the Government of the United States recognizes a state of civil war to exist between a foreign nation and her colonies, but remaining itself neutral, the Courts are bound to consider as lawful all those acts which the new Government may direct against the enemy, and we admit the President who conducts the foreign relations of the Government may fitly recognize or refuse to do so, the existence of civil war in the foreign nation under the circumstances stated.

But this is a very different question from the one before us, which is whether the President can recognize or declare a civil war, under the Constitution, with all its belligerent rights, between his own Government and a portion of its citizens in a state of insurrection. That power, as we have seen, belongs to Congress. We agree when such a war is recognized or declared to exist by the war-making power, but not otherwise, it is the duty of the Courts to follow the decision of the political power of the Government.

The case of *Luther vs. Borden et al.*, (7 How., 45,) which arose out of the attempt of an assumed new government in the State to overthrow the old and established Government of Rhode Island by arms. The Legislature of the old Government had established martial law, and the Chief Justice in delivering the opinion of the Court observed, among other things, that "if the Government of Rhode Island deemed the armed opposition so formidable and so ramified throughout the State as to require the use of its military force, and the declaration of martial law, we see no ground upon which this Court can question its authority. It was a state of war, and the established Government resorted to the rights and usages of war to maintain itself and overcome the unlawful opposition."

But it is only necessary to say, that the term "war" must necessarily have been used here by the Chief Justice in its popular sense, and not as known to the law of nations, as the State of Rhode Island confessedly possessed no power under the Federal Constitution to declare war.

Congress on the 6th of August, 1862, passed an Act confirming all acts, proclamations, and orders of the President, after the 4th of March, 1861, respecting the army and navy, and legalizing them, so far as was competent for that body, and it has been suggested, but scarcely argued, that this legislation on the subject had the effect to bring into existence an *ex post facto* civil war with all the rights of capture and confiscation, *jure belli*, from the date referred to. An *ex post facto* law is defined, when, after an action, indifferent in itself, or lawful, is committed, the Legislature then, for the first time, declares it to have been a crime and inflicts punishment upon the person who committed it. The principle is sought to be applied in this case. Property of the citizen or foreign subject engaged in lawful trade at the time, and illegally captured, which must be taken as true if a confirmatory act be necessary, may be held and confiscated by subsequent legislation. In other words trade and commerce authorized at the time by acts of Congress and treaties, may, by *ex post facto* legislation, be changed into illicit trade and commerce with all its penalties and forfeitures annexed and enforced. The instance of the seizure of the Dutch ships in 1803 by Great Britain before the war, and confiscation after the declaration of war, which is well known, is referred to as an authority. But there the ships were seized by the war power, the orders of the Government, the seizure being a partial exercise of that power, and which was soon after exercised in full.

The precedent is one which has not received the approbation of jurists, and is not to be followed. See W. B. Lawrence, 2d ed. Wheaton's Element of Int. Law, pt. 4, ch. 1. sec. 11, and note. But, admitting its full weight, it affords no authority in the present case. Here the captures were without any Constitutional authority, and void; and, on principle, no subsequent ratification could make them valid.

Upon the whole, after the most careful consideration of this case which the pressure of other duties has admitted, I am compelled to the conclusion that no civil war existed between this Government and the States in insurrection till recognized by the Act of Congress 13th of July, 1861; that the President does not possess the power under the Constitution to declare war or recognize its existence within the meaning of the law of nations, which carries with it belligerent rights, and thus change the country and all its citizens from a state of peace to a state of war; that this power belongs exclusively to the Congress of the United States, and, consequently, that the President had no power to set on foot a blockade under the law of nations, and that the capture of the vessel and cargo in this case, and in all cases before us in which the capture occurred before the 13th of July, 1861, for breach of blockade, or as enemies' property, are illegal and void, and that the decrees of condemnation should be reversed and the vessel and cargo restored.

> Mr. Chief Justice TANEY, Mr. Justice CATRON and Mr. Justice CLIFFORD, concurred in the dissenting opinion of Mr. Justice Nelson.

Ex Parte Vallandigham

Supreme Court of the United States
February 15, 1864
1 Wallace (68 U.S.) 243 (1864)

    Antiwar Democrat and negrophobe Clement L. Vallandigham became the center of national attention because of his arrest for his political activities. In early 1863, General Ambrose Burnside took command of the Department of the Ohio and decided to clamp down on "Copperhead" (or pro-Southern) activity in the area along the Ohio River. He issued orders that anyone committing "expressed or implied" treason would be subject to arrest and trial by military authorities. As a Democratic candidate for the Ohio governorship, Vallandigham saw an opportunity to draw attention to his cause. On May 1, 1863, in Mount Vernon, Ohio, he delivered a well-publicized speech denouncing the war and warning of a society of racial equality if the Union won. In response, Burnside ordered his arrest, with Vallandigham brought into custody in the middle of the night and taken to Cincinnati after soldiers broke down the door to his house. A military commission met on May 6 and convicted Vallandigham of violating Burnside's orders and sentenced him to imprisonment. Vallandigham then applied for a writ of habeas corpus, which the local federal district court judge refused, noting that President Abraham Lincoln had suspended the writ in that area of the country.
    Burnside undertook his actions—both issuing orders limiting political speech and arresting Vallandigham—without consulting the president. Vallandigham's arrest and the ensuing uproar in both Democratic and Republican newspapers caused unneeded embarrassment for Lincoln. To deal with the situation, the president commuted Vallandigham's sentence from imprisonment to banishment to Confederate lines. Once sent into the Confederacy, Vallandigham made his way to the southern coast, took a blockade runner to Canada, and continued on to Windsor, Ontario, where

he continued his in-exile campaign for the Ohio governorship. In time Vallandigham returned to Ohio, where he hoped to be rearrested; instead, the Lincoln administration ignored him.

In 1863, Vallandigham applied to the United States Supreme Court seeking a writ of certiorari (a request to a court to undertake some action) for the purpose of annulling his conviction by military tribunal. Associate Justice James M. Wayne wrote the unanimous opinion of the Court, holding that the Supreme Court did not possess jurisdiction over direct appeals from military courts. In this manner, the justices sidestepped any conflict with the chief executive over the arrest and trials of such political opponents of the administration and its policies. Proceeding during the war, *Ex parte Vallandigham* provided the military authorities the leeway they needed to deal with potential dissent in areas of military actions. After the war, in *Ex parte Milligan*, 71 U.S. 2 (1866), the justices reached a different conclusion.

THIS case arose on the petition of Clement L. Vallandigham for a *certiorari*, to be directed to the Judge Advocate General of the Army of the United States, to send up to this court, for its review, the proceedings of a military commission, by which the said Vallandigham had been tried and sentenced to imprisonment; the facts of the case, as derived from the statement of the learned Justice (WAYNE) who delivered the opinion of the court, having been as follows:

Major-General Burnside, commanding the military department of Ohio, issued a special order, No. 135, on the 21st April, 1863, by which a military commission was appointed to meet at Cincinnati, Ohio, on the 22d of April, or as soon thereafter as practicable, for the trial of such persons as might be brought before it. There was a detail of officers to constitute it, and a judge advocate appointed.

The same general had, previously, on the 13th of April, 1863, issued a general order, No. 38, declaring, for the information of all persons concerned, that thereafter all persons found within his lines who should commit acts for the benefit of the enemies of our country, should be tried as spies or traitors, and if convicted should suffer death; and among other acts prohibited, was the habit of declaring sympathies for the enemy. The order issued by General Burnside declared that persons committing such offences would be at once arrested, with a view to being tried as above stated, or to be sent beyond his lines into the lines of their friends; that it must be distinctly understood that treason, expressed or implied, would not be tolerated in his department.

On the 5th of May, 1863, Vallandigham, a resident of the State of Ohio, and a citizen of the United States, was arrested at his residence and taken to Cincinnati, and there imprisoned. On the following day, he was arraigned before a military commission on a charge of having expressed sympathies for those in arms against the Government of the United States, and for having uttered, in a speech at a public meeting, disloyal sentiments and opinions, with the object and purpose of weakening the power of the Government in its efforts for the suppression of an unlawful rebellion.

The specification under the charge was, that he, the said Vallandigham, a citizen of Ohio, on the 1st of May, 1863, at Mount Vernon, in Knox County, Ohio, did publicly address a large meeting of persons, and did utter sentiments, in words or to the effect, "that the present war was a wicked, cruel, and unnecessary war, one not waged for the preservation of the Union, but for the purpose of crushing out liberty and to erect a despotism; a war for the freedom of the blacks and the enslavement of the whites; and that if the administration had not wished otherwise, that the war could have been honorably terminated long ago; that peace might have been honorably made by listening to the proposed intermediation of France; that propositions, by which the Southern States could be won back, and the South guaranteed their rights under the Constitution, had been rejected the day before the late battle of Fredericksburg by Lincoln and his minions, meaning the President of the United States, and those under him in authority. Also charging that the Government of the United States was about to appoint military marshals in every district to restrain the people of their liberties, and to deprive them of their rights and privileges, characterizing General Order No. 38, from headquarters of the Department of the Ohio, as a base usurpation of arbitrary authority, inviting his hearers to resist the same, by saying, the sooner the people inform the minions of usurped power that they will not submit to such restrictions upon their liberties, the better; and adding, that he was at all times and upon all occasions resolved to do what he could to defeat the attempts now being made to build up a monarchy upon the ruins of our free government, and asserting that he firmly believed, as he had said six months ago, that the men in power are attempting to establish a despotism in this country, more cruel and oppressive than ever existed before."

The prisoner, on being arraigned, denied the jurisdiction of the military commission, and refused to plead either to the charge or specification. Thereon, the members of the commission, after private consultation, directed the judge advocate to enter a plea of Not Guilty, and to proceed with the trial, with an allowance to the petitioner to call witnesses to rebut the evidence which might be introduced against him to establish the charge. The next day the commission proceeded with the trial. Seven members of it were present, and tried the charge in due form of military law. The prisoner exercised his right to call witnesses, and to cross-examine those who were sworn for the prosecution. At his request he had the aid of counsel, and the court adjourned to enable him to procure it. Three gentlemen of his own choice attended; but for some cause, only known to themselves and their client, they remained in an adjoining room during the trial, without having been introduced before the commission, though it expressly authorized it to be done, saying that it had adjourned to permit the prisoner to obtain their presence. The prisoner was informed by the judge advocate, when he closed his evidence, that no other witnesses would be introduced. He then offered the Hon. S. S. Cox as a witness in his behalf. This gentleman was interrogated in chief, without being cross-examined, and it was admitted by the judge advocate, that if three other persons who had been summoned to appear as witnesses for the prisoner had appeared, but who were not in court, that their evidence would have been substantially the same as Mr. Cox had given. Here the accused closed his testimony, and then read to the commission a statement, which, with the other proceedings of the trial, was forwarded to the judge advocate general, and was inserted in the record.

It began with the declaration, that he had been arrested without due process of law, without a warrant from any judicial officer; that he was then in a military prison, and had been served with a charge and specifications, as in a court-martial or military commission; that he was not either in the land or naval forces of the United States, nor in the militia in the actual service of the United States, and, therefore, not triable for any cause by any such court; that he was subject, by the express terms of the Constitution, to arrest only by due process of law or judicial warrant, regularly issued upon affidavit by some officer or court of competent jurisdiction for the trial of citizens; that he was entitled to be tried on an indictment or presentment of a grand jury of such court, to a speedy and public trial, and also by an impartial jury of the State of Ohio, to be confronted with witnesses against him, to have compulsory process for witnesses in his behalf, the assistance of counsel for his defence, by evidence and argument according to the common law and the usages of judicial courts;—all those he demanded as his right as a citizen of the United States, under the Constitution of the United States. He also alleged that the offence of which he is charged is not known to the Constitution of the United States, nor to any law thereof; that they were words spoken to the people of Ohio, in an open and public political meeting, lawfully and peaceably assembled under the Constitution, and upon full notice; that they were words of criticism upon the policy of the public servants of the people, by which policy it was alleged that the welfare of the country was not promoted. That they were used as an appeal to the people to change that policy, not by force, but by free elections and the ballot-box; that it is not pretended that he counselled disobedience to the Constitution or resistance to the law or lawful authority; that he had never done so, and that beyond this protest he had nothing further to submit.

The judge advocate replied, that so far as the statement called in question the jurisdiction of the commission, that had been decided by the authority convening and ordering the trial, nor had the commission, at any time, been willing to entertain the objection; that as far as any implications or inferences designed or contemplated by the statement of the accused, his rights to counsel and to witnesses for his defence, he had enjoyed the allowance of both, and process for his witnesses, which had been issued; and that as to the facts charged in the specification, they were to be determined by the evidence;—that his criminality was a question peculiarly for the commission, and that he had submitted the case to its consideration. The commission was then cleared for consideration.

The finding and sentence were, that Vallandigham was guilty of the charge and specification, except so much of the latter, "as *that propositions by which the Southern States could be won back and guaranteed in their rights under the Constitution had been rejected the day before the battle of Fredericksburg,* by Lincoln and his minions, meaning the President of the United States, and those under him in authority;" and the words, *"asserting that he firmly believed, as he had asserted six months ago, that the men in power are attempting to establish a despotism in this country more oppressive than ever existed before."* As to those words the prisoner was not guilty; but of the charge he was guilty, and the commission, therefore, sentenced him to be placed in close confinement in some fortress of the United States, to be designated by the commanding officer of this department, there to be kept during the war.

The finding and sentence were approved and confirmed by General Burnside, in an order bearing date the 16th of May, 1863, and Fort Warren was designated as the place of imprisonment. On the 19th of May, 1863, the President, in commutation of the sentence, directed Major-General Burnside to send the prisoner, without delay, to the headquarters of General Rosecrans, then in Tennessee, to be by him put beyond our military lines; which order was executed.

In support of the motion for the certiorari, and against the jurisdiction of the military commission, it was urged that the latter was prohibited by the act of March 3d, 1863, for enrolling and calling out the national forces (§ 30, 12 *Stat. at Large,* 736), as the crimes punishable in it by the sentence of a court-martial or military commission, applied only to persons who are in the military service of the United States, and subject to the articles of war. And also, that by the Constitution itself, § 3, art. 3, all crimes, except in cases of impeachment, were to be tried by juries in the State where the crime had been committed, and when not committed within any State, at such place as Congress may by law have directed; and that the military commission could have no jurisdiction to try the petitioner, as neither the charge against him nor its specifications imputed to him any offence known to the law of the land, and that General Burnside had no authority to enlarge the jurisdiction of a military commission by the General Order No. 38, or otherwise.

The Supreme Court of the United States has no power to review by *certiorari* the proceedings of a military commission ordered by a general officer of the United States Army, commanding a military department.

> Mr. Justice WAYNE after stating the case, much as precedes, delivered the opinion of the court:

General Burnside acted in the matter as the general commanding the Ohio Department, in conformity with the instructions for the government of the armies of the United States, approved by the President of the United States, and published by the Assistant Adjutant-General, by order of the Secretary of War, on the 24th of April, 1863.[1]

It is affirmed in these instructions, that military jurisdiction is of two kinds. First, that which is conferred and defined by statute; second, that which is derived from the common law of war. "Military offences, under the statute, must be tried in the manner therein directed; but military offences, which do not come within the statute, must be tried and punished under the common law of war. The character of the courts which exercise these jurisdictions depends upon the local law of each particular county."

In the armies of the United States, the first is exercised by courts-martial, while cases which do not come within the "rules and regulations of war," or the jurisdiction conferred by statute or court-martial, are tried by *military commissions.*

These jurisdictions are applicable, not only to war with foreign nations, but to a rebellion, when a part of a country wages war against its legitimate government, seeking to throw off all allegiance to it, to set up a government of its own.

Our first remark upon *the motion for a certiorari* is, that there is no analogy between the power given by the Constitution and law of the United States to the Supreme Court, and the other inferior courts of the United States, and to the judges of them, to issue such processes, and the prerogative power by which it is done in England. The purposes for which the writ is issued are alike, but there is no similitude in the origin of the power to do it. In England, the Court of King's Bench has a superintendence over all courts of an inferior criminal jurisdiction, and may, by the plenitude of its power, award a certiorari to have any indictment removed and brought before it; and where such certiorari is allowable, it is awarded at the instance of the king, because every indictment is at the suit of the king, and he has a prerogative of suing in whatever court he pleases. The courts of the United States derive authority to issue such a writ from the Constitution and the legislation of Congress. To place the two sources of the right to issue the writ in obvious contrast, and in application to the motion we are considering for its exercise by this court, we will cite so much of the third article of the Constitution as we think will best illustrate the subject.

"The judicial power of the United States shall be vested in one Supreme Court, and in such inferior courts as the Congress may, from time to time, ordain and establish." "The judicial power shall extend to all cases in law and equity, arising under the Constitution, the laws of the United States, and treaties made or which shall be made under their authority; to all cases affecting ambassadors, other public ministers and consuls," &c., &c., and "*in all cases affecting ambassadors, other ministers and consuls, and those in which a State shall be a party, the Supreme Court shall have original jurisdiction.* In all the other cases before mentioned, the Supreme Court shall have appellate jurisdiction, both as to law and fact, with such exceptions and under such regulations as the Congress shall make." Then Congress passed the act to establish the judicial courts of the United States, and in the 13th section of it declared that the Supreme Court shall have exclusively all such jurisdiction of suits or proceedings against ambassadors or other public ministers or their domestics or their domestic servants as a court of law can have or exercise *consistently with the laws of nations,* and original, but not exclusive jurisdiction, of suits brought by ambassadors, or other public ministers, or in which a consul or vice-consul shall be a party. In the same section, the Supreme Court is declared to have appellate jurisdiction in cases hereinafter expressly provided. In this section, it will be perceived that the jurisdiction given, besides that which is mentioned in the preceding part of the section, is an exclusive jurisdiction of suits or proceedings against ambassadors or other public ministers or their domestics or domestic servants, as a court of law can have or exercise consistently with the laws of nations, and original but not exclusive jurisdiction of all suits *brought by ambassadors or other public ministers,* or in which a consul or vice-consul shall be a party, thus guarding them from all other judicial interference, and giving to them the right to prosecute for their own benefit in the courts of the United States. Thus substantially reaffirming the constitutional declaration, that the Supreme Court had original jurisdiction in all cases affecting ambassadors and other public ministers and consuls, and those in which a State shall be a party, and that it shall have appellate jurisdiction in all other cases before mentioned, both as to law and fact, with such exceptions and under such regulations as the Congress shall make.

The appellate powers of the Supreme Court, as granted by the Constitution, are limited and regulated by the acts of Congress, and must be exercised subject to the exceptions and regulations made by Congress. In other words, the petition before us we think not to be within the letter or spirit of the grants of appellate jurisdiction to the Supreme Court. It is not in law or equity within the meaning of those terms as used in the 3d article of the Constitution. Nor is a military commission a court within the meaning of the 14th section of the Judiciary Act of 1789. That act is denominated to be one to establish the judicial courts of the United States, and the 14th section declares that all the "before-mentioned courts" of the United States shall have power to issue writs of *scire facias, habeas corpus,* and all other writs not specially provided for by statute, which may be necessary for the exercise of their respective jurisdictions, agreeably to the principles and usages of law. The words in the section, "the before-mentioned" courts, can only have reference to such courts as were established in the preceding part of the act, and excludes the idea that a court of military commission can be one of them.

Whatever may be the force of Vallandigham's protest, that he was not triable by a court of military commission, it is certain that his petition cannot be brought within the 14th section of the act; and further, that the court cannot, without disregarding its frequent decisions and interpretation of the Constitution in respect to its judicial power, originate a writ of certiorari to review or pronounce any opinion upon the proceedings of a military commission. It was natural, before the sections of the 3d article of the Constitution had been fully considered in connection with the legislation of Congress, giving to the courts of the United States power to issue writs of *scire facias, habeas corpus,* and all other writs not specially provided for by statute, which might be necessary for the exercise of their respective jurisdiction, that by some members of the profession it should have been thought, and some of the early judges of the Supreme Court also, that the 14th section of the act of 24th September, 1789, gave to this court a right to originate processes of *habeas corpus ad subjiciendum,* writs of certiorari to review the proceedings of the inferior courts as a matter of original jurisdiction, without being in any way restricted by the constitutional limitation, that in all cases affecting ambassadors, other public ministers and consuls, and those in which a State shall be a party, the Supreme Court shall have original jurisdiction. This limitation has always been considered restrictive of any other original jurisdiction. *The rule of construction of the Constitution being, that affirmative words in the Constitution, declaring in what cases the Supreme Court shall have original jurisdiction, must be construed negatively as to all other cases.*[2] The nature and extent of the court's appellate jurisdiction and its want of it to issue writs of *habeas corpus ad subjiciendum* have been fully discussed by this court at different times. We do not think it necessary, however, to examine or cite many of them at this time. We will annex a list to this opinion, distinguishing what this court's action has been in cases brought to it by appeal from such applications as have been rejected, when it has been asked that it would act upon the matter as one of original jurisdiction.

In the case *Ex parte Milburn*, Chief Justice Marshall said, as the jurisdiction of the court is appellate, it must first be shown that it has the power to award a *habeas corpus. In re Kaine,* the court denied the motion, saying that the court's jurisdiction to award the writ was appellative, and that the case had not been so presented to it, and for the same cause refused to issue a writ of certiorari, which in the course of the argument was prayed for. In *Ex parte Metzger,* it was determined that a writ of certiorari could not be allowed to examine a commitment by a district judge, under the treaty between the United States and France, for the reason that the judge exercised a special authority, and that no provision had been made for the revision of his judgment. So does a court of military commission exercise a special authority. In the case before us, it was urged that the decision in Metzger's case had been made upon the ground that the proceeding of the district judge was not judicial in its character, *but that the proceedings of the military commission* were so; and further, it was said that the ruling in that case had been overruled by a majority of the judges in Raines' case. There is a misapprehension of the report of the latter case, and as to the judicial character of the proceedings of the military commission, we cite what was said by this court in the case of *The United States* v. *Ferreira.*

"The powers conferred by Congress upon the district judge and the secretary are judicial in their nature, for judgment and discretion must be exercised by both of them, but it is not judicial in either case, in the sense in which judicial power is granted to the courts of the United States." Nor can it be said that the authority to be exercised by a military commission is judicial in that sense. It involves discretion to examine, to decide and sentence, but there is no original jurisdiction in the Supreme Court to issue a writ of *habeas corpus ad subjiciendum* to review or reverse its proceedings, or the writ of certiorari to revise the proceedings of a military commission.

And as to the President's action in such matters, and those acting in them under his authority, we refer to the opinions expressed by this court, in the cases of *Martin* v. *Mott*, and *Dynes* v. *Hoover*.

For the reasons given, our judgment is, that the writ of certiorari prayed for to revise and review the proceedings of the military commission, by which Clement L. Vallandigham was tried, sentenced, and imprisoned, must be denied, and so do we order accordingly.

CERTIORARI REFUSED.

NELSON, J., GRIER, J., and FIELD, J., concurred in the result of this opinion. MILLER, J., was not present at the argument, and took no part.

Notes

1. They were prepared by Francis Leiber, LL.D., and were revised by a board of officers, of which Major-General E. A. Hitchcock was president.

2. *Marbury v. Madison*, 1 Cranch, 137; *State of New Jersey v. State of New York*, 5 Peters, 284; *Kendall v. The United States*, 12 Id., 637; *Cohens v.* Virginia, 6 Wheaton, 264.

GELPCKE ET AL. V. THE CITY OF DUBUQUE

Supreme Court of the United States
January 11, 1864
1 Wallace (68 U.S.) 175 (1864)

In the middle to late nineteenth century, cities sought to entice railroads to build lines connecting to them to tie the city to markets and the larger world, which provided income generated from jobs and taxes. Cities often issued bonds to raise money to build and support railroad facilities or to purchase land to encourage the railroad to invest in their municipality. But, in their determination to support the railroads, some cities, like Dubuque, Iowa, authorized bonds in excess of the spending limits imposed on cities by the state constitution. When challenged in state court for overspending, the state courts generally upheld Dubuque's actions, but a reforming state Supreme Court struck down the bonds as a violation of the state constitution. Bond holders appealed to the United States Supreme Court urging the Court to uphold the validity of the bonds on the grounds that in commercial matters, the state Supreme Court could construe the state's constitution when the state's Supreme Court decisions were inconsistent. Associate Justice Noah Swayne reversed the state Supreme Court's finding and upheld the validity of the bonds in spite of the state constitution's restrictions and the varying decisions of the Iowa Supreme Court. In this fashion, Swayne increased the tension between the federal courts and elected state court judges. Swayne's suspicions about the actions of the state foreshadow the second-guessing of the state courts and their decisions by the federal courts later in the century, a type of judging now labeled "substantive due process." Yet, at the time, this decision was highly praised by railroad investors and city boosters for supporting economic development. Even the United States Supreme Court's own reporter, John William Wallace, drew readers' attention to the decision. He noted that the majority decision constituted an instance "where high moral duties were enforced upon a whole community, seeking apparently to violate them." Iowan Associate Justice Samuel F. Miller dissented, arguing that only the Iowa Supreme Court could interpret the Iowa state constitution, not the federal courts.

THE Constitution of the State of Iowa, adopted in 1846, contains the following provisions, to wit:

"ART. 1. § 6. All laws of a general nature shall have a uniform operation."

"ART. 3. § 1. The legislative authority of the State shall be vested in a Senate and House of Representatives, which shall be designated the General Assembly of the State of Iowa," &c.

"ART. 7. The *General Assembly* shall not *in any manner create any debt* or debts, liability or liabilities, which shall, singly or in the aggregate, with any previous debts or liabilities, exceed the sum of *one hundred thousand dollars*, except in case of war, to repel invasion, or suppress insurrection."

"ART. 8. § 2. Corporations shall *not be created in this State by special laws, except for political or municipal purposes;* but the General Assembly shall provide, by *general laws*, for the organization of all other corporations, except corporations with banking privileges, the creation of which is prohibited. The stockholders shall be subject to such liabilities and restrictions as shall be provided by law. *The State shall not directly or indirectly become a stockholder in any corporation.*"

With these *constitutional* provisions in existence and force, the *legislature* passed certain *statutes*. One,—incorporating the city of Dubuque, passed February 24, 1847,—provided, in its 27th section, as follows:

"That *whenever*, in the *opinion of the City Council*, it is expedient to *borrow money* for any particular purpose, the question shall be submitted to the citizens of Dubuque, the nature and object of the loan shall be stated, and a day fixed for the electors of said city to express their wishes; the like notice shall be given as in cases of election, and the loan shall not be made unless two-thirds of all the votes polled at such election shall be given in the affirmative."

By an act passed January 8, 1851, this charter was "so amended as to empower the City Councils to levy annually a special tax to pay interest on such loans as are authorized by the 27th section of said act;" that is to say, by the section just quoted. A subsequent act,—one passed 28th January, 1857,—enacts thus:

"The *city of Dubuque* is hereby *authorized and empowered* to aid in the construction of the *Dubuque Western*, and Dubuque, St. Peter's and St. Paul Railroad Companies, *by issuing* $250,000 *of city bonds to each,* in pursuance of a vote of the citizens of said city, taken in the month of December, A.D. 1856. *Said bonds shall be legal and valid,* and the City Council is authorized *and required* to levy a special tax to meet the principal and interest of said bonds, in case it shall become necessary from the failure of funds from other sources."

"The proclamation, the vote, *bonds issued or to be issued, are hereby declared valid, and the said railroad companies are hereby authorized to expend the moneys aris-*

ing from the sale of said bonds, without the limits of the city and county of Dubuque, in the construction of either of said roads; and *neither the city of Dubuque nor any of the citizens shall ever be allowed to plead that the said bonds are invalid."*

With this Constitution, as already mentioned, in force, and after the incorporation of the city and the passage of acts of Assembly, as just mentioned,—*and after certain decisions of the Supreme Court of Iowa as to the constitutionality of these acts, the character and value of which decisions* make the principal subject of discussion in this case,—the city of Dubuque issued a large amount of coupon bonds, which were now in the hands of the plaintiffs. The bonds bore date on the 1st of July, 1857, and were payable to Edward Langworthy, *or bearer,* on the 1st of January, 1877, at the Metropolitan Bank, in the city of New York. The coupons were for the successive half year's interest accruing on the bonds respectively, and were payable at the same place. The bonds recited that they were given "for and in consideration" of stock of the Dubuque Western Railroad Company,—(one of the roads to which, by the act last mentioned, the city was authorized to subscribe),—and that for the due payment of their principal and interest, "the said city is hereby pledged, in accordance with the code of Iowa, and an act of the General Assembly of the State of Iowa, of January 28, 1857,"—the act just referred to. The coupons on the bonds not being paid, the plaintiffs sued the city of Dubuque in the District Court of the United States for the District of Iowa, claiming to recover the amount specified in the coupons, with the New York rate of interest from the time of their maturity, and exchange on the city of New York.

The city set up the following grounds of defence:

1. That the bonds were issued by the city to aid in the construction of a railroad extending *beyond its limits into the interior of the State.*
2. That at the time of issuing the bonds and coupons, the indebtedness of the city *exceeded one hundred thousand dollars.*
3. That at the time of issuing the bonds and coupons, the indebtedness of *the State of Iowa exceeded one hundred thousand dollars.*
4. That at the time of issuing the bonds and coupons, the indebtedness of *the cities and counties of Iowa exceeded,* in the aggregate, *one hundred thousand dollars.*

The plaintiffs demurred. The demurrer was overruled, and judgment entered for the defendant. On error, the question in this court was, whether the judgment had been rightly given?

Mr. S. V. White and Mr. Allison for the bondholders: In one point of view, the question before the court is a narrow one; a question as to the number and relative weight of decisions of the Supreme Court of Iowa alone, and in its own constitution and statutes; a settlement of the balance on an account domestic simply. It is a question whether this court will regard seven solemn decisions, made by the Supreme Court of Iowa, beginning in A.D. 1853, and ending in A.D. 1859, on the faith of which decisions, strangers have lent their money for the improvement of the State itself, or of cities which adorn and enrich it, so overruled by a decision made in A.D. 1860, or decisions of a later date, as that bonds issued payable to BEARER, are now void in the hands of bearers who, between the said years of 1853 and 1859, and on the faith of those decisions, bought them in good faith and for value. Undoubtedly we shall ask that this question be decided; that this settlement of the account domestic simply be settled. The case involves, as a necessity, perhaps no other question. The court may possibly confine itself much to these limits. In some points of view, however, the issue is of greater dignity. It concerns the honor, not of Iowa only, but of all the States; the value of millions of securities issued by nearly every State of the Union, and by cities and counties and boroughs in them all. Yet, more: we shall ask this court to treat as contradicting precedents made by the Supreme Court of Iowa itself, and so as subversive of regard for authority,—as erroneous, therefore, in the law, and of no obligation,—the latest decisions of a State of this Union; the decision, we mean, in *The State of Iowa, ex relatione*, v. *The County of Wapello*, and any decisions which, to the disregard of earlier and settled precedents, follow it. On all these accounts the subject deserves an examination on a wider view of precedents than those of Iowa alone. Time is not wasted in appropriating much of it to an inquiry as to American decisions universally. We propose, therefore, to examine

1. By a series of decisions of the Supreme Court of Iowa prior to that, A. D. 1859, in *The State of Iowa, ex relatione, v. The County of Wapello (13 Iowa, 388)*, the right of the legislature of that State to authorize municipal corporations to subscribe to railroads extending beyond the limits of the city or county, and to issue bonds accordingly, was settled in favor of the right; and those decisions, meeting with the approbation of this court, and being in harmony with the adjudications of sixteen States of the Union, will be regarded as a true interpretation of the constitution and laws of the State so far as relate to bonds issued and put upon the market during the time that those decisions were in force. The fact that the said Supreme Court of Iowa *now* holds that those decisions were erroneous, and ought not to have been made, and that the legislature of the State had no such power as former courts decided that they had, can have no effect upon transactions in the past, however it may affect those in the future.
2. Although it is the practice of this court to follow the latest settled adjudications of the States courts giving constructions to the laws and Constitutions of their own States, it will not necessarily follow decisions which may prove but oscillations in the course of such judicial settlement. Nor will it follow any adjudication to such an extent as to make a sacrifice of truth, justice, and law.
3. Municipal bonds, with coupons payable to "bearer," having, by universal usage and consent, all the qualities of commercial paper, a party recovering on the coupons will be entitled to the amount of them, with interest and exchange at the place where, by their terms, they were made payable.

1. The adjudications of courts of the different States upon the same or similar questions, prior to its adjudication by the courts of Iowa.
2. The adjudications of the courts of the State of Iowa, upon such questions; and,
3. The adjudications of the courts of the United States, and of the several States, since the question was first decided by the courts of Iowa.
1. And first, we may admit that all courts have held uniformly, that such acts and contracts as those to be considered in this case do not arise from any legislative power delegated to the municipal corporations, but that they arise only from powers conferred *by legislative act of the State.*

The first case upon the subject arose in Virginia, and was decided by the Court of Appeals of that State, A. D. 1837, in *Goddin* v. *Crump.* The legislature of that State had authorized the city of Richmond to subscribe for stock in a company incorporated for the improvement of the navigation of James River, and for building a road to the Falls of the Kanawha River, and to borrow money to pay the same, and to levy and collect a tax for the payment of principal and interest so borrowed. Under these acts the Common Council of the city of Richmond passed an ordinance subscribing for such stock, and for levying a tax, as authorized by such acts, and the collector of the city had levied upon a slave, the property of complainant, to satisfy the tax due from him under such levy. The complainant exhibited his bill in equity, in behalf of himself and others, citizens of the city of Richmond, who were property-holders therein, and who had not consented to the passage of the acts of the legislature, nor the acts of the council in passing the ordinance and in levying the tax, and prayed to be relieved from the payment of such tax; and that the collector, who, with the Common Council of Richmond, was made a party defendant, might be enjoined and restrained from the collection of such tax, perpetually; upon the ground that the law authorizing such subscription and levy was unconstitutional and void.

Upon this case the Court of Appeals of Virginia (Brooke, J., dissenting) decided:

I. That an act, to be within the legitimate scope of a municipal corporation, need not be performed in the corporate limits, but might properly be extended to objects beyond the limits of the corporation.

II. That the true test of the corporate character of the act, was the *interest* of the corporation.

III. That the citizens themselves were the judges of what was the interest of the corporation, and not the judges of the court, and however much a court might doubt the wisdom of the citizens in determining that question, they would not interfere with it.

IV. That the majority of such citizens could bind a dissenting minority, and properly charge them and their property with the payment of tax, to which they had given no assent.

V. That the laws in question are not repugnant to the Constitution, and the bill was accordingly dismissed with costs.

The next case in point arose, A. D. 1843, before the Supreme Court of Errors of the State of Connecticut, *City of Bridgeport* v. *Housatonic R. R. Co.* In that case, in March, 1837, the city of Bridgeport voted to take stock in the Housatonic Railroad Company, and to procure loans of money, pledging the faith of the city therefor. In May, 1838, the legislature confirmed and legalized such acts; and on June 15th, 1838, the bonds sued on were duly issued. The court unanimously decided:

I. The legislature can give power to municipal corporations to subscribe stock in railroads passing through or terminating in them;

II. That the legislature may, by act or resolution, confirm and render valid, prior voidable acts of such corporations;

III. That the fact of a municipal corporation becoming stockholders in a railroad, and therefore, *pro tanto*, going beyond the legitimate ends for which the corporation was constructed, is only an incident to the general power to provide for the interests of the citizens of the corporation, and does not, therefore, take it out of the scope of its corporate acts;

IV. That a majority of such citizens can constitutionally decide upon the acts of the corporation, and compel a minority to contribute, by taxation, to objects to which such minority are opposed.

The next case was in the Supreme Court of Tennessee, *Nichol* v. *Mayor of Nashville*, December Term, A. D. 1848. The legislature of Tennessee had incorporated a railroad company, and by subsequent act the town of Nashville was authorized to subscribe 20,000 shares of its stock, and to borrow money, and to levy taxes to pay principal and interest on such loan. A bill was filed in equity to enjoin the borrowing of money under said act, and to prevent the issue of bonds and the levy of a tax, the ground assigned being, the acts were unconstitutional and void. Demurrer to bill. The court decide:

I. That the building of a railroad or aiding therein, by subscription to the stock, which railroad shall terminate in, or pass through or *near* a municipal corporation, is within the legitimate scope of corporate acts, and for such purposes a tax may be levied and collected by the delegated authorities of such corporation;

II. That such act neither contravenes the provisions of the Constitution of the United States, nor of the State of Tennessee.

The same questions came before the Court of Appeals in Kentucky, in *Talbot* v. *Dent*, A. D. 1849, and again, A. D. 1852, in *Slack* v. *Maysville R. R. Co.*

The chief justice delivered the opinion of the court in both cases, and in both, the foregoing decisions of Virginia, Connecticut, and Tennessee were cited, argued, approved, and followed, at length.

The same questions came before the Supreme Court of Pennsylvania, in *The Commonwealth* v. *McWilliams*, May Term, 1849, and again in *Sharpless* v. *Mayor*, and in *Moers* v. *City of Reading*. All these cases decide the questions as former and other courts had done, and hold the bonds binding.

The Supreme Court of Illinois, A. D. 1849, held an act of the legislature, giving the right of taxation to a certain precinct, to keep up a bridge across Rock River, to be constitutional, and sustained a tax levied by the local authorities under such law; and the Supreme Court of New York, May Term, 1840, made a similar ruling in behalf of a law authorizing a municipal tax, for the purpose of paying the excess of expenses for bringing a canal to such corporation, although private individuals had given bond for the payment of such excess to the canal company.

The same questions came before the Supreme Court of Ohio, A. D. 1852, and A. D. 1853, in two cases, in which the questions were decided as in all the cases already named. Comment may therefore be spared.

Thus there had then been decisions of the highest appellate courts of eight States of the Union, extending through a period of sixteen years, and numbering in all twelve such decisions.

2. *As respects the Courts of Iowa*. And here, we premise, that so far as *cities* are concerned, there has never been a decision made upon the question in Iowa, but the principle has been repeatedly settled in the case of *counties*, upon principles, however, equally binding upon cities.

The question came before the Supreme Court of Iowa, at the June Term, 1853, in the case of *Dubuque Co.* v. *Dubuque and Pacific R. R. Co.*, and the court held:

I. That a county has the constitutional right to aid in building a railroad within its limits.

II. That the provision of the Constitution, which limited the State debts to the sum of $100,000, and also the provision which declares that the State shall not directly nor indirectly become a stockholder in any corporation, applied only to the *State* in its *sovereign* capacity.

III. That § 114 of the Code of 1851, applied as well to railroads as to ordinary roads, and that proceedings regularly had, under that and subsequent sections, to § 124 inclusive, were regular and legal, and authorized the issue of bonds for railroad purposes, and that said railroad bonds were valid and binding upon the county. This opinion is written by Greene, J.; Kinney, J. dissenting.

At the June Term, 1854, in *The State* v. *Bissell*, the same question was raised, together with minor questions, about the regularity of the proceedings. It was a proceeding in Chancery to prohibit the county judge of Cedar County from issuing bonds to a certain railroad company. The county judge in response set out his action in the premises, to which the relators filed a demurrer, which was sustained by the court below, and the defendant prohibited from levying the tax by perpetual injunction. From this decree the defendant, the county judge, appealed, and the case was heard in the Supreme Court, the decree reversed, and the county judge permitted to issue bonds and levy and collect a tax therefor. In this case the opinion was written by Hall, J., and the decision last but one cited is followed without comment. Although Greene, J., dissented on a minor question, growing out of the facts in the case, there was no dissenting opinion on the constitutionality of the bonds.

Next in order, in the course of the history of this question, in the State of Iowa, are two acts of the legislature of the State, passed at the session of December, A. D. 1854, both approved January 28th, 1855.

By the first of these it is enacted, "*That wherever* any [railway] company shall have received, or may hereafter receive, the bonds of any city or county *upon subscription of stock,* by such city or county, such bonds may have interest at any rate not exceeding ten per cent., and may be sold by the company, at such discount as may be deemed expedient."

By the second it is enacted, "that in all cases where county or town or city incorporations have or may hereafter become stockholders in railroads, or other private companies or incorporations, it shall not be lawful for the county judges, mayors, or other agents of such cities or counties, to issue the bonds of their counties, or cities, until they are satisfied that the contemplated improvements will be constructed through or to their respective cities or counties, within thirty-six months from the issuing and delivery of said bonds; and the proceeds of such bonds shall, in all cases, be expended within the limits of the county in which said city may be situated; *Provided*, that nothing in this act shall in any way affect corporation rights, for any contracts or subscriptions heretofore made with any railroad company or corporation, for the issuing of county corporation bonds."

These acts show the construction of the State authorities at that time, and are themselves a legislative acknowledgment that under prior laws such municipal corporations had the right to issue bonds to railroads and to take stock in them, and afforded general authority of law for such actions on the part of such corporations in future.

The next case that came before the Supreme Court of the State, was that of *Clapp* v. *The County of Cedar,* a suit brought on the same bonds, the issue of which was sought to be enjoined in the case of *The State* v. *Bissell,* and was determined before the court at the June Term, A.D. 1857, by a court composed entirely of different judges from those on the bench when the last cause was decided. In that case the majority of the court hold:

I. That the question of the constitutionality of the bonds is decided by the prior decisions, upon which the public and the world have acted, and that a change of ruling would be "the worst of all repudiation,—judicial repudiation."

II. That such bonds and coupons were negotiable as under the law merchant.

Other questions foreign to this subject were also discussed, but it is unnecessary to refer to them. Wright, C. J., dissented, to use his own words, "very reluctantly," on the question of the constitutionality of such bonds.

The question again was decided three times at the June Term, 1858, in *Ring* v. *The County of Johnson,* in *McMillen* v. *Boyles,* and in *McMillen* v. *The County Judge and Treasurer of Lee County.* The opinions in the first two cases were written by Woodward (Wright, C. J., dissenting in the first case); in the second case no one dissented; and the opinion in the third case was written by Wright, former dissenting judge. Each case holds,

I. That the question is *settled* by the Supreme Court *by former* adjudications, that the counties have the right, constitutionally, to take stock in a railroad, and to issue their bonds therefor.

II. And the second and third cases decide that the legislature by a curative act had made the bonds of Lee County binding upon the county, although from an informality they were irregularly issued.

In one of the cases, *Ring* v. *The County of Johnson,* which was decided a few days before the others, Chief Justice Wright wrote a short dissenting opinion.

Next in order in the decisions of this question comes *Games* v. *Robb,* June Term, 1859, and the opinion is here written by Chief Justice Wright, who says: "That the judge had the power to submit a vote to take subscription on a railroad, to the people, and to levy a tax therefor, *we understand to be settled* in favor of the power by the cases of *Clapp* v. *Cedar County, Ring* v. *The County of Johnson,* and *McMillen* v. *Boyles,* and the cases there referred to." Thus, all the judges concur in the decision of this question, as they did in *McMillen* v. *Boyles,* holding the constitutionality of the bonds to be decided by the former cases, the opinion of the court being, in each case, written by the learned judge who alone had dissented.

We thus have the decisions of the Supreme Court of Iowa, given to the world through a period of six years, by two different benches, in seven different decisions of the court, upon the questions now made before this court, and although two judges had dissented during that time, yet in the opinion of the Chief Justice of the State, written by him who alone had before that time "very reluctantly" dissented, the great commercial world, whose money was at that very moment building up the commerce of the State by extending railroads through it, were assured that the question was settled, and that, too, in favor of the legality and negotiability of these bonds. Whether, in view of the Constitution of Iowa, it was or was not rightly settled in the first instance, is a matter not important at all to inquire into. It was settled by a tribunal which had power to settle it; and on the faith of judicial decisions the bonds were sold.

Before examining decisions since made by the Supreme Court of Iowa, let us mention the decisions of other courts, down to the date when, at December Term, 1859, the Supreme Court just named took that first step, in *Stokes* v. *The County of Scott,* in overthrowing its decision, which was consummated in *The State, ex relatione,* v. *The County of Wapello,* at the June Term, 1862.

In Ohio, the Supreme Court, at different dates, has affirmed its ruling in five different decisions. In Missouri, its court followed, in 1856, previous rulings also.

In this, the Supreme Court of the United States, the question was decided twice at December Term, 1858, and once in 1859, and once in 1860.

The District Court of the United States for the District of Wisconsin, in A. D. 1861, made similar decisions, in *Smith* v. *Milwaukee & Superior R. R. Co.*, and *Mygatt* v. *City of Green Bay*.

The Supreme Court of New York, at June Term, 1857, in *Clarke* v. *The City of Rochester*, in a review of the question, after an elaborate argument before them, made the same ruling, which was affirmed by the Court of Appeals of that State at the September Term, 1858, *nemine dissentiente*.

The Supreme Court of Indiana, at the May Term, 1857, made the same ruling.

The Supreme Court of Illinois made a similar ruling, in April Term, 1858, which was, in April Term, 1860, affirmed in two cases.

The same question, after elaborate discussion, was also unanimously decided in the same way, at the January Term, 1857, of the Court of Appeals of South Carolina.

The Supreme Court of Wisconsin, at the December Term, 1859, in the two cases, made the same ruling, and decided every constitutional question in this case under a Constitution the same as that of the State of Iowa, in favor of the legality of such bonds; and that, too, by the unanimous concurrence of the whole bench. There are other cases, in others of the States of the Union, which might be cited, but it would only tend to lengthen the list, rather than to make it stronger.

Nowhere, in short, can an authority be found, save the subsequent ruling of the State of Iowa, where the highest appellate court of a State, or of the United States, has held such bonds to be invalid, in the hands of *bonâ fide* holders for value; and at the time when that decision was rendered, decisions had been made by the Supreme Court of the United States, and of fifteen of the different States of the Union, of which Iowa was one, running through a quarter of a century of time, and all going to establish the obligation.

But upon what grounds was this contrarient decision finally based?

In *Stokes* v. *The County of Scott*, the majority of the court held, where the bonds had been negotiated, and rights had become vested, by purchase, by innocent holders, that there they were valid; but that where the question was presented prior to the issue of such bonds, the court might properly interfere to restrain the issue. Wright, C. J., took his former position, holding such bonds to be unconstitutional and void, in the hands of all parties. Stockton, J., held the bonds constitutional, but not warranted by law; that they might be enforced by innocent third parties, but that it was properly within the province of a court of equity to restrain the issue thereof, where the question was presented *in limine*.

Woodward, J., dissented from both the other judges, holding that the question was settled in the State, and that it was the duty of the court to abide by precedents.

Of the immediate effect of this decision, the world had no right to complain, as no money had been invested, and it was only so far as it tended to cast loose from the accepted decisions of the State of Iowa, and of other States, and to render vested rights insecure, that it tended to work a hardship upon the commercial world.

We come now to *The State of Iowa, ex relatione,* v. *The County of Wapello,* June Term, 1862. The court there decided:

I. That section 114 of the Code of 1851, did not afford the authority of law for issuing of county bonds, overruling the case of 1853,—*Dubuque County* v. *Dubuque and Pacific Railroad Co.*

II. That certain statutes relied on, did not afford such authority, nor legalize such acts already performed; but—

III. That if a constitutional question did not preclude it, the court would feel bound by the construction of the statute by former courts, and would follow such decisions.

IV. That such a law, however passed, would not confer the authority, because unconstitutional.

[The counsel then examined this case on principle, arguing that independently of precedents it was wrongly decided.]

Now in the face of this history of decisions in Iowa and everywhere, of what value is this case, *The State of Iowa, ex rel.,* v. *The County of Wapello,* so much relied on? By whom, after all, is law to be settled among us? By the Supreme Court of the United States, or of the State of Iowa? By the supreme tribunal of fifteen States or of one? By the Supreme Court of Iowa for *seven* years or for *two?* By *six* judges of that State or by *three?* Are you to hold, in the face of the fact that millions of dollars have been invested, under the law which enters into and forms a part of every contract as it was interpreted by the courts of the whole country, that you yourselves were mistaken? That for twenty-five years all the tribunals of the whole country were mistaken? That for *seven years the Supreme Court of Iowa was mistaken?* Because it appears now that that tribunal has *reversed its long-established rulings?* Had the question been presented to you one year ago to-day, you would not have hesitated an hour on the proposition, for then there was no diversity of rulings anywhere. Because the Supreme Court of Iowa has chosen thus to disregard its own precedents, are millions of property, treasured on the banks of the Delaware, the Hudson, the Thames, the Seine, and the Rhine; are the decisions *of this State of Iowa* itself, as of all the States; the reputation of *that people,* as of Americans generally, to be swept away? swept away by a "surge of judicial opinion?" Is the sway of law among us thus to "shake like a thing unfirm?" This cannot be. At best there is no settled law in Iowa upon the subject. The court of this year has reversed the decisions of former years; and has but taught instructions which will return, hereafter, to plague it. Assuredly, this high tribunal of the United States, whose opinion has been expressed with clearness, will not vary its opinion and cut loose from its own, and from accepted decisions of the whole country, at a time when, above all times, change would be unwarranted in principle and freighted with disaster.

Mr. Bissell, for the City of Dubuque:
The question is, Whether a subscription to an extra-territorial railway,—made by a city corporation under authority of an act of the legislature,—is valid under the *Constitution and decisions of the State of Iowa?* It is not here important for us to inquire what other courts, acting under other constitutions and under other laws, may have decided. And, first, it is conceded by the other side that a city corporation has no power by virtue of its ordinary franchises to make such subscription. If the power exist at all, it is now admitted that it comes only from legislation directly authorizing it. How, then, stands the case?

1. Let it be considered irrespectively of precedents anywhere. Under our form of government, the legislature, unlike parliament, is not omnipotent. Irrespectively of all constitutions, bills of right, or anything of that sort, it will be conceded that the legislature cannot directly take the property of one man and give it to another, or compel one man, or any number of men, to engage in particular pursuits, or to invest their money in particular securities. Nor can it take private property for even public purposes, without *just* compensation; compensation of some kind or in some way. What it cannot do in one form it cannot do in another. What it cannot do by command, it cannot do by taxation. If the legislature should tax the property of individuals in one city for all the expenses of another, such legislation would be void. And even in regard to improvements of a kind really public, if more than any citizen's just share of the expense of them is taken, the legislation is null. If power is given to take property in one place which concerns the public at large, property not being proportionably taken from that public at large, or if property is taken from one place only for objects which concern another, the power is not one conformed to the principles of constitutional republican government. Now a man's property is as much taken by a tax as by any other form. Indeed of all modes of taking property it is the most effective, as also the most difficult to analyze and oppose. It has always been the instrument of unconstitutional legislation, and, therefore, should be watched and guarded. It is of the essence of taxation, therefore, that it be just. And wherein does this justness consist? Plainly in a just apportionment of taxes; that is to say, an apportionment which brings to the party, *in some form,* just compensation for this property taken away. In regard to a man's property taken by tax and applied to purposes purely local and about him, he gets the just recompense, by the application itself. Where the application is to purposes of a wider and more public kind,—for the purposes of his State, or the United States,—he gets a just recompense, provided all others are taxed *proportionably* with him. But just in so far as he is taxed *above* them, he gets no just recompense at all. The principles are readily applied to a case like the present.

It is almost unnecessary to say, that what the legislature cannot do directly, it cannot do indirectly. The stream can mount no higher than its source. The legislature cannot create corporations with illegal powers, nor grant unconstitutional powers to those already granted.

Again: Counsel of the other side do not distinguish well between private corporations and public ones.

Private corporations are only created with the assent of the corporators. They, by becoming corporators, *voluntarily* enter into a *contract,* by which they put their money or property into a common fund, to be controlled in accordance with rules to which they have assented, and which cannot be changed without their assent. The legislature cannot change the terms of their charter, neither can the majority of the corporators, unless it has been so prescribed in the contract, to which each corporator has given his assent. It is therefore right that these corporations should be permitted to enter into such speculations as they may choose. Each member has placed just so much of his property under the control of the corporation, as he has deemed best for his interest, and no more. With *public* corporations it is different. The corporation is created by the legislature without necessarily consulting the will of the inhabitants, and often, in fact, in opposition to said will. The rights, duties, and powers of public corporations may be altered or taken away at any time by legislative enactment, or greater powers may be conferred upon the corporation in the same manner. The inhabitants of such corporation have no voice in accepting the charter; they have no power of electing how much of their property they will subject to the control of the corporation; they cannot transfer their stock, and thus cease to be members of such corporation. The legislature has power to create such corporation, in opposition to the will of the corporators, because such corporation is a portion of the government of the State itself, and every man yields up to the State just so many of his inherent rights, as are necessary to carry on the government which protects him. As said before, every citizen of a State yields up to the State all those rights which are necessary to carry on the government. He yields up the right *without his individual assent,* to be united, with other citizens, into cities, towns, counties, &c., as the legislature may deem proper. As it is necessary to have roads, wharves, waterworks, &c., for the use of the citizens of such corporations, he yields his assent to be taxed for the creation of such works. Such works, however, when created, are under the control of the corporation. They are for the sole use of the corporation.

In regard to the State of Iowa, its Constitution comes in aid of general principles. It declares (i) that all laws of a general nature shall have a uniform operation. Is not a law which authorizes a great public improvement—one running over the State—a law of a general nature? Does it have a uniform operation when the cost of it is laid on the people living at one terminus, all those along its line being exempt? It declares (ii) that the legislative power of the *State* shall be vested in the *Assembly* of the State; meaning, of course, that it shall not be delegated. But is it not delegated when, by statute, you give a city power to legislate in a manner, which, but for the statute, it confessedly would not have? It declares (iii) that the Assembly shall not "in *any* manner create *any* debt, ... which shall singly or in the *aggregate*, ... exceed $100,000." The restraint is not against the creation of a debt in behalf of the State, any more than on behalf of her subdivisions. The language is broad. When the State authorizes the cities, counties, townships, boroughs, which cover her whole surface, to lay debts on every respective part of her, is not the purpose of the restraint violated? A construction which renders practically vain a *constitutional* provision which a different interpretation, not forced, will preserve, can not be a sound one. It declares (iv) that corporations shall not, be created by general laws, except for political or municipal purposes. Here is a law, in fact creating a corporation for a purpose which is neither. It declares in the same section that the State shall not directly nor *indirectly* become a stockholder in any corporation. But does not the State become indirectly a stockholder in a corporation, when she authorizes a portion of her people to enter into an organization, *which, but for her statute, they cannot have,* and allows them in such form to become a stockholder in a corporation?

It is urged that the courts of the different States of the Union have decided this question so uniformly in favor of the power of the legislature to confer the authority claimed, that it is no longer an open question. We may observe in passing that it is [a] matter of difficulty for professional men or judges—if not belonging to a State—perfectly to understand the value of decisions made under local constitutions and local statutes in that State. They may run into great error if they read them by lights in which they are accustomed to see elsewhere. But assuming all that is claimed for them, such decisions are not binding upon this court; and if the decisions of other courts are not in accordance with the law as understood by this court, they will not be followed. If a dissenting opinion of said courts is based upon correct legal principles, this court will follow such principles, rather than an erroneous decision of a court. Let us see if the decisions of the courts of the different States do establish the principle, that a legislature, with power like that of the State of Iowa, can confer upon municipal corporations the right to purchase stock in railroad corporations.

In the first case cited, *Goddin* v. *Crump*, it was decided that the legislature of Virginia had power to authorize the city of Richmond to levy a tax, to aid in removing a bar from James River, to open navigation to the city, and to take stock in a private corporation, organized to perform such work. This river was a navigable stream, under the laws of Virginia. The court held that the levy of the tax to pay for such stock was legal, and also held that the interest of the corporation was the true test of the corporate character of the act, and that the legislature was the sole judge of what would conduce to the interest of the city. The act giving the power to aid in the construction of said work, was passed at the request of a majority of the citizens of the city. The majority of the court seem to have lost sight of the fact that an interest in an improvement is entirely different from an incidental benefit arising from the same improvement. But there is a dissenting opinion by Brooke, J., which places the question upon the true grounds. He holds that such legislation violated the bill of rights; that the power of such corporations to tax the people must be limited to objects of purely a local character. This case arose under an express act of the legislature, giving the specific power claimed.

In the next case relied on, *Bridgeport* v. *Housatonic Railroad Co.*, it was decided that the legislature, upon request of a city, may authorize such city to subscribe for and take stock in a railroad leading to such city, provided such act be approved by the people of the city. The only clause in the Constitution, which was claimed to restrict the legislature, was that which forbade private property being taken for public use without compensation. This was also under an express act of the legislature.

In Tennessee it has been decided—the third case cited, shows—that under the provision of the Constitution of that State, which provides that "the legislature has power to grant to counties and incorporated towns the right to impose taxes for *county* and *corporation purposes*," the legislature may authorize a city to aid in the construction of a railroad *to such corporation*, and when the expenditure is by a county, the expenditure must be *within* the county. The Constitution of that State does not limit the grant to an expenditure municipal for *municipal purposes*, but for corporate purposes.

In Kentucky, it has been decided that the legislature had power to authorize municipal corporations to take stock in railroad corporations, and levy taxes to assist in building said road to such corporation. There is an able dissenting opinion in this case. This decision is founded upon the fact that there was no limitation to the legislative power in their Constitution, and that it was, therefore, omnipotent.

In Pennsylvania, this doctrine was carried to its extreme limit in one case,—*Sharpless* v. *The Mayor of Philadelphia*,—where it was decided that a municipal corporation may aid in the construction of a railroad, miles away, if it can be supposed that it may benefit the corporation; and that the legislature is the judge of the question. But in another,—*Diamond* v. *The County of Lawrence*,—when suit was brought on bonds, like those here, in the hands of holders who had paid value for them, the court declared that they were open to defences of every kind; and a recovery was not had.

In Illinois, where there is no constitutional limitation, it has been held that a municipal corporation may, under legislative authority, aid in the construction of railroads within the corporation.

In Florida, under a similar provision of the Constitution to that of Tennessee, it was held that a county might aid in constructing a railroad *through the county*.

Other States have followed the decisions we dissent from; some following them to a full extent, and some limiting the application to a narrower compass.

All of the decisions, we believe, are where there was no constitutional restriction, or where the power was expressly given, as in Tennessee and Florida.

In many of the decisions, the courts seem to have been imbued with the frenzy of the day, and to have lost sight of the well-defined distinction between the powers and liabilities of municipal and private corporations.

This question, it is believed, has not been decided by this court as an independent question; but its decisions so far are based upon the decisions of the courts of the State in which the cases originated, and upon the rule that this court will follow the decisions of State courts, as to the construction of their own Constitution or statutes. If this question has been settled by the courts in the State of Iowa, then this court will follow such ruling; but if they have not settled it, then it is an open question for determination by this court. What is the history of these decisions?

The Supreme Court of Iowa, in the case of *The Dubuque and Pacific Railroad Co.* v. *Dubuque County*, which is claimed to be decisive of this question, decided that the Constitution of the State had not *deprived* the *citizens* of the county of the right to vote the credit of said county to build a railroad within the county limits. That court uses the following language: "As the people have not, in the Constitution, delegated this power, to vote upon such propositions, nor in any way conceded or divested themselves of this right, but have in express terms affirmed, in the bill of rights, that 'all political power is inherent in the people' (Art. I, Sec. 2), we conclude that the people may, with constitutional propriety, vote the credit of the county to aid in the construction of a railroad within its limits;" one judge dissenting as to the power of the county to take stock in railroads. That court has thus decided that the Constitution has not conferred upon the legislature of the State any power to authorize such an expenditure. That this power is not in the people in their aggregate capacity, either as a town, city, county, or State, but in their individual capacity. It holds virtually that the legislature has no such power, but that it is inherent in the people. There is nothing said about the power of the legislature to confer this authority on a city or county.

The next case relied on is the *State* v. *Bissell*. In that case the question was not raised, and the court say: "This decision is not intended to sanction or deny the legal validity of the decision in the foregoing case, but to leave that question where that decision has left it."

The next case is *Clapp* v. *County of Cedar*. The court disposes of the constitutional question with the following remarks: "The second step would be, whether a legislature possesses the power to confer this authority upon a county? Few have doubted the existence of this power, the question having generally been, whether the power had been exercised, or whether a county possessed the desired authority without a special grant?" The court, however, say that "this power is not, as far as the court can see, derived from any legislative enactment," but, upon the strength of the judgment of the court in the above case of *The Dubuque and*

Pacific Railroad Co. v. *Dubuque County,* it decides that the counties have power to aid in the construction of railroads within the limits of such county; one judge dissenting.

In *Ring* v. *Johnson Co.,* and *McMillen* v. *Boyles,* the last cases cited on the other side, the question was not directly raised nor decided, the court conceding that counties had the right to aid in the construction of railroads to be constructed *within their limits.*

But confessedly the Iowa decisions in favor of these bonds end here. They were never quite unanimous, and have never given satisfaction to either profession or courts. In *Stokes* v. *The County of Scott,* a majority of the court assumed tenable ground, and restrained an issue about to be made. Then came *The State, ex relatione,* v. *The County of Wapello,* a case fully argued, much considered, and unanimously decided. That this case does decide these bonds to be void, that such is now the law in the State of Iowa, is undeniable, we think. The court in that great case remarks, that although some fourteen or fifteen States had expressed their opinions upon this exercise of power by municipal corporations, they had not reached satisfactory conclusions. Hence, it declares, the renewed agitation on the subject; an agitation, it remarks, which "will continue to obtrude itself upon the courts of the country, year after year, until they have finally settled it upon principles of adjudication which are known to be of the class of those that are laid up among the fundamentals of the law: and which will leave the capital of private individuals where the railroad era, when it dawned upon the world, found it, namely, under the control and dominion of those who have it, to be employed in whatever field of industry and enterprise they themselves might judge best." The court then speaks of the decisions of Iowa from the first, *Dubuque Co.* v. *The Dubuque, &c., R. R.,* in 1853, where by a divided court the power was held to have been given, to the last, *Stokers* v. *County of Scott,* in 1859, where by a like court it was to a degree decided otherwise. "The intermediate decisions," it declares, "were an acquiescence in the former of these, by two members of the court, not upon the ground that the legislature had in fact authorized the exercise of any such power by the cities or counties in this State (for this they had expressed very great doubts about, and affected not to believe), but because they felt themselves so much committed and trammelled by the previous decision and subsequent legislative recognition, that they did not feel themselves at liberty, from public considerations, to unsettle the construction which the first decision had given to the code on the subject."

"In this aspect of the case," the court continues, "it will be perceived that the question now under consideration is an entirely open one in this State, and that this court as now constituted must pass upon it as an original question, wholly unaffected by the doctrine of *stare decisis;* or, if influenced at all by prior decisions, we should be inclined to follow the later rather than the earlier opinions." The court then examines the history of legislation in Iowa, and shows that important features in it have escaped the notice of judges who first gave a construction to the code. It then inquires whether the legislature *can* pass laws like those in question, and considers the question on the principles of State and of municipal governments, and on the character and responsibilities, the risks and liabilities, of railroad corporations; declaring that the legislature cannot. The court was conscious of the importance of the decision they were making. They say, in denying the validity of these bonds: "We are not insensible that in doing so, at this late day, we are liable to expose ourselves and our people to the charge of insincerity and bad faith, and perhaps that which is still worse, inflict a great wrong upon innocent creditors and bondholders: consequences which we would most gladly have avoided, if we could have done so and been true to the obligations of conscience and principle." But they declare that the legislative power assumed "practically overturns one of the reserved and fundamental rights of the citizen, that of making his own contracts, choosing his own business pursuits, and managing his property and means in his own way, and which, under the Constitution of this State, however it may be elsewhere, entitles him to the intervention and protection of the courts, we are willing to risk the consequences resulting from the exercise of such a power as furnishing a sufficient answer in itself to all the reasons which have been or may be assigned in favor of its exercise." In answer to the cry about improvement and trade, they declare that if any person "who believes the law to possess the dignity of a science, and hold an exalted rank in the empire of reason," will "analyze the question with reference to the principles and theory of our own political organization, he will discover that it implicates a right which in importance is above all or any interest connected with the business relation or the physical improvements of the county." And rendering everything to its proper sphere, and leaving to the law its duties, and to conscience hers, they end with this declaration: "We know, however, that there is such a thing as a moral sense and a public faith which may be successfully appealed to, when the law is impotent to afford relief. These sentiments, we cannot but believe, still reside in the hearts and consciences of our people, and may be invoked to save themselves and their State from seeming bad faith." The case may be avoided or evaded. Answered, on principle, it cannot be.

Amey v. *Alleghany City,* decided in this court in 1859, is one of the decisions relied on to support the plaintiff's case; but that decision is against it. The case, a Pennsylvania one, acknowledged the force of the argument we have used as to the proper objects of legislation, and the constitutionality or unconstitutionality of statutes accordingly. But the court considered that constitutionality was not *there* open for discussion; it having been affirmed by the State court. If it had been open, such legislation would not have been supported. "We have not," say the court, "discussed that position of the learned counsel. *Agreeing with him in the main, as to the foundations upon which the correctness of legislation should be tested, and the objects for which it ought to be approved,* we cannot, with the respect which we have for the judiciary of his State, discuss the imputed unconstitutionality of the acts; it having been repeatedly decided by the judges of the courts of Pennsylvania, including its Supreme Court, that acts for the same purposes as those are which we have been considering were constitutional."

If this court considers, as the court of Iowa has done, that the constitutionality of the Iowa acts is open for consideration, they will decide that constitutionality does not exist, and that the bonds are void.

Then, the question is, whether the constitution and laws of a State are to be construed by the State courts of other States, or by its own courts? whether, in a case where no power to interpret *above* the State's court is given to the Supreme Court of the United States—as such power is given in certain other cases, where a writ of error lies to the highest State court from this—this court will determine that the constitution and statutes of a State mean one thing, when the courts of the State itself have solemnly adjudged that they mean another? whether this court will say, that the State courts have decided a question, when the judges who sit on the bench of that court are declaring unanimously that "the question is an entirely open one," and to be passed upon as an "original question?" whether, because dealers upon change, whose daily bread, like that of underwriters, is "risk;" people upon the "Rhine"—the respectable citizens of the Juden-Gasse of Frankfürt-am-Maine,—have bought these bonds at large discounts, *on account of those doubts of their legality* which everywhere have attended the issue of them, shall have them enforced in the face of constitutions and solemn decisions of the State courts, simply because they *have* bought and yet hold them? These are the questions; some of them grave ones,—if resolved in the affirmative.

>Mr. Justice SWAYNE delivered the opinion
>of the court:

The whole case resolves itself into a question of the power of the city to issue bonds for the purpose stated.

The act incorporating the city, approved February 24, 1847, provides as follows:

"SECT. 27. That whenever, in the opinion of the City Council, it is expedient to borrow money for any public purpose, the question shall be submitted to the citizens of Dubuque, the nature and object of the loan shall be stated, and a day fixed for the electors of said city to express their wishes, the like notice shall be given as in cases of election, and the loan shall not be made unless two-thirds of all the votes polled at such election shall be given in the affirmative."

"By an act approved January 8th, 1851, the act of incorporation was so amended as to empower the City Council to levy annually a special tax to pay interest on such loans as are authorized by the 27th section of said act."

An act approved January 28th, 1857, contains these provisions:

"That the city of Dubuque is hereby authorized and empowered to aid in the construction of the Dubuque Western and the Dubuque, St. Peter's & St. Paul

Railroad Companies, by issuing $250,000 of city bonds to each, in pursuance of a vote of the citizens of said city, taken in the month of December, A. D. 1856. Said bonds shall be legal and valid, and the City Council is authorized and required to levy a special tax to meet the principal and interest of said bonds, in case it shall become necessary from the failure of funds from other sources."

"The proclamation, the vote, and bonds issued or to be issued, are hereby declared valid, and the said railroad companies are hereby authorized to expend the money arising from the sale of said bonds, without the limits of the city and county of Dubuque, in the construction of either of said roads, and neither the city of Dubuque, nor any of the citizens, shall ever be allowed to plead that said bonds are invalid."

By these enactments, if they are valid, ample authority was given to the city to issue the bonds in question. The city acted upon this authority. The qualifications coupled with the grant of power contained in the 27th section of the act of incorporation are not now in question. If they were, the result would be the same. When a corporation has power, under any circumstances, to issue negotiable securities, the *bonâ fide* holder has a right to presume they were issued under the circumstances which give the requisite authority, and they are no more liable to be impeached for any infirmity in the hands of such a holder than any other commercial paper. If there were any irregularity in taking the votes of the electors or otherwise in issuing the bonds, it is remedied by the curative provisions of the act of January 28, 1857.

Where there is no defect of constitutional power, such legislation, in cases like this, is valid. This question, with reference to a statute containing similar provisions, came under the consideration of the Supreme Court of Iowa, in *McMillen* v. *Boyles,* and again in *McMillen et al.* v. *The County Judge and Treasurer of Lee County.* The validity of the act was sustained. Without these rulings we should entertain no doubt upon the subject.

It is claimed "that the legislature of Iowa had no authority under the Constitution to authorize municipal corporations to purchase stock in railroad companies, or to issue bonds in payment of such stock." In this connection our attention has been called to the following provisions of the Constitution of the State:

"ART. 1. § 6. All laws of a general nature shall have a uniform operation."

"ART. 3. § 1. The legislative authority of the State shall be vested in a Senate and House of Representatives, which shall be designated as the General Assembly of the State of Iowa," &c.

"ART. 7. The General Assembly shall not in any manner create any debt or debts, liability or liabilities which shall, singly or in the aggregate, exceed the sum of one hundred thousand dollars, except," &c. The exceptions stated do not relate to this case.

"ART. 8. § 2. Corporations shall *not be created in this State by special laws, except for political or municipal purposes,* but the General Assembly shall provide by general laws for the organization of all other corporations, except corporations with banking privileges, the creation of which is prohibited. The stockholders shall be subject to such liabilities and restrictions as shall be provided by law. The State shall not, directly or indirectly, become a stockholder in any corporation."

Under these provisions it is insisted,—

1. That the general grant of power to the legislature did not warrant it in conferring upon municipal corporations the power which was exercised by the city of Dubuque in this case.
2. That the seventh article of the Constitution prohibits the conferring of such power under the circumstances stated in the answer,—debts of counties and cities being, within the meaning of the Constitution, debts of the State.
3. That the eighth article forbids the conferring of such power upon municipal corporations by special laws.

All these objections have been fully considered and repeatedly overruled by the Supreme Court of Iowa: *Dubuque Co. v. The Dubuque & Pacific R. R. Co.* (4 Greene, 1); *The State v. Bissel* (4 Id., 328); *Clapp v. Cedar Co.* (5 Iowa, 15); *Ring v. County of Johnson* (6 Id., 265); *McMillen v. Boyles* (6 Id., 304); *McMillen v. The County Judge of Lee Co.* (6 Id., 393); *Games v. Robb* (8 Id., 193); *State v. The Board of Equalization of the County of Johnson* (10 Id., 157). The earliest of these cases was decided in 1853, the latest in 1859. The bonds were issued and put upon the market between the periods named. These adjudications cover the entire ground of this controversy. They exhaust the argument upon the subject. We could add nothing to what they contain. We shall be governed by them, unless there be something which takes the case out of the established rule of this court upon that subject.

It is urged that all these decisions have been overruled by the Supreme Court of the State, in the later case of the *State of Iowa, ex relatione, v. The County of Wapello,* and it is insisted that in cases involving the construction of a State law or constitution, this court is bound to follow the latest adjudication of the highest court of the State. *Leffingwell v. Warren* is relied upon as authority for the proposition. In that case this court said it would follow "the latest *settled* adjudications." Whether the judgment in question can, under the circumstances, be deemed to come within that category, it is not now necessary to determine. It cannot be expected that this court will follow every such oscillation, from whatever cause arising, that may possibly occur. The earlier decisions, we think, are sustained by reason and authority. They are in harmony with the adjudications of sixteen States of the Union. Many of the cases in the other States are marked by the profoundest legal ability.

The late case in Iowa, and two other cases of a kindred character in another State, also overruling earlier adjudications, stand out, as far as we are advised, in unenviable solitude and notoriety. However we may regard the late case in Iowa as affecting the future, it can have no effect upon the past. "The sound and true rule is, that if the contract, when made, was valid by the laws of the State as then expounded by all departments of the government, and administered in its courts of justice, its validity and obligation cannot be impaired by any subsequent action of legislation, or decision of its courts altering the construction of the law."

The same principle applies where there is a change of judicial decision as to the constitutional power of the legislature to enact the law. To this rule, thus enlarged, we adhere. It is the law of this court. It rests upon the plainest principles of justice. To hold otherwise would be as unjust as to hold that rights acquired under a statute may be lost by its repeal. The rule embraces this case.

Bonds and coupons, like these, by universal commercial usage and consent, have all the qualities of commercial paper. If the plaintiffs recover in this case, they will be entitled to the amount specified in the coupons, with interest and exchange as claimed.

We are not unmindful of the importance of uniformity in the decisions of this court, and those of the highest local courts, giving constructions to the laws and constitutions of their own States. It is the settled rule of this court in such cases, to follow the decisions of the State courts. But there have been heretofore, in the judicial history of this court, as doubtless there will be hereafter, many exceptional cases. We shall never immolate truth, justice, and the law, because a State tribunal has erected the altar and decreed the sacrifice.

The judgment below is reversed, and the cause remanded for further proceedings in conformity to this opinion.

JUDGMENT AND MANDATE ACCORDINGLY.

Mr. Justice MILLER, dissenting:

In the opinions which have just been delivered, I have not been able to concur. But I should have contented myself with the mere expression of dissent, if it were not that the principle on which the court rests its decision is one, not only essentially wrong, in my judgment, but one which, if steadily adhered to in future, may lead to consequences of the most serious character. In adopting that principle, this court has, as I shall attempt to show, gone in the present case a step in advance of anything heretofore ruled by it on the subject, and has taken a position which must bring in into direct and unseemly conflict with the judiciary of the States. Under these circumstances, I do not feel at liberty to decline placing upon the records of the court the reasons which have forced me, however reluctantly, to a conclusion different from that of the other members of the court.

The action in the present case is on bonds of the city of Dubuque, given in payment of certain shares of the capital stock of a railroad company, whose road runs from said city westward. The court below held, that the bonds were void for want of authority in the city to subscribe and pay for such stock. It is admitted that the legislature had, as to one set of bonds, passed an act intended to confer such authority on the city, and it is claimed that it had done so as to all the bonds. I do not propose to discuss this latter question.

It is said, in support of the judgment of the court below, that all such grants of power by the legislature of Iowa to any municipal corporation is in conflict with the Constitution of the State, and therefore void. In support of this view of the subject, the cases of *Stokes* v. *Scott County,* and *The State of Iowa, ex relatione,* v. *The County of Wapello,* are relied on.

In the last-mentioned case, the County of Wapello had agreed to take stock in a company whose road passed through the county, but had afterwards refused to issue the bonds which had been voted by the majority of the legal voters. The relator prayed a writ of mandamus to compel the officers of the county to issue the bonds. One question raised in the discussion was, whether section 114 of the code of Iowa, of 1851, was intended to authorize the counties of the State to take stock in railroad companies? And another was, that conceding such to be the fair construction of that section of the code, was it constitutional?

The Supreme Court, in a very elaborate and well-reasoned opinion, held that there was no constitutional power in the legislature to confer such authority on the counties, or on any municipal corporation. This decision was made in a case where the question fairly arose, and where it was necessary and proper that the court should decide it. It was decided by a full bench, and with unanimity. It was decided by the court of highest resort in that State, to which is confided, according to all the authorities, the right to construe the Constitution of the State, and whose decision is binding on all other courts which may have occasion to consider the same question, until it is reversed or modified by the same court. It has been followed in that court by several other decisions to the same point, not yet reported. It is the law administered by all the inferior judicial tribunals in the State, who are bound by it beyond all question. I apprehend that none of my brethren who concur in the opinion just delivered, would go so far as to say that the inferior State courts would have a right to disregard the decision of their own appellate court, and give judgment that the bonds were valid. Such a course would be as useless, as it would be destructive of all judicial subordination.

Yet this is in substance what the majority of the court have decided.

They have said to the Federal court sitting in Iowa, "You shall disregard this decision of the highest of the State on this question. Although you are sitting in the State of Iowa, and administering her laws, and construing her constitution, you shall not follow the latest, though it be the soundest, exposition of its constitution by the Supreme Court of that State, but you shall decide directly to the contrary; and where that court has said that a statute is unconstitutional, you shall say that it is constitutional. When it says bonds are void, issued in that State, because they violate its constitution, you shall say they are valid, because they do *not* violate the constitution."

Thus we are to have two courts, sitting within the same jurisdiction, deciding upon the same rights, arising out of the same statute, yet always arriving at opposite results, with no common arbiter of their differences. There is no hope of avoiding this, if this court adheres to its ruling. For there is in this court no power, in this class of cases, to issue its writ of error to the State court, and thus compel a uniformity of construction, because it is not pretended that either the statute of Iowa, or its constitution, or the decision of its courts thereon, are in conflict with the Constitution of the United States, or any law or treaty made under it.

Is it supposed for a moment that this treatment of its decision, accompanied by language as unsuited to the dispassionate dignity of this court, as it is disrespectful to another court of at least concurrent jurisdiction over the matter in question, will induce the Supreme Court of Iowa to conform its rulings to suit our dictation, in a matter which the very frame and organization of our Government places entirely under its control? On the contrary, such a course, pursued by this court, is well calculated to make that court not only adhere to its own opinion with more tenacity, but also to examine if the law does not afford them the means, in all cases, of enforcing their own construction of their own constitution, and their own statutes, within the limits of their own jurisdiction. What this may lead to it is not possible now to foresee, nor do I wish to point out the field of judicial conflicts, which may never occur, but which if they shall occur, will weigh heavily on that court which should have yielded to the other, but did not.

The general principle is not controverted by the majority, that to the highest courts of the State belongs the right to construe its statutes and its constitution, except where they may conflict with the Constitution of the United States, or some statute or treaty made under it. Nor is it denied that when such a construction has been given by the State court, that this court is bound to follow it. The cases on this subject are numerous, and the principle is as well settled, and is as necessary to the harmonious working of our complex system of government, as the correlative proposition that to this court belongs the right to expound conclusively, for all other courts, the Constitution and laws of the Federal Government.

But while admitting the general principle thus laid down, the court says it is inapplicable to the present case, because there have been conflicting decisions on this very point by the Supreme Court of Iowa, and that as the bonds issued while the decisions of that court holding such instruments to be constitutional were unreversed, that this construction of the constitution must now govern this court instead of the later one. The moral force of this proposition is unquestionably very great. And I think, taken in connection with some fancied duty of this court to enforce contracts, over and beyond that appertaining to other courts, has given the majority a leaning towards the adoption of a rule, which in my opinion cannot be sustained either on principle or authority.

The only special charge which this court has over contracts, beyond any other court, is to declare judicially whether the statute of a State impairs their obligation. No such question arises here, for the plaintiff claims under and by virtue of the statute which is here the subject of discussion. Neither is there any question of the obligation of contracts, or the right to enforce them. The question goes behind that. We are called upon, not to construe a contract, nor to determine how one shall be enforced, but to decide whether there ever was a contract made in the case. To assume that there was a contract, which contract is about to be violated by the decisions of the State court of Iowa, is to beg the very question in dispute. In deciding this question the court is called upon, as the court in Iowa was, to construe the constitution of the State. It is a grave error to suppose that this court must, or should, determine this upon any principle which would not be equally binding on the courts of Iowa, or that the decision should depend upon the fact that certain parties had purchased bonds which were supposed to be valid contracts, when they really were not.

The Supreme Court of Iowa is not the first or the only court which has changed its rulings on questions as important as the one now presented. I understand the doctrine to be in such cases, not that the law is changed, but that it was always the same as expounded by the later decision, and that the former decision was not, and never had been, the law, and is overruled for that very reason. The decision of this court contravenes this principle, and holds that the decision of the court makes the law, and in fact, that the same statute or constitution means one thing in 1853, and another thing in 1859. For it is impliedly conceded, that if these bonds had been issued since the more recent decision of the Iowa court, this court would not hold them valid.

Not only is the decision of the court, as I think, thus unsound in principle, but it appears to me to be in conflict with its former decisions on this point, as I shall now attempt to show.

In the case of *Shelby* v. *Guy*, a question arose on the construction of the statute of limitations of Tennessee. It was an old English statute, adopted by Tennessee from North Carolina, and which had in many other States received a uniform construction. It was stated on the argument, however, that the highest court of Tennessee had given a different construction to it, although the opinion could not then be produced. The court said, that out of a desire to follow the courts of the State in the construction of their own statute, it would not then decide that question, but as the case had to be reversed on other points, it would send it back, leaving that question undecided.

In the case of *The United States* v. *Morrison*, the question was, whether a judgment in the State of Virginia was, under the circumstances of that case, a lien on the real estate of the judgment debtor. In the Circuit Court this had been ruled in the negative, I presume by Chief Justice Marshall, and a writ of error was prosecuted to this court. Between the time of the decision in the Circuit Court and the hearing in this court, the Court of Appeals of Virginia had decided, in a case precisely similar, that the judgment was a lien. This court, by Chief Justice Marshall, said it would follow the recent decision of the Court of Appeals without examination, although it required the reversal of a judgment in the Circuit Court rendered before that decision was made.

The case of *Green* v. *Neal,* is almost parallel with the one now under consideration, but stronger in the circumstances under which the court followed the later decision of the State courts in the construction of their own statute. It is stronger in this, that the court there overruled two former decisions of its own, based upon former decisions of the State court of Tennessee, in order to follow a later decision of the State court, after the law had been supposed to be settled for many years. The case was one on the construction of the statute of limitations, and the Circuit Court at the trial had instructed the jury, "that according to the present state of decisions in the Supreme Court of the United States, they could not charge that defendant's title was made good by the statute of limitations." The decisions here referred to were the cases of *Patton* v. *Easton,* and *Powell* v. *Harman.*

The first of these cases was argued in the February Term, 1815, by some of the ablest counsel of the day, and the opinion delivered more than a year afterwards. In that opinion Chief Justice Marshall recites the long dispute about the point in North Carolina and Tennessee, and says it has at length been settled by the Supreme Court of the latter State by two recent decisions, made after the case then before it had been certified to this court, and the court follows those decisions. This is reaffirmed in the second of the abovementioned cases.

In delivering the opinion in the case of *Green* v. *Neal,* Justice McLean says that the two decisions in Tennessee referred to by Judge Marshall were made under such circumstances that they were never considered as fully settling the point in that State, *there being contrariety of opinion among the judges.* The question, he says, was frequently raised before the Supreme Court of Tennessee, but was never considered as finally settled, until 1825, the first decision having been made in 1815. The opinion of Judge McLean is long, and the case is presented with his usual ability, and I will not here go into further details of it. It is sufficient to say that the court holds it to be its duty to abandon the two first cases decided in Tennessee, to overrule their own well-considered construction in the case of *Patton* v. *Easton,* and its repetition in *Powell* v. *Green,* and to follow without examination the later decision of the Supreme Court of Tennessee, which is in conflict with them all.

At the last term of this court, in the case of *Leffingwell* v. *Warren,* my very learned associate, who has just delivered the opinion in this case, has collated the authorities on this subject, and thus on behalf of the whole court announces the result:

"The construction given to a State statute by the highest judicial tribunal of such State, is regarded as a part of the statute, and is as binding upon the courts of the United States as the text. . . . If the highest judicial tribunal of a State adopt new views as to the proper construction of such a statute, and reverse its former decision, this court will follow the latest settled adjudications."

It is attempted, however, to distinguish the case now before us from those just considered, by saying that the latter relate to what is rather ambiguously called a rule of property, while the former concerns a matter of contract. I must confess my inability to see any principle on which the distinction can rest. All the statutes of the States which prescribe the formalities and incidents to conveyances of real estate would, I presume, be held to be rules of property. If the deed by which a man supposes he has secured to himself and family a homestead, fails to comply in any essential particular with the statute or constitution of the State, as expounded by the most recent decision of the State court, it is held void by this court without hesitation, because it is a rule of property, and the last decision of the State court must govern, even to overturning the well-considered construction of this court. But if a gambling stockbroker of Wall Street buys at twenty-five per cent. of their par value, the bonds issued to a railroad company in Iowa, although the court of the State, in several of its most recent decisions, have decided that such bonds were issued in violation of the Constitution, this court will not follow that decision, but resort to some former one, delivered by a divided court, because in the latter case it is not a rule of property, but a *case of contract*. I cannot rid myself of the conviction that the deed which conveys to a man his homestead, or other real estate, is as much a contract as the paper issued by a municipal corporation to a railroad for its worthless stock, and that a bond when good and valid is property. If bonds are not property, then half the wealth of the nation, now so liberally invested in the bonds of the government, both State and national, and in bonds of corporations, must be considered as having no claim to be called property. And when the construction of a constitution is brought to bear upon the questions of property or no property, contract or no contract, I can see no sound reason for any difference in the rule for determining the question.

The case of *Rowan* v. *Runnels*, is relied on as furnishing a rule for this case, and support to the opinion of the court. In that case the question was on the validity of a note given for the purchase of slaves, imported into the State of Mississippi. It was claimed that the importation was a violation of the Constitution of the State, and the note therefore void. In the case of *Groves* v. *Slaughter* this court had previously decided that very point the other way. In making that decision it had no light from the courts of Mississippi, but was called on to make a decision in a case of the first impression. The court made a decision, with which it remained satisfied when *Rowan* v. *Runnels* came before it, and which is averred by the court to have been in conformity to the expressed sense of the legislature, and the general understanding of the people of that State. The court therefore in *Rowan* v. *Runnels* declined to change its own rulings, under such circumstances, to follow a single later and adverse decision of the Mississippi court.

In the case now before the court it is not called on to retract any decision it has ever made, or any opinion it has declared. The question is before this court for the first time, and it lacks in that particular the main ground on which the judgment of this court rested in *Rowan* v. *Runnels*. It is true that the chief justice, in delivering the opinion in that case, goes on to say, in speaking of the decision of the State courts on their own constitution and laws: "But we ought not to give them a retroactive effect, and allow them to render invalid contracts entered into *with citizens of other States*, which, in the *judgment of this court*, were lawfully made." I have to remark, in the first place, that this dictum was unnecessary, as the first and main ground was, that this court could not be required to overrule its own decision, when it had first occupied the ground, and when it still remained of the opinion then declared. Secondly, that the contract in *Rowan* v. *Runnels*, was between a citizen of Mississippi, on the one part, and a citizen of Virginia on the other, and the language of the chief justice makes that the ground of the right of this court to disregard the later decision of the State court; and in this case the contract was made between the city of Dubuque and a railroad company, both of which were corporations existing under the laws of Iowa, and citizens of that State, in the sense in which that word is used by the chief justice. And, thirdly, the qualification is used in the Runnels case that the *"contracts were, in the judgment of this court, lawfully made."* In the present case, the court rests on the former decision of the State court, declining to examine the constitutional question for itself.

The distinction between the cases is so obvious as to need no further illustration.

The remaining cases in which the subject is spoken of, may be mentioned as a series of cases brought into the Supreme Court of the United States by writ of error to the Supreme Court of Ohio, under the twenty-fifth section of the Judiciary Act. In all these cases the jurisdiction of the Supreme Court of the United States was based upon the allegation that a statute of Ohio, imposing taxes upon bank corporations, was a violation of a previous contract made by the State with them, in regard to the extent to which they should be liable to be taxed. In the argument of these cases it was urged that the very judgments of the Supreme Court of Ohio, which were then under review, being the construction placed by the courts of that State on their own statutes and constitution, should be held to govern the Supreme Court of the Union, in the exercise of its acknowledged right of revising the decision of the State court in that class of cases. It requires but a bare statement of the proposition to show that, if admitted, the jurisdiction of the Federal Supreme Court to sit as a revisory tribunal over the State courts, in cases where the State law is supposed to impair the obligation of a contract, would be the merest sham.

It is true that in the extract, given in the opinion of the court just read, from the case of the *Ohio Trust Company* v. *Debolt*, language is used by Chief Justice Taney, susceptible of a wider application. But he clearly shows that there was in his mind nothing beyond the case of a writ of error to the Supreme Court of a State, for he says in the midst of the sentence cited, or in the immediate context, "The writ of error to a State court would be no protection to a contract, if we were bound to follow the judgment which the State court had given, and which the court brings up here for revision." Besides, in the opinion thus cited, the chief justice says, in the commencement of it, that he only speaks for himself and Justice Grier. The remarks cited, then, were not the opinion of the court, were outside the record, and were evidently intended to be confined to the case of a writ of error to the court of a State, where it was insisted that the judgment sought to be revised should conclude this court.

But let us examine for a moment the earlier decisions in the State court of Iowa, on which this court rests with such entire satisfaction.

The question of the right of municipal corporations to take stock in railroad companies, came before the Supreme Court of Iowa, for the first time, at the June Term, A.D. 1853, in the case of *Dubuque County* v. *The Dubuque and Pacific Railroad Company*. The majority of the court, Kinney J., dissenting, affirmed the judgment of the court below, and in so doing must necessarily have held that municipal corporations could take stock in railroad enterprises. The opinions of the court were by law filed with the clerk, and by him copied into a book kept for that purpose. The dissenting opinion of Judge Kinney, a very able one, is there found in its proper place, in which he says, he has never seen the opinion of the majority. No such opinion is to be found in the clerk's office, as I have verified by a personal examination. Nor was it ever seen, until it was published five years afterwards, in the volume above referred to, by one of the judges, who had ceased to be either judge or official reporter at the time it was published. Shortly after this judgment was rendered, Judge Kinney resigned, and his place was supplied by Judge Hall. The case of the *State* v. *Bissell* then came before the court in 1854. In this case, after disposing of several questions relating to the regularity of the proceedings in issuing bonds for a railroad subscription, Judge Hall, who delivered the opinion of the court, then refers to the right of the county to take stock and issue bonds for railroad purposes. He says: "This point is not urged, and the same question having been decided at the December Term of this court in 1853, in the case of the *Dubuque and Pacific Railroad Company* v. *Dubuque County*, is not examined. This decision is not intended to sanction or deny the legal validity of that decision, but to leave the question where that decision left it." It is clear that if Judge Hall had concurred with the other two judges, no such language as this would have been used, but they would have settled the question by a unanimous opinion. In the case of *Clapp* v. *Cedar County*, the question came up again in the same court, composed of new judges. The Chief Justice, Wright, was against the power of the counties to subscribe stock, and delivered an able dissenting opinion to that purport. The other two judges, however, while in substance admitting that no such power had been conferred by law, held that they must follow the decision in [the] Dubuque case. Several other cases followed these, with about the same result, up to 1859, Wright always protesting, and the other judges overruling him. In 1859, in the case of *Stokes* v. *Scott County*, which was an application to restrain the issue of bonds voted by the county, Judge Stockton said that, in a case like that, where the bonds had not passed into the hands of *bonâ fide* holders, he felt at liberty to declare them void, and concurring with Judge Wright that far, they so decided; Judge Wright placing his opinion upon a want of constitutional power in the legislature. Finally, in the case of the *State of Iowa, ex relatione, v. Wapello County,* the court, now composed of Wright, Lowe, and Baldwin, held unanimously that the bonds were void absolutely, because their issue was in violation of the Constitution of the State of Iowa. The opinion in that case, delivered by Judge Lowe, covers the whole ground, and after an examination of all the previous cases, overrules them all, except *Stokes* v. *Scott County.* It is exhausting, able, and conclusive, and after a struggle of seven or eight years, in which this question has been always before the court, and never considered as closed, this case may now be considered as finally settling the law on that subject in the courts of Iowa. It has already been repeated in several cases not yet reported. It is the first time the question has been decided by a unanimous court. It is altogether improbable that any serious effort will ever be made to shake its force in that State; for of the nine judges who have occupied the bench while the matter was in contest, but two have ever expressed their approbation of the doctrine of the Dubuque County case.

Comparing the course of decisions of the State courts in the present case with those upon which this court acted in *Green* v. *Neal,* how do they stand?

In the latter case the court of Tennessee had decided by a divided court in 1815, and that decision was repeated several times, but with contrariety of opinion among the judges, up to 1825, when the former decisions were reversed. In the cases which we have been considering from Iowa, the point was decided in 1853 by a divided court; it was repeated several times up to 1859, by a divided court, under a continuous struggle. In 1859 the majority changed to the other side, and in 1862 it became unanimous. In the Tennessee case, this court had twice committed itself to the decision first made by the courts of that State; yet it retracted and followed the later decision made ten years after. In the present case, this court, which was not committed at all, follows decisions which were never unanimous, which were struggled against and denied, and which had only six years of judicial life, in preference to the later decisions commenced four years ago, and finally receiving the full assent of the entire court.

I think I have sustained, by this examination of the cases, the assertion made in the commencement of this opinion, that the court has, in this case, taken a step in advance of anything heretofore decided by it on this subject. That advance is in the direction of a usurpation of the right, which belongs to the State courts, to decide as a finality upon the construction of State constitutions and State statutes. This invasion is made in a case where there is no pretence that the constitution, as thus construed, is any infraction of the laws or Constitution of the United States.

The importance of the principle thus for the first time asserted by this court, opposed, as it is, to my profoundest convictions of the relative rights, duties, and comities of this court, and the State court, will, I am persuaded, be received as a sufficient apology for placing on its record, as I now do, my protest against it.

Ex parte Milligan

Supreme Court of the United States
April 3, 1866
4 Wallace (71 U.S.) 2 (1866)

In this decision, controversial at the time and since, the justices of the United States Supreme Court held that the military trial of civilians in areas not directly in war zones and in times of crisis when the civilian courts were open was unconstitutional, but the justices disagreed on the grounds for the decision. Further, while *Milligan* has been hailed by civil libertarians as a major advance of individual liberties, such a reading of the ruling is not warranted by the decision or the subsequent history of its rule. Thus, *Milligan* remains controversial for what it did and what it did not.

In 1864, military authorities in Indiana arrested a number of antiwar Democrats, including Lambdin P. Milligan. The army charged Milligan and his conspirators with planning to seize federal weapons arsenals and use the weapons to liberate Confederates from prison camps and begin an uprising behind Union Army lines. For an area known to exhibit "Copperhead" or pro-Southern sympathies, the military decided against using the Indiana state courts or the federal courts (both of which were open and well behind the lines of military conflict) and instead opted to try the defendants by military commissions. This military tribunal found Milligan and his fellow defendants guilty of the charges against them and sentenced them to hang for their crimes. Milligan appealed to the federal circuit court for a writ of habeas corpus to be released from his confinement as a military prisoner, and challenged the trial of civilians in areas outside war zones by military commissions. When the judges on the circuit court could not agree, they certified the request for the writ to the United States Supreme Court. As a result, the justices of the Supreme Court did not hear arguments on the case until March 1866, after the war had ended; they decided the case in April, but did not hand down their decision until December of that year.

Because of the importance of the issues raised in this case about the limits of a president's powers in times of war, and whether the president can authorize the trial of civilians by military authorities even when the local, state, and federal courts are open, the Supreme Court reprinted the briefs of the attorneys who appeared on behalf of Milligan and the federal government. As a result, the first sixty-plus pages of this decision are the arguments and evidence presented by the lawyers in the case, with the last twenty-plus pages constituting the decision by the unanimous court.

The justices disagreed on their reasons for overturning Milligan's trial and conviction. Associate Justice David Davis argued that even in times of emergency, the Constitution and the laws of the United States were not suspended. His famous phrase is that the Constitution was "a law for rulers and people, equally in times of war and peace." Davis emphasized that when the courts are open, then neither Congress nor the president could authorize the trial of civilians by military authorities. Although Chief Justice Salmon P. Chase agreed with the result that Justice Davis reached, arguing that the 1863 Habeas Corpus Act had guaranteed a trial of civilians in civil court with procedural safeguards, he disagreed that the Congress or the president could not authorize such trials. Chase argued that if the civilian court were unable or incapable of trying civilians on charges such as treason, then Congress could authorize the military trials of civilians. While the *Milligan* rule prohibiting the military trial of civilians when civilian courts are open has been much hailed in post-*Milligan* cases and years, the rule has not always restrained the actions of the federal government in war time and, thus, casts doubt on the significance and weight of *Ex parte Milligan*.

THIS case came before the court upon a certificate of division from the judges of the Circuit Court for Indiana, on a petition for discharge from unlawful imprisonment.

The case was thus:

An act of Congress—the Judiciary Act of 1789, section 14—enacts that the Circuit Courts of the United States[:]

1. Circuit Courts, as well as the judges thereof, are authorized, by the fourteenth section of the Judiciary Act, to issue the writ of *habeas corpus* for the purpose of inquiring into the cause of commitment, and they have jurisdic-

tion, except in cases where the privilege of the writ is suspended, to hear and determine the question, whether the party is entitled to be discharged.
2. The usual course of proceeding is for the court, on the application of the prisoner for a writ of *habeas corpus,* to issue the writ, and on its return to hear and dispose of the case; but where the cause of imprisonment is fully shown by the petition, the court may, without issuing the writ, consider and determine whether, upon the facts presented in the petition, the prisoner, if brought before the court, would be discharged.
3. When the Circuit Court renders a final judgment refusing to discharge the prisoner, he may bring the case here by writ of error; and if the judges of the Circuit Court, being opposed in opinion, can render no judgment, he may have the point upon which the disagreement happens certified to this tribunal.
4. A petition for a writ of *habeas corpus,* duly presented, is the institution of a cause of [on] behalf of the petitioner; and the allowance or refusal of the process, as well as the subsequent disposition of the prisoner, is [a] matter of law and not of discretion.
5. A person arrested after the passage of the act of March 3d, 1863, "relating to *habeas corpus* and regulating judicial proceedings in certain cases," and under the authority of the said act, was entitled to his discharge if not indicted or presented by the grand jury convened at the first subsequent term of the Circuit or District Court of the United States for the district.
6. The omission to furnish a list of the persons arrested, to the judges of the Circuit or District Court as provided in the said act, did not impair the right of such person, if not indicted or presented, to his discharge.
7. Military commissions organized during the late civil war, in a State not invaded and not engaged in rebellion, in which the Federal courts were open, and in the proper and unobstructed exercise of their judicial functions, had no jurisdiction to try, convict, or sentence for any criminal offence, a citizen who was neither a resident of a rebellious State, nor a prisoner of war, nor a person in the military or naval service. And Congress could not invest them with any such power.
8. The guaranty of trial by jury contained in the Constitution was intended for a state of war as well as a state of peace; and is equally binding upon rules and people, at all times and under all circumstances.
9. The Federal authority having been unopposed in the State of Indiana, and the Federal courts open for the trial of offences and the redress of grievances, the usages of war could not, under the Constitution, afford any sanction for the trial there of a citizen in civil life, not connected with the military or naval service, by a military tribunal, for any offence whatever.
10. Cases arising in the land or naval forces, or in the militia in time of war or public danger, are excepted from the necessity of presentment or indictment

by a grand jury; and the right of trial by jury, in such cases, is subject to the same exceptions.
11. Neither the President, nor Congress, nor the Judiciary can disturb any one of the safeguards of civil liberty incorporated into the Constitution, except so far as the right is given to suspend in certain cases the privilege of the writ of *habeas corpus*.
12. A citizen not connected with the military service and resident in a State where the courts are open and in the proper exercise of their jurisdiction cannot, even when the privilege of the writ of *habeas corpus* is suspended, be tried, convicted, or sentenced otherwise than by the ordinary courts of law.
13. Suspension of the privilege of the writ of *habeas corpus* does not suspend the writ itself. The writ issues as a matter of course; and, on its return, the court decides whether the applicant is denied the right of proceeding any further.
14. A person who is a resident of a loyal State, where he was arrested; who was never resident in any State engaged in rebellion, nor connected with the military or naval service, cannot be regarded as a prisoner of war.

'Shall have power to issue writs of *habeas corpus*. And that either of the justices of the Supreme Court, as well as judges of the District Court, shall have power to grant writs of *habeas corpus* for the purpose of an inquiry into the cause of commitment.

Another act—that of March 3d, 1863, "relating to *habeas corpus*, and regulating judicial proceedings in certain cases"—an act passed in the midst of the Rebellion—makes various provisions in regard to the subject of it.

The first section authorizes the suspension, during the Rebellion, of the writ of *habeas corpus*, throughout the United States, by the President.

Two following sections limited the authority in certain respects.

The second section required that lists of all persons, being citizens of States in which the administration of the laws had continued unimpaired in the Federal courts, who were then held, or might thereafter be held, as prisoners of the United States, under the authority of the President, otherwise than as prisoners of war, should be furnished by the Secretary of State and Secretary of War to the judges of the Circuit and District Courts. These lists were to contain the names of all persons, residing within their respective jurisdictions, charged with violation of national law. And it was required, in cases where the grand jury in attendance upon any of these courts should terminate its session without proceeding by indictment or otherwise against any prisoner named in the list, that *the judge* of the court should forth-with make an order that such prisoner, desiring a discharge, should be brought before him or the court to be discharged, on entering into recognizance, if required, to keep the peace and for good behavior, or to appear, as the court might direct, to be further dealt with according to law. Every officer of the United States having custody of such prisoners was required to obey and execute *the judge's* order, under penalty, for refusal or delay, of fine and imprisonment.

The third section enacts, in case lists of persons other than prisoners of war then held in confinement, or thereafter arrested, should not be furnished within twenty days after the passage of the act, or, in cases of subsequent arrest, within twenty days after the time of arrest, that any citizen, after the termination of a session of the grand jury without indictment or presentment, might, by petition alleging the facts and verified by oath, obtain *the judge's* order of discharge in favor of any person so imprisoned, on the terms and conditions prescribed in the second section.

This act made it the duty of the District Attorney of the United States to attend examinations on petitions for discharge.

By proclamation, dated the 15th September following the President reciting this statute suspended the privilege of the writ in the cases where, by his authority, military, naval, and civil officers of the United States "hold persons in their custody either as prisoners of war, spies, or aiders and abettors of the enemy, . . . or belonging to the land or naval force of the United States, or otherwise amenable to military law, or the rules and articles of war, or the rules or regulations prescribed for the military or naval services, by authority of the President, or for resisting a draft, or for any other offence against the military or naval service."

With both these statutes and this proclamation in force, Lamdin [*sic*] P. Milligan, a citizen of the United States, and a resident and citizen of the State of Indiana, was arrested on the 5th day of October, 1864, at his home in the said State, by the order of Brevet Major-General Hovey, military commandant of the District of Indiana, and by the same authority confined in a military prison, at or near Indianapolis, the capital of the State. On the 21st day of the same month, he was placed on trial before a "military commission," convened at Indianapolis, by order of the said General, upon the following charges; preferred by Major Burnett, Judge Advocate of the Northwestern Military Department, namely:

1. "Conspiracy against the Government of the United States;"
2. "Affording aid and comfort to rebels against the authority of the United States;"
3. "Inciting insurrection;"
4. "Disloyal practices;" and
5. "Violation of the laws of war."

Under each of these charges there were various specifications. The substance of them was, joining and aiding, at different times, between October, 1863, and August, 1864, a secret society known as the Order of American Knights or Sons of Liberty, for the purpose of overthrowing the Government and duly constituted authorities of the United States; holding communication with the enemy; conspiring to seize munitions of war stored in the arsenals; to liberate prisoners of war, &c.; resisting the draft, &c.; . . . "at a period of war and armed rebellion against the authority of the United States, at or near Indianapolis, [and various other places specified] in Indiana, a State within the military lines of the army of the United States, and the theatre of military operations, and which had been and was constantly threatened to be invaded by the enemy." These were amplified and stated with various circumstances.

An objection by him to the authority of the commission to try him being overruled, Milligan was found guilty on all the charges, and sentenced to suffer death by hanging; and this sentence, having been approved, he was ordered to be executed on Friday, the 19th of May, 1865.

On the 10th of that same May, 1865, Milligan filed his petition in the Circuit Court of the United States for the District of Indiana, by which, or by the documents appended to which as exhibits, the above facts appeared. These exhibits consisted of the order for the commission; the charges and specifications; the findings and sentence of the court, with a statement of the fact that the sentence was approved by the President of the United States, who directed that it should "be carried into execution without delay;" all "by order of the Secretary of War."

The petition set forth the additional fact, that while the petitioner was held and detained, as already mentioned, in military custody (and more than twenty days after his arrest), a grand jury of the Circuit Court of the United States for the District of Indiana was convened at Indianapolis, his said place of confinement, and duly empanelled, charged, and sworn for said district, held its sittings, and finally adjourned without having found any bill of indictment, or made any presentment whatever against him. That at no time had he been in the military service of the United States, or in any way connected with the land or naval force, or the militia in actual service; nor within the limits of any State whose citizens were engaged in rebellion against the United States, at any time during the war; but during all the time aforesaid, and for twenty years last past, he had been an inhabitant, resident, and citizen of Indiana. And so, that it had been "wholly out of his power to have acquired belligerent rights, or to have placed himself in such relation to the government as to have enabled him to violate the laws of war."

The record, in stating who appeared in the Circuit Court, ran thus:

"Be it remembered, that on the 10th day of May, A.D. 1865, in the court aforesaid, before the judges aforesaid, comes Jonathan W. Gorden, Esq., of counsel for said Milligan, and files here, in open court, the petition of said Milligan, to be discharged." . . . "At the same time comes John Hanna, Esquire, the attorney prosecuting the pleas of the United States in this behalf. And thereupon, by agreement, this application is submitted to the court, and day is given, &c."

The prayer of the petition was that under the already mentioned act of Congress of March 3d, 1863, the petitioner might be brought before the court, and either turned over to the proper civil tribunal to be proceeded with according to the law of the land, or discharged from custody altogether.

At the hearing of the petition in the Circuit Court, the opinions of the judges were opposed upon the following questions:

I. On the facts stated in the petition and exhibits, ought a writ of *habeas corpus* to be issued according to the prayer of said petitioner?

II. On the facts stated in the petition and exhibits, ought the said Milligan to be discharged from custody as in said petition prayed?

III. Whether, upon the facts stated in the petition and exhibits, the military commission had jurisdiction legally to try and sentence said Milligan in manner and form, as in said petition and exhibit is stated?

And these questions were certified to this court under the provisions of the act of Congress of April 29th, 1802, an act which provides "that whenever any question shall occur before a Circuit Court, upon which the opinions of the judges shall be opposed, the point upon which the disagreement shall happen, shall, during the same term, upon the request of *either party* or their counsel, be stated under the direction of the judges, and certified under the seal of the court to the Supreme Court, at their next session to be held thereafter; and shall by the said court be *finally* decided: and the decision of the Supreme Court and their order in the premises shall be remitted to the Circuit Court, and be there entered of record, and shall have effect according to the nature of the said judgment and order: *Provided,* That nothing herein contained shall prevent the *cause* from proceeding, if, in the opinion of the court, further proceedings can be had without prejudice to the merits."

The three several questions above mentioned were argued at the last term. And along with them an additional question raised in this court, namely:

IV. A question of jurisdiction, as—1. Whether the Circuit Court had jurisdiction to hear the case there presented?—2. Whether the case sent up here by certificate of division was so sent up in conformity with the intention of the act of 1802? In other words, whether *this* court had jurisdiction of the questions raised by the certificate?

Mr. J. E. McDonald, Mr. J. S. Black, Mr. J. H. Garfield, and Mr. David Dudley Field, for the petitioner. Mr. McDonald opening the case fully, and stating and examining the preliminary proceedings.

Mr. Speed, A. G., Mr. Stanbery, and Mr. B. F. Butler, special counsel of the United States, contra. Mr. Stanbery confining himself to the question of jurisdiction under the act of 1802.

ON THE SIDE OF THE UNITED STATES.

I. JURISDICTION.
1. *As to the jurisdiction of the Circuit Court.*—The record shows that the application was made to the court in open session. The language of the third section contemplates that it shall be made to a "judge."

But, independently of this, the record does not state the facts necessary to bring the case within the act of 1863. It does not show under which section of the act it is presented; nor allege that the petitioners are state or political prisoners otherwise than as prisoners of war; nor that a list has been brought in, or that it has not been brought in. If a list had been brought in containing the name of one of these petitioners, it would have been the judge's duty to inquire into his imprisonment; if no list had been brought in, his case could only be brought before the court by some petition, and the judge, upon being satisfied that the allegations of the petition were true, would discharge him. But there is no certificate in the division of opinion that the judges were or were not satisfied that the allegations of these petitioners were true; nor were the petitions brought under the provisions of that duty. But conceding, for arguments sake, this point, a graver question exists.

2. *As to the jurisdiction of this court.*—If there is any jurisdiction over the case here, it must arise under the acts of Congress which give to this court jurisdiction to take cognizance of questions arising in[a] case pending in a Circuit Court of the United States and certified to the court for its decision, and then to be remanded to the Circuit Court. This is appellate jurisdiction, and is defined and limited by the single section of the act of April 29, 1802. The case is not within the provisions of this section.

First. The question in the court below arose upon *the application* for a *habeas corpus,* before there was a service upon the parties having the petitioner in custody, before an answer was made by those parties, before the writ was ordered or issued, while yet there was no other party before the court, except the petitioner. The case was then an *ex parte* case, and is so still. The proceeding had not yet ripened into a "cause."

No division of opinion in such a case is within the purview of the section. The division of opinion on which this court can act, must occur in the progress of a case where the parties on *both* sides are before the court, or have a status in the case. The right to send the question or point of division to this court can only arise upon the motion of the *parties, or either of them,*—not by the court on its own motion or for its own convenience. The record hardly exhibits the Attorney of the United States, Mr. Hanna, as taking any part.

The parties have an equal right to be heard upon the question in the court below. It must appear to them in open court that the judges are divided in opinion. They must have an equal right to move for its transfer to this court. They must have an equal opportunity to follow it here and to argue it here,—not as volunteers, not as *amici curioe,* not by permission, but *as parties on the record,* with equal rights.

This record shows no parties, except the petitioner. Its title is *Ex parte* Milligan. The persons who are charged in the petition as having him in wrongful custody are not made parties, and had, when the question arose, no right to be heard as parties in the court below, and have no right to be heard as parties in this court.

In such a case, this court cannot answer any one of the questions sent here, especially the one, "Had the Military Commission jurisdiction to try and condemn Milligan?" For if the court answer that question in the negative, its answer is a *final decision*, and, as it is asserted, settles it for all the future of the case below; and when, hereafter, that case shall, in its progress, bring the parties complained of before the court, silences all argument upon the vital point so decided. What becomes of the whole argument which will be made on the other side, of the right of every man before being condemned of crime, to be heard and tried by an impartial jury?

Second. This being an *ex parte* application for a writ of *habeas corpus* made to a court, the division of opinion *then* occurring was in effect a decision of the case.

The case was ended when the court declined to issue the writ. It was not a division of opinion occurring in the progress of a case or the trial of a case, and when it was announced to the petitioner that one judge was in favor of granting the writ, and that the other would not grant it—*that* settled and ended the case. The case had not arisen within the meaning of the statute, when from necessity the case and the progress of the case must stop until the question should be decided. And as Milligan was sentenced to be hanged on the 19th May, for aught that appears, we are discussing a question relating to the liberty of a dead man. Having been sentenced to be hanged on the 19th, the presumption is that he was hanged on that day. Any answer to the question raised will therefore be answers to moot points—answers which courts will not give.

Third. If the parties had all been before the court below, and the case in progress, and then the questions certified, and the parties were now here, the court would not answer these questions.

1. Every question involves matters of fact not stated in an agreed case, or admitted on demurrer, but alleged by one of the parties, and standing alone on his *ex parte* statement.
2. All the facts bearing on the questions are not set forth, so that even if the parties had made an agreed state of facts, yet if this court find that other facts important to be known before a decision of the question do not appear, the questions will not be answered.
3. The main question certified, the one, as the counsel for the petitioners assert, on which the other two depend, had not yet arisen for decision, especially for final decision, so that if the parties had both concurred in sending that question here, this court could not decide it.

If it be said this question did arise upon the application for the writ, it did not then arise for final decision, but only as showing probable cause, leaving it open and undecided until the answer should be made to the writ. A case, upon application for the writ of *habeas corpus*, has no status as a case until the service of the writ on the party having the petitioner in custody, and his return and the production of the body of the petitioner. No issue arises until there is a return, and when that is made the issue arises upon it, and in the courts of the United States it is conclusive as to the facts contained in the return.

4. The uniform practice in this court is against its jurisdiction in such a case as this upon *ex parte* proceedings.

All the cases (some twenty in number) before this court, on certificates of division, during all the time that this jurisdiction has existed, are cases between parties, and stated in the usual formula of A. *v.* B., or B. *ad sectam* A.

So, too, all the rules of this court as to the rights and duties of parties in cases before this court, exclude the idea of an *ex parte* case under the head of appellate jurisdiction.

II. THE MERITS OR MAIN QUESTION.

Mr. Speed, A. G., and Mr. Butler: By the settled practice of the courts of the United States, upon application for a writ of *habeas corpus,* if it appear upon the facts stated by the petitioner, all of which shall be taken to be true, that he could not be discharged upon a return of the writ, then no writ will be issued. Therefore the questions resolve themselves into two:

I. Had the military commission jurisdiction to hear and determine the case submitted to it?

II. The jurisdiction failing, had the military authorities of the United States a right, at the time of filing the petition, to detain the petitioner in custody as a military prisoner, or for trial before a civil court?

1. A military commission derives its powers and authority wholly from martial law; and by that law and by military authority only are its proceedings to be judged or reviewed.
2. Martial law is the will of the commanding officer of an armed force, or of a geographical military department, expressed in time of war within the limits of his military jurisdiction, as necessity demands and prudence dictates, restrained or enlarged by the orders of his military chief, or supreme executive ruler.
3. Military law is the rules and regulations made by the legislative power of the State for the government of its land and naval forces.
4. The laws of war (when this expression is not used as a generic term) are the laws which govern the conduct of belligerents towards each other and other nations, *flagranti bello.*

These several kinds of laws should not be confounded, as their adjudications are referable to distinct and different tribunals.

Infractions of the laws of war can only to punished or remedied by retaliation, negotiation, or an appeal to the opinion of nations.

Offences against military laws are determined by tribunals established in the acts of the legislature which create these laws—such as courts martial and courts of inquiry.

The officer executing martial law is at the same time supreme legislator, supreme judge, and supreme executive. As necessity makes his will the law, he only can define and declare it; and whether or not it is infringed, and of the extent of the infraction, he alone can judge; and his sole order punishes or acquits the alleged offender.

But the necessities and effects of warlike operations which create the law also give power incidental to its execution. It would be impossible for the commanding general of an army to investigate each fact which might be supposed to interfere with his movements, endanger his safety, aid his enemy, or bring disorder and crime into the community under his charge. He, therefore, must commit to his officers, and in practice, to a board of officers, as a tribunal, by whatever name it may be called, the charge of examining the circumstances and reporting the facts in each particular case, and of advising him as to its disposition—the whole matter to be then determined and executed by his order.

Hence arise *military commissions,* to investigate and determine, not offences against military law by soldiers and sailors, not breaches of the common laws of war belligerents, but the quality of the acts which are the proper subject of restraint by martial law.

Martial law and its tribunals have thus come to be recognized in the military operations of all civilized warfare. Washington, in the Revolutionary war, had repeated recourse to military commissions. General Scott resorted to them as instruments with which to govern the people of Mexico within his lines. They are familiarly recognized in express terms by the acts of Congress of July 17th, 1862, chap. 201, sec. 5; March 18th, 1863, chap. 75, sec. 36; Resolution No. 18, March 11th, 1862; and their jurisdiction over certain offences is also recognized by these acts.

But, as has been seen, military commissions do not thus derive their authority. Neither is their jurisdiction confined to the classes of offences therein enumerated.

Assuming the jurisdiction where military operations are being in fact carried on, over classes of military offences, Congress, by this legislation, from considerations of public safety, has endeavored to extend the sphere of that jurisdiction over certain offenders who were beyond what might be supposed to be the limit of actual military occupation.

As the war progressed, being a civil war, not unlikely, as the facts in this record abundantly show, to break out in any portion of the Union, in any form of insurrection, the President, as commander-in-chief, by this proclamation of September 24th, 1862, ordered:

"That during the existing insurrection, and as a necessary means for suppressing the same, all rebels and insurgents, their aiders and abettors, within the United States, and all persons discouraging volunteer enlistments, resisting militia drafts, or guilty of any disloyal practice, affording aid and comfort to rebels, against the authority of the United States, shall be subject to martial law, and liable to trial and punishment by courts martial or military commission.["]

"Second. That the writ of *habeas corpus* is suspended in respect to all persons arrested, or who now, or hereafter during the Rebellion shall be, imprisoned in any fort, camp, arsenal, military prison, or other place of confinement, by any military authority, or by the sentence of any court martial or military commission."

This was an exercise of his sovereignty in carrying on war, which is vested by the Constitution in the President.

This proclamation, which by its terms was to continue during the then existing insurrection, was in full force during the pendency of the proceedings complained of, at the time of the filing of this petition, and is still unrevoked.

While we do not admit that any legislation of Congress was needed to sustain this proclamation of the President, it being clearly within his power, as commander-in-chief, to issue it; yet, if it is asserted that legislative action is necessary to give validity to it, Congress has seen fit to expressly ratify the proclamation by the act of March 3d, 1863, by declaring that the President, whenever in his judgment the public safety may require it, is authorized to suspend the writ of *habeas corpus* in any case throughout the United States, and in any part thereof.

The offences for which the petitioner for the purpose of this hearing is confessed to be guilty, are the offences enumerated in this proclamation. The prison in which he is confined is a "military prison" therein mentioned. As to him, his acts and imprisonment, the writ of *habeas corpus* is expressly suspended.

Apparently admitting by his petition that a military commission might have jurisdiction in certain cases, the petitioner seeks to except himself by alleging that he is a citizen of Indiana, and has never been in the naval or military service of the United States, or since the commencement of the Rebellion a resident of a rebel State, and that, therefore, it had been out of his power to have acquired belligerent rights and to have placed himself in such a relation to the government as to enable him to violate the laws of war.

But neither residence nor propinquity to the field of actual hostilities is the test to determine who is or who is not subject to martial law, even in a time of foreign war, and certainly not in a time of civil insurrection. The commander-in-chief has full power to make an effectual use of his forces. He must, therefore, have power to arrest and punish one who arms men to join the enemy in the field against him; one who holds correspondence with that enemy; one who is an officer of an armed force organized to oppose him; one who is preparing to seize arsenals and release prisoners of war taken in battle and confined within his military lines.

These crimes of the petitioner were committed within the State of Indiana, where his arrest, trial, and imprisonment took place; within a military district of a geographical military department, duly established by the commander-in-chief; within the military lines of the army, and upon the theatre of military operations; in a State which had been and was then threatened with invasion, having arsenals which the petitioner plotted to seize, and prisoners of war whom he plotted to liberate; where citizens were liable to be made soldiers, and were actually ordered into the ranks; and to prevent whose becoming soldiers the petitioner conspired with and armed others.

Thus far the discussion has proceeded without reference to the effect of the Constitution upon war-making powers, duties, and rights, save to that provision which makes the President commander-in-chief of the armies and navies.

Does the Constitution provide restraint upon the exercise of this power?

The people of every sovereign State possess all the rights and powers of government. The people of these States in forming a "more perfect Union, to insure domestic tranquillity, and to provide for the common defence," have vested the power of making and carrying on war in the general government, reserving to the States, respectively, only the right to repel invasion and suppress insurrection "of such imminent danger as will not admit of delay." This right and power thus granted to the general government is in its nature entirely *executive,* and in the absence of constitutional limitations would be wholly lodged in the President, as chief executive officer and commander-in-chief of the armies and navies.

Lest this grant of power should be so broad as to tempt its exercise in initiating war, in order to reap the fruits of victory, and, therefore, be unsafe to be vested in a single branch of a republican government, the Constitution has delegated to Congress the power of originating war by declaration, when such declaration is necessary to the commencement of hostilities, and of provoking it by issuing letters of marque and reprisal; consequently, also, the power of raising and supporting armies, maintaining a navy, employing the militia, and of making rules for the government of all armed forces while in the service of the United States.

To keep out of the hands of the Executive the fruits of victory, Congress is also invested with the power to "make rules for the disposition of captures by land or water."

After war is originated, whether by declaration, invasion, or insurrection, the whole power of conducting it, as to manner, and as to all the means and appliances by which war is carried on by civilized nations, is given to the President. He is the sole judge of the exigencies, necessities, and duties of the occasion, their extent and duration.

During the war his powers must be without limit, because, if defending, the means of offence may be nearly illimitable; or, if acting offensively, his resources must be proportionate to the end in view,—"to conquer a peace." New difficulties are constantly arising, and new combinations are at once to be thwarted, which the slow movement of legislative action cannot meet.

These propositions are axiomatic in the absence of all restraining legislation by Congress.

Much of the argument on the side of the petitioner will rest, perhaps, upon certain provisions—not in the Constitution itself, and as originally made, but now seen in the Amendments made in 1789: the fourth, fifth, and sixth amendments. They may as well be here set out:

4. The right of the people to be secure in their persons, houses, papers, and effects, against unreasonable searches and seizures, shall not be violated,

and no warrants shall issue but upon probable cause supported by oath or affirmation, and particularly describing the place to be searched and the persons or things to be seized.

5. No person shall be held to answer for a capital or otherwise infamous crime, unless on a presentment or indictment of a grand jury, except in cases arising in the land or naval forces, or in the militia when in actual service in time of war or public danger; nor shall any person be subject for the same offence to be twice put in jeopardy of life or limb; nor shall be compelled in any criminal case to be a witness against himself, nor be deprived of life, liberty, or property, without due process of law; nor shall private property be taken for public use without just compensation.

6. In all criminal prosecutions the accused shall enjoy the right to a speedy and public trial, by an impartial jury of the State and district wherein the crime shall have been committed, . . . and to be informed of the nature and cause of the accusation; to be confronted with the witnesses against him; to have compulsory process for obtaining witnesses in his favor, and to have the assistance of counsel for his defence.

In addition to these, there are two preceding amendments which we may also mention, to wit: the second and third. They are thus:

2. A well-regulated militia being necessary to the security of a free State, the right of the people to keep and bear arms shall not be infringed.

3. No soldier shall in time of peace be quartered in any house without the consent of the owner, nor in time of war, but in a manner to be prescribed by law.

It will be argued that the fourth, fifth, and sixth articles, as above given, are restraints upon the war-making power; but we deny this. All these amendments are in *pari materiâ*, and if either is a restraint upon the President in carrying on war, in favor of the citizen, it is difficult to see why all of them are not. Yet will it be argued that the fifth article would be violated in "depriving if life, liberty, or property, without due process of law," armed rebels marching to attack the capital? Or that the fourth would be violated by searching and seizing the papers and houses of persons in open insurrection and war against the government? It cannot properly be so argued, any more than it could be that it was intended by the second article (declaring that "the right of the people to keep and bear arms shall not be infringed") to hinder the President from disarming insurrectionists, rebels, and traitors in arms while he was carrying on war against them.

These, in truth, are all peace provisions of the Constitution and, like all other conventional and legislative laws and enactments, are silent amidst arms, and when the safety of the people becomes the supreme law.

By the Constitution, as originally adopted, no limitations were put upon the war-making and war-conducting powers of Congress and the President; and after discussion, and after the attention of the country was called to the subject, no other limitation by subsequent amendment has been made, except by the Third

Article, which prescribes that "no soldier shall be quartered in any house in time of peace without consent of the owner, nor in *time of war,* except in a manner prescribed by law."

This, then, is the only expressed constitutional restraint upon the President as to the manner of carrying on war. There would seem to be no implied one; on the contrary, while carefully providing for the privilege of the writ of *habeas corpus* in time of peace, the Constitution takes it for granted that it will be suspended "in case of rebellion or invasion (*i. e.,* in time of war), when the public safety requires it."

The second and third sections of the act relating to *habeas corpus,* of March 3d, 1863, apply only to those persons who are held as "state or political offenders," and not to those who are held as prisoners of war. The petitioner was as much a prisoner of war as if he had been taken in action with arms in his hands.

They apply, also, only to those persons, the cause of whose detention is not disclosed; and not to those who, at the time when the lists by the provisions of said sections are to be furnished to the court, are actually undergoing trial before military tribunals upon written charges made against them.

The law was framed to prevent imprisonment for an indefinite time without trial, not to interfere with the case of prisoners undergoing trial. Its purpose was to make it certain that such persons should be tried.

Notwithstanding, therefore, the act of March 3, 1863, the commission had jurisdiction, and properly tried the prisoner.

The petitioner does not complain that he has been kept in ignorance of the charges against him, or that the investigation of those charges has been unduly delayed.

Finally, if the military tribunal has no jurisdiction, the petitioner may be held as a prisoner of war, aiding with arms the enemies of the United States, and held, under the authority of the United States, until the war terminates, then to be handed over by the military to the civil authorities, to be tried for his crimes under the acts of Congress, and before the courts which he has selected

ON THE SIDE OF THE PETITIONER.

Mr. David Dudley Field:

Certain topics have been brought into this discussion which have no proper place in it, and which I shall endeavor to keep out of it.

This not a question of the discipline of camps; it is not a question of the government of armies in the field; it is not a question respecting the power of a conqueror over conquered armies or conquered states.

It is not a question, how far the *legislative* department of the government can deal with the question of martial rule. Whatever has been done in these cases, has been done by the *executive* department alone.

Nor is it a question of the patriotism, or the character, or the services of the late chief magistrate, or of his constitutional advisers.

It is a question of the rights of the citizen in time of war.

Is it true, that the moment a declaration of war is made, the executive department of this government, without an act of Congress, becomes absolute master of our liberties and our lives? Are we, then, subject to martial rule, administered by the President upon his own sense of the exigency, with nobody to control him, and with every magistrate and every authority in the land subject to his will alone? These are the considerations which give to the case its greatest significance.

But we are met with the preliminary objection, that you cannot consider it for want of JURISDICTION.

The objection is twofold: first, that the Circuit Court of Indiana had not jurisdiction to hear the case there presented; and, second, that this court has not jurisdiction to hear and decide the questions thus certified.

First. *As to the jurisdiction of the Circuit Court.* That depended on the fourteenth section of the Judiciary Act of 1789, and on the *Habeas Corpus* Act of 1863. The former was, in Bollman's case, held to authorize the courts, as well as the judges, to issue the writ for the purpose of inquiring into the cause of commitment.

The act of March 3d, 1863, after providing that the Secretaries of State and of War shall furnish to the judges of the Circuit and District Courts a list of political and state prisoners, and of all others, except prisoners of war, goes on to declare, that if a grand jury has had a session, and has adjourned without finding an indictment, thereupon "it shall be the duty of the judge of said court forthwith to make an order, that any such prisoner desiring a discharge from said imprisonment be brought before him to be discharged."

Upon this act the objection is, first, that the application of the petitioner should have been made to one of the judges of the circuit, instead of the court itself; and, second, that the petitioner does not show whether it was made under the second or the third section.

To the former objection the answer is, first, that the decision in Bollman's case, just mentioned, covers this case; for the same reasoning which gives the court power to proceed under the fourteenth section of the act of 1789, gives the court power to proceed under the second and third sections of the act of 1863. The second answer is that, by the provisos of the second section, the court is expressly mentioned as having the power.

The other objection to the jurisdiction of the Circuit Court is, that the petition does not show under which section of the act it was presented. It states that the petitioner is held a prisoner under the authority of the President; that a term has been held, and that a grand jury has been in attendance, and has adjourned without indicting. It does not state whether a list has been furnished to the judge by the Secretary of State and the Secretary of War, and, therefore, argues the learned counsel, the court has no jurisdiction. That is to say, the judges, knowing themselves whether the list has, or has not been furnished, cannot proceed, because we have not told them by our petition what they already know, and what we ourselves might not know, and perhaps could not know, because the law does not make it necessary that the list shall be filed, or that anybody shall be informed of it but the judges.

Second. *As to the jurisdiction of this court.* Supposing the Circuit Court to have had jurisdiction, has this court jurisdiction to hear these questions as they are certified? There are various objections. It is said that a division of opinion can be certified only in a cause, and that this is not a cause.

It was decided by this court, in *Holmes v. Jennison*, that a proceeding on *habeas corpus* is a suit, and suit is a more comprehensive word than cause. The argument is, that it is not a cause until the adverse party comes in. Is not a suit commenced before the defendant is brought into court? Is the defendant's appearance the first proceeding in a cause? There have been three acts in respect to this writ of *habeas corpus*. The first of 1789; then the act passed in 1833; and, finally, the act of 1842. The last act expressly designates the proceeding as a cause.

Another objection is, that there must be parties; that is, at least two parties, and that here is only one. This argument is derived from the direction in the act, that the point must be stated "upon the request of either party" or their counsel. It is said that "either party" imports two, and if there are not two, there can be no certificate. This is too literal: *"qui haeret in litera haeret in cortice."* The language is elliptical. What is meant is, "any party or parties, his or their counsel." Again: "either," if precisely used, would exclude all over two, because "either" strictly means "one of two;" and if there are three parties or more, as there may be, you cannot have a certificate. It is not unusual, in proceedings *in rem*, to have several intervenors and claimants: what are we to do then? The answer must be, that "either" is an equivalent word for "any;" and that who ever may happen to be a party, whether he stand alone or with others, may ask for the certificate.

The words "either party" were introduced, not for restriction but enlargement. The purpose was to enable any party to bring the case here; otherwise it might have been argued, perhaps, that all parties must join in asking for the certificate. The purpose of the act was to prevent a failure of justice, when the two judges of the Circuit Court were divided in opinion. The reason of the rule is as applicable to a case with one party as if there were two. Whether a question shall be certified to this court, depends upon the point in controversy. If it concerns a matter of right, and not of discretion, there is as much reason for its being sent *ex parte* as for its being sent *inter partes*. This very case is an illustration. Here a writ is applied for, or an order is asked. The judges do not agree about the issue of the writ, or the granting of the order. Upon their action the lives of these men depend. Shall there be a failure of justice? The question presented to the Circuit Court was not merely a formal one; whether an initial writ should issue. It is the practice, upon petitions for *habeas corpus*, to consider whether, upon the facts presented, the prisoners, if brought up, would be remanded. The presentation of the petition brings before the court, at the outset, the merits, to a certain extent, of the whole case. That was the course pursued in *Passmore Williamson's* case; in *Rex* v. *Ennis;* in the case of the *Three Spanish Sailors;* in *Hobhouse's* case; in *Husted's* case; and in *Ferguson's* case; and in this court, in *Watkins's* case, where the disposition of the case turned upon the point whether, if the writ were issued, the petitioner would be remanded upon the facts as they appeared.

There may, indeed, be cases where only one party can appear, that are at first and must always remain *ex parte*. Here, however, there were, in fact, two parties. Who were they? The record tells us:

"Be it remembered, that on the 10th day of May, A.D. 1865, in the court aforesaid, before the judges aforesaid, comes Jonathan W. Gordon, Esq., of counsel for said Milligan, and files here in open court the petition of said Milligan to be discharged. At the same time comes, also, John Hanna, Esq., the attorney prosecuting the pleas of the United States in this behalf. And thereupon, by agreement, this application is submitted to the court, and day is given," &c.

The next day the case came on again, and the certificate was made.

In point of fact, therefore, this cause had all the solemnity which two parties could give it. The government came into court, and submitted the case in Indiana, for the very purpose of having it brought to Washington.

A still additional objection made to the jurisdiction of this court is, that no questions can be certified except those which arise upon the trial.

The answer is, first, that there has been a trial, in its proper sense, as applicable to this case. The facts are all before the court. A return could not vary them. The case has been heard upon the petition, as if that contained all that need be known, or could be known. The practice is not peculiar to *habeas corpus;* it is the same on application for *mandamus,* or for attachments in cases of contempt; in both which cases the court sometimes hears the whole matter on the first motion, and sometimes postpones it till formal pleadings are put in. In either case, the result is the same.

But, secondly, if it were not so, is it correct to say that a certificate can only be made upon a trial? To sustain this position, the counsel refers to the case of *Davis* v. *Burden*. But that case expressly reserves the question.

It is admitted that the question of jurisdiction is a question that may be certified. The qualification insisted upon is, that no question can be certified unless it arose upon the trial of the cause, or be a question of jurisdiction. This is a question of jurisdiction. It is a question of the jurisdiction of the Circuit Court to grant the writ of *habeas corpus,* and to liberate these men; and that question brings up all the other questions in the cause.

Yet another objection to the jurisdiction of this court is, that the case must be one in which the answer to the questions when given shall be final; that is to say, the questions come here to be finally decided. What does that mean? Does it mean that the same thing can never be debated again? Certainly not. It means that the decision shall be final for the two judges who certified the difference of opinion, so that when the answer goes down from this court they shall act according to its order, as if they had originally decided in the same way.

Another objection to the jurisdiction of this court is, that the *whole* case is certified. The answer is, that no question is certified except those which actually arose before the court at the time, and without considering which it could not move at all. That is the first answer. The second is, that if too much is certified, the court will divide the questions, and answer only those which it finds to be properly certified, as it did in the *Silliman* v. *Hudson River Bridge Company* case.

The last objection to the jurisdiction of this court is, that the case is ended; because, it is to be presumed that these unfortunate men have been hanged. Is it to be presumed that any executive officer of this country, though he arrogate to himself this awful power of military government, would venture to put to death three men, who claim that they are unjustly convicted, and whose case is considered of such gravity by the Circuit Court of the United States that it certifies the question to the Supreme Court?

The suggestion is disrespectful to the executive, and I am glad to believe that it has no foundation in fact.

All the objections, then, are answered. There is nothing, then, in the way of proceeding to

II. [III] THE MERITS AND MAIN QUESTION.

The argument upon the questions naturally divides itself into two parts:

First. Was the military commission a competent tribunal for the trial of the petitioners upon the charges upon which they were convicted and sentenced?

Second. If it was not a competent tribunal, could the petitioners be released by the Circuit Court of the United States for the District of Indiana, upon writs of *habeas corpus* or otherwise?

The discussion of the competency of the military commission is first in order, because, if the petitioners were lawfully tried and convicted, it is useless to inquire how they could be released from an unlawful imprisonment.

If, on the other hand, the tribunal was incompetent, and the conviction and sentence nullities, then the means of relief become subjects of inquiry, and involve the following considerations:

1. Does the power of suspending the privilege of the writ of *habeas corpus* appertain to all the great departments of government concurrently, or to some only, and which of them?
2. If the power is concurrent, can its exercise by the executive or judicial department be restrained or regulated by act of Congress?
3. If the power appertains to Congress alone, or if Congress may control its exercise by the other departments, has that body so exercised its functions as to leave to the petitioners the privilege of the writ, or to entitle them to their discharge?

In considering the first question, that of the competency of the military tribunal for the trial of the petitioners upon those charges, let me first call attention to the *dates* of the transactions.

Let it be observed next, that for the same offences as those set forth in the charges and specifications, the petitioners could have been tried and punished by the ordinary civil tribunals.

Let it also be remembered, that Indiana, at the time of this trial, was a peaceful State; the courts were all open; their processes had not been interrupted; the laws had their full sway.

Then let it be remembered that the petitioners were simple citizens, not belonging to the army or navy; not in any official position; not connected in any manner with the public service.

The evidence against them is not to be found in this record, and it is immaterial. Their guilt or their innocence does not affect the question of the competency of the tribunal by which they were judged.

Bearing in mind, therefore, the nature of the charges, and the time of the trial and sentence; bearing in mind, also, the presence and undisputed authority of the civil tribunals and the civil condition of the petitioners, we ask by what authority they were withdrawn from their natural judges?

What is a military commission? Originally, it appears to have been an advisory board of officers, convened for the purpose of informing the conscience of the commanding officer, in cases where he might act for himself if he chose. General Scott resorted to it in Mexico for his assistance in governing conquered places. The first mention of it in an act of Congress appears to have been in the act of July 22, 1861, where the general commanding a separate department, or a detached army, was authorized to appoint a military board, or *commission,* of not less than three, or more than five officers, to examine the qualifications and conduct of commissioned officers of volunteers.

Subsequently, military commissions are mentioned in four acts of Congress, but in none of them is any provision made for their organization, regulation, or jurisdiction, further than that it is declared that in time of war or rebellion, spies may be tried by a general court-martial or military commission; and that "persons who are in the military service of the United States, and subject to the Articles of War," may also be tried by the same, for murder, and certain other infamous crimes.

These acts do not confer upon military commissions jurisdiction over any persons other than those in the military service and spies.

There being, then, no act of Congress for the establishment of the commission, it depended entirely upon the executive will for its creation and support. This brings up the true question now before the court: Has the President, in time of war, upon his own mere will and judgment, the power to bring before his military officers any person in the land, and subject him to trial and punishment, even to death? The proposition is stated in this form, because it really amounts to this.

If the President has this awful [lawful] power, whence does he derive it? He can exercise no authority whatever but that which the Constitution of the country gives him. Our system knows no authority beyond or above the law. We may, therefore, dismiss from our minds every thought of the President's having any prerogative, as representative of the people, or as interpreter of the popular will. He is elected by the people to perform those functions, and those only, which the Constitution of his country, and the laws made pursuant to that Constitution, confer.

The plan of argument which I propose is, first to examine the text of the 'Constitution. That instrument, framed with the greatest deliberation, after thirteen years' experience of war and peace, should be accepted as the authentic and final expression of the public judgment, regarding that form and scope of government, and those guarantees of private rights, which legal science, political philosophy, and the experience of previous times had taught as the safest and most perfect. All attempts to explain it away, or to evade or pervert it, should be discountenanced and resisted. Beyond the line of such an argument, everything else ought, in strictness, to be superfluous. But, I shall endeavor to show, further, that the theory of our government, for which I am contending, is the only one compatible with civil liberty; and, by what I may call an historical argument, that this theory is as old as the nation, and that even in the constitutional monarchies of England and France that notion of executive power, which would uphold military commissions, like the one against which I am speaking, has never been admitted.

What are the powers and attributes of the presidential office? They are written in the second article of the Constitution, and, so far as they relate to the present question, they are these: He is vested with the "executive power;" he is "commander-in-chief of the army and navy of the United States, and of the militia of the several States when called into the actual service of the United States;" he is to "take care that the laws be faithfully executed;" and he takes this oath: "I do solemnly swear that I will faithfully execute the office of President of the United States, and will, to the best of my ability, preserve, protect, and defend the Constitution of the United States." The "executive power" mentioned in the Constitution is the executive power of the United States. The President is not clothed with the executive power of the States. He is not clothed with any executive power, except as he is specifically directed by some other part of the Constitution, or by an act of Congress.

He is to "take care that the laws be faithfully executed." He is to execute the laws by the means and in the manner which the laws themselves prescribe.

The oath of office cannot be considered as a grant of power. Its effect is merely to superadd a religious sanction to what would otherwise be his official duty, and to bind his conscience against any attempt to usurp power or overthrow the Constitution.

There remains, then, but a single clause to discuss, and that is the one which makes him commander-in-chief of the army and navy of the United States, and of the militia of the States when called into the federal service. The question, therefore, is narrowed down to this: Does the authority to command an army carry with it authority to arrest and try by court-martial civilians—by which I mean persons not in the martial forces; not impressed by law with a martial character? The question is easily answered. To command an army, whether in camp, or on the march, or in battle, requires the control of no other persons than the officers, soldiers, and camp followers. It can hardly be contended that, if Congress neglects to find subsistence, the commander-in-chief may lawfully take it from our own citizens. It cannot be supposed that, if Congress fails to provide the means of recruiting, the commander-in-chief may lawfully force the citizens into the ranks. What is called the war power of the President, if indeed there be any such thing, is nothing more than the power of commanding the armies and fleets which Congress causes to be raised. To command them is to direct their operations.

Much confusion of ideas has been produced by mistaking executive power for kingly power. Because in monarchial countries the kingly office includes the executive, it seems to have been sometimes inferred that, conversely, the executive carries with it the kingly prerogative. Our executive is in no sense a king, even for four years.

So much for that article of the Constitution, the second, which creates and regulates the executive power. If we turn to the other portions of the original instrument (I do not now speak of the amendments) the conclusion already drawn from the second article will be confirmed, if there be room for confirmation. Thus, in the first article, Congress is authorized "to declare war, and make rules concerning captures on land and water;" "to raise and support armies;" "to provide and maintain a navy;" "to make rules for the government and regulation of the land and naval forces;" "to provide for calling forth the militia to execute the laws of the Union, suppress insurrections, and repel invasions;" "to provide for organizing, arming, and disciplining the militia, and governing such part of them as may be in the service of the United States, reserving to the States respectively the appointment of the officers, and the authority of training the militia according to the discipline prescribed by Congress;" "to exercise exclusive legislation in all cases whatsoever over . . . all places purchased . . . for the erection of forts, magazines, arsenals, dock-yards;" "to make all laws which shall be necessary and proper for carrying into execution the . . . powers vested by this Constitution in the Government of the United States, or in any department or officer thereof."

These various provisions of the first article would show, if there were any doubt upon the construction of the second, that the powers of the President do not include the power to raise or support an army, or to provide or maintain a navy, or to call forth the militia, to repel an invasion, or to suppress an insurrection, or execute the laws, or even to govern such portions of the militia as are called into the service of the United States, or to make law for any of the forts, magazines, arsenals, or dock-yards. If the President could not, even in flagrant war, except as authorized by Congress, call forth the militia of Indiana to repel an invasion of that State, or, when called, govern them, it is absurd to say that he could nevertheless, under the same circumstances, govern the whole State and every person in it by martial rule.

The jealousy of the executive power prevailed with our forefathers. They carried it so far that, in providing for the protection of a State against domestic violence, they required, as a condition, that the legislature of the State should ask for it if possible to be convened.

I submit, therefore, that upon the text of the original Constitution, as it stood when it was ratified, there is no color for the assumption that the President, without act of Congress, could create military commissions for the trial of persons not military, for any cause or under any circumstances whatever.

But, as we well know, the Constitution, in the process of ratification, had to undergo a severe ordeal. To quiet apprehensions, as well as to guard against possible dangers, ten amendments were proposed by the first Congress sitting at New York, in 1789, and were duly ratified by the States. The third and fifth are as follows:

"ART. III. No soldier shall, in time of peace, be quartered in any house, without the consent of the owner, nor in time of war, but in a manner to be prescribed by law."

"ART. V. No person shall be held to answer for a capital or otherwise infamous crime, unless on a presentment or indictment of a grand jury, except in cases arising in the land or naval forces, or in the militia when in actual service, in time of war or public danger; nor shall any person be subject, for the same offence, to be twice put in jeopardy of life or limb, nor shall be compelled in any criminal case to be a witness against himself, nor be deprived of life, liberty, or property, without due process of law, nor shall private property be taken for public use without just compensation."

If there could have been any doubt whatever, whether military commissions or courts-martial for the trial of persons not "in the land or naval forces, or the militia" in actual service, could ever be established by the President, or even by Congress, these amendments would have removed the doubt. They were made for a state of war as well as a state of peace; they were aimed at the military authority, as well as the civil; and they were as explicit as our mother tongue could make them.

The phrase "in time of war or public danger" qualifies the member of the sentence relating to the militia; as otherwise, there could be no court-martial in the army or navy during peace.

This is the argument upon the text of the Constitution.

I will now show that military tribunals for civilians, or non-military persons, whether in war or peace, are inconsistent with the liberty of the citizen, and can have no place in constitutional government. This is a legitimate argument even upon a question of interpretation; for if there be, as I think there is not, room left for interpretation of what seem to be the plain provisions of the Constitution, then the principles of liberty, as they were understood by the fathers of the Republic; the maxims of free government, as they were accepted by the men who framed and those who adopted the Constitution; and those occurrences in the history of older states, which they had profoundly studied, may be called in to show us what they must have meant by the words they used.

The source and origin of the power to establish military commissions, if it exist at all, is in the assumed power to declare what is called martial law. I say what is called martial law, for strictly there is no such thing as martial law; it is martial rule; that is to say, the will of the commanding officer, and nothing more, nothing less.

On this subject, as on many others, the incorrect use of a word has led to great confusion of ideas and to great abuses. People imagine, when they hear the expression martial law, that there is a system of law known by that name, which can upon occasion be substituted for the ordinary system; and there is a prevalent notion that under certain circumstances a military commander may, by issuing a proclamation, displace one system, the civil law, and substitute another, the martial. A moment's reflection will show that this is an error. Law is a rule of property and of conduct, prescribed by the sovereign power of the state. The Civil Code of Louisiana defines it as "a solemn expression of legislative will." Blackstone calls it "a rule of civil conduct prescribed by the supreme power in the state;" . . . "not a transient, sudden order from a superior to or concerning a particular person, but something permanent, uniform, and universal." Demosthenes thus explains it: "The design and object of laws is to ascertain what is just, honorable, and expedient; and when that is discovered, it is proclaimed as a general ordinance, equal and impartial to all."

There is a system of regulations known as the Rules and Article of War, prescribed by Congress for the government of the army and navy, under that clause of the Constitution which empowers Congress "to make rules for the government and regulation of the land and naval forces." This is generally known as military law.

There are also certain usages, sanctioned by time, for the conduct towards each other of nations engaged in war, known as the usages of war, or the *jus belli*, accepted as part of the law of nations, and extended from national to all belligerents. These respect, however, only the conduct of belligerents towards each other, and have no application to the present case.

What is ordinarily called martial law is no law at all. Wellington, in one of his dispatches from Portugal, in 1810, in his speech on the Ceylon affair, so describes it.

Let us call the thing by its right name; it is not martial law, but martial rule. And when we speak of it, let us speak of it as abolishing all law, and substituting the will of the military commander, and we shall give a true idea of the thing, and be able to reason about it with a clear sense of what we are doing.

Another expression, much used in relation to the same subject, has led also to misapprehension; that is, the declaration, or proclamation, of martial rule; as if a formal promulgation made any difference. It makes no difference whatever.

It may be asked, may a general never in any case use force but to compel submission in the opposite army and obedience in his own? I answer, yes; there are cases in which he may. There is a maxim of our law which gives the reason and the extent of the power: *"Necessitas quod cogit defendit."* This is a maxim not peculiar in its application to military men; it applies to all men under certain circumstances.

Private persons may lawfully tear down a house, if necessary, to prevent the spread of a fire. Indeed, the maxim is not confined in its application to the calamities of war and conflagration. A mutiny, breaking out in a garrison, may make necessary for its suppression, and therefore justify, acts which would otherwise be unjustifiable. In all these cases, however, the person acting under the pressure of necessity, real or supposed, acts at his peril. The correctness of his conclusion must be judged by courts and juries, whenever the acts and the alleged necessity are drawn in question.

The creation of a commission or board to decide or advise upon the subject gives no increased sanction to the act. As necessity compels, so that necessity alone can justify it. The decision or advice of any number of persons, whether designated as a military commission, or board of officers, or council of war, or as a committee, proves nothing but greater deliberation; it does not make legal what would otherwise be illegal.

Let us proceed now to the historical part of the argument.

First. As to our own country. The nation began its life in 1776, with a protest against military usurpation. It was one of the grievances set forth in the Declaration of Independence, that the king of Great Britain had "affected to render the military independent of and superior to the civil power." The attempts of General Gage, in Boston, and of Lord Dunmore, in Virginia, to enforce martial rule, excited the greatest indignation. Our fathers never forgot their principles; and though the war by which they maintained their independence was a revolutionary one, though their lives depended on their success in arms, they always asserted and enforced the subordination of the military to the civil arm.

The first constitutions of the States were framed with the most jealous care. By the constitution of New Hampshire, it was declared that "in all cases, and at all times, the military ought to be under strict subordination to, and governed by the civil power;" by the constitution of Massachusetts of 1780, that "no person can in any case be subjected to law martial, or to any penalties or pains by virtue of that law, except those employed in the army or navy, and except the militia in actual service, but by the authority of the legislature;" by the constitution of Pennsylvania of 1776, "that the military should be kept under strict subordination to, and governed by the civil power;" by the constitution of Delaware of 1776, "that in all cases, and at all times, the military ought to be under strict subordination to, and governed by the civil power;" by that of Maryland of 1776, "that in all cases, and at all times, the military ought to be under strict subordination to, and control of the civil power;" by that of North Carolina, 1776, "that the military should be kept under strict subordination to, and governed by the civil power;" by that of South Carolina, 1778, "that the military be subordinate to the civil power of the State;" and by that of Georgia, 1777, that "the principles of the *habeas corpus* act shall be part of this constitution; and freedom of the press, and trial by jury, to remain inviolate forever."

Second. As to England, the constitutional history of that country is the history of a struggle on the part of the crown to obtain or to exercise a similar power to the one here attempted to be set up. The power was claimed by the king as much in virtue of his royal prerogative and of his feudal relations to his people as lord paramount, as of his title as commander of the forces. But it is enough to say that, from the day when the answer of the sovereign was given in assent to the petition of right, courts-martial for the trial of civilians, upon the authority of the crown alone, have always been held illegal.

Third. As to France—as France was when she had a constitutional government. I have shown what the king of England cannot do. Let me show what the constitutional king of France could not do.

On the continent of Europe, the legal formula for putting a place under martial rule is to declare it in a state of siege; as if there were in the minds of lawyers everywhere no justification for such a measure but the exigencies of impending battle. The charter established for the government of France, on the final expulsion of the first Napoleon, contained these provisions:

"ART. The king is the supreme chief of the state; he commands the forces by sea and land; declares war; makes treaties of peace, alliance, and commerce; appoints to every office and agency of public administration; and makes rules and ordinances necessary for the execution of the laws, without the power ever of suspending them, or dispensing with their execution."

"ART. The king alone sanctions and promulgates the laws."

"ART. No person can be withdrawn from his natural judges."

"ART. Therefore there cannot be erected commissions or extraordinary tribunals."

When Charles the Tenth was driven from the kingdom the last article was amended, by adding the words, "under what name or denomination soever;" Dupin giving the reason thus:

"In order to prevent every possible abuse, we have added to the former text of the charter 'under what name or denomination soever,' for specious names have never been wanting for bad things, and without this precaution the title of 'ordinary tribunal' might be conferred on the most irregular and extraordinary of courts."

Now, it so happened, that two years later the strength of these constitutional provisions was to be tested. A formidable insurrection broke out in France. The king issued an order, dated June 6, 1832, placing Paris in a state of siege, founded "on the necessity of suppressing seditious assemblages which had appeared in arms in the capital, during the days of June 5th and 6th; on attacks upon public and private property; on assassinations of national guards, troops of the line, municipal guards and officers in the public service; and on the necessity of prompt and energetic measures to protect public safety against the renewal of similar attacks." On the 18th of June, one Geoffroy, designer, of Paris, was, by a decision of the second military commission of Paris, declared "guilty of an attack, with intent to subvert the government and to excite civil war," and condemned to death.

He appealed to the Court of Cassation. Odilon Barrot, a leader of the French bar, undertook his case, and after a discussion memorable forever for the spirit and learning of the advocates, and the dignity and independence of the judges, the court gave judgment, thus:

"Whereas Geoffroy, brought before the second military commission of the first military division, is neither in the army nor impressed with a military character, yet nevertheless said tribunal has implicitly declared itself to have jurisdiction and passed upon the merits, wherein it has committed an excess of power, violated the limits of its jurisdiction, and the provisions of articles 53 and 54 of the charter and those of the laws above cited: On these grounds the court reverses and annuls the proceedings instituted against the appellant before the said commission, whatsoever has followed the form, and especially the judgment of condemnation of the 18th of June, instant; and in order that further proceedings be had according to law, remands him before one of the judges of instruction of the court of first instance of Paris," &c.

Thereupon the prisoner was discharged from military custody.

This closes my argument against the competency of the military commission.

It remains to consider what remedy, if any, there was against this unlawful judgment and its threatened execution.

The great remedy provided by our legal and political system for unlawful restraint, whether upon pretended judgments, decrees, sentences, warrants, orders, or otherwise, is the writ of *habeas corpus*.

The authority to suspend the privilege of the *habeas corpus* is derived, it is said, from two sources: first, from the martial power; and, second, from the second subdivision of the ninth section of the first article of the Federal Constitution.

As to the martial power, I have already discussed it so fully that I need not discuss it again.

How, then, stands the question upon the text of the Constitution? This is the language: "The privilege of the writ of *habeas corpus* shall not be suspended, unless when, in cases of rebellion or invasion, the public safety may require it."

The clause in question certainly either grants the power, or implies that it is already granted; and in either case it belongs to the legislative, executive, and judicial departments concurrently, or to some excluding the rest.

There have been four theories: one that it belongs to all the departments; a second, that it belongs to the legislature; a third, that it belongs to the executive; and the fourth, that it belongs to the judiciary.

Is the clause a *grant* or a *limitation* of power? Looking only at the form of expression, it should be regarded as a limitation.

As a grant of power, it would be superfluous, for it is clearly an incident of others which are granted.

Then, regarding the clause according to its place in the Constitution, it should be deemed a *limitation;* for it is placed with six other subdivisions in the same section, every one of which is a limitation.

If the sentence respecting the *habeas corpus* be, as I contend, a limitation, and not a grant of power, we must look into other parts of the Constitution to find the grant; and if we find none making it to the President, it follows that the power is in the legislative or the judicial department. That it lies with the judiciary will hardly be contended. That department has no other function than to judge. It cannot refuse or delay justice.

But if the clause in question were deemed a *grant* of power, the question would then be, to whom is the grant made? The following considerations would show that it was made to Congress:

First. The debates in the convention which framed the Constitution seem, at least, to suppose that the power was given to Congress, and to Congress alone.

Second. The debates in the various State conventions which ratified the Constitution do most certainly proceed upon that supposition.

Third. The place in which the provision is left indicates, if it does not absolutely decide, that it relates only to the powers of Congress. It is not in the second article, which treats of the executive department. It is not in the third, which treats of the judicial department. It is in the first article, which treats of the legislative department. There is not another subdivision in all the seven subdivisions of the ninth section which does not relate to Congress in part, at least, and most of them relate to Congress alone.

Fourth. The constitutional law of the mother country had been long settled, that the power of suspending the privilege of the writ, or, as it was sometimes called, suspending the writ itself, belonged only to Parliament. With this principle firmly seated in the minds of lawyers, it seems incredible that so vast a change as conferring the grant upon the executive should have been so loosely and carelessly expressed.

Fifth. The prevailing sentiment of the time when the Constitution was framed, was a dislike and dread of executive authority. It is hardly to be believed, that so vast and dangerous a power would have been conferred upon the President, without providing some safeguards against its abuse.

Sixth. Every judicial opinion, and every commentary on the Constitution, up to the period of the Rebellion, treated the power as belonging to Congress, and to that department only.

And so we submit to the court, that the answers to the three questions, certified by the court below, should be, to the first, that, on the facts stated in the petition and exhibits, a writ of *habeas corpus* ought to be issued according to the prayer of the petition; to the second, that, on the same facts, the petitioner ought to be discharged; and to the third, that the military commission had not jurisdiction to try and sentence the petitioner, in manner and form as in the petition and exhibits is stated.

Mr. Garfield, on the same side.

Had the military commission jurisdiction legally to try and sentence the petitioner? This is the main question.

The Constitution establishes the Supreme Court, and empowers Congress—

"To constitute tribunals inferior to the Supreme Court."

"To make rules for the governments of the land and naval forces, and to provide for governing such part of the militia as may be employed in the service of the United States."

For all cases not arising in the land or naval forces, Congress has provided in the Judiciary Act of September 24th, 1789, and the acts amendatory thereof. For all cases arising in the naval forces, it has fully provided in the act of March 2d, 1799, "for the government of the navy of the United States," and similar subsequent acts.

We are apt to regard the military department of the government as an organized despotism, in which all personal rights are merged in the will of the commander-in-chief. But that department has definitely marked boundaries, and all its members are not only controlled, but also sacredly protected by definitely prescribed law. The first law of the Revolutionary Congress, passed September 20th, 1776, touching the organization of the army, provided that no officer or soldier should be kept in arrest more than eight days without being furnished with the written charges and specifications against him; that he should be tried, at as early a day as possible, by a regular military court, whose proceedings were regulated by law, and that no sentence should be carried into execution till the full record of the trial had been submitted to Congress or to the commander-in-chief, and his or their direction be signified thereon. From year to year Congress has added new safeguards to protect the rights of its soldiers, and the rules and articles of war are as really a part of the laws of the land as the Judiciary Act or the act establishing the treasury department. The main boundary line between the civil and military jurisdictions is the muster into service. In *Mills v. Martin,* a militiaman, called out by the Governor of the State of New York, and ordered by him to enter the service of the United States, on a requisition of the President for troops, refused to obey the summons, and was tried by a Federal court-martial for disobedience of orders.

The Supreme Court of the State of New York decided, that until he had gone to the place of general rendezvous, and had been regularly enrolled, and mustered into the national militia, he was not amenable to the action of a court-martial composed of officers of the United States.

By the sixtieth article of war, the military jurisdiction is so extended as to cover those persons not mustered into the service, but necessarily connected with the army. It provides that:

"All sutlers and retainers to the camp, and all persons whatsoever, serving with the armies of the United States in the field, though not enlisted soldiers, are to be subject to orders according to the rules and articles of war."

That the question of jurisdiction might not be doubtful, it was thought necessary to provide by law of Congress that spies should be subject to trial by court-martial. As the law stood for eighty-five years, spies were described as "persons not citizens of, or owing allegiance to, the United States, who shall be found lurking," &c. Not until after the Great Rebellion began, was this law so amended as to allow the punishment by court-martial of *citizens of the United States* who should be found lurking about the lines of our army to betray it to the enemy.

It is evident, therefore, that by no loose and general construction of the law can citizens be held amenable to military tribunals, whose jurisdiction extends only to persons mustered into the military service, and such other classes of persons as are, by express provisions of law, made subject to the rules and articles of war. But even within their proper jurisdiction, military courts are, in many important particulars, subordinate to the civil courts. This is acknowledged by the leading authorities on the subject, and also by precedents, to some of which I refer:

1. A Lieutenant Frye, serving in the West Indies, in 1743, on a British man-of-war, was ordered by his superior officer to assist in arresting another officer. The lieutenant demanded, what he had, according to the customs of the naval service, a right to demand, a written order before he would obey the command. For this he was put under arrest, tried by a naval court-martial, and sentenced to fifteen years' imprisonment. In 1746 he brought an action before a civil court against the president of the court-martial, and damages of £1000 were awarded him for his illegal detention and sentence; and the judge informed him that he might also bring his action against any member of the court-martial. Rear Admiral Mayne and Captain Rentone, who were members of the court that tried him, were at the time, when damages were awarded to Lieutenant Frye, sitting on a naval court-martial. The lieutenant proceeded against them, and they were arrested by a writ from the Common Pleas. The order of arrest was served upon them one afternoon, just as the court-martial adjourned. Its members, fifteen in number, immediately reassembled and passed resolutions declaring it a great insult to the dignity of the naval service that any person, however high in civil authority, should order the arrest of a naval officer for any of his official acts. Lord Chief Jus-

tice Willes immediately ordered the arrest of all the members of the court who signed the resolutions, and they were arrested. They appealed to the king, who was very indignant at the arrest. The judge, however, persevered in his determination to maintain the supremacy of civil law, and after two months' examination and investigation of the cause, all the members of the court-martial signed an humble and submissive letter of apology, begging leave to withdraw their resolutions, in order to put an end to further proceedings. When the Lord Chief Justice had heard the letter read in open court, he directed that it be recorded in the Rememberance Office, "to the end," as he said, "that the present and future ages may know that whosoever set themselves up in opposition to the law, or think themselves above the law, will in the end find themselves mistaken."

2. In *Wilson* v. *McKenzie* it was proved that a mutiny of very threatening aspect had broken out; and that the lives of the captain and his officers were threatened by the mutineers. Among the persons arrested was the plaintiff, Wilson, an enlisted sailor, who being supposed to be in the conspiracy, was knocked down by the captain, ironed, and held in confinement for a number of days. When the cruise was ended, Wilson brought suit against the captain for illegal arrest and imprisonment. The cause was tried before the Supreme Court of New York; Chief Justice Nelson delivered the judgment of the court, giving judgment in favor of Wilson.

A clear and complete statement of the relation between civil and military courts may be found in *Dynes* v. *Hoover,* in this court:

"If a court-martial has no jurisdiction over the subject-matter of the charge it has been convened to try, or shall inflict a punishment forbidden by the law, though its sentence shall be approved by the officers having a revisory power of it, civil courts may, on an action by a party aggrieved by it, inquire into the want of the court's jurisdiction and give him redress."

"The courts of common law will examine whether courts-martial have exceeded the jurisdiction given them, though it is said, 'not, however, after the sentence has been ratified and carried into execution.'"

It is clear, then, that the Supreme Court of the United States may inquire into the question of jurisdiction of a military court; may take cognizance of extraordinary punishment inflicted by such a court not warranted by law; and may issue writs of prohibition or give such other redress as the case may require. It is also clear that the Constitution and laws of the United States have carefully provided for the protection of individual liberty and the right of accused persons to a speedy trial before a tribunal established and regulated by law.

To maintain the legality of the sentence here, opposite counsel are compelled not only to ignore the Constitution, but to declare it suspended—its voice lost in war—to hold that from the 5th of October, 1864, to the 9th of May, 1865, martial law alone existed in Indiana; that it silenced not only the civil courts, but all the laws of the land, and even the Constitution itself; and that during this silence the executor of martial law could lay his hand upon every citizen; could not only suspend the writ of *habeas corpus*, but could create a court which should have the exclusive jurisdiction over the citizen to try him, sentence him, and put him to death.

Sir Matthew Hale, in his History of the Common Law, says:

"Touching the business of martial law, these things are to be observed, viz.:

"First. That in truth and reality it is not a law, but something indulged rather than allowed as a law; the necessity of government, order, and discipline in an army, is that only which can give those laws a countenance: *quod enim necessitas cogit defendit.*

"Secondly. This indulged law was only to extend to members of the army, or to those of the opposed army, and never was so much indulged as intended to be executed or exercised upon others, for others who had not listed under the army had no color or reason to be bound by military constitutions applicable only to the army, whereof they were not parts, but they were to be ordered and governed according to the laws to which they were subject, though it were a time of war.

"Thirdly. That the exercises of martial law, whereby any person should lose his life, or member, or liberty, may not be permitted in time of peace, when the king's courts are open for all persons to receive justice according to the laws of the land. This is declared in the Petition of Right (3 Car. I), whereby such commissions and martial law were repealed and declared to be contrary to law."

In order to trace the history and exhibit the character of martial law, reference may be made to several leading precedents in English and American history.

1. *The Earl of Lancaster.* In the year 1322, the Earl of Lancaster and the Earl of Hereford rebelled against the authority of Edward II. They collected an army so large that Edward was compelled to raise forty thousand men to withstand them. The rebellious earls posted their forces on the Trent, and the armies of the king confronted them. They fought at Boroughbridge; the insurgent forces were overthrown; Hereford was slain and Lancaster taken in arms at the head of his army, and amid the noise of battle was tried by a court-martial, sentenced to death, and executed. When Edward III came into power, eight years later, on a formal petition presented to Parliament by Lancaster's son, setting forth the facts, the case was examined and a law was enacted reversing the attainder, and declaring: "1. That in time of peace no man ought to be adjudged to death for treason or any other offence without being arraigned and held to answer. 2. That regularly when the king's courts are open it is a time of peace in judgment of law; and 3. That no man ought to be sentenced to death, by the record of the king, without his legal trial *per pares.*"

So carefully was the line drawn between civil and martial law five hundred years ago.

2. *Sir Thomas Darnell.* He was arrested in 1625 by order of the king, for refusing to pay a tax which he regarded as illegal. He was arrested and imprisoned. A writ of *habeas corpus* was prayed for, but answer was returned by the court that he had been arrested by special order of the king, and that was held to be a sufficient answer to the petition. Then the great cause came up to be tried in Parliament, whether the order of the king was sufficient to override the writ of *habeas corpus*, and after a long and stormy debate, in which the ablest minds in England were engaged, the Petition of Right, of 1628, received the sanction of the king. In that statute it was decreed that the king should never again suspend the writ of *habeas corpus;* that he should never again try a subject by military commission; and since that day no king of England has presumed to usurp that high prerogative, which belongs to Parliament alone.
3. *The Bill of Rights of 1688.* The house of Stuart had been expelled and William had succeeded to the British throne. Great disturbances had arisen in the realm in consequence of the change of dynasty. The king's person was unsafe in London. He informed the Lords and Commons of the great dangers that threatened the kingdom, and reminded them that he had no right to declare martial law, to suspend the writ of *habeas corpus*, or to seize and imprison his subjects on suspicion of treason or intended outbreak against the peace of the realm. He laid the case before them and asked their advice and assistance. In answer, Parliament passed the celebrated *habeas corpus* act. Since that day, no king of England has dared to suspend the writ. It is only done by Parliament.
4. *Governor Wall.* In the year 1782, Joseph Wall, governor of the British colony at Goree, in Africa, had under his command about five hundred British soldiers. Suspecting a mutiny about to break out in the garrison, he assembled them on the parade-ground, held a hasty consultation with his officers, and immediately ordered Benjamin Armstrong, a private, and supposed ringleader, to be seized, stripped, tied to the wheel of an artillery-carriage, and with a rope one inch in diameter, to receive eight hundred lashes. The order was carried into execution, and Armstrong died of his injuries. Twenty years afterward Governor Wall was brought before the most august civil tribunal of England to answer for the murder of Armstrong. Sir Archibald McDonald, Lord Chief Baron of the Court of Exchequer, Sir Soulden Lawrence, of the King's Bench, Sir Giles Rooke, of the Common Pleas, constituted the court. Wall's counsel claimed that he had the power of life and death in his hands in time of mutiny; that the necessity of the case authorized him to suspend the usual forms of law; that as governor and military commander-in-chief of the forces at Goree, he was the sole judge of the necessities of the case. After a patient hearing before that high court, he was found guilty of murder, was sentenced and executed.

I now ask attention to precedents in our own colonial history.

5. On the 12th of June, 1775, General Gage, the commander of the British forces, declared martial law in Boston. The battles of Concord and Lexington had been fought two months before. The colonial army was besieging the city and its British garrison. It was but five days before the battle of Bunker Hill. Parliament had, in the previous February, declared the colonies in a state of rebellion. Yet, by the common consent of English jurists, General Gage violated the laws of England, and laid himself liable to its penalty, when he declared martial law. This position is sustained in the opinion of Woodbury, J., in *Luther* v. *Borden*.

6. On the 7th of November, 1775, Lord Dunmore declared martial law throughout the commonwealth of Virginia. This was long after the battle of Bunker Hill, and when war was flaming throughout the colonies; yet he was denounced by the Virginia Assembly for having assumed a power which the king himself dared not exercise, as it "annuls the law of the land, and introduces the most execrable of all systems, martial law." Woodbury, J., declares the act of Lord Dunmore unwarranted by British law.

7. The practice of our Revolutionary fathers on this subject is instructive. Their conduct throughout the great struggle for independence was equally marked by respect for civil law, and jealousy of martial law. Though Washington was clothed with almost dictatorial powers, he did not presume to override the civil law, or disregard the orders of the courts, except by express authority of Congress or the States. In his file of general orders, covering a period of five years, there are but four instances in which civilians appear to have been tried by a military court, and all these trials were expressly authorized by resolutions of Congress. In the autumn of 1777, the gloomiest period of the war, a powerful hostile army landed at Chesapeake Bay, for the purpose of invading Maryland and Pennsylvania. It was feared that the disloyal inhabitants along his line of march would give such aid and information to the British commander as to imperil the safety of our cause. Congress resolved "That the executive authorities of Pennsylvania and Maryland be requested to cause all persons within their respective States, notoriously disaffected, to be forthwith apprehended, disarmed, and secured till such time as the respective States think they can be released without injury to the common cause." The governor authorized the arrests, and many disloyal citizens were taken into custody by Washington's officers, who refused to answer the writ of *habeas corpus* which a civil court issued for the release of the prisoners. Very soon afterwards the Pennsylvania legislature passed a law indemnifying the governor and the military authorities, and allowing a similar course to be pursued thereafter on recommendation of Congress or the commanding officer of the army. But this law gave authority only to arrest and hold—not to try; and the act was to remain in force only till the

end of the next session of the General Assembly. So careful were our fathers to recognize the supremacy of civil law, and to resist all pretensions of the authority of martial law!

8. *Shay's Rebellion in 1787.* That rebellion, which was before the Constitution was adopted, was mentioned by Hamilton in the Federalist as a proof that we needed a strong central government to preserve our liberties. During all that disturbance there was no declaration of martial law, and the *habeas corpus* was only suspended for a limited time and with very careful restrictions. Governor Bowdoin's order to General Lincoln, on the 19th of January, 1787, was in these words: "Consider yourself in all your military offensive operations constantly as under the direction of the civil officer, save where any armed force shall appear to oppose you marching to execute these orders."

9. I refer too to a case under the Constitution, the Rebellion of 1793, in Western Pennsylvania. President Washington did not march with his troops until the judge of the United States District Court had certified that the marshal was unable to execute his warrants. Though the parties were tried for treason, all the arrests were made by the authority of the civil officers. The orders of the Secretary of War stated that "the object of the expedition was to assist the marshal of the district to make prisoners." Every movement was made under the direction of the civil authorities. So anxious was Washington on this subject that he issued orders declaring that "the army should not consider themselves as judges of executioners of the laws, but only as employed to support the proper authorities in the execution of the laws."

10. I call the attention of the court also to the case of General Jackson, in 1815, at New Orleans. In 1815, at New Orleans, General Jackson took upon himself the command of every person in the city, suspended the functions of all the civil authorities, and made his own will for a time the only rule of conduct. It was believed to be absolutely necessary. Judges, officers of the city corporation, and members of the State legislature insisted on it as the only way to save the citizens and property of the place from the unspeakable outrages committed at Badajos and St. Sebastian by the very same troops then marching to the attack. Jackson used the power thus taken by him moderately, sparingly, benignly, and only for the purpose of preventing mutiny in his camp. A single mutineer was restrained by a short confinement, and another was sent four miles up the river. But after he had saved the city, and the danger was all over, he stood before the court to be tried by the law; his conduct was decided to be illegal, and he paid the penalty without a murmur. The Supreme Court of Louisiana, in *Johnson v. Duncan*, decided that everything done during the siege in pursuance of martial rule, but in conflict with the law of the land, was void and of none effect, without reference to the circumstances which made it necessary. In 1842, a bill was

introduced into Congress to reimburse General Jackson for the fine. The debate was able and thorough. Mr. Buchanan, then a member of Congress, spoke in its favor, and no one will doubt his willingness to put the conduct of Jackson on the most favorable ground possible. Yet he did not attempt to justify, but only sought to palliate and excuse the conduct of Jackson. All the leading members took the same ground.

11. I may fortify my argument by the authority of two great British jurists, and call attention to the trial of the Rev. John Smith, missionary at Demerara, in British Guiana. In the year 1823, a rebellion broke out in Demerara, extending over some fifty plantations. The governor of the district immediately declared martial law. A number of the insurgents were killed, and the rebellion was crushed. It was alleged that the Rev. John Smith, a missionary, sent out by the London Missionary Society, had been an aider and abettor of the rebellion. A court-martial was appointed, and in order to give it the semblance of civil law, the governor-general appointed the chief justice of the district as a staff officer, and then detailed him as president of the court to try the accused. All the other members of the court were military men, and he was made a military officer for the special occasion. Missionary Smith was tried, found guilty, and sentenced to be hung. The proceedings came to the notice of Parliament, and were made the subject of inquiry and debate. Smith died in prison before the day of execution; but the trial gave rise to one of the ablest debates of the century, in which the principles involved in the cause now before this court were fully discussed. Lord Brougham and Sir James Mackintosh were among the speakers. In the course of his speech Lord Brougham said:

"No such thing as martial law is recognized in Great Britain, and courts founded on proclamations of martial law are wholly unknown. Suppose I am ready to admit that, on the pressure of a great necessity, such as invasion or rebellion, when there is no time for the slow and cumbrous proceedings of the civil law, a proclamation may justifiably be issued for excluding the ordinary tribunals, and directing that offences should be tried by a military court, such a proceeding might be justified by necessity, but it could rest on that alone. Created by necessity, necessity must limit its continuance. It would be the worst of all conceivable grievances, it would be a calamity unspeakable, if the whole law and constitution of England were suspended one hour longer than the most imperious necessity demanded. I know that the proclamation of martial law renders every man liable to be treated as a soldier. But the instant the necessity ceases, that instant the state of soldiership ought to cease, and the rights, with the relations of civil life, to be restored."

Sir James Mackintosh says:

"The only principle on which the law of England tolerates what is called 'martial law,' is necessity. Its introduction can be justified only by necessity; its continuance requires precisely the same justification of necessity; and if it survives the necessity, in which alone it rests, for a single minute, it becomes instantly a mere exercise of lawless violence. When foreign invasion or civil war renders it impossible for courts of law to sit, or to enforce the execution of their judgments, it becomes necessary to find some rude substitute for them, and to employ for that purpose the military, which is the only remaining force in the community."

The next paragraph lays down the chief condition that can justify martial law, and also marks the boundary between martial and civil law:

"While the laws are silenced by the noise of arms, the rulers of the armed force must punish, as equitably as they can, those crimes which threaten their own safety and that of society, but no longer; every moment beyond is usurpation. As soon as the laws can act, every other mode of punishing supposed crimes is itself an enormous crime. If argument be not enough on this subject—if, indeed, the mere statement be not the evidence of its own truth—I appeal to the highest and most venerable authority known to our law."

He proceeds to quote Sir Matthew Hale on Martial Law, and cites the case of the Earl of Lancaster, to which I have already referred, and then declares:

"No other doctrine has ever been maintained in this country since the solemn parliamentary condemnation of the usurpations of Charles I, which he was himself compelled to sanction in the Petition of Right. In none of the revolutions or rebellions which have since occurred has martial law been exercised, however much, in some of them, the necessity might seem to exist. Even in those most deplorable of all commotions which tore Ireland in pieces in the last years of the eighteenth century, in the midst of ferocious revolt and cruel punishment, at the very moment of legalizing these martial jurisdictions in 1799, the very Irish statute, which was passed for that purpose, did homage to the ancient and fundamental principles of the law in the very act of departing from them. The Irish statute (39 George III, chap. 3), after reciting "that martial law had been successfully exercised to the restoration of peace, so far as to permit the course of the common law partially to take place, but that the rebellion continued to rage in considerable parts of the kingdom, whereby it has become necessary for Parliament to interpose," goes on to enable the Lord Lieutenant 'to punish rebels by courts-martial.' This statute is the most positive declaration, that where the common law can be exercised in some parts of the country, martial law cannot be established in others, though rebellion actually prevails in those others, without an extraordinary interposition of the supreme legislative authority itself."

After presenting arguments to show that a declaration of martial law was not necessary, the learned jurist continues:

"For six weeks, then, before the court-martial was assembled, and for twelve weeks before that court pronounced sentence of death on Mr. Smith, all hostility had ceased, no necessity for their existence can be pretended, and every act which they did was an open and deliberate defiance of the law of England. Where, then, are we to look for any color of law in these proceedings? Do they derive it from the Dutch law? I have diligently examined the Roman law, which is the foundation of that system, and the writings of those most eminent jurists who have contributed so much to the reputation of Holland. I can find in them no trace of any such principle as martial law. Military law, indeed, is clearly defined; and provision is made for the punishment, by military judges, of the purely military offences of soldiers. But to any power of extending military jurisdiction over those who are not soldiers, there is not an allusion."

Many more such precedents as I have already cited might be added to the list; but it is unnecessary. They all teach the same lesson. They enable us to trace, from its far-off source, the progress and development of Anglo-Saxon liberty; its conflicts with irresponsible power; its victories, dearly bought, but always won—victories which have crowned with immortal honors the institutions of England, and left their indelible impress upon the Anglo-Saxon mind. These principles our fathers brought with them to the New World, and guarded with vigilance and devotion. During the late Rebellion, the Republic did not forget them. So completely have they been impressed on the minds of American lawyers, so thoroughly ingrained into the fibre of American character, that notwithstanding the citizens of eleven States went off into rebellion, broke their oaths of allegiance to the Constitution, and levied war against their country, yet with all their crimes upon them, there was still in the minds of those men, during all the struggle, so deep an impression on this great subject, that, even during their rebellion, the courts of the Southern States adjudicated causes, like the one now before you, in favor of the civil law, and against courts-martial established under military authority for the trial of citizens. In Texas, Mississippi, Virginia, and other insurgent States, by the order of the rebel President, the writ of *habeas corpus* was suspended, martial law was declared, and provost marshals were appointed to administer military authority. But when civilians, arrested by military authority, petitioned for release by writ of *habeas corpus*, in every case, save one, the writ was granted, and it was decided that there could be no suspension of the writ or declaration of martial law by the executive, or by any other than the supreme legislative authority.

The military commission, under our government, is of recent origin. It was instituted, as has been frequently said, by General Scott, in Mexico, to enable him, in the absence of any civil authority, to punish Mexican and American citizens for offences not provided for in the rules and articles of war. The purpose and character of a military commission may be seen from his celebrated order, No. 20, published at Tampico. It was no tribunal with authority to punish, but merely a committee appointed to examine an offender, and advise the commanding general what punishment to inflict. It is a rude substitute for a court of justice, in the absence of civil law. Even our own military authorities, who have given so much prominence to these commissions, do not claim for them the character of tribunals established by law. In his "Digest of Opinions" for 1866, the Judge Advocate General says:

"Military commissions have grown out of the necessities of the service, but their powers have not been defined nor their mode of proceeding regulated by any statute law."

Again:

"In a military department the military commission is a substitute for the ordinary State or United States Court, when the latter is closed by the exigencies of war or is without the jurisdiction of the offence committed."

The plea set up by the Attorney-General for this military tribunal is that of the necessity of this case. But there was in fact no necessity. From the beginning of the Rebellion to its close, Congress, by its legislation, kept pace with the necessities of the nation. In sixteen carefully considered laws, the national legislature undertook to provide for every contingency, and arm the executive at every point with the solemn sanction of law. Observe how the case of the petitioner was covered by the provisions of law.

The first *charge* against him was "conspiracy against the government of the United States." In the act approved July 31st, 1861, that crime was defined, and placed within the jurisdiction of the District and Circuit Courts of the United States.

Charge 2. "Affording aid and comfort to the rebels against the authority of the United States." In the act approved July 17th, 1862, this crime is set forth in the very words of the charge, and it is provided that "on conviction before any court of the United States, having jurisdiction thereof, the offender shall be punished by a fine not exceeding ten thousand dollars, and by imprisonment not less than six months, nor exceeding five years."

Charge 3. "Inciting insurrection." In Brightly's Digest, there is compiled from ten separate acts, a chapter of sixty-four sections on insurrection, setting forth in the fullest manner possible, every mode by which citizens may aid in insurrection, and providing for their trial and punishment by the regularly ordained courts of the United States.

Charge 4. "Disloyal practices." The meaning of this charge can only be found in the specifications under it, which consists in discouraging enlistments and making preparations to resist a draft designed to increase the army of the United States. These offences are fully defined in the thirty-third section of the act of March 3d, 1863, "for enrolling and calling out the national forces," and in the twelfth section of the act of February 24th, 1864, amendatory thereof. The provost marshal is authorized to arrest such offenders, but he must deliver them over for trial to the civil authorities. Their trial and punishment are expressly placed in the jurisdiction of the District and Circuit Courts of the United States.

Charge 5. "Violation of the laws of war;" which, according to the specifications, consisted of an attempt, through a secret organization, to give aid and comfort to rebels. This crime is amply provided for in the laws referred to in relation to the second charge.

But Congress did far more than to provide for a case like this. Throughout the eleven rebellious States, it clothed the military department with supreme power and authority. State constitutions and laws, the decrees and edicts of courts, were all superseded by the laws of war. Even in States not in rebellion, but where treason had a foothold, and hostile collisions were likely to occur, Congress authorized the suspension of the writ of *habeas corpus,* and directed the army to keep the peace. But Congress went further still, and authorized the President, during the Rebellion, whenever, in his judgment, the public safety should require it, to suspend the privilege of the writ in any State or Territory of the United States, and order the arrest of any persons whom he might believe dangerous to the safety of the Republic, and hold them till the civil authorities could examine into the nature of their crimes. But this act of March 3d, 1863, gave no authority to try the person by any military tribunal, and it commanded judges of the Circuit and District Courts of the United States, whenever the grand jury had adjourned its sessions, and found no indictment against such persons, to order their immediate discharge from arrest. All these capacious powers were conferred upon the military department, but there is no law on the statute book, in which the tribunal that tried the petitioner can find the least recognition.

What have our Representatives in Congress thought on this subject?

Near the close of the Thirty-Eighth Congress, when the miscellaneous appropriation bill, which authorized the disbursement of several millions of dollars for the civil expenditures of the government, was under discussion, the House of Representatives, having observed with alarm the growing tendency to break down the barriers of law, and desiring to protect the rights of citizens as well as to preserve the Union added to the appropriation bill the following section:

"And be it further enacted, That no person shall be tried by court-martial or military commission in any State or Territory where the courts of the United States are open, except persons actually mustered or commissioned or appointed in the military or naval service of the United States, or rebel enemies charged with being spies."

It was debated at length in the Senate, and almost every Senator acknowledged its justice, yet, as the nation was then in the very midst of the war, it was feared that the Executive might thereby be crippled, and the section was stricken out. The bill came back to the House; conferences were held upon it, and finally, in the last hour of the session, the House deliberately determined that, important as the bill was to the interests of the country, they preferred it should not become a law if that section were stricken out.

The bill failed; and the record of its failure is an emphatic declaration that the House of Representatives have never consented to the establishment of any tribunals except those authorized by the Constitution of the United States and the laws of Congress.

A point is suggested by the opposing counsel, that if the military tribunal had no jurisdiction, the petitioners may be held as prisoners captured in war, and handed over by the military to the civil authorities, to be tried for their crimes under the acts of Congress and before the courts of the United States. The answer to this is that the petitioners were never enlisted, commissioned, or mustered into the service of the Confederacy; nor had they been within the rebel lines, or within any theatre of active military operations; nor had they been in any way recognized by the rebel authorities as in their service. They could not have been exchanged as prisoners of war; nor, if all the charges against them were true, could they be brought under the legal definition of spies. The suggestion that they should be handed over to the civil authorities for trial is precisely what they petitioned for, and what, according to the laws of Congress, should have been done.

Mr. Black, on the same side:

Had the commissioners jurisdiction? Were they invested with legal authority to try the petitioner and put him to death for the offence of which he was accused? This is the main question in the controversy, and the main one upon which the court divided. We answer, that they were not; and, therefore, that the whole proceeding from beginning to end was null and void.

On the other hand, it is necessary for those who oppose us to assert, and they do assert, that the commissioners had complete legal jurisdiction both of the subject-matter and of the party, so that their judgment upon the law and the facts is absolutely conclusive and binding, not subject to correction nor open to inquiry in any court whatever. Of these two opposite views, the court must adopt one or the other. There is no middle ground on which to stand.

The men whose acts we complain of erected themselves, it will be remembered, into a tribunal for the trial and punishment of citizens who were connected in no way whatever with the army or navy. And this they did in the midst of a community whose social and legal organization had never been disturbed by any war or insurrection, where the courts were wide open, where judicial process was executed every day without interruption, and where all the civil authorities, both state and national, were in the full exercise of their functions.

It is unimportant whether the petitioner was intended to be charged with treason or conspiracy, or with some offence of which the law takes no notice. Either or any way, the men who undertook to try him had no jurisdiction of the *subject-matter*.

Nor had they jurisdiction of the *party*. The case, not having been one of impeachment, or a case arising in the land or naval forces, is either nothing at all or else it is a simple crime against the United States, committed by private individuals not in the public service, civil or military. Persons standing in that relation to the government are answerable for the offences which they may commit only to the civil courts of the country. So says the Constitution, as we read it; and the act of Congress of March 3d, 1863, which was passed with reference to persons in the exact situation of this man, declares that they shall be delivered up for trial to the proper civil authorities.

There being no jurisdiction of the subject-matter or of the party, you are bound to relieve the petitioner. It is as much the duty of a judge to protect the innocent as it is to punish the guilty.

We submit that a person not in the military or naval service cannot be punished at all until he has had a fair, open, public trial before an impartial jury, in an ordained and established court, to which the jurisdiction has been given by law to try him for that specific offence.

Our proposition ought to be received as true without any argument to support it; because, if that, or something precisely equivalent to it, be not a part of our law, then the country is not a free country. Nevertheless, we take upon ourselves the burden of showing affirmatively not only that it is true, but that it is immovably fixed in the very framework of the government, so that it is impossible to detach it without destroying the whole political structure under which we live.

In the first place, the self-evident truth will not be denied that the trial and punishment of an offender against the government is the exercise of judicial authority. That is a kind of authority which would be lost by being diffused among the masses of the people. A judge would be no judge if everybody else were a judge as well as he. Therefore, in every society, however rude or however perfect its organization, the judicial authority is always committed to the hands of particular persons, who are trusted to use it wisely and well; and their authority is exclusive; they cannot share it with others to whom it has not been committed. Where, then, is the judicial power in this country? Who are the depositaries of it here? The Federal Constitution answers that question in very plain words, by declaring that "the judicial power of the United States shall be vested in one Supreme Court, and in such inferior courts as Congress may from time to time ordain and establish." Congress *has*, from time to time, ordained and established certain inferior courts; and, in them, together with the one Supreme Court to which they are subordinate, is vested all the judicial power, properly so called, which the United States can lawfully exercise. At the time the General Government was created, the States and the people bestowed upon that government a certain portion of the judicial power which otherwise would have remained in their own hands, but they gave it on a solemn trust, and coupled the grant of it with this express condition, that it should never be used in any way but one; that is, by means of ordained and established courts. Any person, therefore, who undertakes to exercise judicial power in any other way, not only violates the law of the land, but he tramples upon the most important part of that Constitution which holds these States together.

We all know that it was the intention of the men who founded this Republic to put the life, liberty, and property of every person in it under the protection of a regular and permanent judiciary, separate, apart, distinct, from all other branches of the government, whose sole and exclusive business it should be to distribute justice among the people according to the wants and needs of each individual. It was to consist of courts, always open to the complaint of the injured, and always ready to hear criminal accusations when founded upon probable cause; surrounded with all the machinery necessary for the investigation of truth, and clothed with sufficient power to carry their decrees into execution. In these courts it was expected that judges would sit who would be upright, honest, and sober men, learned in the laws of their country, and lovers of justice from the habitual practice of that virtue; independent, because their salaries could not be reduced, and free from party passion, because their tenure of office was for life. Although this would place them above the clamors of the mere mob and beyond the reach of executive influence, it was not intended that they should be wholly irresponsible. For any willful or corrupt violation of their duty, they are liable to be impeached; and they cannot escape the control of an enlightened public opinion, for they must sit with open doors, listen to full discussion, and give satisfactory reasons for the judgments they pronounce. In ordinary tranquil times the citizen might feel himself safe under a judicial system so organized.

But our wise forefathers knew that tranquillity was not to be always anticipated in a republic; the spirit of a free people is often turbulent. They expected that strife would rise between classes and sections, and even civil war might come, and they supposed, that in such times, judges themselves might not be safely trusted in criminal cases—especially in prosecutions for political offences, where the whole power of the executive is arrayed against the accused party. All history proves that public officers of any government when they are engaged in a severe struggle to retain their places, become bitter and ferocious, and hate those who oppose them, even in the most legitimate way, with a rancor which they never exhibit towards actual crime. This kind of malignity vents itself in prosecutions for political offences, sedition, conspiracy, libel, and treason, and the charges are generally founded upon the information of spies and delators, who make merchandise of their oaths, and trade in the blood of their fellow men. During the civil commotions in England, which lasted from the beginning of the reign of Charles I to the Revolution of 1688, the best men, and the purest patriots that ever lived, fell by the hand of the public executioner. Judges were made the instruments for inflicting the most merciless sentences on men, the latchet of whose shoes the ministers that prosecuted them were not worthy to stoop down and unloose. Nothing has occurred, indeed, in the history of this country to justify the doubt of judicial integrity which our forefathers seem to have felt. On the contrary, the highest compliment that has ever been paid to the American bench, is embodied in this simple fact, that if the executive officers of this government have ever desired to take away the life or the liberty of a citizen contrary to law, they have not come into the courts to get it done, they have gone outside of the courts, and stepped over the Constitution, and created their own tribunals. But the framers of the

Constitution could act only upon the experience of that country whose history they knew most about, and there they saw the ferocity of Jeffreys and Scroggs, the timidity of Guilford, and the venality of such men as Saunders and Wright. It seems necessary, therefore, not only to make the judiciary as perfect as possible, but to give the citizen yet another shield against his government. To that end they could think of no better provision than a public trial before an impartial jury.

We do not assert that the jury trial is an infallible mode of ascertaining truth. Like everything human, it has its imperfections. We only say that it is the best protection for innocence and the surest mode of punishing guilt that has yet been discovered. It has borne the test of a longer experience, and borne it better than any other legal institution that ever existed among men. England owes more of her freedom, her grandeur, and her prosperity to that, than to all other causes put together. It has had the approbation not only of those who lived under it, but of great thinkers who looked at it calmly from a distance, and judged it impartially: Montesquieu and De Tocqueville speak of it with an admiration as rapturous as Coke and Blackstone. Within the present century, the most enlightened states of continental Europe have transplanted it into their countries; and no people ever adopted it once and were afterwards willing to part with it. It was only in 1830 that an interference with it in Belgium provoked a successful insurrection which permanently divided one kingdom into two. In the same year, the Revolution of the Barricades gave the right of trial by jury to every Frenchman.

Those colonists of this country who came from the British Islands brought this institution with them, and they regarded it as the most precious part of their inheritance. The immigrants from other places where trial by jury did not exist became equally attached to it as soon as they understood what it was. There was no subject upon which all the inhabitants of the country were more perfectly unanimous than they were in their determination to maintain this great right unimpaired. An attempt was made to set it aside and substitute military trials in its place, by Lord Dunmore, in Virginia, and General Gage, in Massachusetts, accompanied with the excuse which has been repeated so often in late days, namely, that rebellion had made it necessary; but it excited intense popular anger, and every colony, from New Hampshire to Georgia, made common cause with the two whose rights had been especially invaded. Subsequently the Continental Congress thundered it into the ear of the world, as an unendurable outrage, sufficient to justify universal insurrection against the authority of the government which had allowed it to be done.

If the men who fought out our Revolutionary contest, when they came to frame a government for themselves and their posterity, had failed to insert a provision making the trial by jury perpetual and universal, they would have proved themselves recreant to the principles of that liberty of which they professed to be the special champions. But they were guilty of no such thing. They not only took care of the trial by jury, but they regulated every step to be taken in a criminal trial. They knew very well that no people could be free under a government which had the power to punish without restraint. Hamilton expressed, in the Federalist, the universal sentiment of his time, when he said, that the arbitrary power of conviction and punishment for pretended offences, had been the great engine of despotism in all ages and all countries. The existence of such a power is incompatible with freedom.

But our fathers were not absurd enough to put unlimited power in the hands of the ruler and take away the protection of law from the rights of individuals. It was not thus that they meant "to secure the blessings of liberty to themselves and their posterity." They determined that not one drop of the blood which had been shed on the other side of the Atlantic, during seven centuries of contest with arbitrary power, should sink into the ground; but the fruits of every popular victory should be garnered up in this new government. Of all the great rights already won they threw not an atom away. They went over *Magna Charta*, the *Petition of Right*, the *Bill of Rights*, and the rules of the *common law*, and whatever was found there to favor individual liberty they carefully inserted in their own system, improved by clearer expression, strengthened by heavier sanctions, and extended by a more universal application. They put all those provisions into the organic law, so that neither tyranny in the executive, nor party rage in the legislature could change them without destroying the government itself.

Look at the particulars and see how carefully everything connected with the administration of punitive justice is guarded.

1. No *ex post facto* law shall be passed. No man shall be answerable criminally for any act which was not defined and made punishable as a crime by some law in force at the time when the act was done.
2. For an act which is criminal he cannot be arrested without a judicial warrant founded on proof of probable cause. He shall not be kidnapped and shut up on the mere report of some base spy who gathers the materials of a false accusation by crawling into his house and listening at the keyhole of his chamber door.
3. He shall not be compelled to testify against himself. He may be examined before he is committed, and tell his own story if he pleases; but the rack shall be put out of sight, and even his conscience shall not be tortured; nor shall his unpublished papers be used against him, as was done most wrongfully in the case of Algernon Sydney.
4. He shall be entitled to a speedy trial; not kept in prison for an indefinite time without the opportunity of vindicating his innocence.
5. He shall be informed of the accusation, its nature, and grounds. The public accuser must put the charge into the form of a legal indictment, so that the party can meet it full in the face.
6. Even to the indictment he need not answer unless a grand jury, after hearing the evidence, shall say upon their oaths that they believe it to be true.

7. Then comes the trial, and it must be before a regular court, of competent jurisdiction, ordained and established for the State and district in which the crime was committed; and this shall not be evaded by a legislative change in the district after the crime is alleged to be done.
8. His guilt or innocence shall be determined by an impartial jury. These English words are to be understood in their English sense, and they mean that the jurors shall be fairly selected by a sworn officer from among the peers of the party, residing within the local jurisdiction of the court. When they are called into the box he can purge the panel of all dishonesty, prejudice, personal enmity, and ignorance, by a certain number of peremptory challenges, and as many more challenges as he can sustain by showing reasonable cause.
9. The trial shall be public and open, that no underhand advantage may be taken. The party shall be confronted with the witnesses against him, have compulsory process for his own witnesses, and be entitled to the assistance of counsel in his defence.
10. After the evidence is heard and discussed, unless the jury shall, upon their oaths, *unanimously* agree to surrender him up into the hands of the court as a guilty man, not a hair of his head can be touched by way of punishment.
11. After a verdict of guilty he is still protected. No cruel or unusual punishment shall be inflicted, nor any punishment at all, except what is annexed by the law to his offence. It cannot be doubted for a moment that if a person convicted of an offence not capital were to be hung on the order of a judge, such judge would be guilty of murder as plainly as if he should come down from the bench, turn up the sleeves of his gown, and let out the prisoner's blood with his own hand.
12. After all is over, the law continues to spread its guardianship around him. Whether he is acquitted or condemned he shall never again be molested for that offence. No man shall be twice put in jeopardy of life or limb for the same cause.

These rules apply to all criminal prosecutions. But in addition to these, certain special regulations were required for *treason*,—the one great political charge under which more innocent men have fallen than any other. A tyrannical government calls everybody a traitor who shows the least unwillingness to be a slave. In the absence of a constitutional provision it was justly feared that statutes might be passed which would put the lives of the most patriotic citizens at the mercy of minions that skulk about under the pay of an executive. Therefore a definition of treason was given in the fundamental law, and the legislative authority could not enlarge it to serve the purpose of partisan malice. The nature and amount of evidence required to prove the crime was also prescribed, so that prejudice and enmity might have no share in the conviction. And lastly, the punishment was so limited that the property of the party could not be confiscated and used to reward the agents of his prosecutors, or strip his family of their subsistence.

If these provisions exist in full force, unchangeable and irrepealable, then we are not hereditary bondsmen. Every citizen may safely pursue his lawful calling in the open day; and at night, if he is conscious of innocence, he may lie down in security, and sleep the sound sleep of a freeman.

They are in force, and they will remain in force. We have not surrendered them, and we never will. The great race to which we belong has not degenerated.

But how am I to prove the existence of these rights? I do not propose to do it by a long chain of legal argumentation, nor by the production of numerous books with the leaves turned down and the pages marked. If it depended upon judicial precedents, I think I could produce as many as might be necessary. If I claimed this freedom, under any kind of prescription, I could prove a good long possession in ourselves and those under whom we claim it. I might begin with Tacitus, and show how the contest arose in the forests of Germany more than two thousand years ago; how the rough virtues and sound common sense of that people established the right of trial by jury, and thus started on a career which has made their posterity the foremost race that ever lived in all the tide of time. The Saxons carried it to England, and were ever ready to defend it with their blood. It was crushed out by the Danish invasion; and all that they suffered of tyranny and oppression, during the period of their subjugation, resulted from the want of trial by jury. If that had been conceded to them, the reaction would not have taken place which drove back the Danes to their frozen homes in the North. But those ruffian sea kings could not understand that, and the reaction came. Alfred, the greatest of revolutionary heroes and the wisest monarch that ever sat on a throne, made the first use of his power, after the Saxons restored it, to re-establish their ancient laws. He had promised them that he would, and he was true to them because they had been true to him. But it was not easily done; the courts were opposed to it, for it limited their power—a kind of power that everybody covets—the power to punish without regard to law. He was obliged to hang forty-four judges in one year for refusing to give his subjects a trial by jury. When the historian says that he hung them, it is not meant that he put them to death without a trial. He had them impeached before the grand council of the nation, the Wittenagemote, the Parliament of that time. During the subsequent period of Saxon domination, no man on English soil was powerful enough to refuse a legal trial to the meanest peasant. If any minister or any king, in war or in peace, had dared to punish a freeman by a tribunal of his own appointment, he would have roused the wrath of the whole population; all orders of society would have resisted it; lord and vassal, knight and squire, priest and penitent, bocman and socman, master and thrall, copyholder and villein, would have risen in one mass and burnt the offender to death in his castle, or followed him in his flight and torn him to atoms. It was again trampled down by the Norman conquerors; but the evils resulting from the want of it united all classes in the effort which compelled King John to restore it by the Great Charter. Everybody is familiar with the struggles which the English people, during many generations, made for their rights with the Plantagenets, the Tudors, and the Stuarts, and which ended finally in the Revolution of 1688, when the liberties of England were placed upon an impregnable basis by the Bill of Rights.

Many times the attempt was made to stretch the royal authority far enough to justify military trials; but it never had more than temporary success. Five hundred years ago Edward II closed up a great rebellion by taking the life of its leader, the Earl of Lancaster, after trying him before a military court. Eight years later that same king, together with his lords and commons in Parliament assembled, acknowledged with shame and sorrow that the execution of Lancaster was a mere murder, because the courts were open, and he might have had a legal trial. Queen Elizabeth, for sundry reasons affecting the safety of the state, ordered that certain offenders not of her army should be tried according to the law martial. But she heard the storm of popular vengeance rising, and, haughty, imperious, self-willed as she was, she yielded the point; for she knew that upon that subject the English people would never consent to be trifled with. Strafford, as Lord Lieutenant of Ireland, tried the Viscount Stormont before a military commission, and executed him. When impeached, he pleaded in vain that Ireland was in a state of insurrection, that Stormont was a traitor, and the army would be undone if it could not defend itself without appealing to the civil courts. The Parliament was deaf; the king himself could not save him; he was condemned to suffer death as a traitor and a murderer. Charles I issued commissions to divers officers for the trial of his enemies according to the course of military law. If rebellion ever was an excuse for such an act, he could surely have pleaded it; for there was scarcely a spot in his kingdom, from sea to sea, where the royal authority was not disputed by somebody. Yet the Parliament demanded, in their petition of right, and the king was obliged to concede, that all his commissions were illegal. James II claimed the right to suspend the operation of the penal laws—a power which the courts denied—but the experience of his predecessors taught him that he could not suspend any man's right to a trial. He could easily have convicted the seven bishops of any offence he saw fit to charge them with, if he could have selected their judges from among the mercenary creatures to whom he had given commands in his army. But this he dared not do. He was obliged to send the bishops to a jury, and endure the mortification of seeing them acquitted. He, too, might have had rebellion for an excuse, if rebellion be an excuse. The conspiracy was already ripe which, a few months afterwards, made him an exile and an outcast; he had reason to believe that the Prince of Orange was making his preparations, on the other side of the Channel, to invade the kingdom, where thousands burned to join him; nay, he pronounced the bishops guilty of rebellion by the very act for which he arrested them. He had raised an army to meet the rebellion, and he was on Hounslow Heath reviewing the troops organized for that purpose, when he heard the great shout of joy that went up from Westminster Hall, was echoed back from Temple Bar, spread down the city and over the Thames, and rose from every vessel on the river—the simultaneous shout of two hundred thousand men for the triumph of justice and law.

The truth is, that no authority exists anywhere in the world for the doctrine of the Attorney-General. No judge or jurist, no statesman or parliamentary orator, on this or the other side of the water, sustains him. Every elementary writer is against him. All military authors who profess to know the duties of their profession admit themselves to be under, not above the laws. No book can be found in any library to justify the assertion that military tribunals may try a citizen at a place where the courts are open. When I say no book, I mean, of course, no book of acknowledged authority. I do not deny that hireling clergymen have often been found to dishonor the pulpit by trying to prove the divine right of kings and other rulers to govern as they please. Court sycophants and party hacks have many times written pamphlets, and perhaps large volumes, to show that those whom they serve should be allowed to work out their bloody will upon the people. No abuse of power is too flagrant to find its defenders.

But this case does not depend on authority. It is rather a question of fact than of law.

I prove my right to a trial by jury just as I would prove my title to an estate, if I held in my hand a solemn deed conveying it to me, coupled with undeniable evidence of long and undisturbed possession under and according to the deed. There is the charter by which we claim to hold it. It is called the Constitution of the United States. It is signed with the sacred name of George Washington, and with thirty-nine other names, only less illustrious than his. They represented every independent State then upon this continent, and each State afterwards ratified their work by a separate convention of its own people. Every State that subsequently came in acknowledged that this was the great standard by which their rights were to be measured. Every man that has ever held office in the country, from that time to this, has taken an oath that he would support and sustain it through good report and through evil. The Attorney-General himself became a party to the instrument when he laid his hand upon the holy gospels, and swore that he would give to me and every other citizen the full benefit of all it contains.

What does it contain? This among other things:

"The trial of all crimes except in cases of impeachment shall be by jury."

Again:

"No person shall be held to answer for a capital or otherwise infamous crime unless on a presentment or indictment of a grand jury, except in cases arising in the land or naval forces, or in the militia when in actual service in time of war or public danger; nor shall any person be subject for the same offence to be twice put in jeopardy of life or limb, nor be compelled, in any criminal case, to be a witness against himself, nor be deprived of life, liberty, or property, without due process of law; nor shall private property be taken for public use without just compensation."

This is not all; another article declares that,

"In all criminal prosecutions, the accused shall enjoy the right to a speedy and public trial by an impartial jury of the state and district wherein the crime shall have been committed, which district shall have been previously ascertained by law; and to be informed of the nature and cause of the accusation; to be confronted with the witnesses against him; to have compulsory process for the witnesses in his favor; and to have the assistance of counsel for his defence."

Is there any ambiguity there? If that does not signify that a jury trial shall be the exclusive and only means of ascertaining guilt in criminal cases, then I demand to know what words, or what collocation of words in the English language would have that effect? Does this mean that a fair, open, speedy, public trial by an impartial jury shall be given only to those persons against whom no special grudge is felt by the Attorney-General, or the judge-advocate, or the head of a department? Shall this inestimable privilege be extended only to men whom the administration does not care to convict? Is it confined to vulgar criminals, who commit ordinary crimes against society, and shall it be denied to men who are accused of such offences as those for which Sydney and Russell were beheaded, and Alice Lisle was hung, and Elizabeth Gaunt was burnt alive, and John Bunyan was imprisoned fourteen years, and Baxter was whipped at the cart's tail, and Prynn had his ears cut off? No; the words of the Constitution are all-embracing, "as broad and general as the casing air." The trial of ALL crimes shall be by jury. ALL persons accused shall enjoy that privilege—and NO person shall be held to answer in any other way.

That would be sufficient without more. But there is another consideration which gives it tenfold power. It is a universal rule of construction, that general words in any instrument, though they may be weakened by enumeration, are always strengthened by exceptions. Here is no attempt to enumerate the particular cases in which men charged with criminal offences shall be entitled to a jury trial. It is simply declared that *all* shall have it. But that is coupled with a statement of two specific exceptions: cases of impeachment; and cases arising in the land or naval forces. These exceptions strengthen the application of the general rule to all other cases. Where the lawgiver himself has declared when and in what circumstances you may depart from the general rule, you shall not presume to leave that onward path for other reasons, and make different exceptions. To exceptions the maxim is always applicable, that *expressio unius exclusio est alterius.*

But we shall be answered that the judgment under consideration was pronounced in time of war, and it is, therefore, at least, morally excusable. There may, or there may not, be something in that. I admit that the merits or demerits of any particular act, whether it involve a violation of the Constitution or not, depend upon the motives that prompted it, the time, the occasion, and all the attending circumstances. When the people of this country come to decide upon the acts of their rulers, they will take all these things into consideration. But that presents the political aspect of the case, with which we have nothing to do here. I would only say, in order to prevent misapprehension, that I think it is precisely in a time of war and civil commotion that we should double the guards upon the Constitution. In peaceable and quiet times, our legal rights are in little danger of being overborne; but when the wave of power lashes itself into violence and rage, and goes surging up against the barriers which were made to confine it, then we need the whole strength of an unbroken Constitution to save us from destruction.

There has been and will be another *quasi* political argument,—necessity. If the law was violated because it could not be obeyed, that might be an excuse. But no absolute compulsion is pretended here. These commissioners acted, at most, under what they regarded as a moral necessity. The choice was left them to obey the law or disobey it. The disobedience was only necessary as means to an end which they thought desirable; and now they assert that though these means are unlawful and wrong, they are made right, because without them the object could not be accomplished; in other words, the end justifies the means. There you have a rule of conduct denounced by all law, human and divine, as being pernicious in policy and false in morals.

Nothing that the worst men ever propounded has produced so much oppression, misgovernment, and suffering, as this pretence of state necessity. A great authority calls it the tyrant's plea; and the common honestly of all mankind has branded it with infamy.

Of course, it is mere absurdity to say that the petitioner was *necessarily* deprived of his right to a fair and legal trial. But concede for the argument's sake that a trial by jury was wholly impossible; admit that there was an absolute, overwhelming, imperious necessity operating so as literally to compel every act which the commissioners did, would that give their sentence of death the validity and force of a legal judgment pronounced by an ordained and established court? The question answers itself. This trial was a violation of law, and no necessity could be more than a mere *excuse* for those who committed it. If the commissioners were on trial for murder or conspiracy to murder, they might plead necessity if the fact were true, just as they would plead insanity or anything else to show that their guilt was not wilful. But we are now considering the legal effect of their decision, and that depends on their legal authority to make it. They had no such authority; they usurped a jurisdiction which the law not only did not give them, but expressly forbade them to exercise, and it follows that their act is void, whatever may have been the real or supposed excuse for it.

If these commissioners, instead of aiming at the life and liberty of the petitioner, had attempted to deprive him of his property by a sentence of confiscation, would any court in Christendom declare that such a sentence divested the title? Or would a person claiming under the sentence make his right any better by showing that the illegal assumption of jurisdiction was accompanied by some excuse which might save the commissioners from a criminal prosecution?

That a necessity for violating the law is nothing more than a mere excuse to the perpetrator, and does not in any legal sense change the quality of the act itself in its operation upon other parties, is a proposition too plain on original principles to need the aid of authority. I do not see how any man is to stand up and dispute it. But there is decisive authority upon the point.

The counsel on the other side will not assert that there was war at Indianapolis in 1864, for they have read *Coke's Institute,* and the opinion of Mr. Justice Grier, in the *Prize Cases,* and they know it to be a settled rule that war cannot be said to exist where the civil courts are open. They will not set up the plea of necessity, for they are well aware that it would not be true in point of fact. They will hardly take the ground that any Kind of necessity could give legal validity to that which they law forbids.

This, therefore, must be their position: that although there was no war at the place where this commission sat, and no actual necessity for it, yet if there was a war anywhere else, to which the United States were a party, the technical effect of such war was to take the jurisdiction away from the civil courts and transfer it to army officers. Nothing else is left them. They may not state their proposition precisely as I state it; that is too plain a way of putting it. But, in substance, it is their doctrine. What else can they say? They will admit that the Constitution is not altogether without a meaning; that at a time of universal peace it imposes some kind of obligation upon those who swear to support it. If no war existed they would not deny the exclusive jurisdiction of the civil courts in criminal cases. How then did the military get jurisdiction in Indiana?

They must answer the question by saying that military jurisdiction comes from the mere existence of war; and it comes in Indiana only as the legal result of a war which is going on in Mississippi, Tennessee, or South Carolina. The Constitution is repealed, or its operation suspended in one state because there is war in another. The courts are open, the organization of society is intact, the judges are on the bench, and their process is not impeded; but their jurisdiction is gone. Why? For no reason, if not because war exists, and the silent, legal, technical operation of that fact is to deprive all American citizens of their right to a fair trial.

That class of jurists and statesmen who hold that the trial by jury is lost to the citizen during the existence of war, must carry out their doctrine theoretically and practically to its ultimate consequences. The right of trial by jury being gone, all other rights are going with it; therefore a man may be arrested without an accusation and kept in prison during the pleasure of his captors; his papers may be searched without a warrant; his property may be confiscated behind his back, and he has no earthly means of redress. Nay, an attempt to get a just remedy is construed as a new crime. He dare not even complain, for the right of free speech is gone with the rest of his rights. If you sanction that doctrine, what is to be the consequence? I do not speak of what is past and gone; but in case of a future war what results will follow from your decision indorsing the Attorney-General's views? They are very obvious. At the instant when the war begins, our whole system of legal government will tumble into ruin, and if we are left in the enjoyment of any privileges at all we will owe it not to the Constitution and laws, but to the mercy or policy of those persons who may then happen to control the organized physical force of the country.

This puts us in a most precarious condition; we must have war often, do what we may to avoid it. The President or the Congress can provoke it, and they can keep it going even after the actual conflict of arms is over. They could make war a chronic condition of the country, and they slavery of the people perpetual. Nay, we are at the mercy of any foreign potentate who may envy us the possession of those liberties which we boast of so much; he can shatter our Constitution without striking a single blow or bringing a gun to bear upon us. A simple declaration of hostilities is more terrible to us than an army with banners.

To me the argument set up by the other side seems a delusion simply. In a time of war, more than at any other time, Public Liberty is in the hands of the public officers. And she is there in double trust; first, as they are citizens, and therefore bound to defend her, by the common obligation of all citizens; and next, as they are her special guardians. The opposing argument, when turned into its true sense, means this, and this only: that when the Constitution is attacked upon one side, its official guardians may assail it upon the other; when rebellion strikes it in the face, they may take advantage of the blindness produced by the blow, to stab it in the back.

The Convention when it framed the Constitution, and the people when they adopted it, could have had no thought like that. If they had supposed that it would operate only while perfect peace continued, they certainly would have given us some other rule to go by in time of war; they would not have left us to wander about in a wilderness of anarchy, without a lamp to our feet, or a guide to our path. Another thing proves their actual intent still more strikingly. They required that every man in any kind of public employment, state or national, civil or military, should swear, without reserve or qualification, that he would support the Constitution. Surely our ancestors had too much regard for the moral and religious welfare of their posterity, to impose upon them an oath like that, if they intended and expected it to be broken half the time.

These statesmen who settled our institutions, had no such notions in their minds. Washington deserved the lofty praise bestowed upon him by the president of Congress when he resigned his commission,—that he had always regarded the rights of the civil authority through all changes and through all disasters. When his duty as President afterwards required him to arm the public force to suppress a rebellion in Western Pennsylvania, he never thought that the Constitution was abolished, by virtue of that fact, in New Jersey, or Maryland, or Virginia.

Opposite counsel must be conscious that when they deny the binding obligation of the Constitution they must put some other system of law in its place. They do so; and argue that, while the Constitution, and the acts of Congress, and *Magna Charta*, and the common law, and all the rules of natural justice remain under foot, they will try American citizens according to what they call the *laws of war*.

But what do they mean by this? Do they mean that code of public law which defines the duties of two belligerent parties to one another, and regulates the intercourse of neutrals with both? If yes, then it is simply a recurrence to the law of nations, which has nothing to do with the subject. Do they mean that portion of our municipal code which defines our duties to the government in war as well as in peace? Then they are speaking of the Constitution and laws, which declare in plain words that the government owes every citizen a fair legal trial, as much as the citizen owes obedience to the government. When they appeal to international law, it is silent; and when they interrogate the law of the land, the answer is a contradiction of their whole theory.

The Attorney-General conceives that all persons whom he and his associates choose to denounce for giving aid to the Rebellion, are to be treated as being themselves a part of the Rebellion,—they are public enemies, and therefore they may be punished without being found guilty by a competent court or a jury. This convenient rule would outlaw every citizen the moment he is charged with a political offence. But political offenders are precisely the class of persons who most need the protection of a court and jury, for the prosecutions against them are most likely to be unfounded both in fact and in law. Whether innocent or guilty, to accuse is to convict them before the men who generally sit in military courts. But this court decided in the *Prize Cases* that all who live in the enemy's territory are public enemies, without regard to their personal sentiments or conduct; and the converse of the proposition is equally true,—that all who reside inside of our own territory are to be treated as under the protection of the law. If they help the enemy they are criminals, but they cannot be punished without legal conviction.

You have heard much, and you will hear more, concerning the natural and inherent right of the government to defend itself without regard to law. This is fallacious. In a despotism the autocrat is unrestricted in the means he may use for the defence of his authority against the opposition of his own subjects or others; and that is what makes him a despot. But in a limited monarchy the prince must confine himself to a legal defence of his government. If he goes beyond that, and commits aggressions on the rights of the people, he breaks the social compact, releases his subjects from all their obligations to him, renders himself liable to be dragged to the block or driven into exile. A violation of law on pretence of saving such a government as ours is not self-preservation, but suicide.

Salus populi suprema lex. This is true; but it is the safety of the *people*, not the safety of the *ruler*, which is the supreme law. The maxim is revolutionary and express simply the right to resist tyranny without regard to prescribed forms. It can never be used to stretch the powers of government *against* the people.

But this government of ours has power to defend itself without violating its own laws; it does not carry the seeds of destruction in its own bosom. It is clothed from head to foot in a panoply of defensive armor. What are the perils which may threaten its existence? I am not able at this moment to think of more than these, which I am about to mention: foreign invasion, domestic insurrection, mutiny in the army and navy, corruption in the civil administration, and last, but not least, criminal violations of its laws committed by individuals among the body of the people. Have we not a legal mode of defence against all these? Military force repels invasion and suppresses insurrection; you preserve discipline in the army and navy by means of courts-martial; you preserve the purity of the civil administration by impeaching dishonest magistrates; and crimes are prevented and punished by the regular judicial authorities. You are not compelled to use these weapons against your enemies, merely because they and they only are justified by the law; you ought to use them because they are more efficient than any other, and less liable to be abused.

There is another view of the subject which settles all controversy about it. No human being in this country can exercise any kind of public authority which is not conferred by law; and under the United States it must be given by the express words of a written statute. Whatever is not so given is withheld, and the exercise of it is positively prohibited. Courts-martial in the army and navy are authorized; they are legal institutions; their jurisdiction is limited, and their whole code of procedure is regulated by act of Congress. Upon the civil courts all the jurisdiction they have or can have is bestowed by law, and if one of them goes beyond what is written its action is *ultra vires* and void. But a military commission is not a court-martial, and it is not a civil court. It is not governed by the law which is made for either, and it has no law of its own. Its terrible authority is undefined, and its exercise is without any legal control. Undelegated power is always unlimited. The field that lies outside of the Constitution and laws has no boundary. So these commissions have no legal origin and no legal name by which they are known among the children of men; no law applies to them; and they exercise all power for the paradoxical reason that none belongs to them right-fully.

How is a military commission organized? What shall be the number and rank of its members? What offences come within its jurisdiction? What is its code of procedure? How shall witnesses be compelled to attend it? Is it perjury for a witness to swear falsely? What is the function of the judge-advocate? Does he tell the members how they must find, or does he only persuade them to convict? Is he the agent of the government, to command them what evidence they shall admit and what sentence they shall pronounce; or does he always carry his point, right or wrong, by the mere force of eloquence and ingenuity? What is the nature of their punishments? May they confiscate property and levy fines as well as imprison and kill? In addition to strangling their victim, may they also deny him the last consolations of religion, and refuse his family the melancholy privilege of giving him a decent grave?

To none of these questions can the Attorney-General or any one make a reply, for there is no law on the subject.

The power exercised through these military commissions is not only unregulated by law but it is incapable of being so regulated. It asserts the right of the executive government, without the intervention of the judiciary, to capture, imprison, and kill any person to whom that government or its paid dependents may choose to impute an offence. This, in its very essence, is despotic and lawless. It is never claimed or tolerated except by those governments which deny the restraints of all law. It operates in different ways; the instruments which it uses are not always the same; it hides its hideous features under many disguises; it assumes every variety of form. But in all its mutations of outward appearance it is still identical in principle, object, and origin. It is always the same great engine of despotism which Hamilton described it to be.

We cannot help but see that military commissions, if suffered to go on, will be used for pernicious purposes. I have made no allusion to their history in the last five years. But what can be the meaning of an effort to maintain them among us? Certainly not to punish actual guilt. All the ends of true justice are attained by the prompt, speedy, impartial trial which the courts are bound to give. Is there any danger than crime will be winked upon by the judges? Does anybody pretend that courts and juries have less ability to decide upon facts and law than the men who sit in military tribunals? What just purpose, then, can they serve? None.

But while they are powerless to do good, they may become omnipotent to trample upon innocence, to gag the truth, to silence patriotism, and crush the liberties of the country. They would be organized to convict, and the conviction would follow the accusation as surely as night follows the day. A government, of course, will accuse none before such a commission except those whom it predetermines to destroy. The accuser can choose the judges, and will select those who are known to be ignorant, unprincipled, and the most ready to do whatever may please the power which gives them pay and promotion. The willing witness could be found as easily as the superserviceable judge. The treacherous spy and the base informer would stock such a market with abundant perjury; for the authorities that employ them will be bound to protect as well as reward them. A corrupt and tyrannical government, with such an engine at its command, would shock the world with the enormity of its crimes.

ON THE SIDE OF THE UNITED STATES. REPLY.

Mr. Butler:

What are the exact facts set forth in the record, and what the exact question raised by it?

The facts of the case are all in the relator's petition and the exhibits thereto attached, and must, for the purposes of this hearing, be taken to be indisputably true; at least as against him. He is estopped to deny his own showing. Now every specification upon which the petitioner was tried by the military commission concludes with this averment:

"This, on or about,' &c.,—the different time and place as applied to the different parties—'at or near Indianapolis, Indiana,' or wherever else it may be, 'a State within the military lines of the army of the United States, and the theatre of military operations, and which had been and was constantly threatened to be invaded by the enemy."

It may be said that these specifications are only the averments of the government against the relator. But they, in fact, are a part of the exhibits of the relator, upon which he seeks relief; are an integral part of the case presented by him, and cannot be controlled by the pretence set up on the other side, that the court should take judicial notice of the contrary. Judicial cognizance of a fact, by the court, as a matter of public notoriety, or of history, is only a mode of proof of the fact; but no proof can be heard, in behalf of the relator, in contradiction of the record.

Therefore, what we at the bar must discuss, and what the court must decide, is, what law is applicable to a theatre of military operations, within the lines of an army, in a State which has been and constantly is threatened with invasion.

Yet a large portion of the argument on the other side has proceeded on an assumption which is itself a denial of the facts stated upon the record. The fact that military operations were being carried on in Indiana, at the places where these occurrences are said to have taken place, is a question that opposite counsel desire to argue, and desire farther that the court should take judicial notice that the fact was not as stated by the record.

Is the question, then, before this court, one of law or of fact? The matter becomes exceedingly important. We do freely agree, that if at the time of these occurrences there were no military operations in Indiana, if there was no army there, if there was no necessity of armed forces there, if there was no need of a military commission there, if there was nothing there on which the war power of the United States could attach itself, then this commission had no jurisdiction to deal with the relator, and the question proposed may as well at once be answered in the negative. What, then, is the state of facts brought here by the record? For, whatever question may have divided the learned judges in the court below, we here at the bar are divided *toto coelo* upon a vital question of fact. If the facts are to be assumed as the record presents them, then much of the argument of the other side has been misapplied.

The facts of record should have been questioned, if at all, in the court below. If the fact, stated in the record, of war on the theatre of these events—which in our judgment is a fact conclusive upon the jurisdiction of the military commission—is not admitted, then it is of the greatest importance to the cause that it be ascertained. If that fact was questioned below, some measures should have been taken to ascertain it, before the certificate of division of opinion was sent up. Otherwise the Circuit Court, in defiance of settled practice, and also of the act of 1802, has sent up a case in which material facts are not stated, and there is no jurisdiction under the act to hear. Certainly we at the bar seem to be arguing upon different cases; the one side on the assumption that the acts of Milligan and his trial took place in the midst of a community whose social and legal organization had never been disturbed by any war at all, the other on the assumption that they took place in a theatre of military operations, within the lines of the army, in a State which had been and then was threatened with invasion.

But the very form of question submitted, "whether upon the *facts stated in the petition and exhibits,* the military commission had jurisdiction to try the several relators in manner and form as set forth;"—not upon any other facts of which the court or anybody else will take notice, or which can be brought to the court in any other way than upon the petition and exhibits,—is conclusive as to the facts or case upon which the argument arises. The question, we therefore repeat—and we pray the court to keep it always in mind—is whether upon the facts stated in the petition and exhibit, the commission had jurisdiction; and the great and determining fact stated, and without which we have no standing in court, is that these acts of Milligan and his felonious associates, took place in the theatre of military operations, within the lines of the army, in a State which had been and then was constantly threatened with invasion. Certainly the learned judges in the court below, being on the ground, were bound to take notice of the facts which then existed in Indiana, and if they were not as alleged in the petition and exhibits, ought to have spread them as they truly were upon the record. Then they would have certified the question to be, whether under that state of facts so known by them, and spread upon the record, the military commission had jurisdiction, and not as they have certified, that the question was whether they had jurisdiction on the state of facts set forth in the relator's petition and exhibits.

The strength of the opposing argument is, that this court is bound to know that the courts of justice in Indiana were open at the time when these occurrences are alleged to have happened. Where is the proper allegation to this effect upon the record, upon which this court is to judge? If the court takes judicial notice that the courts were open, must it not also take judicial notice how, and by whose protection, and by whose permission they were so open? that they were open because the strong arm of the military upheld them; because by that power these Sons of Liberty and Knights of the American Circle, who would have driven them away, were arrested, staid, and punished. If judicial notice is to be taken of the one fact, judicial notice must be taken of the other also;—of the fact, namely, that if the soldiers of the United States, by their arms, had not held the State from intestine domestic foes within, and the attacks of traitors leagued with such without; had not kept the ten thousand rebel prisoners of war confined in the neighborhood from being released by these knights and men of the Order of the Sons of Liberty; there would have been no courts in Indiana, no place in which the Circuit Judge of the United States could sit in peace to administer the law.

If, however, this court will take notice that justice could only be administered in Indiana because of the immediate protection of the bayonet, and therefore by the permission of the commander of her armed forces, to which the safety of the State, its citizens, courts, and homes were committed, then the court will have taken notice of the precise state of facts as to the existence of warlike operations in Indiana, which is spread upon the record, and we are content with the necessary inferences.

As respects precedents. I admit that there is a dearth of precedents bearing on the exact point raised here. Why is this? It is because the facts are unprecedented; because the war out of which they grew is unprecedented also; because the clemency that did not at once strike down armed traitors, who is [*sic*] peaceful communities were seeking to overturn all authority, is equally unprecedented; because the necessity which called forth this exertion of the reserved powers of the government is unprecedented, as well as all the rest. Let opposing counsel show the instance in an enlightened age, in a civilized and Christian country, where almost one-half its citizens undertook, without cause, to over-throw the government, and where coward sympathizers, not daring to join them, plotted in the security given by the protecting arms of the other half to aid such rebellion and treason, and we will perhaps show a precedent for hanging such traitors by military commissions.

This is the value of this case: whenever we are thrown into a war again; whenever, hereafter, we have to defend the life of the nation from dangers which invade it, we shall have set precedents how a nation may preserve itself from self-destruction. In the conduct of the war, and in dealing with the troubles which preceded it, we have been obliged to learn up to these questions; to approach the result step by step.

Opposite counsel (Mr. Black) has admitted that there were dangers which might threaten the life of the nation, and in that case it would be the duty of the nation, and it would be its right, to defend itself. He classed those dangers thus: first, foreign invasion; second, domestic insurrection; third, mutiny in the army and navy; fourth, corruption in civil administration; and last, crimes committed by individuals; and he says further, there were within the Constitution powers sufficient to enable the country to defend itself from each and all these dangers. But there is yet another, a more perilous danger, one from which this country came nearer ruin than it ever came by any or by all others. That danger is imbecility of administration; such an administration as should say that there is no constitutional right in a State to go out of the Union, but that there is no power in the Constitution to coerce a State or her people, if she choose to go out. It is in getting rid of that danger, unenumerated, that we have had to use military power, military orders, martial law, and military commissions.

The same counsel was pleased to put certain questions, difficult as he thinks to be answered, as to the method of proceeding before military commissions; but no suggestion is made upon the record or upon the briefs, that all the proceedings were not regular according to the custom and usages of war. They have all the *indicia* of regularity. There being then nothing alleged why the proceedings are not regular, we are brought back to the main question.

A portion of the argument on the other side has proceeded upon the mistake, that a military commission is a *court*, either under, by virtue of, or without the Constitution. It is not a court, and that question was decided not long ago. A military commission, whatever it may be, derives its power and authority wholly from martial law, and by that law, and by military authority only, are its proceedings to be adjudged and reviewed. In *Dynes* v. *Hoover,* this was decided by this tribunal in regard to a court-martial. The conclusion was sustained in *Ex parte Vallandigham.*

The last quoted case is like the present. Vallandigham was tried by a military commission, and he invoked the aid of the court of get away from it. Why did not this court then decide, as opposing counsel assert the law to be, that under no possible circumstances can a military commission have any right, power, authority, or jurisdiction? No such decision was made. It was decided that a military commission "is not a court within the meaning of the 14th section of the act of 1789:" that this court has no power to issue a writ of *certiorari,* or to review or pronounce any opinion upon the proceedings of a military commission; that affirmative words in the Constitution, giving this court original jurisdiction in certain cases must be construed negatively as to all others. Mr. Justice Wayne, in delivering the opinion of the court, says:

In *Ex parte Metzger* it was determined that a *writ of certiorari* could not be allowed to examine a commitment by a district judge, under the treaty between the United States and France, for the reason that the judge exercised a special authority, and that no provision had been made for the revision of his judgment. So does a court of military commission exercise a special authority. In the case before us, it was urged that the decision in Metzger's case had been made upon the ground that the proceeding of the district judge was not judicial in its character, *but that the proceedings of the military commission* were so; and further, it was said that the ruling in that case had been overruled by a majority of the judges in Raine's case. There is a misapprehension of the report of the latter case, and as to the judicial character of the proceedings of the military commission, we cite what was said by this court in the case of *The United States* v. *Ferreira.*

"The powers conferred by Congress upon the district judge and the secretary are judicial in their nature, for judgment and discretion must be exercised by both of them; but it is not judicial in either case, in the sense in which judicial power is granted to the courts of the United States. Nor can it be said that the authority to be exercised by a military commission is judicial in that sense. It involves discretion to examine, to decide, and sentence, but there is no original jurisdiction in the Supreme Court to issue a writ of *habeas corpus ad subjiciendum,* to review or reverse its proceedings, or the *writ of certiorari* to revise the proceedings of a military commission."

Under such language there is an end of this case.

We have already stated that military commissions obtain their jurisdiction from martial law. What, then, is martial law? We have also already defined it. But our definition has not been observed. Counsel treat it as if we would set up the absolutely unregulated, arbitrary, and unjust caprice of a commanding and despotic officer. Let us restate and analyze it. "Martial law is the will of the commanding officer of an armed force or of a geographical military department, expressed in time of war, within the limits of his military jurisdiction, as necessity demands and prudence dictates, restrained or enlarged by the orders of his military or supreme executive chief." This definition is substantially taken from the dispatches of the Duke of Wellington. When he was called upon to answer a complaint in Parliament for this exercise of military jurisdiction and martial law in Spain, he thus defined it. On another occasion, when speaking of Viscount Torrington's administration as military governor of Ceylon, he said thus:

"The general who declared martial law, and commanded that it should be carried into execution, was bound to lay down distinctly the *rules*, and *regulations*, and *limits* according to which his will was to be carried out. Now he had, in another country, carried on martial law; that was to say, he had governed a large proportion of the population of a country, by his own will. But, then, what did he do? He declared that the country should be governed according to its own national laws, and he carried into execution that will. He governed the country strictly by the laws of the country; and he governed it with such moderation, he [we] must say, that political servants and judges, who at first had fled or had been expelled, afterwards consented to act under his direction. *The judges sat in the courts of law*, conducting their judicial business and administering the law *under his direction.*"

It is the will of the commanding officer. Being to be exercised upon the instant, it can have no other source. The commanding officer of an armed force, is another element of the definition.

Martial law must have another distinguishing quality. It must be the will of the commander, exercised under the limitations mentioned in *time of war*, and that is a portion of the definition which is fatal to the authorities read by my brother Garfield, as I shall show.

When is it to be exercised? "When necessity demands and prudence dictates." That is to say, in carrying on war, when in the judgment of him to whom the country has intrusted its welfare—whose single word, as commander of the army, can devote to death thousands of its bravest and best sons—we give to him, when necessity demands, the discretion to govern, outside of the ordinary forms and constitutional limits of law, the wicked and disloyal within the military lines.

In time of war, to save the country's life, you send forth your brothers, your sons, and put them under the command, under the arbitrary will of a general to dispose of their persons and lives as he pleases; but if, for the same purpose, he touches a Milligan, a Son of Liberty, the Constitution is invoked in his behalf—and we are told that the fabric of civil government is about to fall! We submit that if he is intrusted with the power, the will, the authority to act in the one case, he ought to have sufficient discretion to deal with the other; and that the country will not be so much endangered from the use of both, as it would be if he used the first and not the last.

Martial law is known to our laws; it is constitutional, and was derived from our mother country. De Lolme says:

"In general, it may be laid down as a maxim, that, where the sovereign looks to his army for the security of his person and authority, the same military laws by which this army is kept together, must be extended over the whole nation; not in regard to military duties and exercises, but certainly in regard to all that relates to the respect due to the sovereign and to his orders."

"The martial law, concerning these tender points, must be *universal*. The jealous regulations, concerning mutiny and contempt of orders, cannot be severely enforced on that part of the nation which secures the subjection of the rest, and enforced, too, through the whole scale of military subordination, from the soldier to the officer, up to the very head of the military system, while the more numerous and inferior part of the people are left to enjoy an unrestrained freedom;—that secret disposition which prompts mankind to resist and counteract their superiors, cannot be surrounded by such formidable checks on one side, and be left to be indulged to a degree of licentiousness and wantonness on the other."

Passing from one of the most learned commentators upon England's Constitution, to one who may be said to have lived our Constitution; who came into life almost as the Constitution came into life; whose father was the second chief executive officer of the nation; conversant with public affairs and executing constitutional law in every department of the government from earliest youth, wielding himself chief executive power, and admitted to be one of the ablest constitutional lawyers of his time—what principles do we find asserted?

Mr. John Quincy Adams, speaking of the effect of war upon the municipal institutions of a country, said:

"Slavery was abolished in Columbia, first, by the Spanish General Morillo, and, secondly, by the American General Bolivar. It was abolished by virtue of a military command given at the head of the army, and the abolition continues to be law to this day. It was abolished by the laws of war, and not by municipal enactments; the power was exercised by military commanders, under instructions, of course, from their respective governments. And here I recur again to the examples of General Jackson. What are you now about in Congress? You are about passing a grant to refund to General Jackson the amount of a certain fine imposed upon him by a judge, under the laws of the State of Louisiana. You are going to refund him the money, with interest; and this you are going to do because the imposition of the fine was unjust. Because General Jackson was acting under the laws of war, and because the moment you place a military commander *in a district which is the theatre of war, the laws of war apply to that district.*"

... "I might furnish a thousand proofs to show that the pretensions of gentlemen to the sanctity of their municipal institutions under a state of actual invasion and of actual war, whether servile, civil, or foreign, is wholly unfounded, and that the laws of war do, in all such cases, take the precedence."

"I lay this down as the law of nations. I say that the military authority takes for the time the place of all municipal institutions, and slavery among the rest; and that, under that state of things, so far from its being true that the States where slavery exists have the exclusive management of the subject, not only the President of the United States, but the commander of the army has power to order the universal emancipation of the slaves. I have given here more in detail a principal, which I have asserted on this floor before now, and of which I have no more doubt, than that you, sir, occupy that chair. I give it in its development, in order that any gentleman, from any part of the Union, may, if he thinks proper, deny the truth of the position, and may maintain his denial; not by indignation, not by passion and fury, but by sound and sober reasoning from the laws of nations and laws of war. And if my position can be answered and refuted, I shall receive the refutation with pleasure; I shall be glad to listen to reason, aside, as I say, from indignation and passion. And if, by force of reasoning, my understanding can be convinced, I here pledge myself to recant what I have asserted."

The case of General Jackson's fine was the test case of martial law in this country. What were the facts? On the 15th of December, 1814, General Jackson declared martial law within his camp, extending four miles above and four miles below the city. The press murmured, but did not speak out until after there came unofficial news of peace. Then it was said that the declaration of peace, *ipso facto*, dissolved martial law; that the General had no right to maintain martial law any longer; and murmurs loudly increased. But, the General said, that he had not received any official news of the establishment of peace; and, until it came officially, he should not cease his military operations for safety of the city. Thereupon what happened? One Louallier was arrested by the military, for alleged seditious language, and Judge Hall interposed with his writ of *habeas corpus*. This was on the 5th of March, 1815. The battle of New Orleans, which substantially removed all danger, was fought on the 8th of January. General Jackson sent his aide-de-camp and arrested Judge Hall. The cry then as now was that the necessity for martial law had ceased; why hold Judge Hall, after the news of peace had come? Why not turn him over to the civil authorities? What next took place? Peace was declared in an official manner; the proclamation of martial law was withdrawn; Judge Hall took his seat on the bench, and his first act was to issue an attachment of contempt for General Jackson, who was accordingly brought before him. When General Jackson offered an explanation of his conduct, the Judge refused to receive it, and fined him $1000. The fine was paid in submission to the law. Years afterwards, Congress proceeded not to excuse, not to explain away that act of General Jackson, declaring martial law, but to justify it. I am surprised to hear it said that nobody *justified* General Jackson. Whether General Jackson was to be excused or to be justified was the whole question at issue between the parties in Congress. A bill was brought in "to indemnify Major-General Andrew Jackson for damages sustained in the discharge of his official *duty*." Some who were in the Senate of that day, said: "We will not justify, we will excuse, this action in General Jackson; we move, therefore, to change the title of the bill into a 'bill for the *relief* of General Jackson.'" But Mr. R. J. Walker, speaking for General Jackson, made a minority report, in which he put the whole question upon the ground of justification.

He said:

"That General Jackson, and those united with him in the defence of New Orleans, fully believed this emergency to exist, is beyond all doubt or controversy. If, then, this was the state of the case, it was the duty of General Jackson to have made the arrest; and the act was not merely excusable but justifiable. It was demanded by a great and overruling necessity. . . . This great law of necessity—of defence of self, of home, and of country—never was designed to be abrogated by any statute, or by any constitution. This was the law which justified the arrest and detention of the prisoner; and, however the act may now be assailed, it has long since received the cordial approbation of the American people. That General Jackson never desired to elevate the military above the civil authority is proved by his conduct during the trial, and after the imposition of this fine."

"The title of the bill is in strict conformity with the facts of the case, and, in the opinion of the undersigned, should be retained. The country demands that his money shall be returned as an act of justice. It was a penalty incurred for saving the country, and the country requires that it shall be restored."

The fine was returned with interest.

The case of *Johnson* v. *Duncan*, in the Supreme Court of Louisiana, and cited on the other side, was decided by judges sitting under the excitement of the collision between the military and the judges. As an authority it is of no value. The case of *Luther* v. *Borden*, in which Mr. Justice Woodbury's *dissenting* opinion, strange to say, has been cited by my brother Garfield against the opinion of the court, decides that martial law did obtain in Rhode Island, and sustains General Jackson.

The court say:

"If the government of Rhode Island deemed the armed opposition so formidable, and so ramified throughout the State, as to require the use of its military force and the declaration of martial law, we see no ground upon which this court can question its authority. It was a state of war; and the established government resorted to the rights and usages of war to maintain itself, and to overcome the unlawful opposition. And in that state of things the officers engaged in its military service might lawfully arrest any one, who from the information before them, they had reasonable grounds to believe was engaged in the insurrection, and might order a house to be forcibly entered and searched, when there were reasonable grounds for supposing he might be there concealed."

We have put in our definition of martial law the words, "in time of war," *tempore belli*. That portion of the definition answers every question, as to when this law may obtain.

Now what was the Earl of Lancaster's case, quoted and so much relied on by the other side? The earl raised a rebellion; and was condemned and executed by sentence of a court-martial, *after the rebellion had been subdued*. Thereupon his brother brought a writ of error, by leave of the king, before the king himself in Parliament, for the purpose of reversing the judgment and obtaining his lands, and among the errors assigned, was this:

"Yet the said Earl Thomas, &c., was taken *in time of peace*, and brought before the king himself; and the said our lord and father the king, &c., remembered that the same Thomas was guilty of the seditions and other felonies in the aforesaid contained; without this, that he arraigned him therefor, or put him to answer as is the custom according to the law, &c., and thus, without arraignment and answer, the same Thomas, of error and contrary to the law of the land, was *in time of peace* adjudged to death, notwithstanding that it is notorious and manifest that the whole time in which the said misdeeds and crimes contained in the said record and proceedings were charged against the said earl, and also the time in which he was taken, and in which our said lord and father the king remembered him to be guilty, &c., and in which he was adjudged to death, was *a time of peace*, and the more especially as throughout the whole time, aforesaid, the Chancery and other courts of pleas of our lord the king were open, and in which *right was done to every man, as it used to be;* nor did the same lord the king in that *time ever side with standard unfurled;* the said lord and father the king, &c., *in such time of peace* ought not against the same earl, thus to have remembered nor to have adjudged him to death, without arraignment and answer."

So that the whole record turned upon the question whether the rebellion being ended, peace having come, the Earl of Lancaster was liable to be adjudged by military commission in time of peace, and it was held that that was against common right.

The Petition of Right is referred to; but it was not, as is supposed, because of the ship-money and the trial of Hampden and others, that this great petition was passed. It was because King Charles had quartered in the town of Plymouth, and in the County of Devon, certain soldiers in time of peace, upon the inhabitants thereof; and had issued his commission that those counties should be governed by "martial law," while the soldiers, in time of peace, were quartered there, and therefore came the Petition cited; and it was adjudged that military commissions, issued in time of peace, should never have place in the law of England; and all the people to that, even to this day, heartily agree.

Governor Wall's case shows truly that martial law did not protect him for his action under it; but if there ever was a judicial murder, a case where a man, without cause and without right, was put to death, this was the case. Lord Chief Justice Campbell, speaking of it, says:

"The prosecution brought great popularity to the Attorney-General and the government of which he was the organ, upon the supposition that it presented a striking display of the stern impartiality of British jurisprudence; but after a calm review of the evidence, I fear it will rather be considered by posterity as an instance of the triumph of vulgar prejudice over humanity and justice."

Another case cited is that of the Rev. John Smith, of Demerara, who was tried and convicted by a court-martial, for inciting negroes to mutiny in Demerara, six weeks after a rebellion was wholly quelled, and when there seems to have been no necessity for such proceedings, nor any reason that they should be carried on. The excuse of the governor was, that the planters were so infuriated against Mr. Smith that he thought that trying him by court-martial would secure him better justice. I agree that this was no excuse, that no necessity here existed. Brougham and Mackintosh brought all their eloquence to overturn martial law. Their words have been cited; but the other side forgot to state that upon a division of the House of Commons, Brougham and Mackintosh were in a minority of forty-six. So that after a deliberate argument of many days, the great final tribunal of English justice decided that Mr. John Smith's case was rightly tried under martial law. The case is an authority not for, but against, the side which it is cited to support.

It is said that in 1865, Congress refused to pass an act which would throw any discredit on military commissions, or limit their action wherever a rebel or a traitor, secret or open, was to be found upon whom their jurisdiction should operate. If such tribunals for certain purposes were not lawful in the judgment of the House of Representatives; if military commissions had no place in the laws of the land, why the necessity of action by Congress to repeal them?

Reference has been made by opposing counsel to what they consider the views of General Washington; and an argument has been attempted to be drawn from this. Now, the first military commission upon this continent of which there is any record sat by command of Washington himself. Its proceedings were published by order of Congress, and are well known. I refer to André's case. That was not a "court-martial;" there was no order to adjudicate; no finding; no sentence; only a report of facts to General Washington, and then Washington issued the order, in virtue of his authority as commander-in-chief, which condemned André to death.

But we do not stop there. This may be said to have been the exceptional case of a spy. To give, then, another illustration of what Washington thought of the rights of military commanders in the field, attention may be directed to the trial of Joshua Hett Smith. Smith was the man at whose house Arnold and André met. He was taken and tried by a military court for treasonable practices. The civil courts were open at Tarrytown, at that time; the British Constitution as adopted by our colonial fathers extended over him, but still Washington tried Smith by a military court. In Chandler's Criminal Trials, Smith gives an account of his interview, when he was first brought before Washington, which I cite in order that the court may understand how the Father of his Country regarded the extent of his powers as military commander. Smith says:

"After as much time had elapsed as I supposed was thought necessary to give me rest from my march, I was conducted into a room, where were standing General Washington in the centre, and on each side General Knox and the Marquis de La Fayette, with Washington's two aides-de-camp, Colonels Harrison and Hamilton. Provoked at the usage I received, I addressed General Washington, and demanded to know for what cause I was brought before him in so ignominious a manner? The General answered, sternly, that I stood before him charged with the blackest treason against the citizens of the United States; that he was authorized, from the evidence in his possession, and from the authority vested in him by Congress, to hang me immediately as a traitor, and that nothing could save me but a candid confession who in the army, or among the citizens at large, were my accomplices in the horrid and nefarious designs I had meditated for the last ten days past."

What now, may I ask, is to be thought of the argument of my opposing brethren, who assert that in civil courts the Constitution does not allow any pressure to be brought upon a man to make him confess, at the same time that they eulogize the military conduct of Washington?

But what redress, it is asked, shall any citizen have if this power—so great, so terrible, and so quick in its effects—is abused? The same and only remedy that he can have whenever power is abused. If that power, under martial law, is used for personal objects of aggrandizement, or revenge; of imprisoning, one hour, any citizen, except when necessity under fair judgment demands, he ought to have an appeal to the courts of the country after peace, for redress of grievance.

It has been said that martial law, and its execution by trials by military commission, is fatal to liberty and the pursuit of happiness; but we are only asking for the exercise of military power, when necessity demands and prudence dictates. If the civil law fails to preserve rights, and to insure safety and tranquillity to the country; if there is no intervention of military power to right wrongs and punish crime, an outraged community will improvise some tribunal for themselves, whose execution shall be as swift and whose punishments shall be as terrible as any exhibition of military power; some tribunal wholly unregulated and which is responsible to no one. We are not without such examples on this continent.

The proclamation of 24th September, 1862, by which the President suspended the privilege of the writ of *habeas corpus,* and which proclamation was in full force during these proceedings, was within the power of the President, independently of the subsequent act of Congress, to make. *Brown* v. *The United States* seems full on this point. It says:

"When the legislative authority, to whom the right to declare war is confined, has declared war in its most unlimited manner, the executive authority, to whom the execution of the war is confided, is bound to carry it into effect. He has a discretion vested in him, as to the manner and extent, but he cannot lawfully transcend the rules of warfare established among civilized nations. He cannot lawfully exercise powers or authorize proceedings which the civilized world repudiates and disclaims. The sovereignty, as to declaring war and limiting its effects, rests with the legislature. The sovereignty as to its execution rests with the President."

However, the subsequent act of Congress did ratify what the President did; so that every way the view taken of his powers in the case just quoted stands firm.

And the wisdom of this view appears nowhere more than in the present case. The court, of course, can have no knowledge how extensive was this "Order of Sons of Liberty;" how extensive was the organization of these American Knights in Indiana. It was a secret Order. Its vast extent was not known generally. But the Executive might have known; and if I might step out of the record, I could say that I am aware that he did know, that this Order professed to have one hundred thousand men enrolled in it in the States of Indiana, Ohio, and Illinois, so that no jury could be found to pass upon any case, and that any courthouse wherein it had been attempted to try any of the conspirators, would have been destroyed. The President has judged that in this exigency a military tribunal alone could safely act.

We have thus far grounded our case on the great law of nations and of war. Has the Constitution any restraining clause on the power thus derived?

It is argued that the fourth, fifth, and sixth articles to the amendments to the Constitution are limitations of the war-making power; that they were made for a state of war as well as a state of peace, and aimed at the military authority as well as the civil. We have anticipated and partially answered this argument. As we observed, by the Constitution, as originally adopted, there was no limitation put upon the war-making powers. It only undertook to limit one *incident* of the war-making power,—the *habeas corpus;* and if limit it can be called, observe the way in which that writ is guarded. It is provided that the writ of *habeas corpus,* in *time of peace,* shall not be suspended; it shall only be suspended when, "in case of rebellion or invasion, the public safety requires;" that is, in time of war. It seems to have been taken for granted by the Constitution that the writ is to be suspended in time of war because very different rules must then govern. The language of the Constitution is, that it "shall not be suspended except,"—showing that it was supposed that the war-making power would find it necessary to suspend the *habeas corpus;* and yet no other guard was thrown around it.

By the subsequent amendments there was, as we conceive, but one limitation put upon the war-making power, and that was in regard to the quartering of soldiers in private houses.

In no discussion upon these articles of amendment was there, in any State of the Union, a discussion upon the question, what should be their effect in time of war? Yet every one knew, and must have known, that each article would be inoperative in some cases in time of war. If in some cases, why not in all cases where necessity demands it, and where prudence dictates?

There is, in truth, no other way of construing constitutional provisions, than by the maxim, *Singula singulis reddenda*. Each provision of the Constitution must be taken to refer to the proper time, as to peace or war, in which it operates, as well as to the proper subject of its provisions.

For instance, the Constitution provides that "no person" shall be deprived of liberty without due process of law. And yet, as we know, whole generations of people in this land—as many as four millions of them at one time—people described in the Constitution by this same word, "persons," have been till lately deprived of liberty ever since the adoption of the Constitution, without any process of law whatever.

The Constitution provides, also, that no "person's" right to bear arms shall be infringed; yet these same people, described elsewhere in the Constitution as "persons," have been deprived of their arms whenever they had them.

If you are going to stand on that letter of the Constitution which is set up by the opposite side in the matter before us, how are we to explain such features in the Constitution, in various provisions in which slaves are called persons, with nothing in the language used to distinguish them from persons who were free.

Mr. Black has said, that the very time when a constitutional provision is wanted, is the time of war, and that in time of war, of civil war especially, and the commotions just before and just after it, the constitutional provisions should be most rigidly enforced. We agree to that; but we assert that, in peace, when there is no commotion, the constitutional provisions should be most rigidly enforced as well. Constitutional provisions, within their application, should be always most rigidly enforced. We insist only thing outside of or beyond the Constitution [*sic*]. We insist only that the Constitution be interpreted so as to save the nation, and not to let it perish.

We quote again the solemnly expressed opinion of Mr. Adams, in 1836, in another of his speeches:

"In the authority given to Congress by the Constitution of the United States to declare war, all the powers, incident to war, are by necessary implication conferred upon the government of the United States. Now, the powers incidental to war are derived, not from any internal, municipal source, but from the laws and usages of nations. There are, then, in the authority of Congress and the Executive, two classes of powers, altogether different in their nature, and often incompatible with each other,—the war power and the peace power. The peace power is limited by regulation and restraints, by provisions prescribed within the Constitution itself. The war power is limited only by the law and usages of nations. The power is tremendous. It is strictly constitutional, *but it breaks down every barrier so anxiously erected for the protection of liberty, property, and life."*

It is much insisted on, that the determining question as to the exercise of martial law, is whether the civil courts are in session; but civil courts were in session in this city during the whole of the Rebellion, and yet this city has been nearly the whole time under the martial law. There was martial law in this city, when, in 1864, the rebel chief, Jubal Early, was assaulting it, and when, if this court had been sitting here, it would have been disturbed by the enemy's cannon. Yet courts—ordinary courts—were in session. It does not follow, because the ordinary police machinery is in motion for the repression of *ordinary* crimes, because the rights between party and party are determined without the active interference of the military in cases where their safety and rights are not involved, that, therefore, martial law must have lost its power.

This exercise of civil power is, however, wholly permissive, and is subordinated to the military power. And whether it is to be exercised or not, is a matter within the discretion of the commander. That is laid down by Wellington, and the same thing is to be found in nearly every instance of the exercise of martial law. The commanders of armies, in such exercise, have been glad, if by possibility they could do so, to have the courts carry on the ordinary operations of justice. But they rarely permit to them jurisdiction over crimes affecting the well-being of the army or the safety of the state.

The determining test is, in the phrase of the old law-books, that "the King's courts are open." But the King's Court, using that phrase for the highest court in the land, should not be open under the permission of martial law. In a constitutional government like ours, the Supreme Court should sit within its own jurisdiction, as one of the three great co-ordinate powers of the government, supreme, untrammelled, uncontrolled, unawed, unswayed, and its decrees should be executed by its own high *fiat*. The Supreme Court has no superior, and, therefore, it is beneath the office of a judge of that court, inconsistent with the dignity of the tribunal whose robes he wears, that he should sit in any district of country where martial law is the supreme law of the state, and where armed guards protect public tranquillity; where the bayonet has the place of the constable's baton; where the press is restrained by military power, and where a general order construes a statute. On the contrary, we submit that all crimes and misdemeanors, of however high a character, which have occurred during the progress and as a part of the war, however great the criminals, either civil or military, should be tried upon the scene of the offence, and within the theatre of military operations; that justice should be meted out in such cases, by military commissions, through the strong arm of the military law which the offenders have invoked, and to which they have appealed to settle their rights.

We do not desire to exalt the martial above the civil law, or to substitute the necessarily despotic rule of the one, for the mild and healthy restraints of the other. Far otherwise. We demand only, that when the law is silent; when justice is overthrown; when the life of the nation is threatened by foreign foes that league, and wait, and watch without, to unite with domestic foes within, who had seized almost half the territory, and more than half the resources of the government, at the beginning; when the capital is imperilled; when the traitor within plots to bring into its peaceful communities the braver rebel who fights without; when the judge is deposed; when the juries are dispersed; when the sheriff, the executive officer of law, is powerless; when the bayonet is called in as the final arbiter; when on its armed forces the government must rely for all it has of power, authority, and dignity; when the citizen has to look to the same source for everything he has of right in the present, or hope in the future,—then we ask that martial law may prevail, so that the civil law may again live, to the end that this may be a "government of laws and not of men."

At the close of the last term the CHIEF JUSTICE announced the order of the court in this and in two other similar cases (those of Bowles and Horsey) as follows:

1. That on the facts stated in said petition and exhibits a writ of *habeas corpus* ought to be issued, according to the prayer of the said petitioner.
2. That on the facts stated in the said petition and exhibits the said Milligan ought to be discharged from custody as in said petition is prayed, according to the act of Congress passed March 3d, 1863, entitled, "An act relating to *habeas corpus* and regulating judicial proceedings in certain cases."
3. That on the facts stated in said petition and exhibits, the military commission mentioned therein had no jurisdiction legally to try and sentence said Milligan in the manner and form as in said petition and exhibits are stated.

At the opening of the present term, opinions were delivered.

                        Mr. Justice DAVIS delivered the opinion of
                        the court.

On the 10th day of May, 1865, Lambdin P. Milligan presented a petition to the Circuit Court of the United States for the District of Indiana, to be discharged from an alleged unlawful imprisonment. The case made by the petition is this: Milligan is a citizen of the United States; has lived for twenty years in Indiana; and, at the time of the grievances complained of, was not, and never had been in the military or naval service of the United States. On the 5th day of October, 1864, while at home, he was arrested by order of General Alvin P. Hovey, commanding the military district of Indiana; and has ever since been kept in close confinement.

On the 21st day of October, 1864, he was brought before a military commission, convened at Indianapolis, by order of General Hovey, tried on certain charges and specifications; found guilty, and sentenced to be hanged; and the sentence ordered to be executed on Friday, the 19th day of May, 1865.

On the 2d day of January, 1865, after the proceedings of the military commission were at an end, the Circuit Court of the United States for Indiana met at Indianapolis and empanelled a grand jury, who were charged to inquire whether the laws of the United States had been violated; and, if so, to make presentments. The court adjourned on the 27th day of January, having, prior thereto, discharged from further service the grand jury, who did not find any bill of indictment or make any presentment against Milligan for any offence whatever; and, in fact, since his imprisonment, no bill of indictment has been found or presentment made against him by any grand jury of the United States.

Milligan insists that said military commission had no jurisdiction to try him upon the charges preferred, or upon any charges whatever; because he was a citizen of the United States and the State of Indiana, and had not been, since the commencement of the late Rebellion, a resident of any of the States whose citizens were arrayed against the government, and that the right of trial by jury was guaranteed to him by the Constitution of the United States.

The prayer of the petition was, that under the act of Congress, approved March 3d, 1863, entitled, "An act relating to *habeas corpus* and regulating judicial proceedings in certain cases," he may be brought before the court, and either turned over to the proper civil tribunal to be proceeded against according to the law of the land or discharged from custody altogether.

With the petition were filed the order for the commission, the charges and specifications, the findings of the court, with the order of the War Department reciting that the sentence was approved by the President of the United States, and directing that it be carried into execution without delay. The petition was presented and filed in open court by the counsel for Milligan; at the same time the District Attorney of the United States for Indiana appeared, and, by the agreement of counsel, the application was submitted to the court. The opinions of the judges of the Circuit Court were opposed on three questions, which are certified to the Supreme Court:

1st. "On the facts stated in said petition and exhibits, ought a writ of *habeas corpus* to be issued?"

2d. "On the facts stated in said petition and exhibits, ought the said Lambdin P. Milligan to be discharged from custody as in said petition prayed?"

3d. "Whether, upon the facts stated in said petition and exhibits, the military commission mentioned therein had jurisdiction legally to try and sentence said Milligan in manner and form as in said petition and exhibits is stated?"

The importance of the main question presented by this record cannot be overstated; for it involves the very framework of the government and the fundamental principles of American liberty.

During the late wicked Rebellion, the temper of the times did not allow that calmness in deliberation and discussion so necessary to a correct conclusion of a purely judicial question. *Then,* considerations of safety were mingled with the exercise of power; and feelings and interests prevailed which are happily terminated. *Now* that the public safety is assured, this question, as well as all others, can be discussed and decided without passion or the admixture of any element not required to form a legal judgment. We approach the investigation of this case, fully sensible of the magnitude of the inquiry and the necessity of full and cautious deliberation.

But, we are met with a preliminary objection. It is insisted that the Circuit Court of Indiana had no authority to certify these questions; and that we are without jurisdiction to hear and determine them.

The sixth section of the "Act to amend the judicial system of the United States," approved April 29, 1802, declares "that whenever any question shall occur before a Circuit Court upon which the opinions of the judges shall be opposed, the point upon which the disagreement shall happen, shall, during the same term, upon the request of either party or their counsel, be stated under the direction of the judges and certified under the seal of the court to the Supreme Court at their next session to be held thereafter; and shall by the said court be finally decided: And the decision of the Supreme Court and their order in the premises shall be remitted to the Circuit Court and be there entered of record, and shall have effect according to the nature of the said judgment and order: *Provided*, That nothing herein contained shall prevent the cause from proceeding, if, in the opinion of the court, further proceedings can be had without prejudice to the merits."

It is under this provision of law, that a Circuit Court has authority to certify any question to the Supreme Court for adjudication. The inquiry, therefore, is, whether the case of Milligan is brought within its terms.

It was admitted at the bar that the Circuit Court had jurisdiction to entertain the application for the writ of *habeas corpus* and to hear and determine it; and it could not be denied; for the power is expressly given in the 14th section of the Judiciary Act of 1789, as well as in the later act of 1863. Chief Justice Marshall, in Bollman's case, construed this branch of the Judiciary Act to authorize the courts as well as the judges to issue the writ for the purpose of inquiring into the cause of the commitment; and this construction has never been departed from. But, it is maintained with earnestness and ability, that a certificate of division of opinion can occur only in a *cause;* and, that the proceeding by a party, moving for a writ of *habeas corpus,* does not become a cause *until after the writ has been issued and a return made.*

Independently of the provisions of the act of Congress of March 3, 1863, relating to *habeas corpus,* on which the petitioner bases his claim for relief, and which we will presently consider, can this position be sustained?

It is true, that it is usual for a court, on application for a writ of *habeas corpus,* to issue the writ, and, on the return, to dispose of the case; but the court can elect to waive the issuing of the writ and consider whether, upon the facts presented in the petition, the prisoner, if brought before it, could be discharged. One of the very points on which the case of Tobias Watkins, reported in 3 Peters, turned, was, whether, if the writ was issued, the petitioner would be remanded upon the case which he had made.

The Chief Justice, in delivering the opinion of the court, said: "The cause of imprisonment is shown as fully by the petitioner as it could appear on the return of the writ; consequently the writ ought not to be awarded if the court is satisfied that the prisoner would be remanded to prison."

The judges of the Circuit Court of Indiana were, therefore, warranted by an express decision of this court in refusing the writ, if satisfied that the prisoner on his own showing was rightfully detained.

But it is contended, if they differed about the lawfulness of the imprisonment, and could render no judgment, the prisoner is remediless; and cannot have the disputed question certified under the act of 1802. His remedy is complete by writ of error or appeal, if the court renders a final judgment refusing to discharge him; but if he should be so unfortunate as to be placed in the predicament of having the court divided on the question whether he should live or die, he is hopeless and without remedy. He wishes the vital question settled, not by a single judge at his chambers, but by the highest tribunal known to the Constitution; and yet the privilege is denied him; because the Circuit Court consists of two judges instead of one.

Such a result was not in the contemplation of the legislature of 1802; and the language used by it cannot be construed to mean any such thing. The clause under consideration was introduced to further the ends of justice, by obtaining a speedy settlement of important questions where the judges might be opposed in opinion.

The act of 1802 so changed the judicial system that the Circuit Court, instead of three, was composed of two judges; and, without this provision or a kindred one, if the judges differed, the difference would remain, the question be unsettled, and justice denied. The decisions of this court upon the provisions of this section have been numerous. In *United States* v. *Daniel,* the court, in holding that a division of the judges on a motion for a new trial could not be certified, say: "That the question must be one which arises in a cause depending before the court relative to a proceeding belonging to the cause." Testing Milligan's case by this rule of law, is it not apparent that it is rightfully here; and that we are compelled to answer the questions on which the judges below were opposed in opinion? If, in the sense of the law, the proceeding for the writ of *habeas corpus* was the *"cause"* of the party applying for it, then it is evident that the "cause" was pending before the court, and that the questions certified arose out of it, belonged to it, and were matters of right and not of discretion.

But it is argued, that the proceeding does not ripen into a cause, until there are two parties to it.

This we deny. It was the *cause* of Milligan when the petition was presented to the Circuit Court. It would have been the *cause* of both parties, if the court had issued the writ and brought those who held Milligan in custody before it. Webster defines the word "cause" thus: "A suit or action in court; any legal process which a party institutes to obtain his demand, or by which he seeks his right, or supposed right"—and he says, "this is a legal, scriptural, and popular use of the word, coinciding nearly with case, from *cado,* and action, from *ago,* to urge and drive."

In any legal sense, action, suit, and cause, are convertible terms. Milligan supposed he had a right to test the validity of his trial and sentence; and the proceeding which he set in operation for that purpose was his "cause" or "suit." It was the only one by which he could recover his liberty. He was powerless to do more; he could neither instruct the judges nor control their action, and should not suffer, because, without fault of his, they were unable to render a judgment. But, the true meaning to the term "suit" has been given by this court. One of the questions in *Weston* v. *City Council of Charleston,* was, whether a writ of prohibition was a suit; and Chief Justice Marshall says: "The term is certainly a comprehensive one, and is understood to apply to any proceeding in a court of justice by which an individual pursues that remedy which the law affords him." Certainly, Milligan pursued the only remedy which the law afforded him.

Again, in *Cohens* v. *Virginia,* he says: "In law language a suit is the prosecution of some demand in a court of justice." Also, "To commence a suit is to demand something by the institution of process in a court of justice; and to prosecute the suit is to continue that demand." When Milligan demanded his release by the proceeding relating to *habeas corpus,* he commenced a suit; and he has since prosecuted it in all the ways known to the law. One of the questions in *Holmes* v. *Jennison et al.* was, whether under the 25th section of the Judiciary Act a proceeding for a writ of *habeas corpus* was a "suit." Chief Justice Taney held, that, "if a party is unlawfully imprisoned, the writ of *habeas corpus* is his appropriate legal remedy. It is his suit in court to recover his liberty." There was much diversity of opinion on another ground of jurisdiction; but that, in the sense of the 25th section of the Judiciary Act, the proceeding by *habeas corpus* was a suit, was not controverted by any except Baldwin, Justice, and he thought that "suit" and "cause" as used in the section, mean the same thing.

The court do not say, that a return must be made, and the parties appear and begin to try the case before it is a suit. When the petition is filed and the writ prayed for, it is a *suit,*—the suit of the party making the application. If it is a suit under the 25th section of the Judiciary Act when the proceedings are begun, it is, by all the analogies of the law, equally a suit under the 6th section of the act of 1802.

But it is argued, that there must be *two* parties to the suit, because the point is to be stated upon the request of "either party or their counsel."

Such a literal and technical construction would defeat the very purpose the legislature had in view, which was to enable any party to bring the case here, when the point in controversy was a matter of right and not of discretion; and the words "either party," in order to prevent a failure of justice, must be construed as words of enlargement, and not of restriction. Although this case is here *ex parte*, it was not considered by the court below without notice having been given to the party supposed to have an interest in the detention of the prisoner. The statements of the record show that this is not only a fair, but conclusive inference. When the counsel for Milligan presented to the court the petition for the writ of *habeas corpus*, Mr. Hanna, the District Attorney for Indiana, also appeared; and, by agreement, the application was submitted to the court, who took the case under advisement, and on the next day announced their inability to agree, and made the certificate. It is clear that Mr. Hanna did not represent the petitioner, and why is his appearance entered? It admits of no other solution than this,—that he was informed of the application, and appeared on behalf of the government to contest it. The government was the prosecutor of Milligan, who claimed that his imprisonment was illegal; and sought, in the only way he could, to recover his liberty. The case was a grave one; and the court, unquestionably, directed that the law officer of the government should be informed of it. He very properly appeared, and, as the facts were uncontroverted and the difficulty was in the application of the law, there was no useful purpose to be obtained in issuing the writ. The cause was, therefore, submitted to the court for their consideration and determination.

But Milligan claimed his discharge from custody by virtue of the act of Congress "relating to *habeas corpus*, and regulating judicial proceedings in certain cases," approved March 3d, 1863. Did that act confer jurisdiction on the Circuit Court of Indiana to hear this case?

In interpreting a law, the motives which must have operated with the legislature in passing it are proper to be considered. This law was passed in a time of great national peril, when our heritage of free government was in danger. An armed rebellion against the national authority, of greater proportions than history affords an example of, was raging; and the public safety required that the privilege of the writ of *habeas corpus* should be suspended. The President had practically suspended it, and detained suspected persons in custody without trial; but his authority to do this was questioned. It was claimed that Congress alone could exercise this power; and that the legislature, and not the President, should judge of the political considerations on which the right to suspend it rested. The privilege of this great writ had never before been withheld from the citizen; and as the exigence of the times demanded immediate action, it was of the highest importance that the lawfulness of the suspension should be fully established. It was under these circumstances, which were such as to arrest the attention of the country, that this law was passed. The President was authorized by it to suspend the privilege of the writ of *habeas corpus*, whenever, in his judgment, the public safety required; and he did, by proclamation, bearing date the 15th of September, 1863, reciting, among other things, the authority of this statute, suspend it. The suspension of the writ does not authorize the arrest of any one, but simply denies to one arrested the privilege of this writ in order to obtain his liberty.

It is proper, therefore, to inquire under what circumstances the courts could rightfully refuse to grant this writ, and when the citizen was at liberty to invoke its aid.

The second and third sections of the law are explicit on these points. The language used is plain and direct, and the meaning of the Congress cannot be mistaken. The public safety demanded, if the President thought proper to arrest a suspected person, that he should not be required to give the cause of his detention on return to a writ of *habeas corpus*. But it was not contemplated that such person should be detained in custody beyond a certain fixed period, unless certain judicial proceedings, known to the common law, were commenced against him. The Secretaries of State and War were directed to furnish to the judges of the courts of the United States, a list of the names of all parties, not prisoners of war, resident in their respective jurisdictions, who then were or afterwards should be held in custody by the authority of the President, and who were citizens of states in which the administration of the laws in the Federal tribunals was unimpaired. After the list was furnished, if a grand jury of the district convened and adjourned, and did not indict or present one of the persons thus named, he was entitled to his discharge; and it was the duty of the judge of the court to order him brought before him to be discharged, if he desired it. The refusal or omission to furnish the list could not operate to the injury of any one who was not indicted or presented by the grand jury; for, if twenty days had elapsed from the time of his arrest and the termination of the session of the grand jury, he was equally entitled to his discharge as if the list were furnished; and any credible person, on petition verified by affidavit, could obtain the judge's order for that purpose.

Milligan, in his application to be released from imprisonment, averred the existence of every fact necessary under the terms of this law to give the Circuit Court of Indiana jurisdiction. If he was detained in custody by the order of the President, otherwise than as a prisoner of war; if he was a citizen of Indiana and had never been in the military or naval service, and the grand jury of the district had met, after he had been arrested, for a period of twenty days, and adjourned without taking any proceedings against him, *then* the court had the right to entertain his petition and determine the lawfulness of his imprisonment. Because the word "court" is not found in the body of the second section, it was argued at the bar, that the application should have been made to a judge of the court, and not to the court itself; but this is not so, for power is expressly conferred in the last proviso of the section on the court equally with a judge of it to discharge from imprisonment. It was the manifest design of Congress to secure a certain remedy by which any one, deprived of liberty, could obtain it, if there was a judicial failure to find cause of offence against him. Courts are not, always, in session, and can adjourn on the discharge of the grand jury; and before those, who are in confinement, could take proper steps to procure their liberation. To provide for this contingency, authority was given to the judges out of court to grant relief to any party, who could show, that, under the law, he should be no longer restrained of his liberty.

It was insisted that Milligan's case was defective, because it did not state that the list was furnished to the judges; and, therefore, it was impossible to say under which section of the act it was presented.

It is not easy to see how this omission could affect the question of jurisdiction. Milligan could not know that the list was furnished, unless the judges volunteered to tell him; for the law did not require that any record should be made of it or anybody but the judges informed of it. Why aver the fact when the truth of the matter was apparent to the court without an averment? How can Milligan be harmed by the absence of the averment, when he states that he was under arrest for more than sixty days before the court and grand jury, which should have considered his case, met at Indianapolis? It is apparent, therefore, that under the *Habeas Corpus* Act of 1863 the Circuit Court of Indiana had complete jurisdiction to adjudicate upon this case, and, if the judges could not agree on questions vital to the progress of the cause, they had the authority (as we have shown in a previous part of this opinion), and it was their duty to certify those questions of disagreement to this court for final decision. It was argued that a final decision on the questions presented ought not to be made, because the parties who were directly concerned in the arrest and detention of Milligan, were not before the court; and their rights might be prejudiced by the answer which should be given to those questions. But this court cannot know what return will be made to the writ of *habeas corpus* when issued; and it is very clear that no one is concluded upon any question that may be raised to that return. In the sense of the law of 1802 which authorized a certificate of division, a final decision means final upon the points certified; final upon the court below, so that it is estopped from any adverse ruling in all the subsequent proceedings of the cause.

But it is said that this case is ended, as the presumption is, that Milligan was hanged in pursuance of the order of the President.

Although we have no judicial information on the subject, yet the inference is that he is alive; for otherwise learned counsel would not appear for him and urge this court to decide his case. It can never be in this country of written constitution and laws, with a judicial department to interpret them, that any chief magistrate would be so far forgetful of his duty, as to order the execution of a man who denied the jurisdiction that tried and convicted him; *after* his case was before Federal judges with power to decide it, who, being unable to agree on the grave questions involved, had, according to known law, sent it to the Supreme Court of the United States for decision. But even the suggestion is injurious to the Executive, and we dismiss it from further consideration. There is, therefore, nothing to hinder this court from an investigation of the merits of this controversy.

The controlling question in the case is this: Upon the *facts* stated in Milligan's petition, and the exhibits filed, had the military commission mentioned in it *ju-*

risdiction, legally, to try and sentence him? Milligan, not a resident of one of the rebellious states, or a prisoner of war, but a citizen of Indiana for twenty years past, and never in the military or naval service, is, while at his home, arrested by the military power of the United States, imprisoned, and, on certain criminal charges preferred against him, tried, convicted, and sentenced to be hanged by a military commission, organized under the direction of the military commander of the military district of Indiana. Had this tribunal the *legal* power and authority to try and punish this man?

No graver question was ever considered by this court, nor one which more nearly concerns the rights of the whole people; for it is the birthright of every American citizen when charged with crime, to be tried and punished according to law. The power of punishment is, alone through the means which the laws have provided for that purpose, and if they are ineffectual, there is an immunity from punishment, no matter how great an offender the individual may be, or how much his crimes may have shocked the sense of justice of the country, or endangered its safety. By the protection of the law human rights are secured; withdraw that protection, and they are at the mercy of wicked rulers, or the clamor of an excited people. If there was law to justify this military trial, it is not our province to interfere; if there was not, it is our duty to declare the nullity of the whole proceedings. The decision of this question does not depend on argument or judicial precedents, numerous and highly illustrative as they are. These precedents inform us of the extent of the struggle to preserve liberty and to relieve those in civil life from military trials. The founders of our government were familiar with the history of that struggle; and secured in a written constitution every right which the people had wrested from power during a contest of ages. By that Constitution and the laws authorized by it this question must be determined. The provisions of that instrument on the administration of criminal justice are too plain and direct, to leave room for misconstruction or doubt of their true meaning. Those applicable to this case are found in that clause of the original Constitution which says, "That the trial of all crimes, except in case of impeachment, shall be by jury;" and in the fourth, fifth, and sixth articles of the amendments. The fourth proclaims the right to be secure in person and effects against unreasonable search and seizure; and directs that a judicial warrant shall not issue "without proof of probable cause supported by oath or affirmation." The fifth declares "that no person shall be held to answer for a capital or otherwise infamous crime unless on presentment by a grand jury, except in cases arising in the land or naval forces, or in the militia, when in actual service in time of war or public danger, nor be deprived of life, liberty, or property, without due process of law." And the sixth guarantees the right of trial by jury, in such manner and with such regulations that with upright judges, impartial juries, and an able bar, the innocent will be saved and the guilty punished. It is in these words: "In all criminal prosecutions the accused shall enjoy the right to a speedy and public trial by an impartial jury of the state and district wherein the crime shall have been committed, which district shall have been previously ascertained by law, and to be informed of the nature and cause of the accusation, to be confronted with the witnesses against him, to have compulsory process for obtaining witnesses in his favor, and to have the assistance of counsel for his defence." These securities for personal liberty thus embodied, were such as wisdom and experience had demonstrated to be necessary for the protection of those accused of crime. And so strong was the sense of the country of their importance, and so jealous were the people that these rights, highly prized, might be denied them by implication, that when the original Constitution was proposed for adoption it encountered severe opposition; and, but for the belief that it would be so amended as to embrace them, it would never have been ratified.

Time has proven the discernment of our ancestors; for even these provisions, expressed in such plain English words, that it would seem the ingenuity of man could not evade them, are *now*, after the lapse of more than seventy years, sought to be avoided. Those great and good men foresaw that troublous times would arise, when rulers and people would become restive under restraint, and seek by sharp and decisive measures to accomplish ends deemed just and proper; and that the principles of constitutional liberty would be in peril, unless established by irrepealable law. The history of the world had taught them that what was done in the past might be attempted in the future. The Constitution of the United States is a law for rulers and people, equally in war and in peace, and covers with the shield of its protection all classes of men, at all times, and under all circumstances. No doctrine, involving more pernicious consequences, was ever invented by the wit of man than that any of its provisions can be suspended during any of the great exigencies of government. Such a doctrine leads directly to anarchy or despotism, but the theory of necessity on which it is based is false; for the government, within the Constitution, has all the powers granted to it, which are necessary to preserve its existence; as has been happily proved by the result of the great effort to throw off its just authority.

Have any of the rights guaranteed by the Constitution been violated in the case of Milligan? and if so, what are they?

Every trial involves the exercise of judicial power; and from what source did not military commission that tried him derive their authority? Certainly no part of judicial power of the country was conferred on them; because the Constitution expressly vests it "in one supreme court and such inferior courts as the Congress may from time to time ordain and establish," and it is not pretended that the commission was a court ordained and established by Congress. They cannot justify on the mandate of the President; because he is controlled by law, and has his appropriate sphere of duty, which is to execute, not to make, the laws; and there is "no unwritten criminal code to which resort can be had as a source of jurisdiction."

But it is said that the jurisdiction is complete under the "laws and usages of war."

It can serve no useful purpose to inquire what those laws and usages are, whence they originated, where found, and on whom they operate; they can never be applied to citizens in states which have upheld the authority of the government, and where the courts are open and their process unobstructed. This court has judicial knowledge that in Indiana the Federal authority was always unopposed, and its courts always open to hear criminal accusations and redress grievances; and no usage of war could sanction a military trial there for any offence whatever of a citizen in civil life, in nowise connected with the military service. Congress could grant no such power; and to the honor of our national legislature be it said, it has never been provoked by the state of the country even to attempt its exercise. One of the plainest constitutional provisions was, therefore, infringed when Milligan was tried by a court not ordained and established by Congress, and not composed of judges appointed during good behavior.

Why was he not delivered to the Circuit Court of Indiana to be proceeded against according to law? No reason of necessity could be urged against it; because Congress had declared penalties against the offences charged, provided for their punishment, and directed that court to hear and determine them. And soon after this military tribunal was ended, the Circuit Court met, peacefully transacted its business, and adjourned. It needed no bayonets to protect it, and required no military aid to execute its judgments. It was held in a state, eminently distinguished for patriotism, by judges commissioned during the Rebellion, who were provided with juries, upright, intelligent, and selected by a marshal appointed by the President. The government had no right to conclude that Milligan, if guilty, would not receive in that court merited punishment; for its records disclose that it was constantly engaged in the trial of similar offences, and was never interrupted in its administration of criminal justice. If it was dangerous, in the distracted condition of affairs, to leave Milligan unrestrained of his liberty, because he "conspired against the government, afforded aid and comfort to rebels, and incited the people to insurrection," the *law* said arrest him, confine him closely, render him powerless to do further mischief; and then present his case to the grand jury of the district, with proofs of his guilt, and, if indicted, try him according to the course of the common law. If this had been done, the Constitution would have been vindicated, the law of 1863 enforced, and the securities for personal liberty preserved and defended.

Another guarantee of freedom was broken when Milligan was denied a trial by jury. The great minds of the country have differed on the correct interpretation to be given to various provisions of the Federal Constitution; and judicial decision has been often invoked to settle their true meaning; but until recently no one ever doubted that the right of trial by jury was fortified in the organic law against the power of attack. It is *now* assailed; but if ideas can be expressed in words, and language has any meaning, *this right*—one of the most valuable in a free country—is preserved to every one accused of crime who is not attached to the army, or navy, or militia in actual service. The sixth amendment affirms that "in all criminal prosecutions the accused shall enjoy the right to a speedy and public trial by an impartial jury," language broad enough to embrace all persons and cases; but the fifth, recognizing the necessity of an indictment, or presentment, before any one can be held to answer for high crimes, "*excepts* cases arising in the land or naval forces, or in the militia, when in actual service, in time of war or public danger;" and the framers of the Constitution, doubtless, meant to limit the right of trial by jury, in the sixth amendment, to those persons who were subject to indictment or presentment in the fifth.

The discipline necessary to the efficiency of the army and navy, required other and swifter modes of trial than are furnished by the common law courts; and, in pursuance of the power conferred by the Constitution, Congress has declared the kinds of trial, and the manner in which they shall be conducted, for offences committed while the party is in the military or naval service. Every one connected with these branches of the public service is amenable to the jurisdiction which Congress has created for their government, and, while thus serving, surrenders his right to be tried by the civil courts. *All other persons*, citizens of states where the courts are open, if charged with crime, are guaranteed the inestimable privilege of trial by jury. This privilege is a vital principle, underlying the whole administration of criminal justice; it is not held by sufferance, and cannot be frittered away on any plea of state or political necessity. When peace prevails, and the authority of the government is undisputed, there is no difficulty of preserving the safeguards of liberty; for the ordinary modes of trial are never neglected, and no one wishes it otherwise; but if society is disturbed by civil commotion—if the passions of men are aroused and the restraints of law weakened, if not disregarded—these safeguards need, and should receive, the watchful care of those intrusted with the guardianship of the Constitution and laws. In no other way can we transmit to posterity unimpaired the blessings of liberty, consecrated by the sacrifices of the Revolution.

It is claimed that martial law covers with its broad mantle the proceedings of this military commission. The proposition is this: that in a time of war the commander of an armed force (if in his opinion the exigencies of the country demand it, and of which he is to judge), has the power, within the lines of his military district, to suspend all civil rights and their remedies, and subject citizens as well as soldiers to the rule of *his will;* and in the exercise of his lawful authority cannot be restrained, except by his superior officer or the President of the United States.

If this position is sound to the extent claimed, then when war exists, foreign or domestic, and the country is subdivided into military departments for mere convenience, the commander of one of them can, if he chooses, within his limits, on the plea of necessity, with the approval of the Executive, substitute military force for and to the exclusion of the laws, and punish all persons, as he thinks right and proper, without fixed or certain rules.

The statement of this proposition shows its importance; for, if true, republican government is a failure, and there is an end of liberty regulated by law. Martial law, established on such a basis, destroys every guarantee of the Constitution, and effectually renders the "military independent of and superior to the civil power"—the attempt to do which by the King of Great Britain was deemed by our fathers such an offence, that they assigned it to the world as one of the causes which impelled them to declare their independence. Civil liberty and this kind of martial law cannot endure together; the antagonism is irreconcilable; and, in the conflict, one or the other must perish.

This nation, as experience has proved, cannot always remain at peace, and has no right to expect that it will always have wise and humane rulers, sincerely attached to the principles of the Constitution. Wicked men, ambitious of power, with hatred of liberty and contempt of law, may fill the place once occupied by Washington and Lincoln; and if this right is conceded, and the calamities of war again befall us, the dangers to human liberty are frightful to contemplate. If our fathers had failed to provide for just such a contingency, they would have been false to the trust reposed in them. They knew—the history of the world told them—the nation they were founding, be its existence short or long, would be involved in war; how often or how long continued, human foresight could not tell; and that unlimited power, wherever lodged at such a time, was especially hazardous to freemen. For this, and other equally weighty reasons, they secured the inheritance they had fought to maintain, by incorporating in a written constitution the safeguards which *time* had proved were essential to its preservation. Not one of these safeguards can the President, or Congress, or the Judiciary disturb, except the one concerning the writ of *habeas corpus*.

It is essential to the safety of every government that, in a great crisis, like the one we have just passed through, there should be a power somewhere of suspending the writ of *habeas corpus*. In every war, there are men of previously good character, wicked enough to counsel their fellow-citizens to resist the measures deemed necessary by a good government to sustain its just authority and overthrow its enemies; and their influence may lead to dangerous combinations. In the emergency of the times, an immediate public investigation according to law may not be possible; and yet, the period to the country may be too imminent to suffer such persons to go at large. Unquestionably, there is then an exigency which demands that the government, if it should see fit in the exercise of a proper discretion to make arrests, should not be required to produce the persons arrested in answer to a writ of *habeas corpus*. The Constitution goes no further. It does not say after a writ of *habeas corpus* is denied a citizen, that he shall be tried otherwise than by the course of the common law; if it had intended this result, it was easy by the use of direct words to have accomplished it. The illustrious men who framed that instrument were guarding the foundations of civil liberty against the abuses of unlimited power; they were full of wisdom, and the lessons of history informed them that a trial by an established court, assisted by an impartial jury, was the only sure way of protecting the citizen against oppression and wrong. Knowing this, they limited the suspension to one great right, and left the rest to remain forever inviolable. But, it is insisted that the safety of the country in time of war demands that this broad claim for martial law shall be sustained. If this were true, it could be well said that a country, preserved at the sacrifice of all the cardinal principles of liberty, is not worth the cost of preservation. Happily, it is not so.

It will be borne in mind that this is not a question of the power to proclaim martial law, when war exists in a community and the courts and civil authorities are overthrown. Nor is it a question what rule a military commander, at the head of his army, can impose on states in rebellion to cripple their resources and quell the insurrection. The jurisdiction claimed is much more extensive. The necessities of the service, during the late Rebellion, required that the loyal states should be placed within the limits of certain military districts and commanders appointed in them; and, it is urged, that this, in a military sense, constituted them the theater of military operations; and, as in this case, Indiana had been and was again threatened with invasion by the enemy, the occasion was furnished to establish martial law. The conclusion does not follow from the premises. If armies were collected in Indiana, they were to be employed in another locality, where the laws were obstructed and the national authority disputed. On *her* soil there was no hostile foot; if once invaded, that invasion was at an end, and with it all pretext for martial law. Martial law cannot arise from a *threatened* invasion. The necessity must be actual and present; the invasion real, such as effectually closes the courts and deposes the civil administration.

It is difficult to see how the *safety* for the country required martial law in Indiana. If any of her citizens were plotting treason, the power of arrest could secure them, until the government was prepared for their trial, when the courts were open and ready to try them. It was as easy to protect witnesses before a civil as a military tribunal; and as there could be no wish to convict, except on sufficient legal evidence, surely an ordained and establish court was better able to judge of this than a military tribunal composed of gentlemen not trained to the profession of the law.

It follows, from what has been said on this subject, that there are occasions when martial rule can be properly applied. If, in foreign invasion or civil war, the courts are actually closed, and it is impossible to administer criminal justice according to law, *then,* on the theatre of active military operations, where war really prevails, there is a necessity to furnish a substitute for the civil authority, thus overthrown, to preserve the safety of the army and society; and as no power is left but the military, it is allowed to govern by martial rule until the laws can have their free course. As necessity creates the rule, so it limits its duration; for, if this government is continued *after* the courts are reinstated, it is a gross usurpation of power. Martial rule can never exist where the courts are open, and in the proper and unobstructed exercise of their jurisdiction. It is also confined to the locality of actual war. Because, during the late Rebellion it could have been enforced in Virginia, where the national authority was overturned and the courts driven out, it does not follow that it should obtain in Indiana, where that authority was never disputed, and justice was always administered. And so in the case of a foreign invasion, martial rule may become a necessity in one state, when, in another, it would be "mere lawless violence."

We are not without precedents in English and American history illustrating our views of this question; but it is hardly necessary to make particular reference to them.

From the first year of the reign of Edward the Third, when the Parliament of England reversed the attainder of the Earl of Lancaster, because he could have been tried by the courts of the realm, and declared, 'that in time of peace no man ought to be adjudged to death for treason or any other offence without being arraigned and held to answer; and that regularly when the king's courts are open it is a time of peace in judgment of law," down to the present day, martial law, as claimed in this case, has been condemned by all respectable English jurists as contrary to the fundamental laws of the land, and subversive of the liberty of the subject.

During the present century, an instructive debate on this question occurred in Parliament, occasioned by the trial and conviction by court-martial, at Demerara, of the Rev. John Smith, a missionary to the negroes, on the alleged ground of aiding and abetting a formidable rebellion in that colony. Those eminent statesmen, Lord Brougham and Sir James Mackintosh, participated in that debate; [sic] and denounced the trial as illegal; because it did not appear that the courts of law in Demerara could not try offences, and that "when the laws can act, every other mode of punishing supposed crimes is itself an enormous crime."

So sensitive were our Revolutionary fathers on this subject, although Boston was almost in a state of siege, when General Gage issued his proclamation of martial law, they spoke of it as an "attempt to supersede the course of the common law, and instead thereof to publish and order the use of martial law." The Virginia Assembly, also, denounced a similar measure on the part of Governor Dunmore "as an assumed power, which the king himself cannot exercise; because it annuls the law of the land and introduces the most execrable of all systems, martial law."

In some parts of the country, during the war of 1812, our officers made arbitrary arrests and, by military tribunals, tried citizens who were not in the military service. These arrests and trials, when brought to the notice of the courts, were uniformly condemned as illegal. The cases of *Smith* v. *Shaw* and *McConnell* v. *Hampden* (reported in 12 Johnson), are illustrations, which we cite, not only for the principles they determine, but on account of the distinguished jurists concerned in the decisions, one of whom for many years occupied a seat on this bench.

It is contended, that *Luther* v. *Borden*, decided by this court, is an authority for the claim of martial law advanced in this case. The decision is misapprehended.

That case grew out of the attempt in Rhode Island to supersede the old colonial government by a revolutionary proceeding. Rhode Island, until that period, had no other form of local government than the charter granted by King Charles II, in 1663; and as that limited the right of suffrage, and did not provide for its own amendment, many citizens became dissatisfied, because the legislature would not afford the relief in their power; and without the authority of law, formed a new and independent constitution, and proceeded to assert its authority by force of arms. The old government resisted this; and as the rebellion was formidable, called out the militia to subdue it, and passed an act declaring martial law. Borden, in the military service of the *old* government, broke open the house of Luther, who supported the *new*, in order to arrest him. Luther brought suit against Borden; and the question was, whether, under the constitution and laws of the state, Borden was justified. This court held that a state "may use its military power to put down an armed insurrection too strong to be controlled by the civil authority;" and, if the legislature of Rhode Island thought the period so great as to require the use of its military forces and the declaration of martial law, there was no ground on which *this court* could question its authority; and as Borden acted under military orders of the charter government, which had been recognized by the political power of the country, and was upheld by the state judiciary, he was justified in breaking into and entering Luther's house. This is the extent of the decision. There was no question in issue about the power of declaring martial law under the Federal Constitution, and the court did not consider it necessary even to inquire "to what extent nor under what circumstances that power may be exercised by a state."

We do not deem it important to examine further the adjudged cases; and shall, therefore, conclude without any additional reference to authorities.

To the third question, then, on which the judges below were opposed in opinion, an answer in the negative must be returned.

It is proper to say, although Milligan's trial and conviction by a military commission was illegal, yet, if guilty of the crimes imputed to him, and his guilt had been ascertained by an established court and impartial jury, he deserved severe punishment. Open resistance to the measures deemed necessary to subdue a great rebellion, by those who enjoy the protection of government, and have not the excuse even of prejudice of section to plead in their favor, is wicked; but that resistance becomes an *enormous crime* when it assumes the form of a secret political organization, armed to oppose the laws, and seeks by stealthy means to introduce the enemies of the country into peaceful communities, there to light the torch of civil war, and thus overthrow the power of the United States. Conspiracies like these, at such a juncture, are extremely perilous; and those concerned in them are dangerous enemies to their country, and should receive the heaviest penalties of the law, as an example to deter others from similar criminal conduct. It is said the severity of the laws caused them; but Congress was obliged to enact severe laws to meet the crisis; and as our highest civil duty is to serve our country when in danger, the late war has proved that rigorous laws, when necessary, will be cheerfully obeyed by a patriotic people, struggling to preserve the rich blessings of a free government.

The two remaining questions in this case must be answered in the affirmative. The suspension of the privilege of the writ of *habeas corpus* does not suspend the writ itself. The writ issues as a matter of course; and on the return made to it the court decides whether the party applying is denied the right of proceeding any further with it.

If the military trial of Milligan was contrary to law, then he was entitled, on the facts stated in his petition, to be discharged from custody by the terms of the act of Congress of March 3d, 1863. The provisions of this law having been considered in a previous part of this opinion, we will not restate the views there presented. Milligan avers he was a citizen of Indiana, not in the military or naval service, and was detained in close confinement, by order of the President, from the 5th day of October, 1864, until the 2d day of January, 1865, when the Circuit Court for the District of Indiana, with a grand jury, convened in session at Indianapolis; and afterwards, on the 27th day of the same month, adjourned without finding an indictment or presentment against him. If these averments were true (and their truth is conceded for the purposes of this case), the court was required to liberate him on taking certain oaths prescribed by the law, and entering into recognizance for his good behavior.

But it is insisted that Milligan was a prisoner of war, and, therefore, excluded from the privileges of the statute. It is not easy to see how he can be treated as a prisoner of war, when he lived in Indiana for the past twenty years, was arrested there, and had not been, during the late troubles, a resident of any of the states in rebellion. If in Indiana he conspired with bad men to assist the enemy, he is punishable for it in the courts of Indiana; but, when tried for the offence, he cannot plead the rights of war; for he was not engaged in legal acts of hostility against the government, and only such persons, when captured, are prisoners of war. If he cannot enjoy the immunities attaching to the character of a prisoner of war, how can he be subject to their pains and penalties?

This case, as well as the kindred cases of Bowles and Horsey, were disposed of at the last term, and the proper orders were entered of record. There is, therefore, no additional entry required.

> The CHIEF JUSTICE delivered the following opinion.

Four members of the court, concurring with their brethren in the order heretofore made in this cause, but unable to concur in some important particulars with the opinion which has just been read, think it their duty to make a separate statement of their views of the whole case.

We do not doubt that the Circuit Court for the District of Indiana had jurisdiction of the petition of Milligan for the writ of *habeas corpus*.

Whether this court has jurisdiction upon the certificate of division admits of more question. The construction of the act authorizing such certificates, which has hitherto prevailed here, denies jurisdiction in cases where the certificate brings up the whole cause before the court. But none of the adjudicated cases are exactly in point, and we are willing to resolve whatever doubt may exist in favor of the earliest possible answers to questions involving life and liberty. We agree, therefore, that this court may properly answer questions certified in such a case as that before us.

The crimes with which Milligan was charged were of the gravest character, and the petition and exhibits in the record, which must here be taken as true, admit his guilt. But whatever his desert of punishment may be, it is more important to the country and to every citizen that he should not be punished under an illegal sentence, sanctioned by this court of last resort, than that he should be punished at all. The laws which protect the liberties of the whole people must not be violated or set aside in order to inflict, even upon the guilty, unauthorized though merited justice.

The trial and sentence of Milligan were by military commission convened in Indiana during the fall of 1864. The action of the commission had been under consideration by President Lincoln for some time, when he himself became the victim of an abhorred conspiracy. It was approved by his successor in May, 1865, and the sentence was ordered to be carried into execution. The proceedings, therefore, had the fullest sanction of the executive department of the government.

This sanction requires the most respectful and the most careful consideration of this court. The sentence which it supports must not be set aside except upon the clearest conviction that it cannot be reconciled with the Constitution and the constitutional legislation of Congress.

We must inquire, then, what constitutional or statutory provisions have relation to this military proceeding.

The act of Congress of March 3d, 1863, comprises all the legislation which seems to require consideration in this connection. The constitutionality of this act has not been questioned and is not doubted.

The first section authorized the suspension, during the Rebellion, of the writ of *habeas corpus* throughout the United States by the President. The two next sections limited this authority in important respects.

The second section required that lists of all persons, being citizens of states in which the administration of the laws had continued unimpaired in the Federal courts, who were then held or might thereafter be held as prisoners of the United States, under the authority of the President, otherwise than as prisoners of war, should be furnished to the judges of the Circuit and District Courts. The lists transmitted to the judges were to contain the names of all persons, residing within their respective jurisdictions, charged with violation of national law. And it was required, in cases where the grand jury in attendance upon any of these courts should terminate its session without proceeding by indictment or otherwise against any prisoner named in the list, that the judge of the court should forthwith make an order that such prisoner desiring a discharge, should be brought before him or the court to be discharged, on entering into recognizance, if required, to keep the peace and for good behavior, or to appear, as the court might direct, to be further dealt with according to law. Every officer of the United States having custody of such prisoners was required to obey and execute the judge's order, under penalty, for refusal or delay, of fine and imprisonment.

The third section provided, in case lists of persons other than prisoners of war then held in confinement, or thereafter arrested, should not be furnished within twenty days after the passage of the act, or, in cases of subsequent arrest, within twenty days after the time of arrest, that any citizen, after the termination of a session of the grand jury without indictment or presentment, might, by petition alleging the facts and verified by oath, obtain the judge's order of discharge in favor of any person so imprisoned, on the terms and conditions prescribed in the second section.

It was made the duty of the District Attorney of the United States to attend examinations on petitions for discharge.

It was under this act that Milligan petitioned the Circuit Court for the District of Indiana for discharge from imprisonment.

The holding of the Circuit and District Courts of the United States in Indiana had been uninterrupted. The administration of the laws in the Federal courts had remained unimpaired. Milligan was imprisoned under the authority of the President, and was not a prisoner of war. No list of prisoners had been furnished to the judges, either of the District or Circuit Courts, as required by the law. A grand jury had attended the Circuit Courts of the Indiana district, while Milligan was there imprisoned, and had closed its session without finding any indictment or presentment or otherwise proceeding against the prisoner.

His case was thus brought within the precise letter and intent of the act of Congress, unless it can be said that Milligan was not imprisoned by authority of the President; and nothing of this sort was claimed in argument on the part of the government.

It is clear upon this statement that the Circuit Court was bound to hear Milligan's petition for the writ of *habeas corpus*, called in the act an order to bring the prisoner before the judge or the court, and to issue the writ, or, in the language of the act, to make the order.

The first question, therefore—Ought the writ to issue?—must be answered in the affirmative.

And it is equally clear that he was entitled to the discharge prayed for.

It must be borne in mind that the prayer of the petition was not for an absolute discharge, but to be delivered from military custody and imprisonment, and if found probably guilty of any offence, to be turned over to the proper tribunal for inquiry and punishment; or, if not found thus probably guilty, to be discharged altogether.

And the express terms of the act of Congress required this action of the court. The prisoner must be discharged on giving such recognizance as the court should require, not only for good behavior, but for appearance, as directed by the court, to answer and be further dealt with according to law.

The first section of the act authorized the suspension of the writ of *habeas corpus* generally throughout the United States. The second and third sections limited this suspension, in certain cases, within states where the administration of justice by the Federal courts remained unimpaired. In these eases the writ was still to issue, and under it the prisoner was entitled to his discharge by a circuit or district judge or court, unless held to bail for appearance to answer charges. No other judge or court could make an order of discharge under the writ. Except under the circumstances pointed out by the act, neither circuit nor district judge or court could make such an order. But under those circumstances the writ must be issued, and the relief from imprisonment directed by the act must be afforded. The commands of the act were positive, and left no discretion to court or judge.

An affirmative answer must, therefore, be given to the second question, namely: Ought Milligan to be discharged according to the prayer of the petition?

That the third question, namely: Had the military commission in Indiana, under the facts stated, jurisdiction to try and sentence Milligan? must be answered negatively is an unavoidable inference from affirmative answers to the other two.

The military commission could not have jurisdiction to try and sentence Milligan, if he could not be detained in prison under his original arrest or under sentence, after the close of a session of the grand jury without indictment or other proceeding against him.

Indeed, the act seems to have been framed on purpose to secure the trial of all offences of citizens by civil tribunals, in states where these tribunals were not interrupted in the regular exercise of their functions.

Under it, in such states, the privilege of the writ might be suspended. Any person regarded as dangerous to the public safety might be arrested and detained until after the session of a grand jury. Until after such session no person arrested could have the benefit of the writ; and even then no such person could be discharged except on such terms, as to future appearance, as the court might impose. These provisions obviously contemplate no other trial or sentence than that of a civil court, and we could not assert the legality of a trial and sentence by a military commission, under the circumstances specified in the act and described in the petition, without disregarding the plain directions of Congress.

We agree, therefore, that the first two questions certified must receive affirmative answers, and the last a negative. We do not doubt that the positive provisions of the act of Congress require such answers. We do not think it necessary to look beyond these provisions. In them we find sufficient and controlling reasons for our conclusions.

But the opinion which has just been read goes further; and as we understand it, asserts not only that the military commission held in Indiana was not authorized by Congress, but that it was not in the power of Congress to authorize it; from which it may be thought to follow, that Congress has no power to indemnify the officers who composed the commission against liability in civil courts for acting as members of it.

We cannot agree to this.

We agree in the proposition that no department of the government of the United States—neither President, nor Congress, nor the Courts—possesses any power not given by the Constitution.

We assent, fully, to all that is said, in the opinion, of the inestimable value of the trial by jury, and of the other constitutional safeguards of civil liberty. And we concur, also, in what is said of the writ of *habeas corpus,* and of its suspension, with two reservations: (1.) That, in our judgment, when the writ is suspended, the Executive is authorized to arrest as well as to detain; and (2.) that there are cases in which, the privilege of the writ being suspended, trial and punishment by military commission, in states where civil courts are open, may be authorized by Congress, as well as arrest and detention.

We think that Congress had power, though not exercised, to authorize the military commission which was held in Indiana.

We do not think it necessary to discuss at large the grounds of our conclusions. We will briefly indicate some of them.

The Constitution itself provides for military government as well as for civil government. And we do not understand it to be claimed that the civil safeguards of the Constitution have application in cases within the proper sphere of the former.

What, then, is that proper sphere? Congress has power to raise and support armies; to provide and maintain a navy; to make rules for the government and regulation of the land and naval forces; and to provide for governing such part of the militia as may be in the service of the United States.

It is not denied that the power to make rules for the government of the army and navy is a power to provide for trial and punishment by military courts without a jury. It has been so understood and exercised from the adoption of the Constitution to the present time.

Nor, in our judgment, does the fifth, or any other amendment, abridge that power. "Cases arising in the land and naval forces, or in the militia in actual service in time of war or public danger," are expressly excepted from the fifth amendment, "that no person shall be held to answer for a capital or otherwise infamous crime, unless on a presentment or indictment of a grand jury," and it is admitted that the exception applies to the other amendments as well as to the fifth.

Now, we understand this exception to have the same import and effect as if the powers of Congress in relation to the government of the army and navy and the militia had been recited in the amendment, and cases within those powers had been expressly excepted from its operation. The states, most jealous of encroachments upon the liberties of the citizen, when proposing additional safeguards in the form of amendments, excluded specifically from their effect cases arising in the government of the land and naval forces. Thus Massachusetts proposed that "no person shall be tried for any crime by which he would incur an infamous punishment or loss of life until he be first indicted by a grand jury, except in such cases as may arise in the government and regulation of the land forces." The exception in similar amendments, proposed by New York, Maryland, and Virginia, was in the same or equivalent terms. The amendments proposed by the states were considered by the first Congress, and such as were approved in substance were put in form, and proposed by that body to the states. Among those thus proposed, and subsequently ratified, was that which now stands as the fifth amendment of the Constitution. We cannot doubt that this amendment was intended to have the same force and effect as the amendment proposed by the states. We cannot agree to a construction which will impose on the exception in the fifth amendment a sense other than that obviously indicated by action of the state conventions.

We think, therefore, that the power of Congress, in the government of the land and naval forces and of the militia, is not at all affected by the fifth or any other amendment. It is not necessary to attempt any precise definition of the boundaries of this power. But may it not be said that government includes protection and defence as well as the regulation of internal administration? And is it impossible to imagine cases in which citizens conspiring or attempting the destruction or great injury of the national forces may be subjected by Congress to military trial and punishment in the just exercise of this undoubted constitutional power? Congress is but the agent of the nation, and does not the security of individuals against the abuse of this, as of every other power, depend on the intelligence and virtue of the people, on their zeal for public and private liberty, upon official responsibility secured by law, and upon the frequency of elections, rather than upon doubtful constructions of legislative powers?

But we do not put our opinion, that Congress might authorize such a military commission as was held in Indiana, upon the power to provide for the government of the national forces.

Congress has the power not only to raise and support and govern armies but to declare war. It has, therefore, the power to provide by law for carrying on war. This power necessarily extends to all legislation essential to the prosecution of war with vigor and success, except such as interferes with the command of the forces and the conduct of campaigns. That power and duty belong to the President as commander-in-chief. Both these powers are derived from the Constitution, but neither is defined by that instrument. Their extent must be determined by their nature, and by the principles of our institutions.

The power to make the necessary laws is in Congress; the power to execute in the President. Both powers imply many subordinate and auxiliary powers. Each includes all authorities essential to its due exercise. But neither can the President, in war more than in peace, intrude upon the proper authority of Congress, nor Congress upon the proper authority of the President. Both are servants of the people, whose will is expressed in the fundamental law. Congress cannot direct the conduct of campaigns, nor can the President, or any commander under him, without the sanction of Congress, institute tribunals for the trial and punishment of offences, either of soldiers or civilians, unless in cases of a controlling necessity, which justifies what it compels, or at least insures acts of indemnity from the justice of the legislature.

We by no means assert that Congress can establish and apply the laws of war where no war has been declared or exists.

Where peace exists the laws of peace must prevail. What we do maintain is, that when the nation is involved in war, and some portions of the country are invaded, and all are exposed to invasion, it is within the power of Congress to determine in what states or district such great and imminent public danger exists as justifies the authorization of military tribunals for the trial of crimes and offences against the discipline or security of the army or against the public safety.

In Indiana, for example, at the time of the arrest of Milligan and his co-conspirators, it is established by the papers in the record, that the state was a military district, was the theatre of military operations, had been actually invaded, and was constantly threatened with invasion. It appears, also, that a powerful secret association, composed of citizens and others, existed within the state, under military organization, conspiring against the draft, and plotting insurrection, the liberation of the prisoners of war at various depots, the seizure of the state and national arsenals, armed cooperation with the enemy, and war against the national government.

We cannot doubt that, in such a time of public danger, Congress had power, under the Constitution, to provide for the organization of a military commission, and for trial by that commission of persons engaged in this conspiracy. The fact that the Federal courts were open was regarded by Congress as a sufficient reason for not exercising the power; but that fact could not deprive Congress of the right to exercise it. Those courts might be open and undisturbed in the execution of their functions, and yet wholly incompetent to avert threatened danger, or to punish, with adequate promptitude and certainty, the guilty conspirators.

In Indiana, the judges and officers of the courts were loyal to the government. But it might have been otherwise. In times of rebellion and civil war it may often happen, indeed, that judges and marshals will be in active sympathy with the rebels, and courts their most efficient allies.

We have confined ourselves to the question of power. It was for Congress to determine the question of expediency. And Congress did determine it. That body did not see fit to authorize trials by military commission in Indiana, but by the strongest implication prohibited them. With that prohibition we are satisfied, and should have remained silent if the answers to the questions certified had been put on that ground, without denial of the existence of a power which we believe to be constitutional and important to the public safety,—a denial which, as we have already suggested, seems to draw in question the power of Congress to protect from prosecution the members of military commissions who acted in obedience to their superior officers, and whose action, whether warranted by law or not, was approved by that upright and patriotic President under whose administration the Republic was rescued from threatened destruction.

We have thus far said little of martial law, nor do we propose to say much. What we have already said sufficiently indicates our opinion that there is no law for the government of the citizens, the armies or the navy of the United States, within American jurisdiction, which is not contained in or derived from the Constitution. And wherever our army or navy may go beyond our territorial limits, neither can go beyond the authority of the President or the legislation of Congress.

There are under the Constitution three kinds of military jurisdiction: one to be exercised both in peace and war; another to be exercised in time of foreign war without the boundaries of the United States, or in time of rebellion and civil war within states or districts occupied by rebels treated as belligerents; and a third to be exercised in time of invasion or insurrection within the limits of the United States, or during rebellion within the limits of states maintaining adhesion to the National Government, when the public danger requires its exercise. The first of these may be called jurisdiction under MILITARY LAW, and is found in acts of Congress prescribing rules and articles of war, or otherwise providing for the government of the national forces; the second may be distinguished as MILITARY GOVERNMENT, superseding, as far as may be deemed expedient, the local law, and exercised by the military commander under the direction of the President, with the express or implied sanction of Congress; while the third may be denominated MARTIAL LAW PROPER, and is called into action by Congress, or temporarily, when the action of Congress cannot be invited, and in the case of justifying or excusing peril, by the President, in times of insurrection or invasion, or of civil or foreign war, within districts or localities where ordinary law no longer adequately secures public safety and private rights.

We think that the power of Congress, in such times and in such localities, to authorize trials for crimes against the security and safety of the national forces, may be derived from its constitutional authority to raise and support armies and to declare war, if not from its constitutional authority to provide for governing the national forces.

We have no apprehension that this power, under our American system of government, in which all official authority is derived from the people, and exercised under direct responsibility to the people, is more likely to be abused than the power to regulate commerce, or the power to borrow money. And we are unwilling to give our assent by silence to expressions of opinion which seem to us calculated, though not intended, to cripple the constitutional powers of the government, and to augment the public dangers in times of invasion and rebellion.

>Mr. Justice WAYNE, Mr. Justice SWAYNE, and Mr. Justice MILLER concur with me in these views.

UNITED STATES V. RHODES

Circuit Court, D. Kentucky
1866
27 Fed. Cas. 785, Case #16,151

Associate Justice Noah H. Swayne in this federal Circuit Court decision provided perhaps the first judicial interpretation of the 1866 Civil Rights Act enacted by Congress, over the veto of President Andrew Johnson, to enforce the 1865 Thirteenth Amendment. Section two of the Thirteenth Amendment states, "Congress shall have power to enforce this article by appropriate legislation," the first enforcement clause attached to a constitutional amendment in the nation's history. But, could Congress confer "rights" on persons in their localities, a responsibility that had previously been the domain of the locality or (at most) the states prior to the Civil War? Did the Thirteenth Amendment achieve nothing more than the constitutional end of slavery; or, could Congress, not the localities or the states, then move forward and guarantee the rights of those persons recently emancipated? No one knew, but this decision, heard on circuit, involved a dispute that arose out of Nelson County, Kentucky. Kentucky had a long-standing judicial rule that blacks could not testify against whites. Swayne's opinion demonstrated the potential reach of the Thirteenth Amendment, began the judicial consideration of the thorny issue of the meaning of "citizen," tested the constitutionality of the 1866 Civil Rights Act, and suggests just how revolutionary the Thirteenth Amendment might have been. Swayne held that "We entertain no doubt of the constitutionality of the act in all its provisions." In time, other statutes and amendments overshadowed the Thirteenth Amendment and this decision, especially the crucial 1868 Fourteenth Amendment, which built on the Thirteenth, the 1866 Civil Rights Act, and this decision. *Rhodes* suggests a path not taken in judicial interpretation.

Motion in arrest of judgment.

An indictment for burglary in entering the house of T., in Kentucky, averred that T. was of African descent, and a citizen; that she was, by the laws of Kentucky, denied the right to testify against the defendants, they being white. There was a public statute of Kentucky enabling white persons, under similar circumstances, to testify. *Held,* that the indictment was sufficient, and that the circuit court might take jurisdiction, under section 3 of the act of April 9, 1866, 14 Stat. 27, *28 U.S.C.A. § § 41(14),* 74, 75, 79, 729, known as the "Civil Rights Bill," notwithstanding there was no averment of the statute of Kentucky. The circuit court should take judicial notice of such statute, and the indictment should be construed in the same manner as if the statute were averred.

SWAYNE, Circuit Justice.

This is a prosecution under the act of congress of the 9th of April, 1866 [14 Stat. 27], entitled "An act to protect all persons in the United States in their civil rights, and to furnish the means for their vindication." The defendants having been found guilty by a jury, the case is now before us upon a motion in arrest of judgment.

Three grounds are relied upon in support of the motion. It is insisted: I. That the indictment is fatally defective. II. That the case which it makes, or was intended to make, is not within the act of congress upon which it is founded. III. That the act itself is unconstitutional and void.

I. As to the indictment, if either count be sufficient, it will support the judgment of the court upon the verdict. Our attention will be confined to the second count. That count alleges that the defendants, being white persons, "on the 1st of May, 1866, at the county of Nelson, in the state and district of Kentucky, at the hour of eleven of the clock in the night of the same day, feloniously and burglariously did break and enter the dwelling house there situate of Nancy Talbot, a citizen of the United States of the African race, having been born in the United States, and not subject to any foreign power, who was then and there, and is now, denied the right to testify against the said defendants, in the courts of the state of Kentucky, and of the said county of Nelson, with intent the goods and chattels, moneys and property of the said Nancy Talbot, in the said dwelling house then and there being, feloniously and burglariously to steal, take, and carry away, contrary to the statute in such case made and provided, and against the peace and dignity of the United States."

The objection urged against this count is, that it does not aver that "white citizens" enjoy the right which it is alleged is denied to Nancy Talbot. This fact is vital in the case. Without it our jurisdiction cannot be maintained. It is averred that she is a citizen of the United States, of the African race, and that she is denied the right to testify against the defendants, they being white persons. Section 669 of the Code of Civil Practice of Kentucky gives this right to white persons under the same circumstances. This is a public statute, and we are bound to take judicial cognizance of it. It is never necessary to set forth matters of law in a criminal pleading. The indictment is, in legal effect, as if it averred the existence and provisions of the statute. The enjoyment of the right in question by white citizens is a conclusion of law from the facts stated. Averment and proof could not bring it into the case more effectually for any purpose than it is there already. This right is one of those secured to Nancy Talbot by the first section of this act. The objection to this count cannot be sustained.

II. Is the offense charged, within the statute? The first section enacts:—"That all persons born in the United States, and not subject to any foreign power, excluding Indians not taxed, are hereby declared to be citizens of the United States; and such citizens, of every race and color, without regard to any previous condition of slavery," . . . "shall have the same right in every state and territory in the United States, to make and enforce contracts, to sue, be parties, and give evidence, to inherit, purchase, sell and convey real and personal property; and to full and equal benefit of all laws and proceedings for the security of person and property as is enjoyed by white citizens, and shall be subject to like punishment, pains, and penalties, and to none other, any law, statute, ordinance, regulation, or custom, to the contrary notwithstanding."

The second section provides:—"That any person, who under color of any law, statute, ordinance, regulation, or custom, shall subject, or cause to be subjected, any inhabitant of any state or territory to the deprivation of any right secured or protected by this act, or to different punishment, pains, or penalties on account of such person having at any time been held in the condition of slavery," . . . "or by reason of his color or race, than is prescribed for the punishment of white persons, shall be deemed guilty of a misdemeanor," &c.

The third section declares:—"That the district courts of the United States within their respective districts, shall have, exclusively of the courts of the several states, cognizance of all crimes and offenses committed against the provisions of this act, and also, concurrently with the circuit courts of the United States, of all causes, civil and criminal, affecting persons who are denied or cannot enforce in the courts or judicial tribunals of the state where they may be, any of the rights secured to them by the first section of this act; and if any suit or prosecution, civil or criminal, shall be commenced in any state court against such person, for any cause whatsoever," . . . "such defendant shall have the right to remove such cause for trial to the proper district or circuit court in the manner prescribed by the act relating to habeas corpus, and regulating judicial proceedings in certain cases, approved March 3, 1863, and all acts amendatory thereof."

It will be observed that jurisdiction is given to this court "of all causes, civil and criminal," affecting persons who are denied or cannot enforce in the local state courts "any of the rights secured by the first section of this act." The denial of any one is as effectual as the denial of any other or of all. But it is said the cause set forth in the indictment is not one affecting Nancy Talbot, in the sense of the law, and that therefore this court has no jurisdiction. *U. S. v. Ortega*, 11 Wheat. [24 U.

S.] 467, is relied upon as authority for this proposition. That case is as follows: The constitution provides (article 3, § 2) that—"In all cases affecting ambassadors, other public ministers and consuls and those in which a state shall be a party, the supreme court shall have original jurisdiction."

Ortega was indicted in the circuit court for "infracting the law of nations by offering violence to the person" of Salmon, the charge d'affaires of Spain in the United States. The judges of the circuit court were opposed in opinion upon two questions, which were thereupon certified to the supreme court. They were: (1) Whether the case was one affecting a public minister within the meaning of the constitution; (2) and whether in such cases the jurisdiction of the Supreme Court is exclusive.

The Supreme Court decided only the first question. It was held that the case did not affect the charge d'affaires. This rendered it unnecessary to decide the other question, and it is still unsettled. It will be observed that the language of the statute is different. It is "causes, civil and criminal," and not "cases."

Burrill, in his Law Dictionary, thus defines "cause": "The origin or foundation of a thing, as of a suit or action; a ground of action. 1 Const. 470." The phrase "causes, civil and criminal," must be understood in the sense of causes of civil action and causes of criminal prosecution. These do unquestionably affect the plaintiff in the one case, and the party against whose person or property the crime is committed in the other.

The soundness and authority of the judgment in the case of Ortega are not questioned; but it is by no means true, as a universal proposition, that none are affected in the legal sense of the term, by a case, but those who are parties to the record. The solution of the question must always depend upon the circumstances.

In *Osborn v. Bank of the United States*, 9 Wheat. [22 U. S.] 584, the court said: "If a suit be brought against a foreign minister, the supreme court has original jurisdiction, and this is shown in the record; but suppose a suit be brought which affects the interests of a foreign minister, or by which his servant, or his secretary, becomes a party to the suit, but the actual defendant pleads to the jurisdiction and asserts his privilege. If the suit affects a foreign minister it must be dismissed; not because he is a party to it, but because it affects him."

It may be asked, what is—if this is not—the proper construction of the statute? It has been answered that none are affected in criminal cases but the sovereign prosecuting and the defendants; and that hence colored persons only can be prosecuted under its provisions. When the act was passed there was no state where ample provision did not exist for the trial and punishment of persons of color for all offenses; and no locality where there was any difficulty in enforcing the law against them. There was no complaint upon the subject. The aid of congress was not invoked in that direction. It is not denied that the first and second sections were designed solely for their benefit. The third section, giving the jurisdiction to which this question relates, provides expressly that if sued or prosecuted in a state court under the circumstances mentioned, they may at once have the cause certified into a proper federal court.

The fourth section requires district-attorneys, marshals and their deputies, commissioners, agents of the freedmen's bureau, and other officers specially empowered by the president, to institute proceedings at the expense of the United States, against all persons violating the provisions of the act; and "with a view to affording reasonable protection to all persons in their constitutional rights of equality before the law, without distinction of race or color, or previous condition of slavery or involuntary servitude," it is made the duty of circuit courts of the United States to increase the number of their commissioners.

The fifth section imposes a heavy fine on marshals who shall refuse to receive or neglect to execute any process issued under the act; and it authorizes commissioners to appoint persons to serve such process issued by them.

The sixth section renders liable to fine and imprisonment any person who shall obstruct an officer or other person in the execution of such process; or who shall aid a person arrested to escape; or conceal a person for whose arrest a warrant has been issued.

Section eight authorizes the president to direct the judge, marshal, and district-attorney to attend at such place and for such time as he may designate, "for the purpose of the more speedy arrest and trial of persons charged with violations of this act."

The ninth section authorizes the president to employ such part of the land and naval forces of the United States, and of the militia, as shall be necessary to "prevent the violation and enforce the due execution of this act."

It is incredible that all this machinery, including the agency of the freedmen's bureau, would have been provided, if the intention were to limit the criminal jurisdiction conferred by the third section to colored persons, and exclude all white persons from its operation.

The title of the act is in harmony with this view of the subject. The construction contended for would obviously defeat the main object which congress had in view in passing the act, and produce results the opposite of those intended.

The difficulty was that where a white man was sued by a colored man, or was prosecuted for a crime against a colored man, colored witnesses were excluded. This in many cases involved a denial of justice. Crimes of the deepest dye were committed by white men with impunity. Courts and juries were frequently hostile to the colored man, and administered justice, both civil and criminal, in a corresponding spirit. Congress met these evils by giving to the colored man everywhere the same right to testify "as is enjoyed by white citizens," abolishing the distinction between white and colored witnesses, and by giving to the courts of the United States jurisdiction of all causes, civil and criminal, which concern him, wherever the right to testify as if he were white is denied to him or cannot be enforced in the local tribunals of the state.

The context and the rules of interpretation to be applied permit of no other construction. Such was clearly the intention of congress, and that intention constitutes the law.

This, with the provision which authorizes colored defendants in the state courts to have their causes certified into the federal courts, and the other provisions referred to, renders the protection which congress has given as effectual as it can well be made by legislation. It is one system, all the parts looking to the same end.

Where crime is committed with impunity by any class of persons, society, so far as they are concerned, is reduced to that condition of barbarism which compels those unprotected by other sanctions to rely upon physical force for the vindication of their natural rights. There is no other remedy, and no other security.

It is said there can be no such thing as a right to testify, and that if congress conferred it by this act, a cloud of colored witnesses may appear in every case and claim to exercise it. There is no force in this argument. The statute is to be construed reasonably. Like the right to sue and to contract, it is to be exercised only on proper occasions and within proper limits. Every right given is to be the same "as is enjoyed by white citizens."

It is urged that this is a penal statute, and to be construed strictly. We regard it as remedial in its character, and to be construed liberally, to carry out the wise and beneficent purposes of congress in enacting it.

But if the act were a penal statute, the canons of interpretation to be applied would not affect the conclusion at which we have arrived. This objection to the indictment cannot avail the defendants.

III. Is the act warranted by the constitution? The first eleven amendments of the constitution were intended to limit the powers of the government which it created, and to protect the people of the states. Though earnestly sustained by the friends of the constitution, they originated in the hostile feelings with which it was regarded by a large portion of the people, and were shaped by the jealous policy which those feelings inspired. The enemies of the constitution saw many perils of evil in the center, but none elsewhere. They feared tyranny in the head, not anarchy in the members, and they took their measures accordingly. The friends of the constitution desired to obviate all just grounds of apprehension, and to give repose to the public mind. It was important to unite, as far as possible, the entire people in support of the new system which had been adopted. They felt the necessity of doing all in their power to remove every obstacle in the way of its success. The most momentous consequences for good or evil to the country were to follow the results of the experiment. Hence the spirit of concession which animated the convention, and hence the adoption of these amendments after the work of the convention was done and had been approved by the people. The twelfth amendment grew out of the contest between Jefferson and Burr for the presidency. The thirteenth amendment is the last one made. It trenches directly upon the power of the states and of the people of the states. It is the first and only instance of a change of this character in the organic law. It destroyed the most important relation between capital and labor in all the states where slavery existed. It affected deeply the fortunes of a large portion of their people. It struck out of existence millions of property. The measure was the consequence of a strife of opinions, and a conflict of interests, real or imaginary, as old as the constitution itself. These elements of discord grew in intensity. Their violence was increased by the throes and convulsions of a civil war. The impetuous vortex finally swallowed up the evil and with it forever the power to restore it. Those who insisted upon the adoption of this amendment were animated by no spirit of vengeance. They sought security against the recurrence of a sectional conflict. They felt that much was due to the African race for the part it had borne during the war. They were also impelled by a sense of right and by a strong sense of justice to an unoffending and long-suffering people. These considerations must not be lost sight of when we come to examine the amendment in order to ascertain its proper construction.

The act of congress confers citizenship. Who are citizens, and what are their rights? The constitution uses the words "citizen" and "natural born citizens;" but neither that instrument nor any act of congress has attempted to define their meaning. British jurisprudence, whence so much of our own is drawn, throws little light upon the subject. In Johnson's Dictionary, "citizen" is thus defined: "(1) A freeman of a city; not a foreigner; not a slave; (2) a townsman, a man of trade; not a gentleman; (3) an inhabitant; a dweller in any place."

The definitions given by other English lexicographers are substantially the same. In Jacob's Law Dictionary (Ed. 1783), the only definition given is as follows: "Citizens (cives) of London are either freemen or such as reside and keep a family in the city, etc.; and some are citizens and freemen, and some are not, who have not so great privileges as others. The citizens of London may prescribe against a statute, because their liberties are reinforced by statute" 1 Rolle, 105.

Blackstone and Tomlin contain nothing upon the subject. "The word 'civis,' taken in the strictest sense, extends only to him that is entitled to the privileges of a city of which he is a member, and in that sense there is a distinction between a citizen and an inhabitant within the same city, for every inhabitant there is not a citizen." Scot v. Schwartz, Comyn, 677. "A citizen is a freeman who has kept a family in a city." Roy v. Hanger, 1 Rolle, 138, 149. "The term 'citizen,' as understood in our law, is precisely analogous to the term subject, in the common law; and the change of phrases has entirely resulted from the change of government. The sovereignty has been changed from one man to the collective body of the people, and he who before was a subject of the king is now a citizen of the state." State v. Manuel, 4 Dev. & B. 26.

In *Shanks v. Dupont*, 3 Pet. [28 U. S.] 247, the supreme court of the United States said: "During the war each party claimed the allegiance of the natives of the colonies as due exclusively to itself. The Americans insisted upon the allegiance of all born within the states, respectively; and Great Britain asserted an equally exclusive claim. The treaty of 1783 acted upon the state of things as it existed at that period. It took the actual state of things as its basis. All those, whether natives or otherwise, who then adhered to the American states, were virtually absolved from their allegiance to the British crown, and those who then adhered to the British crown, were deemed and held subjects of that crown. The treaty of peace was a treaty operating between the states on each side, and the inhabitants thereof; in the language of the seventh article, it was a 'firm and perpetual peace between his Britannic majesty and the said states, and between the subjects of one and the citizens of the other.' Who then were subjects or citizens was to be decided by the state of facts. If they were originally subjects of Great Britain and then adhered to her and were claimed by her as subjects, the treaty deemed them such; if they were originally British subjects, but then adhering to the states, the treaty deemed them citizens."

All persons born in the allegiance of the king are natural born subjects, and all persons born in the allegiance of the United States are natural born citizens. Birth and allegiance go together. Such is the rule of the common law, and it is the common law of this country, as well as of England. There are two exceptions, and only two, to the universality of its application. The children of ambassadors are in theory born in the allegiance of the powers the ambassadors represent, and slaves, in legal contemplation, are property, and not persons.

The common law has made no distinction on account of race or color. None is now made in England, nor in any other Christian country of Europe. The fourth of the Articles of Confederation declared that the "free inhabitants of each of these states, paupers, vagabonds, and fugitives from justice excepted, shall be entitled to all the privileges and immunities of free citizens in the United States," &c. On the 25th of June, 1778, when these articles were under consideration by the congress, South Carolina moved to amend this fourth article by inserting after the word "free" and before the word "inhabitants," the word "white." Two states voted for the amendment and eight against it. The vote of one was divided. When the constitution was adopted, free men of color were clothed with the franchise of voting in at least five states, and were a part of the people whose sanction breathed into it the breath of life.

"'Citizens' under our constitution and laws means free inhabitants born within the United States or naturalized under the laws of congress." 1 Kent, Comm. 292, note. We find no warrant for the opinion that this great principle of the common law has ever been changed in the United States. If has always obtained here with the same vigor, and subject only to the same exceptions, since as before the Revolution.

It is further said in the note in 1 Kent, Comm., before referred to: "If a slave born in the United States be manumitted or otherwise lawfully discharged from bondage, or if a black man born in the United States becomes free, he becomes thenceforward a citizen, but under such disabilities as the laws of the several states may deem it expedient to prescribe to persons of color."

In the case of State v. Manuel, supra, it was remarked: "It has been said that by the constitution of the United States, the power of naturalization has been conferred exclusively upon congress, and therefore it cannot be competent for any state by its municipal regulations to make a citizen. But what is naturalization? It is the removal of the disabilities of alienage. Emancipation is the removal of the incapacity of slavery. The latter depends wholly upon the internal regulations of the state. The former belongs to the government of the United States. It would be dangerous to confound them."

This was a decision of the supreme court of North Carolina, made in the year 1836. The opinion was delivered by Judge Gaston. He was one of the most able and learned judges this country has produced. The same court, in 1848, Chief Justice Ruffin delivering the opinion, referred to the case of State v. Manuel, and said: "That case underwent a very laborious investigation by both the bench and the bar. The case was brought here by appeal, and was felt to be one of very great importance in principle. It was considered with an anxiety and care worthy of the principle involved, and which give it a controlling influence upon all questions of similar nature."

We cannot deny the assent of our judgment to the soundness of the proposition that the emancipation of a native born slave by removing the disability of slavery made him a citizen. If these views be correct, the provision in the act of congress conferring citizenship was unnecessary, and is inoperative. Granting this to be so, it was well, if congress had the power, to insert it, in order to prevent doubts and differences of opinion which might otherwise have existed upon the subject. We are aware that a majority of the court, in the case of *Scott v. Sandford*, arrived at conclusions different from those we have expressed. But in our judgment these points were not before them. They decided that the whole case, including the agreed facts, was open to their examination, and that Scott was a slave. This central and controlling fact excluded all other questions, and what was said upon them by those of the majority, with whatever learning and ability the argument was conducted, is no more binding upon this court as authority than the views of the minority upon the same subjects.

The fact that one is a subject or citizen determines nothing as to his rights as such. They vary in different localities and according to circumstances. Citizenship has no necessary connection with the franchise of voting, eligibility to office, or indeed with any other rights, civil or political. Women, minors, and persons non compos are citizens, and not the less so on account of their disabilities. In England, not to advert to the various local regulations, the new reform bill gives the right of voting for members of parliament to about eight hundred thousand persons from whom it was before withheld. There, the subject is wholly within the control of parliament. Here, until the thirteenth amendment was adopted, the power belonged entirely to the states, and they exercised it without question from any quarter, as absolutely as if they were not members of the Union.

The first ten amendments to the constitution, which are in the nature of a bill of rights, apply only to the national government. They were not intended to restrict the power of the states.

Our attention has been called to several treaties by which Indians were made citizens; to those by which Louisiana, Florida, and California were acquired, and to the act passed in relation to Texas. All this was done under the war and treaty making powers of the constitution, and those which authorize the national government to regulate the territory and other property of the United States, and to admit new states into the Union.

These powers are not involved in the question before us, and it is not necessary particularly to consider them. A few remarks, however, in this connection will not be out of place. A treaty is declared by the constitution to be the "law of the land." What is unwarranted or forbidden by the constitution can no more be done in one way than in another. The authority of the national government is limited, though supreme in the sphere of its operation. As compared with the state governments, the subjects upon which it operates are few in number. Its objects are all national. It is one wholly of delegated powers. The states possess all which they have not surrendered; the government of the Union only such as the constitution has given to it, expressly or incidentally, and by reasonable intendment. Whenever an act of that government is challenged a grant of power must be shown, or the act is void.

"The power to make colored persons citizens has been actually exercised in repeated and important instances. See the treaty with the Choctaws of September 27, 1830, art. 14; with the Cherokees of May 20, 1836, art. 12; and the treaty of Guadeloupe Hidalgo, of February 2, 1848, art. 8." *Scott v. Sandford*, 19 Now. [60 U. S.] 486, opinion of Curtis, J.

See also, the treaty with France of April 30, 1803, by which Louisiana was acquired (article 3); and the treaty with Spain of the 23rd of February, 1819, by which Florida was acquired (article 3). The article referred to in the treaty with France and in the treaty with Spain is in the same language. In both the phrase "inhabitants" is used. No discrimination is made against those, in whole or in part, of the African race. So in the treaty of Guadeloupe Hidalgo (articles 8 and 9), no reference is made to color.

Our attention has been called to three provisions of the constitution, besides the thirteenth amendment, each of which will be briefly adverted to.

1. Congress has power "to establish an uniform rule of naturalization." Article 1, § 8. After considerable fluctuations of judicial opinion, it was finally settled by the supreme court that this power is vested exclusively in congress.

An alien naturalized is "to all intents and purposes a natural born subject." Co. Litt. 129. "Naturalization takes effect from birth; denization from the date of the patent." Vin. Abr. tit. "Alien," D. Until the passage of a late act of parliament, naturalization in England was effected by a special statute in each case. The statutes were usually alike. The form appears in Godfrey v. Dickson, Cro. Jac. 539, c. 7. Under the late act a resident alien may accomplish the object by a petition to the secretary of state for the home department.

The power is applicable only to those of foreign birth. Alienage is an indispensable element in the process. To make one of domestic birth a citizen is not naturalization, and cannot be brought within the exercise of that power. There is a universal agreement of opinion upon this subject.

In the exercise of this power congress has confined the law to white persons. No one doubts their authority to extend it to all aliens, without regard to race or color. But they were not bound to do so. As in other cases, it was for them to determine the extent and the manner in which the power given should be exercised. They could not exceed it, but they were not bound to exhaust it. It was well remarked by one of the dissenting judges, in *Scott v. Sandford*, 19 How. [60 U. S.] 586, in regard to the African race:

"The constitution has not excluded them, and since that has conferred on congress the power to naturalize colored aliens, it certainly shows color is not a necessary qualification for citizenship under the constitution of the United States."

It may be added that before the adoption of the constitution, the states possessed the power of making both those of foreign and domestic birth citizens, according to their discretion. This power, as to the former, they surrendered. They did not as to the latter, and they still possess it.

"The powers not delegated to the United States by this constitution, nor prohibited by it to the states, are reserved to the states respectively or to the people." Const. Amend. What the several states under the original constitution only could have done, the nation has done by the thirteenth amendment. An occasion for the exercise of this power by the states may not, perhaps cannot, hereafter arise.

2. "The citizens of each state shall be entitled to all the privileges and immunities of citizens in the several states." Const. art. 14, § 2. This provision of the constitution applies only to citizens going from one state to another. "It is obvious that if the citizens of each state were to be deemed aliens to each other, they could not take or hold real estate, or other privileges, except as other aliens." "The intention of this clause was to confer on them, as one may say, a general citizenship, and to communicate all the privileges and immunities which the citizens of the same state would be entitled to under the same circumstances." 2 Story, Const. § 187.

Chancellor Kent says: "If citizens remove from one state to another, they are entitled to the privileges that persons of the same description are entitled to in the states to which the removal is made, and to none other." 2 Kent, Comm. 36. This provision does not bear particularly upon the question before us, and need not be further considered.

3. "The United States shall guarantee to every state in this Union a republican form of government, and shall protect each of them against invasion, and on application of the legislature or of the executive (when the legislature cannot be convened), against domestic violence." Article 4, § 4.

Mr. Justice Story, adopting the language of the Federalist, says: "That but for this power a successful faction might erect a tyranny on the ruins of order and law, while no succor could be constitutionally afforded by the Union to the friends and supporters of the government." . . . "But a right implies a remedy, and where else could the remedy be deposited than where it is deposited by the constitution?" 2 Story, Const. 559, 560. This topic is foreign to the subject before us. We shall not pursue it further.

Congress, in passing the act under consideration, did not proceed upon this ground. It is not the theory or purpose of that act to apply the appropriate remedy for such a state of things. The constitutionality of the act cannot be sustained under this section.

This brings us to the examination of the thirteenth amendment. It is as follows:

"Article 13, § 1. Neither slavery nor involuntary servitude, except as a punishment for crime, whereof the party shall have been duly convicted, shall exist within the United States or any place subject to their jurisdiction.

"Sec. 2. Congress shall have power to enforce this article by appropriate legislation."

Before the adoption of this amendment, the constitution, at the close of the enumeration of the powers of congress, authorized that body "to make all laws which shall be necessary and proper for carrying into execution the foregoing powers, and all other powers vested by this constitution in the government of the United States, or any department or officer thereof."

In *McCullough* v. *Maryland,* 4 Wheat. [17 U. S.] 421–23, Chief Justice Marshall used the phrase "appropriate" as the equivalent and exponent of "necessary and proper" in the preceding paragraph. He said: "Let the end be legitimate, let it be within the scope of the constitution, and all the means which are appropriate, which are plainly adapted to the end, which are not prohibited, but consistent with the letter and spirit of the constitution, are constitutional." . . . "To use one" (a bank) "must be within the discretion of congress, if it be an appropriate mode of executing the powers of government." . . . "But were its necessity less apparent" (the Bank of the United States), "none can deny its being an appropriate measure; and if it is, the degree of its necessity, as has been justly observed, is to be discussed in another place."

Pursuing the subject, he added: "When the law is not prohibited, and is really calculated to effect any of the objects entrusted to the government, to undertake here to inquire into the degree of its necessity, would be to pass the line which circumscribes the judicial department, and to tread on legislative ground. This court disclaims all pretensions to such a power."

Judge Story says: "In the practical application of government, then, the public functionaries must be left at liberty to exercise the powers with which the people, by the constitution and laws, have entrusted them. They must have a wide discretion as to the choice of means; and the only limitation upon the discretion would seem to be that the means are appropriate to the end; and this must admit of considerable latitude, for the relation between the action and the end, as has been justly remarked, is not always so direct and palpable as to strike the eye of every observer. If the end be legitimate, and within the scope of the constitution, all the means which are appropriate, and which are plainly adapted to that end, and which are not prohibited, may be constitutionally employed to carry it into effect." 1 Story, Const. § 432.

These passages show the spirit in which the amendment is to be interpreted, and develop fully the principles to be applied. Before proceeding further, it would be well to pause and direct our attention to what has been deemed appropriate in the execution of some of the other powers confided to congress in like general terms.

1. "The power to lay and collect taxes, duties, and imposts." This includes authority to build custom houses; to employ revenue cutters; to appoint the necessary collectors and other officers; to take bonds for the performance of their duties; to establish the needful bureaus; to prescribe when, how, and in what the taxes and duties shall be paid; to rent or build warehouses for temporary storing purposes; to define all crimes relating to the subject in its various ramifications, with their punishment; and to provide for their prosecution.
2. "To regulate commerce with foreign nations, among the several states, and with the Indian tribes." This carries with it the power to build and maintain lighthouses, piers, and breakwaters; to employ revenue cutters; to cause surveys to be made of coasts, rivers, and harbors; to appoint all necessary officers, at home and abroad; to prescribe their duties, fix their terms of office and compensation; and to define and punish all crimes relating to commerce within the sphere of the constitution.
3. "To establish post-offices and post-roads." This gives authority to appoint a postmaster-general, and local postmasters throughout the country; to define their duties and compensation; to cause the mails to be carried by contract, or by the servants of the department, to all parts of the states and territories of the Union, and to foreign countries, and to punish crimes relating to the service, including obstructions to those engaged in transporting the mail while in the performance of their duty. The mail penal code comprises more than fifty offenses. All of them rest for their necessary constitutional sanction upon this power, thus briefly expressed.
4. "To raise and support armies." This includes the power to enlist such number of men for such periods and at such rates of compensation as may be deemed proper; to provide all the necessary officers, equipments, and

supplies, and to establish a military academy, where are taught military and such other sciences and branches of knowledge as may be deemed expedient, in order to prepare young men for the military service.

5. "To provide and maintain a navy." This authorizes the government to buy or build any number of steam or other ships of war, to man, arm, and otherwise prepare them for war, and to dispatch them to any accessible part of the globe. Under this power the naval academy has been established.

These are but a small part of the powers which are incidental and appropriate to the main powers expressly granted. It is Utopian to believe that without such constructive powers, the powers expressed can be so executed as to meet the intentions of the framers of the constitution, and to accomplish the objects for which governments are instituted. The constitution, provides expressly for the exercise of such powers to the full extent that may be "necessary and proper." No other limitation is imposed. Without this provision, the same result would have followed. The means of execution are inherently and inseparably a part of the power to be executed.

The constitution declares that "the senators and representatives before mentioned, and the members of the several state legislatures, and all executive and judicial officers, both of the United States and of the several states, shall be bound by oath to support this constitution." No other oath is required, "yet he would be charged with insanity who would contend that the legislature might not superadd to the oath directed by the constitution such other oath of office as its wisdom might suggest." *McCulloch v. Maryland,* 4 Wheat. [17 U. S.] 416.

The Bank of the United States, with all its faculties, was sustained because it was "convenient" and "appropriate" for the government in the management of its fiscal affairs. *McCulloch v. Maryland,* 4 Wheat. [17 U. S.] 316. Perhaps no measures of the national government have involved more doubt of their constitutionality than the acquisition of Louisiana and the embargo. Both were carried through congress by those who had been most strenuous for a strict construction of the constitution. Mr. Jefferson thought the former ultra vires, and advised an amendment of the constitution, but expressed a willingness to acquiesce if his friends should entertain a different opinion. 2 Story, Const. 160.

The Second Bank of the United States was a measure of the same class of thinkers. The acquisition of Florida involved the same question of constitutional power as the acquisition of Louisiana. It was universally acquiesced in; and the constitutional question was not raised.

It is an axiom in our jurisprudence, that an act of congress is not to be pronounced unconstitutional unless the defect of power to pass it is so clear as to admit of no doubt. Every doubt is to be resolved in favor of the validity of the law. "The opposition between the constitution and the law should be such, that the judge feels a clear and strong conviction of their incompatibility with each other." *Fletcher v. Peck,* 6 Cranch [10 U. S.] 128. "The presumption, indeed, must always be in favor of the validity of laws, if the contrary is not clearly demonstrated." *Cooper v. Telfair,* 4 Dall. [4 U. S.] 18. "A remedial power in the constitution is to be construed liberally." *Chisholm v. Georgia,* 2 Dall. [2 U. S.] 476.

"Perhaps the safest rule of interpretation, after all, will be found to be to look to the nature and objects of the particular powers, duties, and rights, with all lights and aids of contemporary history, and to give to the words of each just such operation and force, consistent with their legitimate meaning, as may fairly secure and attain the ends proposed."

Since the organization of the Supreme Court, but three acts of congress have been pronounced by that body void for unconstitutionality.

The present effect of the amendment was to abolish slavery wherever it existed within the jurisdiction of the United States. In the future it throws its protection over every one, of every race, color, and condition within that jurisdiction, and guards them against the recurrence of the evil. The constitution, thus amended, consecrates the entire territory of the republic to freedom, as well as to free institutions. The amendment will continue to perform its function throughout the expanding domain of the nation, without limit to time or space. Present possessions and future acquisitions will be alike within the sphere of its operation.

Without any other provision than the first section of the amendment, congress would have had authority to give full effect to the abolition of slavery thereby decreed. It would have been competent to put in requisition the executive and judicial, as well as the legislative power, with all the energy needful for that purpose. The second section of the amendment was added out of abundant caution. It authorizes congress to select, from time to time, the means that might be deemed appropriate to the end. It employs a phrase which had been enlightened by well-considered judicial application. Any exercise of legislative power within its limits involves a legislative, and not a judicial question. It is only when the authority given has been clearly exceeded, that the judicial power can be invoked. Its office, then, is to repress and annul the excess; beyond that it is powerless.

We will now proceed to consider the state of things which existed before and at the time the amendment was adopted, the mischiefs complained of or apprehended, and the remedy intended to be provided for existing and anticipated evils.

When the late Civil War broke out, slavery of the African race subsisted in fifteen states of the Union. The legal code relating to persons in that condition was everywhere harsh and severe. An eminent writer said: "They cannot take property by descent or purchase; and all they find and all they own belongs to their master. They cannot make contracts, and they are deprived of civil rights. They are assets for the payment of debts, and cannot be emancipated by will or otherwise to the prejudice of creditors." 2 Kent, Comm. 281, 282.

In a note, it is added: "In Georgia, by an act of 1829, no person is permitted to teach a slave, a negro, or a free person of color to read or write. So in Virginia, by a statute of 1830; meetings of free negroes to learn reading or writing are unlawful, and subject them to corporal punishment; and it is unlawful for white persons to assemble with free negroes or slaves to teach them to read or write. The prohibitory act of the legislature of Alabama, passed at the session of 1831-2, relative to the instruction to be given to the slaves or free colored population, or exhortation, or preaching to them, or any mischievous influence attempted to be exerted over them, is sufficiently penal. Laws of similar import are presumed to exist in the other slaveholding states, but in Louisiana the law on the subject is armed with ten-fold severity. It not only forbids any person teaching slaves to read or write, but it declares that any person using language in any public discourse from the bar, bench, stage, or pulpit, or any other place, or in any private conversation, or making use of any sign or actions having a tendency to produce discontent among the free colored population or insubordination among the slaves, or who shall be knowingly instrumental in bringing into the state any paper, book, or pamphlet having a like tendency, shall, on conviction, be punishable with imprisonment or death, at the discretion of the court."

Slaves were imperfectly, if at all, protected from the grossest outrages by the whites. Justice was not for them. The charities and rights of the domestic relations had no legal existence among them. The shadow of the evil fell upon the free blacks. They had but few civil and no political rights in the slave states. Many of the badges of the bondman's degradation were fastened upon them. Their condition, like his, though not so bad, was helpless and hopeless. This is borne out by the passages we have given from Kent's Commentaries. Further research would darken the picture. The states had always claimed and exercised the exclusive right to fix the status of all persons living within their jurisdiction.

On January 1, 1863, President Lincoln issued his proclamation of emancipation. Missouri and Maryland abolished slavery by their own voluntary action. Throughout the war the African race had evinced entire sympathy with the Union cause. At the close of the Rebellion two hundred thousand had become soldiers in the Union armies. The race had strong claims upon the justice and generosity of the nation. Weighty considerations of policy, humanity, and right were superadded. Slavery, in fact, still subsisted in thirteen states. Its simple abolition, leaving these laws and this exclusive power of the states over the emancipated in force, would have been a phantom of delusion. The hostility of the dominant class would have been animated with new ardor. Legislative oppression would have been increased in severity. Under the guise of police and other regulations slavery would have been in effect restored, perhaps in a worse form, and the gift of freedom would have been a curse instead of a blessing to those intended to be benefited. They would have had no longer the protection which the instinct of property leads its possessor to give in whatever form the property may exist. It was to guard against such evils that the second section of the amendment was framed. It was intended to give expressly to congress the requisite authority, and to leave no room for doubt or cavil upon the subject. The results have shown the wisdom of this forecast. Almost simultaneously with the adoption of the amendment this course of legislative oppression was begun. Hence, doubtless, the passage of the act under consideration. In the presence of these facts, who will say it is not an "appropriate" means of carrying out the object of the first section of the amendment, and a necessary and proper execution of the power conferred by the second? Blot out this act and deny the constitutional power to pass it, and the worst effects of slavery might speedily follow. It would be a virtual abrogation of the amendment.

It would be a remarkable anomaly if the national government, without this amendment, could confer citizenship on aliens of every race or color, and citizenship, with civil and political rights, on the "inhabitants" of Louisiana and Florida, without reference to race or color, and can not, with the help of the amendment, confer on those of the African race, who have been born and always lived within the United States, all that this law seeks to give them.

It was passed by the congress succeeding the one which proposed the amendment. Many of the members of both houses were the same. This fact is not without weight and significance.

The amendment reversed and annulled the original policy of the constitution, which left it to each state to decide exclusively for itself whether slavery should or should not exist as a local institution, and what disabilities should attach to those of the servile race within its limits. The whites needed no relief or protection, and they are practically unaffected by the amendment. The emancipation which it wrought was an act of great national grace, and was doubtless intended to reach further in its effects as to every one within its scope, than the consequences of a manumission by a private individual.

We entertain no doubt of the constitutionality of the act in all its provisions. It gives only certain civil rights. Whether it was competent for congress to confer political rights also, involves a different inquiry. We have not found it necessary to consider the subject.

We are not unmindful of the opinion of the court of appeals of Kentucky, in the case of *Brown v. Com.* [4 Metc. (Ky.) 221]. With all our respect for the eminent tribunal from which it proceeded, we have found ourselves unable to concur in its conclusions. The constitutionality of the act is sustained by the supreme court of Indiana, and the chief justice of the court of appeals of Maryland, in able and well-considered opinions.

We are happy to know that if we have erred the supreme court of the United States can revise our judgment and correct our error. The motion is overruled, and judgment will be entered upon the verdict.

Motion overruled.

Chronology

1850
Fugitive Slave Act, September 18, 1850

1854
Kansas-Nebraska Act, May 30, 1854

1856
American (Know-Nothing) Party Platform, February 21, 1856
Democratic Party Platform, June 2, 1856
Republican Party Platform, June 18, 1856

1857
Dred Scott v. *Sanford*, 19 Howard (60 U.S.) 393 (1857), March 5, 1857

1858
Lincoln's House Divided Speech, June 16, 1858

1859
Ableman v. *Booth*, 21 How. (62 U.S.) 506 (1859), March 2, 1859
Virginia Indictment of John Brown, October 16, 1859

1860
Abraham Lincoln, Cooper Union Speech, February 27, 1860
Lemmon v. *People*, 20 NY 562 (1860), March 1860
Frederick Douglass, The American Constitution and the Slave, March 26, 1860
Constitutional Union Party Platform, May 8, 1860
Republican Party Platform, May 17, 1860
Democratic Party Platform (Douglas Faction), June 18, 1860
Democratic Party Platform (Breckinridge Faction), June 18, 1860
Attorney General Jeremiah Black on Secession, November 20, 1860
Crittenden Compromise, December 18, 1860
South Carolina Ordinance of Secession, December 20, 1860

1861

Alabama Ordinance of Secession, January 11, 1861
Georgia Ordinance of Secession, January 19, 1861
President James Buchanan, State of the Union, January 29, 1861
Inauguration Speech of Jefferson Davis, February 22, 1861
Proposed 13th Amendment of 1860, March 2, 1861
First Inaugural of Abraham Lincoln, March 4, 1861
Lincoln's Presidential Order of April 15, 1861
Lincoln's Proclamation of Blockade, April 19, 1861
Robert E. Lee Letter of Resignation, April 20, 1861
Jefferson Davis, Message to Congress: "Our Cause is Just and Holy," April 29, 1861
Ex parte Merryman, 17 Fed. Cas. 144, Case # 9,487 (1861), April 1861
Kentucky Resolution of Neutrality and Governor's Statement, May 16, 1861.
Lincoln's Special Message to Congress, "A People's Contest," July 4, 1861
Crittenden-Johnson Resolutions, July 22/23, 1861
General Benjamin Butler on "Contraband," July 30, 1861
Seditious Conspiracy Act, July 31, 1861
First Confiscation Act, August 6, 1861
General John C. Fremont's martial law/emancipation policy, August 30, 1861
Karl Marx on the Civil War, October 11, 1861

1862

Thaddeus Stevens's Speech on Emancipation, January 22, 1862
Abolishment of Slavery in the District of Columbia Act, April 16, 1862
Confederate Conscription Act, April 17, 1862
Homestead Act, May 20, 1862
Pacific Railroad Act, July 1, 1862
Morrill Land Grant Act, July 2, 1862
Non-Issued Lincoln Veto to Second Confiscation Act, July 12, 1862
Supplement, Abolishment of Slavery in the District of Columbia Act, July 12, 1862
Judiciary Act, July 15, 1862
Militia Act, July 17, 1862
Second Confiscation Act, July 17, 1862
Supplement to Second Confiscation Act, July 17, 1862
Lincoln to Greeley, "I would save the Union," August 22, 1862
Preliminary Emancipation Proclamation, September 22, 1862
Confederate Conscription Act, "Twenty Slave" Amendment, October 11, 1862
President Lincoln's Message to Congress, December 1, 1862
West Virginia Act, December 31, 1862

1863

Emancipation Proclamation, January 1, 1863
National Banking Act, February 25, 1863
Federal Conscription Act of March 3, 1863
Habeas Corpus Act, March 3, 1863
Prize Cases, 2 Black (67 U.S.) 635 (1863), March 10, 1863
General Order 100, Lieber Code, April 23, 1863
Grant to Lincoln on use of African-American troops, August 23, 1863
Lincoln's 10% Plan, December 8, 1863

1864

Gelpke v. *City of Dubuque*, 1 Wallace (68 U.S.) 175 (1864), January 11, 1864
Ex parte Vallandigham, 1 Wallace (68 U.S.) 243 (1864), February 15, 1864
Republican (National Union) Party Platform, June 8, 1864
Wade/Davis Plan of July 2, 1864
Pocket Veto and Wade/Davis Manifesto, August 5, 1864
Grant on Reconstruction, August 16, 1864
Democratic Party Platform, August 29, 1864
Lincoln to Sherman, 'Needs Soldier Vote,' September 19, 1864

1865

Freedman's Bureau Act, March 3, 1865
Lincoln's Second Inaugural, March 4, 1865
Attorney General James Speed, Opinion on Lincoln Murder Trial, April 28, 1865
President Johnson's Proclamation of Amnesty, May 29, 1865
President Johnson's Proclamation of Concerning the Government of North Carolina, May 29, 1865
Attorney General James Speed, Extended Opinion on Lincoln Murder Trial, July—, 1865
Thaddeus Stevens, September 9, 1865, Lancaster Speech
Thirteenth Amendment, December 6, 1865
Thaddeus Stevens, Reconstruction, December 18, 1865
Grant Southern Tour Report, December 18, 1865

1866

U.S. v. *Rhodes*, 27 Fed. Cas. 785, Case # 16,151 (1866), 1866
President Johnson's veto of Freedman's Bureau Act, February 19, 1866
President Johnson's Veto of Civil Rights Act of March 27, 1866
Ex parte Milligan, 4 Wallace (71 U.S.) 2 (1866), April 3, 1866
Civil Rights Act of April 9, 1866

Freedman's Bureau Act, July 16, 1866
President Johnson's Veto of Freedman's Bureau Act, July 16, 1866
Judicial Circuits Act, July 23, 1866
Union Party Convention, August 7, 1866
Republican National Convention, September 3, 1866.

1867

Cummings v. Missouri, 4 Wallace (71 U.S.) 277 (1867), January 14, 1867
Ex parte Garland, 4 Wallace (71 U.S.) 333 (1867), January 14, 1867
Habeas Corpus Act, February 5, 1867
[First] Reconstruction Act, March 2, 1867
President Johnson's Veto of [First] Reconstruction Act, March 2, 1867
Tenure of Office Act, March 2, 1867
President Johnson's Veto of Tenure of Office Act, March 2, 1867
Anti-Peonage Act of March 2, 1867
[Second] Reconstruction Act, March 23, 1867
President Johnson's Veto of the [Second] Reconstruction Act, March 23, 1867
West Chester and Philadelphia Railroad Co. v. Miles, 55 Pa. 209 (1867), April 1, 1867
[Third] Reconstruction Act, July 19, 1867
President Johnson's Veto of the Third Reconstruction Act, July 19, 1867

1868

Georgia v. Stanton, 6 Wallace (73 U.S.) 50 (1867), February 10, 1868
Articles of Impeachment of President Andrew Johnson, February 24, 1868
[Fourth] Reconstruction Act, March 11, 1868
Republican Party Platform, May 20, 1868
Democratic Party Platform, July 4, 1868
Fourteenth Amendment, July 9, 1868

1869

Grant's First Inaugural, March 4, 1869
Texas v. White, 7 Wallace (74 U.S.) 700 (1869), April 12, 1869
Ex parte McCardle, 7 Wallace (74 U.S.) 506 (1869), April 12, 1869
Ex parte Yerger, 8 Wallace (75 U.S.) 85 (1869), December 1869

1870

Fifteenth Amendment, February 3, 1870
Hepburn v. Griswold, 8 Wallace (75 U.S.) 603 (1870), February 7, 1870
Enforcement Acts of May 30, 1870

1871

Enforcement Act of April 20, 1871
Second Legal Tender Cases, 12 Wallace (79 U.S.) 457 (1871), May 1, 1871
Virginia v. *West Virginia*, 11 Wallace (78 U.S.) 39 (1871), December 1871
Blyew v. *U.S.*, 13 Wallace (80 U.S.) 581 (1872), December 1871

1872

Liberal Republican Platform, May 2, 1872
Republican Party Platform, June 5, 1872
Democratic Party Platform, June 9, 1872

1873

Grant's Second Inaugural, March 4, 1873
Slaughterhouse Cases, 16 Wallace (83 U.S.) 36 (1873), April 14, 1873
Bradwell v. *Illinois*, 16 Wallace (83 U.S.) 130 (1873), April 15, 1873

1875

Civil Rights Act of March 1, 1875

1876

U.S. v. *Cruikshank*, 92 U.S. 542 (1876), March 27, 1876
U.S. v. *Reese*, 92 U.S. 214 (1876), March 27, 1876
Republican Party Platform, June 14, 1876
Democratic Party Platform, June 22, 1876

1877

Congressional Electoral Commission, January 29, 1877
Hayes Inaugural, March 5, 1877

1878

Hall v. *DeCuir*, 95 U.S. 485 (1878), January 14, 1878
Posse Comitatus Act of June 18, 1878

1883

U.S. v. *Harris*, 106 U.S. 629 (1883), January 22, 1883
Civil Rights Cases, 109 U.S. 3 (1883), October 15, 1883

1896

Plessy v. *Ferguson*, 163 U.S. 537 (1896), May 18, 1896

Selected Readings

Baker, Jean. *James Buchanan*. Times Books, 2004.

Belz, Herman. *A New Birth of Freedom: The Republican Party and Freedman's Rights, 1861–1866*. Westport, CN.: Greenwood Press, 1976.

———. *Emancipation and Equal Rights: Politics and Constitutionalism in the Civil War Era*. New York: W.W. Norton, 1978.

———. *Reconstructing the Union: Theory and Policy during the Civil War*. Ithaca, NY.: Cornell University Press, 1969.

Benedict, Michael Les. *A Compromise of Principle: Congressional Republicans and Reconstruction*. New York: W.W. Norton, 1974.

———, *The Impeachment and Trial of Andrew Johnson*. New York: W.W. Norton, 1999.

———, *The Fruits of Victory: Alternatives in Restoring the Union, 1865–1877*. Lanham: University Press of America, 1986.

Bentley, George R. *A History of the Freedman's Bureau*. Philadelphia: University of Pennsylvania, 1955.

Bogue, Allen G. *The Congressman's Civil War*. New York: Cambridge University Press, 1989.

———. *The Earnest Men: Republicans of the Civil War Senate*. Ithaca, NY.: Cornell University Press, 1981.

Brodie, Fawn N. *Thaddeus Stevens: Scourge of the South*. New York: W.W. Norton & Co., 1959.

Burlingame, Michael. *Abraham Lincoln: A Life*, 2 Vols. Baltimore, MD.: The Johns Hopkins University Press, 2008.

Burton, Orville Vernon. *The Age of Lincoln*. New York: Hill & Wang, 2007.

Carnahan, Burrus M. *Act of Justice: Lincoln's Emancipation Proclamation and the Law of War*. Lexington: University Press of Kentucky, 2007.

———. *Lincoln on Trial: Southern Civilians and the Law of War*. Lexington: University Press of Kentucky, 2010.

Carter, Dan. *When the War Was Over: The Failure of Self-Reconstruction in the South, 1865–1867*. Baton Rouge: Louisiana State University Press, 1985.

Carwardine, Richard. *Lincoln: A Life of Purpose and Power*. New York: Knopf, 2006.

Castle, Albert. *The Presidency of Andrew Johnson*. Lawrence: Regents Press of Kansas, 1979.

Cooper, Jr., William J. *Jefferson Davis, American*. New York: Knopf, 2000.

Cox, LaWanda. *Lincoln and Black Freedom: A Study in Presidential Leadership*. Columbia: University of South Carolina Press, 1981.

Cox, LaWanda, and John Cox. *Politics, Principle, and Prejudice, 1865–1866: The Dilemma of Reconstruction America*. New York: Free Press of Glencoe, 1963.

Currie, David P. *Constitution in Congress: Descent into the Maelstrom, 1829–1861*. Chicago: University of Chicago Press, 2005.

———. *Constitution in the Supreme Court: The First Hundred Years, 1789–1888*. Chicago: University of Chicago Press, 1985.

Curry, Leonard P. *Blueprint for Modern America: Non-Military Legislation of the First Civil War Congress*. Nashville, TN.: Vanderbilt University Press, 1968.

Curtis, Michael Kent. *No State Shall Abridge: The 14th Amendment and the Bill of Rights*. Durham, NC.: Duke University Press, 1986.

Dollar, Kent T., Larry H. Whiteaker, and W. Calvin Dickinson, eds. *Sister States, Enemy States: The Civil War in Kentucky and Tennessee*. Lexington: University Press of Kentucky, 2009.

Donald, David Herbert. *Civil War and Reconstruction*. New York: W.W. Norton, 2001.

———, ed. *Inside Lincoln's Cabinet: The Civil War Diaries of Salmon P. Chase*. New York: Longmans, Green and Co, 1954.

———. *Liberty and Union: The Crisis of Popular Government, 1830–1890*. Boston: Little, Brown and Co., 1978.

———. *Lincoln*. New York: Simon and Schuster, 1995.

———. *Lincoln's Herndon*. New York: Alfred A. Knopf, Inc., 2007.

———. *Politics of Reconstruction, 1863–1867*. Cambridge: Harvard University Press, 1984.

Epps, Garrett. *Democracy Reborn: The Fourteenth Amendment and the Fight for Equal Rights in Post–Civil War America*. New York: Henry Holt, 2006.

Ehrlich, Walter. *They Have No Rights: Dred Scott's Struggle for Freedom*. Westport, CN.: Greenwood Press, 1979.

Eicher, David J. *The Civil War in Books: An Analytical Bibliography*. Urbana: University of Illinois Press, 1997.

Fairman, Charles. *Reconstruction and Reunion, 1864–1888: Part One*. New York: Macmillin, 1971.

Farber, Daniel. *Lincoln's Constitution*. Chicago: University of Chicago Press, 2003.

Fehrenbacher, Don E. *The Dred Scott Case: Its Significance in American Law and Politics*. New York: Oxford University Press, 1978.

———. *Prelude to Greatness: Lincoln in the 1850s*. Stanford, CA.: Stanford University Press, 1962.

Ferrell, Claudine L. *Reconstruction*. Westport, CN.: Greenwood Press, 2003.

Finkelman, Paul. *An Imperfect Union: Slavery, Federalism, and Comity* (Chapel Hill: University of North Carolina Press, 1980.

———. *Dred Scott v. Sanford: A Brief History with Documents*. Boston: Bedford/St. Martin's, 1997.

———, ed. *His Soul Goes Marching On: Responses to John Brown and the Harper Ferry Raid*. Charlottesville: University Press of Virginia, 1995.

———. *Slavery in the Courtroom: An Annotated Bibliography of American Cases*. Washington, D.C.: Library of Congress, 1985.

Foner, Eric. *The Fiery Trial: Abraham Lincoln and American Slavery*. New York: W.W. Norton, 2010.

———. *Forever Free: The Story of Emancipation and Reconstruction*. New York: Knopf, 2005.

———. *Free Soil, Free Labor, Free Men: The Ideology of the Republican Party Before the Civil War*. New York: Oxford University Press, 1995.

———, *Nothing but Freedom: Emancipation and Its Legacy*. Baton Rouge: Louisiana State University Press, 1983.

———. *Politics and Ideology in the Age of the Civil War*. New York: Oxford University Press, 1980.

———. *Reconstruction: America's Unfinished Revolution, 1863–1877*. New York: Harper & Row, 1988.

———. *Slavery and Freedom in Nineteenth-Century America*. New York: Oxford University Press, 1994.

Foner, Eric, and Olivia Mahoney. *A House Divided: America in the Age of Lincoln*. Chicago: Chicago Historical Society, 1990.

Ford, Lacy K., ed. *A Companion to the Civil War and Reconstruction*. Malden, MA.: Blackwell Publishing, 2005.

Franklin, John Hope. *The Emancipation Proclamation*. Garden City, NY.: Doubleday, 1963.

Fredrickson, George E. *The Inner Civil War: Northern Intellectuals and the Crisis of the Union*. New York: Harper & Row, 1965).

Freehling, William W. *The Road to Disunion: Volume II: Secessionists Triumphant, 1854–1861*. (New York: Oxford University Press, 2007).

Gillette, William. *Retreat from Reconstruction, 1869–1879*. Baton Rouge: Louisiana State University Press, 1979.

———. *The Right to Vote: Politics and the Passage of the Fifteenth Amendment*. Baltimore, MD.: The Johns Hopkins University Press, 1965.

Guelzo, Allen C. *Lincoln's Emancipation Proclamation: The End of Slavery in America*. New York: Simon & Schuster, 2004.

Halliday, Paul D. *Habeas Corpus: From England to Empire*. Cambridge, MA.: Belknap Press of Harvard University Press, 2010.

Hamilton, Daniel W. *The Limits of Sovereignty: Property Confiscation in the Union and Confederacy during the Civil War*. Chicago: University of Chicago Press, 2007.

Harris, William C. *With Charity for All: Lincoln and the Restoration of the Union*. Lexington: University Press of Kentucky, 1997.

Hoffer, Peter Charles, Williamjames Hull Hoffer, and N.E.H. Null. *The Supreme Court: An Essential History*. Lawrence, KS.: University Press of Kansas, 2007.

Holt, Michael L. *By One Vote: The Disputed Election of 1876*. Lawrence: University of Kansas Press, 2008.

Holzer, Harold. *Lincoln at Cooper Union: The Speech That Made Abraham Lincoln President*. New York: Simon and Schuster, 2004.

———. *Lincoln President-Elect: Abraham Lincoln and the Great Secession Winter, 1860–1861*. New York: Simon and Schuster, 2008.

Hoogenboom, Ari Arthur. *The Presidency of Rutherford B. Hayes*. Lawrence: University Press of Kansas, 1988.

———. *Rutherford B. Hayes: Warrior and President*. Lawrence: University Press of Kansas, 1995.

Huebner, Timothy S. *Taney Court: Justices, Rulings, and Legacy*. Santa Barbara, CA.: ABC-Clio, 2003.

Hyman, Harold Melvin. *Era of the Oath: Northern Loyalty Tests During the Civil War and Reconstruction* (Philadelphia: University of Pennsylvania Press, 1954).

———. *A More Perfect Union: The Impact of the Civil War and Reconstruction on the Constitution*. New York: Alfred A. Knopf, Inc., 1973.

———. *The Reconstruction Justice of Salmon P. Chase: In Re Turner and Texas v. White*. Lawrence: University Press of Kansas, 1997.

———. *To Try Men's Souls: Loyalty Tests in American History*. Santa Barbara: Greenwood Press, 1982.

Hyman, Harold Melvin, and William W. Wiecek. *Equal Justice Under Law: Constitutional Development, 1835–1875*. New York: HarperCollins Publishers, 1982.

Kaczorowski, Robert J. *The Politics of Judicial Interpretation: Federal Courts, the Department of Justice, and Civil Rights, 1866–1876*. Dobbs Ferry, NY.: Oceana Publications, 1985).

Keith, LeeAnna. *The Colfax Massacre: The Untold Story of Black Power, White Terror, & The Death of Reconstruction*. New York: Oxford University Press, 2008.

Klein, Phillip Shriver. *James Buchanan, A Biography*. University Park: Pennsylvania State University Press, 1962.

Konig, David T., Paul Finkelman, and Christopher A. Bracey, eds. *The Dred Scott Case: Historical and Contemporary Perspectives on Race and Law*. Athens: Ohio University Press, 2010.

Kutler, Stanley I. *Judicial Power and Reconstruction Politics*. Chicago: University of Chicago Press, 1968.

Labbé, Ronald M. and Jonathan Lurie. *The Slaughterhouse Cases: Regulation, Reconstruction, and the Fourteenth Amendment*. Lawrence: University Press of Kansas, 2003.

Lewis, H. H. Walker. *Without Fear or Favor: A Biography of Chief Justice Roger B. Taney*. Boston: Houghton Mifflin, 1965.

Lofgren, Charles A. *The Plessy Case: A Legal-Historical Interpretation*. New York: Oxford University Press, 1987.

Maltz, Earl M. *Civil Rights, the Constitution, and Congress, 1863–1869*. Lawrence: University Press of Kansas, 1990.

———. *Slavery and the Supreme Court, 1825–1861*. Lawrence: University Press of Kansas, 2009.

Mantell, Martin E. *Johnson, Grant, and the Politics of Reconstruction*. New York: Columbia University Press, 1973.

Masur, Louis P. *Lincoln's Hundred Days: The Emancipation Proclamation and the War for the Union*. Cambridge, MA.: Belknap Press of the Harvard University Press, 2012.

McFeeley, William S. *Frederick Douglass*. New York: W. W. Norton & Co., 1991.

———. *Grant: A Biography*. New York: W. W. Norton & Co., 1981.

McGinty, Brian. *John Brown's Trial*. Cambridge, MA.: Harvard University Press, 2009.

———. *Lincoln & the Court*. Cambridge, MA.: Harvard University Press, 2008.

McPherson, James M. *Abraham Lincoln*. Oxford: Oxford University Press, 2009.

———. *Abraham Lincoln and the Second American Revolution*. New York: Oxford University Press, 1990.

———. *Battle Cry of Freedom: The Civil War Era*. New York: Oxford University Press, 1988.

———. *Lincoln and the Strategy of Unconditional Surrender*. Gettysburg: Gettysburg College, 1984.

———. *Marching Toward Freedom: Blacks in the Civil War, 1861–1865*. New York: Facts on File, 1965.

———. *The Negro's Civil War: How American Negroes Felt and Acted during the War for the Union*. New York: Ballantine Books, 1991.

———. *Ordeal by Fire: The Civil War and Reconstruction*. New York: Knopf, 1982.

———. *The Struggle for Equality: Abolitionists and the Negro in the Civil War and Reconstruction*. Princeton: Princeton University Press, 1964.

———. *Tried by War: Abraham Lincoln as Commander in Chief*. New York: Penguin Press, 2008.

Morris, Thomas D. *Southern Slavery and the Law, 1619–1860*. Chapel Hill: University of North Carolina Press, 1996.

Neely, Mark E., Jr. *The Fate of Liberty: Abraham Lincoln and Civil Liberties*. New York: Oxford University Press, 1991.

———. *The Last Best Hope of Earth: Abraham Lincoln and the Promise of America*. Cambridge, MA.: Harvard University Press, 1993.

———. *Southern Rights: Political Prisoners and the Myth of Confederate Constitutionalism*. Charlottesville: University of Virginia Press, 1999.

Neff, Stephen C. *Justice in Blue and Gray: A Legal History of the Civil War*. Cambridge, MA.: Harvard University Press, 2010.

Nelson, William E. *The Fourteenth Amendment: From Political Principle to Judicial Doctrine*. Cambridge: Harvard University Press, 1998.

Niven, John. *Salmon P. Chase: A Biography*. New York: Oxford University Press, 1995.

Nevins, Allan. *Ordeal of the Union*, 8 Vols. New York: Charles Scribner's Sons, 1947–71.

Newmyer, R. Kent. *Supreme Court under Marshall and Taney*. New York: Cromwell, 1968.

Nieman, Donald G. *Promises to Keep: African-Americans and the Constitutional Order, 1776 to the Present*. New York: Oxford University Press, 1991.

———. *To Set the Law in Motion: The Freedman's Bureau and the Legal Rights of Blacks, 1865–1868*. Millwood, NY.: KTO Press, 1979.

Oates, Stephen B. *To Purge This Land With Blood: A Biography of John Brown*. Amherst: University of Massachusetts Press, 1970.

———. *With Malice Toward None: A Life of Abraham Lincoln*. New York: Harper & Row, 1977.

Paludan, Phillip Shaw. *A Covenant With Death: The Constitution, Law, and Equality in the Civil War Era*. Champaign: University of Illinois Press, 1975.

———. *"A People's Contest": The Union and Civil War 1861–1865*. Lawrence: University Press of Kansas, 1996.

———. *The Presidency of Abraham Lincoln*. University Press of Kansas, 1994.

Perman, Michael. *Reunion Without Compromise: The South and Reconstruction, 1865–1868*. Cambridge: Cambridge University Press, 1973.

Polakoff, Keith Ian. *The Politics of Inertia: The Election of 1876 and the End of Reconstruction*. Baton Rouge: Louisiana State University Press, 1973.

Potter, David. *The Impending Crisis, 1848–1861*. New York: Harper & Row, 1976.

Rawley, James A. *Race and Politics: "Bleeding Kansas" and the Coming of the Civil War*. Philadelphia: Lippincott, 1969.

Richardson, Heather Cox. *The Death of Reconstruction: Race, Labor, and Politics in the Post–Civil War North, 1865–1901*. Cambridge, MA.: Harvard University Press, 2001.

———. *The Greatest Nation of the Earth: Republican Economic Policies During the Civil War*. Cambridge, MA.: Harvard University Press, 1997.

———. *West from Appomattox: The Reconstruction of America after the Civil War*. New Haven, CT.: Yale University Press, 2007.

Riddleberger, Patrick W. *1866: The Critical Year Revisited*. Carbondale: Southern Illinois University Press, 1979.

Russo, Peggy A. and Paul Finkelman, eds. *Terrible Swift Sword: The Legacy of John Brown*. Athens: Ohio University Press, 2005.

Sefton, James E. *Andrew Johnson and the Uses of Constitutional Power*. Boston: Little, Brown, 1980.

———. *The United States Army and Reconstruction, 1865–1877*. Baton Rouge: Louisiana University Press, 1967.

Sibley, Joel H. *A Respectable Minority: The Democratic Party in the Civil War Era, 1860–1868*. New York: W.W. Norton & Co., 1977.

Siddali, Silvanna R. *From Property to Person: Slavery and the Confiscation Acts, 1861–1862*. Baton Rouge: Louisiana State University Press, 2005.

Silver, David M. *Lincoln's Supreme Court*. Urbana: University of Illinois Press, 1956.

Simon, John F. *Lincoln and Chief Justice Taney: Slavery, Secession and the President's War Power*. New York: Simon & Schuster, 2006.

Simpson, Brooks D. *Let Us Have Peace: Ulysses S. Grant and the Politics of War and Reconstruction, 1861–1868*. Chapel Hill: University of North Carolina Press, 1991.

———. *The Reconstruction Presidents*. Lawrence: University Press of Kansas, 1998.

Swisher, Carl B. *Roger B. Taney*. New York: Macmillan Co., 1935.

Tap, Bruce. *Over Lincoln's Shoulder: The Committee on the Conduct of the War*. Lawrence: University Press of Kansas, 1998.

TenBroeck, Jacobus. *Equal Under Law: Anti-Slavery Origins of the Fourteenth Amendment*. New York: Collier, 1965.

Trefousse, Hans L. *Andrew Johnson: A Biography*. New York: W.W. Norton, 1997.

———. *Benjamin Franklin Wade: Radical Republican from Ohio*. New York: Twayne Publishers Inc., 1963.

———. *Causes of the Civil War: Institutional Failure or Human Blunder*. Malabar: Krieger Publishing Co., 1983.

———. *First Among Equals: Abraham Lincoln's Reputation During His Administration*. Bronx: Fordham University Press, 2005.

———. *Impeachment of a President: Andrew Johnson, the Blacks, and Reconstruction*. Bronx: Fordham University Press, 1999.

———. *The Radical Republicans: Lincoln's Vanguard for Racial Justice*. Baton Rouge: Louisiana State University Press, 1969.

———. *Reconstruction: America's First Effort at Radical Democracy*. Malabar: Krieger Publishing Co., 1999.

———. *Rutherford B. Hayes*. Times Books, 2002.

———. *Thaddeus Stevens: Nineteenth-Century Egalitarian*. Knoxville: University of Tennessee Press, 1982.

Trefousse, Hans L. and Arthur M. Schlesinger, Jr., ed. *Rutherford B. Hayes*. New York: Times Books, 2002.

U.S. War Department. *The War of the Rebellion: A Compilation of the Official Records of the Union and Confederate Armies*, 70 Vols. Washington, D.C.: Government Printing Office, 1880–1901.

Vorenberg, Michael. *Final Freedom: The Civil War, the Abolition of Slavery, and the Thirteenth Amendment*. New York: Cambridge University Press, 2001.

Waugh, Joan. *U.S. Grant: American Hero, American Myth*. Chapel Hill: University of North Carolina Press, 2009.

Weigley, Russell F. *A Great Civil War: A Military and Political History, 1861–1865*. Bloomington: Indiana University Press, 2000.

White, Ronald C., Jr. *A. Lincoln: A Biography*. New York: Random House, 2009.

Williams, Lou Falkner. *The Great South Carolina Ku Klux Klan Trials, 1871–1872*. Athens: University of Georgia Press, 1996.

Witt, John Fabian. *Lincoln's Code: The Laws of War in American History*. New York: Free Press, 2012.

Woodward, C. Vann. *The Strange Career of Jim Crow*, 3rd ed. New York: Oxford University Press, 1989.

Wooster, Ralph A. *The Secession Conventions of the South*. Princeton, NJ.: Princeton University Press, 1962.

Index

Abel, Lieutenant William H., 321
Abelman v. *Booth* (1859), 203–18, 533
Ableman, Stephen V. R., 203, 205–6
Abolishment of Slaver in the District of Columbia Act (1862), vii, xvi, 534
Adams, John Quincy, 101, 190, 480, 487
Adams, Samuel, 95, 99–100
Allen, George W., 336
Allison, 391
Allstadt, John H., 221, 223
Allstadt, John M., 220
Amanda (slave), 226
André, John 484
Ann (slave), 226
Arizona Territory Act, Confederate, xviii–xix
Armstrong, Benjamin, 451
Arnold, Benedict, 484

Bacon, Judge William J., 250, 272
Baldwin, Judge Caleb, 418
Baldwin, Associate Justice Henry, 109, 114, 237, 493
Ball, Armstead, 220, 223
Bangs, Edward, 337
Barrot, Odilon, 445
Baylor, Colonel Robert W., 221
Beckham, Fontaine, 220, 222–23
Ben Jerry (slave), 221
Berry, L. A., 285
Betts, Judge Samuel Roissiter, 351
Bill (slave), 221
Bissell, Frederick E., 400
Black, Jeremiah S., 204, 425, 459, 477, 487

Blackstone, William, 170, 231, 327–30, 442, 462, 521
Blair, Associate Justice John, Jr., 307
Blair, Montgomery, 7
Blunt, Joseph, 240
Boerly, Thomas, 220, 222–23
Bodin, Jean, 88, 241
Bolivar, General Simon, 480
Bonaparte, Napoleon, 96, 444
Booth, Sherman M., 203–9
Borcaut, Jean, 241
Bowdoin, James, 453
Boyle, John, 202
Brailsford, Samuel, 307–8
Baxter, Richard, 468
Brooke, Judge, 393, 403
Brougham, Lord Henry, 454, 484, 503
Brown, Charles, 336
Brown, John, xviii, 219– 224, 533
Brown, Robert T., 223
Brus, Joseph A., 223
Buchanan, James, xvii, 454, 534
Bunyan, John, 468
Burnside, General Ambrose, 379–80, 383
Burr, Aaron, 324, 520
Burrill, Alexander Mansfield, 518
Butler, Benjamin F., 425, 428, 474

Cadwalader, Judge John, 351
Cadwalader, General George, 319–23
Campbell, Associate Justice John A., DS concurrence 85–105, 247
Campbell, George W., 202
Carlisle, James M., 337
Catesby (slave), 221

Catron, Associate Justice John, DS concurrence 105–15, 236, 378
Charlemagne, 87
Charles I, 329, 455, 461, 466, 483
Charles II, 504
Charles X, 444
Charlotte (slave), 283, 285–86
Chase, Chief Justice Salmon P., xiv, xvi, 226, 420, 505
Chase, Associate Justice Samuel, 92, 94
Civil Rights Act (1866), xii, xiv, xvii, 3, 5, 515–16, 535
Civil Rights Act (1875), 3, 537
Clay, Henry, 121
Clerke, Judge Thomas W., 250, 272
Clifford, Associate Justice Nathan, 378
Clinton, George, 95
Cochrane, Admiral Thomas, 119
Cockburn, Admiral George, 241
Coke, Lord Edward, 361, 462, 470
Commonwealth v. *Aves* (1836), 152, 167, 228, 243, 245
Comstock, Chief Judge George F., 250, 272, 281
Confederate Conscription Act (1862), xvii, 534
Confiscation Act (1861), xvii, 534
Confiscation Act (1862), xvii, 534
Cook, John E., 221
Cooper, 288
Copland, John, 220–23
Coppie, Edwin, 220–23
Cox, Samuel Sullivan, 382
Currie, David, 336, 362
Currie, William, 336
Curtis, Associate Justice Benjamin R., 53, 115; DS dissent, 144–202, 239, 524
Curtis, George T. [incorrectly listed in case as "F."], 7
Curtis, George Ticknor, 276–77
Cushing, Caleb, 25
Cushing, Associate Justice William, 307

Dagget, Chief Justice, Connecticut Supreme Court, David, 20

Dana Richard Henry, 337, 345
Dangerfield, John E. P., 220, 223
Daniel, Associate Justice Peter V., DS concurrence 65–85, 193, 239
Darnall, Nicholas, 27–28
Darnell, Thomas, 451
Davies, Judge Henry E., 250, 272
Davis, Associate Justice David, 420, 489
Davis, Jefferson, xv–xviii, 534; Letters of Marque, xvi
Dennison, Governor William, 283, 288–90, 293, 297
De Lafayette, Marquis (Gilbert du Mortier), 485
De Lolme, Jean-Louis, 480
De Tocqueville, Alexis-Charles-Henri Clérel Alexis, 462
Dickinson, John, 99
Denio, Judge Hiram, 250
Donoho, John, 220
Douglas, Stephen, 5
Downey, W. S., 285
Dred Scott v. *Emerson* (1852), 86, 134, 137, 142, 144, 175
Dred Scott v. *Sandford* (1857), xv, xviii, 3, 5–202, 226, 228, 239, 247–48, 267, 278, 284, 533; plea of abatement, 6–11, 30–32, 54–56, 65, 67–70, 76, 84, 105–6, 115, 117, 147; Missouri Compromise (1820), 5, 6, 53, 80, 106, 112, 114, 129–30, 136, 139–40, 142, 165, 202; "they have no rights," 13
Dunlap, James, 336
Dunlop, Judge James, 351
Dunmore, Lord (Thomas Murray), 99, 443, 452, 462, 503
Dupin, André Marie Jean Jacques, 444

Eames, Charles, 337
Early, General Jubal, 488
Edmonds, Robert, 336
Edward (slave), 226
Edward II, 289, 450, 466
Edward III, 450, 503

Edwards, Charles, 337
Eldon, Lord (John Scott), 230
Elizabeth I, 89, 466
Emancipation Proclamation (1863), xii–xiii, xvii, 336, 535
Emeline (slave), 226
Emerson, Dr. John, 33–34, 55–56, 64, 66–67, 85–86, 113–16, 134, 136–37, 140, 142, 144, 171–78
Eustis, William, 202
Evarts, William M., 246, 337
Ex parte Merryman (1861), xviii, 3, 317–33, 534
Ex parte Milligan (1866), 3, 380, 419–513, 535
Ex parte Vallandigham, xviii, 379–87, 478, 535

Federal Conscription Act (1863), xvii, 535
Field, Roswell M., 67
Field, David Dudley, 425, 433
Field, Associate Justice Stephen Johnson, 387
Fifteenth Amendment, xvii, 3, 536
Fleta, 361
Fort Snelling, 33–34, 55–6, 60, 63, 66–67, 85, 114–16, 133, 136, 140, 168, 171–73
Fourteenth Amendment, xii, xvi–xviii, 3, 5, 515, 536
Francisque (slave), 241
Franklin, Benjamin, 99
Frye, Lieutenant, 448
Fugitive Slave Act (1850), xvi, 203–4, 207, 209, 217, 533

Gage, General Thomas, 443, 452, 462, 503
Gamble, Missouri Chief Justice Hamilton Rowan, 135–36, 176
Garfield, J. H., 425, 447, 479, 482
Garland, Benjamin S., 203
Garland, Hugh, A., 67
Gaston, Judge William, 151, 523

Gaunt, Elizabeth, 468
Gelpcke v. *Dubuque* (1864), 389–418
Geoffroy, 445
George (slave), 221
George III, 90, 99, 375, 455
Geyer, Henry S., 7
Gibbons, Edward, 202
Gibson, Colonel John Thomas, 221
Giles, Judge William Fell, 351
Glover, Joshua, 203
Gorden, Jonathan, 424, 436
Grant, Ulysses, xvii, 535–37
Green, Shields, 220–23
Greene, Judge, 396
Grenville, George, 99
Grier, Associate Justice Robert C., DS concurrence 65, 143, 236–37, 335, 337, 355, 387, 417, 470
Groves v. *Slaughter* (1841), 98, 121, 237, 247, 253, 265–68, 415
Gual, Julian, 337

Hale, Matthew, 450, 455
Hall, Judge Dominic Augustin, 481
Hall, Judge Jonathan C., 396, 417
Hall v. *DeCuir* (1878), xviii, 4, 537
Hamilton, Alexander, 87, 99, 122, 453, 463, 474, 485
Hanan, John, 319–20
Hancock, John, 100
Hanna, John, 424, 426, 436, 494
Hardwicke, Lord (Phillip Yorke), 120
Hargrave, Francis, 228, 230
Harrison, Colonel Benjamin, 485
Hayes, Rutherford B., xvii, 537
Henikin, Gustave, 366
Henry (slave), 221
Henry VIII, 89
Henry, Patrick, 95, 99–100
Hillsborough, Viscount (Willis Hill), 99
Hitchcock, General Ethan A., 387
Holmes, Oliver Wendell, Jr., xi–xii, xx
Holt, Lord Chief Justice John, 228
Homestead Act (1862), xv, xvii, 534
Hovey, General Alvin Peterson, 423, 489

Hutchinson, Thomas, 99
Hyde, Sir Nicholas, 329

Iredell, Associate Justice James, 307
Irven, Samuel, 366

Jacob, Giles, 521
Jackson, General Andrew, 453–54, 480–82
James II, 375, 466
Jay, John, 99, 122, 277, 307
Jefferson, Thomas, 99–100, 122, 181, 202, 244, 324, 520, 528
Jim (slave), 221
John, King, 465
Johnson, President Andrew, xvi–xvii, 515, 535–36
Johnson, Reverdy, 7
Johnson, Samuel, 521
Johnson, William, 223
Johnson, Associate Justice William, 43–44
Judicial Circuits Act (1866), xv, 536
Julia v. *McKinney* (1833), 133, 176, 242

Kagi, John, 221
Keim, General William High, 319, 321, 323
Kelly, Alexander, 223
Kent, Chancellor James, 21, 78, 370, 525. 530
Kentucky v. *Dennison* (1861), 283–316
Kinney, Judge John F., 417
Kitzmiller, Archibald M., 220, 223
Knight (slave), 241
Knox, General Henry, 485

Lago, Willis, 283–88, 303–4, 309, 314
Lagrange v. *Chouteau* (1828), 133
Lancaster, Earl Thomas, 450, 455, 466, 483, 503
Langworthy, Edward, 391

Lawrence, Soulden, 451
Lee, Richard Henry, 94, 202
Lee, Robert Edward, xvii, 534
Legrand v. *Darnell* (1829), 27–28, 165, 174
Le Grand, Claudius F., 27–28
Lemmon, Jonathan, 225–27, 261
Lemmon, Juliet, 225–27, 246, 251. 253, 259, 261–62
Lemmon v. *People* (1860), 225–281
Levi (slave), 221
Lewis (slave), 226
Leiber, Francis, xvii, 535; General Order 100, xvii, 387, 535
Lincoln, Abraham, xii–xviii, 3, 5, 283, 317, 335, 338–40, 379–81, 383–84, 453, 501, 506, 530, 533–34, and passim; Proclamation on Blockade (1861), xvi, 362, 364–65; Message to Congress, December 1, 1862, xiii, 534
Lincoln, General Benjamin, 453
Lisle, Alice, 468
Lord, Daniel, 337
Lortin, R. H., 365
Louallier, 481
Louisiana Purchase (1803), 33–34, 96, 100, 111, 114, 138, 184, 201
Lowe, Judge Ralph P., 418
Lucas, [John Baptiste Charles?], 202
Ludlam, Henry, 366
Lydia (slave), 242
Lyons, Lord Richard, 359, 362

Mackintosh, James, 454, 484, 503
Macon, Nathanial, 202
Madison, James, 46, 83–84, 87, 89, 94, 100, 108–9, 112, 121–23, 127–29, 181, 188, 202, 243–44, 267, 290, 300. 302, 306, 387
Magoffin, Governor Beriah, xv, 283, 288
Mansfield, Lord Chief Justice (William Murray), 63, 88–90, 119–20, 131, 229–30, 236, 241, 254–55, 271, 305
Marshall, 288
Marshall, Chief Justice John, 93, 99, 124, 126, 182, 185, 192, 201, 234, 237,

239, 260, 307, 331, 369, 386, 413–14, 491–93, 526
Martin, Luther, 64, 95
Marvin, Judge William, 351
Marx, Karl, xvii, 534
Mason (slave), 221
Mason, George, 100
Mayne, Rear Admiral Richard Charles, 448
McCulloch v. *Maryland* (1819), 125, 528
McDonald, Archibald, 452
McDonald, J. E., 425
McLean, Associate Justice John, 53, 98; DS dissent, 115–44, 228, 236–37, 266, 296, 414
Merryman, John, 317–23, 331
Mifflin, Governor Thomas, 295
Miller, Associate Justice Samuel Freeman, 387, 390, 410, 513
Milligan, Lambdin P., 419–20, 423–27, 437, 476, 480, 489–99, 504–8, 511
Mills, Judge Benjamin, 120, 143
Mills, Benjamin J., 220
Monroe, James, 129
Montesquieu, Baron Charles-Louis de Secondat, 262, 462
Morilla, General Pablo, 480
Morris, Gouverneur, 97, 109, 123, 182

Nancy (slave), 226
Napoleon, Louis, 226
Nelson, Associate Justice Samuel, 53; DS concurrence, 55–64, 65, 106, 247, 335, 337, 367, 378, 387, 449
North, Lord Frederick, 99
Northington, Lord (Robert Henley), 241
Nuckols, C. W., 285–86

O'Conor, Charles, 227
Ortega, Juan Gualberto de, 517–18

Pacific Railroad Act (1862), xvii, 534
Paine, Judge, 226–27, 232, 234, 243

Pendergrast, Commodore Garrett J., 362, 364, 367–68
Penn, William, 109
Phil (slave), 221
Phipps, John L., 336
Pinckney, Charles Cotesworth, 121, 243
Plessy v. *Ferguson* (1896), xviii, 4, 537
Posse Comitatus Act (1878), xvi, 537
Powell, Judge John, 228
Preciat, Don Rafael, 337–38, 364
Preliminary Emancipation Proclamation (1862), xvii, 534
Prigg v. *Pennsylvania* (1842), 119, 130, 188, 194, 247, 265–66, 294, 296, 304
Prize Cases, 335–78, 470, 472
Prynn, William, 468

Queen, Victoria, 358
Quinn, Luke, 220, 222

Rachel v. *Walker* (1836), 133–34, 136, 169, 176, 242
Randolph, John, 128
Randolph, Edmund, 108, 122–23, 128, 181, 244
Reconstruction Acts, xvii, 536
Rentone, Captain James, 448
Richard II, 89
Robert (slave), 226
Rooke, Giles, 451
Rosecrans, General William, 383
Ruffin, Chief Judge Thomas, 523
Russell, Lord William, 468
Rutherford, Thomas, 224

Sam (slave), 221
Sandford, John F. A., 3, 5–6, 33, 56, 115, 134, 147–48, 226, 228, 247–48, 523–25
Scott, Eliza, 33–34, 55–56, 67, 115–16, 140, 173
Scott, Harriet, 33–34, 55–56, 66–67, 115–16, 140, 173

Scott, Lizzie, 33–34, 55, 67, 115–16, 173
Scott, General Winfield, 429, 438, 456
Sedgwick, Charles B., 337
Sedgwick, Theodore, 87
Selden, Judge Samuel L, 250, 272, 281, 329
Seward, William, 340
Shaw, Massachusetts Chief Judge Lemuel, 63, 167, 232, 235–36, 243
Sheppard, Haywood, 219–20, 222
Slaughter-House Cases (1873), xii, xviii, 3, 357
Sloan, James, 202
Smith, Abram D., 205
Smith, Rev. John, 454, 484, 503
Smith, Joshua Hett, 484–5
Smith, Winfield, 205
Somersett, Lewis, 63–64, 79, 88–89, 119–20
Somerset v. Stewart (1772), 63,–64, 79, 88–89, 119–20, 228–30, 236, 241, 246, 254–55, 263, 266
Spangler, Emanuel, 223
Speed, Attorney General James, xvii, 425, 428, 535; Opinion, Lincoln Murder Trial, xvii, 535
Spencer v. Negro Dennis (1849), 141
Spicer, Thomas, 320–21
Sprague, Judge Peleg, 351
Stanbery, Henry, 425
Starry, Lewis P., 223
Stephen, Aaron C., (alias Aaron D. Stephens), 220–23
Stevens, Thaddeus, xvii, 534–35
Stevenson, John W., 288
Stockton, Judge Lacon D., 398, 417
Stormont, Viscount, 466
Story, Associate Justice Joseph, 57–58, 63, 245, 250, 266, 269, 272, 330, 359, 526–7
Stowell, Lord (1st Baron, William Scott), 63–64, 79, 90, 120, 131, 140–41, 166–67, 228, 240, 357
Strader v. Graham (1851), 51–52, 59–60, 62, 83, 141, 247, 265, 267

Strafford, Lord (Thomas Wentworth), 466
Stringham, Flag Officer Silas, 365
Swan, Judge Joseph Rockwell, 239
Swayne, Associate Justice Noah, 389, 407, 513, 515–16
Sydney, Algernon, 463, 468
Sylvia v. Kirby (1853), 136

Talbot, Lord (Charles Talbot), 120
Talbot, Nancy, 516–17
Taliaferro, Major, 33, 55, 64, 66, 115
Taney, Chief Justice Roger B., 5; DS Opinion 7–52, 169, 203–4, 226, 234, 245, 268–69, 278, 283–84, 306, 317–18, 320–23, 377–78, 416, 493
Tapping, Thomas, 289, 305
Tellfair, Governor Edward, 308
Texas v. White (1869), xiv, xvi, xviii, 3, 536
Thirteenth Amendment, xii, xvii, 3, 5, 515, 520, 523–26, 535
Tidd, Charles, 221
Tomlins, Thomas Edlyne, 521
Torrington, Viscount (George Byng), 479
Turner, George W., 220, 222–23

Vallandigham, Clement L., 379–80, 383, 385, 387, 478
Varnum, James Bradley, 202
Vattel, Emer de, 71, 77–78, 138, 238, 245, 248, 292, 341, 356

Walker, R. J., 482
Wall, Joseph, 451, 484
Wallace, John William, 389
Walsh, Robert, 202
Warwick, Abraham, 336
Washington, George, 87, 94, 99, 188, 190, 202, 312, 429, 452–53, 467, 471, 484–85, 501
Washington, Lewis W., 220–23
Watkins, Tobias, 436, 492

Watson, G. F., 366–67
Wayne, Associate Justice James Moore, DS concurrence 52–55, 202, 236–37, 380, 383, 478, 513
Webster, Daniel, 121
Webster, Noah, 493
Welles, Judge Henry, 250, 272
Wellington, Duke of (Arthur Wellesley), 442, 479, 488
West Chester and Philadelphia Railroad Co. v. Miles (1867), xviii, 4, 536
Wheaton, Henry, 167, 309, 371, 378, 387
White, S. V., 391
Willes, Lord Chief Justice Edward, 449
William III, 451, 466
William, the Conqueror, 88, 101
Williams, George H., 319
Wilmot, Jonathan Eardley, 229
Wilson, Associate Justice James, 307
Wilson v. Melvin (1835), 134, 176, 242
Winny v. Whitesides (1824), 133, 136
Winthrop, Governor Jonathan, 310
Wirt, William, 25, 125
Wittimore, Adjutant James, 321
Wolcott, Attorney General, Ohio, C[hristoipher] P[arsons], 287–88, 298
Worchester, Joseph Emerson, 125
Woodbury, Associate Justice Levi, 452, 482
Woodward, Judge William G., 397–98
Wright, Iowa Chief Justice George G., 396–98, 417–18
Wright, Judge William B., 250, 261

Yohe, Colonel Samuel, 321